The Slavs
in European History
and Civilization

The Slavs
in European History
and Civilization

By Francis Dvornik

RUTGERS UNIVERSITY PRESS
New Brunswick   *New Jersey*

OTAKARO ODLOŽILÍK

olim Pragensis Caroli IV, nunc Pennsylvaniae

Universitatis professori,

necnon

ROMANO JAKOBSON

olim Brunensis, nunc Harvardianae

Universitatis professori,

consortibus laborum.

Copyright © 1962 by Rutgers, The State University

Library of Congress Catalogue Card Number: 61-10259

ISBN: 0-8135-0403-1

Manufactured in the United States of America

M 9 8 7 6 5 4 3 2 1

PREFACE

During the school year of 1956-57 I gave a course at the Slavic Department of Harvard University on Slavic history and civilization from the thirteenth to the seventeenth centuries. My colleagues in that department, especially Professor A. B. Lord, then its Chairman, urged me to complete and enlarge the course and to publish it in book form. I thank them for their encouragement and interest. The present book is also, in some way, the continuation of another study of mine, *The Slavs, Their Early History and Civilization*, published in 1956 by The American Academy in Boston, which was based on a course given by me in 1951 at the same department of Harvard University.

Since many of the problems treated in my course deserved a more profound study, I extended considerably my research on Slavic problems during that most difficult and often misunderstood period, from the thirteenth to the eighteenth century. Because the present book is also intended to encourage a more detailed study of the many problems discussed, I have added to each chapter a bibliography in non-Slavic languages, indicating the most important sources. Students who are able to use publications in Slavic will find in the footnotes references to works in which a more exhaustive bibliography in those languages may be found. The bibliographical indications—especially those given in the last chapter—are not, of course, complete, but I trust that they will be useful.

I was fortunate in receiving help and encouragement from my many friends and colleagues. A former colleague from Charles IV University in Prague, now Professor of Central European History at Pennsylvania University, read the complete manuscript and gave me invaluable advice on the division of the book into chapters, and also on problems of Czech, Polish and German history. Professor R. Jakobson of Harvard University, a zealous promoter of Slavic studies in the United States, read the chapters on Czech and Russian literature. I was fortunate in being able to consult at the British Museum, Professor S. Kot, the well-known specialist in the history of the Reformation, about certain problems connected with the spread of the Reformation in Slavic lands, especially in Poland. Professor V. Weintraub of Harvard University was kind enough to read the chapters on Polish literature, and I am grateful for his suggestions. I. Ševčenko,

Professor at Columbia University, gave me much useful information about Ukrainian and Russian History, and G. C. Soulis, now Professor at Indiana State University and a specialist in Balkan history, read the chapters on Serbian and Bulgarian History and Literature. D. R. Hitchcock, now an assistant professor at the University of Maryland, helped me with the transliteration of Slavic words and compiled the transliteration and pronunciation tables. The maps were planned by my friend Mr. G. Scheele, to whom I express my most sincere thanks, and executed by Mr. Myron Otrok of the Geography Department of Rutgers University.

I am indebted to Professor P. Charanis, who recommended this book to the Rutgers University Press. I wish to express my thanks also to the Director of Dumbarton Oaks, Mr. J. S. Thacher, for granting a subsidy towards its publication.

I am most grateful to the Director of the Rutgers University Press, William Sloane, who, with his very competent staff, supervised the printing of this book, a difficult task which, owing to the unfamiliarity of the subject, demanded unusual skill and experience on the part of both publisher and printer.

I dedicate this work to two friends and colleagues of mine, as an acknowledgment of the help I received from them.

Dumbarton Oaks
Autumn, 1960

CONTENTS

tion—Tsar Asen II, Rome, Hungary, and the Latin Empire—
Disastrous consequences in the Balkans of the Mongol invasion—A new Balkan political combination and the triumph of
Michael Palaeologus—Hungary and the southern Slavs—
Croatian national expansion and the rise of Bosnia—Emperor
Michael VIII's duplicity at the Council of Lyons, the decline
of Bulgaria—Serbian leadership in the Balkans—Serbia's victorious progress under Tsar Stephen Dušan—Serbia's decline,
the Turkish conquest of Bulgaria, and defeat of the Serbians
at Kosovo

The old Slavic principle of division overcome in Bohemia—
Oldest political organization in Bohemia—Origins of the
Czech nobility—Special features of Czech feudalism, the "right
of the land"—Evolution of the nobility into a special class—
Position of the higher clergy and of the burghers in Bohemia
—Bohemia, a dualistic state—Attempts at the creation of a new
juridical code—The *Maiestas Carolina,* the crown, symbol of
the state—Characteristic traits in the origin of the Polish
nobility—Position of the higher clergy and of the burghers in
Poland—The Polish nobility as a ruling class—*Corona regni
Poloniae, regnum*—Succession to the Polish throne, Casimir's
reforms—Administrative reforms—The Slovenes—The Slovaks
and the political evolution of Hungary—Mathias Csak and the
Slovaks—The reforms of the Angevins and the Slovaks—The
political status of the Croats—Croatian assemblies, Hungarian
influences in Slavonia—Survival of Romano-Byzantine law in
Dalmatia—Ragusa (Dubrovnik)—Organization of the Second
Bulgarian Empire on the Byzantine model—Byzantine and
Western elements in medieval Serbia—Origins of the Serbian
aristocracy, the *pronoia,* religious situation, Serbian cities,
Dušan's code

The westernization of Czech Christianity, Latin religious
poetry in Bohemia—Original Latin works in Bohemia—Czech
translations of Latin writings—Czech compositions in verse
and prose—Czech epic poetry and prose, its Western patterns
—The Old Czech secular lyric and its relationship to the

ers of Slovene literature—Catholic Counter-Reformation follows methods of the Protestant reformers—Spread of the
Reformation among the Croats—Protestant Croatian literature—Flacius and Vergerius, Croatian reformers—Catholic
Counter-Reformation, creation of Serbo-Croatian literary language—Protestant and Catholic Pan-Slavic ideas, Križanić—
Protestant propaganda among Orthodox Slavs—Protestantism
and the eastern Slavs—Protestantism and Muscovy

Rise of the Habsburgs—First contacts with Muscovy—Muscovite-Habsburg alliance—Sigismund, Basil III, and the Habsburgs—Congress of Vienna (1515)—The Habsburgs and
Muscovy profit by mutual friendship—Maximilian II, Ivan IV,
and the Polish interregnum—Stephen Bathory's succession,
Rudolf II, Fedor—The Habsburgs, Zamoyski, and Boris
Godunov—Zamoyski, the Habsburgs, and the Danubian prin-
cipalities—Charles V's attempts at imperialism—Philip II's
political conceptions and their failure—Leading ideas of Span-
ish monarchic absolutism—Austrian Habsburgs adopt the
Spanish conception—Its application in Bohemia—Ferdinand
II's monarchic plans in Germany opposed by Denmark,
France, and Sweden—End of the Thirty Years' War, peace of
Westphalia (1648), ruin of Bohemia—Literary activity of
Czech exiles, Komenský, Žerotín—Czech literature of the
Counter-Reformation—Czech patriots, decadence of Czech
national life—Czech and Slovak baroque art

Failure of Sigismund III in Sweden and of plans for reform—
Boris Godunov, the false Dmitrij, Šujskij—The Poles in Moscow—Losses on the Baltic, origins of the Cossacks, first Polish
clash with Turkey—The Cossacks as defenders of Orthodoxy
—Chmel'nyćkyj's insurrection, Muscovy and the Ukraine, the
pact of Perejaslavl'—Polish reaction, Union of Hadjač, division
of Ukraine between Poland and Muscovy—Dorošenko's adventure, Poland threatened by Turkey—King John Sobieski's
victories and disappointments—Polish economic and cultural
setbacks—Polish baroque literature reflects the nation's cultural and political ideas—Peculiarities of Polish baroque art

INTRODUCTION

The most complicated period in the history of Central and Eastern Europe is the late Middle Ages and the beginning of modern times, from the thirteenth to the eighteenth century. Although the Slavic element predominated, at least in Eastern Europe, many non-Slavic peoples such as the Germans, Magyars, Lithuanians, Balts, Tatars, Turks, Rumanians, and others, took part in the political, cultural, and economic history of this part of Europe; and certain of them held, at least for a time, a dominant role among some of the Slavic peoples.

No wonder then, that because of the complexity of these problems the study of this period is neglected, particularly in the West. To an observer, familiar with the growth of what we call Western Europe, where, at that time, Latin and Germanic nations were establishing their states and laying the solid groundwork for a flourishing civilization, the development of the eastern part of Europe must appear very strange and unfamiliar, nay, at times almost chaotic. It presents difficulties also to those who are trying to find a central basis for the comprehensive history of this part of Europe, which is so different from the West in its geographical, ethnic, and cultural aspects.

There can be no objection to taking the Slavic nations as the central basis for the study of the medieval and the early modern period of Eastern Europe and to treating them as an organic unity. Not only do they form the dominating ethnic elements in these parts, but although divided geographically and culturally, all of them have many common traits in their political history, their civilization, their national character, and language. Moreover, Slavic unity manifested itself not only during the early stages of their history, but also during the Middle Ages and in modern times. Even religious separation could not suppress this unity.

Although the Czechs were more exposed to Western influence and German domination than the other Slavic peoples, the sentiment of Slavic solidarity manifested itself in the thirteenth century during the struggle of the Czech king with Rudolf of Habsburg and at the beginning of the fourteenth century in the attempt to create a Czech-Polish state. Charles IV, although Roman emperor, supported the Slavic idea in his realm and looked upon the Serbian king as a member of the same Slavic family. The Hussites exploited the linguistic affinity when trying to win over the

Slovaks, the Poles, and the Croats, and also when trying to gain the sympathy of the Slavic East.

The idea that Poland was a part of the Slavic world resounds in all the early Polish chronicles. Czech, Ukrainian, and White Russian influences on the development of modern Polish literary language show the affinity of these nations one with the other. The true common Slavic spirit manifested itself during the Polish Renaissance by the foremost Polish writers Kochanowski and Bielski. The affinity between the Russians and the Poles showed itself, in spite of political and religious differences, in the attempts made to create a common state.

Even the reformists, and after them the counter-reformists, exploited the idea of Slavic unity for their religious propaganda. During the Turkish occupation the Croats and other southern Slavs looked first toward the Poles and then to the Russians, brotherly nations, in their hopes for deliverance. Serbian and Bulgarian influences on Muscovite literature at that time were remarkable. Even the Catholic enthusiast, the Croat Križanić, went to Moscow hoping to convert the tsar to the idea of national and religious unity.

Thus, this idea of Slavic unity did not originate in the nineteenth century in the Russian Pan-Slavic movement, as is often believed. It was alive from the beginning of the history of the Slavic nations and persisted through the Middle Ages on up to modern times.[1]

It is, therefore, clear that there is a unifying factor which justifies treating the history of all Slavic peoples as a unity, the more so as they played a dominant role in the fate of eastern and southeastern Europe at this crucial time. Because, however, the history of the Slavs is intimately associated with the many non-Slavic nations, we cannot exclude these nations from our investigations. Nor can the history of the Slavs and their neighboring nations be treated in isolation from the history of the rest of Europe. They were often very closely involved with the Western nations, and their history is a part of the history of the whole of Europe.

In the last decades the problem of the division of European history into Eastern and Western spheres and the limits of these spheres have been the object of numerous scholarly discussions, and these discussions are still continuing. Many different theories have been advanced as to the division of East European history into distinctive periods.[2] We cannot enter into the details of these discussions here. The concept of "eastern Europe"

[1] Compare, for details, R. Jakobson's study "Comparative Slavic Studies" in *The Review of Politics*, 16 (1954), pp. 67-90.

[2] These problems and the discussions have been thoroughly investigated by the Czech historian J. Macůrek in his *Dějepisectví evropského východu* ("Historiography of the European East," Prague, 1946), pp. 1-128.

changed throughout different periods, and its definition varies according to the convictions or prejudices of the historian dealing with this problem.

With regard to these different periods, we can discern, in spite of apparent confusion in the historical background of southeastern Europe, certain salient factors which divide its history into well-delineated periods. The first phase is characterized by the influence of the Byzantine Empire and its civilization on the Slavic nations. This influence extended not only over the Bulgarians and Serbians, but also over the Croats, Czechs, and Slovaks, and touched slightly upon the Poles. The Russians with their center in Kiev were definitely won for the Byzantine religion and civilization, although they still kept in touch with the Latin West. Early Slavic history presents a remarkable unity characterized by a common literary language, the Old Slavonic. I described this period of Slavic history in my book *The Slavs: Their Early History and Civilization,* published in 1956 (by the American Academy, Boston, Mass., 280 Newton Street). But even in the thirteenth and fourteenth centuries Byzantine influence was noticeable in the Balkans in the renovated states of the Bulgarians and Serbians and in Muscovy. Even Poland was partly involved by its occupation of Orthodox Galicia. Moreover, as we shall see, the policy of the Árpád dynasty of Hungary, which at the beginning of its history had also come under the spell of Byzantium, gravitated at this time toward the Balkan Slavs in an effort to replace Byzantine political supremacy with its own.

Among the Czechs, the last vestige of Byzantine cultural influence—the Slavic liturgy—disappeared at the end of the eleventh century, but the memory of it remained alive although from the tenth century on, Bohemia was part of the renovated Western Roman Empire. Poland, holding to her independent position, won prominence in the fourteenth century both in the Slavic world and in Europe and thus inaugurated the second phase of eastern European history, which was characterized by Polish-Lithuanian leadership in the East and Turkish domination in the South. The Osman Turks in many ways replaced the Byzantines and expanded their empire not only over the Balkans, but also over a part of Croatia, over Hungary, and over the two Rumanian principalities of Moldavia and Wallachia to the Black Sea. The Polish-Lithuanian commonwealth had attracted also the Czechs and Hungary, but was unable to stop the progress of the Turks, who influenced also the life of the Russians, liberated from the Mongol yoke but endangered by the Tatars of Crimea, who were vassals of the Turks.

Another characteristic of this period is the attempts at a union of Poland-Lithuania with the growing Muscovy, either by the election of a common ruler or by the conquest of Moscow. The attempts failed, and from the end of the seventeenth century on, a new phase in eastern European history began, characterized by the growth of Muscovy, which gathered into its empire the Ukrainian and White Russian principalities and thus caused the disappearance of the Polish kingdom. Muscovy claimed more influence in European affairs and liked to think of herself as holding a protectorate over all Orthodox nations.

However, we cannot limit ourselves only to the study of eastern Europe. There were other political factors which dominated Central Europe, and at times also affected Western Europe, influencing profoundly the history of the Slavic nations and the whole East. First of all there was the Western Roman Empire, renovated by the Saxon King Otto I in the tenth century. Bohemia was part of this empire, as were also the Alpine lands inhabited partly by the Slovenes. The struggle of the emperor with the feudal lords had strong repercussions in Bohemia and in the Alpine lands, and was echoed also in Poland. The claims of the Empire to the Baltic lands, where the Teutonic Knights were laying the foundations of the future Prussia, provoked a strong reaction in Poland, which led to the establishment of the Polish-Lithuanian commonwealth. Even Russia, barred from access to the Baltic Sea, was eventually involved, and there was a sharp conflict, successfully ended by Peter the Great.

The gradual disintegration of the Empire into a state of almost independent principalities; the colonization of Slavic lands on the Baltic shores and between the Elbe and the Vistula; the growth of German cities; the settling of German burghers and peasants in Bohemia, Poland, and Hungary—all had a profound influence on the economic, national, and cultural life of the Czechs, Slovaks, Slovenes, and Poles. Even the Ukrainians accepted German laws in the organization of their cities. The importance of the German element in the modernization of Muscovy should not be forgotten.

Also to be considered was a principle of medieval papacy, established under Gregory VII in the eleventh century, which put forward the idea of the superiority of the spiritual over the temporal. This was a defense against the encroachment of the secular princes in Church affairs, and was opposed by the German emperors more vehemently than by other European rulers. The question as to whether the secular princes had the right to choose their ecclesiastical dignitaries and to what extent the latter were bound to fulfill their feudal duties to their lay masters in return for the lands with which they had been invested by them, or the so-called investiture conflict, shattered the basis of the Western Roman Empire and brought about the downfall of the mighty dynasty of the Hohenstaufens.

The victory of the Papacy under Innocent III impressed even the Bulgarians and the Serbians. The founders of their newly resuscitated kingdoms asked to receive their crowns in Rome. The prestige which the

Papacy enjoyed in the Middle Ages was of help to the Poles in their struggle for unity and independence. A tax called "Peter's Pence," to the payment of which all Polish leaders bound themselves soon after the conversion of their nation, was, together with Church organization, the sole reminder of national unity during the dismemberment of the kingdom into numerous principalities, and ensured Poland of protection against the emperors after the resuscitation of the Polish kingdom. Bohemia's position was different. The first attempts at the Reformation were made in Bohemian lands by the Hussites and led to a protracted conflict with the Papacy.

The division of Christianity into the Roman Catholic and Orthodox Churches proved fatal to Slavic cultural unity and had profound repercussions on the life of all the Slavic nations. The efforts at Church union made by the Roman Curia were, for a short time, favorably received by the Serbians and Bulgarians. The vehement rejection by Muscovy under Basil II of this attempted union widened the gap between the Orthodox East and the Catholic West, strengthened Muscovy's cultural and political isolation, and heightened the tension with Poland-Lithuania, which, alone among the Ukrainian and White Russian peoples, favored the union. Repercussions of this animosity toward the Uniats were evident even in recent years in the new order of things in the East.

Another important factor was that the Habsburg dynasty, which had inherited the spoils of the Czech kings in the Alpine lands, won the crowns of both Bohemia and Hungary, and now held the scepter of the emperors. More than once did the Habsburgs look to the crown of Poland, hoping that it would rest on the head of one of their scions. Diplomatic relations with the last of the Rurik rulers and the hopes they were awakening in Vienna and in Moscow are little known, but should not be forgotten.

Finally, when the Habsburgs, with the help of the German, Czech, Slovak, and Croatian armies, freed the whole of Hungary from the Turkish yoke, it looked as if they would become the heirs of the Byzantines and the Turks in the Balkans. This possibility, however, did not become reality. The eyes of the southern Slavs were turning toward Moscow, regarded as the Third Rome and champion of the Orthodox world. The newly awakened interest of the Russian rulers in the fate of the southern Slavs and their penetration of the South Danube basin halted the progress of the armies of the Habsburgs, who were forced to content themselves with the conquest of Croatia, with Dalmatia, and the occupation of Bosnia.

Besides the political and religious factors, there were other elements of a different nature, many of which originated in the western states, which stimulated the evolution of the Slavic and other nations of central, eastern, and southern Europe. We must see, for example, how the French and German feudal system affected their social life and what repercussions the growing monarchic idea in the West produced in the states founded by the Slavs, or inhabited by them. A considerable contribution was made by Poland to the history of political philosophy in the Renaissance period, and by her "parliamentary" system, so different from that of the English and the French. This should be examined according to its merits, as should the less commendable sides, which became disastrous for the kingdom. Muscovy's monarchic idea sprang from a different background than had that of western Europe: it had its roots in Byzantine political theories and was influenced by Mongol practice.

We must also pay due attention to the cultural incentives coming from western, southern, and central Europe. From the thirteenth century on, the West had begun to compete with the still culturally superior Byzantine East. A new kind of literature was originating in France and Provence using the vernacular, and this genre was beginning to spread over the whole of Europe. Gothic art was born, and the chivalrous spirit was cultivated in the West. These new trends penetrated into the lands inhabited by the Slavs from France, Italy, and Germany, although in the South and East the Byzantine cultural elements still predominated.

Then came the mighty wave of humanism and the Renaissance from Italy. It engulfed the Czechs and created a golden age in Polish literature; it was also echoed in Russia. In the South in the Slavic independent oasis of Dubrovnik (Ragusa), great literary masterpieces were created, which, with other native elements, helped to build up modern Croatian, Serbian, and Bulgarian literature.

Of course, the lands of the Slavs could not escape another mighty wave which swept over Europe from Germany, France, and Switzerland—that of the Reformation. There are many features in the influence this had on the Slavic peoples which are not too well known. The reformers created the Slovene literary language and letters and were the first to begin to cultivate the All-Slavic idea. This wave profoundly shook the Slavic inhabitants of Bohemia, Poland, and Hungary. It reached out also to the Croats, who gave some of their most prominent men to the cause of the Reformation. Again, the echo of this movement was heard in Moscow and in Rumania.

In trying to combat the reformers, the counter-reformers had to accept many of the methods used by the former in the spread of their doctrines. The use of the vernacular in literature, a method used by the reformers, thus preserved the new genre of baroque literature and helped the Czechs survive the most depressing era of their national life, during the eighteenth century. The baroque style, which became so characteristic of the Counter-Reformation, came from Italy, Germany, and Vienna to Bohemia, Hungary, and Poland. It flourished especially in Czech lands, and was accepted in Muscovy.

All these elements must be examined in order to see to what extent the Slavic nations had responded to the incentives coming from western Europe in the period from the thirteenth to the eighteenth century. At the same time, we should ask ourselves to what degree the Slavic nations contributed to the political, cultural, and religious development of Europe. They slowed down and finally stopped the Turkish advance into the center of Europe, and they contributed much to European civilization during the period of humanism and the Renaissance, and during the Reformation.

This will explain the division of this book into its different chapters. It seemed necessary to give in the introductory chapter a short review of the emergence of the Slavs in European history and to sketch in a few sentences the situation in Europe at the beginning of the thirteenth century, particularly the different phases of the struggle between the Papacy and the Empire. This explains also why in the third and fourth chapters I found it necessary to go into some detail in describing the situation of the Empire and the rest of Europe. It is the period in which Bohemia, through her kings, John of Luxemburg and particularly his son, Charles IV, played an important, nay, decisive role in the Empire, and in which her influence extended into France, England, and Italy. It is impossible, when describing the reign of the Emperor Charles IV, not to speak of his plans and deeds in Germany. Although he thought of himself as a Slav, he made serious attempts to establish a peaceful modus vivendi between his Slavic subjects and the German people.

The complications of Polish history during the Jagiellonian period induced me into devoting several separate chapters to Polish-Lithuanian problems which seem to have little coherence even among themselves: the Turkish danger, which the Jagiellonians tried to prevent, and the complications in the Baltic with Prussia and with growing Muscovy.

It was my intention to devote this study only to the period from the thirteenth to the eighteenth century as it is these centuries which are more often neglected in the general histories of Europe and of the Slavic nations, for the events during this particular phase of history are very difficult to master. I have added, however, in the last chapter, a short history of Peter the Great together with a sketch of the influence of imperial Russia on the other Slavic nations and on the rest of Europe, up to modern times. I have found it superfluous to go into greater detail as the history of the modern period of Russia and of other Slavic nations is fully described in historical handbooks and specialized studies. It is the medieval and early modern period which is less well known. When I added this chapter, it was because I felt it necessary to show how the political developments, together with many ideas, have survived from the earlier period, and to what degree they have influenced the modern history of these parts of Europe.

In order to show the influence of the rest of Europe on the Slavs and the contribution of the Slavs to the political and cultural growth of the world, I have followed the chronological, not the schematic, method. This has the disadvantage, for example, that the literature and the system of political organization of the different nations are dealt with in separate chapters. In order to overcome this disadvantage and to facilitate the use of this book to readers interested in special questions, I have prepared a very detailed index. This will enable the student to confine his reading to those problems in which he is particularly interested. For the same reason, and in order to avoid too many cross references, I have found it necessary in some chapters to give a brief review of certain problems which have already been discussed more fully in other parts of the book.

I think that every specialist will agree with me that writing the history of the Slavic peoples and their neighbors during the Middle Ages and on up to the early modern period is a great and difficult task. There will be readers who would have preferred to find their particular problems examined in greater detail, but certain limits must be observed. I have tried to give the important problems the consideration they deserve.

It has become the custom to entrust the treatment of such complicated historical and cultural problems, which extend over a long period, to a team of scholars specializing in the different sectors involved. However, experience has shown that such collective works have many disadvantages. Lack of unity is the main one, together with contradictory perspectives and unnecessary repetition. These reasons will, I hope, justify my attempt to treat, in a coherent fashion, the various and complex problems of the history of the Slavic peoples as a unity and, of necessity, within the framework of the entire European history and civilization, whence they began, from this time on, to play an ever increasing role.

Chapter I

EUROPE TO THE THIRTEENTH CENTURY

The appearance of Slavic and Germanic nations on the European political scene—The Moravian empire and the consequences of its destruction—German political leadership in Central Europe. The Slavs in the Western and Eastern cultural spheres—Rise and crisis of Kievan Russia—Growth of the Papacy until the thirteenth century—Debasement of the imperial idea—Henry VI and Frederick II—The Papacy fails to establish the political supremacy of the sacerdotium—*Political disintegration of Germany—German progress on the Baltic, in Prussia and Livonia—Economic progress in Germany and Italy—Intensification of cultural life in Europe—Spread of a secular spirit in literature—The West competing with the East*

The emergence of the Slavic nations into the foreground of European history was belated and rather slow. Their primitive habitats were most probably in the region between the Vistula and Dnieper rivers. From there some of the tribes began early to penetrate the lands beyond the Dnieper and to follow the course of the rivers, toward the Black Sea, the Danube, and beyond it. One group of them, probably led by a Sarmatian upper class called Antês, was the first which came into contact with the Byzantine Empire, but their organization was destroyed, in the sixth century A.D., by the Turkic invaders, the Avars. The tribes on the Dnieper and beyond, later called Russians, after being subdued by other invaders, especially by the Turkic Khazars, found help and protection in an alliance with the Scandinavian warriors who had founded a solid state in the ninth century with its center at Kiev.

When the Germanic tribes from the Baltic coast began to migrate toward the south, Slavic tribes, in the sixth century, crossed the Vistula and the Oder rivers and spread over the Baltic shores as far as the Elbe river, crossing it in many places. These tribes, called Baltic Slavs, Polabians, Pomeranians, and Sorbs or Sorbians (in modern Saxony), were

1

almost doomed to extinction when the Franks and then the Germans began their expansion to the north and the east.

The Czechs and the Slovaks occupied Bohemia, Moravia, and Slovakia, where they now live, definitely only in the sixth century A.D. At the same time the Slovenes pressed on into the Alpine lands toward the Adriatic. The Turkic Avars, who had settled in the Danube basin, subdued the Slavs, and together they invaded the Byzantine Empire during the sixth and seventh centuries, destroying the flourishing provinces of Pannonia and Illyricum. The Slavs, settled in what is now modern Yugoslavia, were liberated from the Avars in the seventh century by the Croats and Serbians, who came from beyond the Carpathian Mountains, from the country now called Galicia, at the invitation of the Emperor Heraclius (610-664). They laid the foundations of the political organization of the southern Slavs—Croatia and Serbia. The Slavs, settled between the Danube and the Balkans, were organized into a solid political structure by the Turkic Bulgars, who named their state Bulgaria.

The tribes which stayed on in the primitive settlements spread to the Vistula and Oder and into the neighborhood of the Polabians, Pomeranians, and Sorbians. They were called Poles after their most important tribe, but only came into prominence in the tenth century.

The early history of the Slavic nations is full of tragic incidents, of brilliant hopes, and promising possibilities which seldom found realization owing to the varying circumstances and events beyond control of the Slavic rulers.

In this respect the Germanic peoples were more fortunate since they had appeared on the European scene several centuries earlier. After breaking through the defenses of the western part of the Roman Empire, the Germanic nations took possession of its flourishing provinces and established their own realms in Gaul, Germany, Spain, Africa, Italy, and Britain.

Thus, long before the Slavs, they emerged into the sphere of Western and Latin culture, and after accepting quite docilely the Christian faith, the Germanic peoples became the determining factor in the Christian West. Although Roman missionaries were successful in imposing on their Germanic converts the Roman form of Christianity, and also its Latin liturgical language, they failed to persuade them to accept the Roman mentality in its entirety. In fact, the impelling force of the vigorous young race was so strong that the Church in western Europe could not prevent a profound Germanization of some features of its organization. This was most visible in the new system of proprietary churches introduced in all Germanic lands. According to this system, kings and noblemen claimed not only the ownership of sanctuaries established by them, but also the right to appoint both higher and lower clergy in ecclesiastical institutions endowed by them. This was a dangerous breach with the old Roman conceptions which had hitherto been followed by the Church in both the western and the eastern parts of the Roman Empire. Moreover, this new course in Western Christianity could not but promote the estrangement between East and West.

The Franks, the most vigorous among these Germanic peoples, made this new system the backbone of their state. Soon, after having extended their empire from Spain to the Elbe and from the Danube to the Apennines, the Franks under their ruler Charlemagne (771-814) assumed the leadership of the West and the protection of the Church in the renovated Roman Empire.

Christianity penetrated, however, slowly among the Croats, Serbians, Bulgarians, Slovenes, and Czechs. They were Christianized completely only in the ninth century. Although Frankish, Roman, and Irish, as well as Byzantine, missionaries worked among the Slavs, it appeared for some time that not only the southern but also the western Slavs would all come under the direct influence of Eastern Christianity and of Byzantine culture. Their first political organization in Central Europe was Great Moravia, comprising modern Moravia with Slovakia and part of Austria to the Danube River. Recent archeological finds in Moravia have shown that from the beginning of the ninth century Byzantine cultural influence was strongly felt in the new Moravian state. This fact explains why the Moravian ruler Rastislav (846-870) concluded a kind of political and cultural alliance with Byzantium. This alliance helped the Byzantines to stop Frankish expansion toward the Balkans, to win another new Slavic state—Bulgaria—over to their civilization, and to extend their sway over the Slavic tribes of future Serbia.

The consolidation of Christianity in Moravia by Byzantine missionaries in the ninth century seemed to open the way to a bright future, not only for the Slavs but also for the whole of the West. The introduction of the vernacular into the liturgy by the Greek apostles of Moravia, St. Cyril and Methodius, a concession which was sanctioned by Rome, promised a more rapid spread of the Christian faith among new nations and easier access for the common man to the religious mysteries. The rapid rise of Old Slavonic literary activity in Moravia, and later in Bohemia, illustrates vividly what other nations could have gained by the development of their vernacular literature if the new example had been imitated. The interpenetration of Byzantine and Latin culture in Moravia also augured well for a better understanding between East and West.

Some of these possibilities would have perhaps been realized if the Moravian experiment had taken place in happier circumstances. In fact, it was used by the Moravian rulers to stop the penetration of the Franks into the Moravian and Danubian basins, and by the Papacy to undermine the power of the East Frankish (German) Church in the new lands. The Franks were too powerful to be easily overcome, and the new political and cultural power in Moravia was too young to impose its will. The new state succumbed to the German swords and was stamped into the ground by the hoofs of Magyar horses (906). The access to Byzantine cultural treasures which seemed to be opening for western Europe along the Danube was closed once more. The new invaders of Central Europe, the Magyars, established themselves definitively in the Danubian basin and drove a wedge between the western and eastern Slavic groups. Bohemia, which had joind the East Frankish Empire, was saved from the disaster and inherited the cultural achievements of Great Moravia.

Thus it was that the Slavs lost their best opportunity of becoming an important political and cultural power in Central Europe. The leadership was taken over by the Regnum Teutonicorum—the eastern part of the declining Frankish Empire, or Germany. The Slavs between the Elbe and the Oder were the first to feel the consequences of the change. The conquest of their lands by Henry I (919-936) and Otto I (936-973) and the introduction of the Germanic church system among them were of bad augury for their freedom and existence.

This also initiated the passionate feud between Germans and Slavs, which was destined to last for centuries. Only once did there appear to be a possibility of peaceful collaboration between Slavs and Germans—in the renovated Roman Empire of Otto III (983-1002). Then it seemed that Germany would take over the role of Great Moravia and become the intermediary between the Byzantine East and the Roman West. But the premature death of the young emperor dashed all these hopes.

Fate did not favor another attempt to create a Slavic empire by uniting Poland and Bohemia into one state under the leadership of the great Polish statesman and ruler, Boleslav I (992-1018). This circumstance sealed the fate of the Slavic peoples between the Elbe and the Oder rivers and opened the way for a new phase of the German push toward the East, but also for the penetration of Western culture among the Czechs and Poles through the German intermediary.

Again the Papacy sought to break the dangerous system of proprietary churches and to reduce the influence of the Reichskirche. But Gregory VII's (1073-1085) attempt at the encirclement of Germany by its neighboring states failed owing to the Czech refusal, the Czech Duke Vratislav remaining faithful to the excommunicated Emperor Henry IV.

The Germans were given new opportunities to secure their position among the Slavs along the Baltic and the Elbe. The foundations of the new colonial Germany, of Berlin, and of Prussia were laid by the dukes Henry the Lion and Albert the Bear and by the introduction of the Teutonic Order into Poland for the purpose of converting and fighting the Baltic Prussians and Lithuanians and the Finnic Estonians. Only the diversion of imperial interest toward Sicily and southern Italy, under the last Hohenstaufen, probably saved Bohemia and Poland from the fate of the Polabian Slavs.

The result of this development was to incorporate the western Slavs definitively into the sphere of Roman and Latin culture. Byzantine cultural influence could maintain itself only in Bulgaria, owing to the fact that it was propagated through Slavic letters and liturgy. From Bulgaria it spread to Serbia, but the Byzantines did not succeed in extending their political and cultural influence into Croatia. So it happened that the southern Slavs were divided, the Croats and the Slovenes developing within the Roman and Latin world, the Bulgarians and Serbians within that of Byzantium.

In spite of the circumstance that the Byzantine Church tolerated the use of national liturgies and favored the development of national literatures, the relationship between the Bulgarians and Byzantium did not evolve amicably. The Byzantines ruined the only opportunity of incorporating Bulgaria into their empire on the basis of mutual collaboration and consent when the proud Empress Zoë refused to accept the Greek-educated Symeon the Great of Bulgaria (893-927) as father-in-law for her son Constantine Porphyrogennitus. The resulting feud assumed the character of a bloody national war between Slavs and Greeks. It led to the tragic end of the First Bulgarian Empire and the incorporation of Bulgaria as a conquered province of Byzantium. The Bulgarians never accepted this as a definitive end of their independence.

A happier relationship was established between the Byzantines and their new converts, the Russians. The Kievan state, built with the help of Norsemen, soon became a mighty power beyond the Carpathian Mountains. Its capital, Kiev, became an important commercial center between Byzantium, the Arab world, and western Europe, particularly Germany and Scandinavia. A lively cultural activity developed there, fostered by Slavonic literary influences from Bulgaria and from Bohemia. Byzantine artists taught the Russians the secrets of their crafts, and Byzantine bishops instructed them in Eastern theology and spiritual life. In a short time the Russians mastered their methods and achieved an unusually high degree of civilization. In spite of its Byzantine Christianity and civilization, the State of Kiev maintained a lively contact with the Latin West, regarding itself as an active partner in the European commonwealth of nations. The distance from Byzantium guaranteed Kiev against imperial intervention in its internal affairs; while recognizing the Byzantine emperor as the supreme authority in the Christian commonwealth, the Kievans developed their own political system, a curious combination of democratic city-states with monarchic principles.

This loose political system, however, proved fatal to Kiev. Weakened by internal strife between the princes of the ruling dynasty and by invasions of new Asiatic nomads, the Turkic Cumans, which cut it off from access to the Black Sea, Kiev declined steadily. The Mongols rapidly annihilated Russian political freedom, and for two centuries Russia disappeared from the European scene.

A new era began for all the Slavic nations with the thirteenth century. This century is regarded as a period in which medieval civilization was reaching its peak. Many features which had hitherto characterized European life were maturing, and others were appearing to herald progress in new directions.

This is particularly evident in the development of relations between the Papacy and secular power. Here the ideological process which had already started in the ninth century under Nicholas I, and was especially promoted by Gregory VII in the eleventh century, reached its apogee with Innocent III (1198-1216). The principle of the superiority of the spiritual power over the temporal had been boldly launched by Gregory VII. It was defended by his followers, the reformers, who were hostile to any intervention of laymen in Church affairs, and was further elaborated by the canonists until it became the basis of relationships between the Papacy and the rulers of medieval Europe. This relationship was described by the canonists in allegoric comparisons with the sun and the moon, the soul and the body, gold and lead.

This new political theory represented a complete reversal of the earlier Christian political speculation on the basis of Hellenistic ideas on kingship. In this political order it was the emperor who was regarded as the representative of God on earth, charged with the care not only of secular but also of divine things and thus of leading his subjects to God. In the West these imperial prerogatives were gradually being transferred to the Pope, and with the conquest of Constantinople by the Latins in 1204, even the Eastern imperial dignity seemed to have been deprived of its former superiority and to be overshadowed by the dignity of the supreme pontiff. One of the canonists defined this new situation in the following words: [1] "The Pope is above the emperor, because he is himself the true emperor."

Innocent III was aware of an historical connection between the old and the new balance of powers. He traced this transformation to Charlemagne, pretending that when crowning Charlemagne emperor (800), the Pope had transferred the imperium from the Greeks to the Germans.[2] The weakness of this explanation must have been realized already by

Innocent IV, who declared in 1245 that Christ, the true king and the true priest, had given to Peter and to his successors two keys, those of the sacerdotal and royal monarchies.[3] These ideas, which the reformists were popularizing in their treatises on the fullness of the papal power, were further elaborated by the canonists.

These new theories were first tested during the investiture contest. Thanks to the fervent activity of the reformists, who were passionately opposed to any intervention by secular princes in Church affairs, the Papacy was able to win this long and bitter struggle and to drive a wedge into the Germanic system of proprietary churches. The Concordat of Worms (1122) gave back to the popes the free disposal of ecclesiastical benefices in Italy, and during the weak rule of Lothair II (1125-1137) and Conrad III (1138-1152) the Roman Curia was also able to bring the Reichskirche under its direct supervision. The newly established practice of appointment to rich ecclesiastical offices appeared to be a source of important income for the Curia. So it happened that the Papacy not only became the most important factor in the Middle Ages both in the ecclesiastical and in the political sphere, but could also dispose of rich financial resources beyond the means of any of the contemporary rulers.

The main consequence of this new situation was, of course, the debasement of the imperial idea, which was now represented by the German kingdom. In spite of that, it had not lost its claims to universality. Lombardy, the Kingdom of Arles, and Bohemia—all non-German lands—were still part of the Empire. The emperors themselves were to be blamed in great part for this debasement. They neglected to strengthen the ideological basis of the imperium in the face of the growing prestige of the sacerdotium, enhanced by the work of the promoters of the canon law, who also made extremely able use of some principles of Roman jurisprudence to sustain the importance of the sacerdotium and of the supreme pontiff.

The great Hohenstaufen ruler Frederick I Barbarossa (1152-1190) made a bold attempt to restore the dignity of the imperial idea. With the help of his jurists, headed by his chancellor, Rainald of Dassel, Frederick I revived the traditions of royal theocracy initiated by Charlemagne and defended passionately the divine origin of the secular power and its ascendancy over the ecclesiastical power. He succeeded through feudal bonds in recovering a complete hold on the Reichskirche and in securing on this basis his royal rights against the German dukes and princes.

These old Germanic conceptions of kingship proved, however, inadequate to re-establish the imperial authority in Lombardy. Frederick had underestimated the rising power of the Lombard cities and their quick-witted burghers, and it never occurred to him that they presaged a revolution in national life. He wanted to force the Lombard cities back to the ancient feudal status and to reduce them to mere vassalage. The result was that the cities joined the papal party, and a long, fierce, and bloody struggle between the Ghibellines, or the imperials, and the Guelfs, or anti-imperials, followed.

During this struggle Frederick I lost the possible ideological support of the experts in Roman law, the study of which had started to flourish in Bologna. When he scored his first victory over Milan, the students of Roman law expected him to proclaim it once more to be the foundation of justice in Italy, the framework of the administrative system, and the inspiration of imperial rule. Frederick remained blind to these possibilities and, instead, ordered the law experts to study and interpret the old feudal customs. Revolt followed revolt until Frederick's defeat by the Lombard League at Legnano in 1176 and the peace of Constance in 1183, which secured for the Lombard cities recognition as great corporate vassals and feudal investiture for their consuls—an irrevocable break with the old traditions and one more step in the direction of a new order in Europe.

The emperor's capitulation to Alexander III (1177) left the issue between the imperium and the sacerdotium undecided. The Papacy retained its independence, and the Third Council of the Lateran (1179) demonstrated once again that the Pope's leadership of the West was an uncontested reality.

The greatest diplomatic success of Frederick I was the negotiation of a marriage between Constance, a posthumous daughter of Roger II and the heiress presumptive to the Norman Kingdom of Sicily, and his son Henry. Henry VI, after affirming his authority in Sicily and failing to improve upon his father's regime in Germany, decided to make Italy the center and backbone of his power and to this end divided it into provinces under the rule of officials directly responsible to him. He even planned to extend the system to the Papal States. Under his energetic rule the complete victory of the imperium over the sacerdotium seemed imminent. Not satisfied with Sicily and his western empire, Henry VI harbored the design of rebuilding the Mediterranean empire of ancient Rome, embracing Syria, Palestine, and even Constantinople. Henry VI's sudden death (1197), however, turned over a new page in the history of the contest between the imperium and the sacerdotium. It was indeed an event of supreme importance, for it brought about a change in the general situation such as seldom occurs in history. The Papacy, which seemed to have reached its lowest ebb, recovered and rose to undreamed-of heights under Innocent III.

The new Pope, a born ruler, denied the royal theocracy and improved upon the theoretical supremacy of the sacerdotium by calling himself Vicar of God, or Vicar of Christ, i.e., less than God but more than man.[4] He had the opportunity of putting his principles into practice by reserving to himself the right to give definitive recognition as emperor during the strife of the two rivals—the Welf Otto of Brunswick and the Hohenstaufen Philip. When Otto IV had started to follow in the footsteps of Henry VI, the Pope engineered the election of Henry's son, Frederick II, whose guardian he had been during his infancy. With the help of France he sealed the fate of Otto IV at Bouvines. The Fourth Council of the Lateran (1215), which ratified the deposition of Otto IV and the election of Frederick II, made it clear to contemporary Europe that the Papacy had the right to dispose of the imperial crown.

Despite his intellectual qualities and high statesmanship, Frederick II (1211-1250) did not succeed in saving the imperial idea from steady degeneration. He was, above all, king of Sicily. He was less successful in confirming his power in Germany than Henry VI, and his attempt to make Italy the basis of his empire and to establish there a monarchic and absolutist regime was thwarted by the Papacy in alliance with the Guelfs.[5] The popes displayed their strength by repeated excommunication of Frederick II and his son Conrad IV (1250-1254). The great interregnum (1254-1273), characterized by the double election in 1257 of two foreigners, Richard of Cornwall and Alfonso X of Castile, was a sad epilogue to the victory of the sacerdotium over the imperium, which made the lofty imperial title almost meaningless. Finally, papal supremacy also became evident in Italy when, in 1266, Urban IV offered the crown of Sicily, regarded as a papal fief, to Charles of Anjou, brother of Louis IX of France. With him a new factor entered into the medieval history of Europe. The ambitions of the Anjous soon led them to other scenes than Sicily—to Italy, to the Balkans, to Hungary, and to Poland, where their interests often conflicted with those of Slavic nations.

After the decline of the imperium, only the Papacy seemed to be able to realize the idea of political universality which had been so intimately connected with the Roman Empire. However, in spite of intensive theoretical propaganda for the beliefs that there was only one source of all kingship in the world and that this source was the sacerdotium, the Papacy did not succeed in making its theocracy a reality. Although some of its representatives came very near to their goal, their work was often interrupted by long interregna such as that of 1268, which lasted more than three years. The electoral practice was also a handicap. It was natural that the college of cardinals would be in favor of an oligarchic rule rather than of a full development of the papal autocracy.

The main reason for this failure lay, however, in the growth of the idea of sovereign states, especially in the territories which were not parts of the new Roman Empire, as renovated by the German kings—namely in England, France, Aragon,⁶ Castile, and Portugal. The kings of these realms were able to strengthen the dynastic ties uniting their subjects and to stabilize their rule by consolidating the feudal system and improving the primitive administrative means inherited from the early Middle Ages.

The gradual division of the population into four estates—those of the higher clergy, the aristocracy, the burghers, and the common people—facilitated administration. It appears that the Normans were the main pioneers in the formation of a new conception of state, one with a centralized administration and a dependable bureaucracy. At least such improvements in government are to be found in Norman Sicily and also in the Anglo-Norman state. Similar features can be detected in the system which the Hohenstaufens Henry VI and Frederick II wanted to introduce into Italy.

A latent opposition can be detected also in these states to the acceptance of the papal theocracy. It flared up particularly in the Sicilian kingdom under Henry VI and Frederick II and also under Manfred and the Anjous, but it was equally strong in England, as the English struggle over investiture clearly shows. On the other hand, because the Roman Curia needed the help of the French kings in its struggle with the Hohenstaufens, it was obliged to attenuate its claims in France. Furthermore, the national sentiment based on community of language which was slowly awakening in the thirteenth century helped to make those states increasingly conscious of their national sovereignty.

In this respect a most spectacular change was being enacted in France. Philip II Augustus (1180-1223) continued the work of the early Capetians by further consolidating the monarchy and laying solid bases for an organized state. Thus France reached its medieval golden age under St. Louis IX (1226-1270), regarded as the ideal medieval king. After his brother, Charles of Anjou, had in 1266 accepted the Pope's offer of the crown of Sicily, France became more and more interested in Italian affairs. As king of Sicily and Naples (1268-1285), Charles conceived a grandiose plan for a revival of the Latin Empire in the East, which would replace the Byzantine Empire. The second crusade of his brother, St. Louis, against Tunis (1270) was probably inspired by Charles, who harbored plans of domination over the Mediterranean. The scheme ended in disaster with the death of the saintly king in Tunisia. The revolt of the Sicilians against the French, inaugurated by the massacre of the Sicilian Vespers (1282), put an end to all such ambitious ventures, while Sicily became an independent kingdom under the rule of the Spanish House of Aragon.

France's leading position in the West became manifest under Philip

IV the Fair (1285-1314). Defying Boniface VIII's prohibition on the levying of taxes on the clergy, Philip found support in public opinion in France. This had been prepared by the writings of Philip's legists, especially Peter Dubois. Moreover, in his opposition to the Pope, Philip found an ally in Edward I of England, and the Pope was forced to give way. When, however, Boniface VIII published his famous bull *Unam Sanctam* (1302), in which he set out quite uncompromisingly his claim to superiority over all national states and rulers, Philip protested most vehemently and ordered his councilor, Nogaret, to bring the Pope to France, that he might be tried by a council to be convoked by the king. Death saved Boniface from further humiliation. But the reign of Clement V (1305-1314), a Frenchman, initiated a new epoch in the history of the Papacy known as the Babylonian Captivity (1309-1376). During this period the popes resided on French soil at Avignon and were generally strongly influenced by the French kings.

It was this new conception of state sovereignty and centralized government which had given France the courage to assert its national interests and to defy the claims of papal theocracy. Of course, in spite of this spectacular appearance in political history, the new idea of sovereignty and of an organized state had not yet fully developed according to modern conceptions. The central authority which had started so successfully to assert itself in Naples and Sicily, England and France, could only be weakened by prolonged wars. These brought about a decline of the Sicilian state, while the Hundred Years' War between France and England allowed the high aristocracy of both kingdoms to claim an important share in government. This development was foreshadowed by the concession of the Magna Carta in 1215 in England. In this way another conception of government was introduced into medieval Europe.

Because of the disastrous contest between the emperors and the popes, the German kingdom suffered a greater loss in sovereignty than any other state. Under the Ottonian dynasty, the royal power was rooted, above all, in an immense royal estate which allowed the kings to support a great number of knights. The royal domains were considerably diminished during the investiture struggle and became the property of mighty nobles, whose help was indispensable to the kings. Frederick I started to rebuild the royal domains with the money he obtained from Italy, but what he won was lost again in the ensuing phases of the struggle. The Hohenstaufen family estates in Swabia were an important asset, but not sufficient for all needs. After the extinction of the dynasty they were divided among neighboring noble families, and so the future kings lost even this base on which to build their power. In proportion as the royal power was being weakened, that of the dukes and counts grew in importance. The extension of the old tribal duchies was diminished by division. Bavaria, for example, was gradually divided into four dukedoms: Bavaria proper, Austria, Styria, and Carantia. Bavaria proper passed into the hands of the Wittelsbachs, Austria into those of the Babenbergs. The great Duchy of Saxony was dismembered by Frederick Barbarossa after he had defeated its duke, Henry the Lion. Only Brunswick and Lüneburg remained in the possession of Henry and his descendants, the Guelfs. The major western part was added to the archbishopric of Cologne, and the remainder, which continued to be called the Duchy of Saxony, was given to the son of Albert the Bear, who became the founder of a new Saxon line. About the middle of the thirteenth century even this duchy was divided into two lines, those of Wittenberg and Lauenburg.

The Wittelsbach family, which acquired the Rhenish Palatinate, also divided into two branches about 1255. These divisions coincided with an important development in Germany's political life. Until the middle of the thirteenth century territories usually remained undivided among the princes' descendants. The reason for this lay in the fact that although the private fiefs were hereditary in the princely families, the offices of margrave, count, and duke were, at least in theory, at the king's disposal. The weakening of the royal authority during the interregnum, however, caused this principle to fall into oblivion. So it happened that not only the private fiefs but also territories and offices were regarded as hereditary in the princely families, which disposed of them as they pleased without awaiting the king's approval. As a consequence, Germany broke up into a multitude of hereditary principalities. The hereditary principle was further strengthened by private treaties among the princely houses to further their own interest.

The other tribal duchies had a similar fate. Swabia and Franconia lost their dukes. Lorraine was divided into the duchy of Brabant and other smaller territories. The new cities, which had been granted many privileges by the kings and nobles, also became self-governing and almost independent. Unable to count on the protection of the royal authority, they were forced to form leagues among themselves for protection against the encroachment of princes. The most important were the Rhenish Confederation on the Rhine and the Hanseatic League, headed by Lübeck in North Germany.

The territories which are particularly important for the medieval history of the Slavs were the Margraviate of Brandenburg, in the hands of the Ascanians; Lusatia, divided into Lower and Upper Lusatia; and Meissen. These territories still contained a high proportion of their original Slavic populations; their number was, however, steadily diminishing through German colonization and assimilation. The margraviates of Meissen and Thuringia, together with the Saxon Palatinate, were in the hands of the Wettin family from 1261 on. These territories were often coveted by the kings of Bohemia and Poland. Poland was, moreover, anxious to regain the possession of western Pomerania, on the Baltic, which was still ruled by a Slavic dynasty and, although nominally part of the Empire, was practically independent. The Slavic population in the counties of Holstein and Mecklenburg was also being rapidly absorbed by the influx of German colonists.

In spite of the continuous divisions which went on, the importance of the great family estates increased. The smaller extent of the territory permitted more effective government, and so it came about that during the second half of the twelfth century there had already emerged in Germany a number of these territorial states whose rulers exercised the administrative and judicial rights which belonged to the king. This situation was sealed by Frederick II, who granted to the territorial rulers full sovereignty in their lands. The dynastic idea could not, of course, develop in these circumstances as well as it did in other western kingdoms. The great nobles insisted on their right to approve royal successions. Thus Germany became an electoral kingdom, the right of election being reserved to the seven most important princes—the Kurfürsten.[7]

At the beginning of the thirteenth century a new territory was being added to the empire on the Baltic. There, the neighbors of the Slavic Pomeranians, the Poles, and the Russians were the Baltic Prussians, Lithuanians, and Letts, speaking a tongue which had no affinity to those of the Slavs or the Germans. Being remote from the Western and Latin centers of civilization, they were still pagans in the thirteenth century. German influence first took firm root in these lands in 1198, when some merchants from Bremen founded the city of Riga at the mouth of the river Dvina as a storehouse for their merchandise. The first missionary to the Letts was the Augustinian monk Meinhart, who also became their first bishop. As the Christianization of the Letts made little progress, Bishop Albert of Livonia (1199-1229) conceived the idea of founding a military order for the promotion of Christianity, the Knights of the Sword (Fratres militiae Christi). With the help of a crusading army of German knights, he succeeded in conquering the whole of Latvia. King Philip of Swabia gave the country as a fief to Albert and the order. German political and cultural influence penetrated even farther toward the north when, between 1207 and 1217, Albert and his order conquered Estonia with the help of the Danish king Waldemar. This country was inhabited by a people racially akin to the Finns. The city of Dorpat (Yurjev, Tartu), of Slavic foundation, was conquered and became the seat of the German bishop of Estonia and a new focus of German political and cultural influence.

The Poles were more interested in the Christianization of their neighbors, the Prussians and the Lithuanians. Some success had been achieved in Prussia by the Cistercian monks of Lekno, in Great Poland, and of Oliva, near Gdańsk (Danzig). Christian, one of these missionaries, became the first bishop of Prussia in 1215. The missions, however, did not progress well because of the jealousy between the Papacy and the Polish princes who protected the missions. The latter planned to extend their domination over the whole land to be converted, but the Papacy desired to gain direct authority over the territories of the Prussian missions and to keep the converts under its own rule. A pagan reaction ruined a great deal of the first results. Even the Abbey of Oliva was destroyed and the Polish district of Chełmno (Kulm) suffered from repeated incursions.

This led the Polish duke, Conrad of Mazovia, to conceive an idea similar to that of Albert of Livonia, and supported by Bishop Christian, he founded in 1228 a new military order, the Brotherhood of Dobrzyń Knights. At the same time he was also negotiating with the Teutonic Order, which had been founded during the siege of Acre in Palestine by the crusaders (1191) and which, from 1197, had also been established in Europe.

It was Conrad's intention to entrust to the Teutonic Knights the protection of Chełmno and to keep this land unler his sovereignty. The grand-master of the order, Hermann von Salza, intended, however, to bring this territory under the sovereignty of the order and to attach it, together with the territories which he hoped to conquer, to the empire. Therefore, at the opening of the negotiations with the Polish duke, the grand-master asked the Emperor Frederick II to confirm the grants of land to be given by Conrad and to confer on him the privileges of German princes in the Prussian territories to be conquered.

The first detachment of the Knights arrived in Prussia in 1230. With the help of a falsified document pretending that Conrad had granted them full sovereignty over Chełmno, the Knights obtained the confirmation of those rights from the Pope. They were further strengthened by the fusion of the Brotherhood of Dobrzyń Knights with their order. Furthermore, when in 1237, the military forces of the Knights of the Sword were annihilated by the pagan Lithuanians, the Teutonic Order absorbed the remnant of the Knights of the Sword and assumed the task of pacifying Livonia and Estonia. From that time on, the power of the order grew constantly. Aided by crusaders from Germany, the order founded in conquered Prussian lands a new German state on the Baltic.[8]

This was an odd result of the crusading idea, which had lost much of its flavor by the thirteenth century while its unchristian basis became increasingly apparent. Just as the application of this idea in the Near East had provoked a reaction on the part of the "infidel" Arabs and Turks, so did its application in the North provoke a remarkable reaction by the pagan Lithuanians. Constantly harassed by the Knights and the armies of crusaders from Germany, Bohemia, and Poland, the Lithuanians, reinforced by the refugee Prussians, became fierce warriors. Under unceasing pressure from the northwest, the Lithuanians learned the advantage of a more solid political organization. Their first great ruler, the Grand Duke Mendovg, succeeded about 1240 in uniting the different tribes into a single political unit. By accepting Christianity—he received a royal title from Pope Innocent IV—Mendovg gained a respite for his nation and continued to extend his rule over neighboring Russian principalities, still under Mongolian rule. Mendovg's relapse into paganism should have shown the pious crusaders how ineffective their missionary methods were. Although still pagans, the Lithuanians became a major power in northern Europe and were able to influence Polish and Russian history profoundly during the thirteenth and fourteenth centuries.

This expansion of German influence in the Baltic is intimately connected with economic evolution in Germany and in the rest of the empire. In this respect, despite their disturbing and almost chaotic political situation, Germany and Italy were registering a steady and sometimes even unexpected progress in economic development. The colonization of the Slavic lands on the Baltic opened great possibilities for German commerce. The new cities became commercial centers and their number grew constantly. Wisby, on the island of Gotland, was founded about 1160, Rostock about 1218, Stralsund and Gdańsk (Danzig) about 1230, Wismar about 1269, Greifswald in Pomerania in 1240. The old town of Lüneburg rose to prominence as a commercial center at the end of the twelfth century. The oldest of these foundations, Lübeck (1158), took the initiative of inviting the merchants of all the Baltic cities into a powerful commercial organization—the Hanseatic League—which took over the flourishing commerce with Novgorod, the Baltic lands, England, and the rest of Europe.[9] The bases of operation of the league were the steelyard in London, which existed from the middle of the twelfth century on, and the comptoir in Bruges. The latter city was the most important international commercial center in Europe at this period. Merchants of all prominent trading centers established their comptoirs in this Flemish town. There Flanders and Brabant obtained the English wool which their burghers needed for the manufacture of cloth, which was exported from Bruges by the Hanse toward the north and by other merchants into France, Germany, Spain, and Italy. Bruges was also the terminal port to which the Venetians exported spices and luxury articles from the East for distribution in the northern parts of Europe.

Italian merchandise was reaching Bruges and northern France not by sea, but overland. The cities on the Rhine, of course, profited from this trade in addition to commerce in their own products and the Rhine and Moselle wines. Maritime relations with Bruges and northern France were inaugurated by Genoa and Venice only in the first half of the fourteenth century.

In Italy itself, the political desolation and bloody feuds between cities jealous of one another and between the Ghibellines and the Guelfs did not stop economic progress. It is true that this provoked some unorthodox movements like the fraternities of the Flagellants, which also spread over southern Germany and reached Bohemia; but on the whole, despite political insecurity, economic life flourished. Industry made considerable progress in the Lombard cities, where the appearance of some capitalistic elements can already be discerned.

The towns became city-states, extending their sway also over neighboring villages while they continued to accumulate riches, and commercial exchanges flourished, thanks to the opening of new markets in the Near East. The patricians of Venice and Genoa, with their vast fleets, were masters of the Mediterranean sea routes. They ruled over important colonies on the territory of the Byzantine Empire, and their daring seamen had reached the shores of the Black Sea on one side and the Azores on the other. With the crusaders, they had penetrated into Syria and Palestine. The reconquest by the Moslems of most of the Christian states founded by the crusaders did not stop their commercial progress. From Egypt and from Syria they extended their relations into the interior of the Islamic world, retaining a very lucrative monopoly of commercial intercourse between the Middle East and western Europe.

The kind of merchandise they were exporting from the East—spices and luxury wares—assured them much larger profits than the merchandise in which the Hanseatic League dealt. They had learned commercial methods from the Byzantines and the Arabs and developed these further by their own experience. Their explorers had penetrated even into the interior of Asia. Franciscan missionaries were opening possibilities of intercourse with the Mongolian Empire, extending from the Volga region as far as the shores of the Pacific. The Venetian brothers Niccolo and Matteo Polo even reached China and brought back Kubla Khan's request to the Pope for a body of learned men to instruct his people in Christian religion and in the liberal arts. The long interregnum of 1269 was in great part responsible for Rome's failure to meet the Khan's request. The young Marco Polo's description of his experiences in China and in India, in his *Il Milione,* gave medieval scholars the first glimpse into the strange cultures of the Far East.

Economic progress was accompanied by a considerable advance in cultural life. In this respect the thirteenth century was able to build on the foundations laid by the Renaissance of the twelfth century.[10] The best political conditions for this advance developed in France, thanks to the consolidation of the royal power. The French Capetians not only were able to assert their rights in face of overweening vassals, but also soon perceived the importance in national life of the rising cities and quickly learned how to control them. France also enjoyed the lion's share in the contact with Eastern culture during the First Crusade. Through its barons, established in the conquered lands, it was in touch with the culture of Byzantium and the Near East. It was no wonder, then, that so many cultural initiatives in the thirteenth century came from this country. The Gothic style of architecture which is so characteristic of the thirteenth and fourteenth centuries originated in France. With the lofty spires of its cathedrals it expressed so appropriately the ideals of this period, especially the mystical craving for the divine and the desire for a more popular approach to Christian teaching. From France the new style spread to England and to Germany. It represents the best cultural achievements of the Middle Ages, being one of the most perfect forms of architecture of all times; it symbolized fittingly Catholic universality and spread also from Germany to the Slavic lands and, through the Baltic and Poland, reached the confines of native and Byzantine culture in Russia. The Gothic style penetrated into Italy only in a sporadic way. The Italians preferred to develop further the artistic forms of their Roman inheritance.

On the other hand, the Norman and Hohenstaufen kings of Sicily favored an artistic style blending old Christian, Romanesque, Byzantine, and Islamic elements.

France also gave Europe one of its first universities, that of Paris, founded about 1200. Higher learning was, however, not a French monopoly. Similar foundations were made at Bologna and Oxford at about the same time. These universities were soon joined by those of Naples (1224), Toulouse (1229), Salamanca (1243), and Rome (1294-95). The new institutions of advanced learning became the centers of the scholastic philosophy, which, based on Aristotle's philosophical system, was exploring and explaining the depths of Christian teaching. Its leader was St. Thomas Aquinas, but the names of Alexander of Hales, St. Albert the Great, and St. Bonaventure and of others were also famous.

A more humanistic and popular interpretation of Christianity was attempted by the founders of two great new orders—St. Francis and St. Dominic. The Franciscan and Dominican houses were built not in the country, like the abbeys of the Benedictines and the Cistercians, but in the cities, where their friars ministered to the new class of burghers, another new feature in the development of religious life.

Learning and the writing of books were, however, no longer limited, as in previous centuries, almost exclusively to religious subjects and to the clergy. For the first time the monopoly of the Latin language was questioned, during the twelfth and thirteenth centuries. In this direction, too, France took the lead. The movement started in French aristocratic circles and soon became an important factor influencing the cultural progress of the Middle Ages. The chivalrous spirit which characterizes this movement supplied, for the first time, norms of social behavior to be observed by the upper classes.[11] This chivalrous spirit gave the main impulse to the creation of a new genre of French poetry which was soon to inspire and to dominate the literary activity of other nations. The poets looked for inspiration first in their national tradition. Their phantasy transformed King Arthur and his knights into legendary figures celebrated as ideals of the chivalrous spirit. The poets were, however, also attracted by the figures of classical tradition, already rediscovered in the twelfth century, especially by Alexander the Great, Aeneas, and the legends of Troy and Thebes. Oriental legends also captivated their imagination.

French poetry spread to Germany under Frederick I. The German counterpart of the French Christian of Troyes was Wolfram von Eschenbach with his Parzival. On the other hand, this literary movement gave the Germans the greatest epic song of the Middle Ages, the *Nibelungenlied,* whose definitive edition dates from the very end of the twelfth century.

Besides epic poetry, lyrics also won great popularity. This kind of poetry was first cultivated by the troubadours of Provence, who composed not only love songs but also biting verses criticizing the political situation. From Provence the love epic (*Minnesang*) spread to the north of France, to England, Germany, Italy, Catalonia, and Portugal.

But not only epic and lyric poetry were cultivated in national languages. France took the lead in vernacular prose history with Godeffroy de Villehardouin, whose *Conquête de Constantinople* chronicled the Fourth Crusade (1204). It is one of the oldest French compositions in prose. He was followed by Jean de Joinville, whose history of St. Louis IX gave France its first memoirs. Giovanni Villani was the first Italian vernacular historian. Eike von Repgow composed in the Saxon dialect, between 1215 and 1235, the oldest law book of the Middle Ages, the *Sachsenspiegel.*

This literary development testifies, at the same time, to a surprising growth of the secular spirit. This impression is strengthened even more when account is taken of the existence of another literary genre very popular among wandering clerics and students, who liked to relieve their feelings in lusty drinking songs and ribald love ditties. This kind of literature may have been, of course, outweighed by the numerous and remarkable religious hymns composed at the same period. It is, nonetheless, interesting to notice such a growth of secular literary motifs at this period and the popularity which they enjoyed, not only in aristocratic circles but also among the burghers. This kind of literature offered a serious competition to religious literature and broke the monopoly of the clergy and of the Latin language in letters: this growth of secularism may provide an additional reason for the failure of the papal theocracy to find full realization.

The progress in cultural fields during this period was so spectacular that the West started to compete with Byzantine culture and to outshine Islamic civilization. Dante and Petrarch were the forerunners of the great Western Renaissance. However, in many respects Byzantium was still leading. It is true that it had lost most of its importance in European history when it had fallen into the hands of the Latins and when its empire was limited only to its possessions in Asia Minor. But even so, the emperors of Nicaea and the despots of Epirus played an important role in the Balkans and influenced strongly the rise of the Balkan Slavic states. Byzantium rose once more into prominence when, in 1261, Michael VIII Palaeologus reconquered Constantinople and a great part of the Empire from the Latins. Byzantine culture then experienced a new period of renascence, and the mosaics and frescoes of the time of the Palaeologan dynasty, recently rediscovered and restored, delight the specialists with their freshness and their lively composition. This new wave of Byzantine cultural revival overflowed into Bulgaria and Serbia, leaving in both these lands numerous monuments which are still their pride. Its waters also reached Italy, where they fertilized the receptive Italian artistic spirit. This new Byzantine renascence even reached Russia, still submerged beneath the Mongolian flood but seeking its unification and liberation.

This gives a hasty sketch of the framework inside which the Slavs had to build their political, cultural, and economic life in the thirteenth and fourteenth centuries. Their lands were part of Europe, and all that happened among other nations in the West and in the South was bound to influence their history and the growth of their civilization. Naturally, these influences were not always equally marked among all Slavic nations and did not leave the same impression on all features of their life. Two Slavic nations were, however, particularly exposed to Western influences and to all happenings in the Empire and in Germany—the Czechs and the Poles.

NOTES

1. The anonymous author of the *Summa Coloniensis*, published by J. F. v. Schulte, "Zur Geschichte der Literatur über das Dekret Gratians" in *Sitzungsberichte* of the Acad. of Vienna, Phil. histor. Kl. 69 (1870), p. 111. Cf. however M. Stickler, *Imperator vicarius Papae* (see Bibl.). Similar declarations cannot be always understood in the strict hierocratic sense.

2. Cf. F. Kempf, *Papsttum und Kaisertum bei Innocent III* (Rome, 1954), pp. 65-84.

3. In his letter to Frederick II published by E. Winkelmann, *Acta imperii inedita* (Innsbruck, 1885), vol. II, p. 698, No. 1035.

4. Especially in his *Sermo secundus consecr. pontificis*, P. L., vol. 217, col. 658A.

5. E. Kantorowicz, *Kaiser Friedrich der Zweite* (Berlin, 1928), pp. 340 ff.

6. For the growth of the royal power in Aragon see the recent study by P. E. Schramm, "Der König von Aragon: Seine Stellung im Staatsrecht (1276-1410)," *Histor. Jahrbuch*, 74 (1955), pp. 99-123.

7. For more details concerning this transformation of Germany's constitution and economic evolution see G. Barr. lough's *Mediaeval Germany, 911-1250* (Oxford, 1938). In vol. I the author i views the history of Germany from the election of the first king to the Hohenstaufens. Vol. II contains translations of essays by prominent German scholars on different problems in German history. The essays are well related and give a clear picture of the problems reviewed here.

8. A short history of the order and of its relationship with Poland is given by Z. Wojciechowski, *Territorial Development of Prussia in Relation to the Polish Homeland* (Toruń, 1936) and by St. Zajączkowski, *Rise and Fall of the Teutonic Order in Prussia* (Toruń, 1935). The latter publication is a resumé of the author's Polish work, *Polska a Zakon Krzyzacki* (Lwów, 1929). The most recent work on the order's history is that by Rudolf ten Haaf, *Deutschordenstaat und Deutschordensballeien: Untersuchungen über Leistung und Sonderung der Deutschordensprovinzen in Deutschland vom 13 bis zum 16. Jht.* (Göttingen, 1951, 2nd ed., 1954). The same author gave useful bibliographical information in his booklet *Kurze Bibliographie zur Geschichte des Deutschen Ordens 1198 bis 1561* (Kitzingen, 1949). Recent works on the order's history and collections of source material are reviewed by M. Hellmann, "Neue Arbeiten zur Geschichte des Deutschen Ordens" in *Historisches Jahrbuch*, 75 (1956), pp. 201-13. See also Ch. IX.

9. A useful bibliographical survey of Hanseatic history to the year 1937 was given by W. Vogel in *Revue historique*, vol. 179 (1937), "La Hanse d'après les publications récentes," pp. 1-33. Cf. also K. Pagel, *Die Hanse* (Oddenburg, 1943).

10. Cf. C. H. Haskins, *The Renaissance of the Twelfth Century* (Cambridge, Mass., 1939). See also *Twelfth-Century Europe and the Foundations of Modern Society*, ed. by M. Clagett, G. Post, R. Reynolds (Madison, Wis., 1961).

11. Cf. S. Painter, *French Chivalry: Chivalric Ideas and Practices in Mediaeval France* (Baltimore, 1948).

Chapter II

THE LAST PŘEMYSLIDES, BOHEMIA, AND POLAND

Přemysl I of Bohemia obtains the royal title—Blessed Agnes of Bohemia, the emperor's son, and the King of England—King Wenceslas I and Austria—Přemysl II, Poland, and Lithuania—Union of Austria with Bohemia —Přemysl II and Rudolf of Habsburg—"Manifesto to the Poles"—Wenceslas II, king of Bohemia and of Poland—A Czech-Polish Hungarian empire?—After the extinction of the Czech national dynasty

The countries of the Czechs—Bohemia and Moravia—were part of the Roman Empire renovated by the German Emperor Otto I (962), and naturally, the political developments in Germany had a profound influence on their national life. The strengthening of imperial power under Frederick Barbarossa and the quarrels among the members of the reigning native dynasty, the Přemyslides, made the Czechs feel the weight of the imperial power in their lands. Fortunately, Barbarossa and his successor Henry VI could not fully exploit this opportunity because they became entangled in Lombardy and Sicily.

Moreover, the Czechs were lucky to have found in their Duke Přemysl Otakar I (1197-1230) a gifted ruler whose statesmanship helped him to exploit the struggles for the German throne, after the death of Henry VI, for the benefit of his state and his dynasty.[1] The weakening of the royal authority in Germany enhanced the position of the Czech duke among German princes. He ruled over a vast realm which exceeded any of the territorial states then forming in Germany. Perfectly conscious of the fact that his country was a part of the Empire, he strove like its other great princes to take advantage of the conditions prevailing after Henry's death.

Přemysl was, moreover, fortunate to have found in his brother Vladislav III an understanding partner who not only resigned the throne of Bo-

21

hemia in his favor but, as margrave of Moravia, continued loyally to support all the moves of the ambitious Přemysl.

The latter made use of his right as one of the Kurfürsten—the emperor's cupbearers—to take part in the election of a new emperor, and charged his brother Adalbert, archbishop of Salzburg, to vote for Philip of Swabia. He then personally attended the coronation ceremony in Mainz (1198) and pledged his help to Philip against his rival Otto in return for the conferment of the royal title on the Přemyslide dynasty in the name of the emperor and his successors. He obtained, moreover, a confirmation of the boundaries of his kingdom, with the inclusion of Moravia, and the right of investiture of his bishops. It was a great success, especially when the interventions of Frederick I Barbarossa and of Henry VI into Bohemian affairs are recalled, interventions which had threatened to disintegrate the Bohemian dukedom into several territorial units directly dependent on the German king and Roman emperor.

Přemysl was, however, not unaware of the pretensions of the Papacy in the Empire, and when Innocent III, after some hesitation, had sided with Philip's adversary Otto IV, he realized that it would not be easy to obtain papal confirmation of the privileges granted by Philip of Swabia, the less so as the Curia could find an easy pretext for interfering in Bohemian affairs. Though Přemysl had several children by his wife Adleta, a member of the famous Wettin family of Meissen, he transferred his affections to Constance, sister of the Hungarian king Emmerich, and obtained annulment of his marriage from the bishop of Prague on the grounds of prohibited relationship. The repudiated wife appealed to the Roman Curia against the Bohemian bishop's decree, and the incident threatened to develop into the tragedy that marked the case of Philip II of France, when Innocent III treated him with so little mercy.

But the realization of Bohemia's importance in the Empire and in the contest for the imperial throne made the Pope deal with the Czech king somewhat differently. He invited him to join the party of Otto and to obtain his royal title from somebody who was in full possession of the imperial dignity and enjoyed, moreover, the Pope's approval. In spite of the hidden threat which accompanied this invitation, Přemysl hesitated and transferred his allegiance to Otto IV only when the latter's chances had altered for the better. The Pope confirmed the privileges bestowed on Přemysl by Otto IV, but was unwilling to grant his request to make Prague the seat of an archbishop. The king was prompted by the Přemyslides' previous experiences with the bishops of Prague, and the emperors' constant interference in this matter, as long as the bishopric of Prague was subordinated to the archbishopric of Mainz. Unwilling to grant as much as this, the Pope allowed him, at least, to proceed with the canonization (1204) of St. Procopius, abbot of Sázava, which had been the last stronghold of the Slavonic liturgy in Bohemia.

However, in the conflict that followed Přemysl's defection, Philip obtained the upper hand and moreover threatened to put another candidate on the Bohemian throne. But when Přemysl returned to his party, Philip dropped his candidate, and the two sovereigns sealed their friendship by pledging their infant children in marriage.

The Pope, disappointed, tried vainly to win the Czech back to his candidate for the imperial throne. Even when Philip was assassinated (1208), Přemysl continued his dynastic tradition of loyalty to the Hohenstaufens despite papal pressure. But Otto was excommunicated by the Pope for his attempt to invade Sicily in 1211, and Přemysl had become free from the threat which the Curia used against him because his repudiated wife had died. He was, therefore, the first among the princes to throw Otto over and to make his obeisance to the Hohenstaufen Frederick II, the Pope's new candidate. Přemysl's promptness turned the balance in Frederick's favor, and the young emperor recognized this service by confirming on September 26, 1212, "in the noble city of Basel" all the privileges conferred on the Czech king by Philip and dispensing him and his successors from attendance at the Reichstags, with the exception of those held near Bohemia in Bamberg, Nürnberg (Nuremburg), and Merseburg. The kings of Bohemia were further asked to provide three hundred knights for the imperial coronation in Italy, with the option of paying three hundred silver marks in lieu. This bull, stamped with the golden seal of the Sicilian kingdom, became the most valuable document in the royal archives of Bohemia. It opened a new phase in Bohemia's history.

Anxious to avert the last possible danger to his succession, Přemysl presented his son Wenceslas to the nobles for election as his successor, subject to confirmation by the emperor, which he duly obtained. Thus the right of primogeniture was at last established more firmly in the house of the Přemyslides, doing away with the incessant succession conflicts that had become the common feature of Bohemian history. These had been constantly provoked by the old order of succession, favoring the oldest member of the dynasty. Thanks to Přemysl's diplomatic skill, the realm was again regarded as one single unit, Moravia was integrated with Bohemia, and the title of margrave lost the ominous sound with which it had previously been associated. It was the starting point for unprecedented growth and development.

Bohemia's prestige increased rapidly in the empire and throughout contemporary Europe. Přemysl's first great success was the betrothal of his eight-year-old daughter, Agnes, to the fourteen-year-old King Henry, son and heir of Frederick II (1219).²

Agnes' betrothal, however, initiated a complicated chain of events which affected not only Bohemia's foreign relations, but also Europe's political and religious conditions. The matrimonial arrangement between the Czech king and the emperor did not accord with the views of Engelbert, archbishop of Cologne, who was the de facto ruler of Germany in the name of the young king. However much Frederick II's interests demanded friendly relations with France in order to obtain the necessary support at the Roman Curia, Engelbert, prompted no doubt by the traditional jealousy of the archbishops of Cologne toward their neighbor, worked for a rapprochement between Germany and France's rival, England. He won over Leopold of Babenberg, Duke of Austria, to his plan and proposed a marriage between the English king Henry III and Margaret, daughter of the duke. At the same time, he planned a union between the young German king and Henry III's youngest sister, Isabella. Engelbert imagined he had outwitted Přemysl by inducing the young King Henry to break the engagement with the Czech princess. But both the Czech king and the archbishop were outdone by the Duke of Austria, who, fearing complications with the emperor in the event of a union between the Babenbergs and the Plantagenets, secured the hand of Frederick II's son (1225) for his own daughter Margaret.

War broke out between Bohemia and Austria (1226). In the meantime, however, Přemysl did not reject the overtures made in Prague by Henry III of England for the hand of his daughter and was not unwilling to negotiate with the Plantagenets, but he was too anxious to avoid a conflict with the emperor to go to all lengths with the English king.³ The war with Austria, however, gave the Czechs very little satisfaction. All that Přemysl Otakar I was able to achieve was to prevent the Austrian duke from becoming a member of the regency after Engelbert's assassination and to obtain for his ally, Louis of Bavaria, a place among Henry's councilors.

Negotiations between London and Prague went on even after this incident, but without any tangible results. While an alliance between England and the empire was being projected by Engelbert's successor in Cologne and the Duke of Bavaria, Frederick II incurred excommunication for the repeated postponement of his promised crusade. Pope Gregory IX, seeking a substitute for the German throne, found his man, apparently with English encouragement, in the nephew of the late Emperor Otto IV, Otto of Brunswick. The old feud between the Ghibellines and the Guelfs threatened to flare up again on German soil. Louis of Bavaria, who had joined the combination, tried to attract Přemysl to his side, but the Czech king preferred to remain faithful to Frederick II.⁴

Thus once again the Curia's schemes were thwarted by Czech loyalty to the emperor and the Přemyslides' traditional sympathy for the Hohenstaufens. Otto of Brunswick abandoned his candidature, Louis of Bavaria made his submission to the emperor-king, and the *pourparlers* between the king of England Henry III and Přemysl Otakar I broke down. Princess Agnes had lost her second suitor.

Such was the position in Bohemia and in the empire when Přemysl died on December 15th, 1230, and was succeeded as sole ruler by Wenceslas I. The latter had already been crowned king in 1228 by the Archbishop of Mainz, who was the metropolitan of Prague. He received investiture from the emperor only in 1231, having applied for it not personally, but through an embassy. The method showed how far Bohemia had progressed: the investiture, which had been the stormy petrel of Bohemian history and supplied the emperors with ever-recurring opportunities to meddle with Bohemian affairs, had now degenerated into a mere formality.

It looked at the outset as though Wenceslas I would defeat the plans of the Babenberg of Austria. Young King Henry had tired of his wife, who besides being much older than himself, was still waiting for the payment of her dowry, an important consideration for a husband who was constantly short of money. It so happened that Louis, duke of Bavaria, whose wife was a Czech princess, had recovered favor with Henry and used his influence to induce the young man to abandon his alliance with the Babenberg for a rapprochement with the Přemyslides; as Henry's relations with his father had gone from bad to worse and the young man was impatient to come to power, the duke was sure of an easy hearing. An alliance with Bohemia seemed the best way out. To help matters, the young king was actually in love with the Czech princess and sorely regretted having transferred his affections to Margaret.[5]

In 1231 Henry openly revealed his intention of divorcing his wife and marrying the Czech princess. The news filled many German princes with horror and dismay because of its political consequences. However, the emperor, who could not afford open hostilities with the mighty Austrian duke, took prompt action and paid Margaret's dowry out of his own pocket. King Wenceslas I, much as he and his sister appreciated Henry's romance, wisely refrained from action. Henry yielded to persuasion and submitted to his father.

Disappointed in earthly love,[6] the Czech princess resolved to renounce the world. She chose the severe rule of the Order of Saint Clare, St. Francis' most fervent follower, and entered a convent she had founded in Prague. Being of the first generation of St. Francis' disciples, she was numbered among the enthusiasts who tried to adhere as strictly as possible to the humble Saint of Assisi's ideals of poverty and abnegation, and for twenty years she was a personal friend of St. Clare.[7] She shared with the convent she had founded the task of spreading St. Francis' ideals over Central and Eastern Europe, and inspired the foundation of a new Czech order, the Knights of the Cross.

But the princess' disappearance from court and public life into a convent did not settle the Austro-Bohemian conflict. Frederick, the new duke of Austria, vindictive and unprincipled, succeeded in making an alliance with his brother-in-law Přemysl, margrave of Moravia, and the king's own brother. With his help the duke planned to avenge the devastation of Austria and to overthrow the king. He was successful until a sudden illness forced him to suspend operations, and the rebellious margrave had to make his submission. The quarrelsome duke soon got into difficulties with the Hungarians, who had formed an alliance with the Czechs, and the two kings, Andrew II and Wenceslas I, set out together in 1235 to work havoc on Austrian territory.

In the meantime, the emperor, who suspected the duke of having had a hand in his son Henry's recent plot, condemned his son to the loss of his crown and to banishment (1235) and determined to put an end to the duke's mischievous activities. New incidents and suspicious contacts between the Austrian duke and the Lombard cities forced the emperor to precipitate action: the refractory duke was stripped of his dukedom, and King Wenceslas and Otto, who had succeeded Louis of Bavaria after his assassination, were made executors of the imperial ban, or Reichsacht (1236). They penetrated as far as Vienna, and then the whole country abandoned its troublesome duke, the emperor winding up the campaign the following year in Vienna, where he caused his son Conrad to be elected king of Germany.[8]

Frederick II was then at the height of his power, having crushed all opposition in Germany and forced the Lombard cities to accept his sovereignty. It is possible that he harbored a plan to reduce Bohemia again to its previous humiliating status in the Empire. This would explain why Wenceslas I joined the papal party for a short time. But, swayed by the Přemyslides' traditional sympathies for the Hohenstaufens, he soon returned to the imperial party. The conflict with Frederick of Austria, now reconciled with the emperor, continued, however, and only the common Mongol danger that threatened Central Europe forced the two rivals to come to an agreement. The Austrian consented to the marriage of his niece Gertrude to Wenceslas' son Vladislav (1241).

The Mongols, who had devastated Silesia, were, fortunately, halted in the passes leading to Bohemia. Only Moravia and Austria had suffered devastation. When the Mongolian danger had disappeared, the conflict with Austria was renewed. It seems that after the death of his English wife, Frederick II himself turned his thoughts if not his affections to

Gertrude, with an eye to Austrian lands for the promotion of his family policy in Germany. He is said to have promised Duke Frederick in 1245 to raise Austria and Styria to the rank of a kingdom. In the face of this new danger, Wenceslas I adhered to Pope Innocent IV and his candidate to the imperial throne, William of Holland. Fortunately, Frederick of Austria died suddenly in the course of another war with the Hungarians (1246). The Czech prince Vladislav married Gertrude, but died a few months after the wedding.

This was a blow to the Czech king, and another disappointment soon followed—a revolt of the Czech nobility dissatisfied with the King's curialist policy. Czech Ghibellines elected the king's son Přemysl margrave and governor of Moravia, as co-regent. The civil war lasted until 1250, when Wenceslas I became reconciled with his son. The struggle was an aftermath on Bohemian soil of the conflict between Guelfs and Ghibellines and developed to the ultimate benefit of the Guelfs and their curialist program.

But this reverse in policy finally helped the king to realize his Austrian ambitions. In 1251 Gertrude's second husband Herrmann of Baden died, and Czech prospects in Austria again rose high. Přemysl, governor of Moravia, was elected duke by the Estates of Austria and was able, with the help of the Archbishop of Salzburg, the Czech king's nephew, to take over the duchy. In order to confirm his claims and to silence any possible opposition, Přemysl decided to marry King Henry VII's widow, Margaret, though she was old enough to be his mother and was seriously considering retiring to a convent. The ill-matched couple were united in their political nuptials in 1254.

Complications arose with Béla IV of Hungary, who claimed Styria, which was politically united with Austria. After some bloody conflicts a peace treaty was signed, thanks to the intervention of the Curia, giving Austria and a part of Styria to Přemysl and Styria in its present limits to Béla's son Stephen.

Přemysl Otakar II (1253-1278) was the most powerful ruler in Central Europe. The dynastic ties binding the Czech lands to their ruler had been considerably strengthened during the reign of his two predecessors. As he was the only surviving male member of the dynasty, he did not have to share the administration of the Margraviate of Moravia with any other member. The racial unity of his subjects gave a solid basis to his realm. This basis was strengthened by the remarkable economic prosperity caused by the discovery of silver mines in Bohemia and Moravia under Wenceslas I and by a vast colonization of the borderlands. The colonists —miners, artisans, and peasants—came mostly from the north of Germany, from Thuringia, Brandenberg, Swabia, and Saxony. Přemysl entertained very friendly relations with all the leading families of these principalities, the Wettins, the Ascanians, the Guelfs, and even with the counts of Schauenburg ruling over Holstein.

Perhaps because of these good relations with the princes of northern Germany, Přemysl, instead of trying to expand his power in that direction among the Slavic nations still living there, turned, at the beginning of his reign, toward the northeast. The situation in Poland seemed particularly inviting for Přemysl's intervention. Divided into several principalities ruled by members of the Piast dynasty, Poland had been badly hit by the Mongol invasion of 1241 and was unable to organize a common defense against the inroads of the Mongols on the one side and of the Baltic Prussians and Lithuanians on the other side.[9] Přemysl was fully aware of this situation, and in his letter to Prandol, Bishop of Cracow (1255), he promised his help and assistance to the Duke of Cracow and to all other Polish dukes against their enemies. His words echoed the crusading idea which still dominated the minds of many. He must have been regarded by his contemporaries as a promoter of Christianity among the infidels, and he is praised as such by the author of *Alexander the Great,* a contemporary Czech epic.

His crusading spirit led Přemysl II to the Baltic in 1255, where he gave welcome assistance to the Teutonic Order in its attempts to subdue Samland. The city of Königsberg (now Kaliningrad), which was founded by Přemysl II in the conquered part of Prussia, still recalls the memory of this valiant Czech, called the Iron King by his contemporaries.

Another expedition was planned for 1267 against the pagan Lithuanians. The king conceived the bold idea of keeping all the conquered lands as fiefs of the Czech crown and of subordinating all newly founded bishoprics to Olomouc, where Bruno, of the family of Schauenburg, a faithful councilor of the king, was bishop. Olomouc (Olmütz in German) would thus eventually become a missionary metropolis for the North, in line with the plans which Otto I had formerly cherished for Magdeburg.[10] It was a grandiose plan characteristic of the king's enterprising and romantic spirit, but it miscarried. The Roman Curia was unwilling to assign such an unusual role to Bruno and his bishopric, and Clement IV needed the help of Přemysl II in German interior affairs. Some of the Polish princes were also unwilling to back such a plan, although Přemysl had intended to give some of the conquered lands to Polish princes as Czech fiefs. Although it needed help, the Teutonic Order could hardly welcome Czech competition on the Baltic. In the face of such opposition the Czech king had to abandon his plan and sent only a small body of knights to help the Teutonic Order. The expedition could, however, accomplish little because of unexpected climatic conditions.

Nevertheless, the Czech king seemed to have had excellent chances of penetrating Poland successfully had he persisted in his eastern expansion, although several Polish princes looked rather to Hungary for help and alliance. Přemysl II, however, limited himself to winning the friendship of the Polish princes of Silesia, where the Duke of Wrocław (Breslau) was especially favorable to the Czech cause. Instead of continuing his expansion eastward, Přemysl II concentrated on the South in an effort to create a vast demesne for his house in the German Alpine lands.

A welcome occasion for further expansion in the South offered itself in 1259, when the Styrian nobles revolted against Béla IV of Hungary. Přemysl II took possession of Styria.

Béla's home country had suffered terribly during the Mongol invasion, and whole districts in central Hungary were depopulated. Béla IV settled the Turkic Cumans and Sarmatian Yazigs there and used these fierce pagan warriors against his enemies. Thanks to his efforts and diplomatic skill, Hungary quickly recovered from the devastation and expanded its influence in the Slavic states in the Balkans.[11] Béla IV did not intend to abandon his possessions in the Alpine lands and marched with his Cumans against Přemysl II. In the battle of Kressenbrun (1260), however, the Czech army proved its superiority over the fierce hordes of the Cumans. The battle ended in a slaughter of Béla's men. In order to strengthen his influence in Hungary, Přemysl II, who had obtained the annulment of his marriage with Margaret, who had become a nun, married Cunigunda, the grandchild of Béla IV, and arranged the marriage of Béla's son with his niece, Cunigunda of Brandenburg.[12]

Other great successes soon followed. As heir to his nephew Henry, duke of Carinthia, Přemysl added that duchy, with Carniola, Istria, and the town of Pordenone, to his Alpine possessions in 1269. Carinthia and Carniola were still in great part Slavic lands inhabited by the Slovenes. The king's influence was soon felt in Lombardy.[13] In this way Přemysl II became the true creator of the modern Austrian Empire. Thanks to him, the idea of the union of Bohemia and the Alpine lands was introduced into the history of Central Europe.

All these acquisitions were fiefs of the Empire, and, naturally, Přemysl's rise to become one of the most powerful rulers in contemporary Europe provoked much jealousy among other princes. Přemysl had achieved something which had eluded all the efforts of the Hohenstaufen emperors: the creation of a vast demesne which would secure their position vis-à-vis the feudal aristocracy. Had Přemysl II become emperor, he would have wielded an influence unwelcome to many jealous princes. It seems that Přemysl II did originally harbor such intentions. His chances of being elected emperor after his military success of 1255 were spoiled by the Curia, which supported William of Holland and, after his death, Richard of Cornwall. Přemysl II first hesitated between Richard and Alfonso X of Castile,[14] but in order to prevent the election of Conradin, Frederick II's grandson, he declared for Richard and accepted Austria and Styria from him as fiefs of the Empire. Přemysl II seems also to have prepared the candidacy to the German throne of Frederick of Meissen, to whom he betrothed his daughter Cunigunda, a plan which was again spoiled by the Curia.[15] After the death of Richard (1272), Přemysl hoped that the Curia would favor his candidature. Gregory X, however, gave the German princes liberty to elect whomsoever they wished. As was to be expected, the jealous princes chose a rival of Přemysl II, Count Rudolf of Habsburg (1273), who obtained from them the confirmation of his decision that all imperial fiefs acquired since the death of Frederick II should be given back to the Empire, a measure directly aimed against the Czech king. Přemysl II had only one choice—to reject Rudolf's election and to declare himself for Alfonso of Castile. When, however, in 1275 Alfonso, pressed by the Curia, had to recognize Rudolf, Přemysl II was isolated and the only issue was war. Abandoned by his supporter Henry of Bavaria, Přemysl was unable to defend his Alpine possessions. Only Vienna refused to open its gates to Rudolf. The king hastened to its help, but before the decisive battle, he was betrayed by the Bohemian aristocracy, who, enriched by the economic progress in their domains, seem to have followed the example of their German confreres in seeking greater independence from the royal crown. Záviš of Falkenstein was their leader.[16] Přemysl II had to surrender. He was obliged to renounce all his possessions in the Alps and to accept his own lands from Rudolf as fiefs of the Empire.

A final conflict was provoked by Rudolf himself, who was curtailing the king's rights in intervention in favor of the rebelled Czechs and against Přemysl's royal rights. When the fateful decision was made, Přemysl II lost his cause and his life on the battlefield of the Marchfeld in Austria.[17] It was a Swabian, the impoverished Count Rudolf of Habsburg, now king of the Germans, who became the chief beneficiary of Přemysl's labors in the Alpine lands and so brought Austria and the Habsburgs upon the European scene.

It was a tragic end, and it is not yet quite clear why Přemysl II was unable to attain his supreme goal. The main reason seems to have been the jealousy of the princes of the Empire, who did not want an emperor with such wide dominions and economic wealth. Then, Přemysl, although he had generally followed the policy of the Curia, was denied its support when he needed it. The question of nationality does not seem to have been of paramount importance. Přemysl's court was full of German adventurers and courtiers, German colonists and German cities were numerous in his realm, and many German mercenaries fought under his flag. Richard of Cornwall and Alfonso of Castile were not Germans either, and the universal character of the Empire was still acknowledged.

In spite of that, the Slavic character of the king and of his realm must have been resented by many in Germany. An anti-Slavic tone can be discovered in a contemporary panegyric of Rudolf, and the burghers of Vienna were blamed for having sided with a Slav.[18] A contemporary satiric poet, Seifried Helbling,[19] mockingly rebuked the Austrian nobles for their imitation of Czech manners. They had learned to greet each other in Czech and preferred Czech words of abuse to German. The Austrian Germans should learn from the Czechs how to love their native tongue. This is characteristic, but the poet's rebukes testify at the same time to the fact that Přemysl's rule, although short, had already taken some solid roots in Austria.

Anti-German sentiment may also have been manifested at Přemysl's court. It is quite possible that Přemysl II finally realized that he had made a mistake in concentrating on the Alpine lands and neglecting the Poles. An echo of such sentiments prevailing at the Czech court before or after the tragic conflict is to be heard in the "Manifesto to the Poles," written by the Italian Henry of Isernia, a Ghibelline refugee from southern Italy who had sought his fortune at the Czech court. It appears that the manifesto was only a stylistic composition, one of the many written by the eloquent Italian, but the ideas expressed by its author are highly interesting. The Czech king is presented in this document as addressing the Poles as kinsmen of the Czechs, bound to them by the bonds of common blood and similar tongue. He promises his aid to Polish princes in the defense of their rights, wishes them prosperity, and expresses the hope that in case of necessity he also can count on their help.[20] It is surprising to find such a Slavic consciousness at that period.

National sentiment was greatly strengthened in Bohemia after Přemysl II's death, when Rudolf of Habsburg, after reserving the administration of Moravia to himself, had entrusted the government of Bohemia and the guardianship of Přemysl's young son Wenceslas II to Otto of Brandenburg. The latter greatly misused his power and with his mercenaries exploited Bohemia shamelessly. Rudolf had to intervene (1280) to stop the civil war, restore order, and give some satisfaction to the discontented Czechs.

The young king was only twelve years old when Otto finally had let him return to his country in 1283. The main influence in the administration of affairs was exercised by a former enemy of his father's policy,

Záviš of Falkenstein, an ambitious man of great talent who had won the love of Přemysl II's widow, Queen Cunigunda. Záviš followed an anti-Habsburg policy, and the young king listened to him; but when in 1287 he married Rudolf's daughter Guta, Záviš' influence ceased. Young Wenceslas feared that Záviš intended to seize the Czech throne for himself. Záviš was imprisoned and executed during the reprisals against his relatives, who had revolted (1290) under tragic circumstances.

Dante has written in his *Purgatorio* a few verses (VII, 97-103) which are not flattering to Wenceslas II and which influenced the opinion of contemporaries concerning the king. It is true that the young king, who was physically weak and in poor health and who therefore preferred a quiet life, seemed out of place in the age of chivalry, but he proved to be an intelligent and able ruler. He had some ideas on government which outstripped the method used by the chanceries of his neighbors. He seemed to have derived his inspiration from France, where Philip the Fair, with his legists, was modernizing old administrative methods. Wenceslas' administration was more bureaucratic, and there are some signs indicating that he was seeking a solid basis for legislation not in custom law but in Roman law, the study of which had been revived in Italy. His attempts at a codification of the Czech law on this basis were thwarted by the aristocracy, which feared the curtailment of its rights. Wenceslas II was, however, able to publish, at least, a code of mining law, and some of his declarations testify that his conception of kingship was rooted in late Roman law, which gave to the ruler the exclusive right to legislate.[21]

In his foreign policy Wenceslas had also shown great wisdom. He refused the opportunity which was offered to him in 1291 to be elected emperor, and contrary to the policy of his father, which Záviš wanted him to follow, he abandoned the idea of conquests in the South, concentrating his effort on the North and Northeast. He first established a firm footing in Meissen, where the Slavic Sorbs were still living, and concentrated all his efforts on Poland. With the help of a strong pro-Czech party among the Polish princes, he first of all occupied Cracow (1291). The idea of the renascence of the Polish kingdom had gained ground recently, and two dukes, Henry IV and Przemysl of Gniezno, made serious attempts to bring it to realization.[22] After the death of the latter, the Czech king entered Gniezno and was crowned king of Poland, in 1300, by the Archbishop of Gniezno, James Swińka, one of the principal promoters of the restoration of the Polish kingdom. In order to strengthen his position, Wenceslas II married the daughter of Przemysl, Ryksa. From that time onward, Wenceslas proudly referred to himself as *Dei gratia Bohemiae et Poloniae Rex.*

Until the present the reign of the Czech king in Poland has generally been unfavorably treated by Polish historians.[23] Their criticisms have been largely actuated by national bias, and they have neglected to consider certain aspects of the situation which throw quite a different light upon Czech-Polish union. It is true that Wenceslas II had consented to accept Poland as a fief of the Empire; but this fact did not have the same significance at that time as it would have had if it had happened under the Hohenstaufens. The Empire was in decline, and Wenceslas II ruled Poland without paying any regard to the Empire. It was, in fact, a necessary precaution to safeguard the new Slavic Empire against foreign intervention. Moreover, the influx of Polish elements into Bohemia served to outweigh German influence at the Czech court, where, thanks to earlier German colonization, that influence was very great.

Recent research has shown that the short reign of the Czech king in Poland was most beneficial to that country. Wenceslas II was a good administrator, and he brought some order to the disorganized Polish economy. His reign should be regarded as a progressive step toward the definitive consolidation of the Polish lands in the fourteenth century.

This might have been a development of immense importance for the Czechs, the Poles, and all Europe. Had this union of Poland and Bohemia lasted longer, history would have witnessed in this part of Europe something similar to what happened in France. There the North and the South were fused into one nation using the same literary language, although their idioms were much more different from each other than were Polish and Czech in the fourteenth century. This was, indeed, the last opportunity the Czechs and Poles had to amalgamate into a single nation.

The reign of Wenceslas II is also important in another respect. For the first time in history the idea of a great Central European monarchy, in which even the Magyars would have been included, appeared a possibility. After the death of Andrew, the last ruler of the Árpád dynasty (1301), the Hungarian crown, with which was united that of Croatia, was offered to the young son of the Czech king. The Hungarian supporters of the Přemyslides won a victory over the partisans of the Angevins of Naples, and young Wenceslas was crowned king of Hungary.[24]

The acquisition of three crowns by a single dynasty provoked many jealousies. Pope Boniface VIII, invoking the fact that Hungary was a fief of the Papacy, started openly to favor the candidature of the Angevins and to support the Polish antagonist of the Czech king, Władysław Łokietek the Short. The Emperor Albert I joined this coalition and asked for a share in the wealth of the Czech silver mines. Wenceslas II found an ally in Philip the Fair of France, and mutual help was pledged (1303 or 1304) in the event of an attack by the emperor or the Pope. When, however, the French king had come to terms with Boniface VIII, Wenceslas II had to bear the brunt of Albert's attack alone, and guerrilla warfare brought him full success.

The alliance of the emperor, the Pope, and the Angevins of Naples proved, however, to be too weighty for the Czech king. He saw himself forced to abandon Hungary, at least temporarily, and to bring his son back to Prague. Wenceslas II was, however, not able to resume his fight for Hungary. He died in June, 1305. After a disappointing start, his young son Wenceslas III began to show some of his father's determination and wisdom. He obtained an honorable peace treaty from the emperor; and yielding to the pressure of the Angevins, he gave up his pretentions to the Hungarian throne, which was occupied by the Angevin Charles Robert. In Poland, Wenceslas III showed a firm determination to continue his father's policy of promoting the union between Bohemia and Poland. But here again, fate struck a decisive blow. When he was on his way to Poland to crush a revolt led by Władysław Łokietek against the Czechs, Wenceslas III was assassinated, probably by an unknown discontented noble, in Olomouc in 1306. That was the end of the Přemyslide dynasty, and from that time onward Poland and Bohemia developed on separate lines.

After the extinction of its national dynasty, Bohemia witnessed some dire struggles for the possession of its coveted throne. First of all, the Habsburgs, following the tradition of the founder of their Hausmacht in Austria, Rudolf, laid their greedy hands on the crown of Bohemia. The Emperor Albert I declared that Bohemia was a fief of the Empire, and persuaded the Czech nobles to elect his son Rudolf as king. The latter married the widow of Wenceslas II, the Polish Ryksa, called Rejčka by the Czechs, thus indicating that the Czech Polish claims were still alive. His father, in order to secure Bohemia for the Habsburgs and to curtail the electoral rights of the Czech nobility, recently confirmed by him, stipulated that Rudolf should be followed on the throne by his brothers. This fact and the parsimonious habits of Rudolf made the Habsburgs very unpopular, and when Rudolf died suddenly in 1307, the Czechs elected Duke Henry of Carinthia, who was married to the eldest sister of Wenceslas III. The warlike complications with the Habsburgs which followed this election were only terminated by the sudden assassination of the Emperor Albert by one of his relatives in 1308.

Henry of Carinthia was liberated from the Habsburg menace, but he was unable to win the support of the Czech nobility, who were angered by the favoritism which he showed toward the German cities. The burghers, in order to force their admission into the Diet of the kingdom, had dared to seize and imprison Czech nobles holding the highest offices.

A new course in Czech history was inaugurated by two men who had played an important role at the court of Wenceslas II. Peter of Aspelt, his former chancellor and now archbishop of Mainz, continuing Wenceslas's pro-French policy, engineered the election of Henry, count of Luxemburg, to the Roman and German throne (1308-1313). Peter and the Czech Cistercian monks, who had exerted great influence on Wenceslas II, won the consent of the Czech nobility for their candidate, King Henry's son John, and also arranged the marriage of the youthful John with Elizabeth, second daughter of Wenceslas II. Henry of Carinthia was driven from Prague, and John of Luxemburg, founder of a new Czech dynasty, became king (1310-1346).

NOTES

1. Cf. chapter I, pp. 8 ff. and Dvornik, *The Slavs*, pp. 321 ff.

2. It was the absence of Přemysl at King Henry's election that prompted Eike of Repgow, the author of the collection of Saxon laws, the famous *Sachsenspiegel*, to deny the Czech king's right to participate in the imperial election: he may have been the emperor's cupbearer, but he was not a German. This was a personal opinion of the famous jurist and was shared in some German circles about the year 1235, when this collection was written, but it did not reflect the general conviction of the German princes. For detailed literature on the evolution of the German electoral college, see B. Wunderlich, *Die neueren Ansichten* (see Bibl.) and W. Neumann, *Die deutschen Königswahlen* (see Bibl.).

3. These details are derived from, among other sources, a report presented by Walter, Bishop of Carlisle, to King Henry III on his embassy to Germany, written on February 10, 1225. W. W. Shirley, *Royal and Other Historical Letters Illustrative of the Reign of Henry III* (*Chronicles and Memorials of Great Britain and Ireland*, vol. 27), 1, 252.

4. From another English source, a letter written between October, 1228, and 1229, we learn that the Czech king was spreading news about Frederick's exploits in the Holy Land and was pretending to have received a letter from him giving an account of his doings. This proves that the Czech had no intention of exchanging the emperor's service for any combination. This English source was written by Duke Henry of Lotharingia-Brabant to Henry III, and is reprinted by W. W. Shirley, *ibid.*, p. 343.

5. Among the love songs composed by the many *Minnesänger* of this period there are two of outstanding beauty and romance, which in some manuscripts are attributed to "Kaiser Heinrich." They speak of tender love for a beautiful lady the lover can never possess though he is ready to forfeit his crown for her. It is now generally admitted that the songs were the work of King Henry pouring out his heart to Agnes.

6. The legend of St. Agnes relates of the second marriage of Frederick II that Isabella, King Henry III's sister, had taken the place which Agnes had refused. This would indicate that Frederick II had tried to marry his son's beloved, the Czech princess. This is possible, but it cannot be demonstrated to

a certainty. A confusion between father and son was only too easy since Isabella had been destined for Henry before being allotted to Frederick.

7. There still exist three letters which St. Clare wrote to the Czech princess. Agnes stood by Clare in the effort to obtain the papal approval for a rule that would assure to their sisters the life of poverty such as St. Francis had in mind. It is known that both Blessed Agnes and St. Clare failed this. The letters were published by W. Seton (see Bibl.). Cf. the Czech monograph by J. K. Vyskočil, *The Legend of the Blessed Agnes and the Four Letters of Saint Clare* (Prague, 1932).

8. The imperial decree issued for the occasion marked the definite progress made by the Kurfürsten, or Prince-Electors, in the establishment of their rights and privileges.

9. For more details see F. Dvornik, *The Slavs: Their Early History*, pp. 312 ff.

10. Cf. F. Dvornik, *The Slavs: Their Early History*, pp. 109-113.

11. For details see below:

12. A well-known Czech historian V. Chaloupecký ("Uherská politika Přemysla Otakara II," *Pekařův Sborník*, Prague, 1930, pp. 138-88) thought to have discovered in Přemysl's Hungarian policy plans aiming at joining northern Hungary—modern Slovakia—with the Kingdom of Bohemia and of Pannonia with the Alpine lands. J. Šusta (*Soumrak Přemyslovců a jejich dědictví*, Prague, 1935, pp. 45 ff.), however, refused to go as far as that in the interpretation of Přemysl's Hungarian policy. He contends, with apparent correctness, that Přemysl II was only anxious to strengthen his influence in Hungary and to secure Hungarian help in case of need. He occupied parts of northern Hungary only after Béla's death, during the political disorders reigning in that country, in order to protect his lands against the invasions of the Cumans. Šusta's work is of paramount importance for the history of the last Přemyslides. A French review of this work was given by B. Mendl ("Les derniers Přemyslides," *Revue historique*, vol. 179, 1937, pp. 34-62).

13. The city of Pordenone was under his sovereignty. The famous medieval traveler, the Blessed Odoricus de Pordenone, seems to have been the son of a member of the Czech garrison stationed by Otakar in the city.

14. For more details on Otakar's role at the double election, see F. R. Lewis, "Ottokar II of Bohemia and the Double Election of 1257," *Speculum*, 12 (1937), pp. 512-15.

15. The most detailed study of this problem is to be found in J. Šusta, *Soumrak Přemyslovců*, pp. 57 ff. The author has shown the weakness of O. Redlich's presentation of Rudolf of Habsburg's election (*Rudolf von Habsburg*, see Bibl.), and Lorenz's suspicions that Přemysl II wanted to atomize the imperial power (*Deutsche Geschichte im 13. und 14. Jahrhunderte*, vol. 1).

16. On Záviš, see below, p. 146.

17. Šusta, *op. cit.*, pp. 271 ff., after examining all available evidence, comes to the conclusion that there is no certainty in the reports of the treason of Czech aristocrats during the second conflict.

18. See Šusta, *op. cit.*, p. 204.

19. Poem XIV, verses 20-23, poem VIII, verses 783 ff., ed. J. Seemüller (Halle/Saale, 1886), pp. 1, 2, 210. (See Bibl.)

20. The Kingdom of Bohemia is said to be a wall created for the defense of Poland: "If the Roman King will destroy us, then the insatiable mouths of

the Germans will open even more freely, and their insatiable greediness will stretch out its shameless hands toward your country. We are your solid wall, and if this wall will not hold, a great danger will threaten you. . . . O, what kind of oppression will your numerous nation, which is so much hated by the Germans, have to suffer? Oh, how hard will be the yoke of slavery which free Poland will have to bear . . ." It should be added that similar sentiments of Slavic solidarity and of mistrust toward the Germans had been voiced also by Magister Bohuslav, chancellor of Přemysl's spouse Cunigunda, in a letter addressed to Agnes, abbess of the Polish Abbey of Trzebnica. The queen reproached the abbess for favoring German monks instead of Polish brethren: "Instead of having—because of love of your origin—sympathies with the difficulties of poor men, of your tongue, you do the contrary, in supporting German brethren. . . . You should rather patronize and defend brethren of our (Czech) and your (Polish) tongue . . ." The letter is again only a stylistic composition. The appeal to the Poles was published in *Codex epistolaris Primislai Ottocari* (see Bibl.), pp. 93 ff. The letter attributed to the Queen was published in vol. 1 of F. Palacký's *Formelbücher* (see Bibl.). On Bohuslav see the study by J. B. Novák in Goll's *Festschrift* (*Sborník* . . . *J. Golla,* Prague, 1906), pp. 124-152.

21. Cf. also below.

22. See F. Dvornik, *The Slavs,* pp. 316, 320.

23. Namely, by the prominent Polish historian Oswald Balzer in his work, *Krolewstwo Polskie 1295-1370* ("The Polish Kingdom 1295-1370"), 2 vols. (Lwów, 1919). Czech answers to Polish criticisms were made by J. Šusta. These were printed in his *Úvahy a drobné spisy historické* ("Studies and Short Writings on History"), 2 vols. (Prague, 1934).

24. Cf. below.

Chapter III

JOHN OF BOHEMIA, EMPEROR LOUIS IV, AND POLAND

Emperor Henry VII of Luxemburg, France, and Italy—John of Luxemburg, king of Bohemia, a knight-errant—Pope John XXII, his fiscal and Italian policy, France's interest in Italy—First conflict between Louis IV and the Pope, John of Bohemia as mediator—Louis IV's coronation in Rome, Marsilius of Padua and his revolutionary ideas—King John's Italian adventure—John's unsuccessful attempt at new mediation between the emperor and the Pope—John's claims to the Kingdom of Poland, Łokietek's difficult position in Poland—Łokietek's coronation and alliance with Hungary and Lithuania—John of Bohemia, Poland, and the Teutonic Order—Casimir of Poland, the loss of Silesia to Bohemia and of Pomerelia to the order—New crisis in Polish-Czech relations—Louis IV, John of Bohemia, and the Declaration of Rense—Final break between Louis IV and Bohemia—Clement VI chooses John's son Charles as candidate for the German throne—Charles elected king of Germany—John's death at the Battle of Crécy and evaluation of his reign in Bohemia

With the election of a Luxemburg to the German royal dignity a new era seemed to open for the Empire. It is true that the election of Henry VII had blocked French hopes of winning the imperial crown for the French royal house, but Henry was himself more French than German and he was permeated with the ideas of the imperium which were firing the imagination of contemporary Frenchmen. Since the reign of St. Louis, France had become a first-rate power in Europe, and the imperial idea had found new appreciation there during the conflict between Philip the Fair and Boniface VIII. The legist Peter Dubois [1] voiced the new ideas most clearly when declaring that the Christian world would be pacified and organized only when the French had saved the imperial idea from the degradation into which the German nobility had allowed it to fall in the last sixty years, and when they had realized the Christian and universal inspiration which should be its mainspring. The growing interest of the French in Italy and the acquisition of Naples by the Angevins were awakening hopes that the French were predestined to renovate the old imperial idea so sadly debased.

Philip the Fair's hopes of establishing his brother Charles of Valois on the imperial throne were thwarted by the election of 1308. It was a poor Count of Luxemburg, also impregnated with the new French imperial ideals, who made a supreme attempt at another *renovatio imperii.* His chances of success had certainly been enhanced by the acquisition of the Kingdom of Bohemia by his dynasty. He also found a powerful ally in his brother Baldwin, who became archbishop and Elector of Trier. Hailed by the Italian patriots, whose hopes were so forcefully expressed by Dante,[2] Henry VII entered Italy in order to be crowned in Rome by the legates of Clement V. The latter, although staying at Avignon under the "protection" of the powerful French king, had rather welcomed the fact that he was not obliged to place the imperial crown on the brow of a Capetian. Unfortunately Henry VII became involved in great difficulties in northern Italy and in Rome, against which he battled courageously. But before his son John could bring substantial help from his kingdom, Henry VII died suddenly and was buried at Pisa, which had stayed faithful to him.[3]

This was the end of Henry's imperial dreams. The hopes of his supporters that his young son would be able to continue his work were thwarted by the emergence of the Habsburgs, who sought the imperial dignity for one of their members. The most which John's principal supporters—the archbishops of Trier and Mainz—could achieve was to rally the majority of the Electors to a Bavarian Wittelsbach, Louis IV (1314-1347). The minority of the Electors, however, voted for the Habsburg duke Frederick of Austria. This double election led to a bloody contest between the two rivals during which the imperial idea lost much of its value and the prestige of the German crown suffered a new decline.

John of Bohemia sided with the Wittelsbachs against the Habsburgs. He obtained from Louis IV confirmation of all the rights of his kingdom and the promise of recognition of all fiefs and acquisitions which he might gain in the future. The fact that Czech claims to the Kingdom of Poland were not forgotten showed that the new dynasty sought to continue the policy of the Přemyslides.

John's wife Elizabeth was completely devoted to the traditions of government and foreign policy established by the last Přemyslides and especially by her father Wenceslas II. These she wished her younger husband to follow, and she particularly resented the encroachments on the royal authority during recent years by the Czech nobility. Henry of Lípa, who held the highest office in the kingdom, that of marshal, was its leader. His influence seemed the more dangerous in that he had won the favor of Wenceslas II and of Rudolf's widow, Queen Elizabeth Rejčka (Ryksa). King John imprisoned him in an attempt to break his influence and that of the nobility. He overrated his own power, however, and had to call in the help of King Louis to subdue the revolt of the nobility (1318). Henry of Lípa regained his offices, and the importance of the nobility in the kingdom was reinforced. Thus John's only attempt to strengthen the royal powers was unsuccessful.

It was a pity that John had lost his father at the very beginning of his reign in Bohemia. The guidance of his father's wise advice, together with the influence of Queen Elizabeth, would perhaps have curbed his somewhat adventurous character and helped him to strengthen his links with Bohemia. The efforts of Queen Elizabeth to inculcate in her husband the ideas on kingship and government which she had inherited from her father were vain. After his impulsiveness and imprudence had ruined his attempt to assert his authority in Bohemia, John left its administration in the hands of Henry of Lípa and other nobles, preferring to make prolonged stays in Luxemburg and at the court of France.

His estrangement from the queen even led him to believe the suggestions of her enemies among the Czech nobility that she intended to dethrone him and to reign alone in the name of their son Wenceslas Charles.[4] He therefore interned his queen and imprisoned his child, ignoring the sympathies which the last member of the Přemyslide dynasty enjoyed in Bohemia. John was therefore obliged to give way to the citizens of Prague, who spiritedly defended their queen, and to reconcile himself with Elizabeth and free his child. Fearing, however, that such a plot might materialize in the future, he brought his son to Paris in 1323 so that he might be educated at the court of Charles IV.

So it came about that John [5] never felt at home in Bohemia, which he only visited for the purpose of obtaining financial resources for his adventures abroad. He became a knight-errant for whom the ideal of chivalry was everything. His attempt to make Prague a center of chivalry by establishing there the Round Table of King Arthur was impeded by the failure of his "international" tournament there in 1319. Thereupon King John transferred all his sympathies to France, where the spirit of chivalry found more appreciation. There was hardly a major warlike conflict in contemporary Europe in which John did not seek to draw his sword, so that it was said that "nothing could have been done without the help of God and of the King of Bohemia."

The most spectacular of these military expeditions was John's intervention in the battle of Mühldorf in 1322. He contributed largely to the victory of Louis IV over the Habsburgs, which was crowned by the capture of the pretender Frederick and of his brother Duke Henry. This catastrophe eliminated the Habsburgs for more than a century from playing a leading role in the Empire.

In recognition of his signal help John of Bohemia obtained from Louis IV, among other favors, the imperial fief of Cheb (Eger). But he also became intimately involved in the conflict between Louis IV and Pope John XXII, which was soon to flare up with unprecedented fury.

John XXII (1316-1334), a native of Cahors, then known as the center of southern French financiers and usurers, has the merit of having perfected the centralizing policy of the Curia and of having subordinated all the clergy to its fiscal policy through a new practice of conferring ecclesiastical benefices in all the lands of western Christendom. The Pope was adamant in the enforcement of his bureaucratic fiscalism, basing his claims on the theocratic character of his office and on new stipulations of canon law. Thus he created a kind of absolutist state to which all Christians were subject through the government of a hierarchy completely subordinated to the judicial power and fiscal rights of its head. He was thus one of the first to realize the importance of sound finances for any political power in a world which was rapidly changing over to a money economy. All this resulted in the debasement of the spiritual forces which the Papacy had to protect and propagate, and provoked fanatic opposition from some of the followers of St. Francis, who stressed the necessity for the absolute poverty of monastic institutions. William of Ockham, the famous English Franciscan philosopher, was one of the fiercest opponents of John XXII's policies. John's supreme goal seems to have been the restoration of papal political authority in Lombardy and central Italy with the help of the Angevins of Naples and of the French kings. He hoped thus to make possible his own victorious return from Avignon to Rome. This implied, of course, the elimination of German influence from Italy. In this respect a new current of thought had arisen in Naples and Avignon since the death of Henry VII. Many prominent canonists sought to discontinue the union of Germany with the kingdoms of Arles and Lombardy. The rule of the German king, elected by the Kurfürsten, should be limited to Germany proper. It was argued that the Pope should refuse the imperial crown to any German king who wished to extend his rule over Italy.

French pretentions to a share in this new organization were also revived. Two possible solutions were suggested to the Pope: the extension of Angevin supremacy over the rest of Italy, or the creation of a new kingdom of Lombardy for a member of the Capetian dynasty.

John XXII never took up a clear position toward these suggestions although he may have considered all of them at different stages of his pontificate. Profiting from the disorders to which the double election had given rise in Germany, John XXII claimed, as the emperor's feudal lord, the exclusive right to exercise imperial functions in Italy until the succession should be settled. He appointed Robert of Naples as his vicar-general in Italy and tried to strengthen the party of the Guelfs in Lombardy by sending his legates there with military forces. He even tried to influence the French prince Philip in the fight for Lombardy, but with little success. In spite of the stubborn resistance of the Ghibellines, the Pope was able greatly to improve his chances for the pacification of Lombardy. All this was changed, however, by the direct intervention of Louis IV in Italy after his victory at Mühldorf.

Encouraged by his victory over the Habsburgs, Louis IV made a daring attempt to strengthen the position of his house by giving the March of Brandenburg with its electoral dignity to his son after the extinction of the Ascanian dynasty, which had won this valuable territory for Germany. When the Pope refused to recognize his right to the throne, Louis sent his vicar to Lombardy. The latter, with a force of German knights, improved the chances of the Ghibellines and stopped the progress of the papal legate.

The Pope in his disappointment accused Louis the Bavarian of exercising royal and imperial powers illegally without the approval of the Holy See. Under the threat of excommunication the king was invited to cease exercising royal and imperial functions within a time limit of three months. The Pope is also said to have been determined to break "the iron snake of the Empire" into three pieces: Germany, the Kingdom of Arles, and Italy. Louis IV answered by an appeal to the Pope "better informed," [6] and the threat of a sharp conflict between the two heads of western Christendom moved some influential rulers to act as mediators between them. The most prominent among these mediators was John of Bohemia. The compromise which he proposed was very characteristic and revealed the currents of opinion which were then manifesting themselves in western Europe. Louis IV should remain king of Germany; he should, however, renounce the imperial dignity in favor of the French king. In order to win the French king Charles IV for this solution, the mediators offered the Kingdom of Arles to his uncle Charles of Valois. The project echoed the ideas propagated some time previously by Peter Dubois and illustrates the difficult position of the Bohemian king in his desire to reconcile his loyalty to the Empire with his sympathies for France.[7]

All such projects, however, undermined the very basis on which the Roman Empire had been renovated by Otto I in 962, and could hardly expect to find acceptance in responsible German circles. Neither did they satisfy the courts of Paris and Naples. The attempts at reconciliation having failed, the Pope pronounced the sentence of excommunication against Louis IV. The latter issued a new appeal against the Pope, accusing him of usurpation of the rights of the German electoral princes and of the emperor, and launched against him the charge of heresy because he rejected the doctrine of poverty spread by some of the disciples of St. Francis. The unjust judgment of the Pope should be re-examined by a future general council.

These were very strong words and recalled the accusations launched against Boniface VIII by Philip the Fair of France. But neither the papal bulls against the king nor Louis' appeals achieved their full effect in Germany, which was exhausted by the repeated struggles between emperors and popes. Only the Habsburgs were manifesting a determined opposition to Louis IV. They were even willing to work for the election of the French king to the German throne. Louis IV, however, nullified this alliance between France and the Habsburgs by releasing his prisoner Frederick and accepting him as a second king of Germany. A new rapprochement with John of Luxemburg [8] made it possible for Louis to accept the urgent invitation of the Ghibellines and to accomplish his Roman expedition in 1327.

He was received with enthusiasm by the Lombard Ghibellines and was crowned at Milan with the iron crown of Lombardy. Rome was in full revolt against the Pope. Its leader Sciarra Colonna in the name of the Roman Commune invited Louis IV to receive the imperial crown and as supreme head of Christendom to reform the Papacy, which John XXII had so much debased by his fiscalism. Louis entered Rome in triumph and received from the representatives of the Roman people the dignity of Senator and Lord of Rome. In the name of the Roman people he was crowned emperor. The ceremony ended with a banquet offered to the emperor by the people of Rome on the Capitol, the symbol of ancient Roman greatness built by the sovereign Roman people.

All this echoed the revolutionary ideas which Marsilius of Padua had expressed in his *Defensor Pacis,* the most daring treatise of medieval political thought. Against papal theocratic principles he stressed the sovereignty of the people as the foundation on which the state is built. The competence of the hierarchy was there limited to providing for spiritual needs under the surveillance of the state. The Pope's actions should be controlled by general councils in which laymen and states should be represented. Marsilius of Padua, together with his friend the Frenchman John of Jandun, influenced Louis IV, to whom he had presented his work, and they were both present at Louis' triumphs in Rome. The logical conclusion of the revolutionary act was, of course, the condemnation of John XXII and the election—by the people of Rome—of an anti-Pope, Martin V, one of the condemned fanatic sons of St. Francis.

The time was, however, not yet ripe for the realization of such revolutionary ideas. It is indeed questionable whether Louis IV himself was aware of the real significance of the radical innovations preached by Marsilius. Moreover, the appointment of an anti-Pope was a mistake which failed to win Louis new supporters. Pressed by Robert of Naples, he had to quit Rome amidst the curses of the people who had recently hailed him, and for two more years he battled vainly in Lombardy to secure victory for the Ghibellines.

At the beginning of 1330 he returned to Germany promising his supporters a new Italian expedition, for which he had also won over the Czech king.

John of Bohemia had again assumed the role of mediator between the emperor and the Pope. With his uncle the Archbishop of Trier, he had remained deaf to the Pope's invitation to work for the election of a new king of Germany, and now, eager for new adventures in Italy, he accepted Louis' authorization to approach the Pope with proposals for a compromise. John won over even the Habsburgs for a reconciliation with the emperor: Louis should abandon his anti-Pope and revoke his appeal to a general council and all his actions and utterances against the Pope; he should then submit himself to the Pope, but without detriment to his royal and imperial authority.

The Pope, however, refused to accept any compromise, demanding a complete capitulation by the emperor and his renunciation of the royal and imperial dignities. The French king, Philip VI, also came forward with his aspirations to a Lombard kingdom for a member of his dynasty. In spite of this failure King John continued to make preparations for his Italian expedition. The final agreement with Duke Henry of Carinthia was an important step toward the realization of his plans. Henry not only surrendered all his pretensions to the Kingdom of Bohemia, but gave his daughter Margaret in marriage to John's young son John Henry, who was to inherit the Duchy of Carinthia with Tyrol. When staying in Trent, John of Bohemia received an embassy from the commune of Brescia offering him the lordship of the city if he would help the citizens to stop the invasion of their territory by the Ghibellines. John accepted the offer, although he had learned that the emperor had given another proof of his unstable character by concluding an agreement with the Habsburgs aimed at excluding the Luxemburgs from the Alpine lands.

So began John's Italian adventure. It was inspired not only by his own adventurous spirit, but also by the dynastic interests of the Luxemburgs. The possibility of establishing a Luxemburg secundogeniture in Carinthia tempted the enterprising king to create in its neighborhood a vast new domain for his house in the sunny lands of Lombardy. He enjoyed, however, neither imperial, papal, nor French authoritization for the role which he intended to play in Lombardy. But he masked this shortcoming by stressing his good relations with the emperor, the Pope, and the French court. The desire for more peaceful conditions in Lombardy was so great that John, who presented himself as a peacemaker, was soon recognized as sovereign of a great number of communes including Brescia, Verona, Cremona, Milan, Modena, and Lucca. His success was so unexpected that even the Pope preferred to observe a neutral attitude toward John, satisfied for the time being with the fact that Lombardy had not been seized again by Louis IV. In order to strengthen his position in Italy, John ordered his son Charles, who was then in Luxemburg, to join him in Lombardy, thus expressing his hope that the sovereign position he had gained in Lombardy would be hereditary in his house.

It was to be expected that Louis IV would not welcome the spectacular success won by John in Italy. When news reached John that the emperor was about to encourage Habsburg threats to Bohemia, he was forced to leave the direction of affairs in Italy to his young son and to pacify Louis IV. After a prolonged discussion he succeeded in coming to an agreement with the emperor in August 1331 at Nürnberg. The emperor sanctioned John's conquests in Italy, giving him Brescia and Lucca as hereditary imperial fiefs and releasing to him nine communes (Milan, Bergamo, Novara, Pavia, Cremona, Parma, Modena, Reggio, and Bobbio) to be held as an imperial pledge. French support was secured by John's promise of military assistance in French campaigns against England and any other attacker, with the exception of the emperor. The Franco-Bohemian friendship was to be strengthened by the marriage of John's daughter Guta to Prince John, the heir to the French throne.

With the help of the French king, John was also able to come to an agreement with John XXII, but at that moment the Bohemian dominions in Italy were already in great peril. The despots of Milan and Verona—the Visconti and the Scaligeri—started the reaction, and Brescia was the first commune to defect from Charles of Luxemburg. A new Lombard League was formed by the despots of different communes, and the victory which young Charles won over them at San Felice was soon rendered ineffective by other successes of the league. King John hastened to Italy with a contingent of knights from France, but the support which the papal legate gave to the Luxemburgs was rendered useless when their army was defeated at Ferrara. The Bohemian domination in Italy was shrinking constantly. Lucca in Tuscany was held by Charles, who built a fort there still known as Monte Carlo. Charles saw clearly that the Italian dominions could not be held and persuaded his father to allow him to return to Bohemia. John left small contingents in Parma and some other cities and quitted Italy in October 1333.[9] The only result of John's adventure in Italy was the strengthening of animosity there against foreign domination. John failed to establish warmer relations with the Lombard communes and remained a stranger in Italy as he was in Bohemia. Petrarch likened John's attitude in Italy to that of a hungry wolf eager for a rich bounty.[10]

When leaving Italy, John probably still hoped that he would be able to return and to make another attempt to establish an Italian dominion for his house. He immediately resumed his role of mediator between the emperor and the Pope. According to the new plan for whose realization John started to work, Louis would abdicate in favor of his nephew, Henry of Lower Bavaria, who was also John's son-in-law. The latter would give the necessary guarantees for the integrity of all the possessions which Louis IV had acquired so far for his house. The Pope would then absolve Louis from his condemnation. John of Luxemburg won the agreement of Philip VI of France in return for a promise by Henry, on his assumption of the German crown, to conclude a treaty of friendship and alliance with France and to cede to the French king all imperial possessions in the Kingdom of Arles. It seems that Philip VI also expected to receive from the Pope the vicariate in Lombardy. John of Luxemburg may thus have hoped to renew his attempt in Italy with the help and under the protectorate of France.

The Pope was too slow in giving his consent in principle to initiate negotiations with Louis. He did not welcome the increase in French influence and had to reckon with the opposition of Robert of Naples. When at last he had decided to send his legates to Louis, it was too late. In the meantime the emperor had been approached by Cardinal Orsini, who was preparing a new stroke against John XXII. The Pope was about to be accused of having favored heretical teaching, and was threatened with judgment by a general council. The shrewd emperor, who was also aware of the criticism which rumors of the plans for his abdication had provoked in some German circles, declared these rumors groundless. Thus the plan for a reconciliation between the emperor and the Pope failed. John of Bohemia, disappointed in his hopes, wished to advise the Pope to detach the Kingdom of Arles from the Empire, and volunteered to work for the election of his son-in-law to the German throne. The sud-

den death of the nonagenarian Pope on December 4, 1334, however, put
an end to all these schemes.

In this way ended the first phase of John's interventions on the international stage of Europe. During the second phase he was to be guided
by his son Charles, whose more balanced spirit was able to curb the
adventurous and impetuous character of his father.

The affairs of the Empire were not the only object of John's preoccupations during this period. The relations of Bohemia with Poland provided another problem which demanded a solution and moreover directly affected his own royal aspirations. Although John preferred to stay
in Germany or France rather than to reside in his own kingdom, he was
in no way willing to abandon the claims which he had inherited from
the Přemyslides, including that to the crown of Poland.

However, although John's claims to the Polish crown were confirmed
by Louis IV, he did little enough for many years to realize them. This
gave Wenceslas III's opponent, Władysław Łokietek,[11] more time to
consolidate his position in Poland. When Łokietek began his activities
there, he encountered many difficulties. Although he was the only one
of the Piast dukes who was in any position to attempt the reunion of the
duchies into a single political unit, he was at first welcomed only in
the Duchy of Sandomierz. It was only thanks to the death of Wenceslas II
that he was able to overcome the opposition in Little Poland and to
occupy Cracow in 1306. In Great Poland, however, the Silesian duke
Henry of Głogów dominated the situation. In these circumstances it
was quite possible that Łokietek would have been crushed, had not
Wenceslas III's army disintegrated after his assassination on August 8,
1306. This helped Łokietek to occupy the eastern part of Pomerania
called by the Germans Pomerelia, which was also coveted by the Ascanians of Brandenburg, who had obtained a legal title to this country
from Wenceslas III. When, however, the Brandenburgers in a new
invasion in 1308 had penetrated as far as Danzig, Łokietek appealed to
the Teutonic Knights for help. The latter betrayed the duke and treacherously occupied the whole of Pomerelia. They came to an agreement with
Brandenburg, which was a great blow to Łokietek and to the whole of
Poland. The revolt of some towns in Little Poland in 1311 and the difficulties which Łokietek had with the Bishop of Cracow showed how precarious was his position. John of Luxemburg, however, profited little by
this situation in 1312. Łokietek's position became more secure when,
after the death of Henry of Głogów, he was able to expel Henry's sons
from Great Poland into Silesia, becoming master of the duchy in 1314.
Again the Bohemian king missed an opportunity for intervening, although

the dukes of Glogów continued to press their claims to the crown of Poland.

As previously under Wenceslas II, the Polish higher clergy were the warmest supporters of the renovation of the Kingdom of Poland. They now gave their sympathies and help to Łokietek and worked for the recognition of his pretensions by the Pope. Peter's Pence, the contribution which the Poles were paying to the Papacy, proved to be the best means to win the sympathies of a financier like John XXII. At the assembly of Sulejów in 1318 Łokietek and his bishops accepted the Pope's demand that the rate of Peter's Pence should be raised from threepence per household to a penny per head. Thereupon the Pope not only gave his consent to the coronation of Łokietek, which took place at Cracow in 1320, but also opened a lawsuit against the Teutonic Order, which ended in a verdict that Pomerelia should be restored to Poland. Although the order avoided the execution of the sentence by an appeal, its prestige had suffered a setback.[12]

The King of Bohemia protested at Avignon against the Pope's decision concerning the coronation of Łokietek. He did it, however, in such a way that the Pope could accept the fait accompli after having declared that nobody's rights should be violated by Łokietek's initiative.[13]

However, the new King of Poland still encountered opposition to his authority, especially on the part of the Mazovian and Silesian dukes. The latter, claiming the title *duces Poloniae,* regarded themselves as sovereign, and when some of them protested against Łokietek's acceptance of the higher rate of Peter's Pence, they made it clear that they regarded their duchies as being outside the bounds of the Polish crown.[14]

In spite of this opposition Łokietek's authority continued to grow. His greatest success was the conclusion of an alliance between Poland and Hungary, which was cemented by the marriage of the widowed Hungarian king Charles Robert with Łokietek's daughter Elizabeth (1320). In 1325 Łokietek reached an agreement with the Lithuanians, who were still pagans, and his son Kazimierz married Anne (Aldona), daughter of the Lithuanian duke Gedymin.

With the help of the Lithuanians, Łokietek made an inroad in 1326 into Brandenburg, which was now in the hands of the young son of the Emperor Louis IV, against whom John XXII was mobilizing all available forces. However, intelligence of the devastation wrought by the pagan Lithuanians in a Christian land turned the public opinion of Europe against Łokietek. The Teutonic Order entered into closer relations with the young Wittelsbach and also won the alliance of the Duke of Wrocław (Breslau).

But Łokietek was more endangered by the initiative taken in this connection by John of Luxemburg. Renewing his claims to the Kingdom of Poland, John attacked and advanced as far as Cracow. It was only the intervention of Łokietek's Hungarian ally that brought John's campaign to a halt. The immediate consequence was, however, that at least five, if not all eight, of the dukes of Upper Silesia recognized John of Bohemia as their sovereign. More important was the fact that Henry VI, duke of Wrocław, mainly owing to the initiative of the German burghers of the city, concluded an agreement with John, acknowledging him as his heir. The king appeared personally in Wrocław and acted as its supreme sovereign.

The war against Łokietek's allies the Lithuanians was continued by the order, aided by an influx of knights from Germany still under the spell of the crusading idea. They were joined at the end of 1328 by the King of Bohemia, who probably sought in this way to fulfill his vow to participate in the crusade against Granada, the last Islamic stronghold in Spain. With the forces of the order he invaded the territory of the Lithuanians from Toruń, and together they took the important fort of Medelvagen. The attack launched by Łokietek against the order gave John another opportunity to renew his claims to Polish lands. He concluded a treaty of friendship with the Teutonic Order directed against the Lithuanians and Łokietek, "King of Cracow." Moreover, acting as king of Poland, he ceded to the order Pomerelia, whose possession was still in dispute between the order and Łokietek. John then penetrated into the district of Dobrzyń, which was a part of Kujavja, and forced the Duke of Płock in Mazovia to become his vassal. Before leaving for Silesia, John gave to the order half of the territory of Dobrzyń, together with a promise of half of the territory which he hoped to conquer in the future in Mazovia.

The knights of the order continued their offensive in Kujavja and in Mazovia. Several important cities were occupied by them. This was a sad consequence of Łokietek's attack on the territory of the order. To prevent complications with Brandenburg, which would have aggravated his serious situation, Łokietek had to make peace with its Wittelsbach ruler.

John's military success in Poland had its repercussions in Silesia. The Bohemian king not only was able to put a stop to attacks on the Duke of Wrocław by other Silesian dukes dissatisfied with Henry VI's arrangement with John, but he also forced a number of the petty dukes to recognize his overlordship.[15] The Duke of Glogów resisted, but after his death in 1331 even this duchy became a Bohemian fief. Moreover, that part of Upper Lusatia which had remained in the hands of the Silesian Duke of

Jawor, after the extinction of the Ascanians, submitted to the authority of
the King of Bohemia.

Łokietek continued to do battle against the order with varying success
in 1330 and 1331. But the position of the order was too strong, and he
had to abandon the hope of recovering Pomerelia for Poland. He died
in 1333 without succeeding in uniting all the lands which had been in
the possession of the Piast dynasty. The difficulties which he encountered
show that his task would have been even more arduous if John of Luxemburg had concentrated on conquests in the East. John's lack of genuine
interest in his kingdom and his preference for adventures in the West
facilitated Łokietek's task considerably. Łokietek's greatest merit was to
have revived definitively the idea of Polish unity under a national king.

Łokietek's son and successor, Casimir the Great (1333-1370),[16] saw
clearly that he could not continue the war against his two powerful
neighbors, the Teutonic Order and the King of Bohemia—the less so as
there was also the danger of complications with the Wittelsbach Henry of
Brandenburg, supported by his father the Emperor Louis IV. He therefore contented himself with an extension of the armistice with the order
and King John and started negotiations for a rapprochement with the
Wittelsbachs. This turn of affairs was, however, dangerous for John of
Bohemia, and so his son Charles, margrave of Moravia, prepared the way
for new negotiations between the Czech and Polish kings. Thanks to the
mediation of Charles Robert, king of Hungary, the negotiations began
in Trenčín, then in Hungary. In recognition of John's readiness to renounce all claims to the crown of Poland, Casimir declared his willingness
to accept the situation in Silesia, where most of the princes had accepted
the sovereignty of the Czech king. It was an important diplomatic success for Casimir because John abandoned his alliance with the order and
promised to act as joint arbiter with the Hungarian king in the conflict
between the order and Poland.[17]

The result of the negotiations was solemnly proclaimed in November
1335 at Visegrád, the residence of Charles Robert, where the three kings
had met. John surrendered definitively his title as "King of Poland" in return for the payment by Casimir of a considerable sum of money. The
two arbiters then decided that the order should be given Pomerelia as a
Polish "Alm," but that it should cede Kujavja and Dobrzyń to Casimir.[18]

Casimir, although aware that in the circumstances he could hardly have
obtained a better solution, hesitated to sign the surrender of Silesia to
Bohemia. He only did so in 1339 on the occasoion of another meeting at
Visegrád. So ended an important phase in the relationship of the two
Slavic states. Silesia, for whose possession Poles and Czechs had striven,
became a land of the Bohemian crown. The prestige of the Czech king-

dom was considerably enhanced by this acquisition, and the danger that some at least of the Silesian dukes might become direct vassals of the emperor was averted. Time has, however, shown that the surrender of Silesia to Bohemia weakened considerably the Slavic element in this area. German colonization, which had already begun under the Polish dukes of Silesia, made considerable progress especially in Lower Silesia, where most of the towns were founded by German burghers. German burghers were also John's principal supporters during his campaigns in Silesia. However, it cannot be said that John favored the germanization of Silesia in his own interest. It is not sure that this process would have been slowed down if the province had remained under Poland, although the Polish higher clergy always resisted German penetration more than any other element.

Painful as the surrender of Silesia was to Casimir, he resented even more the loss of Pomerelia. He saw clearly that his country was being cut off from the sea, thus precluding any expansion of Polish interests in that direction. He first tried to avoid this surrender by initiating another legal process. The suit against the order was opened with the Pope's consent in Warsaw in 1339. Its records are of great importance for our knowledge of fourteenth century Poland. But although the order was condemned to cede all conquered Polish territory to Casimir, the decision remained a dead letter. Not even the Pope dared to insist on the execution of the verdict. At last Casimir saw himself forced to give way, and he signed a peace treaty with the order in 1343 at Kalisz based on the arbitrary decisions of 1335. Having thus ensured more peaceful conditions for his kingdom, Casimir concentrated his efforts on the political and economic consolidation of his lands. This enabled him also to initiate Polish expansion toward the East.

The relations between the Czech and Polish kingdoms would probably have developed more amicably had the marriage of Charles' sister Margaret with Casimir been concluded. The marriage was planned by the Margrave Charles, who was already making the strengthening of relations between Bohemia, Poland, and Hungary into one of his principal aims in politics. The wedding should have taken place in Prague in 1341. Unfortunately, Margaret became ill and died, to the great grief of her fiancé, who could be present only at her funeral. Instead of the Czech princess Casimir married Adelaide of Hesse. Even this marriage was arranged by Charles, who desired to attach Casimir to the party among the German princes which was opposed to Louis IV.

In this respect Charles was not fully successful. At the beginning of 1345 Casimir was won over by the emperor to an alliance directed against the House of Luxemburg, which should be sealed by the marriage of

Casimir's second daughter with Louis' son. The first Polish act of hostility against the Czechs was Casimir's attempt to take Charles prisoner on his return from another unsuccessful Lithuanian crusade, in which he had taken part with his father and the young Hungarian king Louis. Charles, however, learning of Polish intentions to capture him while he stayed in Kalisz, escaped from the trap with the help of German burghers of the town.

Casimir thus lost a good opportunity of demanding some territorial concessions in return for the release of a princely prisoner. He then invaded the principality of Racibórz in Silesia. The Czech king quickly retorted, and soon his army stood under the walls of Cracow. Casimir was forced to ask for an armistice, and the Czech-Polish conflict was soon settled thanks to the intervention of the Curia. In order to strenghten good relations with Hungary, Poland's ally, Charles visited the young King Louis in order to prepare the marriage of his daughter Margaret with the Hungarian heir.

The Polish-Czech incident was intimately connected with the second phase of John's intervention in the conflict of Louis IV with the Papacy. The new Pope Benedict XII (1334-1342) was more inclined to a reconciliation with the emperor, and he paid no heed to the suggestions of John and the French king to proceed against Louis of Bavaria on the basis agreed upon before John XXII's death. Emboldened by this, Louis IV dared to launch a new stroke against the Luxemburgs. After the death of Henry of Carinthia (1335), disregarding the late duke's will bequeathing his duchy and Tyrol to his daughter Margaret, who was married to John Henry, the youngest son of the Czech king, the emperor conferred Carinthia with Carniola on the Habsburgs as an imperial fief, reserving to himself the northern part of the Tyrol. However the loyalty of the nobility of Tyrol saved this country, at least, for Margaret. John of Bohemia protested in vain against this unjust decision. The military conflict with the Habsburgs and the emperor, in which John was supported by Hungary, brought no clear decision. The Margrave Charles was only able to consolidate his possession of the Tyrol. In order to weaken the position of the emperor, John made an agreement with the Habsburgs renouncing his rights to the Duchy of Carinthia on condition that Margaret and her boy husband should be left in possession of the Tyrol. In 1337, when Charles had lost for a few months the confidence of his father, he again appeared in the Tyrol and was even able to extend his authority over two Italian cities—Belluno and Feltre.

However, the emperor's position was not weakened by John's entente with the Habsburgs. Hoping for a reconciliation with the Pope through the help of Philip VI, he cultivated good relations with France. But when his attempts proved unsuccesful, Louis IV turned to King Edward III of England, who had renewed his claims to the French throne and was determined to defend his rights to the province of Guyenne in southern France and his trade with Flanders. The Pope tried desperately to reconcile the two rivals, fearing the consequences for western Christendom of an armed conflict between them. John of Luxemburg, acting in the interests of his French ally, made a futile attempt to dissuade the emperor from an alliance with England.

Public opinion in Germany, tired of the prolonged rivalries between the emperor and the Pope, was becoming increasingly hostile in its attitude toward Avignon and Rome. Profiting by this change in public opinion, Louis IV won the Electors for an important act in defense of their rights, and of the rights of the emperor elected by them, against the pretensions of the Curia. This was achieved at the meeting at Rense.[19] The Electors declared that the emperor elected by them did not need any approbation or confirmation on the part of the Curia. He was fully entitled to use his royal and imperial rights when elected, and the Pope enjoyed only the privilege of crowning him and giving him the imperial title.

John of Bohemia was the only electoral prince who was not present at Rense. A formal alliance between England and the Empire was concluded in the summer of 1338, when Edward III met Louis IV at Coblenz and was given the title of general vicar in Germany. When not only John's uncle, the Archbishop of Trier, but also his son-in-law Henry of Lower Bavaria sided with the emperor against France, John remained isolated and was forced to capitulate to the emperor. In the spring of 1339 he did homage to Louis IV in Frankfurt and formally accepted his possessions from him as fiefs of the Empire. A treaty of alliance was then concluded between the Wittelsbachs and the Luxemburgs. John succeeded, however, in safeguarding his obligations toward France.

But this alliance was not fated to last for long, and indeed the first cracks appeared in the autumn of the same year. After the unexpected death of John's son-in-law, Henry of Lower Bavaria, the emperor himself assumed the regency in order to exclude John's widowed daughter Margaret from exercising it in the name of her son John. When at the end of 1340 the eleven-year-old orphan died, Louis IV simply added the whole duchy to his own, even depriving the widow of her appanage. The last blow which completely shattered the alliance came in 1342. The position of John Henry in the Tyrol had been deteriorating for some time. The nobility of the country felt disappointed with the Luxemburgs, from whom more resolute help had been expected in the defense of the late duke's lands. More dangerous was the estrangement between Margaret

—to whom posterity has given the unflattering epithet of "Maultasch" (Sackmouth)—and her much younger husband John Henry. She willingly accepted the suggestion of turning toward the emperor and offering her hand to his widowed son Louis of Brandenburg. John Henry's brother Charles prevented the implementation of these plans by his military intervention in the Tyrol in 1340. At the end of the next year, however, Margaret, aided by her nobles, succeeded in expelling her husband from the Tyrol. The emperor hastened to accept the invitation, and in February 1342 his son married Margaret, nowithstanding the fact that her former marriage was regarded as canonically valid,[20] and took possession of the country. The alliance between the Wittelsbachs and the Luxemburgs was, of course, ended, and armed clashes ensued on the borders of Bohemia and Bavaria.

Although the emperor had violated the Church's prescriptions concerning the sacredness of marriage and had acted without Church authorization, the Luxemburgs would hardly have obtained full support from Benedict XII, who was not ready to aggravate the conflict of the Curia with the emperor. Fortunately Benedict XII died in April of the same year and was succeeded as Pope by Pierre de Rosiers, a favorite of the French court and a friend of the Luxemburgs—he had once been tutor to the Margrave Charles.

The new Pope Clement VI (1342-1352) was determined to bring about the downfall of Louis IV by the election of a new German king. Louis made further attempts at reconciliation, sending embassies to Avignon, asking the Electors for support, and offering the Luxemburgs Lower Lusatia in compensation for the loss of the Tyrol (1345). John's sons, however, mistrusting the emperor, prevented their father from accepting the offer. In the middle of new negotiations between the emperor and the Luxemburgs in 1346, however, the Pope made up his mind, summoned John and his son to Avignon, and disclosed to them his intention of preparing the election of his former pupil Charles as emperor. John's own candidature would not have been opportune, not only because of his unstable character but also because he had gone completely blind.[21]

The Pope proceeded very cautiously with the realization of his plan. Without rejecting completely the possibility of a reconciliation with the excommunicated emperor, he continued to strengthen the position of the Luxemburgs, giving them more time to win over the Electors for the plan of a new imperial election. One of his measures intended to consolidate the position of Charles was the promotion of the bishopric of Prague to metropolitan status, while the bishopric of Olomouc and a new foundation at Litomyšl were to be subject to it. In giving this privileged position to the capital of Bohemia, Clement VI was also taking action against the

Archbishop of Mainz, who had hitherto been metropolitan of Prague and who had sided with Louis IV.

In the meantime the emperor's popularity was declining steadily. German public opinion, which had welcomed Louis' alliance with England against France, was turning slowly against him because of his ambiguous position during the first military conflicts between the two kings and because of his willful transgression of Church doctrine concerning the indissolubility of marriage. The princes resented Louis' cumulation of imperial fiefs in the hands of his family regardless of the rights of former holders. A new case of this kind arose in 1345 when the emperor seized the lands of the Count of Lower Holland after the latter's death. So it came about that Louis failed to find the same support among the princes that he did at Rense. His attempts at encircling the Luxemburgs failed when John and his son forced Casimir of Poland to abandon his hopes of territorial gains in alliance with the emperor.

In view of the danger which the unpredictable Bavarian might provoke if he were given more time for his intrigues, the Pope decided to come into the open. In April 1346 he renewed all former sentences against the "Antichrist" Louis of Bavaria, deprived him of all his rights, and invited the Electors to proceed immediately to a new election, threatening that if they hesitated he would be forced to nominate a new German king and Roman emperor. At the same time he announced to the German princes that Charles of Bohemia was his candidate.

Before this announcement, however, Clement VI made a special agreement with Charles. This agreement has often been criticized as a surrender of imperial rights to the Papacy. Today, however, the opinion seems to prevail that in his negotiations with the Pope, Charles tried successfully to salvage what could still be saved of the imperial idea and of the functions of the emperor. As a good observer of the recent evolution in Germany, he had realized how important the imperial idea with its appeal to universality was for the German people and the German kingdom. For lack of a stricter monarchic regime based on dynastic ties, the imperial idea was the only bond which could give a kind of cohesion and national unity to the many quasi-sovereign states into which Germany had disintegrated. Mindful of the sentiments recently expressed by the Electors at Rense, Charles could not accept the curial view manifested by John XXII that only papal approbation legitimized the exercise of royal power by the elected monarch. He promised to ask for this approbation only before exercising imperial rights in Italy. In the same spirit he avoided any declaration invalidating Louis IV's acts as German king. In many other points his agreement with the Pope recalls the text of Louis' declaration (procuratorium) of 1336, in which the Bavarian enumerated the concessions which he was ready to make in order to be reconciled with the Pope.[22]

French consent to the new arrangement could not be obtained publicly because Philip VI (1328-1350) was at war with England and did not wish to provoke Louis to direct intervention against France. Charles, however, was assured of France's tacit consent by his brother-in-law the Dauphin John. Charles's uncle, the archbishop of Trier, was his main agent in Germany. The Pope had facilitated the situation by appointing a new archbishop of Mainz who was favorable to the Luxemburgs. Although the number of princes who promised to support Charles was small, the election effected on July 11 at Rense was peaceful. Charles was elected Roman king by all the five Electors present.

Louis of Bavaria would probably have placed the Luxemburgs and the Pope in a very difficult position if he had taken immediate and energetic measures against the anti-king. He seems, however, to have overestimated his chances in view of the small number of princes of the Empire who had adhered to Charles. He was also confident of the support of the German cities. In this respect he was not mistaken, as was demonstrated by the refusal of the city of Aachen, where the royal coronations habitually took place, to admit the anti-king within its walls. The coronation was, therefore, only performed in Bonn by the Archbishop of Cologne on November 26, after Charles's election had been approved by the Pope.

Moreover, Louis IV could count on the help of England with whose king, Edward III (1327-1377), he was on friendly relations. The latter had just invaded France, and Philip VI was summoning his vassals to his banner. John and the newly elected King Charles were making a vain attempt to win the sympathies of the Rhine lands when the news reached them. Mindful of his obligations to France and to Philip VI and hoping that a French victory over England would weaken Louis IV and strengthen the position of his son, John hastened to France with his Luxemburg and Czech knights. Charles led his own detachment of knights under the banner of a Roman king. But their hopes were shattered at the decisive battle near the village of Crécy, which proved disastrous for the French army. The English demonstrated for the first time the importance of well-trained infantry experienced in handling the longbow against attacking knights. The losses sustained by the French knights were terrific, and among the slain was the King of Bohemia.[23]

The French historian Jean Froissart has preserved in his chronicle, composed after 1370, a very touching description of the last battle and death of the chivalrous King John. His words show that contemporaries were impressed by the tragic end of a blind king who preferred a noble death to ignominious flight.[24] Froissart's description is not supported in all its details by other chronicles, but his touching picture of the heroic death of a blind knight-errant is a monument which French chivalry has erected to the memory of the King of Bohemia.

It is said that when King Edward heard of his death, he exclaimed with tears in his eyes: "The crown of chivalry has fallen today. Never was anyone equal to this King of Bohemia." It is also said that Edward's son, the Black Prince, assumed the three ostrich feathers from John's crest together with his motto "Ich dien" (I serve). These have remained the crest and motto of the princes of Wales to this day.[25]

The profound echo left by the tragic death of the Bohemian king in contemporary chronicles indicates how well John was known in the courts of fourteenth century Europe. It is at the same time a symbol of the homage paid by the Age of Chivalry to its "Crown of Knighthood." John's Bohemian subjects could, however, hardly remember his reign with satisfaction. Although Bohemia was the basis of all his political combinations and warlike enterprises, John remained a stranger in his own kingdom. He visited his realm only at long intervals and for short periods, and the main aim of his visits was to obtain more money for his adventurous enterprises abroad. The result of this neglect of his royal duties was the diminution of royal authority and the growth of the nobility's influence on the administration of the realm. The constant drain of money from the royal estates and other revenues and the imposition of high taxes ruined the kingdom financially. This is best illustrated by the description of the state of affairs in 1333 made by John's son Charles, when he became margrave of Moravia. He says: "We found the kingdom in such a state of deterioration that we failed to find one of the royal castles which had not been pawned with all its royal estates. We could therefore stay nowhere other than in burghers' houses as an ordinary citizen."

This sad decline in Bohemia's economic position during the reign of John seems all the more depressing when compared with developments in Hungary, which was also ruled by a king of a foreign dynasty, Charles Robert of Anjou (1308-1342). After a protracted struggle this Frenchman subdued the powerful aristocracy and then devoted all his energies to the economic development of his kingdom. It was not the Czech but the Hungarian king who profited by the experience and the reforms of the last Přemyslides. Charles Robert organized the exploitation of Hungary's mineral wealth on the Czech model, and following the example of Wenceslas II, he introduced a successful monetary reform. In regulating taxation and supporting the rising cities, Charles Robert ensured a new era of prosperity for his realm.[26]

The same cannot be said of John of Luxemburg. Nevertheless his reign was not completely sterile for the growth of the Bohemian kingdom. His lasting acquisition for the crown of Bohemia lay in the sovereignty over the Cheb (Eger), Upper Lusatia, and the greater part of Silesia. It was the task of his son and successor Charles to consolidate these acquisitions and to raise Bohemia to new financial and economic heights.

NOTES

1. For more details see E. Zeck, *Der Publizist Pierre Dubois* (see Bibl.); cf. also F. Bock, *Reichsidee und Nationalstaaten* (see Bibl.), pp. 147-48 (Deutscher Thronkampf und französisches Papsttum). On Dubois cf. *ibidem,* pp. 486 ff.

2. Dante's letters to Henry VII were published by P. Toynbee, *Dantis Alagherii Epistolae* (Oxford, 1920).

3. Rich indications of source material and complete bibliographical data on Henry VII are given by F. Schneider, *Kaiser Heinrich VII.* (See Bibl.)

4. John gave his son the name of Wenceslas in deference to the Přemyslide saint and in memory of Elizabeth's father, Wenceslas II. He was, however, called Charles, after his uncle Charles IV the Fair (1322-1328), king of France, who acted as his godfather at his confirmation.

5. The most important work in Czech on John of Luxemburg was written by J. Šusta in České dějiny, vol. 2, part 2 (*Král cizinec*—"The Foreigner King"— Prague, 1939), and in vol. 2, part 3 (*Karel IV: Otec a syn, 1333-1346*—"Charles IV: Father and Son, 1333-1346"—Prague, 1946). There more detailed Czech bibliography will be found.

6. For more details on the papal lawsuits against Louis IV and on his appeals see R. Moeller: *Ludwig der Bayer und die Kurie* (see Bibl.), pp. 36 ff. The author mentions the role of the Bohemian king as mediator only briefly on p. 80, for the year 1330. Cf. also Th. Lindner (see Bibl.), vol. I, pp. 284, 411 ff.

7. Some German historians saw in John's mediation an intention to dispossess Louis of his throne and to prepare the way to the imperial dignity for himself or his son. J. Šusta (*Král cizinec,* pp. 370 ff.) shows clearly that at that time John did not intend to compete for the imperial crown.

8. Louis IV sent a most friendly letter to John in which he offered him the dignity of his vicar in Germany during his absence from the kingdom. The Italian Ghibellines had also appealed to John to second Louis' imperial plans, recalling the memory of his father Henry VII. The letters were published by E. E. Stengel, *Nova Alamaniae* (Berlin, 1921), vol. I, pp. 93 ff. The letter of the Italian Ghibellines (*ibid.,* pp. 95 ff.) is addressed to John "Bohemie et Polon(ie) regi" (sic!).

9. For more details see the study by L. Pöppelmann, *Johann von Böhmen in Italien (1330-1333)* (see Bibl.), pp. 249-462. The author quotes the main Italian and Bohemian sources important for this period of John's reign. These are completed by E. Schiecher in his study "Příspěvky k dějinám politiky Jana Lucemburského. Podle pramenů z italských archivů," *Zprávy českého zemského archivu,* vol. 7 (1927), a contribution to the history of John, based on material found in Italian archives. See also A. Lehleiter, *Die Politik K. Johanns von Böhmen in den Jahren 1331-1334* (Bonn, 1908), and J. Šusta,

Král cizinec, pp. 481-573. On the Italian policy of the Curia, see H. Otto, *Zur italienischen Politik Johanns XXII* (see Bibl.).

10. Cf. L. Pöppelmann, pp. 390-392. Petrarch was then living at Avignon. He described the sad situation of Italy in a letter in hexameters to Aeneas Tolomei di Siena.

11. The reign of Łokietek has not yet been the object of a scholarly monograph. The best Polish study on the thirteenth century in Poland and on Łokietek is that by S. Zachorowski, "Wiek XIII i panowanie Wld. Łokietka," in *Encyklopedya Polska*, vol. 5, part 1, pp. 134-309. On pp. 302-309, the author gives a detailed Polish bibliography on this period. J. Roepell and J. Caro's *Geschichte Polens*, vol. 2 (Gotha, 1863) can still be read with profit, although it is outdated in many ways.

12. The main sources concerning the disputes between the order and Poland were published in two volumes in Poznań in 1890 (*Lites et res gestae inter Polonos Ordinemque Cruciferorum*). For a more complete bibliography see St. Zajączkowski, *Polska a Zakon Krzyzacki* (Archivum Tow. Nauk, Lwów, 1929).

13. The Polish historian O. Balzer in his standard work on the Polish history of this period (*Królewstvo polskie 1295-1370*, Lwów, 1919-20, vol. II, pp. 281 ff.) put forward the thesis that John of Luxemburg had pretensions only to Great Poland when speaking of his rights to the Polish kingdom. J. Šusta (*Král cizinec*, pp. 426, 468) shows clearly that John always had the whole Kingdom of Poland in mind.

14. On the many problems concerning Peter's Pence see the monograph by E. Maschke, *Der Peterspfennig* (see Bibl.).

15. The famous French poet Guillaume de Machaut, a great admirer of John of Luxemburg, in whose service he stayed from 1323 on, speaks in "Le Confort d'ami" of thirteen Silesian dukes paying homage to John. This work also gives highly interesting information on John's Lithuanian campaign (Hoepffner, *Oeuvres de Guillaume de Machaut*, vol. 3 (1921), pp. 103 ff.). Cf. also Comte de Puymaire, "Une campagne de Jean de Luxembourg, roi de Bohême," *Revue des questions historiques*, vol. 42 (1887), pp. 168 ff.

16. On Casimir the Great, see O. Halecki, "Kazimierz Wielki," in the *Encyklopedya Polska*, vol. 5, part 1 (Cracow, 1920), pp. 310-409. Minute indications on the sources of Casimir's reign and much Polish bibliographical data will be found in the monograph by Z. Kaczmarczyk, *Kazimierz Wielki, 1330-1370* (Warsaw, 1948), pp. 388-394. Cf. also his book *Monarchia Kazimierza Wielkiego. Organizacja kościoła, sztuka i nauka* (Poznań, 1946).

17. The documents signed at Trenčín were published by O. Bauer, "Poznámky k mírovým smlouvám československým z roku 1335" (Comments on the Czech-Polish treatises from 1335), *Sborník Friedrichův* (Prague, 1931), pp. 9-22.

18. During the new Lithuanian expedition which he had undertaken as another crusade in 1336, John made another attempt to reconcile the order with Casimir. His son Charles visited the grand master of the order in October 1341 on a similar mission.

19. For more details on this important meeting and on the conflict between Louis IV and the popes in general see E. E. Stengel: *Avignon und Rhens* (see Bibl.).

20. The emperor was aided in this respect by his two advisors Marsilius of Padua and William of Ockham. The first pretended that the emperor had

the right to dissolve unsuccessful marriages in the interests of the welfare of his subjects. Ockham regarded the marriage with John Henry as invalid. Without denying the Church's right to give judgment on the validity of a marriage, as did Marsilius, Ockham ascribed to the emperor the same right in exceptional cases. John Henry later obtained a declaration of the nullity of his marriage with Margaret on the ground of nonconsummation of the union. For details see E. Werunsky, *Geschichte Kaiser Karls IV* (see Bibl.), vol. I, pp. 451 ff.

21. John had suffered from bad eyesight since his boyhood. He lost the sight of one eye in 1337 on his crusading expedition against the Lithuanians. In 1340 he went to Montpellier to consult some specialists, but they could not save the sight of his second eye. The cause of his misfortune is not clear. The loss of his eyesight was probably brought about by glaucoma, for which, of course, medieval doctors knew no remedy.

22. This is evident from K. Zeumer's edition of Charles' acts (*M. G. H. Constitutiones VIII*, pp. 12-17). The words and phrases copied by Charles from Louis' procuratorium are there printed in smaller type.

23. On the battle of Crécy see especially the study by J. Viard: "La Campagne de juillet-aout 1346 et la bataille de Crécy" (*Le Moyen Age*, 36, 1926), pp. 1-84, where earlier bibliographical data will be found.

24. *Chroniques abrégées*, ed. Kervynda Lettenhove, *Oeuvres de Froissart* (Bruxelles, 1872), vol. 17.

25. J. Šusta (*Karel IV, otec a syn*, pp. 505-512), after reviewing the principal reports on John's death, expresses his doubts as to the reliability of these traditions. It is doubtful whether John wore ostrich feathers in his crest on the day of the battle. One source speaks rather of hawk's feathers. There seems to be no evidence that John used the motto "Ich dien." Edward III ordred a funeral service to be held for the king and sent his body to Luxemburg. John's bodily relics also experienced a troubled history. After several transfers they were found in 1833 by King Frederick William IV of Prussia in a collection of curiosities. He caused them to be deposited in a chapel at Castel on the Saar, whence they were transported on August 26, 1946, the six hundredth anniversary of his death, back to Luxemburg.

26. It is the merit of the Hungarian historian B. Hóman to have thrown new light on the economic reforms of the first Angevin king of Hungary. For details see B. Hóman: *Gli Angiovini di Napoli* (see Bibl.), pp. 149-243.

Chapter IV

CHARLES IV, EMPEROR AND KING
OF BOHEMIA, AND CASIMIR THE GREAT,
KING OF POLAND

Charles's education and character—Struggle for the imperial throne—Charles's rule in Germany—Charles's Italian policy—Charles and Cola di Rienzo in Prague—Charles's first Italian expedition, Petrarch's criticism—Charles's second Italian expedition—Emperor Charles and the Kingdom of Arles—The Golden Bull—Juridical and economic reforms in Bohemia, the Maiestas Carolina— *Territorial additions to the Kingdom of Bohemia—Charles's commercial policy, control of the Oder and Elbe waterways—Prague, capital of the Empire—Charles and the Habsburgs—Polish expansion toward the East under Casimir—Casimir's consolidation of Poland—Casimir, Charles IV, and the Teutonic Order—The Congress of Cracow—Casimir's success in the East and against Brandenburg—Casimir's succession—Louis of Anjou, king of Poland—The Luxemburg candidacy for the Polish throne—Charles secures the German throne for his son Wenceslas—Charles's imperial policy*

Charles was well prepared for the difficult tasks ahead of him. Although in his youth he had sometimes felt the adventurous impulses that had prompted his father to become a knight-errant, he had inherited undoubtedly a more stable nature from his Přemyslide mother. Moreover, he regarded not Luxemburg but Bohemia as his native country and had learned his mother's Czech tongue well. He spent his youth in Paris, at the most brilliant court of contemporary Europe. There he not only received a good education, but also became acquainted with the administrative machinery of the French monarchy, modernized and perfected by the last Capetians. Paris was also the seat of a famous university and the center of Christian learning as expounded by the great teachers of scholastic philosophy. All this stimulated his eagerness for learning and his interest in religious questions.[1]

His experiences in Italy, where he had fought for two years under most difficult conditions, could only sharpen his sensitive mind. There he was thrown into the intricate complications of Italian diplomacy, with all its brilliant as well as repulsive aspects, and he had shown his ability to learn both quickly and well. The contrast between the political chaos in Lombardy and the firm monarchic and feudal regime in France taught him to appreciate the value of a stable central administration for the welfare of the realm. Lombardy also taught him the importance of stable finances, while the wealth of its cities led him to appreciate the significance of commerce for the prosperity of a state. There, at Lucca, Charles tasted also some of the seductions of vice. But a lively dream in which he saw one of his friends indulging in the same excesses and then punished by an angel, who threatened Charles with the same fate, made such a deep impression on his young soul that it became a moral lodestar for the rest of his life. His profound religious sentiment, also inherited from his mother, manifested itself in a lively interest in theological discussions, in a true appreciation of good relations between the imperium and the sacerdotium, and in a passion for collecting religious relics. In this respect he succumbed to the mood of his time, but although his zeal may today appear exaggerated, Charles was in no way bigoted. He was, at bottom, a realist, able to examine even Church affairs coolly, bearing in mind the interests of his realm.[2]

After his father's death and his own coronation, Charles lost no time in organizing a military expedition against Louis IV. At the height of the crisis, however, he received the news that his Bavarian rival had died suddenly of apoplexy when hunting bears. Charles's situation improved greatly, because he could now justifiably claim to be the legitimate king. The Wittelsbach party was weakened, and looked in vain for a suitable successor to Louis IV. Charles won over to his side Rudolf, the Elector of the Palatinate, a Wittelsbach, whose daughter Anne he married after the death of his first wife, Blanche.

A curious incident enabled him to win over the other Wittelsbachs definitively. In Brandenburg, where Louis' regime was very unpopular, an old man called Müller suddenly appeared, claiming to be the Ascanian Margrave Waldemar, who had died in 1319. He pretended to have spent in Palestine the years since his simulated burial and to be returning to claim his land. Because he probably bore some resemblance to the late Waldemar and because Louis of Bavaria was unpopular in Brandenburg, this adventurer found numerous adherents among the simple people. This incident was cleverly exploited by Brandenburg's neighbors, the

Archbishop of Magdeburg, the Duke of Saxony, and the Count of Anhalt, who hoped that after the death of the old pretender, they would be able to "inherit" his lands. Invited by Charles to examine the trustworthiness of the pretender's story, the three neighbors declared it true and invaded Brandenburg. Their military operations, however, were not as successful as they had hoped. Charles, who had accepted the pretender's claims and hoped to inherit Lusatia from him, changed sides, abandoned his former allies, and started secret negotiations with the Wittelsbachs. He succeeded in inducing them to abandon their candidate as Louis' successor, the Count Günther, and to pay him homage after he had confirmed them in the possession of Brandenburg and of Tyrol. When Günther died, Charles attended his burial in person, a gesture which won him new supporters and also gave the opposition the satisfaction of seeking the confirmation of his royal dignity by a second coronation, this time in the traditional manner, at Aix-la-Chapelle (Aachen) on June 18, 1349. The Wittelsbachs surrendered to Charles the crown and other imperial insignia in February, 1350, when, after rejecting Waldemar, he had at Bautzen (Budyšin) solemnly confirmed them in the possession of their lands as fiefs of the Empire.

Charles had thus shown unusual diplomatic adroitness in the liquidation of so many difficulties which had blocked the way to his definite recognition as German and Roman king. Some of his moves show that he had been an apt pupil of the crafty Lombards. On the whole, he had sized up well the situation in Germany, where people were tired of the continuous struggles for the throne and anxious for more peaceful times. This was one of the reasons why Charles had so often preferred to circumvent or win over his adversaries by money or grants of new favors.

Another reason for his restraint in handling the dangerous situation lay in the new social scourges of Germany. The Black Death, a pestilence which had originated in the Orient, had spread in 1348 from Italy into Germany and was depopulating the unhygienic medieval cities. A religious epidemic accompanied the spread of this scourge. Processions of frantic penitents trying to pacify God and to avert the Black Death by flagellation wandered from city to city spreading panic, hysteria, and the epidemic. These religious fanatics propagated the nonsensical accusation that the Jews had poisoned the wells and caused the epidemic. This agitation ended in wholesale massacres of Jews in the cities. The bloodbaths were often welcomed by the burghers, jealous of the economic prosperity of Jewish merchants and financiers, and were tolerated by the nobles, who thus liquidated their debts to Jewish bankers and enriched themselves with the fortunes of murdered Jews. The pogroms provoked such disorder and unrest that any military conflicts would have aggravated the situation beyond measure. The country needed peace, and the first task of the new king was to stop the agitation. Charles acted, however, without haste and did not refuse certain profits which the death of rich merchants brought to the royal finances. He only became more energetic when the agitation reached his hereditary domains.[3] He also asked Clement VI to condemn and ban the fraternities of the flagellants.

Charles's rule in Germany was also characterized by peaceful methods. He was too realistic a statesman to overlook the fact that the disintegration of the Empire into independent principalities had gone too far and that unity could not be brought about by force of arms. He used his regal power to stop armed conflicts between territories and cities, and imposed peace conventions called Landfriede for different parts or for the whole of the Empire. In this way he induced the different classes of his subjects to remember that they belonged to one political unit and that there was still a central authority which should be obeyed. He therefore made a personal appearance as often as possible in the different parts of Germany, imposing the Landfriede and contributing to a better appreciation of the idea of the Empire.

This was, of course, only a poor substitute for the nonexistent central power in the Empire, but it was all that Charles could do and wished to do in the circumstances. Such methods best suited his personal character. He was not a warrior, and the serious attack of gout which he had suffered in 1350 made him even more inclined to peaceful methods. In order to render his government more effective he reserved to himself the direct government over the eastern territories of Germany, appointing his uncle, the Archbishop of Trier, as his vicar in the western part.[4] He extended this system to Lombardy and to the Kingdom of Arles, where, of course, the imperial authority was almost forgotten.

With regard to Italy, Charles knew from his own experience the dangers which might arise from involvement in the intricate political situation there. In his Italian policy he was not willing to follow the examples of his grandfather Henry VII or of Louis IV. His only aim was to obtain the imperial title through coronation in Rome and to induce the many political bodies there to recognize the authority of the emperor by rendering him homage and paying an imperial tax. He had no intention of wasting the resources of Germany and Bohemia to obtain any more from this tangle of political intrigues and feuds.

He realized that the gulf between imperial Italy and Germany had grown considerably in recent years and that it would be more than hazardous to try to stop the process of alienation. The animosity between Ghibellines and Guelfs had subsided since the time of Louis' appearance in Italy, but the groups remained basically the same. They had gained more compactness without, however, being able to make any marked progress toward building up a single Italian political unit. In Tuscany the group of Guelf cities—Florence, Lucca, Siena, with their dependencies—stood opposed to the local aristocracy, who mostly cherished Ghibelline sympathies. The *popolo grasso*—the "fat" class of merchants and industrialists which governed those cities—was jealous of its freedom and was opposed, in principle, to any outside authority, especially to that of the emperor. In the North the Visconti family, which dominated Milan, had made the most progress toward a unification of Italy by extending their power over the whole of Lombardy, Genoa, and papal Bologna. Profiting by the attack of King Louis of Hungary, who claimed the heritage of the Kingdom of Naples for the Hungarian branch of the Angevins, the Visconti occupied some cities in Piedmont belonging to Queen Joanna of Naples. The Visconti were the fiercest opponents of papal political power in Italy. In this constant struggle with the Visconti, the popes of Avignon sought through their legates, nominally acting as imperial vicars, to protect their state and the rights of the Empire.

It would have been natural, therefore, for Clement VI to work for an agreement between the Tuscan Guelfs—since Florence felt endangered by the expansion of the Visconti—and Charles against the rulers of Milan. Charles, however, was not willing to engage his forces in Italy for the political profit of the Papacy, and dismissed the Florentine embassy with vague promises. The Pope on his part had lost some of his earlier enthusiasm for Charles, who had given him so many proofs of his independence and had especially disappointed him by his reconciliation with the excommunicated Wittelsbachs. Fearing that Charles's Italian expedition might have some unexpected ending, the Pope preferred to accept the Visconti offer to recognize his authority rather than conclude a pact with the Florentines and Charles. He also deliberately delayed his permission for Charles' Roman coronation.

The Pope may have been alarmed also by the approaches which were made to Charles by Cola di Rienzo, who had for a short time, in defiance of the Pope, set up his rule in Rome as tribune of the Roman people. After his downfall, at the end of 1347, Cola, a fierce believer in Roman greatness, lived in seclusion with Franciscan monks in the mountains. There he came to the conviction that Roman glory could only be revived by a new Augustus, whose forerunner he should himself be. So in 1350 he appeared in Prague and disclosed to Charles some secret prophecies to the effect that he, the new Roman king, was selected by Providence to renew the old glory of Rome and to unite all Christendom under his scepter.[5] Charles was impressed by the enthusiasm of the dreamer although Cola's prophecies and ideas left him unmoved. Fearing that the presence in Prague of an excommunicate, who was accused of heresy, might spoil his chances further with the Pope, Charles placed Cola under the supervision of the Archbishop of Prague. But even from the castle of Roudnice, where Cola was interned, he continued to exhort Charles in letters and treatises to a *renovatio imperii* for which he had been chosen by God. The fierce tribune even claimed to be an illegitimate son of Henry VII.

It is characteristic of Charles that he answered Cola's letters, showing appreciation for his education, style, and rhetorical talent.[6] When Charles was invited by Petrarch to make his Roman expedition and to follow in the footsteps of his grandfather, he asked Rienzo to compose the answer to Petrarch's letter. Finally, on the Pope's insistence, Charles had to send Rienzo to Avignon. The proceedings against Rienzo had, however, not yet been concluded when Clement VI died. Under his successor Rienzo was even given the satisfaction of trying to realize his ideas with the help and for the profit of the Papacy. Sent by Innocent VI (1352-62) to Rome as senator, Rienzo was, however, killed during the revolt provoked against him by the Roman aristocracy (1354).

The sending of Rienzo to Rome was inspired by the policy of the new Pope, who abandoned the idea of papal supremacy over the whole of Italy and tried to pacify and regain at least the papal state. For this purpose he needed the help of Charles against the Visconti, who were threatening papal territories. Innocent VI was therefore not opposed to Charles's Roman expedition.[7] Charles concluded treaties with all the enemies of the Visconti but was not at all enthusiastic for the idea that his entry into Italy should mean war. He was rescued from this unpleasant situation by the unexpected accident of the death of John, archbishop of Milan, the fiercest leader of the Visconti, which left the other members of the clan more ready for peaceful negotiations. For the price of the imperial vicariate which Charles had conferred on them, they recognized his imperial supremacy and assured him free passage across their territory. Charles could enter Milan in great state and was crowned there with the iron crown of the Lombard kings.

Making use of his diplomatic talents, Charles advanced southward, accepting the homage of the ruling classes of the cities and collecting imperial taxes. He even won over Florence, the fiercest enemy of imperial power, and collected a huge sum from that city. Arriving before Rome, Charles visited the holy places in disguise as a pilgrim but entered the city officially only on the day of his coronation, Easter Sunday, 1355, and, according to his promises to the Pope, he left it before the end of the day.

Charles's Roman expedition gave him what he sought—the imperial title and the re-establishment of his authority over imperial Italy without fighting. This was, however, not what some of his contemporaries in Italy had expected. Cola di Rienzo was not the only one who had dreamed of a renovation of the Roman Empire. There was yet another, more brilliant, thinker and writer who had hoped that Charles would follow in the footsteps of his grandfather, Henry VII, by realizing the pacification of Italy and become a true successor of the great Roman Caesars—Petrarch. Charles was enchanted by the brilliance of this forerunner of humanism and invited him to visit him during his Roman journey. They met in Mantua, and Charles, fascinated by Petrarch's extraordinary personality, listened patiently to the poet's exhortations to imitate the virtues of the great Roman Caesars and to renew old Roman greatness. Although Charles appreciated the poet's talents, he was in no way persuaded by his arguments. Disillusioned in his expectations, Petrarch greeted the returning emperor with bitter words of reproach, echoing the sentiments of many other Italian patriots. The Ghibellines could not forgive Charles his submission to the Pope's wishes and saw in his short stay in Rome an affront to the imperial dignity. The disappointment spread, and in Pisa Charles had a narrow escape from the enraged populace, which had set fire to the royal palace. All this, however, only served to make Charles hasten his return from Italy.

Charles's attitude is often criticized by historians. It is true that he often had recourse, on his Roman expedition, to cunning diplomacy, and his attitude could hardly fire the imagination of some Italian patriots. On the whole, however, Charles made a good appreciation of the situation and, in the circumstances, saved for the Empire what could still be saved. It would have been pure folly for Charles to endeavor to realize Henry VII's plans, as Petrarch had expected. Rienzo was more realistic in his dreams than Petrarch. His dream of a federation of Italian cities and peoples under the supremacy of a national emperor residing in Rome had at least some practical basis, but Petrarch limited himself to phantasies on the greatness of ancient Rome, which should be renovated by Charles. The Italians still respected the imperial idea but were opposed, at the same time, to any effective imperial power. Rienzo and Petrarch with their followers were isolated, and their dreams were actually supported by none of the numerous city-states and sovereign territories, which preferred their own local interests to any general ones. Charles saw clearly through the dust of Italian political tempests and intrigues and as a realistic statesman contented himself with what could be attained without arms. It must be admitted that not even Henry VII and Louis IV had been able to accomplish by force of arms what Charles achieved with diplomacy, especially the submission of Guelf Florence.[8]

This was not the only Italian expedition organized by Charles. In 1368 he felt called to Rome again by his duty as emperor to protect the Papacy.[9] Charles was not unaware of the growing desire among sincere Christians for the return of the papacy from Avignon to Rome. As long as the prestige of France was on the wane, because of the disasters of the Hundred Years' War against England, the need for the return of the Papacy to Rome was not so urgent. When, however, King Charles V the Wise (1364-1380) had strengthened the French monarchy again, the Avignon "captivity" encountered increasing resentment outside France, especially in England and in Germany.

Pope Urban V (1362-1370), previously a Benedictine abbot, was zealous for the reform of the Church. So, attentive to passionate exhortations, from Petrarch among others, he was willing to return to Rome. However, he needed the help of the emperor to realize his plan. The Papal States were again threatened by the Visconti, whose defiance forced the emperor to take away the vicariate he had previously conferred on them. Moreover, Italy was plagued by the bands of soldiers who had just served in the French and English armies and had transferred their activity to Italy after the peace of Bretigny (1360); offering their services to the many warring cities and political parties, they ravaged the land and extorted huge sums of money from the unfortunate population. The Pope founded a special league for defense against the wandering companies of soldiers, but without the help of the emperor there was no hope of pacifying the Papal States and securing the return of the Pope to Rome.

The emperor gave Urban firm assurances of help when he visited him in Avignon in 1365, and obtained the imperial assembly's approval for an Italian expedition to help the Pope, who had returned to Rome in 1367. The imperial army attacked the Visconti and their allies, but again Charles's diplomacy proved more effective than his armed forces. The emperor concluded a favorable peace with the Visconti in Modena and conferred on them anew the imperial vicariate in Lombardy. He persuaded them to adhere to the league formed by the Pope, and obtained a considerable military contingent for his march on Rome, where he was greeted by the Pope in 1368.

Although Charles rendered all customary honors to the Pope, acknowledging the supremacy of the sacerdotium, he was not prepared to follow the advice of the papalists to extend the Papal States and further to restrain the Visconti. On the contrary, he induced the Pope to make peace with the Visconti, and only with reluctance did he appoint a cardinal as imperial vicar of Tuscany, knowing how unpopular such a measure would be. Events confirmed his fears. In general, Charles limited his diplomatic efforts to reinforcing peaceful relations between the territories and the city-states (*signorias*). He recognized that the *signorias* represented forces of order which it would be a mistake to combat. He showed hostility only toward the unruly elements, represented especially by the companies of the mercenaries, and defeated one of the most dangerous bands near Arezzo. Thanks to his diplomacy Charles obtained in Italy results similar to those of his first expedition. Once again, even Florence recognized Charles's supremacy, and the taxes paid by his Italian subjects financed the costs of the expedition.

Unfortunately, almost everything collapsed again after his departure in the summer of 1369. The Visconti revolted, and feuds between the *signorias* recommenced. The Pope, feeling isolated in Rome, returned to Avignon, where he soon died (1370). After these experiences, Charles returned to his previous tactics in Italy, limiting himself to diplomatic intervention and to the appointment of imperial vicars.

Charles followed a similar policy in the Kingdom of Arles, still nominally a part of the Empire although deeply influenced by France, whose kings coveted its possession. French ascendancy made another important inroad there when the Count of Dauphiné—the dauphin, who was in debt—ceded his lands to the French heir apparent (1343), an arrangement which entered into effect in 1349. Charles was, at that time, still struggling for his crown in Germany. All he could do to protect the interests of the Empire against further encroachment was to conclude a treaty of friendship with France in 1347, followed in the next year by a similar treaty with England.[10] He also separated Savoy and the county of Geneva from the Kingdom of Arles and made them immediately subject to the Empire. To safeguard the rights of the Empire in Dauphiné, Charles induced the French heir apparent to accept the county from the emperor an as imperial fief. When the dauphin, as heir apparent, ascended the French throne in 1364, the emperor let himself be crowned in 1365 as king of Burgundy in order to demonstrate that it was still a part of the Empire. All Charles's predecessors since Frederick Barbarossa had omitted the performance of this ceremony. Charles only surrendered the imperial rights over Avignon to the Papacy after the Pope had acquired this district from Joanna, queen of Naples, who held the southern part of the Kingdom of Arles as an imperial fief. Charles also renewed his claims to sovereignty over the county of Burgundy, the Franche-Comté, which was already firmly in French hands, when he conferred it (1362) on Prince Philip as an imperial fief.

These actions could retard, but not stop, the gravitation of this part of the Empire toward eventual union with the Kingdom of France. Charles himself gave considerable impetus to this development later. In order to win French approval for the succession of his son Wenceslas to the German throne and for the marriage of his son Sigismund to the Angevin princess, Mary, heiress to the crown of Hungary, he had to confer on the French heir apparent not only the vicariate of Dauphiné and of the neighboring dioceses, but also that of the whole Kingdom of Arles (1378). He thought it necessary to make this sacrifice because the French dynasty could otherwise have voiced claims to the throne of Hungary, which Charles planned to secure for his son Sigismund.[11]

Charles had clearly recognized that the dreams of the Hohenstaufens concerning the expansion of the Empire were definitely out of date, and that not even the noble attempts of his grandfather to resuscitate the imperial ideal could be repeated because the situation in Germany and Italy had undergone profound changes. As a realist he modeled his foreign and imperial policy accordingly. But the situation had also changed profoundly in Germany itself since the times of the Hohenstaufens. Even here Charles acted as a realistic statesman, trying through peaceful means to save what could be saved.

In some ways the situation which Charles had found in Germany was also a legacy from the Hohenstaufens. Frederick II, unable to rule alone over the growing number of princes pretending to be masters in their own lands, felt obliged to grant sovereign rights to the most important imperial princes in the hope of controlling the kingdom with their help. However, it proved impossible to restrict these privileges to only a few territorial rulers. More and more princes acquired the same rights. Fortunately, some imperial princes were able to maintain a privileged position which entitled them, as electoral princes, to play a prominent role during the interregnum after the extinction of the Hohenstaufens. Under the reign of Louis IV the electoral princes gained even more importance as defenders of imperial rights against the pretensions of the Curia.

Charles, following to some extent the method of Frederick II, made the college of Electors his close allies in governing the tangle of quasi-sovereign principalities, towns, and ecclesiastical territories. But as this situation had developed gradually and the rights of the Electors were based only on custom, the emperor decided to give their position a more solid legal basis. The special code embodying this was carefully prepared by Charles and promulgated in 1356, after prolonged discussions with the Electors and other princes at the imperial assemblies in Nürnberg and Metz. The document containing this law, which was meant to provide some sort of constitution for the Empire, was sealed with the imperial Golden Bull, after which it is known.

First of all the number of Electors was definitely fixed, and any doubt as to which branch of a family was entitled to exercise the vote was removed. Besides the archbishops of Mainz, Trier, and Cologne, four secular princes were confirmed in the possession of electoral rights—the King of Bohemia, the Count Palatine of the Rhine, the Duke of Saxony, and the Margrave of Brandenburg. Hitherto the dignity had often been in dispute between different branches of the princely families, especially between the Bavarian and Palatine branches of the Wittelsbachs and in Saxony between the houses of Wettin and Lauenburg. In both cases Charles secured the dignity for the branch which had supported him. In order to prevent such splits in the future, it was specified that secular electorates should be indivisible and be inherited by the principle of primogeniture. Should the princely family in possession of the electorate die out, the succession was to be settled by the king or, in the case of Bohemia, by election by the local princes. Moreover, in order to prevent double imperial elections, it was specified that elections should be effected by majority and without delay. The Archbishop of Mainz was entitled to convoke the Electors to Frankfurt, where the elections should take place. The coronation should be performed at Aix-la-Chapelle (Aachen), and the first imperial assembly should convene at Nürnberg.

The Electors were, moreover, given certain privileges which distinguished them from other princes. They were given regalian rights over salt and mines, over the Jews and the coinage. Their courts were accorded final jurisdiction without right of appeal. Only in exceptional cases of refusal of justice could the royal court intervene. Bohemia was, however, completely exempted from the jurisdiction of the imperial courts. The persons of the Electors were even protected by the extension to them of the privilege given to the senators by Justinian.

It is significant that there is no trace in the Golden Bull of the papal claims against the Empire and the emperor. Here Charles accepted the stipulations of Rense (Rhens, Rhense) defending the rights of the Electors and rejecting the Pope's claims to approve the election and to exercise a papal vicariate during an interregnum. In such an eventuality the affairs of the Empire were to be administered by the Count Palatine of the Rhine and the Duke of Saxony. The Count Palatine should also sit in judgment over the king. This, however, the king could avoid by nonappearance.

It is thus clear that Charles's intention was to transform the German monarchy into an aristocratic oligarchy. This intention is indicated even more clearly by another measure contained in the Golden Bull. Charles planned yearly meetings with the Electors in order to discuss the most important affairs of the Empire. Owing to the distances separating the lands of the Electors and the primitive means of transportation, this measure could not be put into practice. Charles was also anxious to induce the Electors to share his idea of the Empire as a nonnational state with a pretension to universality. For this reason he specified in the

Golden Bull that the heirs of the Electors should learn not only German but also Italian and Czech.

The clauses of the Bull dealing with other princes and with the cities generally favored feudal customs and rights. Confederations of cities might be concluded only with the permission of the territorial lords. The cities were permitted to grant citizenship only to their residents, and fugitives from other jurisdictions were not to be admitted. Other regulations were destined to prevent private wars and to encourage Landfriede confederations, including both territorial lords and cities.[12]

In general, in the Golden Bull Charles was not enacting new laws, but only codifying and stressing what was good in the old laws and customs. He had attained his main goals—the definitive elimination of double elections, so disastrous for Germany and the Empire, and the building up of the government on a new basis, the aristocratic oligarchy of the college of Electors. His code remained the basic law of the Empire until 1806.

Bearing in mind that the emperor's authority in the Empire depended mainly on the solidity and prosperity of his family estate (*Hausmacht*), Charles devoted most of his efforts to consolidating the strength and prosperity of his Bohemian kingdom. Already during the life of his father, as margrave of Moravia and then as governor of Bohemia, Charles had helped to reorganize the economic and financial strength of the kingdom, so badly depleted by his father. One of his first thoughts when he became king of Bohemia was to give the country a new juridical basis. This Czech "Golden Bull"—the lawbook known as *Maiestas Carolina* [13] —was ready for promulgation in 1355. His principal aims were to strengthen the authority and administration of the royal court, to stop abuses in the local courts, which were in the hands of the nobility, to reform the criminal law, and to stop private wars. The power of the Bohemian nobility had grown considerably during John's reign, and the degree of this growth became apparent at the assembly of the Estates in 1355. The Estates rejected the lawbook, fearing that their old and newly acquired rights would be curtailed by its stipulations. Charles did not insist on acceptance, which he could not have obtained without the use of force. Instead, he decided to achieve his aims in other ways, conscious of his own growing power and relying on the help of the Church and the cities.

In reality, Charles later succeeded in introducing some of the reforms in this document into practice by administrative means. For some stipulations he was, however, able to obtain the agreement of the Estates. He himself valued most the impartial administration of justice and was merciless against unruly elements in his realm. He led in person the expeditions against bands of robbers who were rendering the highroads insecure and whose number had grown during his prolonged absence from his kingdom at the beginning of his reign. This activity must have especially impressed his subjects. One of the chronicles of the period, Beneš of Veitmíle (Weitmühl), describes with delight how Charles hung the rope round the neck of one of the fiercest robber knights, after having destroyed his castle. The same man had previously been awarded a golden chain by Charles for bravery.[14] This time the king presented him with a rope, remarking that he had not only golden chains to distribute.

Charles was mindful above all of the economic prosperity of his lands. He not only watched over the growth of the cities but also introduced new industries and was most anxious to raise the productivity of agriculture. He introduced wines from Burgundy and plum trees from Lorraine into Bohemia. He established orchards, founded new ponds for fish breeding, and watched over forestry. Such activity on the part of a king must also have attracted attention outside Bohemia. One Italian, dissatisfied with Charles's Italian policy, remarked sarcastically that the emperor, instead of vying with Augustus, Otto I, or the Hohenstaufens for imperial glory, preferred to sit in Bohemia, planting vines and figs. All these measures, combined with intensive care for commerce and for good and safe communications, led to unprecedented economic prosperity for the country.

This prosperity ensured Charles of the necessary financial means for the further extension of his Hausmacht. He was not satisfied with the territorial gains realized by his father, but worked according to a careful plan for the further extension of his lands at the expense of his immediate neighbors. This plan is also reflected in his request to the Pope to grant the distinction of a papal legate to the Archbishop of Prague, to whom the neighboring bishoprics of Bamberg, Regensburg, and Meissen would be subject. This dignity was conferred by the Pope on Archbishop Očko of Vlašim.

Charles's first great success in this policy of expansion was the incorporation into his kingdom of the last Silesian duchy still outside the Czech political orbit. He acquired it through his third marriage, with Anne, daughter of the Duke of Svídnice and Jawor (Schweidnitz, Jauer). He then proceeded, with the agreement of the Silesian Estates, to draw up a legal statute for the whole of the duchy.

Another of Charles's preoccupations was to secure and extend the Chebsko (Egerland). From his second father-in-law, the Count Palatine, who was in debt, Charles bought important properties which he extended toward the Danube, the middle Main in the direction of Frankfurt, and the Neckar. Nürnberg and Frankfurt were given new privileges and brought into the sphere of influence of the Bohemian king.

In the North, Charles extended his dominions toward Dresden and

Leipzig. His acquisitions in these parts were so substantial that the Margrave of Meissen, hitherto Charles's stout supporter, began to fear for the safety of his own lands. However, Charles's main goal was not Meissen but Brandenburg. Profiting by a serious estrangement between the Bavarian and Brandenburg branches of the Wittelsbachs, Charles induced the Brandenburgers to conclude a treaty according to which his son Wenceslas should inherit their lands should they die without heirs. When Louis of Brandenburg died (1365), Charles, in order to secure the heritage for his house, gave his widowed daughter Catherine in marriage to the surviving Margrave Otto, called the Lazy. He then purchased possession of Lower Lusatia (1367) and joined it (1370) "for ever" to the lands of the crown of Bohemia.

The other Wittelsbachs dreaded such an expansion of the Luxemburg power and therefore looked for help to Poland and Hungary, while they won the Margrave Otto over to their camp. This gave Charles a pretext for military intervention. Finally he persuaded his son-in-law to sell him the margraviate for a huge sum of money and to accept as compensation Charles's lands in the Palatinate (1373).

Brandenburg was Charles's most important acquisition. The emperor had proceeded quite unscrupulously when realizing it, but he devoted much of his time to improving the economic conditions of the new territory. Here too he drew up a legal statute for the whole margraviate and devoted great care to the safety and prosperity of the inhabitants. His rule in the margraviate was so beneficial that the Estates expressed their desire to remain under Luxemburg rule forever (1374).[15]

At the same time that he planned the acquisition of Brandenburg, Charles was also extending his influence over western Pomerania through a fourth marriage with Elisabeth, daughter of Bogislaus V, duke of Pomerania-Wolgast (1363). It seems evident that this was all part of a carefully laid plan. Thanks to his new acquisitions and to his friendly relations with the Saxon Ascanians and the Wettins of Meissen, Charles controlled the river Oder from Silesia to its mouth and most of the course of the Elbe. The proposal which Charles made to Venice in 1364 testifies to the grandiosity of his plans. He asked the republic to direct its commerce through Austria and Bohemia and to use, instead of the Rhine, the Vltava (Moldau) and the Elbe for the transport of its merchandise to the medieval commercial centers of Bruges and London. Some say that he even planned a water canal connecting these rivers with the Danube. But the project could not be realized although it offered a longer waterway which was both safer and cheaper. Charles's residence in Brandenburg, Tangermünde, was to be granted the right of staple; this was, however, strongly opposed by Magdeburg, which already possessed this right. Also, medieval merchants were less interested in cheaper communications than in touching on their way as many centers of population as possible. The future was to show, however, that Charles's plan was ingenious. The Elbe ultimately became the most important river route of Germany, and Hamburg, which was "discovered" by Charles and received its first great privileges from him, became the greatest emporium of the later German Empire.

Charles was mindful of good communications on other occasions also. He seems to have supplied the initiative for the construction of a canal linking the Elbe with the Baltic, which was later realized (the Stecknitzkanal). This occurred in 1375 when he visited Lübeck, the leading city of the Hanseatic League. Although Charles was unfavorable to the conclusion of leagues of cities, he was fully alive to the importance of the Hansa, which had secured complete supremacy in the Baltic after its victory over Waldemar IV of Denmark (1370). He honored Lübeck with many privileges, including the German vicariate.[16]

From the beginning of his reign Charles paid special attention to the aggrandizement and embellishment of his capital, Prague, which was also the capital of the Empire. The cities of Central Europe could rarely, at that time, vie with Paris or the towns of Lombardy in the magnificence of their monuments. Charles was captivated by the splendor of Paris, Lucca, and Bologna, which he had admired in his youth, and he wished Prague to rival them. He founded a new city (1348) near the old one and in its construction used all the experience of city building which had been gained so far in medieval Europe. A new stone bridge was to unite the two cities, which were adorned with new churches and the castle of Hradčany. On the other side of the new city on the Vyšehrad Hill, Charles built another royal castle. In order to relieve the unemployment and hardship caused by a series of bad harvests, Charles ordered the construction of a wall around Hradčany and its suburb (Malá Strana). It is still called the "Hunger Wall."

Charles also made Prague the intellectual center of the Empire by the foundation of the first university of Central Europe (1348). Here again he was influenced by the example of Paris. The central position of Bohemia in the Empire was also symbolized by the fact that the crown jewels of the Empire were to be deposited in Bohemia in a large fortress which Charles built for this purpose and which was called Karlův Týn (Karlstein).[17, 18] The two burgraves who were appointed as governors of the castle were soon ranked among the highest dignitaries of the realm. A similar idea was also expressed by Charles when he began to build a new cathedral in Prague and deposited there the relics of the patron saints of different imperial territories. The unparalleled prosperity of his kingdom allowed Charles to assemble in Bohemia prominent architects and artists of contemporary Europe, who built and decorated the many ecclesiastical foundations and monuments founded by him, by the burghers of the flourishing cities, and by ecclesiastics.[19]

In his foreign policy as king of Bohemia, Charles faced problems similar to those of his predecessors. He had to regulate the relations of his kingdom with the Habsburgs in Austria, with Hungary, and with Poland. Charles had decided that the Habsburgs were less dangerous to his imperial plans than the Wittelsbachs. He could not fight both rival houses, and so he chose the Habsburgs as his allies and married his daughter Catherine to Duke Rudolf IV of Austria.[20] As long as Charles had no male heir he even thought of bequeathing his lands to his Austrian son-in-law. The pride and vanity of the duke, however, made friendly relations between the two rather difficult. Charles had first to persuade Rudolf to abandon some titles to which he had no right. Then the duke felt very much offended that he was not included among the electoral princes. In 1359 he presented to his father-in-law some old documents with genuine seals, conferring on the dukes of Austria titles and privileges much exceeding those accorded to the Electors in the Golden Bull. Some of the privileges went back to Caesar and Nero. It was easy for Charles to see through these falsifications, but in order to obtain expert judgment on their validity, he asked Petrarch, as a specialist, to examine them. The latter was then rewarded by Charles with a golden cup for his rejection of their genuineness.

The relations between Charles and Rudolf deteriorated when the emperor's first son Wenceslas was born (1361), and Rudolf joined the emperor's foes, Hungary and the Wittelsbachs. Charles answered by threatening to call his enemies before the imperial tribunal and by recognizing the Swiss federation formed against the Habsburgs, which he had hitherto rejected. Finally, anxious to settle his accounts with the Wittelsbachs first, Charles came to a new agreement with Rudolf, after helping him to obtain the Tyrol, which was in the possession of the Wittelsbachs.

The agreement was sealed in Brno (Brünn) (1364) with the stipulation that each house should inherit the lands of the other in case of its extinction. Charles could not foresee, at that time, that it would not be his house but the rival Habsburgs who would one day profit by this agreement and would rule his lands from the fifteenth to the twentieth centuries. Fortunately for Charles, Rudolf died the year after, and his successor Albrecht III, also Charles's son-in-law, continued to entertain friendly relations with the emperor.

Relations between Bohemia and Poland improved considerably during the reign of Charles. It is true that Casimir,[21] king of Poland, could only with difficulty reconcile himself to the loss of Silesia, but although he never abandoned completely the hope of one day recovering that wealthy province, he was too much of a realist to allow this to embroil him with his powerful neighbor. Moreover, he soon found a welcome opportunity for expansion in the East. His cousin, Bolesław of Mazovia, had been elected (about 1325) prince of Galicia and Volhynia after the extinction of the native dynasty, to which he had been related.[22] This part of the former Kievan state, also called Western Russia, was still under Mongol supremacy, and its possession was much coveted by the Lithuanians. Bolesław received confirmation from the Khan of the Mongols and inaugurated friendlier relations with the Lithuanians. The native nobility, however, disliked his rule, and he was murdered by them in 1340. Casimir claimed the succession and occupied the city of Lwów. The boyars, however, favored as Bolesław's successor the Lithuanian prince Lubart, one of the seven sons of Gedymin, the founder of Lithuanian greatness, who had, moreover, married a Russian princess. Lubart occupied Volhynia and forced the Polish king to withdraw from Galicia. He recognized the supremacy of the Tatars and received support from them in his struggle with the Poles.

In this conflict Casimir was supported by Hungary. The Hungarian kings also coveted the possession of Galicia and Volhynia, which they termed *regnum Galiciae et Lodomeriae*. In order to obtain Hungarian support, Casimir had to negotiate first with Charles Robert and then with his son and successor, Louis of Anjou, who was Casimir's own nephew. In the final agreement Casimir, who had no male heirs, combined the question of the lands coveted by both with that of Louis' succession to the throne of Poland. It was agreed that if Louis did not become king of Poland, he should be allowed to recover Galicia and Volhynia from the Polish kings.

In spite of Hungarian help, Casimir had to await his chance until it was provided by the intervention of the Teutonic Order into Lithuanian affairs. Profiting by the weakening of Lithuanian power after the death of Gedymin (1341) and the division of the grand duchy among his seven sons and his brother, the Knights began new attacks against the Lithuanians. The grand ducal dignity was assumed in 1345 by the energetic Olgerd (1341-1377), who was supported by his brother Keistut, but it was too late. The Lithuanian army, reinforced by their Russian subjects, was finally completely defeated (1348). Casimir seized this occasion to occupy Galicia with Lwów in 1349. In spite of a prolonged struggle, however, Casimir and Louis of Anjou were unable to conquer the rest of the country. But this already represented a considerable success and showed the direction of further Polish expansion.

After the conclusion of peace with the Lithuanians in 1352, Casimir devoted all his attention to consolidating his authority in the rest of Poland. In 1355 the last prince of Mazovia recognized his sovereignty, thus attaching this province firmly to the Polish crown. Casimir was also successful in uniting the whole of Kujavja under his rule. But he encountered more difficulty in Great Poland, where the old separatism and lack of interest in the unity of the realm seemed most deeply rooted. However, he showed great skill and patience in reducing the opposition of the nobility to the surrender of illegally alienated crown property. Finally, in 1358 he was able to break the last stronghold of Great Polish separatism.

Like Charles IV in Bohemia, Casimir received staunch support from the Church in his efforts at unification and at raising the economic and cultural level of Poland. There are many other traits in the rule of both kings which are similar. Casimir too was very much alive to the importance of trade, and thanks to his commercial policy, Poland soon became an important link between the Baltic and the Black seas. He supported the rise of cities, but defended Polish interests in them more successfully than Charles IV did Czech interests. In order to curtail appeals to German tribunals from Polish cities founded according to German law, he erected in Cracow a court of appeal for all Polish cities using German law. He favored colonization and protected the peasantry against abuses by the nobility.

In cultural progress, also, Casimir followed the same line as Charles IV. His greatest achievement in this respect was the foundation in Cracow of a law school, which became the university, the second in this part of Europe. Casimir also followed Charles IV's example in favoring learning, introducing new religious orders, and constructing churches.[23]

It was natural that Charles should seek to maintain good relations with Poland when he was still fighting the Wittelsbachs in Brandenburg. Fortunately, Casimir was also more interested in his conquests in the East and not at all inclined to risk a conflict with Charles for the sake of a problematical friendship with the Wittelsbachs. So it was easy for both to come to an agreement as early as 1348. The text of the treaty shows that Casimir had not lost hope of recovering from the Teutonic Order and from Brandenburg the lost Polish territories. Casimir promised Charles to support him militarily against any enemy, with the exception of the King of Hungary, but only after he had restored with Charles's help the old Polish frontiers in the North.

This treaty was renewed in 1356, when Casimir visited Charles in

Prague. The main subject of their discussions was again that of relations with the Teutonic Order. The order was then at the height of its power under its grand master, Winrich of Kniprode (1351-1382). Casimir knew that alone he could not risk any major conflict with the order, but local friction could not be avoided. Neither could Charles open hostilities against the order, which claimed to work in the interests of Christendom and of the Empire. But he never enjoyed such friendly relations with the order as his father had had. As emperor he limited himself to the confirmation of all the privileges granted to the order by his predecessors, and released it from imperial taxes. At the meeting in Prague Casimir also confirmed an agreement made by the King of Hungary, acting as his proxy in 1353, by which Charles renounced sovereignty over Polock in Mazovia, conquered by his father, while Casimir accepted the fait accompli in Silesia, which was then incorporated under the crown of Bohemia.

Casimir had also shown a lively interest in the conversion of the Lithuanians to Christianity by peaceful means, rather than by the violence favored by the Teutonic Order. On Casimir's initiative, one of Gedymin's sons went to Germany to negotiate with Charles about the conditions on which the conversion could be effected. The Lithuanians hoped that if they embraced Christianity, they would be given back the territories which the order had taken away from them. Of course, at a period when the order was at the apogee of its military power it was impossible to consider the realization of such a condition. Despite Charles's good will, Casimir's initiative therefore had no positive result. However, it alarmed the order, and the fact that Charles was willing to negotiate with the Lithuanians on the Polish initiative showed that he was fully alive to the questionable aspects of the methods used by the order in pagan Lithuania.

This good understanding between Bohemia and Poland was troubled in 1362, when the Hungarian king, Louis of Anjou, persuaded his Polish uncle to join the coalition which Rudolf of Habsburg was organizing against Charles. The latter, however, prevented the bloody clash of armies which threatened to occur in Upper Hungary—modern Slovakia—by negotiating an armistice. Thanks to Casimir's mediation, an understanding was soon reached between Charles and Louis. The friendly relations between Charles and Casimir were strengthened in 1363, when the widowed Charles asked Casimir for the hand of his granddaughter Elisabeth, the Princess of Western Pomerania, who was being educated at Casimir's court. The marriage was even celebrated at Cracow. Casimir then acted as an intermediary between the Duke of Austria and his new relative, Charles. The reconciliation which he helped to bring about was then sealed by the famous Treaty of Brno (1364) mentioned above.

The friendship between Charles, Casimir, and Louis of Anjou emerged considerably strengthened from the first international congress held at Cracow in the autumn of the same year.[24] The initiative for this assembly came from Peter, king of Cyprus, who was visiting all the European courts in an endeavor to interest the various rulers in a new crusade against the Turks. In August he was received in Prague with great honor by Charles, but the emperor hesitated to make any firm promises, suggesting instead a preliminary meeting with the kings of Poland and Hungary. He proposed Cracow as the venue for the meeting, stressing to the Cypriot monarch the importance of both kings.

The emperor and the three kings were joined in Cracow by Waldemar II of Denmark, with whom Casimir had concluded an alliance. However, only the King of Hungary showed a real interest in the crusade because his possessions were most exposed to the Ottoman Turks, who had occupied Adrianople and Philippopolis in 1363. The emperor limited himself to a promise to commend the crusade to the Electors, princes, and cities of the Empire. The time for such enterprises was already past, and a crusade no longer aroused in Europe the enthusiasm of the twelfth or thirteenth centuries. The only king who was still romantic enough to take such an enterprise seriously was John II, king of France. When he died in April, 1364, it became clear that the whole plan for which the King of Cyprus was working was stillborn.[25]

The five kings who had met in Cracow profited by this occasion to strengthen the ties of friendship between their countries. Charles also concluded a pact of friendship with Hungary and obtained from Louis of Anjou confirmation of the agreement made with the Habsburgs at Brno. For Casimir himself the meeting of five kings and many other nobles in his capital represented a great personal success. Poland, almost negligible as a power under Łokietek, was now recognized by the emperor and the rest of Europe as an important factor in European politics. Casimir's neighbors could also see on this occasion how far his country had progressed culturally and economically under his wise direction.

Perhaps inspired by the crusading ideals discussed at Cracow, Casimir undertook in 1366 his own small crusade against the Lithuanians. It was more successful than that of the King of Cyprus. Casimir induced some Lithuanian nobles to become his vassals and conquered the western part of Volhynia. The Lithuanians replied with an invasion of Mazovia in 1368. Nevertheless, relations between the two countries became more friendly because they faced a common enemy, the Teutonic Knights.

In this respect Casimir was unable to realize his ambition of restoring to Poland the lands taken by the order. He was more successful on the Polish frontier with Brandenburg. In friendly negotiations with some local lords he brought some important fortresses and small territories under his authority. These small gains were important for Poland because they separated the possessions of the order from Brandenburg and restored contact between Poland and Western Pomerania. This land was nominally a dependency of the Empire, but its dukes still enjoyed a great degree of independence. In this way Casimir gained access to the sea through a friendly land. To achieve this had been one of his main preoccupations. He knew how important it was for Polish interests. Even in this respect Casimir had some traits in common with Charles.

Charles's interest in Poland was reinvigorated when it became apparent that Casimir would leave no male heirs. In his marital life Casimir was less fortunate than Charles. His first wife, a Lithuanian, died, and his second marriage, with Adelaide of Hesse, was childless, ending in divorce. He had some trouble before his third marriage, with a Silesian princess whom he had met in Prague, was recognized by the Church. From his first and third marriages he had only daughters, one of whom might well become his heiress. Charles therefore planned to marry one of his sons to one of Casimir's daughters in the hope of inheriting the Polish kingdom after his death. But Casimir had decided that his nephew Louis of Anjou should inherit his throne.

However, he did not appear happy about this solution of his succession. Casimir must have foreseen that Louis, in order to obtain the consent of the Polish nobility, would be bound to grant them privileges which would be detrimental to the royal authority in Poland. This was evident from the demands already presented to Louis by the nobility in 1351 and 1355, during Casimir's lifetime. The arrangement with Hungary had, however, been made at a time when Poland needed an ally and could only find one in Hungary. There was also the problem of Louis' own succession, because Louis so far also had no male heirs. For this reason Casimir adopted in 1368 his grandson, Casimir of Szczecin (Stettin), thus indicating that he would like him to succeed Louis on the Polish throne. This choice is very characteristic of Casimir. It shows once more how anxious he was to secure for Poland access to the sea, which had been blocked by the conquests of the order. Unable to reconquer Gdańsk (Danzig) and Eastern Pomerania, he never missed an opportunity to strengthen the ties between Poland and Western Pomerania, hoping that one day this part at least of the lost region of Pomerania would be reunited with Poland.

Fate, however, prevented him from doing more in this direction. He died, a sexagenarian, on November 5, 1370, as a result of a hunting accident. Posterity has called him "the Great," and Casimir fully deserved this title. He laid the foundations in so many respects for the future greatness of Poland.

It appeared soon after Casimir's death that the solution he had chosen for the succession was not the best for Polish interests. The new king, Louis of Anjou (1370-1382), paid little attention to the government of Poland. He appeared in Poland only at long intervals and for short periods. Meanwhile, he left the regency in the hands of his mother Elizabeth, and after her death he appointed a council of regency, presided over by the Bishop of Cracow. Neither of these solutions was a happy one.[26] One of the Mazovian princes, Ziemowit, regained his independence, and Louis encountered an unsuccessful pretender in the last member of the Piast dynasty in Kujavja. In the fight against him Casimir of Szczecin (Stettin) lost his life in 1377. He had given a splendid example of loyalty to Louis although the king, afraid of a possible pretender, had curtailed considerably the benefits which Casimir the Great had bestowed on him.

In foreign policy Louis also neglected Polish interests. Nothing was done to promote Polish expansion in the North or to secure direct access to the Baltic. Peace was maintained with the Teutonic Order, but relations with Western Pomerania were not strengthened. On the northwestern frontier the important fortress of Santok was lost, and on the eastern frontier Vladimir was conquered by the Lithuanians. Louis even failed to protect Hungarian interests in the Balkans in the face of the steady progress of the Turks. His neglect of these vital interests of his realms was motivated by his plan to conquer the Kingdom of Naples and Sicily for his branch of the Anjou family and by his renewal of hostilities with the Venetians. Thus the ways opened by Casimir became neglected.

There was, furthermore, the question of Louis' succession. Having no male heirs, Louis desired to obtain from the nobility a revision of the agreements concluded with Casimir so as to secure the succession to the Polish throne for one of his daughters. His regime had found most support in Little Poland, whose nobility had always been in closer contact with their Hungarian neighbors. Louis' dynastic policy was quite readily accepted by them but was opposed by the nobility and higher clergy of Great Poland, more remote from Hungary and jealous, moreover, of the rise of Cracow over Gniezno (Gnesen).

Louis invited the representatives of the Polish nobility to discuss the matter with him on Hungarian soil at Košice (Kassa) in modern Slovakia. After protracted negotiations during three meetings, an understanding was reached between the king and the nobles in September, 1374, and embodied in a special charter, which marked a new period in Polish constitutional history. The nobles promised to accept as their queen any one of Louis' daughters whom the king, his mother, or his wife might choose. They agreed to this, however, only after having obtained from Louis new and far-reaching privileges. The king had to exempt the gentry from all but a few symbolic taxes, to give an assurance that only nobles of the provinces concerned would be appointed to official posts, and to promise that only natives would be placed in charge of the royal castles.

The agreement marked another milestone on the road to the rule of the gentry in Poland. On the other hand it illustrated the national consciousness of the Polish nobility and their opposition to the rule of foreigners. In this respect the Polish nobility defended the national interests of the kingdom more vigilantly than did their Czech counterparts.

For some time it looked as if the Polish kingdom would be governed by a Luxemburg. Charles IV was, of course, following developments attentively, vigilant for possible openings for his house in Poland and Hungary. He succeeded in negotiating the marriage of his second son Sigismund, whom he had appointed margrave of Brandenburg, with Louis' daughter Mary. It was this princess who, after the death of her sister Catherine in 1378, was designated by Louis as his heiress in Poland. The decision met with stubborn opposition from a part of the Polish gentry. But Louis was adamant and induced the gentry to render homage not only to Mary (1379), but also to Sigismund (1382).

This arrangement was, however, nullified in the same year, soon after Louis' death. He had appointed his daughter Jadwiga as his successor in Hungary and had married her at the age of five to William of Habsburg, hoping to achieve in this way a more intimate collaboration between Hungary and Austria. In spite of this agreement the unpredictable Hungarian nobility elected not Jadwiga but Mary as "King of Hungary." It seemed, therefore, that the personal union between the two kingdoms would continue. But the Polish nobility had had their fill of such a union, whose disadvantages they had experienced to the full during Louis' reign. They therefore persuaded Louis' widow to designate, in accordance with the charter of 1374, the younger Jadwiga as Louis' successor in Poland. This gave rise, however, to a new problem. The nationally conscious Poles rejected the idea of a German prince as their ruler. This dislike had been a powerful contributory reason for the rejection of Sigismund, margrave of Brandenburg, and so the candidature of William of Austria was even less welcome.

The attention of the Poles had in 1377 once more been concentrated on Lithuania. A great victory of Louis' combined army over the Lithuanians not only ended their series of raids, but also extended Polish sovereignty over Volhynia and over some Lithuanian princes. New possibilities were opening on the eastern frontiers, and the new grand duke of Lithuania, Jagiello, was seriously considering the possibility of accepting Christianity in order to achieve a more peaceful coexistence with his Polish neighbors.

Many of the Polish nobles turned their attention to him, and the nobility of Mazovia especially began to give serious consideration to the possibility of a union between Jadwiga and the Lithuanian grand duke.

Charles IV was prevented by his death in 1378 from witnessing this development. He had, however, done all he could to secure for his son Sigismund at least the crown of Hungary, if not that of Poland also. It was certainly a master stroke of his diplomatic genius. There was one further important matter which preoccupied the emperor during the last years of his life. It was his wish to secure the succession, not only in Bohemia but also in Germany, to his eldest son Wenceslas. The latter was recognized in 1363 already as king of Bohemia by the assembly of the nobles. To obtain his recognition in Germany was, however, beset with difficulties. For more than a hundred years no successor to the German throne had been recognized during the lifetime of a reigning king. Charles had himself contributed considerably to the increased self-consciousness of the Electors, who naturally resented any limitation of their electoral rights. The Papacy, moreover, had not yet abandoned its claim to control the election by papal approbation, even though this claim had been rejected by the Declaration of Rense and had been shrewdly bypassed by Charles himself in the Golden Bull.

Pope Gregory XI (1370-1378), on learning of Charles' intentions, hastened once more to voice the papal claims. Charles, however, had already won the consent of the Electors for his son, after bestowing new privileges on them. Now he cleverly exploited the discontent provoked among them by the Pope's intervention. Wenceslas was unanimously elected in 1376, and his first act was to confirm the privileges of the Electors.

This did justice to the stipulations laid down at Rense and in the Golden Bull, but it was still necessary to give satisfaction to the Pope. The latter was in a difficult position and needed the emperor's help because he had only recently left Avignon and found affairs in Rome and in Italy still most unsettled. On the other hand Charles needed the Pope's cooperation for the eventual coronation of his son. They both took refuge in a face-saving concession. Charles asked only then in an antedated letter for the Pope's approval of his son's election, promising at the same time, in his own and his son's name, to abstain from seeking the election of a successor in their lifetime. The Electors were, of course, not bound by Charles's promise, and even when, after Charles's death, Wenceslas had to make the same promise for himself in order to appease the Papacy (1379), the great Western Schism with its consequences prevented the popes from taking advantage of Charles's and Wenceslas' concessions.

Thus, owing to Charles's initiative, the succession to the German throne became altogether hereditary and electoral.

It must be acknowledged that Charles's imperial policy was well coordinated and farsighted. The Emperor Maximilian was certainly exaggerating when he accused Charles of being a good father to his Bohemian kingdom but a stepfather to the Empire. In his Golden Bull he gave the Empire a juridical basis which, in the absence of a constitution, attempted to save what could be saved of the royal authority, to put an end to the recurring contests for the throne, and to ensure at least a minimum of order in Germany.[27] It was a good foundation and might have been of considerable benefit to the German nation and the imperial idea if it had been properly developed by his successors.

Nor can he be blamed for the care which he lavished on the aggrandizement and prosperity of his Bohemian kingdom. Here Charles fell back upon the policy of most German kings and emperors and concentrated upon creating a strong dynastic power or *Hausmacht,* which would provide the principal support for his authority in the Empire and in Europe. It is, moreover, evident from the way in which Charles directed his dynastic policy that he intended to create in Central Europe a mighty political structure, founded on strong dynastic principles, which would be a leading factor in European affairs for years to come. For this reason he was also interested in Hungary, which he sought to secure for his son Sigismund, while he made considerable financial sacrifices to secure the election of his son Wenceslas as king of the Romans, in order to ensure leadership in the Empire and in Europe for his dynasty. Thus he laid the basis for a mighty political edifice, which was, however, ultimately to be realized, not by the House of Luxemburg, but by that of Habsburg.

It is also important to appreciate Charles's constant stress on the fact that Bohemia was an independent and most important part of the Empire. Therefore, in the Golden Bull he confirmed all the privileges granted to Bohemia by previous emperors and defined once and for all the position of the kingdom within the Empire. There is some evidence here to show that Charles regarded the Empire as a supranational formation with an appeal to universality and that he believed that this political structure offered the possibility for a peaceful symbiosis of the Germans with the Czechs. This is the more interesting because Charles IV was not unaware of the rise of a national spirit in Bohemia and indeed did everything in his power to ensure to the Czech language its due place of honor in his kingdom. He even urged the Electors to learn Czech. Subsequent events, however, showed that Charles's idea could not be realized because of circumstances which he could not foresee. Had he lived ten years longer, history might perhaps have judged his aims more favorably, but it is at least gratifying to record that Charles had such broad conceptions.

NOTES

1. W. Klein's dissertation deals with Charles's boyhood spent in Paris (see Bibl.).

2. Although Charles's reign is of great importance, not only for the history of the Bohemian kingdom but also for the evolution of the imperial idea and for the development of the relations between the imperium and the sacerdotium, a complete history of his life has still to be written. There exist, of course, many monographs concerning his age and his reign. The first of this kind to merit special mention was the study by H. Friedjung, *Kaiser Karl IV und sein Anteil am geistigen Leben seiner Zeit* (Vienna, 1876). This was followed by K. Höfler's work, *Kaiser Karl IV und Kaiser Karl V. Eine Parallele* (Prague, 1891, *Mitteilungen des Vereines für Geschichte der Deutschen in Böhmen*, vol. 29). Höfler's disciple, E. Werunsky, made the most remarkable attempt at a history of Charles's reign in his work *Geschichte Kaiser Karls IV und seiner Zeit* (Innsbruck, 1880-1892). His detailed and unbiased work remained, however, unfinished. In his three volumes he was able to go only to the year 1368. Th. Lindner's *Deutsche Geschichte unter den Habsburgern und Luxemburgern* (Halle, 1890-1893, 2 vols.), vol. II, pp. 3-100 can be consulted with profit for the study of Charles's reign in Germany. Short but instructive sketches of Charles's life were given by two prominent German historians. In the collection *Meister der Politik* (1922) by Fritz Vigener and especially by K. Hampl in *Herrschergestalten des deutschen Mittelalters* (Heidelberg, 1927, 6th ed. 1955, pp. 298-315; to this sixth edition was added a most recent bibliography). J. Pfitzner's *Kaiser Karl IV* in the collection *Deutsche Könige und Kaiser* (ed. W. Reese, Potsdam, 1938) is written under the biased influence of Nazi racial theories. A short sketch of Charles's imperial ideas was given by G. Groveland Walsh, S.J. under the title *The Emperor Charles IV 1316-1378. A study in Holy Empire Imperialism* (London, 1924). The biography by B. Jarrett, O.P. (*The Emperor Charles IV*, London, 1935) is disappointing and not based on original research. J. Šusta wrote the life of Charles for the monumental Czech history which was started by J. Novotný in 1912. He published two volumes, the first one covering the period from 1333 to 1346 (*Karel IV. Otec a syn, České dějiny*, díl II, část 3, Prague, 1946) and the second from 1346 to 1355 (*Za císařskou korunou, ibidem*, díl II část 4, Prague, 1948). The second volume is a posthumous work. It is a pity that J. Šusta was unable to bring his work to an end because he seemed to be particularly well equipped for such a difficult task. Useful bibliographical indications on Czech literature are given by O. Odložilík in the collection *Československá Vlastivěda*, vol. 7 (History). Some summary indications on editions of sources are given by J. Pfitzner (*Kaiser Karl IV*, pp. 108 ff.). A complete specification of sources will be found in Werunsky's three volumes. A short appreciation of J. Šusta's work was given by O. Odložilík in *Speculum*, vol. 24 (1949) pp. 143-48, vol. 25 (1951) pp.

215-17 ff. Cf. also the sketch by H. Heimpel in *Handbuch der Deutschen Geschichte,* ed. by A. O. Meyer (Potsdam, 1936), vol. I, pp. 309-26, 398 (useful bibliography) and O. Fischer, *Karl IV deutscher Kaiser, König von Böhmen* (Bremen, 1941).

3. A particularly detailed study of the spread of the pestilence, the Jewish pogroms in Germany, and the excesses of the flagellants was given by E. Werunsky (*Geschichte Kaiser Karls IV,* vol. I, pp. 239-324. On Charles's attitude see ibid., pp. 271 ff.).

4. On Charles's vicars in Germany see L. Huttenbranker (see Bibl.), pp. 546-68.

5. On Cola di Rienzo, his ideas and prophecies see K. Burdach, P. Piur, *Briefwechsel des Cola di Rienzo* in K. Burdach's collection *Vom Mittelalter zur Reformation,* vol. II, part I (Berlin, 1913): K. Burdach, *Rienzo und die geistige Wandlung seiner Zeit.*

6. The letters are published by K. Burdach, P. Piur, *op. cit.,* vol. II, part III (Berlin, 1912), pp. 191 ff.

7. For details see W. Scheffer, *Karl IV und Innozenz VI, 1355-1360* (Berlin, 1912, *Histor. Studien,* Heft. 101).

8. A very realistic appreciation of Charles's Italian policy is given by E. Werunsky, *Geschichte Kaisers Karls IV,* vol. 2, pp. 613 ff. J. Šusta (*Karel IV. Za císařskou korunou,* pp. 298, 300, 380) rightly criticizes the biased presentation of Charles's attitude toward Petrarch's ideas given by J. Pfitzner (*Kaiser Karl IV,* pp. 60 ff.).

9. For details cf. the monograph by G. Pirchan, *Italien und Kaiser Karl IV in der Zeit seiner zweiten Romfahrt* (see Bibl.).

10. On Charles's relations with England see the remarks by R. Salomon *Zur Geschichte der englischen Politik Karls IV* (see Bibl.).

11. On the kingdom of Arles see the monograph by R. Grieser, *Das Arelat in der europäischen Politik* (see Bibl.), where a bibliography of earlier works will be found. On Charles's policy, *ibid.,* pp. 56-63.

12. The most extensive study of the Bull is that written by K. Zeumer, *Die Goldene Bulle Kaiser Karls IV,* "Quellen und Studien zur Verfassungsgeschichte des Deutschen Reichs in Mittelalter und Neuzeit," vol. II (Weimar, 1908), in two parts, the text in part 2.

13. See the study by E. Werunsky, "*Maiestas Karolina*" (see Bibl.). A Czech bibliography is given by J. Šusta (*Karel IV. Za cís. korunou,* pp. 186-224).

14. Chronicle, book IV, *F.R.B.,* vol. IV, p. 525.

15. On the methods by which Charles IV incorporated the new acquisition into the Kingdom of Bohemia see Hedwig Saunmann-von Bülow, *Die Inkorporationen Karls IV* (see Bibl.), pp. 34-66.

16. On Charles's relations with the Hansa see the monograph by H. Reincke, *Kaiser Karl IV und die deutsche Hanse* (see Bibl.).

17. Charles chose a special day when the jewels were exposed each year for inspection and veneration by the public. On this day hosts of pilgrims from Bohemia and Germany were attracted to Karlstein.

18. However, J. Pirchan in his study, "Karlstein," *Prager Festgabe für Theodor Mayer* (see Bibl.)., thinks that the castle was built not for the imperial insignias, but for the relics of the Lord's Passion, kept in the cross which was part of the royal insignias of Bohemia.

19. On the cultural progress of Bohemia during Charles's reign see below, pp. 159 ff.

20. There is a monograph on the duke by E. K. Winter, *Rudolf IV* (Vienna, 1934-36), 2 vols. On his relationship with Charles, *ibid.* vol. I, pp. 290 ff.

21. For the most recent study on Casimir's monarchy and the organization of Church, art, and science during his reign see chapter VII, p. 170. For a full bibliography in Polish, see Z. Kaczmarczyk, *Kazimierz Wielki* (Warsaw, 1948), pp. 388-394. Cf. also vol. 2 of J. Dąbrowski, *Dzieje Polski średniowicznej* (Cracow, 1926). On Casimir's Russian policy, see H. Paszkiewicz, *Polityka ruska Kazimierza Wielkiego* (Warsaw, 1925), Rozprawy histor. towar. nauk, vol. 4.

22. For more details on Galicia and Volhynia see chapter IX, pp. 213 ff.

23. For further details on Casimir's cultural achievements, see below, pp. 168 ff.

24. There is a monograph on the Congress of Cracow by R. Grodecki, *Kongres Krakowski w roku 1364* (Warsaw, 1939). Cf. the most recent publication on Casimir the Great by J. Sieradzki, *Polska wieku XIV. Studium z czasów Kazimierza Wielkiego* (Warsaw, 1959).

25. Interesting reports on King Peter's visit to Prague and on the Cracow conference are given by the famous contemporary French poet and writer Guillaume de Machaut in his description of the capture of Alexandria (*La Prise d'Alexandrie,* ed. by Mas Latrie, Genève, 1877. "Publications de la Société de l'Orient latin," *serie hist.* vol. I, pp. 27 ff.). Charles's plan to employ on this crusade the bands of mercenary soldiers roaming through Italy proved impossible of realization. Charles then abandoned the whole idea. In the next year Peter of Cyprus, with a small army consisting mostly of French knights, attacked Alexandria, which was taken and plundered by the crusaders. The enterprise ended in a complete failure, however, and the crusaders fled before the advancing Turkish army. As a reprisal the sultan imprisoned all Christian merchants in Egypt and Syria and confiscated their property.

26. The most severe critic of Louis' rule in Poland was Casimir's vice-chancellor, Janko of Czarnków. His chronicle is published in vol. II of the SRS pp. 78-155.

27. Bryce is also too severe on Charles in his *Holy Roman Empire* with his comment on the publication of the Golden Bull: "He legalized anarchy and called it a constitution" (p. 246, ed. of 1922).

Chapter V

THE SECOND BULGARIAN EMPIRE,
THE RISE OF SERBIA

The Balkans between East and West—Serbians, Bulgarians, and the Western Empire—Latin and Byzantine influences in Serbia—Bulgaria, the Papacy, and the Latin Empire—Serbia, Rome, and Nicaea—King Stephen's dual action, an explanation—Tsar Asen II, Rome, Hungary, and the Latin Empire—Disastrous consequences in the Balkans of the Mongol invasion —A new Balkan political combination and the triumph of Michael Palaeologus—Hungary and the southern Slavs—Croatian national expansion and the rise of Bosnia—Emperor Michael VIII's duplicity at the Council of Lyons, the decline of Bulgaria—Serbian leadership in the Balkans— Serbia's victorious progress under Tsar Stephen Dušan—Serbia's decline, the Turkish conquest of Bulgaria, and defeat of the Serbians at Kosovo

In the thirteenth century southeastern Europe witnessed the rise of two new and independent Slav states, Bulgaria and Serbia. In this part of Europe, the principal political power was, of course, not the western but the Byzantine Empire. The Emperor Basil II, called Bulgaroktonos— the Bulgar-slayer, had shattered the First Bulgarian Empire, and from the beginning of the eleventh century Bulgaria existed only as a Byzantine province.

The first attempt by the Serbian Slavs to create an independent political unit had been frustrated at the end of the eleventh century, when the Emperor Alexius I Comnenus had annexed the lands of the Slavic Kingdom of Dioclea [1] to Byzantium.

The Emperor Manuel Comnenus (1143-1180) thwarted a similar attempt by Uroš II, župan of Serbia proper, then called Rascia, and forced his successor the Župan Nemanja (c. 1167-1196) to abandon his alliance with the Venetians and to recognize Byzantine overlordship. Manuel also defeated the Hungarians, who had gained suzerainty over the territory of Bosnia, and added that country to the Empire. He also extended his sway over a large portion of Croatia and expelled the Venetians from Dalmatia. Such was the political situation in the Balkans at the end of the twelfth century.

But Byzantium was not the only power vitally interested in southeastern Europe. The Hungarian kings had also been kings of Croatia since the end of the eleventh century. It was natural that they should endeavor to extend their influence into the neighboring Slavic lands to the south. Bosnia, the nearest to Croatia, had joined Hungary voluntarily, following the example of the Croats, in 1120. From Bosnia it seemed easy to reach Hum (the modern Hercegovina) and Raška (Rascia). Later, when the antagonism between Latin and Orthodox Christians had grown—especially after the conquest of Constantinople by the crusaders in 1204—the Hungarian kings succumbed to the temptation to pose as the champions of the Papacy and of Latin civilization in the Balkans.

Furthermore, the maritime power of Venice was growing constantly, and with it her desire to be mistress of the Adriatic and to secure a firm foothold in Dalmatia. The Venetians were principally responsible for the diversion of the Fourth Crusade from its original purpose and for the foundation of the Latin Empire of the East. It must be remembered that the whole enterprise started with the conquest of Zadar (Zara) in Dalmatia by the crusaders for the Venetians in 1202. It is hardly surprising, therefore, that Venetian diplomats should have tried to interfere at every opportunity in the affairs of the southern Slav states.

Another competitor for influence in the Balkans was the Norman Kingdom of Sicily, which came under the rule of the Angevins in the thirteenth century. Charles Robert of Anjou dreamed of a mediterranean empire and was therefore also interested in the Slavic states on the Adriatic.

The western emperors were too much engaged in Germany, Italy, and Central Europe to be able to spare much attention for Balkan affairs. There remained the other great power, the Papacy, with its vast spiritual and political influence in western Europe. The echoes of the victory of the sacerdotium over the imperium penetrated into the Orthodox lands in the Balkans and even resounded on the walls of Constantinople. The Serbians and the Bulgarians, fighting for their freedom against the Byzantines, were naturally eager for help from the West and for moral support from the popes. But their Byzantine religious formation precluded them from understanding fully the ideological transformation which had taken place in the West. All these elements naturally influenced the political and cultural changes which were taking place in southern Europe during the thirteenth and fourteenth centuries. It is no wonder that despite the different cultural and religious outlook inherited from Byzantium, medieval Serbia and Bulgaria show some features similar to those already observed among the western Slavs.

It was thus to be expected that as long as Manuel Comnenus lived, the Serbians had no chance of achieving self-government. This great warrior and diplomat made a final daring bid from Constantinople to revive the Roman Empire. He was the last Byzantine emperor to adorn his name by adding to it, in the true Roman fashion, the pompous title of Ruler of Dalmatia, Bosnia, Croatia, Serbia, Bulgaria, and Hungary.

But the position altered completely with Manuel's death. Profiting by the dynastic quarrels in Byzantium, Béla III of Hungary (1172-1196) occupied all the Byzantine possessions in Dalmatia and Croatia. Nemanja made short work of the Dioclean kingdom, then under Byzantine supremacy. The grand župans of Rascia had long coveted its possession and had continually intervened in its internal affairs when it was weakened by dynastic troubles. Now all traces of the descendants of King Constantine Bodin, its founder, disappeared. Nemanja also captured Ulcinium, Antibari, and Cattaro on the Adriatic. Only Ragusa resisted successfully, and when it made an agreement with the Normans of Sicily, Nemanja desisted from further attempts to conquer it. He made peace and confirmed the commercial privileges of the Ragusans in Dioclea and Rascia. Thus the foundations of medieval Serbia were laid.

In 1186 a revolution broke out in Bulgaria, when the boyars of the Danube region rose against Byzantium. The coup succeeded and inaugurated the Second Bulgarian Empire under the brothers Peter (Kalopeter) and Asen (Asěn, Assen, Asan),[2] who held court as tsars at Trnovo. Despite certain initial successes, the Emperor Isaac II Angelus (1185-1195) was hampered by the revolt of one of his best generals and was unable to crush the rebels, who were reinforced by their allies the Cumans, a Turkic tribe.

Nemanja, who had a keen eye to his own advantage, promptly concluded an alliance with the new Slavic state, at the same time adding slices of neighboring territories as far as Niš to his own possessions. Then, needing other allies to legalize these acquisitions, he turned characteristically to Germany and the western emperor. On learning that Frederick Barbarossa was contemplating a new crusade, he sent envoys to him with assurances of good will and promises of support if the emperor and his army would march through Serbian territory. Nemanja's Bulgarian allies supported this initiative, and Kalopeter promised Frederick 40,000 Vlach and Cuman archers for an attack on Constantinople. Nemanja even seems to have asked the emperor to crown him "with the diadem of the realm of Greece." The attack was timed for the spring of 1190. Frederick was flattered by all these marks of respect, and there was a moment during a period of tension between Frederick's army and the Greeks when it seemed that the attack on Constantinople might be launched. But Barbarossa was primarily intent upon the success of his crusade, and so he made peace with the Byzantine emperor.

The Slav allies were then obliged to settle their differences with the Greeks on their own. The Bulgarians were lucky and in 1191 inflicted a severe defeat on the Greek army, which enabled them to occupy Serdica (Sofia). Nemanja, after being seriously defeated on the river Morava, had to compound with the Greeks and was fortunate to secure highly satisfactory terms. Belgrade, Ravno, Niš, Skoplje, Prizren, Kroja, and Alessio were made frontier cities of the Byzantine Empire. For the last time Byzantine cavalry watered its horses at the confluence of the Sava and the Danube, when Issac met his father-in-law, Béla III of Hungary, at Belgrade, the old Singidunum. Isaac gave his niece in marriage to Nemanja's son and heir Stephen. His successor, Alexius III, anxious to save at least the semblance of Serbian dependence on Byzantium, conferred upon Stephen the highest honor of the Empire, the title of Sebastocrator.

It was natural that in their struggle against Byzantium both Slavic states should look to the West for allies. If they still expected any support from Frederick Barbarossa, their hopes were drowned with the emperor himself in the icy waters of the Saleph river in Asia Minor. He seems to have had some schemes for the Balkans, which he might have attempted to put into operation after his return from the crusade. He appears at least to have charged Berthold IV of Andechs, margrave of Istria, to continue negotiations with the Serbians. The margraves of Andechs fancied themselves as the leading champions of the Empire in south-eastern Europe and took great pride in their title of "Duke of Croatia and Dalmatia (Merania)."

There was another possibility under Barbarossa's successor, Henry VI (1190-1197). With the Sicilian kingdom, Henry VI had also inherited the far-reaching ambitions of the great Norman kings, Robert Guiscard, Roger II, and William II. More than once the lust for power had driven the fleets and armies of the Normans of Sicily along the Adriatic coast or into Greece. Their arrival in those parts always stirred in the Slavic populations a hope of regaining their independence from Byzantium. Henry's Sicilian chancellery was, of course, alive to these interesting possibilities, and Barbarossa's experiences in the Balkans had been shared by his gallant knights, who did not fail to report upon them to his son and successor. It is probable that this practical, stern, and shrewd diplomat counted upon these opportunities in the Balkans when he was drawing up his daring plans for a new Mediterranean empire, with himself as the ruler of Byzantium.

However, the treacherous Sicilian climate made an end of Henry's life and plans. All his Balkan schemes were wasted, and Niš, where Barbarossa had met Serbians and Bulgarians for the last time, had to wait until 1916 before another German emperor, William II, met another Bulgarian tsar, Ferdinand, as his ally there in a new drive for German world supremacy.

But Nemanja took care to remain on good terms with the other mighty power in the West which wielded an enormous moral and political influence, the Papacy. His son Stephen records in his biography of his father that Nemanja used to send rich presents to all those churches of East and West which were held in deep veneration by the Christians of his time—the churches of Jerusalem and Constantinople and those of St. Demetrius in Thessalonica, SS. Peter and Paul in Rome, and St. Nicholas in Bari. After his conquest of the Kingdom of Dioclea and the three coastal cities, Nemanja came into direct contact with the Latin culture of those regions. This was represented principally by Antibari, whose archbishop had extended his jurisdiction in the times of kings Michael and Bodin, even over Rascia.

Unfortunately for Antibari, the decline of the Dioclean kingdom under Bodin's successors had also undermined the prestige of its metropolitan, who found a dangerous competitor in Ragusa. From the beginning of the twelfth century onward, Ragusa, enjoying ever increasing prosperity, repeatedly received papal confirmation of its privileges and metropolitan status. It then also claimed jurisdiction over all the lands which had formerly been subject to Antibari, including the bishopric of Rascia. In the letters of popes Alexander III (1167) and Clement III (1188), who were the last to confirm Ragusa's privileged position, Antibari figured as a bishopric only.

The bishops of Antibari, of course, tried to reverse the situation. At the time when Nemanja was about to conquer the city, its bishop, Gregory, did in fact style himself Archbishop. It would have been more expedient for relations between Rome and the new rulers of Dioclea and Rascia if the former status of Antibari had been restored. As this city fell within their new political creation, it was natural that Nemanja and his brothers would prefer to have the metropolitan of Antibari exercising jurisdiction over their territory rather than the archbishop of Ragusa, whose see lay outside. It seems, however, that Rome was not quick enough to appreciate the changed situation. Pope Clement III sent a cordial letter in 1189 to Nemanja and his brothers introducing the new archbishop of Ragusa, Bernard, whose jurisdiction extended, according to the Pope, over the whole of Dioclea, Serbia, and Hum. The Pope seems to have assumed that the princes he was addressing were subject to the Holy See, whose counsels they were expected to obey, and that the archbishop of Ragusa was the supreme religious authority in their realm.

In reality the situation was not as favorable for Rome as the papal documents of the time represented it to be. The jurisdiction of the Latin archbishop of Antibari might have been effective even in Orthodox Rascia when that province was part of the Dioclean kingdom; but this situation definitely changed during the decline of that kingdom, when the influence of the great župans of Rascia came to be felt more keenly. To shift supremacy from Antibari to Ragusa did nothing to strengthen Roman influence in Rascia. The great župans of Rascia regarded their Orthodox bishop of Ras as their own bishop, and relations between Ras and Ochrida were strengthened by the fact that the Serbians of Rascia obtained all their holy books in Slavonic, together with other literary treasures, from this center of old Slavonic culture. It was thus natural that the ecclesiastical dependence of the see of Ras upon the autonomous archbishopric of Ochrida came to be both renewed and strengthened.

How profoundly the Serbians of Rascia were influenced by the Slavonic liturgy and literature and by Byzantine ways in spiritual life is well illustrated by the example of Nemanja. In spite of his sympathetic attitude toward Rome and the West, all his religious foundations were set up for the Orthodox Church. The monks of Mount Athos were frequent guests at his court, and his son Rastko (Rastislav) was so impressed by their accounts of this center of Byzantine piety and by his readings in Slavonic and Greek religious works that he secretly left his father's court and became a monk in the monastery of Vatopedi on Mount Athos under the name of Sabbas or Sava. Instead of being shocked by this, Nemanja followed his son's example. In 1196 he handed over the supreme government of the Serbian lands to his eldest son Stephen, placing his younger son Vlk or Vlkan under his authority as župan of the coastal province, the former Dioclean kingdom, and entered the monastery of Studenica, one of his own foundations. Soon after, the new monk, who took the name Symeon, joined his son on the Holy Mountain where they founded the famous Serbian monastery of Chilandari.

The new Bulgarian rulers were the first to solicit the support of Rome. A letter addressed in 1199 by Pope Innocent III to "the noble man Joannica," who ruled in Bulgaria after the assassination of Asen and Peter, shows that a request of this sort must have been made to Rome by the addressee, who was also called Kalojan (John the Fair) (1197-1207), or by his brothers. Incidentally this letter, in which the Pope says that Joannica's ancestors were of Roman origin, or rather the latter's reaction to this allusion, provides further evidence that the Bulgarian rulers were Vlachs (Rumanians) and not Bulgarians. The Bulgarian rulers must have made a suggestion that they were ready to join the Roman Church, and an interesting correspondence developed between Rome and Bulgaria.

The astute Bulgarian who called himself "Emperor of the Bulgarians and the Vlachs," felt flattered by the Pope's compliment and thanked him warmly for recalling his Roman origin. After profuse expressions of respect, Kalojan asked the Pope to send him an imperial crown and to promote the bishop of his residential capital, Trnovo, to patriarch, with power to consecrate and to rule over the bishops of his realm. To improve his own case and also the Pope's knowledge of Bulgarian history, Kalojan reminded him that his predecessors, in particular Peter and Samuel, had been invested with the imperial dignity.

This passage of Kalojan's letter has often been misunderstood, and many historians, especially ecclesiastical historians, have read into it evidence proving that all the Bulgarian tsars had asked Rome for recognition. This is false, and it is evident from the context that Kalojan never said anything of the kind (P.L., vol. 214, col. 1113): "The first favor we are asking from the Roman Church, our mother, as her beloved son, is the crown and the dignity as our imperial predecessors of old possessed them. One was Peter, another was Samuel, besides others who preceded them on the throne, as we find it written in our books."

Clear though it is that Kalojan did not say that the Bulgarian tsars had ever received their title from Rome, the Roman chancellery of Innocent III was the first to draw this conclusion—as the Pope's reply clearly shows: "You have humbly asked that the Roman Church should grant you the crown as it did to Peter and Samuel of glorious memory, and to other predecessors of yours, according to your books."

In another letter Kalojan hinted to the hesitant Pope that he could without difficulty obtain the favor he asked from the Greeks, who had actually approached him on the subject. His next step was to dispatch the proposed patriarch, Basil, to Rome; but Basil was detained in Dyrrhachium by the Greeks as he was on the point of embarking for Italy. In a third letter Kalojan accepted the Pope's interpretation of Bulgarian history and naively confessed that after rereading his books, he had himself come to the conclusion that all his predecessors had received the imperial crown from Rome. He added the promise, as Boris had previously done, that he would remain forever under Roman jurisdiction and would subject any lands he might conquer to Rome.

In the meantime, Kalojan was taking the fullest advantage of the general confusion reigning in the Balkans as a result of the Latin expedition against Constantinople (1204) and occupied the whole region from Sofia to the frontier of Thessaly.[3] In the north he advanced toward the rivers Morava and Danube. His lightning successes must have impressed Rome and lent weight to his pledges of fidelity; as it would have been rash to alienate such a powerful neighbor of the nascent Latin Empire, Kalojan obtained his crown from Rome in 1204, with a scepter and a banner of SS. Peter and Paul thrown in for good measure. But the Pope behaved with caution and cunning: he granted the royal dignity and no more, while the Bishop of Trnovo was made primate of Bulgaria. The Pope explained that this was almost the same as making him a patriarch. The distinction did not embarrass Kalojan, who coolly continued to call himself Emperor (Tsar) and his primate Patriarch.

But the Bulgaro-Roman rapprochement came to nothing. The Bulgarian's outlook was too Byzantine, and he could not adjust himself to the mentality of the western new order which the Romans would have liked to force upon him. Resentful of the summons from the Latin emperor of Constantinople to accept his sovereignty from the Latins, Kalojan turned again to the Greeks, who were revolting against the Latin domination. In 1205 he concluded an alliance with the Greeks and bled the Latin Empire almost to extinction. Indeed, Baldwin I, the first Latin emperor of Constantinople, died in Bulgarian captivity. Kalojan's hesitation in attacking Constantinople robbed him of the opportunity to oust the Latins from the Bosphorus and to make a reality of the title which had been assumed in the tenth century by Symeon, "Basileus of the Bulgarians and the Romans." He died in 1207, the victim of a palace revolution, just as he was about to attack Thessolonica.

The Papacy was no more successful with Kalojan's successor Boril (1207-1218). Although a usurper who needed the Pope's help, Boril administered his Church on Byzantine lines, convoking the Synod of Trnovo against the heretical Bogomil movement, a counterpart of the Cathars of the West. To judge from the Acts of this Synod, the Bulgarian princes were copying the ecclesiastical policy of the emperors of Constantinople, and although the Pope sent a cardinal to Bulgaria at the time of the Synod, its procedure was purely Eastern. Roman methods meant little to the Bulgarians, and as soon as they felt that Rome could be of no further benefit to them, they reverted to Byzantine ideals.

Among the Serbians, Nemanja's successor, the Grand Župan Stephen, displayed through his long reign from 1196 to 1228 the qualities of a resourceful general and a supple diplomat. He was gifted with an uncommon political flair, and as soon as he discerned signs of the approaching decline of Byzantium, he turned his back on the Greek capital, severed all connection with the Emperor Alexius III, and repudiated his wife Eudokia, the emperor's daughter. He then approached the

Papacy, represented by the indomitable Innocent III, seeking confirmation of his independence.

It would appear that by this time Rome had at last arrived at a better understanding of the new situation in Serbia. Innocent III recognized the rights of Antibari, and his legates carried to John of Antibari the pallium—a small piece of vestment—which was the prerogative of Latin archbishops or metropolitans. From the correspondence between the Pope and Vlkan, who administered Dioclea under his brother, the grand župan, it is clear that the initiative came from Vlkan, who supported the request of John of Antibari. The Acts of the Synod of Antibari, presided over by the legates, were signed by six suffragans, all from Vlkan's "kingdom." No mention is made of jurisdiction over Rascia, the dominion of the grand župan.

The Pope, however, had not forgotten this part of the new realm. He did not fail to send a letter to Stephen by the hand of his legates. Stephen took advantage of the occasion to send a cordial letter to the Pope, saluting him as his spiritual father and assuring him that he intended to follow in the footsteps of his father Nemanja and "always to observe the precepts of the Roman Church." He also promised to send his own envoys to Rome. When this embassy was dispatched, it was charged to request the Pope to grant Stephen a royal crown, in return for which the grand župan announced his readiness to place his country under Roman supremacy.

The Pope was willing to oblige, but his legates were prevented from reaching Serbia by the Hungarian king Emmerich (1196-1204). It seems evident from the correspondence exchanged between the Pope and the Hungarian king that Emmerich must have contemplated establishing a sort of protectorate over the whole of southeastern Europe. He objected to the Pope's plans for Bulgaria and went so far as to detain the papal legate, Cardinal Leo, who was carrying the royal crown to Kalojan. In the case of Bulgaria, Emmerich had eventually to yield to the Pope's pressure, but he did not abandon his hopes of intervening in Serbia. He plotted with Stephen's ambitious brother Vlkan, who had assumed the royal title of the former rulers of Dioclea and aspired to become the sole ruler of all Serbia. In order to win over the Pope, Vlkan declared through the mediation of Emmerich that he was willing to submit to Rome. Stephen was forced to leave the country. Emmerich himself assumed the title of King of Serbia (*Rex Rasciae*)—which all Hungarian kings were to use until the year 1918—leaving Vlkan in possession of all the Serbian lands under Hungarian suzerainty.

Stephen was saved by the Bulgarians, who resented Hungarian interference in Serbia. Vlkan was forced to submit to Stephen, but Sava succeeded in reconciling his two brothers. Stephen then took advantage of an opportunity which occurred in 1217, when Emmerich's successor Andrew II (1205-1235) left Hungary on a crusade. He approached Rome once more, probably through the mediation of the Venetians, and according to a report made by Thomas, archdeacon of Spalato, he asked Honorius III for a royal crown. In 1218 a cardinal was sent to Serbia to perform the coronation ceremony. From that time on Stephen is called in Serbian annals "the First Crowned" (*Prvovenčani*).

Here again the expectations of Rome were somewhat disappointed. The Romans naturally anticipated that the Serbian hierarchy would be subordinated to a Latin archbishop. Antibari seemed particularly qualified for the new role: it was in Serbian hands, its metropolitan status had been re-established, it could claim a glorious record from the time of the Dioclean kingdom, when its jurisdiction had extended over the whole of Rascia. The claims of Antibari were, however, still being contested by the mighty city-republic of Ragusa, which continued, with the support of Venice, to press for recognition. The popes, especially Gregory IX and Innocent IV, had to intervene time and again in defense of the rights of Antibari without hurting the feelings of the powerful Ragusans.

This uncertainty about the position of Antibari was not likely to induce the new king of Serbia to enter into a more intimate ecclesiastical relationship with its metropolitan. Moreover, Antibari was part of the province of Dioclea and was under the governorship of Stephen's brother Vlkan. In spite of the reconciliation which had been effected at the instance of Sava, Stephen Nemanja II was most unlikely to forget the past, and he regarded it as unwise to place his realm under the jurisdiction of an archbishop who was likely to be on the side of his jealous brother.

Another problem had also to be solved. Stephen's bishop of Ras was nominally under the supremacy of the Greek archbishop of Ochrida. This relationship had been considerably strengthened during the reign of Stephen's father. As long as Ochrida was politically neutral, this was immaterial; but after the disruption of the Byzantine Empire, Ochrida belonged to the Greek Despotate of Epirus, Stephen's rival.

In order to neutralize the possible danger arising from this situation, Stephen had to find a way of making his bishop independent. A transfer of jurisdiction to Rome would have created new difficulties with Ochrida and the rest of the Greeks. Stephen could think of but one solution: to obtain permission for the creation of an independent Serbian Church from the Byzantine patriarch, who was then residing in Nicaea and was regarded as head of the Orthodox Church with suzerainty over Ochrida. He charged his brother Sava with the negotiations.

The Emperor of Nicaea, Theodore I Lascaris, saw the political significance of such a move. He was jealous of his Greek rival in Epirus and was prepared to welcome an alliance with the Serbians. He therefore granted the request and his patriarch, Manuel Sarentenus, consecrated Sava as the first archbishop of Serbia (1219). After Sava's return several new bishoprics were founded in Serbian lands. The Greek archbishop of Ochrida, the learned Demetrius Chomatianus, protested in vain. The Despot of Epirus, about to take the imperial title and to launch an offensive against Thessalonica and Constantinople, wisely abstained from any action and even gave his daughter Anne in marriage to Stephen's son and heir Radoslav.

Stephen's dual action in sending an embassy to Rome for the royal title and applying to the Greek patriarch for the independence of the Serbian Church has been treated as the most obscure puzzle in Serbian history. To modern eyes these two acts seem incapable of being reconciled. They have provoked endless criticism among historians, particularly ecclesiastical historians. Later Serbian tradition, even as early as the *Life of St. Sava*, written in 1254 by the Serbian monk Domentijan, tried to minimize the significance of the Roman intervention, attributing the coronation, with a crown blessed by the Pope, to St. Sava. In order to reconcile the two traditions and to save the Orthodox honor of St. Sava, Serbian and Russian writers have imagined two coronations, one performed by the papal legate with the crown sent by the Pope and the other by St. Sava with a crown brought from Nicaea, although contemporary accounts make no mention of either a second ceremony or a second crown.

As a matter of fact this can be a problem only for those who prejudge the issue by starting from the assumption that there was hatred and distrust between East and West—a prejudice prevalent among later generations. But at the beginning of the thirteenth century, the position in Serbia and Bulgaria was quite different, so much so that it would be an anachronism to attribute to the Serbians or the Bulgarians of that period the same feelings that animated the Greeks toward the West. It has been shown how Serbian and Bulgarian princes tried more than once to make contact with the great western powers, whether popes or German emperors. Moreover the Fourth Crusade of the Latins and the ensuing sack of Constantinople in 1204 could not possibly provoke among the Serbians and Bulgarians the same feelings of distrust, exasperation, and hatred that they did among the Greeks. Byzantium, from which the Serbians and Bulgarians had derived the foundations of their national culture, was nevertheless their political foe, and antagonism must have been at its strongest at the end of the twelfth and beginning of the thirteenth century. For it was just at this time that the Serbian and Bulgarian rulers were straining hardest to secure their political independence and to liberate their nations from the Byzantine yoke. They did not feel the same distrust toward the Emperor of Nicaea in distant Asia Minor, who had been defeated by the Latins, as toward the more dangerous Despot of Epirus. The difference in rites could not at that time have provoked any feeling of distrust where westerners were concerned, for it must be remembered that the two rites then coexisted even in Italy.

It is therefore not surprising that the Serbian king sincerely believed his two actions to be perfectly logical.[4] It is quite incorrect to make Stephen the champion of Latin traditions in his own country and Sava the jealous defender of the "Orthodox" side. There seems to have been no divergence in political outlook between the two brothers, and responsibility for the Nicaean embassy should not be attributed to Sava, as many would aver, but to the king himself.

The case is of unique interest in the study of relations between East and West, and the whole incident shows how the original Christian instinct was still alive at this period in this part of Europe, where people knew little and cared less about differences between the two Churches and where they cherished the naive conviction that one should remain on speaking terms with both the great Christian centers. The incident also shows how erroneous it is to imagine that there was a complete separation between the two Churches after the regrettable episode of 1054, or to think that the whole of Eastern Christianity had since then been irreparably severed from the West. Many avenues which would have led to mutual understanding were at that time still open; they were blocked only later as a result of divergences in evolution.

One of the principal differences lay in the varying attitudes toward national Churches. In this field, the Serbians and the Bulgarians were pupils of the Eastern Church, and the whole development of the Papacy since the eleventh century was strange to them. Their desire to secure the independence of their national Churches under their own patriarchs, or at least under autonomous archbishops, diverged in many respects from the development of Christianity in the West, where national Churches were things of a remote past and where, for all practical purposes, the Pope governed every single diocese. This hankering after independent national Churches was essentially Byzantine, not Roman, and this is the principal factor in explaining why all the numerous attempts at reunion between the thirteenth and fifteenth centuries were frustrated and why eventually the Serbian and Bulgarian Churches remained more than any others under Byzantine obedience.

These differences generated among the Latins in Greece a distrust of the Bulgarians, although Bulgaria was still canonically under Roman supremacy. In the end the Latins had to pay very dearly for this distrust. The new Bulgarian tsar, John (Ivan) Asen II (1218-1241), who had defeated the usurper Boril, would have liked to remain at peace with the Latins, and the Frankish barons in Constantinople were fully alive to the influential position of the Bulgarian tsar. So when the incompetent Latin Emperor Robert died, the plan was mooted of betrothing his young son Baldwin II (1228-1261) to the Bulgarian tsar's daughter. This proposal was welcomed by Asen II, who hoped thereby to realize his predecessors' cherished dream of becoming regent of Constantinople.

The project was repugnant, however, to Theodore of Epirus (1224-1230), who had considerably extended his possessions and had assumed the imperial title after having taken Thessalonica from the Latins. Counting on the eventual help of the new king of Serbia, his son-in-law Radoslav (1228-1233), he attacked John Asen II in complete disregard of his pact of friendship with Bulgaria, hoping thereby to nullify the marriage project. However, the element of surprise failed to work as Theodore had hoped, and in the spring of 1230 he was deservedly defeated at Klokotnica, on the Marica River. His army was routed, and he himself was taken prisoner, together with his staff and family. John Asen II treated his captives with commendable forbearance and was rewarded for his humanity by the Greeks' spontaneous submission to his rule. He annexed Adrianople and the lands of the lower Marica and Mesta rivers, the territory of Northern Albania together with Dyrrhachium (Durazzo) and Croja, leaving Thessalonica, Thessaly, and Epirus to his son-in-law Manuel, the brother of the unfortunate Theodore.

This great victory completely altered the whole situation in the Balkans. In Serbia Radoslav was forced to hand over his crown to his brother Stephen Vladislav (1233-1242) and fled to Ragusa and thence to Durazzo.[5]

Hungary was alarmed and Andrew II attacked the Bulgarians, but Asen's brother was able to cope with him. A more unexpected sequel to Asen's victory occurred in the Latin Empire. The barons, with their instinctive dislike of strong rulers in Constantinople and their dread of another foreign prince gaining mastery over the city, had been watching the tsar's growing power with profound uneasiness, while the Latin clergy gave every sign of loathing the idea of the young emperor's marriage to an Orthodox princess. Bearing in mind that in accordance with canon law, the Bulgarians were still in communion with the Pope, the Latin clergy's refusal to have anything to do with Bulgaria's Orthodox ruler seems quite extraordinary. The issue was submitted to the Pope, who, unfortunately, sided with the Latin clergy. As a result, John de

Brienne (1231-1237), the ex-king of Jerusalem, was made regent of Constantinople with the imperial title, and it was arranged that his daughter should marry the young emperor.

Even supposing that there was a danger of Asen II's ultimately securing the throne of Constantinople, the risk was worth taking because there was no alternative for the Latins. But in refusing the Bulgarian alliance, the barons signed the death warrant of the Latin Empire. Asen II was furious, and from that moment he sought means to make a clean sweep of the Latin Empire. With this end in view he approached its bitterest enemy, the Greek emperor of Nicaea, John III Ducas Vatatzes (1222-1254). The Empire of Nicaea had already made considerable progress in Asia Minor, whence the Latins had been almost expelled. The new allies were only foiled from capturing Constantinople in 1236 by the last minute intervention of the Venetian fleet, supported by other Italian city-republics and by a contingent sent by the Latin prince of Achaia.

Offended by the attitude of the Pope, Asen followed the Serbian example and opened negotiations with the Patriarch of Nicaea; but when the Greeks started to make difficulties, he simply chose a new archbishop of Trnovo and proclaimed the ecclesiastical independence of his Church. However, after the conclusion of the Bulgaro-Greek alliance, the Orthodox Synod of Gallipoli sanctioned his ecclesiastical arrangement and agreed to the creation of a Bulgarian patriarchate.

The Pope was alarmed by these events and appointed the Hungarian king and the Hungarian archbishop as his agents in southeastern Europe to deal with "the Nobleman Asen," but Asen succeeded in calming the Pope for a time by new assurances of submission to Rome and by a new alliance with the Latins. However, when Asen's words were not followed by deeds, Pope Gregory IX with a flourish of trumpets proclaimed a crusade against the schismatic tsar, charging Béla IV of Hungary with its organization.

This crusade, the burning topic of many papal letters to Hungary in the years 1238 and 1239, petered out and all the efforts spent upon it came to nought—except for the historian, who will find in the pontifical missives many interesting details concerning Hungary's international standing at that time.[6]

These complications forced Asen to maintain his good relations with the Serbians. These were immeasurably improved by the fact that on his return from a pilgrimage to the Holy Land, Sava paid a visit to Asen II, who received him with unusual cordiality. It was indeed at Trnovo that Sava died on January 12, 1236. He was buried there in the Church of the Forty Martyrs, which Asen had built to commemorate his great victory near Klokotnica. Here also in the following year King Vladislav visited his father-in-law and transferred the body of his saintly uncle to the monastery of Mileševo, the king's own foundation. Serbia's great national hero thus contributed greatly to a closer union between his countrymen and the Bulgarians.

After the fiasco of the crusade, Asen II was able to end his days in peace (1241) as a mighty figure who had shed the luster of unrivaled distinction upon the Bulgarian throne and people. But after his death a period of slow decadence set in, a period of waste and petty struggles for the succession. Then, on top of domestic wrangles, there came the life and death struggle against the Mongols under their leaders Batu and Sabutai. Batu attacked Poland and Bohemia, while Sabutai invaded Hungary, where he ravaged the countryside, cut Béla IV's army to pieces in 1241, and pursued the fugitive king past Zagreb as far as Split (Spalato). Croatia, Bosnia, Serbia, and Bulgaria suffered severely. The Khanate of the Golden Horde, founded by Batu, which held Russia under its sway, extended to the lower Danube. The Bulgarians escaped complete destruction and subjugation only through the offer of an annual tribute, which they paid to the Khan from 1242 to 1300, long enough for Mongol influence to make itself felt in Bulgaria more than once. Moreover, Bulgaria lost forever her leading position in the Balkans.

It is quite possible that had the Mongols been given a free hand in the Balkans for a longer period, they would have completed their conquest before the arrival of the Ottoman Turks, but in reality they were merely the harbingers of the second conquerors. Curiously enough, the Turks embarked upon their conquest of the Balkans at the end of the fourteenth century from Bulgaria, the very country which the Mongols had selected a century earlier as their base for further operations.

Once more leadership in the Balkans passed from the Serbians and the Bulgarians to the Greeks, who were the least affected by the Mongol incursion. The Emperor John III Ducas Vatatzes of Nicaea (1222-1254) took advantage of the decline of Bulgaria during the reign of Asen II's successors Kaloman I (1241-1246) and Michael Asen (1246-1256) to occupy all Bulgarian territory south of Adrianople as far as the river Vardar. At the same time, the Despot of Epirus annexed territory which included the towns of Veles, Prilep, and Ochrida. Vatatzes was able to count upon the support of the new Serbian king Stephen Uroš I (1242-1276), to whom his brother Stephen Vladislav (1233-1242), shaken by the Mongol invasion, had surrendered the reins of power. Encouraged by this support, the Emperor of Nicaea took Thessalonica (1246), occupied western Macedonia and Albania with its capital Croja, and made preparations to liquidate his Greek rival, Michael II, despot of Epirus.

The Serbians seem to have turned their friendship with Vatatzes to profit. When the Bulgarian tsar Michael Asen (1246-1256) made an alliance with the Republic of Ragusa, whose importance was steadily growing, and invaded Serbia,⁷ the invasion seems to have been stopped by the intervention of Vatatzes. Michael's attempt to recover the territory lost to the Greeks was arrested by Vatatzes' successor, his son Theodore II Lascaris (1254-1258). The Bulgarian tsar then fell a victim to a revolt of the discontented boyars. He scarcely benefited at all from the assistance given to him by his brother-in-law Rastislav, a Russian prince, who, after his expulsion from Galicia by the Mongols, received the Banat of Slavonia with Belgrade from the Hungarians. Koloman II Asen was Michael's successor and shared Michael's fate. Rastislav then tried to seize the vacant throne of Bulgaria, which, together with the territories he held under Hungarian suzerainty, would have formed quite a considerable state; but he had to desist from his attempt because the fierce and proud boyars objected to having a foreign prince and a vassal of Hungary as their tsar. Eventually a relative of the House of Nemanja named Constantine Tich enlisted the help of Nicaean diplomacy, divorced his wife, and married Irene—the daughter of Theodore II Lascaris, a granddaughter of John Asen II, and great-granddaughter of Andrew II of Hungary—and held the Bulgarian throne from 1257 to 1277.

The accession of a tsar who claimed relationship with both the Serbian and Greek dynasties was the last outcome of Serbo-Greek collaboration, for shortly afterward Uroš I (1242-1276) abandoned the Greeks in order to join a new Balkan political combination originated by the Despot of Epirus, Michael II (1237-1271). The latter, jealous of the more progressive Nicaeans, had secured the cooperation of his sons-in-law, William of Villehardouin, prince of Achaia, and Manfred, king of Sicily, who was also the administrator of the dowry of his wife Helen, consisting of the island of Corfu with Dyrrhachium (Durazzo), Berat, and Valona. The first results of the operations initiated by this coalition were satisfactory. All the land between the Adriatic and the Vardar was occupied by the despot, while the Serbians annexed Skoplje and Prilep, where the Greek historian George Akropolites, at that time the imperial governor, was taken prisoner.

With the death of Theodore II Lascaris, whose son and heir John was a minor, the prospects looked even rosier; but General Michael Palaeologus retrieved the Greek position by imposing himself first as co-regent, then as co-emperor, and finally as sole ruler of the Empire. His usurpation turned out to be a stroke of good fortune for the Greeks. Michael of Epirus was already threatening Thessalonica when Palaeologus turned the tables on the coalition, expelled Michael from Macedonia, and marched towards Albania, the despot's own territory. On the plain of Pelagonia, Palaeologus defeated the army of Michael II and his allies in 1259 in so decisive a manner as to discourage them permanently. The Empire of Nicaea again crushed the once mighty Despotate of Epirus out of existence as a power in the Balkans.

There remained still the task of expelling the Latins from their strongholds around Constantinople and from the city itself. Palaeologus started operations in 1260, and in the following year, by an unexpected stroke of luck, his general Alexius Strategopulus captured Constantinople by a stratagem which cost scarcely a drop of blood. The Latin emperor Baldwin II fled in such haste that he left all his imperial insignia behind, and Michael Palaeologus, after a triumphal entry, was crowned in St. Sophia on August 15. Such was the inglorious end of the Latin Empire.

After such a resounding success, Michael Palaeologus felt himself to be in a position to settle the fate of the boy emperor John IV without fear of encountering trouble from supporters of the Lascaris dynasty. In accordance with Byzantine custom, John was therefore blinded and imprisoned, and the way was clear for the Palaeologus dynasty to rule the restored Empire for two centuries. Constantinople began to rise again toward the heights of fame which it had known before the Latin occupation. But it never reached them again because the wounds inflicted by the Westerners were too deep and its economic and political life had been bled white.

The Mongol invasion and the recapture of Constantinople by the Greeks can be regarded as the two main events which closed a long period of evolution in southeastern Europe. But whereas the fall of the Latin Empire affected the Balkans generally, the Mongol invasion touched the interests of Hungary more particularly and terminated an interesting period in Hungarian history which was of vital concern to the southern Slavs. When the Hungarian kings became kings of Croatia and suzerains of Bosnia, it was to be expected that they would show a lively interest in events among the other southern Slavs. The rulers of the Árpád dynasty gave evidence of this interest more than once. They were bold enough to claim an overlordship over the liberated Serbians and Bulgarians.

In the eleventh, twelfth, and even thirteenth centuries there were possibilities that the Magyars would be able to group several Slavonic nations around themselves in a mighty federation. The monarchs of the Árpád dynasty favored a very liberal policy toward other nations and adhered to the principle which St. Stephen had given to his son: "Monoglot kingdoms are never strong." Such a rallying center would have been welcome to the southern Slavs, who were seeking allies in the West in their fight for independence. Unfortunately, some essential conditions for such a development were not fulfilled by the Hungarians, who remained racially alien to all their neighbors. This made it difficult for Slavic elements to make contact with the center of authority, the king and his council of nobles, and to leave their mark on the political life of Hungary proper. However much the kings of Hungary tried to impose their authority on the Slavic states, events conspired to harden the Magyar element and to preclude any sort of racial amalgamation which might have brought the Magyars and the Slavs together for their common good.

At this period Hungary needed colonists for the development of her territory. Among the Slavs only the Czechs and the Croats could give the Magyars the cultural finish they were seeking, but neither of these nations was at that time in a position to send colonists, artisans, or priests to Hungary. So it came about that the most numerous and zealous pioneers of Western civilization in Hungary were the Germans, who settled in large numbers in the Hungarian counties contiguous to the Ostmark, made their way into the northern districts, modern Slovakia, where rich silver mines had been discovered, and founded large colonies in Transylvania.

In this way Hungary, which had in earlier centuries welcomed Byzantine cultural influences, became so thoroughly westernized as to be incapable of understanding the eastern religious mentality of her Slavic neighbors in the Balkans. It was utterly wrong for her to pose as the protagonist of the Papacy and of Western civilization in southeastern Europe or to organize crusades against the schismatics.

The foreign, non-Slavic element in Hungary was greatly strengthened by the Hungarian kings, who were in the habit of admitting "guests" from the wild Turkic tribes. Just as in the eleventh century the Pechenegs, fleeing before the Cumans, had found a home in Hungary, so in the thirteenth century the Cumans were welcomed by Béla IV after their defeat by the Mongols, and their chieftain Kuthen was settled with forty thousand of his warriors between the Danube and the Tisza in enjoyment of full Magyar rights. Béla himself married a Cuman princess, and his son Ladislas IV favored them in many other ways since their presence benefited the Magyars by considerably reinforcing the non-European element in the land. Though the first years of their stay in Hungary were fairly lively, they were assimilated in the course of the fourteenth century, thus giving the Magyars extra powers of resistance against German and Slavic infiltration. The fusion of Cumans and Magyars marked the end of any chance of Slavic penetration of the Magyars or of any closer relationship between the two races. And yet, this was a requisite condition for the success of the designs of the Hungarian kings for hegemony among the Slavic populations. It is the main reason explaining their failure—although at that time it could hardly occur to anyone to associate racial and national problems with the evolution of Europe. The situation could not be changed by the new dynasty of Anjou, which followed on the extinction of the Árpáds in 1301.

The consequences of Hungary's internal development soon became evident in Croatia and Dalmatia, for it was at that time that the Croatian nobility began to take an active interest in national expansion. There were many instances in which Dalmatian cities had to come to terms with influential Croatian families established in the neighborhood, which even ruled the countryside around the city walls. The ramparts of Zadar (Zara), destroyed in 1202 by the crusaders in the hire of Venice, were rebuilt by Croat lords. Although the city was under Venetian suzerainty, the wealthy family of the Svačić played the leading role within its walls. Other Croat families such as the Šubić and the Kačić were the de facto rulers along the whole Adriatic coast. They cared nought for the claims of the Patrician Republic of Venice, and the predominance of the Croat nobles, especially in the Dalmatian districts, was sufficient proof that the sense of Croatian kingship, entailed though it was on a foreign dynasty, was still very much alive.

The loss of Zadar was a great blow to Hungarian prestige. There was no possibility of retaliation, and in 1216 King Andrew II, being too short of money and means of transport to finance and move his army on a private crusade, relinquished his rights over Zadar and acknowledged the Venetian hold on that city.

The power of the Croat nobility in Dalmatia and the corresponding royal weakness there underwent their severest test during the Mongol invasion, when Count Stephen Šubić looked after the defense of Trogir, whereas Béla IV, king of Hungary and Croatia, lost his best chance to recover Zadar in 1243. The burghers had refused allegiance to Venice and taken refuge in the old Croat city of Nin (Nona), but Béla needed Venetian money and could not interfere. So Venice tightened its grip on the city and took strong measures to prevent any influx of Croat elements.

At the same time Hungary was permitting her hold on Bosnia to relax. It will be remembered that the Emperor Manuel I Comnenus (1143-1180) succeeded in bringing Bosnia, which had been Hungarian from 1120 onward, under his own sovereignty. After Manuel's death, the ruler of Bosnia, Ban Kulin (1168-1204), acknowledged Hungarian suzerainty nominally, while trying secretly to achieve his country's complete independence. He did wonders for the economic development of Bosnia and reopened the silver mines, which had not been worked since the days of the Roman occupation. Bosnia's earliest historical document is a commercial treaty concluded between Kulin and Ragusa. To keep his country on its feet and to counteract the influence of both Catholics and Orthodox, Kulin embraced Bogomilism and tried to elevate it to the rank of a state religion. Frightened by the intervention of Pope Innocent III, who had invited King Emmerich to drive the promoter of heresy out of the country, Kulin recanted and allowed a synod to be held in Bosnia in 1203, which condemned Bogomilism.

But the heresy continued to spread in Bosnia, and under Ninoslav (1232-1250) almost the whole populace embraced it. Two crusades were necessary to break the resistance of the heretics and to re-establish Hungarian authority in the land. But no sooner had the crusaders turned their backs than Ninoslav reoccupied the country. Thanks to the Mongol invasion he maintained his position, in spite of a few crusading experiments, until his death in 1250. After Ninoslav's death Béla IV succeeded in bringing Bosnia and Hum under his control. But Bogomilism was never exterminated, and the Bogomils again took matters into their own hands in the fourteenth century.

With the re-establishment of the Greek Empire in Byzantium, the old mistrust toward all things Byzantine again became evident in Bulgaria and Serbia. Michael VIII Palaeologus tried in vain to remain on good terms with his Slavic neighbors because he was menaced by a new and dangerous foe, Charles I of Anjou (1268-1285), king of Sicily. This ambitious French prince had obtained a firm foothold in modern Albania, where he called himself King, and gave every sign of a desire to revive the Latin Empire of Constantinople. In Bulgaria, Irene, the wife of Constantine Tich and sister of the unfortunate John IV Lascaris, blinded and dethroned by Michael VIII, incited her husband against the new Greek emperor.

The tsar, having allied himself with the Tatars, invaded Greek territory. He was, however, outmaneuvered by Michael VIII, who incited against him the Despot Svetislav, a mighty boyar, who seems to have inherited a part of Rastislav's lands. Svetislav, encouraged by the Greeks, married Irene's sister, proclaimed himself tsar, and occupied a great part of Bulgarian territory south of the Danube. When Svetislav, emboldened by success, attempted to annex some Hungarian territory, he was defeated by the Hungarians and forced to recognize Hungarian sovereignty.[8] Michael VIII, angered at the Hungarian intervention, tried to win the friendship of Constantine Tich, who had recently become a widower, by giving him the hand of his niece Mary in marriage. But Mary had personal accounts to settle with her uncle, who had refused to cede to Bulgaria the cities of Anchialus and Mesembria, promised as Mary's dowry, and it was only by enlisting Tatar help himself that the emperor was able to beat off this new danger from the Bulgaro-Angevin alliance.

The Serbian king Stephen Uroš I also gave support to Charles of Anjou. In order to gain time and to split the forces of the westerners, the shrewd Michael VIII sought to placate Pope Gregory X by an offer of union with the Western Church. At the Council of Lyons in 1274 he obtained the suppression of the Bulgarian patriarchate and of the autonomy of the Serbian Church by shrewdly asserting that both these institutions had been created without the papal consent and in curtailment of the rights of Ochrida, which had succeeded to Justiniana Prima. The rights of this latter foundation had been confirmed not only by the Emperor Justinian, but also by Pope Vigile. It was an extremely astute move, and the Latins were completely deceived until it became clear to all that Michael VIII was indulging in political trickery, whereupon enmity against him increased in the West.

The enormity of this mistake on the part of the Latins is illustrated by the fact that before the convocation of the Council there seems to have been a certain willingness on the part of the Bulgarians to enter into a more intimate relationship with Rome. A letter written in 1291 by Pope Nicholas IV (1288-1292) indicates that when he—at that time Jerome of Ascoli, a simple Franciscan friar—came to Constantinople in 1272 to prepare the Greek participation in the Council of Lyons, the Bulgarian patriarch Ignatius declared in his and the Emperor Michael's presence, in the Palace of Blachernae, that he claimed to be directly subordinate to the Pope of Rome.[9] Of course, after the official suppression of Bulgarian and Serbian ecclesiastical autonomy by the council, all efforts of Nicholas IV to induce Bulgaria and Serbia to accept the union were useless.

The troubles which broke out in Bulgaria thanks to the intrigues of the Tsaritsa Mary,[10] to whom the ailing tsar had entrusted the regency, saved Michael VIII and even gave him several opportunities for interfering in Bulgarian affairs. The unfortunate country was repeatedly attacked by the Tatars and now found a national hero in Ivajlo, a simple swineherd who organized the defense of the land, killed Tsar Constantine, and himself became tsar (1278-1279). John (Ivan) Asen III (1279-1280), whom the boyars and the emperor supported in opposition to Ivajlo, proved to be a poor choice, and George I Terter (1280-1292), founder of the new dynasty of Terter, had no option but to become a vassal of the Tatars. The state began to disintegrate under these blows, and the governors of some border provinces started to behave as though they were independent rulers. The Tatar Khan Nogay appointed Smilec (1292-1298), one of the pro-Tatar boyars, as ruler under Tatar supremacy. Even when the Tatar danger became less menacing after Nogay's death, George's son Theodore Svetoslav (1300-1322) got rid of Nogay's son Čaka, pretender to the Bulgarian throne; but he fought in vain to re-establish the prestige of Bulgaria and its tsars. His son George II Terter (1322-1323) was even less fortunate. The slow but sure decline of the country continued under the new dynasty of the Šišmans, which was founded by Michael III (1323-1330).[11]

Leadership in the Balkans was passing slowly but surely to the Serbians. The new period in Serbia's history was initiated by Stephen Uroš II Milutin (1282-1321), to whom his brother Stephen Dragutin (1276-1282) had freely surrendered the crown.[12] He continued the struggle against Michael VIII and conquered the important area around Skoplje, but meanwhile the power of his ally Charles of Anjou, already undermined by Michael's victory at Berat, had been definitely broken by a revolution in Sicily ensuing on the massacre of Angevin supporters in the bloody Sicilian Vespers (1282). The timely death of Michael VIII in 1282 and the incapacity of his son and successor Andronicus II (1282-1328) allowed Uroš II to retain and extend his gains, not only in Macedonia but also along the Adriatic. He also made important advances in the North toward the Danube and the Sava. He was not, however, able to reunite with the Serbian realm the territories which his brother had administered. Uroš II was not a good diplomat, and his policy was not stable. He changed sides between the Greeks and the Latins as lightly as he changed his wives. When he married the six-year-old Byzantine princess Simonis,[13] he even began to cherish the dream of a dynastic union of Byzantium and Serbia. He had trouble with Ragusa and Hungary and also with his brother, because of his pro-Greek policy. His own son Stephen revolted against him and was blinded in punishment.[14] But he was a good general, and luck was on his side. For his consistent good fortune he considered himself beholden to St. Nicholas of Bari, in whose honor he erected in 1319 a massive altar in silver bearing a Latin inscription in which he described himself as "master of all lands from the Adriatic Sea to the great river Danube."

The fact that an Orthodox ruler showed such devotion to a saint buried in a Catholic church is significant as well as illustrative of the mentality of the Serbians of that time. In this respect, the attitude of Uroš' mother Helen is even more to the point. She was French, and although married to an Orthodox ruler, she remained a Catholic. Yet she was held in high esteem by the Orthodox Serbians. The Orthodox Archbishop Daniel pays the highest tribute to her intelligence and her pious Christian life. After the death of her husband, she lived on the large estate on the Adriatic coast between Ragusa and Scutari which her son had given her. She not only set up numerous Catholic foundations in the coastal cities, but also founded the Orthodox monastery of Gradac on the river Ibar. She remained in constant communication with the popes, who used her as an intermediary in their efforts to win over the Serbians and Bulgarians to Rome. But Uroš II and George Terter paid no heed to the invitations which came from Nicholas IV (1288, 1291) and Benedict XI (1303) to join the Roman Church.[15] When Uroš II began to negotiate with Charles of Valois in 1308, he approached Clement V with a proposal for union. But he eventually abandoned both the French prince and the Pope as soon as he realized that no political profit was obtainable by continuing the association, and remained with the Greeks.

It is possible that the blunder of the Romans at the Council of Lyons, in allowing themselves to be deceived by Michael VIII's strategic move against the Serbian and Bulgarian Churches, stiffened the attitude of the Serbians and Bulgarians against Rome and made them suspicious of papal intentions. They valued the autonomy of their national Churches too highly to jeopardize it.

The work of Uroš II was continued by his illegitimate son Stephen Uroš III, also called Stephen Dečanski (1321-1331). He appointed his younger son Stephen as co-ruler and defeated the two pretenders to the throne, his half-brother Constantine and his cousin Vladislav. These troubles were exploited by Bosnia, where the Bogomil leader, Kotromanić (1322-1353), had emancipated himself from the Hungarian yoke and begun to extend his territory. The Bosnians broke through the Serbian territory of Hum (Hercegovina) to the Adriatic, and the Serbian kings strove in vain to recover this valuable possession. The Bosnians were even able to extend their sway over Dalmatia, thus creating a new Slavic power whose religious fanaticism tended unfortunately to complicate the situation in the Balkans.

Serbian losses on the Adriatic were compensated by gains in Bulgaria. Tsar Michael III Šišman (1323-1330), who took an active part in the revolt of Prince Andronicus against his grandfather Andronicus II, made an alliance with the Byzantines against the Serbians. But Uroš III surprised the Bulgarian army on its march to join its Byzantine allies near Velbužd (Küstendil) in 1330, defeating it completely. The tsar himself perished. Uroš III was enabled to extend his sovereignty over the greater part of the Vardar valley. The Byzantines abandoned their conquests on Serbian territory but, profiting by the disorder in Bulgaria, occupied some places on the Bulgarian frontier. The beautiful monastery of Dečani still recalls this great Serbian victory.

In spite of his victory over the Bulgarians, Uroš III was dethroned in the following year by his son and the nobles, and he died soon afterward, possibly by assassination. The reign of his son Stephen Dušan

(1331-1355) marks the most glorious period of Serbian history. The young king was a gifted and energetic ruler and a good general. He introduced an efficient system of administration, effected a new codification of the law, and developed communications with an eye to improving commerce and trade. He established excellent relations with the great commercial republics of Ragusa and Venice and was made an honorary citizen of the latter city.[16] He had a flair for discovering good administrators and financial experts and winning their loyal support. His court was full of "specialists" from all the countries of Europe, and he profited greatly from their services. All these things contributed to the considerable material welfare which was evident in Serbia during his reign.

Hungary under Louis the Great of Anjou (1342-1382) constantly showed a suspiciously lively interest in Serbia and continued to play the trouble-making role of defender of Western Christianity and the Papacy against the schismatic Slavs. Yet Dušan very wisely did all he could to keep peace on his northern frontiers, in order to leave his hands free for action in the South. A dynastic struggle in the shape of a civil war between the Palaeologi and John Cantacuzenus was shaking the very foundations of the Greek Empire. In the early days of the conflict John had found refuge at Dušan's court. Dušan's first act in 1340 was to turn against the Angevins and conquer the Albanian littoral as far as Valona. He then extended his rule over the rest of Albania and over Macedonia. By 1348 he was master also of Epirus and Thessaly, reaching the boundary of the Catalan Duchy of Athens. Dušan was on friendly terms with the Bulgarian tsar John (Ivan) Alexander (1331-1371), whose sister Helen he married. In fact, since its great defeat by the Serbians in 1330, Bulgaria had been in some measure under Serbian supremacy.

These military and political successes gave Dušan the idea of replacing the Byzantine emperors in Constantinople. As a first step toward implementing this plan, he proclaimed himself in 1346 "Emperor of the Serbs and Greeks (Romaioi), of Bulgars and Albanians." He was solemnly crowned by Archbishop Ioannikos of Peć, who was promoted to the rank of patriarch, and established a splendid court on the Byzantine pattern at Skoplje. Byzantine titles and much Byzantine ceremonial were introduced into Serbia.

One of the first acts of the new emperor was to publish his *Zakonik,* the famous legal code, which is also one of the most important documents extant illustrative of Serbian social conditions and culture in the fourteenth century.

Dušan was also presented with good opportunities for reconquering the lost provinces of Hum and Bosnia. Stephen, the Ban of Bosnia, who had attacked Serbia in 1349, had forfeited the sympathy of many of the Bogomils because of his negotiations with the Papacy, and many of his subjects would have preferred to have the Serbian emperor as their lord and master. Dušan was making good progress in Hum, when two attacks, one by Cantacuzenus in the South and the other by the Hungarians, forced him to change his scene of operations. Eventually, after he had defeated Louis of Hungary and his crusaders in 1353, Belgrade was occupied by the Serbians.

Now Dušan thought that the moment had come for him to dispose of his rival in Constantinople and to occupy the imperial city on the Bosphorus. He knew that many Greeks, exhausted by the protracted civil war, alarmed by the menace of the Ottoman Turks, and discontented with their rival rulers, would welcome a strong man capable of saving the tottering Empire. But fate decided against Dušan and cut him off in his prime at the age of 48, when he was allegedly in the midst of preparations for the attack on Constantinople (1355).

His untimely death was a disaster for the whole of the Balkans. He was one of the few who at that time clearly foresaw the danger menacing Christianity from the Turks. In 1353, John VI Cantacuzenus had appealed to the Turks for help against John V Palaeologus and his allies, then represented by one Bulgarian and one Serbian detachment. The Turks cut these two allied bodies to pieces near Dimotika, the Serbians suffering even more than the Bulgarians. This was the first warning, and Dušan did not fail to observe it. When the Turks afterward established themselves at Gallipoli, Dušan saw quite clearly what portended. He made his intention clear to become the military leader of the whole of Christianity against the Turks, proving his seriousness by sending a solemn embassy to Pope Innocent VI at Avignon. He professed his readiness to recognize the Pope as the father of all Christians and as Peter's successor. He was ready also to promote peace and friendly intercourse between the Catholics and the Orthodox in his realms. The Pope welcomed Dušan's offer with eagerness and expressed his willingness to appoint Dušan "captain of the whole of Christendom." [17] The Pope's legates, Bishop Bartholemew of Trogir (Trau) and the learned Frenchman, Peter Thomas of Périgord, met the Emperor Charles IV, king of Bohemia, in Pisa on their way to Serbia, and Charles gave them a letter in which he welcomed Dušan's intentions and greeted him as a fellow Slavic ruler.

Unfortunately, Louis of Hungary spoiled the plan by his untimely attack upon Serbia, possibly launched out of jealousy for the new champion of Christendom. Dušan's death shortly after put an end to all projects of this kind.

After Dušan's death, the weaknesses of the new Serbian Empire soon became apparent. The great extension of the realm naturally gave more independence to the rulers of the different provinces. Only a firm hand could hold them together. Dušan's son and successor, Stephen Uroš IV (1355-1371), was an incompetent youth, unable to restrain the disruptive ambitions of the powerful magnates. The realm became an oligarchy of petty lordlings, who established themselves in different provinces and ruled them after their own wishes and without regard for the central power of the true tsar. Uroš' uncle Symeon entrenched himself in Epirus and Thessaly, Vukašin in Macedonia (Prilep, Prizren, and Skoplje), Lazar Hrbeljanović in Rudnik, and the Balša family in Zeta (Montenegro), while Uroš had to content himself with the old province of Rascia.

In the meantime the Turks made steady progress in Greece. They established themselves in Thrace, and in about 1363 they seized Adrianople, which became their capital. Instead of allying themselves in the face of the common danger, the Greeks and Bulgarians chose to go to war against each other. The Tsar John (Ivan) Alexander (1331-1371) was, moreover, attacked by Louis of Hungary, who occupied the province of Vidin and imprisoned Sracimir, the tsar's son, who was then ruling there. It was not until 1369 that the tsar was able to set his son free and install him once more in Vidin. The division of the tsardom into two parts, Trnovo and Vidin, had the effect of rendering the territory near the Danube delta independent under its own despots. All this considerably weakened Bulgarian powers of resistance. Then internal troubles under Alexander's successor, John (Ivan) Šišman (1371-1393), opened the way for further Turkish successes. Their next smashing blow was delivered in 1371 against Vukašin, who styled himself King of Macedonia. In a battle on the Marica River, the Turks annihilated the troops of the king and of the Serbian nobles. This was the beginning of Turkish rule in the Balkans.

Vukašin perished in the battle, and the whole of Macedonia as far as Thessaly and Albania lay open to the Turks. Serbian and Greek lordlings submitted meekly to their rule. Vukašin's son Marko (1371-1394) continued to bear the royal title, but he was nothing more than an insignificant Turkish vassal. He died in a battle in Wallachia, fighting in the Turkish army, and after his death his realm became a Turkish province. Nevertheless, he achieved fame in Serbian folklore and is celebrated in numerous epics as a great national hero.

Uroš IV died in the same year as Vukašin, and the Serbian kingdom continued to disintegrate. The Balša family, which was established in Zeta (Montenegro), declared that province a separate principality. Other magnates, particularly the Branković family, began to behave as independent rulers. The strongest of the Serbian rulers was Lazar I of the dynasty of the Hrebeljanović (1371-1389); but although he regarded himself as the successor of the Nemanjas, he contented himself with the title of "knez" (prince). He succeeded in repairing the rift with the Emperor and Patriarch of Constantinople which had existed ever since Dušan's imperial proclamation and the establishment of the Serbian patriarchate. In 1375 Constantinople recognized the Serbian patriarchate and revoked the anathema against the memory of Stephen Dušan.

Lazar was, however, unable to maintain his independence. In 1386, after having lost Niš to the Turks, he was forced to recognize Murad's suzerainty.

Parts of western Serbia were occupied by Tvrtko I, the Ban of Bosnia (1353-1391), who profited by the death of Louis of Anjou, king of Hungary, in 1382 and the regency of his widow Elisabeth, to extend his rule over a great part of the coastal region and much of Croatia, assuming the title "By the Grace of God, King of Serbia (Rascia), Bosnia, Dalmatia, Croatia, and the coastal region." [18] A new political foundation, the strongest in the Balkans, was introduced into the annals of history; but in spite of the imposing title of its founder, indicative of his grandiose intention to unite all the southern Slavs in one state, the new foundation proved evanescent and failed unfortunately to leave any enduring consequences.

Weakened by the struggle with Sracimir, the Bulgarian tsar John (Ivan) Šišman had to come to terms with the Turks and gave his own sister in marriage to the sultan in 1375. In 1382 he lost Sofia to the Turks. Then, encouraged by a fleeting military success achieved by the Serbians under Lazar, he thought that the moment was at hand when the Turks might be successfully defied. In putting this to the test, however, he was defeated and owed his life to the intervention of his sister, the sultan's wife. Bulgaria became a Turkish province and at the same time lost its ecclesiastical independence. The patriarchate was suppressed, and the Bulgarian Church was subordinated to the direct jurisdiction of the Oecumenical Patriarch of Constantinople. It was not until 1870 that the autonomous Exarchate of Bulgaria was founded, and even then it was not recognized by the oecumenical patriarch. [19]

Then came the great catastrophe, the battle of Kosovo on June 15, 1389. Prince Lazar succeeded in assembling a coalition of Serbians, Bosnians, Albanians, and Rumanians of Wallachia in an heroic attempt to arrest the progress of the Turks. In spite of initial successes, disaster overtook his army. Murad was killed by a Serbian warrior. A mosque, still to be seen on the battlefield, recalls his death. His son Bayazid, however, routed the Serbian army, captured Lazar, and put him to death together with many other Serbian nobles.

This was the end of independent Serbia. Lazar's son Stephen Lazarević (1389-1427) became a Turkish vassal. The Serbians were permitted to live for a few decades under the shadow of the crescent, but before the end of the fifteenth century the last vestiges of Serbian political independence were eradicated for centuries.[20]

NOTES

1. For details, see F. Dvornik, *The Slavs*, pp. 279 ff. See *ibid.*, pp. 353-357 for the bibliography on the history and the civilization of the southern Slavs to the thirteenth century. There are only a few scholarly works on the history of the Serbians, Croats, and Bulgarians written in Slavic languages. On the history of the Yugoslavs, only the handbooks by A. Melik (*Zgodovina Srbov, Horvatov in Slovencev*, 2 vols., Ljubljana, 1919-20) and by M. Prelog (*Pregled povijesti Južnikh Slavena Srba, Hrvata i Slovenaca*, 2 vols., Sarajevo, 1920-21) should be mentioned. St. Stanojević's short synthetic review (*Istorija Srba, Hrvata i Slovenaca*, Belgrad, 1928, 3rd ed.) was issued also in Russian (1917) and in French (1919). The best history of the Serbians of this period is still that by K. Jireček (see Bibl.), published also in Serbian in 1952 with additions by J. Radonić. S. Stanojević published in Serbian a history of the Serbians (*Istorija srpskog naroda*, Belgrad, 1928, 3rd ed.) and short biographies on the main rulers of the Nemanjid dynasty (Nemanja, 1933, Stefan Prvovenčani, 1934, Kralj Uroš, 1935, Kralj Dragutin, 1936, Kralj Milutin, 1937, Tsar Dušan, 1921). A more complete bibliography on the Serbians and Croats will be found in *Historija naroda Jugoslavije*, ed. by B. Grafenauer, D. Perović, and J. Šidak (Zagreb, Belgrade, 1953), pp. 533-53, 800-12. This is also the most extensive synthesis on the history of the lands and peoples of present-day Yugoslavia. There is no synthetic work on Croatian history of this period which would satisfy all modern requirements. V. Klaić, *Povijest Hrvata* (Zagreb, 1899, 1900) deals with our period in vol. 1 and vol. 2. A. Dabinović, *Hrvatska državna i pravna povijest* (Zagreb, 1940) goes to the year 1526. By far the best treatment of Bosnian history during this period is by V. Ćorović, *Historija Bosne* (Belgrade, 1940), of which only the first volume has appeared posthumously covering the period up to the end of the fifteenth century. The third volume of V. I. Zlatarski, *Istorija na b'lgarskata d'ržava* (Sofia, 1940) treats Bulgarian history from 1187 to 1280 only. For the following period, Jireček's Czech and German edition of his *History* (see Bibl.) is still most useful. Additional notes and corrections made by the author were published by St. Argirov (K. J. Jireček, *Istorija na bŭlgaritê; popravki i dobavki ot samija avtor*, Sofia, 1939). The most up-to-date and most extensive treatment of the period under discussion is to be found in P. Mutafčiev's *Istorija na bŭlgarskija narod* (Sofia, 1943), 2 vols. A shorter account is included in I. S. Deržavin's *Istorija Bolgarii* (Moscow, 1946), vol. II, pp. 128-161. One finds also very useful F. Hýbl's *Dějiny národa bulharského* (Prague, 1930), and F. I. Uspenskij's monograph on the formation of the Second Bulgarian Empire (*Obrazovanie vtorogo bolgarskogo carstva*, Odessa, 1879).

2. The origin of the brothers is a matter of passionate controversy between Bulgarian and Rumanian scholars, the former declaring them to be pure Bulgarians, the latter defending their Vlach origin. The Vlachs, who spoke a Latin dialect akin to the Rumanian tongue, were mostly nomads living a pastoral life in the Balkans under Byzantine or Bulgarian supremacy. They were descendants of the Dacian population evacuated by the Romans to the Latin provinces on the right bank of the Danube (see F. Dvornik, *The Slavs*, pp. 186 ff.). Their Latinization, which had been begun in Dacia, was concluded in their new habitat. Some of them probably settled in parts of Transylvania, the country of their forefathers, which was then under Bulgarian rule, prior to the irruption of the Magyars into the Danube basin. The Magyars were not interested in the mountainous regions and left them unmolested. Their numbers increased later when the Hungarian kings started to colonize the depopulated regions after the Mongol invasion. As regards the origins of Peter and Asen, it seems to be established that they were Vlachs. The state they founded was, however, in all respects mainly Bulgarian. For a clear exposé of the controversy and an exhaustive bibliography on the subject with important new contributions see R. Lee Wolff's study, "The Second Bulgarian Empire. Its Origin and History to 1204" in *Speculum*, vol. 24 (1949), pp. 167-206.

3. The establishment of a Latin Empire completely changed the political situation in the Balkans. As is shown in map no. 3, the fiefs of the Latin emperor were the Latin Kingdom of Salonika, the Latin Duchy of Athens, and the Latin Principality of Achaia, the Venetians having established themselves in the Aegean islands. The Byzantine Despotate of Epirus, founded by Michael Angelus Comnenus, was nearest to the Slavic states and vied with the Byzantine Empire of Nicaea to re-establish the Greek Empire in Constantinople. Some members of the family of the Comneni established the Empire of Trebizond on the Black Sea coast of Asia Minor. This lasted until the fifteenth century. Greek seignories were founded at Rhodes, in Philadelphia, and in Greece.

4. There is evidence for this in a letter preserved in the Register of Honorius III and published by Cardinal C. Baronius in his *Annales Ecclesiastici* (Ed. Od. Raynald, A. Theiner, Bar-le-Duc, 1870, vol. 20, year 1220, no. 37): "Just as all Christians love and honor you and look up to you as their father and lord, so we also wish to be considered as a loyal son of the Roman Church of yours, confident that God's blessing and sanction as well as yours be ever visibly granted to our crown and our country; for which purpose we send you our bishop, Methodius by name, that you may oblige us by replying in writing if it please you, through the bearer of the present letters, whatever your Holiness and Kindness may decide." This letter seems to have reached Rome in March, 1220. If this be so, it would not be inadmissible to conclude that King Stephen sent a special envoy, probably the Bishop of Ras, to the Pope in 1219, to reiterate expressions of reverence and loyalty and to assure him that the application to the Patriarch of Nicaea should not be taken as a slight on Rome.

5. In Durazzo, the unfortunate ex-king lost his Greek wife, who ran away with a French baron. Heartbroken, Radoslav is said to have returned to his native land, where he assumed the name John and died as a monk in the monastery of Studenica. His unfaithful wife repented and became a nun in a Greek convent. These incidents well illustrate the manners and mentality of the period.

6. For instance, Béla IV in a long letter (no. 308 in A. Theiner's collection—

see bibliography to this chapter) asked the Pope for an assurance that he alone should be apostolic legate to Bulgaria, with power to determine the limits of the new dioceses in the conquered country and to nominate its bishops—"since all these privileges were once conferred on St. Stephen, our predecessor of blessed memory." That is how in 1238 the Hungarians understood the privileges which Pope Sylvester II and Emperor Otto III had conferred upon Stephen I, when the Duke of Hungary had joined the new Roman Empire, as restored by Otto (for details see F. Dvornik, *The Slavs,* pp. 261 ff.). This interpretation may easily have given rise to a Hungarian legend to the effect that the first Hungarian king was the Pope's legate and that his dignity was hereditary. The Pope was visibly embarrassed by such a request, but he at least granted the privilege that the symbol of the cross should be carried before the king and his army—"to foster the people's devotion." Even this concession was made much of in Hungarian legend to support the claim that the Hungarian king, by special privilege, was always to be preceded by the cross.

7. The advance of the Bulgarians and their Cuman troops was so swift that the Serbian archbishop considered it desirable to move his residence from Žiča to Peć (Ipek), which remained from then until 1766 the center of the Serbian autonomous Church.

8. Svetislav kept the title of tsar, but as a Hungarian vassal. Béla's son Stephen, who had defeated Svetislav, added to his royal titles on ascending the Hungarian throne in 1270 that of "King of Bulgaria." All his successors continued to use this title down to the year 1918.

9. A. Theiner, ed., *Vetera Monumenta* (see Bibl.), vol. I, pp. 376 ff: . . . "olim quondam magnifico viro Michaele Palaeologo . . . eo tempore Constantinopoli residente, professus fueris, in palatio Blaskavia (sic) coram nobis . . . oraculo vive vocis te pape Romano immediate subesse." On Jerome of Ascoli's mission in 1272 see Potthast: *Regesta pontif. Rom.* (see Bibl.), vol. 2, p. 1826. See *ibid.* the instructions given to Jerome by Gregory X, nos. 20633, 20638, 20766, 20810. F. Hýbl in his Czech history of the Bulgarian nation (*Dějiny národa bulharského,* Prague, 1930), vol. I, p. 203 attributes the history of submission to Mary's initiative after the Council, which is an error. Jerome was elected general of his order in 1274, while still in Constantinople. It is true that he was sent once more to Constantinople by Innocent V in 1276 in order to obtain the definite acceptance of the union (Potthast, *ibid.,* vol. II, p. 1708, nos. 21142 ff.). Jerome with his companions did not reach Constantinople this time because before they had taken boat at Ancona, they learned that the Pope who had sent them had died. His successor, John XXI, had chosen two Dominicans and two bishops for the transmission of Innocent V's messages to the emperor. Jerome could not therefore have been in Constantinople in 1276. (Cf. W. Norden: *Das Papsttum und Byzanz,* Berlin, 1903, pp. 566, 572.) F. Hýbl overlooked these details (see also his remarks "K dějinám cirkevní unie lyonské" in the *Český Časopis historický* ("Czech Historical Review"), vol. 29, 1923, pp. 181-83).

10. The most repulsive of her intrigues was the assassination of Svetislav, whom she had invited to Trnovo and recognized as her "son" who should reign with her natural son, Svetislav's "brother" Michael.

11. See the recent monograph on the Šišman dynasty by A. Burmov: *Istorija na Bŭlgarija prěz vremeneto na Šišmanidov 1323-1396,* part I published in the *Godišnik* of the University of Sofia, Hist. phil. Fakult., vol. 43 (Sofia, 1947).

12. It is not known whether he retained any Serbian lands for himself. Some contemporary writers regarded King Dragutin as a legitimate ruler and Milutin only as a regent, who was supposed to surrender the reins of government to Dragutin's sons. However, Dragutin is given the royal title by all contemporaries until his death in 1316. In 1284 he received from his brother-in-law, the Hungarian king, the lands which had been administered under Hungarian suzerainty by the Russian prince Rastislav. These comprised the territory of Srem (formerly the famous Roman city of Sirmium), with Belgrade, the territory of Mačva, and the northeastern part of Bosnia. Dragutin became a fervent Roman Catholic and pursued a very strong anti-Bogomil policy in his realm. He called the Franciscans into Bosnia, and from that time onward, even under Turkish rule, they played an important role in the political and cultural evolution of that country. Dragutin gave his daughter in marriage to Stephen Kotroman, who governed the rest of Bosnia as Ban, under the suzerainty of Hungary and Dragutin. This relationship with the Nemanjads was exploited after their extinction by Stephen's grandson, the Ban Tvrtko, who assumed the royal title and claimed the succession to the Serbian throne.

13. On the Byzantine princesses in medieval Serbia see the monograph by M. Laskaris, *Vizantijske princeze u srednjevekovnoj Srbiji* (Belgrad, 1926).

14. Happily the operation was not successful, and Stephen had wit enough to conceal the fact.

15. The papal letters (A. Theiner, *op. cit.*, vol. I, pp. 359 ff., 410 ff.) make interesting reading. Nicholas IV also sent a letter to the Patriarch of Bulgaria—calling him Archbishop—and took Stephen Uroš II and his realm under the protection of the Holy See. All was, however, of no avail.

16. Dušan's effort to win Venice's maritime support for his plans for the conquest of Constantinople proved fruitless, however. The Venetians preferred to deal in Constantinople with a weak Greek government rather than with a powerful Serbian ruler.

17. The Pope's correspondence reveals that the project was a serious one. He not only responded to Dušan's embassy and gave minute instructions to his own legates concerning the reforms to be introduced in the "Kingdom of Rascia, Albania, and Serbia," but he also addressed himself to Queen Helen, John, Patriarch (sic) of Serbia, the hierarchy of the three countries, and all the leading ministers of Dušan's court. (A. Theiner, *op. cit.*, vol. II, pp. 8-17.) Dušan's initiative is the more interesting as in his *Zakonik* he had shown a particularly unfavorable attitude toward Latin Catholicism.

18. Tvrtko was crowned king of Serbia and Bosnia in 1377 at Milečevo. On the ceremony of his coronation read N. Radojčić, *Obred krunisanja bosanskoga kralja Tvrtka I; prilog istoriji krunisanja srpskih vladara u srednjem veku* (Belgrade, 1948). See in V. Klajić, *Geschichte Bosniens* (Leipzig, 1884), pp. 202 ff., the translation of Tvrtko's royal declaration. Cf. V. Ćorović, short study, *Kralj Tvrtko i Kotamić* (Belgrade, 1925). On the history of Bosnia and Hercegovina to 1463 see the work *Poviest Hrvatskih zemalja Bosne i Hercegovine . . . do g. 1463* (Sarajevo, 1942), written by prominent Croatian historians.

19. A kind of schism existed thenceforward between the oecumenical patriarchate and the Bulgarian exarchate, promoted to a patriarchate after World War I. Relations between the two patriarchates were only normalized in 1945.

20. See below Chapter X.

Chapter VI

THE POLITICAL ORGANIZATION
OF MEDIEVAL SLAVIC STATES

The old Slavic principle of division overcome in Bohemia—Oldest political organization in Bohemia—Origins of the Czech nobility—Special features of Czech feudalism, the "right of the land"—Evolution of the nobility into a special class—Position of the higher clergy and of the burghers in Bohemia—Bohemia, a dualistic state—Attempts at the creation of a new juridical code—The Maiestas Carolina, *the crown—symbol of the state—Characteristic traits in the origin of the Polish nobility—Position of the higher clergy and of the burghers in Poland—The Polish nobility as a ruling class—*Corona regni Poloniae, regnum—*Succession to the Polish throne, Casimir's reforms—Administrative reforms—The Slovenes—The Slovaks and the political evolution of Hungary—Mathias Csak and the Slovaks—The reforms of the Angevins and the Slovaks—The political status of the Croats—Croatian assemblies, Hungarian influences in Slavonia—Survival of Romano-Byzantine law in Dalmatia. Ragusa (Dubrovnik)—Organization of the Second Bulgarian Empire on the Byzantine model—Byzantine and Western elements in medieval Serbia—Origins of the Serbian aristocracy, the* pronoia, *religious situation, Serbian cities, Dušan's code*

From the twelfth century onward the fate of the Czechs, the Slovaks, the Poles, the Croats, and the Slovenes was definitely and intimately linked with that of western Europe, which provided most of the patterns to inspire and influence their social, religious, literary, and cultural progress. It was thus to be expected that the political organization of their states would also be inspired by Western institutions.

In their political and social evolution, the Czechs and the Poles were handicapped during the eleventh and twelfth centuries by the old Slavic principle that the country was a kind of appanage of the reigning house, all of whose members were entitled to a share in its government.[1] This principle led to the division of the countries into small principalities which slowly lost the conception of common interest in a common realm. The application of this principle was particularly disastrous for Poland and finally resulted in the loss of two valuable provinces, Silesia and Pomerania. But in Bohemia also, the rivalry of the Přemyslide princes nearly caused the disintegration of the country, placing temporarily all the separate dukes in a position of direct dependence upon the emperor. The danger became greatest during the reign of the Emperor Frederick Barbarossa.

This fate was fortunately averted at the last moment by Přemysl I. The circumstance that the members of the Přemyslide dynasty were not as numerous as the Polish Piasts, and that the system of appanages disappeared between 1200 and 1204, saved the Bohemian state from sharing, in this respect, the fate of Poland or of the Kievan state.[2] As has been shown, the relationship of Bohemia to the Empire was finally settled, and the sovereign status of the kingdom confirmed, by the Golden Bull of Sicily and the Golden Bull of Charles IV. The hereditary character of the Czech succession was thus defined although the principle of primogeniture, established more firmly by Přemysl I in 1216, was only made definitive in 1341. It was necessary even then, however, for the heir's rights to be confirmed by the assembly of the nation, represented by the nobility, and to be acknowledged by the emperor.

The power of the duke of Bohemia was originally absolute, and he was not obliged to share it with anybody. He nominated the officers of his court and the governors of the provinces, which were probably organized on the basis of the unification of the Slavic tribes in Bohemia in the ninth and tenth centuries. In Moravia the system of princely appanages gave a special character to the division into provinces. The dukes alone controlled the *župans* (*supanis beneficiarius*), later called *comes, praefectus, castellanus,* to whom the administration of the provinces was entrusted. The duke selected all his officers from among his own retinue. The provinces were administered from castles which were the residences of the *župans*, or governors.[3] The provincial *župan* commanded the castle garrison and also, in the event of war, any body of troops raised by levy in the province. At court, various offices were gradually introduced on the Western pattern. The function of the first of them, called *župan* of the court (*comes palatinus*), disappeared at an early period, but that of the *summus camerarius*, the first chamberlain, retained its importance.

The governors of the castles also exercised control over the provincial police, finances, and justice. Only from the first half of the thirteenth century on were special royal officials (*villici*) appointed to relieve the governors of judicial functions and to act as police commissioners of the districts. The governors were remunerated for their services by the use of some ducal benefices and by a share of the taxes they collected.

The origin of the Czech nobility and the growth of its importance in the state were also influenced by Western usage. Some individuals among the freemen were raised above the level of the common people through being in the immediate service of the prince, or through wealth acquired in war or in the service of the prince. The rise of the nobility seems, however, to have been tardy in Bohemia and Poland. The Czech name for nobility, *šlechta*, indicates the German influence on the rise of this class,[4] as it is formed from the old Germanic *slahta* (modern German *Geschlecht*), meaning "race." Moreover, time brought a distinction between the higher and lower nobility, the latter being that class of freemen who were able to do their military service on horseback. But this development came rather more slowly than elsewhere in Europe. In the twelfth and thirteenth centuries the freemen serving on horseback were still called simply "soldiers of second order" (*milites secundi ordinis*), and they were not regarded as nobles. They were recognized as nobles only in the fourteenth century and were called *rytíři* or *vladyky*, knights or nobles, to distinguish them from the older and higher nobility, whose members were called barons (*barones, domini*). Following the German custom, the dukes and higher nobles started making use of their bondmen to perform various duties in their courts and household, or in the administration of their properties (*villici, ministeriales*). German influence is shown also by such customs as the introduction of the crest, the building of castles, the assumption of family titles.

The influence of the higher nobility in the administration of the state developed on lines similar to those followed in Germany and the rest of western Europe. There is, however, one important difference peculiar to Bohemia. Feudalism had, of course, also penetrated into the Bohemian dukedom, but its institutions never developed in Bohemia to the same degree as in the rest of western Europe. As has been shown, feudalism had split Germany and Italy into numerous principalities, but in France and in England it became, at least for a time, the basis of a new and solid political order. No such development materialized in Bohemia. The noble families were less interested in fiefs and functions which were not hereditary. Their members were anxious to acquire allodia which would remain hereditary in their families.

The Western feudal system offered the nobles certain guarantees against abuses of royal absolutism, protected their liberties and privileges, and assured them a part in the actual government of the realm. In Bohemia the higher nobility succeeded in achieving similar results by stressing and defending the rights and liberties which had developed either on the basis of old native customs and general conceptions or from concessions and guarantees obtained from the dukes and kings. These liberties and rights were termed the "right of the land" (*Zemské právo, ius terrae*). This development had the advantage that it prevented the Duchy of Bohemia from becoming a loose conglomeration of quasi-independent baronies. On the other hand, the codification of territorial rights was bound to limit considerably the ruler's power.

The first confirmation of these privileges was obtained by the nobles from Duke Conrad Otto, in 1189. The originals of the statutes are no longer extant. But documents of Conrad's successors confirming the Statutes of Conrad, *iura Conradi*, gave the freemen some guarantees against abuses of the royal power and against encroachment by the provincial tribunals in the hands of the mighty ducal *župans*. They contained an important change in the rights of heredity by extending these also to daughters and brothers of a deceased nobleman. Moreover, they gave increased security to the nobles by stating that they could only be banished or suffer confiscation of their property after a long judicial procedure in accordance with the established custom of the land.

The promulgation of Conrad's statutes definitely terminated for Bohemia the period of what might be termed the patriarchal despotism of the dukes. Although these changes were intended for all freemen and were obtained by the nobles with the help of the lower class of the knights, it was the higher nobility which profited most from the new situation. Its liberties and privileges were confirmed and increased by the last Přemyslides and became a basis on which the Estates of Bohemia were to develop.

The freemen with less property also profited from this situation. Having obtained important guarantees for the security of their property and of their status as freemen, they were not obliged to seek these guarantees by placing themselves under the protection of the higher nobility and accepting feudal bonds. The consequence of this was the growth of the number of free knights who could claim a lesser degree of nobility.

This, however, does not mean that feudal bonds were despised by the higher nobility. The possession of a court dignity or of a provincial office brought a considerable increase of influence and power. So the nobles sought not only to augment their hereditary patrimonies but also to augment their power by obtaining royal benefices. Soon, however, they started to regard the benefices attached to the feudal office and the office itself as hereditary. In this way patrimonial jurisdiction developed, and during the thirteenth century, the nobles generally exercised direct jurisdiction over the subjects of their patrimonies.

In spite of this development the king was, of course, still regarded as the only source of law, and he expressed his supreme power by granting many exemptions from the jurisdiction of the officers who were supposed to act as his functionaries. Thus he sanctioned indirectly the new state of affairs, limiting his own power.

Emboldened by its success, the nobility revolted against King Wenceslas I, allying itself with his son Přemysl. Although the king was able to maintain his position, from that time on the nobles formed a special Estate, which replaced the former *župans* and was distinguished from the rest of the population by the noble origin of its members, their wealth, and their privileges in private and public life. Nobles who did not exercise any function were also admitted later to this Estate. The class of the nobility, with its brilliant courts and numerous retinues, arose thus.[5]

The other Estate which started to take form was that of the higher clergy. Bohemia had witnessed a stormy aftermath of the investiture struggle during the reign of Přemysl I. After returning from Rome, where he had attended the Council of the Lateran (1215) convoked by Innocent III, Andrew, bishop of Prague, started a struggle for the complete emancipation of the Church in Bohemia from any interference by laymen. The struggle was long and passionate. But in spite of his interdicts and of direct intervention by Rome, Andrew was unable to attain his goal completely. The Bohemian Church did not obtain exemption from taxes and from other public duties. It succeeded, however, in securing to a certain degree its own particular jurisdiction (*privilegium fori*) and greater freedom in appointments to ecclesiastical offices. Of course, like the higher nobility, the higher clergy also got into its hands civil jurisdiction over the inhabitants of its patrimonies.

The burghers of the new cities which started to grow in the kingdom from the end of the twelfth century on did not succeed in attaining recognition as a separate Estate during this period. The cities were mostly founded by German colonists, called in by the last Přemyslides, and were organized on the German model, using in their administration either the law of Madgeburg or that of Nürnberg. They were exempt from the jurisdiction of the župans and from public burdens, and possessed their own jurisdiction and the right to maintain armed forces.

The burghers of Prague and of Kutná Hora (Kuttenberg), a most important silver mining center in Bohemia, became particularly wealthy and made a daring attempt in 1309 at obtaining a share in the government of the country by imprisoning the principal offices of the realm. The attempt failed, however, and the class of burghers was only recognized as a special Estate in 1421. As in Germany, the burghers and the higher clergy were the best allies of the kings in their struggle against the growing influence of the higher nobility.

The most important consequence of the development of the *ius terrae* was that, from the beginning of the thirteenth century on, the Czech state can be described as dualistic because political power was vested not only in the king, but also in the privileged classes, referred to as the Nation. A striking illustration of this evolution is given by the fact that thenceforward the higher nobility as a class, joined later by the Estates, called together the Nation, used its own seal, which was impressed upon state documents alongside the royal seal. In due course, also, the offices and the tribunal of the royal court were transformed into the offices and the tribunal of the land. The latter, which was controlled by the nobility, replaced temporarily the institution of the Diet, which became developed fully only during the fifteenth century. The introduction of the *tabulae terrae*—register of landed property, a Czech *Domesday Book*—also illustrates clearly this interesting development, peculiar to the Kingdom of Bohemia.

As previously mentioned, the foundations of the "law of the land" lay in the local customs as they had developed down to the end of the twelfth century. There were, however, three royal attempts at creating a new juridical code. The first attempt was made by Přemysl II in 1271. Unfortunately, no information is extant about the motives and character of this initiative. Přemysl II may have been inspired by the example of the French court, or he may have been trying to codify the royal rights in process of curtailment by the *ius terrae*.[6] His initiative remained sterile, however, because of the opposition of the higher nobility.

The second attempt, made by Wenceslas II, is more interesting, and more information is available concerning its motives and character. The young king was notoriously influenced by French example and was a great admirer of the new school of Roman law which had begun to flourish in Bologna. He invited one of the Italian jurists, Gozzio of Orvieto, to Prague to advise him on the planned codification. But Wenceslas II was no more fortunate than King Edward I of England (1272-1307), who planned similar reforms for his realm. The English nobility, satisfied with the English custom law and with the Magna Carta, rejected the king's proposal and declared categorically: "*Nolumus leges Angliae mutari.*" The Czech nobility, without knowing it, followed the English example.

Gozzio's stay at the Bohemian court was, however, not without importance for Czech legislative history. The mining code,[7] an admirable piece of jurisprudence published by Wenceslas II, was, in great part, Gozzio's work. In his introduction to the work, Wenceslas betrays his enthusiasm for the Roman law, calling himself, after the fashion of Roman emperors, *lex animata*, the living law.

The third attempt at the codification of Bohemian law was made by Charles IV. His code, the *Maiestas Carolina*,[8] does not seem to have been influenced by the new school of Roman law, although Charles was well acquainted with it. In the introduction to his code, Charles referred as his source to Frederick II's introduction to his *Constitutiones regni Siciliae*. In the composition of the 109 statutes Charles was inspired by native customs and by his desire not only to strengthen the royal power but also to inculcate in his subjects a higher conception of the state, placing its interests above the selfish aims of the nobles or the mere whim of rulers.

Besides dispositions of public and constitutional law, the code contains regulations concerning penal and civil law, and also rules of procedure in law suits. Charles was particularly anxious to speed up procedure in penal law, and stipulated that penal offenses should be exempted from the jurisdiction of the land and provincial tribunals and be judged by the so-called executors (*popravčí*). These officers seem to have existed prior to Charles's reign, but it was the emperor who, by his code, gave them a wider scope of jurisdiction in penal offenses.

Although the code was not a systematic exposition of the law of Bohemia and although it had not been accepted as an official handbook because of some innovations which the nobles resented, the *Maiestas Carolina* had great importance in strengthening the monarchic element in the constitution of the Bohemian realm.[9] It was also Charles's merit to have strengthened the ties of the monarchic idea with a higher conception of the state, symbolized by the royal crown of Bohemia. It is known that this conception originated in the West [10] but was already in use in Bohemia in the second half of the twelfth century. The crown became all the more important as a symbol of the realm when, after the extinction of the Přemyslides, the dynastic principle uniting the lands and the people had disappeared. Even John of Luxemburg was well aware of the significance of this symbol. Charles had learned in France to appreciate the symbolic importance of the crown and of the coronation ceremony, and used these symbols to express his higher idea of the state. He had this in mind when, for the coronation, he ordered a new crown, which should be deposited on the skull of St. Wenceslas (died in 929), the "heir of the land of Bohemia," and when he composed, with such pious care, a new order of coronation.[11] This idea of the crown of the realm (*corona regni*) as symbolizing a higher conception of the state also reached Poland from Bohemia. There too it contributed to the revival and consolidation of the kingdom by Łokietek and Casimir the Great.

The social and political development of medieval Poland presents certain features of similarity with that of Bohemia, but in other respects it differs considerably from anything achieved in this period by other Central European nations. As in Bohemia, the power of the duke was absolute, once the unification of the tribes had been effected by the Piast dynasty in the early history of Poland. This period of patriarchal absolutism lasted in Poland, as in Bohemia, down to the thirteenth century. During the tenth and eleventh centuries, the great Piasts, from Mieszko I (960-992) to Boleslas III Wry-mouth (1102-1138), created a monarchic system of great strength and vigor, exploited with intelligence.[12]

In the social sphere, primitive Poland knew neither nobility nor feudalism. All members of the clans were free, with the exception of prisoners of war and slaves. Class distinction, however, showed itself at an early date. It was natural that the elders of the clans (*starosta*) should begin to regard themselves as being superior to the rest of the people. All freemen were potential soldiers, but the princes maintained their own retinues (*drużyna*) or guards. The members of these were not only warriors and commanders of freemen in the field, but also governors of the duke's fortified castles (*gródy*), which were the centers of political administration in the country.

In this way, there began slowly to emerge a class of privileged men, distinguished by their wealth or by the prominent positions which the ruler had called upon them to occupy. The number of the privileged grew considerably during the period when Poland disintegrated into separate duchies, as each duke had his own court and his own retinue. The necessity to defend the frontier and wage war called for a plentiful supply of knightly warriors, who were better trained than the ordinary freemen. The dukes used to reward them for their services by gifts of land, and they soon began to regard themselves as distinct from the people. This was the origin of the class of the lower nobility. The free peasants became gradually more closely attached to the noble families or to ecclesiastical institutions. A fairly sharp division into classes—magnates, knights, and the people, still freemen in principle—gradually became more clearly marked although, in contrast to the Bohemian development, the knights enjoyed the same privileges of nobility as the magnates. The distinction of the noble class from the people was accentuated by the adoption of the German custom of using crests and family titles. The use of crests was introduced into Poland later than into Bohemia, in fact, only during the second half of the thirteenth century, and it became general only towards the end of that period.[13]

In contrast to the development in Bohemia, it was the higher clergy which first established itself as a special Estate in Poland, thus achieving an important position in the state. The clergy formed the educated class. It was they who looked after the duke's correspondence with other rulers and composed his legal documents and juridical pronouncements. They were also the first to secure important privileges and guarantees against encroachment by the state. The first privileges for the clergy were voted at the Synod of Łęczyca in 1180 and were extended in 1211 (1210) and 1214-1215, thanks to Henry Kietlicz, archbishop of Gniezno (Gnesen) (1199-1219). He was the foremost protagonist in Poland of ecclesiastical reforms in the spirit of Gregory VII. Ecclesiastical property was exempted from almost all public charges, and the clergy received complete autonomy to regulate its affairs through its own synods. Important judicial privileges were also granted to the clergy thanks to the beneficent influence which the Church exercized as the main defender of Poland's unity in division and to the role which the Papacy had often played in the defense of Polish independence against the claims of the emperors. The high dignitaries of the Church were thus able to obtain and to maintain their position as a privileged class—in contrast to events in Bohemia.

The organization of the burghers as a special Estate followed upon that of the higher clergy. Their cities developed partly from the suburbs which had sprung up around castles, partly from settlements established near monasteries and churches, partly from simple villages. As in Bohemia, the first burghers were German colonists. They were soon granted extensive privileges and exemption from public charges. They enjoyed an autonomous status based on the law of Magdeburg. The laws of Środa or Chełmno, which derived from it, were followed by new city foundations in Mazovia.[14]

The higher nobility, which possessed vast estates and traditionally occupied the principal offices both locally and at court, and the lower nobility, which was far more numerous, suddenly became conscious of their personal privileges and liberties and of their position as a class at the time when the Piast dynasty died out on the Polish throne. Casimir the Great, anxious to secure the succession for his nephew, Louis of Anjou, king of Hungary, had to permit the nobility to associate themselves with the negotiations. The nobility duly exploited this occasion to obtain from Louis a promise of further extensive privileges in exchange for accepting him as king of Poland (1355).

These privileges were confirmed and extended still further to the entire nobility as a class in the "Charter of Košice" (Kaschau, Kassa) in 1374. In exchange for the nobility's willingness to accept one of Louis' daughters as their sovereign, the king exempted them from all taxes, save a merely nominal levy on their property at twopence an acre. On the other hand, the king promised that official posts in the provinces would be occupied only by members of the nobility residing in the province concerned and that the royal governors (*starostas*) of the twenty-three important castles would always be members of the Polish nobility.

The self-confidence of the nobility increased considerably during the interregnum (1382-1384) following the death of Louis and during the first two years of the reign of the ten-year-old "King" Jadwiga. Another opportunity for increasing their privileges presented itself to the nobles when they accepted as the new king of Poland Jagiello of Lithuania, whose marriage with the "Maiden-King" they had engineered. They obtained yet further concessions in 1399, when Jadwiga died without issue.

So it came about that the ruling class in Poland was composed of the higher nobility, which not only owned the largest estates but also occupied all the principal offices at court and in the provinces. This class, together with the higher clergy, provided the Council of State, through which it exercised great influence over the king. This exclusive and privileged position was not guaranteed by any special document, but was nevertheless recognized and respected because the magnates formed a firm and solid group.

As has already been mentioned, the custom of regarding the royal crown as a symbol of the state penetrated into Poland from Bohemia. Hungary had developed the same conception, and the circumstance that Poland enjoyed friendly relations with Hungary contributed to the ready acceptance of this custom in Poland, where it acquired particular importance. Prior to the unification of Poland, the succession in the many Piast dukedoms was hereditary but was limited only to the single principalities. When initiating his work of unification, Łokietek could properly claim sovereignty only over his own duchy. Fortunately, the idea of a Polish kingdom had already been resuscitated before Łokietek by Henry IV, Przemysl II (1295), and Wenceslas II of Bohemia.[15] Only after his coronation could Łokietek make valid his claims to suzerainty over the other duchies. The symbol of the royal crown helped considerably to bridge the transfer of suzerainty. The expression *Corona regni Poloniae* was thus used to designate all Polish territories subject to the royal authority, but the word *regnum* designated only the territory which was directly subject to the king.[16]

All this shows how important the actual coronation of the king became in the Polish constitution. The ceremony was performed during the fourteenth century according to the Roman coronation rite, which was adapted to Polish custom in the fifteenth century after the model of the Czech coronation order. Although the coronation ceremony had to be performed in Cracow, it continued to be the prerogative of the Archbishop of Gniezno. Only after the coronation did the king enjoy the full exercise of his royal functions.

Because feudalism was originally unknown in Poland, the first two national kings faced a difficult problem in obtaining a more express acknowledgment of their supremacy. Casimir, however, was quick to see the advantage which the feudal system had offered to John of Bohemia in his gradual incorporation of the Silesian duchies into the crown of Bohemia. Casimir learned the lesson and applied it in his successful attempts at incorporating Mazovia, with Polock and Warsaw, still governed by a Piast duke, in the Polish royal domains.

The Polish crown remained hereditary after the revival of the kingdom. Unfortunately, the political changes of the second half of the fourteenth century also paved the way for the transformation of the hereditary succession into an electoral kingdom. Casimir the Great may have hoped that after the death of his nephew and acknowledged successor, Louis of Hungary, the throne would be occupied by his grandchild and adopted son Casimir, the Pomeranian duke of Słupsk.[17] If this had come to pass, the hereditary principle would probably have been saved. However, Louis' request that one of his daughters should be recognized as his successor, and the death of Jadwiga without issue, opened the way for the direct intervention of the nobility in the succession to the Polish throne. Such interventions were bound ultimately to bring about basic changes in the succession.

The supreme power of the Polish rulers was considerably reduced from the end of the twelfth century on by exemptions and privileges which they were forced by circumstances to grant to churchmen, religious orders, nobles, and knights. Casimir the Great made several bold attempts to arrest this process and to reinforce the royal power. He stabilized the system of territorial taxes, called *poradlne,* re-established royal rights over state property, and reclaimed the *regalia* revenues from customs duties, mines, and mints. Special importance should be attached to his monetary reforms and to his attempted codification of Polish law. Hitherto the Polish legal system and judicial procedure had been based exclusively on customary law, which often varied between the different duchies. Casimir collected and systematized these laws after a fashion, adding new ordinances and statutes. He had, however, to respect the local differences of the former duchies. The statute for Little Poland was made public in 1346 or 1347 at the assembly of nobles at Wiślica, the statute for Great Poland in the same year, at the assembly of Piotrków. The Mazovian duke Ziemovit III followed this example, publishing a statute for Mazovia in 1377 which was based on Casimir's statute.[18]

In his codification of Polish law Casimir followed the example of Charles IV of Bohemia. Czech influences are evident in this codification, but Casimir seems to have been more influenced by Roman and canon law than was Charles IV. He seems to have been particularly anxious to strengthen the basis of Polish jurisprudence, which he had saved from its previous chaotic condition. In order to secure a sufficient number of good lawyers and legal theorists for his country, he founded the law school in Cracow, which was to develop into a Polish university.

Another important problem which faced the first rulers of the restored kingdom was that of bringing the different provinces into a closer dependence on the king. The former principalities were still ruled by their palatines or *wojewodas,* who controlled the administration through their own officials. Wenceslas II of Bohemia had faced the same problem when he became king of Poland, and he attempted to solve it by the institution of special officials called *starostas* for each province, who were dependent on the king. Łokietek had to follow his example, and Casimir perfected the new system. *Starostas* were established in each province of Greater Poland as representatives of the king. They were entrusted with control of the administration and of military and judicial matters. The administration of Lesser Poland was reserved directly to the king, who gradually instituted different officers to help him in the exercise of his duties. The offices of the *wojewodas* and of the *kasztelans*—commanders of royal castles, which were controlled by local noble families and were often regarded already as hereditary, were not abolished but lost their importance. As the king's authority in the provinces grew, thanks to the activity of the *starostas,* so a more centralized government for the whole kingdom developed. The most important royal officers of Lesser Poland —the king's *regnum,* the chancellor, the deputy chancellor, and the treasurer—were increasingly regarded as holding office for the whole kingdom.

The *wojewodas,* however, soon found compensation for the loss of their authority in the administration of the provinces. In order to find support for some new measure or to seek advice on important matters, the king continued the practice of convoking the officials and nobles of each province in order to discuss its problems. Such assemblies, called *wiec,* could also be convoked by the *starostas.* At such assemblies the *wojewodas* acted as heads of the territorial officials and of the nobility of the provinces. It was natural that this new function enhanced their prestige considerably. It was from these assemblies that the famous Polish parliamentary institution was to develop.

The Slovenes were another Slavic nation whose history was intimately connected with that of the Empire. Their political independence was of short duration.[19] The provinces which they inhabited—Styria, Carinthia, Carniola, and Istria—came first under the rule of Bavaria (745-788), then of the Franks, and then, for a short period, of the Magyars (907-955). When the Empire had extended its domination over all Alpine lands, the Slovene areas suffered the fate of the Duchy of Bavaria, which was subdivided into smaller duchies and territories. From the eleventh to the thirteenth century small German dynasties ruled over the Slovene country—the Babenbergs, the Andechs-Merans, the Spanheims, the counts of Cilli, the patriarchs of Aquileia, and the counts of Gorizia. Only for a short period were the Slovenes again under a Slavic ruler, when Přemysl II of Bohemia took over the heritage of the Babenbergs and the Spanheims. After his failure, the Habsburgs became rulers over all the Slovene lands.

The memory of their primitive political independence survived in the ceremony of installation of the dukes of Carinthia on the stone throne near Krnskigrad and Gospa Sveta (Maria Saal) in the basin of Celje (Cilli). The ceremonial, which fell into disuse under the Habsburgs, is described in detail in the Austrian chronicle in verse of Otakar.[20]

The division of the population into nobles and freemen had started, as among their German neighbors, during the ninth and tenth centuries. In the documents of this period and of the early eleventh century, several nobles of Slovene nationality are mentioned as functionaries of the German dukes. During the first half of the eleventh century, however, most of the Slovene noble families disappeared and were replaced by Germans.

Some of the old Slovene customs, common to all Slavic peoples, survived during the Middle Ages in spite of the germanization of the administration. For example, the heads of the Slovene villages in southern Styria and in Friuli have preserved the old Slavic title of *župans* (*supane*), and traces of an autonomous organization can be detected among them.[21] In other social and political aspects the Slovenes had to follow the customs which had developed among their German masters, while the area which they occupied was slowly shrinking through the influx of German colonists.

Two other Slavic nations, the Slovaks and the Croats, shared during this period the social and political development of the non-Slavic nation with which they were united in a common state, the Hungarians. The Croats preserved their autonomous status and were only linked by the identity of the king with Hungary. The Slovaks were not so privileged. There are, indeed, some indications that after the definite annexation of the Slovak lands in the early eleventh century,[22] the Hungarian kings used to bestow the territory in northern Hungary, which covered most of modern Slovakia, as a *ducatus* or dukedom on their sons. Yet, the Slovaks and their lands never achieved a status in Hungary similar to that enjoyed by Croatia.

The westernization of Hungary, which started under St. Stephen at the beginning of the eleventh century, continued during the following period. The higher nobility, consisting of the oldest and richest Magyar families, the chiefs of the Magyar tribes, started to form a powerful group which, like the nobility elsewhere, consolidated its lands and disrupted the organization of the country centered administratively and juridically around royal castles. The lower nobility, composed of royal soldiers (*milites*), royal representatives (*ministeriales*), and "king's servants" (*servientes regis*), freemen dwelling on royal property, also began to appear in the twelfth century. To this class should be added the garrisons of the royal castles (*milites castri, iobbagiones*), who were achieving a higher status among the freemen and becoming landowners. They were mostly stationed near the frontiers of the realm, and their importance was growing steadily. At this period the colonization of Hungary by German settlers was also initiated.

The practice of bestowing estates upon their friends and supporters, inaugurated by St. Stephen, was continued on a larger scale by his successors. As a result a large class of territorial magnates gradually grew up, whose rank was similar to that of the families of the original tribal chiefs. The rapid growth of this oligarchic class also affected increasingly the position of the freemen. Many of them were forced into dependence on the magnates, while the royal authority was considerably diminished. This development reached its peak at the beginning of the thirteenth century. King Andrew II (1205-1235), who had accelerated this evolution by his largess to the magnates, was forced to issue the famous "Golden Bull" (1222) in order to defend the liberties of the freemen and to confirm the privileges of the nobility. The "king's servants" and the *iobbagiones* were granted the same status of nobility as the magnates. The magnates were denied the right to arrest them without due process. All nobles were exempted from taxation of any kind, could refuse military service abroad, and were subject to a legal process which was meticulously defined in order to prevent any abuses. All nobles were also guaranteed the right to appear at the court held annually by the king or his supreme officer, the palatine, and to voice their grievances. Similar exemptions were granted to the clergy and were further extended in 1282. The privilege of resisting the king if he should order something contrary to the liberties granted in the Bull was also given to the nobles and to the clergy.

After the promulgation of the Golden Bull, which in many ways recalls the English Magna Carta, the influence of the lower nobility on the government of the state grew considerably, and the kings often sought for their support against the encroachment of the magnates. In the counties, whose number increased from 45 in the eleventh century to 72 in the thirteenth, only the lord-lieutenant (*foispan*) continued to be appointed by the king, and his office, according to the stipulations of the Golden Bull, was not hereditary. The deputies, judges, assessors, notaries, and all other members of the local administration were, however, elected by the assemblies of the local nobility. Laws were also promulgated by county assemblies and enforced by county officials. The king's appeal to arms was also addressed to the county assemblies.

After 1435 even the royal taxes were collected by the counties, which had also to provide for the royal troops. So it came about that, side by side with the magnates, the members of the lower nobility, although often impoverished, also enjoyed a share in the administration of the realm.

The Golden Bull was meant to guarantee the liberties of the descendants of the original Magyar conquerors. They were protected from becoming serfs of the magnates. Not only Magyars but many Slovaks and Rumanians were also admitted, in the subsequent period, into the class of nobles. Whole villages were sometimes ennobled by the kings. Although the members of the lower aristocracy were, therefore, very numerous, they were heavily outnumbered by the unfree population, living in serfdom and comprising as much as nine-tenths of the inhabitants.

On the other hand it must be admitted that the Golden Bull opened the doors for a feudalization of Hungary and so to the enforcement of serfdom. Béla IV (1235-1270) saw the danger and endeavored to arrest the spread of feudalism and to curb the misrule of the barons. The Tatar invasion spoiled his efforts. The colonization of the depopulated country by the pagan Cumans finally strengthened the non-Slavic element in the realm and precluded the last possibility of the Slavic population's playing a major role in the Hungarian kingdom. During the reign of the last Árpáds the barons continued to grow in power. The ancient county system was absorbed by them, and they held the many "king's servants" by feudal bonds. The whole country was divided into quasi-independent units ruled by groups of barons. Only the central part of the country, with two other small districts, was directly subject to the king. This was the period of oligarchic rule, which lasted from 1301 to 1310.

If Slovakia had formed a single unit within the Hungarian realm, there would have been a possibility for one of the mighty barons to form a kind of quasi-independent fief in the North of Hungary. An attempt of this kind was in fact made by Mathias Csak, one of the powerful magnates, who was an influential member of the oligarchic group which decided the succession to the Hungarian throne after the extinction of the Árpád dynasty.

Mathias Csak created a quasi-independent territory in the western and central part of modern Slovakia. From 1299 on he established the center of his power at the castle of Trenčín. After becoming palatine, Csak established his own court and, through feudal ties, extended his rule over many freemen. It was Csak who won over a great part of the Hungarian nobility to the Czech candidate to the Hungarian throne, Wenceslas III. Csak's defection was also the main cause which forced the Czechs to evacuate Hungary. Charles Robert was victorious thanks to the support of Csak. But the magnate soon revolted against the Angevin king, who in a continuous struggle with the oligarchs won back most of the territory ruled by Csak. But only after Csak's death (1321) could Charles Robert occupy Trenčín, the center of Csak's power.

Although Csak ruled over a great part of Slovakia, he never intended to create anything like a Slovak dukedom, and he hardly made any appeal to the national sentiment of his subjects to consolidate his rule. He was only one of the powerful Magyar oligarchy of magnates anxious for the extension of their influence and power.

Many other magnates disappeared with Csak during the wars waged against them by the new Angevin king Charles Robert (1308-1342), who was determined to curb their power and to consolidate the royal authority. He succeeded and created a new aristocracy, more subservient to the king, by conferring the confiscated lands on those, often of foreign descent, who had supported him in his struggle with the oligarchs. From these magnates, high functionaries, and prelates, the king formed the royal council, which was loyal to him. He also reorganized his court and his chancery, reserving judicial affairs to a special body headed by a secretary, subordinate, however, to a supreme chancellor (*supremus cancellarius*), who also presided over other affairs.

Charles Robert also introduced into Hungary the customs of French and Italian chivalry. He regulated the position of the new higher nobility on a feudal basis, obliging the nobles to furnish special contingents to the royal army, according to the extent of their territory, and to lead them into battle under their own banner (*banderia*). The military units of the lesser nobles were integrated into the *banderia* of the counties. His successor, Louis the Great (1342-1382), continued this policy and codified the rights and the obligations of the Hungarian nobility anew in 1351. In order not to endanger the new military organization, he restricted the right of the nobles to dispose freely of their property and thus prevented the division of the great domains into smaller estates.

Charles Robert also reformed the royal finances and placed the Hungarian economy on a sound footing, thanks to his successful monetary reform based on the gold standard. The Slovaks were, of course, profoundly affected by these reforms. The discovery of silver and gold mines in northern Hungary gave rise to the foundation of flourishing new mining towns in what is now Slovakia. Charles Robert organized mining in Slovakia on the Czech model. Kremnica (Kremnitz), the most important of the new cities, was given the mining code of Kutná Hora (Kuttenberg), Banská Štiavnica was provided with that in use in Jihlava (Iglau) in Moravia. Other mining cities founded among the Slovak population were Banská Bystrica, Gelnica, Rožňava (Rosenau), Pukanec.

The first miners and burghers of the new foundations were, naturally, German colonists, who regulated city affairs according to the laws of Magdeburg or of Nürnberg. The native population soon began, however, to penetrate the towns, and slowly changed their aspect. The town of Žilina, for example, already obtained a special "privilege for the Slavs" (*privilegium pro Slavis*) from Louis I, which shows that the Slovak population must have grown in the new cities. Besides these, new agricultural settlements were founded in the country as Slovak colonists started to penetrate deeper and deeper into the wooded lands. At the same time, Ukrainian colonists were moving into northern Hungary, adding to the numbers of the Slavic population which had already started to cross the Carpathian Mountains during the tenth century. They did not enjoy a special status, as did many other colonists, especially the Cumans, the Siculi (Szekelyek), the Saxons, or Rumanians in Transylvania, because they did not settle en masse in Hungary at the same time. They had, however, their own mayors, called *soltész*, who functioned as magistrates of their villages.

The political status of the Croats was quite different from that of other nations and colonists in Hungary. The successors of King Koloman respected the stipulations of the treaty concluded in 1102 with the representatives of the Croat nobility, who had accepted him as king of Croatia. So the lands of the Croats were regarded not as conquered lands (*partes subiugatae*), but as annexed lands (*partes adnexae*). The exceptional status of Croatia was also emphasized by a special coronation ceremony of the Hungarian king as king of Croatia. This special Croatian coronation was omitted in the thirteenth century, however—probably in 1205, on the succession of King Andrew II—but even afterwards the independent status of Croatia was respected. As Croat kings, the Hungarian rulers used the title "King of Croatia and Dalmatia" (*rex Croatiae et Dalmatiae*). Croatia was administered by a "ban," the supreme officer of the realm, representing the king. Sometimes the kings chose to send their sons or younger brothers to Croatia as administrators, called dukes (*voivoda, dux*). The dukes or bans used the title "Duke or Ban of Slavonia" (*dux, banus Slavoniae*), sometimes also "of all Slavonia" (*totae Slavoniae*), in order to emphasize that their administration extended over the whole Croat kingdom.

From the second half of the thirteenth century, however, the kings started to appoint two bans, one for that part of Croatia which used to be called Pannonian Croatia and comprised the lands between the river Drava, the mountains of Gvozd, and the river Sava, and the other for the rest of the realm. From that time on the first mentioned part of the country was called Slavonia, the name of Croatia and Dalmatia designating the lands between the Gvozd and the Adriatic.

The dukes acted as true kings, calling themselves "Duke by the Grace of God." They appointed also their bans and bishops, confirmed the royal privileges, acted as supreme judges, minted their own coins, directed the finances of the realm, and convoked the diets. The power of the ban was also extensive, although not as extensive as that of the dukes. His representative was the vice-ban (*vicebanus*), and his seal was guarded by a protonotary who had to be elected by the assembly of nobles.

The assemblies were originally, as in Bohemia and Poland, not proper diets, but judicial sessions. Besides the magnates and the higher clergy, the lesser nobility and the representatives of the towns were also members of the assemblies. They were presided over by the king, the duke, or the ban. Although, from the thirteenth century on, there used to be two diets, one for Slavonia and one for Croatia and Dalmatia, diets were sometimes convoked for the whole of the realm (*congregatio totius regni Slavoniae*). Only from the fifteenth century on, however, did the assemblies acquire the character of political diets.

The country continued to be divided into *župas* administered by the *župans*. The *župan* presided over the court of his *župa*, but it was possible to appeal from his court to that of the ban. The garrisons of the royal castles were commanded by castellans called *gradšćik*. The territories of the Church and of the hereditary aristocracy (*perpetui comites, knežije*) were exempt from the jurisdiction of the *župans* and directly subject to that of the bans.

The last Árpád kings had granted many exemptions from the jurisdiction of the bans. Charles Robert suppressed all such exemptions in 1325, allowing only an appeal to the king from the court of the ban. Unfortunately, this measure resulted in a curtailment of Croat independence. The kings presented such appeals to the supreme court of Hungary, which thus achieved a kind of supremacy over the court of the bans. This situation aroused protests from the Croats.

Hungarian influences penetrated Croatia more and more. This was particularly visible in Slavonia, nearest to Hungary proper. For example, although the tribal *župas* in Croatia proper remained intact until the fourteenth century, the tribal *župas* in Slavonia were soon united into larger units on the Hungarian pattern. Also, Hungarian aristocratic families soon began to appear in Slavonia, and a new aristocracy of functionaries was introduced by Charles Robert. Croatia proper, however, was able to preserve its own national aristocracy. Other Hungarian customs were penetrating Slavonia, sometimes even reaching Croatia and Dalmatia. New towns and villages were founded in Slavonia according to German law, as was done in Hungary proper. Little by little a magyarization of Croatian society and Croatian customs was giving Slavonia an increasingly Hungarian character. This assimilation developed further in the fifteenth century when, from 1442 on, the diets of Slavonia started to send their deputies (*nuntii, oratores regni Slavoniae*) to the Hungarian diets.

The territory of the second part of the realm, Croatia and Dalmatia, continued to show a more independent spirit. One of the reasons for this was that this region was able to develop its own judicial statutes not only on the basis of custom law, but also on that of Romano-Byzantine law. The latter had been preserved in the towns of the littoral and on the Adriatic islands which had formed part of the Byzantine Empire and whose possession had always been coveted by the national Croatian kings.[23] Slavic elements soon penetrated the islands and the cities, and the intimate relations between these remnants of the Romano-Byzantine Empire and Croatia proper influenced the development of Croatian public and private law.

The coastal cities were able to preserve their autonomous status even through the period of Venetian occupation and under Croatian or Hungarian supremacy. They were usually governed by a chief called *comes, knez,* often nominated by the Venetians, who was assisted by a vice-chief (*vicarius*) and by judges elected by the city assemblies. Ragusa (Dubrovnik) had three kinds of council—a grand council, a council of appeal similar to a senate, and a lesser council dealing with the administration. The cities had also preserved since the Byzantine period their general assemblies of the whole population, but these were falling into disuse toward the end of the fourteenth century. In Ragusa, for example, the functions of the assembly passed to the grand council.

All these cities possessed their own statutes, based on old traditions dating from the Roman and Byzantine periods but supplemented with Slavic customary law and strongly influenced by Italian and especially by Venetian juridical traditions. The most important is the Statute of Ragusa, the *liber statutorum civitatis Ragusii*, which dates from 1272 although it is only preserved in copies of a later date. Split (Spalato) also possessed its own statute, dating from 1240, although only the Statute of 1312, which derives from it, is preserved, showing a strong infiltration of Roman and canon law beside the custom law. It was re-edited and supplemented in the second half of the fourteenth century.

The statute of Zara (Zadar) also dates from the beginning of the fourteenth century. It betrays some Italian influences, and one of its books contains the maritime law of Zara. The city of Šibenik (Sebenico) also possessed an old statute, which is reflected in a composition from between 1305 and 1322. It was gradually added to between the fourteenth and the sixteenth centuries. This statute is the more interesting in that it is largely of Slavic origin. The city of Šibenik was a Croatian settlement. There also exist special statutes of the Adriatic islands, especially those of Korčula (Curzola), of Brač (Brazza), of Hvar (Lesina), of Lastovo (Lagosta), and of Mljet (Meleda). These statutes have a more Slavic aspect, and they contain laws and prescriptions concerning agriculture, viticulture, and fishing. The most ancient of these statutes is that of Korčula, which already existed in part in 1214.[24]

The most important for Croatian juridical history is the Statute of Vinodol, which was composed in the Croat language in 1288. The *župa* of Vinodol extended, in the thirteenth century, along the Croat littoral from Novi (Novigrad) to Rijeka (Fiume), and its statute had a great influence on Croatian legal history. It contains prescriptions of public law concerning the obligations of the citizens toward the chief of the *župa* and toward the Church and is more interested in penal than in civil law. It contains, also, interesting indications concerning the customary judicial procedure.[25]

At this period one of the cities on the Adriatic littoral, Ragusa, started to develop into a quasi-independent city-republic. Ragusa (Dubrovnik) was founded in the seventh century by Roman refugees from Epidaurum, a Roman town destroyed by the invading Avars and Slavs. The primitive inhabitants were Latins, but Slavic elements began to penetrate into the city from the tenth century on. In 1199 the chief (*comes*) of Ragusa was a Slav—Dobroslav. The city was under Byzantine suzerainty until 1205, and from then until 1358 under Venice, but from 1358 to 1526 its nominal suzerain was the king of Hungary and Croatia.

Already during the twelfth century the city began concluding commercial treaties with Italian cities. Its importance grew during the thirteenth century, when several islands—Lokrum (Lacroma), Koločep (Calamota), Lopud (Dalafota), Lastovo (Lagosta), and Mljet (Meleda) —were acquired by Ragusa. Its territory was enlarged during the fourteenth century thanks to Tsar Dušan and the Bosnian king Stephen, who were favorably disposed toward this growing emporium on the Adriatic. The volume of Ragusa's commerce with the Balkan countries was especially considerable in the fourteenth century; after that period its citizens devoted themselves more to maritime commerce. The term "argosy" derives from the name of the city, whose prosperous status became a solid basis for the growth of Croatian civilization in the following period.

There is not a great deal new to be said concerning the organization of the Second Bulgarian Empire and its social evolution. The organization of the state had been adapted to the Byzantine model by Symeon the Great, and the byzantinization of the administration and of the developing social pattern had been achieved during the two hundred years when Bulgaria was a Byzantine province. In spite of their hostility toward Byzantium, later tsars had no other choice than to continue in the same tradition.

They continued to make use of the title which Symeon the Great had introduced in imitation of the Byzantines, "In Christ the God faithful Tsar and Autocrator of all Bulgarians and Greeks." Also after the Byzantine fashion they used the phrase, when speaking of themselves, "my tsardom." This custom was also followed by the Serbian rulers.

It is rather remarkable that instead of the Greek *basileus*—which is equivalent to the Latin *imperator*—the Bulgarians, followed later by the Serbians and the Russians, used the title of tsar, which is formed from the Latin "Caesar." The clearest indication of this etymology is to be found in old Slavic documents which use the term *cesar'*, later *c'sar'*. The word was coined in the distant days when the Slavs were still in contact with the Romans, and was transmitted to the Slavs, probably, through the intermediary of the Goths.

Although the crown, together with a scepter and a flag bearing a portrait of St. Peter, was given to Kalojan by the Pope, the tsars are often found depicted with a Byzantine diadem. The crown itself is also called by its Byzantine name, *diadema*. The scepter, adorned with a cross or an orb, is often pictured; the orb, with a cross, being shown only on the coins of Asen II. On solemn occasions, the tsars wore a purple robe, a jeweled stole, and a belt adorned with precious stones, all fashioned after the Byzantine ceremonial costume.

The court of the Bulgarian tsars was also patterned on the Byzantine model. The tsars introduced the title of despot, to mark the next rank below the emperor, and they conferred it upon the governors of the various provinces. As in Byzantium, the relations of the tsar were entitled *sebastocrators*. The chancellor of the Empire was called *logothetes* and the minister of finance *protovestiarios*, both after Byzantine usage. Indeed, almost all the Byzantine court titles had their counterpart at the court of Trnovo.

The administrative provinces were designated by the Greek word *chora*, and the principal judicial, administrative, and financial functionaries were called by the Greek word *kefalotes*, meaning chiefs. The system of taxation was almost the same as that operated during the Byzantine occupation, and included taxes on houses, cattle, and fields while a special tax was collected for the maintenance of provincial functionaries.

The tsar was nominally an autocrat; but in reality, as is clear from the political evolution of the Second Bulgarian Empire, the boyars limited his power considerably. The boyars remained divided into two classes, as they had been at the time of the First Empire—the higher and the lower nobility—the latter corresponding to the knightly class of the West. It seems that the distinction between these two classes tended to become more sharply defined during the later period. The number of boyars also increased considerably as many noble Cumans joined their ranks.

Naturally, the tsars chose their officers and functionaries from among the boyars. The boyars were members of the tsar's council, and they participated in the diets convoked by the tsars. During the frequent interregnums, the boyars ruled the state and chose new tsars from among themselves. The members of the higher clergy—bishops and abbots—were also members of the tsar's council and took precedence over the boyars in the diet.

This shows that the higher clergy continued to hold a privileged position, while their numbers diminished. The patriarchate of Trnovo comprised only seven bishoprics, as compared with forty during the reign of Tsar Peter. But the higher clergy enjoyed extensive privileges, including exemption from the jurisdiction of the state and from taxation. There were many monasteries in the land, the most prominent being that of Rila. The Bulgarians also had some monasteries at Mount Athos, of which Zographos was the most important.

The lower ranks of the clergy were recruited from the general populace. Like the artisans or city merchants, they were "free," but they were not privileged as a class.

Most of the peasants were subject to the boyars, either directly as their servants or by cultivating their land. They were known as *paroikoi* (Greek), *pariki* (Bulgarian). There were free peasants (*epoikoi*), who owned land and were subject only to taxation and to the performance of various public services. Their numbers, however, decreased as taxation and other dues became crippling, and many of them preferred to become *paroikoi* of a boyar or an ecclesiastical foundation.

Contrary to the course of events in the medieval West, the cities of Bulgaria did not attain any political status. Most of them were old Roman centers, although some new towns sprang up around fortified places which had become centers of administration. The principal calling of their citizens was commerce, which was far from insignificant at the time of the Second Bulgarian Empire, mainly because of the fact that the country was traversed by some important arteries of trade between Italy and the Adriatic on the one hand and Thessalonica and the Black Sea on the other.[26]

The political and social evolution of the Serbians during this period was more complex than that of the Bulgarians because the Serbians were in direct touch not only with Byzantium but also with the West. Both Western and Eastern influences were therefore naturally to be seen in Serbian development.

The power of the Serbian rulers was more absolute than that of the Bulgarian tsars. This was due to the fact that at the beginning of independent political life in Serbia there was no aristocracy in the land. The only reference to the existence of nobles, as well as the prince, is found in documents concerning the Narentans. Deceased kings were called saints, as was also the case in Bulgaria, a habit which is a form of survival of the title "divine" (*theios*) which was given to Roman and Byzantine emperors. From the thirteenth century onward, living Serbian kings were described as "saintly born" because they were successors and descendants of St. Symeon (Stephen Nemanja), canonized by the Church. This is a Serbian version of the Byzantine *porphyrogennetos*—born in the purple, the title given to the offspring of a reigning emperor.

The Serbian kings also claimed the Byzantine title *autocrator* as an expression of the absolute power of the monarch (*samodrža*, or *carikralj*). Even Stephen Dušan added this title to the pompous "Emperor of Serbia and Romania (Byzantium)," reserving the royal title for the heir to the throne.

The Serbians imitated another Byzantine practice, the appointment of members of the dynasty as co-regents. In some cases, this custom served to offset the disadvantage for the Serbian polity which resulted from the fact that the hereditary principle of royal succession was not fully developed, the king selecting as his successor any member of the dynasty at his choice or on the recommendation of the assembly of nobles representing the people. The principle of election was fully applied in Bosnia and was one of the main reasons for the downfall of the short-lived Bosnian kingdom.

Byzantine and Western elements are also to be found in the symbols of the royal power. The crown was of Western origin, having been given to Stephen Uroš I by the Pope. The throne is often depicted on frescoes and upon coins. The king, sitting upon his throne, holds in one hand a scepter or a sword or an orb surmounted by a cross, sometimes a flag and a cross. He wears a purple mantle and a jeweled belt. Like the Byzantines, the Bulgarians and Serbians did not know any heraldic symbols. A golden eagle with two heads or a lion does, however, appear on the blazon of the despots and was evidently introduced thanks to Western influence. Bosnia, which was in closer contact with Hungary, followed Hungarian custom with regard to heraldry.

As in the earlier period of Serbian history, the country remained divided into provinces called *župa,* each governed by a *župan,* who represented the king and who not only had in his hands the administration of the province but was at the same time the local judge and the commander of the local forces. Finance was administered by special officers, who were also charged with the collection of taxes. At first, all functionaries, from the headman of the village to ministers and members of the dynasty, were called *knez,* a title corresponding to the Latin *comes.* Later, this title was made exclusive to members of the higher nobility, and by the time Serbian political independence came to an end, it was almost equivalent to the royal title. The functionaries were called regents (*vladalac, vladusti*). From the thirteenth century onward some Byzantine titles were introduced, for example, *sevast,* from the Greek *sebastos* (illustrious), and *kefalija,* to designate, at first, military commanders in frontier towns. Court functionaries bore the same titles as their counterparts elsewhere, but with the addition of the epithet "great"—another imitation of Byzantine custom.

Stephen Dušan, in assuming the title Emperor, introduced many Byzantine offices and titles, but he avoided a wholesale imitation of Byzantine court ceremonial. He suppressed the title *župan* and replaced the *župans* by governors with the Greek title of *kefalija,* at the same time creating a new office of judge of the court. Only in Bosnia did the function of the *župan* survive. The chancellery of the Serbian kings and cars was generally organized on the Byzantine model.

An aristocracy only started to develop in Serbia from the end of the twelfth century onward, under both Western and Byzantine influence. The members of the higher nobility, recruited from the families of the *župans,* from other leading functionaries, and from descendants of branches of the royal family, were originally called *velmože* (great men), but later the translation of the word *archon* (commandant, ruler) was adopted—*vlastelin*, pl. *vlastela*. The members of the lower ranks of the nobility were designated, as in Byzantium, as soldiers (*stratiotai: vojnici*). The Serbian *vojnik* was thus also the counterpart of the Western knight.

The influence of the nobility on the royal administration was exercised firstly through the royal council, which was composed of high functionaries recruited exclusively from the nobility, members of prominent families, and the higher clergy, and secondly, through the diets. Serbian diets (*zbor, skupština, stanak*) are mentioned from the reign of Stephen Nemanja on. They were convoked by the king and were composed of high functionaries, members of the higher nobility, military commanders (*voivodes*), some of the lesser nobility, and, with the exception of Bosnia, of prelates. As there was no settled royal residence in either Serbia or Bosnia, the diets were convoked wherever the court might be at the time. They discussed matters relating to the succession to the throne, the enthronement of co-regents, and abdications. Ecclesiastical affairs of importance, such as the election of a new archbishop or the establishment of a new foundation, were also discussed. The diets of Bosnia had more influence on public affairs and maintained the right of the election of new sovereigns.[27]

The famous code (*zakonik*) of Stephen Dušan, the most important Serbian juridical document, was also enacted by a diet held in Skoplje in 1349. The code does not contain the Serbian civil legislation, but specializes in public and penal laws. Some influences of Byzantine legislation can be detected, but its main sources are the laws promulgated by Dušan's predecessors, based on Serbian customary law.[28] Byzantine private and civil legislation predominates in another Serbian compilation of this period, the so-called "Law of Justinian."

Admission to the ranks of the nobility was conditional upon the possession of an hereditary freehold estate, called *baština*. From the end of the thirteenth century onward, the kings adopted the Byzantine practice of conferring upon nobles lands or villages in fief (Greek, *pronoia;* Serbian, *pronija*). The holder of such a fief could not freely dispose of it, although it could be inherited, and he was bound to military service. The system of *pronija* was in use in Serbia and Zeta (Montenegro) until the end of the fifteenth century. It was not practiced in Bosnia.[29]

The Serbian clergy enjoyed great prestige. After the foundation of the archbishopric, eight new bishoprics were created, and this number was increased considerably after the establishment of the patriarchate. Many bishops resided in monasteries, which were particularly numerous and generally better endowed than the bishoprics. The principal monasteries (those of Studenica, Ras, Gradac, Žiča, St. George at Skoplje, and Chilandari at Mount Athos) were called "royal monasteries" and were exempt from the jurisdiction of any bishop—an imitation of the Byzantine custom. Members of the lower clergy obtained a livelihood either from any properties with which their churches might be endowed or from an allotment of "three fields according to the law." Whatsoever they owned was free from taxation. They also received the proceeds of a special tax levied upon their parishioners.

The Roman Catholics, most of whom lived upon the coast, were subject to the Archbishop of Bar (Antibari) and to the Bishop of Cattaro (Kotor). In this region, there were numerous Latin Benedictine monasteries.

The Serbian cities never succeeded in playing a very important part in the country's political evolution. New cities started to develop from the townships which sprang up near fortified castles, that is, centers of administration. This is clearly illustrated by the fact that the same word, *grad*, is used for both city and castle. Some of them became important commercial centers, but they never reached the level of importance which they achieved in the West. They were administered by the governor (*kefalija*) of the castle, by a *knez* who supervised commercial activities, and by a third functionary who was charged with collecting duty. The Greek cities preserved their municipal organization under Serbian rule and were administered by a governor and judges chosen from among prominent citizens.

Only the Latin cities on the coast continued to enjoy their autonomous status. The Statute of Cattaro (Kotor) is preserved. The *knez* or *comes*, who represented the king, was bound to promise faithful observance of the statute. The democratic general assembly of all the citizens was transformed in the fourteenth century into a great council composed of the most prominent citizens, who formed the local nobility.[30]

The peasants, called *sebri* in Serbia and *kmeti* in Bosnia, were almost all settled on territories owned by the king, the aristocracy, or the clergy. They had to bear the same heavy obligations toward both the state and their masters as did the Byzantine and Bulgarian *paroikoi*. The introduction of *pronija* aggravated the situation, for they were then obliged to work two days a week for the *pronijar*. The evolution of the Serbian peasantry followed the same course as the evolution of the peasantry in the West. They were not allowed to change their place of residence as they pleased, while the Code of Dušan prescribed heavy penalties for anyone who sheltered a fugitive peasant without the special written permission of the tsar. Numerous serfs were settled on the estates of the nobles and of the monasteries. The Code of Dušan contains paragraphs regulating the status of serfs.

Byzantine influence was considerable in the organization of Serbian agriculture. Financial administration in Serbia bore many similarities to the system adopted in Bulgaria. There were many taxes of the same kind in both countries, and Byzantine influence is evident in this field also.

Improvements in the exploitation of the country's natural resources from the thirteenth century onward contributed greatly to the enrichment of Serbia and its rulers. Mining in Serbia and Bosnia was mostly done by Germans—Saxons—who came from Hungary, attracted by promises of special privileges. They had an autonomous status, and they introduced into Serbia a Saxon mining law of which the text has survived in a Turkish translation. It gives detailed regulations concerning the rights of miners, their duties, upkeep of the mines, and standard of production.[31] Mining helped considerably in the development of commerce, with the result that medieval Serbia was quite a prosperous state.

NOTES

1. See F. Dvornik, *The Slavs*, pp. 314 ff. for details.
2. For the Kievan State, *ibid.*, pp. 279 ff.
3. Cf. H. F. Schmid, *Die Burgbezirksverfassung bei den slavischen Völkern* (see Bibl.), pp. 81 ff.
4. The Polish word for aristocracy, *szlachta,* is derived from the Czech word *šlechta* and therefore indicates that the origins of the Polish aristocracy are connected with the Bohemian and German example.
5. The most powerful noble family in thirteenth century Bohemia was that of the Vítkovci. They possessed patrimonies and fiefs not only in southern Bohemia but also in neighboring Bavaria, and their intention was to unite all their fiefs and patrimonies into one quasi-independent, political unit. Although of Czech origin, their members were related by marriage to the Bavarian aristocracy. The leader of the revolt against Přemysl II, Záviš, was a Vítkovec, who used the name of one of his Bavarian castles, Falkenstein, and had a German mother. On this revolt see above, p. 32.
6. Most probably Přemysl II was guided in his attempt by the editions of the *Sachsenspiegel,* which were at that time used as a basis for juridical works in northern Germany.
7. Republished in 1900 by A. Zycha, *Das böhmische Bergrecht des Mittelalters* (see Bibl.). The author treats all problems concerning Bohemian mines. Cf. also O. Peterka, *Rechtsgeschichte* (see Bibl.), vol. 1, p. 151, and E. Otto's *Beiträge* (see Bibl.), pp. 62 ff. On the influence of Roman law on Czech jurists, cf. O. Peterka, "Ursachen and Wege der Rezeption" (see Bibl.), pp. 37-55.
8. Published by H. Jireček in *Codex juris bohemici* (1870), vol. II, part 2. A new and more critical edition is desirable. Cf. E. Werunsky, "Die Maiestas Carolina," *Zeitschr. d. Savigny—Stiftung für Rechtsgeschte, German. Abt.* (1888). A Czech bibliography is given by J. Šusta, *Karel IV,* vol. 2, p. 187 (Prague, 1948). See also above, Ch. IV, p. 72.
9. It seems that the norms of the judicial procedure (*Ordo iudicii terrae*),

an important juridical document of this period, was not one of the sources of the *Maiestas Carolina*, but is rather based on Charles's code. The oldest juridical document written in Czech is the anonymous Kniha Rožmberská (Book of Rožmberk) describing mainly the juridical procedure in Bohemia (ed. V Brandl, Prague, 1872).

10. See F. Hartung, *Die Krone als Symbol der monarchischen Herrschaft* (see Bibl.). See also J. Prochno, "Terra Bohemiae, regnum Bohemiae, corona Bohemiae" (see Bibl.), pp. 91-111. The author quotes all documents from 1165 to the half of the fourteenth century in which the above mentioned titles are found. Cf. also A. Soloviev, "Corona regni" in *Przewodnik history cznoprawny,* 4 (Lwów, 1934), pp. 27-48.

11. Charles used the coronation order of the Přemyslide kings, which originated at the beginning of the thirteenth century and was based on the coronation orders of German kings from the tenth century. He also used the French coronation order of 1328 and added some prayers and ceremonies of his own. A critical edition of Charles's coronation order was given by J. Cibulka, *Český řád korunovačni a jeho původ* (Prague, 1934).

12. Cf. F. Dvornik, *The Slavs,* pp. 110 ff., 312 ff.

13. On the origins of Polish knighthood see F. Wojciechowski, *Das Ritterrecht in Polen vor den Statuten Kasimirs des Grosse,* transl. by H. Bellee (see Bibl.).

14. Cf. on Polish urban development in this period the recent work by S. Piekarczyk, *Studia dziejow miast polskech v. XIII-XIV* (Warsaw, 1955). Two works by Polish scholars dealing with colonization in Poland are now available in German translations: Th. Tyc, *Die Anfänge der dörflichen Siedlung* (see Bibl.) and B. Zaborski, *Über Dorfsformen in Polen* (see Bibl.).

15. Polish historians are not unanimous in explaining the conception of the Polish kingdom from 1295 to 1370. S. Kutrzeba, the specialist in the history of the Polish constitution, thinks that the conception of the Polish kingdom was limited to Great Poland only and that this had a purely local and not a national Polish significance. Another specialist, O. Balzer, tries to prove that the conception of *Polonia* was never reduced only to Great Poland, but that, even from the twelfth to the fourteenth centuries, the papal Curia and Poland's neighbors comprised under this name the whole of Poland. Balzer's conception seems preferable.

16. The idea of the unity of the Polish state also found expression in the coat of arms of the kingdom, the figure of an eagle, which started to appear on the national flag and on great state seals under Casimir.

17. Polish historians still differ considerably in their judgment on Casimir's grant to his adopted son of one-eighth of the polish lands, a large district separating Great Poland from Little Poland, as an independent unit. Some think that Casimir was out of his mind when making this bequest.

18. For details, see O. Balzer, *Les Statuts de Casimir le Grand* (Poznań, 1947), Studia nad historią prava polskiego, vol. 19. Two Soviet writers have published studies on Polish feudal institutions from the thirteenth to the fifteenth centuries: K. E. Livancev, *Istorija gosudarstva i prava feodal'noj Pol'ši 13-14 vv.* (Leningrad, 1958), and L. V. Razumovskaja, *Očerki po istorii pol'skikh krest'jan ot drevnikh vremen do 15 v.* (Moscow, 1958) (Outline of the history of the Polish peasants from earliest times to the fifteenth century).

19. On the early history of the Slovenes see F. Dvornik, *The Slavs,* pp. 34, 41 ff., 64, 70 ff.

20. *Oesterreichische Reimchronik* M.G.H., German Chronicles, vol. V, pp. 263-267. Cf. also John Viktring (Joannes Victoriensis), *Liber certarum histor.* All documents concerning this ceremonial have been re-edited and translated into Slovene by B. Grafenauer, *Ustoličevanje koroških vojvod na država karantanskih Slovencev,* published by the Slovene Academy (Razred za zgodov. in družb. vede, Ljubljana, 1952). A more detailed bibliography concerning this ceremonial, whose origin and meaning are still controversial, will also be found there. The ceremonial ceased to be enacted at the beginning of the fifteenth century.

21. Cf. A. Dopsch, *Die ältere Sozial-und Wirtschaftsverfassung der Alpenslaven* (Weimar, 1909). For more details on Slovene history down to the Reformation see M. Kos, *Zgodovina Slovencev od naselitve do reformacije* (Ljubljana, 1933). Kos collected all documents concerning the Slovenes from the eighth century to 1246 in his *Gradivo za zgodovino Slovencev v srednjem veku,* 5 vols. (Ljubljana, 1902-1928).

22. For details, see F. Dvornik, *The Making of Central and Eastern Europe* (London, 1949), pp. 215, 221. The best monograph in Czech on early and medieval Slovakia was written by V. Chaloupecký, *Staré Slovensko* (Bratislava, 1923).

23. For details, see F. Dvornik, *The Slavs,* pp. 152 ff., 174 ff.

24. On the recently discovered "Zavod" book of Trogir, see M. Horvat, "Das Troginer 'Zavod' Buch vom Jahre 1326" (see Bibl.). M. Kostrenčić's history of Croatian law (*Hrvatska pravna povijest,* Zagreb, 1922, 2nd ed.) was inaccessible to me. More accessible is M. Lanović's study, "Ustavno pravo Hrvatske narodne države," in *Rad,* vol. 265 (1938), pp. 167-242.

25. Many of the statutes mentioned here were published or republished by the Academy of Zagreb in its *Monumenta historico—juridica Slavorum meridionalium.* So far eleven volumes have appeared, but some of the statutes are still awaiting a publisher or a new editor. Some of them are only available in editions dating from the sixteenth century. The Statute of Vinodol was re-edited recently by M. Barada (*Hrvatski vlasteoski feudalizam po vinodolskom zakonu,* Zagreb, 1952, Works published by the Academy of Zagreb, vol. 44). There exists also a French translation of this statute, published by J. Preux ("La Loi du Vinodol traduite et annotée," *Nouvelle revue historique du droit français et étranger,* 1896). The Statute of Poljica, similar to that of Vinodol but dating only from 1440, was translated into German by T. Matić, "Statut der Poljica," (see Bibl.). For more details, see K. Kadlec, *Introduction,* see Bibl., pp. 304-15. More recently, H. F. Schmid, "Dalmatinische Stadtbücher" (see Bibl.).

26. Social and economic conditions in the Second Bulgarian Empire need a more thorough investigation. D. Angelov and M. Andreev in their history of the Bulgarian state and law (*Istorija na b"lgarskata država i pravo,* Sofia, 1955) give useful indications in this respect. The agrarian and social situation of the fourteenth century in Macedonia was examined by D. Angelov (*Agrarnite otnošenija v severna i sredna Makedonija pres XIV vek,* Sofia, 1958), French résumé. A more complete bibliography will be found in this book.

27. There is a good monograph on Serbian diets by N. Radojčić, *Srpski državni sabori u srednjem veku* (Belgrade, 1940). On the role of the Serbian nobility under Dušan, see G. Ostrogorsky, "Etienne Dušan et la noblesse serbe dans la lutte contre Byzance," *Byzantion,* 22 (1952), pp. 151-59.

28. An English translation of the code was published by Malcolm Burr in

The Slavonic and East European Review, 28 (1949-50), "The Code of Stephen Dušan," pp. 198-217, 516-39. See there, p. 198, a note on Serbian editions. Cf. also A. Soloviev, "Le droit byzantin dans la codification d'Étienne Douchan" (see Bibl.). See also the *Zbornik* published in commemoration of the sixth centenary of the *Zakonik*, published by the Serbian Academy (Belgrade, 1952). A detailed Yugoslav bibliography on Dušan's code will be found in J. Žontar's survey, published in commemoration of the sixth centenary ("Ob šeststoletnici Dušanovego Zakonika") in *Zgodovinski časopis*, 5 (1951), pp. 209-14. Cf. also Radojčić's study, "Zakonik cara Stefana Dusana," in *Arhiv za pravne i društvene nauke* (1949), pp. 542-556. D. Janković published recently a history of public law in medieval Serbia (*Istorija države i prava feudalne Srbije 12-14 v.*, Belgrade, 1953). F. V. Taranovskij dealt with the history of Serbian medieval public, criminal, and civil law and judicial proceedings in his work, *Istorija srpskog prava v Nemanjičkoj države* (Belgrade, 1931-35), 3 vols.

29. Two paragraphs in the *Code* of Dušan deal with the obligations of the *pronijari*. For details, see G. Ostrogorsky's work (*Pronija*, Belgrade, 1951), published by the Serbian Academy in Serbian with a résumé in German. There is a French translation by H. Grégoire and P. Lemerle (*Pour l'histoire de la féodalité byzantine*, Brussels, 1954).

30. Concerning the evolution of the cities in the Balkans, see for more details not only the works of K. Jireček mentioned in the bibliography, but also S. Novaković's study in the *Archiv für slavische Philologie*, vol. 25 (1903), pp. 321-40. The development of the municipal organization of Cattaro (Kotor) from the second half of the twelfth to the beginning of the fifteenth century was described by I. Sindik, *Komunalno urečenije Kotora* (Belgrade, 1950), with a French résumé.

31. A short description of the mining industry in medieval Serbia is given by M. Dinić in the first volume of his monograph, *Za istoriju rudarstva u srednjevekovnoj Srbiji i Bosni* (Belgrade, 1955), with a French résumé.

Chapter VII

SLAVIC MEDIEVAL CULTURAL
ACHIEVEMENTS

The westernization of Czech Christianity, Latin religious poetry in Bohemia—Original Latin works in Bohemia—Czech translations of Latin writings—Czech compositions in verse and prose—Czech epic poetry and prose, its Western patterns—The Old Czech secular lyric and its relationship to the Provençal and German lyric—Czech national feeling in Bohemia—Historical works, Charles IV's inspiration—Early humanism in Bohemia—Czech devotio moderna, its representatives and links with the Dutch movement—Bohemian Gothic art—Cultural progress in Poland, first compositions in Latin—Slow growth of Polish literature under Czech influence—The fine arts in Poland—Literary activity in Bulgaria—Serbian literature—The Byzantine background of Bulgarian art—Serbian architecture—Originality in Serbian painting

As might be expected, literary production in the early medieval period was, in general, religious in character. The reasons for this are quite obvious. The rich heritage of classical Greece, which was maintained almost intact in the eastern part of the Roman Empire, was almost completely lost in the West owing to the barbarian invasions and to the rupture of political and cultural relations between East and West which followed on them. What was saved was adapted to the purpose of explaining and propagating Christian doctrines and was transmitted to the new western nations by the missionaries, bishops, and monks who converted them to Christianity in the Latin language of their mother Church of Rome.

It is natural, in such circumstances, not only that the main object of the first literary productions in the medieval West should be religious, but also that the vernacular of the converted nations should be little used in the first phase of their cultural life.

The situation was quite different in the East. There the treasures of classical and Hellenistic literary production were kept almost intact and were freely accessible to anyone who desired to enrich his knowledge. The anticlassical bias apparent among the Christians of the first three centuries was overcome in the fourth century: so it came about that Homer's poems and the works of Greek dramatists were read in the schools; Platonic and Aristotelian ideas were freely discussed, applied, or repudiated; the works of Thucydides, Herodotus, and Plutarch were imitated by the Church historians. Even frivolous works, so numerous in the Hellenistic period, especially those of Lucian of Samosata, were copied for preservation.

The new classical renaissance in Byzantium in the ninth century, dominated by the great figure of the Patriarch Photius, made classical lore available also to the Slavic nations, which were at that time entering into the sphere of Byzantine Christianity. But even there, in the Christianization of the Moravians, Bulgarians, and Russians, the first task of the Byzantine missionaries was to transmit to the new converts their own religious literary treasures, which were translated into Old Slavonic. Political catastrophes, which shattered these young Slavic nations in the ninth, eleventh, and thirteenth centuries, prevented them from enriching their literature with nonreligious works, although the translations of the Greek fathers, Greek anthologies, and other works are deeply imbued with classical lore.[1]

Bohemia, which had inherited the Greco-Slavonic culture planted in Moravia by SS. Cyril and Methodius in the ninth century, was completely westernized and latinized toward the end of the eleventh century.[2] But even in the adaptation of Western and Latin cultural treasures, the Czechs made great progress from the twelfth century onward. This progress reached its peak in the fourteenth century.

The first strong wave of Western influence affecting the religious affairs of Bohemia showed itself at the end of the eleventh century in a growing hostility toward the use of the Slavonic language in the liturgy.[3] But, although Latin prevailed during the twelfth century, other disciplinary reforms introduced by Pope Gregory VII, e.g., celibacy of the priesthood, were only accepted after a very hard struggle during the second half of the twelfth century. The Bishop of Olomouc, the learned and zealous Zdík, was the main promoter of these reforms.

The westernization of Czech Christianity was further promoted by the new orders of Premonstratensians and Cistercians. The main foundation of the Premonstratensians was that of Strahov (1142), and of the Cistercians, Sedlec near Kutná Hora (1142) and Velehrad (1205). These orders introduced new agricultural methods, and their foundations became important centers of education providing cultural links with France and Germany.

The introduction of the Franciscans and Dominicans into the new cities of Bohemia, Moravia, and Silesia strengthened these links, extending them also to Italy. On the initiative of Princess Agnes, the leading protagonist of the ideas of St. Francis and St. Clare, a purely Czech order, the Knights of the Cross, was founded in 1237. The Augustinians were settled in Bohemia by Přemysl II in 1263. During the thirteenth century, there was a new wave of enthusiasm for Cistercian religious ideas, which manifested itself in the foundation of five new abbeys. Cistercian influence was so strong in the country that their abbots were very largely responsible—as was already mentioned—for the election of John of Luxemburg to the Czech throne. The latter founded a Carthusian monastery called "Garden of Our Lady" near Prague, which also became an important factor in the spiritualization of Czech religious life.

How deeply these Western influences had penetrated Czech Christianity is best illustrated by the rise of original compositions of Latin religous poetry and prose in Czech lands. Most of the poetry was, of course, of a liturgical character and found its models in the West, in France, Italy, or Germany. One of the oldest documents of this kind is the *Troparium* of St. Guy in Prague, preserved in a manuscript dating from 1235. It contains some liturgical songs called *tropas*, together with some prayers recited during the Mass (e.g., Kyrie, Gloria, Sanctus, etc.), which had been composed in Prague. This shows also that the cathedral church of Prague was the first important center of Latin religious poetry in Bohemia. It is possible that the composition of the *Troparium* coincided with the reform of religious chanting in Prague which is attributed to Dean Vít (Guy). This collection of *tropas* was enlarged later by new compositions, which are preserved in the *Graduale* of St. Guy of 1363.

Other compositions of this kind are hymns in honor of saints, composed for the chapters and monasteries, and sequences which were sung during the Mass. New Latin hymns were composed, not only in honor of Czech saints (SS. Wenceslas, Ludmila, Adalbert, Procopius, Cyril, Methodius, and Hedwig), but also of saints who were particularly venerated in Bohemia and for some popular liturgical feasts. New sequences were composed for the same purpose. They are preserved in the *Missal of Dražice*, dating from 1342, and in the collection of sequences of 1363, which originated in the entourage of Archbishop Ernest of Pardubice. In their form and content these compositions mostly follow the patterns of older Church hymns and sequences, which are copied in these collections together with the new compositions.

Moreover, whole new offices, partly in rhyme, were produced in Bohemia for the same purpose. Some of the offices in honor of Czech saints testify to the patriotic feeling of their authors. The oldest of such offices is that in honor of Christ's crown of thorns, which was probably written in the convent of St. George in Prague at the beginning of the four-teenth century.

Many of the new liturgical compositions are preserved in numerous manuscripts. The most important of them, that of the Monastery of Vyšší Brod, contains forty new songs. The oldest of them are simple, but they soon grew in content and length. Some are complicated poetic composi-tions, adding subjective motives—contemplation, prayer, and invocation —to their epic kernel. This kind of liturgical poetry became particularly popular in Bohemia, and the number of such productions grew, espe-cially in the fifteenth century, and exerted considerable influence on the liturgy of the Hussite period.

Most of the liturgical poems are anonymous. One of the authors is, however, known by name—John of Jenštein, archbishop of Prague (1378-1396). The growing quantity of liturgical poetry in Bohemia in the second half of the fourteenth century can probably be explained by the influx of masters and students to Prague after the foundation of the University (1348).[4]

This Bohemian Latin poetry discloses, also, the extent to which Czech Christianity was westernized and to which Bohemia formed, from the religious aspect, an integral part of medieval western Europe. Czech liturgical poets were attracted by the same mysteries and doctrinal truths as their often more talented Western brothers. The veneration of Our Lady and the cult of Christ's human nature, His infancy, and His suffer-ing, elaborated by St. Bernard and deepened and propagated by St. Francis and his followers, were popular in Bohemia, as in the West, in the later Middle Ages.

An interesting illustration of this spiritual mentality is to be found in the remnants of the library which Cunigunda, daughter of Přemsyl II and abbess of St. George's convent in Prague (1302-1321), collected for herself and her sisters. Besides apocryphal gospels on Christ's infancy and passion, it contains the "Grain of the Passion," ascribed to St. Ber-nard, Pseudo-Anselm's discussion with Mary on Christ's passion, two "lamentations," several Latin writings exalting the virtues of Our Lady, St. Bonaventure's "Tree of Life," prayers of St. Anselm, the famous dia-logue "Synonyma" of St. Isidore of Seville, and the *Soliloquim* of Hugh of St. Victor. The office of Corpus Christi, with many prayers to be said before or after communion, is also preserved in Cunigunda's library, showing that the cult of the Blessed Sacrament, which was so strongly rooted in the West, had also spread in Bohemia.[5]

Cunigunda also inspired original Latin prose compositions in the same spirit. They are preserved in the so-called "Passional of Cunigunda," famous among specialists of medieval art for the splendid illuminations which are the work of Beneš, the canon of St. George. Two of these writings, "The Parable on a Valiant Knight with Mystical Explanation" and "A treatise on Heavenly Dwellings," were written in 1312 and 1314, respectively, by the Dominican Kolda. In the first work Kolda describes, in the spirit of chivalry, Christ's work of redemption on earth, depicting especially minutely the instruments of His passion and using the metaphor of a knight who went through many troubles in order to liberate his betrothed from the power of a seducer who had imprisoned her. The other work is inspired by Pseudo-Areopagite's description of heavenly hierarchies. It is quite possible that two "lamentations," one by Mary, the other by Magdelene, which are copied in the Passional were also written by Kolda.[6]

In this respect a contribution to this kind of literature by the Carthusian prior Albert (died 1397), a friend of Archbishop John of Jenštein, also deserves mention. Albert is the author of a number of Latin prayers, in rhyme, addressed to different saints. They are preserved in a collection of prayers called *Scala coeli* (Ladder to heaven) and contain offices and prayers which were in use in all countries of Central Europe at that time. Albert's prayers are rather meditations on the lives of saints, and his main source was the famous *Legenda Aurea* by James de Voragine. Many prayers contained in the *Scala coeli* can also be read in the collection of prayers called *Oracionale* of Ernest of Pardubice. The main ideas inspiring these prayers are, again, besides the cult of the saints, the cults of Our Lady, of the Passion of Christ, and of the Eucharist.

It seems that the collection containing Albert's prayers had a profound influence on spiritual life in Bohemia in the time of Charles IV. Very many of the prayers contained in the *Scala* were translated into Czech during the second part of the fourteenth century. Because these translations were meant for the simple people, to whom they were read in church, the translations are often not verbatim, many lyric moments being suppressed and didactic explanations added.

These translations were, however, not the first writings composed in Czech during this period. The first contributions to Czech literature are, of course, also of a religious nature.[7] One of the oldest examples of Czech religious lyric poetry is the so-called "Song of Ostrov" celebrating Christ's Incarnation in four strophes.[8] It was composed between the years 1260 and 1290. Two other very popular songs, "God the Almighty" and "Jesus Christ the Generous Prince," probably date from the later fourteenth century. The most beautiful and imaginative of these compositions is the Czech song inspired by St. Thomas Aquinas's eucharistic poem

Lauda Sion Salvatorem, in thirty-eight strophes. The poem is called "Cunigunda's Prayer" because it is copied in one of the manuscripts of Cunigunda's library. Next to this poem is the "Song on St. Dorothy," which describes in 133 verses the martyrdom of the saint and was very popular in medieval Central Europe. Other songs to Our Lady, a Christmas carol, and "Lamentations" also date from this period.

The following Czech compositions in verse date from the beginning of the fourteenth century: "The Legend of Our Lady," "On the Apostles," "On the Sending of the Holy Ghost," and "On Pilate and Judas." They are all based on the Gospels or apocryphal writings. The legends of St. George and of St. Alexius also deserve mention.

A real jewel of this type of composition is provided by the "Legend on St. Catherine," dating from the middle of the fourteenth century. The anonymous author describes in a very vivid manner the history of the popular saint, her conversion, her disputation with the pagan scholars—which enables him to display his scholastic versatility, and her martyrdom. It is quite an imposing epic poem in 3,519 verses.[9]

Such legends in verse also continued to be written during the second half of the fourteenth century. The authors concentrated their attention on native saints, for example St. Procopius, whose popularity had naturally been enhanced by his canonization in 1204, but also on saints whose cult had become popular in Bohemia. Their poetic value is generally equal to that of the earlier rhymed legends.

Czech prose writing also started before the middle of the fourteenth century. Like the first Czech lyric and epic compositions, the first prose writings were anonymous and of a hagiographic nature. This kind of literature was inaugurated by the Czech translations of three Latin works which best characterize the spirit dominating the mind of the Middle Ages. The first of these writings was the "Biographies of the Fathers of the Early Christian Period," which had originated in the thirteenth century and became very popular throughout the West, being translated into Czech in the fourteenth century. Even more important is the *Legenda Aurea,* a collection of lives of saints arranged according to their feasts in the Church calendar. It was composed about the year 1270 by James de Voragine, archbishop of Genoa. James' work is a synthesis of hagiographic achievements of the Middle Ages. His method appealed so well to medieval men that his work became most popular throughout the West and superseded all other works of this kind.

The *Legenda Aurea* must have penetrated into Bohemia soon after its composition because two of its manuscripts copied in Bohemia date from the end of the thirteenth century. The work became very popular and stimulated Czech poetic imitations, and some lives of Czech saints were soon being added to the Latin copies of Czech origin. The Czech translation of this work was called *Passionale*. It was made about the middle of the fourteenth century during the reign of Charles IV, whose Latin Life of St. Wenceslas was chosen by the translator for the feast of this saint. The translator of the *Legenda Aurea* did good work and showed some originality. Unfortunately, a critical edition of the Czech translation does not yet exist.

The third work was the *Meditationes vitae Christi,* wrongly ascribed to St. Bonaventura but in fact written toward the end of the thirteenth century by a Franciscan monk. The *Meditationes* also became very popular and were soon translated into Western vernacular tongues. The Czech version of this work is not a simple translation but rather an independent work inspired by the *Meditationes* and based on them. The author's quotations from the Gospel are important for the study of old Czech translations of the Pericopes, the Sunday readings of the Gospel. It is quite possible that the *Passionale* and the *Meditationes* are the work of the same author, perhaps the Dominican monk called James.[10] To these works should also be added the composition "Anselm," which depicts the Archbishop of Canterbury questioning Our Lady about Christ's passion. The Czech translation was particularly popular.

The epic poetry of the fourteenth century, although devoted mainly to religious themes, should be regarded as forming a transition to the secular verse and prose, which was soon to flourish. To the legends mentioned above should be added that of the "Ten Thousand Knights" of "St. Margaret," or "The Narrative of Christ's Boyhood." In this category there are also other poems with a biblical background, such as "The Life of Adam," "Joseph in Egypt," "The Testament of the Twelve Patriarchs," "Barlaam and Josaphat," "Solphernus," "Belial," and "Asenath."

Czech profane literature reflects, like the religious writings, the main currents in vogue in western Europe during the late Middle Ages. Czech epic poets are inspired by the heroes celebrated in French or German compositions, and the works which were popular in the West were also translated into Czech.

Alexander the Great's life attracted the attention of poets and writers of all medieval Europe. He is also the hero of the best Czech epic poem of this time, the *Alexandreis.* Its anonymous author took as his model the French epic on Alexander by Gautier de Chatillon. He follows his pattern quite closely but shows his originality by interweaving his narrative with his own reflections, which testify to his wide knowledge and wisdom. The language he uses is very rich, and the way in which he handles the verse forms indicates that he was a highly talented poet. He was also a good Czech patriot, allowing himself some satiric remarks on the Germans. The crusading idea must also have influenced him because he wishes that the Czechs might be given a king like Alexander who would bring to the Church all pagan and schismatic nations, enumerating specifically the Lithuanians, Tatars, Prussians, and Russians (sic!).[11]

Other epic poetry often took the form of Czech adaptions of French or German epic compositions. Such are, for example, "The Adventures of Tristram," "The Love of Tandaris for the Indian Girl Floribella," "The Gestes of Stilfrid and Bruncvik," and the tales of Siegfried, Kriemhilde, Attila, and Theodoric.

Two Latin handbooks used in medieval schools, the so-called *Distichs of Cato and Aesop's Fables,* were also translated into Czech verse. There were numerous satiric and moralizing poems, such as "The Explanation of the Ten Commandments" and "Satires on Trades." Among dramatic poems, the most popular was "The Dispute between the Soul and the Body." A number of poems were produced to commemorate current events, for example, the song on the betrayal of the Lord of Šternberk, which is rather a ballad. As in the West, dramatic poetry developed from representations of Christ's Passion and Resurrection. The play "The Quacksalver" is a burlesque addition to one of these dramatic compositions.

The best epic and didactic poems were composed by Smil Flaška of Pardubice and his school. His *New Council* has 2,116 verses. It is an interesting allegory of a parliament of animals giving advice to their king, the lion. It is rather a kind of manual for princes, or a mirror of the good prince. The author must have been familiar with this kind of literature in the West. French and English influence is visible in his composition. Other works of this author are "A Father's Admonition to his Son" and an interesting collection of old Czech proverbs.[12]

Prose works were also inspired by Western patterns. There is the Czech adaptation of the French *Roman de Troie* and the story of Alexander the Great, adapted from late Latin and Greek descriptions of Alexander's life. The cycle *Gesta Romanorum* and the *Romance of Apollonius, King of Tyre* were very popular productions. There was also a legal work written in Czech at the beginning of the fourteenth century, *The Book of the Old Lord of Rosenberg,* which enumerated the customs and the laws existing in Bohemia at that time. At the same period there was composed also, in Czech and in Latin, a collection called *Order of the Tribunal of the Land (Ordo judicii terrae),* a private handbook giving indications on customs and laws observed by the tribunal of the land.

Early Czech lyric poetry of a secular nature has only recently attracted the attention of Czech specialists. The careful analysis of this literary genre led to very interesting discoveries concerning its origins and its connection with the works of the troubadours of Provence and the German *Minnesänger*.[13]

The origins from which the early Czech secular lyric had grown to maturity were popular songs. Two of them, a *dance* "Farewell Little Heart" and a ballad "In Strachota's Grove," are still preserved and show the high standard reached by this early Czech poetry before the penetration of court poetry into Bohemia. The rich crop of folk songs is irretrievably lost, but some of the popular songs were later revised in the spirit of the court poetry. Enough documentary evidence is extant to trace the existence of such popular songs back to pagan times.

Czech production of lyric poetry must also have been rich, but only a minor part of it survives. The poems which have survived show that their authors were well acquainted with all the characteristic qualities of Western court poetry. Among the Czech poems are to be found songs, messages of love, a romance, a ballad, a fragment of a pastoral, and three *albas*. A more detailed examination of these poems has shown that the old Czech *albas* have all the typical qualities of the *aubades* composed by the troubadours during the earliest period of Provençal poetry, in the twelfth and thirteenth century. Bohemia had no direct contact with southern France in that period. How then did knowledge of the old Provençal court poetry reach Bohemia?

Everything seems to point to the Italian courts, whither troubadour poetry had penetrated from Provence. From Italy it was transplanted to the Rhineland, Bavaria, and Austria. The German *Minnesänger* brought this new poetic art to the court of Prague. In reality, there is some evidence to show that the manners of chivalry began to be cultivated at the court of Prague under Wenceslas I (1230-1253) and more so under Přemysl II (1253-1278). During his reign not only did the *Minnesänger* from Austria and Bavaria bring this new art to Bohemia, but also there was direct contact between Bohemia and Italy when the Alpine lands were under the suzerainty of the Czech king.

The most fervent propagator of this poetic art in Prague seems to have been the Italian refugee Henry of Isernia. He was not only an instructor in grammar and rhetoric, but also the author of erotic letters showing all the characteristics of Italian court and love poetry.[14] Under Wenceslas II (1283-1305) chivalrous poetry flourished at the court of Prague. The king himself allegedly composed three love songs in the tongue of the *Minnesänger*.

Czech compositions of this kind became more marked only at the beginning of the fourteenth century. Soon prominent Czech nobles established their own smaller courts, and thanks to these new centers, Czech lyric poetry developed very rapidly. It soon spread also to the lower social strata, especially in the new towns, and flourished particularly during the era of prosperity which characterized Charles IV's reign.

The secular lyrics which have been preserved are anonymous. The name of only one Czech composer has survived—Záviš. He is identified by some with the Master of Arts Záviš of Zap, who was still alive in 1421 as a canon of Olomouc, by others with an Augustinian monk of the same name, a friend of Archbishop Jenštein. In any event his literary activity should be dated from the end of the fourteenth century. Záviš was also a prominent composer of liturgical chants. He is the author of the most famous Old Czech love poem, called "Záviš' Song," for which he also composed a melody. His musical composition is particularly important for the history of Czech music. It shows that under the influence of French music the Czechs had started to emancipate themselves from German musical tradition and to form their own musical school.[15] The literary value of this poem is also very high. It can be compared without hesitation with the best products of the Western medieval lyric, and it is a valuable Czech contribution to this kind of medieval literature.[16]

This rapid efflorescence of Czech literary activity from the second half of the thirteenth century on and the wealth of expression of the Old Czech language [17] presuppose a longer evolution and contradict the opinion that in the twelfth and thirteenth centuries intellectual life in Bohemia was fully germanized.[18] The German *Minnesang* at the court of Přemysl II and Wenceslas II was the work of foreign poets, guests of the Czech kings, and it would be unwarranted to regard their influence as extending over the whole intellectual life of Bohemia. Even from this period numerous expressions of deep-seated Czech national consciousness survive, though there are insufficient indications to show whether in this respect the Czech nobility was following the example of the royal court. On the contrary, as has been seen, the Czech nobles to whom Přemysl II had entrusted the administration of the Alpine lands preferred their own language even in German surroundings. Thus, William Zajíc of Valdek, who played such a prominent role during John of Luxemburg's reign, was celebrated after his death (1319) in a Czech plaint as "friend of the Czech tongue."

Moreover, it seems that the memory of the Slavonic era of Czech Christianity had never completely disappeared from Bohemia. Its echoes survived in some legends of local saints, and its souvenir was again revived in 1204, when Přemysl II obtained the canonization of St. Procopius, founder of the Abbey of Sázava. The consciousness of national kinship between the Czechs and the Poles expressed in Henry of Isernia's manifesto [19] and the stressing of common ties between the Czechs and the Serbians in Charles IV's letter to Tsar Dušan [20] can be fully explained only when the Slavic substratum common to the history of both nations is borne in mind. Charles IV gave more definite expression to this when he asked the Pope to renew the Slavonic liturgy in Bohemia. The Pope gave him permission to found only one abbey of Roman rite but of Slavonic liturgy, that of Emmaus in Prague. It was stocked by monks from Croatia, where the Slavonic liturgy still existed beside the Latin, but monks of Czech origin soon joined their Croat brothers.

To this literary production in Czech verse should also be added the rhymed chronicle of Dalimil, which was composed at the beginning of the fourteenth century, the first chronicle to be written in Czech. Its author was an ardent Czech patriot who never missed an opportunity of venting his patriotic sentiments and his dislike for the Germans. The importance of this chronicle for the better understanding of Hussite nationalism will be discussed later.

Historical works which were destined for intellectual circles were, of course, still written in Latin. The excellent Chronicle of Peter of Zittau (Žitava), abbot of Zbraslav, called also *Chronicon aulae regiae*, covers the reigns of the last Přemyslides and of John of Luxemburg down to 1338. It is a very important historical source, written by a contemporary who was himself active in Bohemian political life.

The learned and patriotic Bishop of Prague, John of Dražice, provided the initiative for the composition of the *Chronicon Pragense*, a synthesis of all historical writings then known in Prague from the oldest chronicle, that of Canon Cosmas, down to the year 1283. This work is particularly important for the study of the thirteenth century. Its continuation was entrusted by the bishop to his chaplain Francis, called "Pragensis." His work is, however, disappointing since the only new information it contains relates to Bishop John, whose glorification the author had primarily in mind. Archbishop Ernest of Pardubice, dissatisfied with this second part of the *Chronicon Pragense*, entrusted Canon Beneš Krabice of Veitmíle with the revision and continuation of Francis' work.[21]

Charles IV [22] read Beneš' work and decided to complete the information given by contemporary historians with his own autobiography. It is the first attempt of this kind by a layman in the Middle Ages in the West. Charles probably wrote his autobiography about 1350, but he only went down to the year 1340.[23] An unknown continuer added to it the description of the six following years of Charles's history. Charles also wrote a Latin legend on St. Wenceslas.

Seeing Charles's interest in historical writings, Francis of Prague produced another edition of his chronicle continued down to 1352, which he presented to the emperor. His second edition is, however, not much better than the first. Charles desired to have the history of Bohemia described against the larger background of world history. For this purpose he selected an Italian friar minor, John Marignola from Florence, who had become famous for his travels in the Far East, where he had spent fifteen years as papal legate. Marignola went to Prague and accepted the task, but his composition proved a dismal failure, as can be judged from the only extant manuscript. A similar attempt made at Charles's invitation by Neplach, abbot of Opatovice, also proved a disappointment.

Anxious to have, at least, a good history of Bohemia, Charles initiated another chronicle, which is known as the Chronicle of Pulkava. Although this work contains some new information—it is important for the history of Brandenburg—it has many defects, but it became very popular and was soon translated into Czech. It only goes down to the year 1330. Beneš Krabice then compiled another edition of his chronicle, extending his narrative to 1374. It is a pity that Charles IV, who was so much interested in historical writing, could not find a historian of the quality of Peter of Zittau. For the later period there remain extant only a few remnants of annals which were made in monasteries for local purposes.

Martin of Opava (1239), a Czech Church historian often regarded as a Pole (Martinus Opaviensis, or M. Polonus), who composed an analytic handbook of world and Roman Church history which became very popular in the Middle Ages, also deserves mention here. His work was translated into Czech from a German adaptation at the end of the fourteenth century by Beneš of Hořovice. This "World Chronicle" was very popular in Bohemia.

An anonymous member of Charles IV's chancellery composed an interesting Latin treatise which is similar to the many "Mirrors of a Good Prince" which were popular in the Middle Ages. In it Charles IV gives instructions to his son Wenceslas IV on the avoidance of certain bad qualities by a good prince. Some allusions to Petrarch's, Cicero's, and Seneca's works—it is said that Charles IV used to carry their writings on his journeys—seem to indicate that some of these might really have been known and read in Prague in Charles's time. The whole work is inspired by humanistic ideas propagated by Petrarch.[24]

This indicates also that the early humanistic movement originating in Italy had reached Bohemia and was quite strong in Charles's reign. The first enthusiastic promoter of this movement in Bohemia was the Bishop of Prague, John IV of Dražice. He had taken part in the Council of Vienne (1311-1312), where he had met the precursors of the humanistic movement and of the Renaissance. Because he defended the rights of his clergy against the Franciscans, who, in Bohemia, were at that time mostly of German origin, they made accusations against him to the papal Curia, and he had to spend eleven years in Avignon before he was acquitted in 1329. The new ideas current in this important center of fourteenth century civilization, where Petrarch, the father of humanism, had reached his spiritual maturity, inspired him to promote humanist and religious studies at home. He introduced the Augustinians into Bohemia and settled them in Roudnice. This foundation was intended to become the focal point in Bohemia for the humanistic studies which the bishop had encountered in France.

Bishop John IV thus became a forerunner of the great cultural and spiritual activity in Bohemia which reached its zenith under Charles IV and Wenceslas IV. His successor, Ernest of Pardubice, the first archbishop of Prague, who had studied in Bologna and other important centers, continued to inspire this movement. The monasteries of the Augustinian canons, which began to multiply in Bohemia and Moravia, became centers of this early humanism. Classical studies acquired a new meaning and were intensified. Latin was spoken and written with elaborate elegance. The cult of beauty found its expression not only in the liturgy but also in the preparation of manuscripts, which were penned and illuminated with impeccable taste, and in other works of art. In the spiritual sphere the intimate relationship of God and man was placed upon a more individualistic basis.

Next to John of Dražice, John of Neumarkt (of Středa, de Novo Foro), the head of the imperial chancery, who died in 1364 as bishop of Olomouc, was a prominent representative of the early Bohemian humanists. Others were the bishops Albrecht of Sternberg and Peter Jelito. John of Neumarkt composed the imperial and royal letters of Charles IV in an elegant and elaborate style.[25] His library contained a great number of Latin classics and the works of Dante. His manuscripts were adorned with magnificent illuminations.[26] One of his disciples was John of Schuttwa (Štiboř), author of the dialogue composition, *"Der Ackermann aus Böhmen"* (*The Bohemian Ploughman*). This is estimated by some specialists as a remarkable example of the influence which the three great forerunners of the Renaissance—Dante, Petrarch, and Cola di Rienzo—had exercised in Europe. The work, written in prose, is regarded as the earliest and best product of German humanism although the author's intention was only to show that such works could be composed in German as well as in Latin. This German composition inspired an anonymous Czech intellectual to write a similar dialogue in Czech. The German author presents his ploughman as accusing death for taking away his wife. In the Czech work, which is particularly important, it is a weaver (*tkadleček*) who disputes with misfortune about the loss of his beloved, who had married another man. Although the Czech author had the German composition as his pattern, he showed an independent spirit and produced a work which is much longer than John of Schuttwa's, richer in expression, and quite original in its ideas and artistic value.

In spite of numerous classical reminiscences and quotations, with which the Czech work abounds even more than its German model, and of the influence which amorous literature exercised on the authors, both works are deeply imbued with the Christian spirit. Their authors also reveal a strong individualistic tendency. This tendency, this straining to find a more intimate association between God and the individual, characterizes the new devotion, called *devotio moderna,* which was cultivated in the fourteenth century in Bohemia and of which the Augustinian canonries and the Carthusian monasteries were the centers. Germans and Czechs were equally affected by this new wave of devotion. Among the Germans, the theologian Mathew of Cracow and the Augustinian Conrad Waldhauser were prominent.

The Czech *devotio moderna* was inaugurated by Milič of Kroměříž, who was also a disciple of John of Neumarkt, under whom he had worked as a notary in the imperial chancery. Adalbertus Ranconis (Vojtěch Raňků), a learned theologian who was rector of the University of Paris in 1355, stood very close to Milič. Later, under Wenceslas IV, Archbishop John of Jenštein became the chief exponent of the Czech *devotio moderna.* Other prominent representatives were Master Matthias of Janov, Thomas Štítný, and Milič' disciples, who formed a new center in the chapel of Bethlehem in Prague, established by their zealous lay supporters. There were other centers in southern Bohemia and in Moravia.

A trait common to all the representatives of the new devotion was a special veneration for the Eucharist. This is found in Mathew of Cracow's works and in those of the Dominican Henry of Bitterfeld, of Thomas Štítný, Milič, and Matthew of Janov.[27] It is known that this devotion to the Eucharist was a most characteristic sign of Western medieval piety. Many specialists wonder why this devotion did not lead the faithful in medieval western Europe to the practice of a more frequent communion. This final deduction was, in fact, made in Bohemia in the fourteenth century. Matthew of Janov was a particularly zealous advocate of daily communion by the laity. Milič also seems to have propagated this idea in his sermons and prayers for laymen.

Another characteristic trait of this movement was the popular appeal of pious works written in the vernacular. In this field, also, John of Neumarkt led the way with German translations of St. Augustine's *Soliloquia* and of a work by St. Jerome and with the composition of prayers for the laity. Milič' Czech prayers are also numerous. From this school also originated the German and Czech translations of the Bible. Among the Czechs, the most prominent in this respect was Thomas Štítný, a lay nobleman, who translated into Czech some religious works which he regarded as classical works, by SS. Augustine, Victor, Bernard, Bonaventura, and Thomas Aquinas. He also popularized scholastic lore in several original Czech compositions—"Of General Christian Matters," "Learned Entertainments," "Sermons for Sundays and Feast Days." He was attacked for this popularization by the masters of Prague University, but defended his initiative vigorously, a unique case in the Middle Ages.

This movement should be linked with that which started in the Netherlands at the end of the fourteenth century. It originated similarly in a sincere desire for Church reform and was stimulated by the spread of early humanism in Bohemia. It is interesting to note that Florentinus Radejwin, the founder of the "Brothers of Common Life," whose monasteries formed the core of the Dutch *devotio moderna,* had studied at the University of Prague, where he might have come into contact with some of the representatives of the Bohemian movement.[28]

The Czech movement also produced some ascetic works which helped to propagate the ideas of the Bohemian *devotio moderna* abroad. Foremost among them is the *Malogranatum,* a handbook of spiritual life, probably written in a Carthusian abbey near Prague. Petrus Clarificator, the provost of Roudnice, also deserves mention in this respect. John of Jenštein propagated some of his ideas in Rome, where he lived in exile after his difference of opinion with Charles's successor Wenceslas IV. Of course, these works cannot match the famous "Imitation of Christ" of Thomas a Kempis, the classical product of the Dutch *devotio moderna.* The troubles of the fifteenth century put an end to further development of this interesting Bohemian religious movement, which has hitherto received but scant attention from historians and students of religious trends.[29]

There were, of course, also some dangerous developments in the evolution of this movement. The sincere desire for Church reform, and the lamentable failure of the Papacy to realize this, had the effect of misleading some religious enthusiasts into indulging in radical criticism of a destructive kind. Some held the view that Antichrist had already established his reign on earth (Milič); others were suspected of heresy in their teachings on the Church (Matthew of Janov and his "Rules of the Old and New Testaments"); but on the whole, the movement remained firmly based on the orthodox Catholic doctrine.

Remarkable progress was also made in the arts in Bohemia, which was profoundly affected by Gothic influences in architecture and art. Gothic architecture penetrated into Bohemia with German colonists after the year 1230. In contrast to German developments, Bohemian Gothic architecture shows no traces of Romanesque survivals. The early Gothic style was accepted in an almost revolutionary way in all its purity. In southern Bohemia, Bavarian Gothic took root, and in the rest of the kingdom Saxon Gothic. One of the first Gothic edifices in Bohemia was the Franciscan monastery and church founded by the Princess Agnes. French influences in later Gothic architecture began to show themselves during the reign of John of Luxemburg. The Gothic style predominated in the new cities, and it was not long before church architecture began to present characteristic features, especially in the length and height of the nave.

The zenith of this architectural evolution was achieved during the reign of Charles IV. The cathedral of St. Guy (Vít) was begun on Charles's initiative by a French architect, Matthias of Arras; but the real pioneer of Bohemian artistic development was his successor, Peter Parler, from Swabia. It was he who developed some of the particular features of the Gothic style which he found in Bohemia, and in stressing unified space at the expense of the usual Gothic verticalism, Parler became the greatest architect of the fourteenth century and one of the creators of the late Gothic style. Not only do St. Guy's cathedral and the churches in Kolín and Kutná Hora testify to the masterly achievements of the school founded by him, but also the church of Karlov in Prague, noted for its remarkable arched ceiling, the Bridge Tower, and St. James's church in Brno. Parler's school exercised a profound influence in Central Europe and reached Vienna, Bavaria, Swabia, Strasbourg, Breslau, Cracow, and even Milan.

Peter Parler also inaugurated a new development in Gothic sculpture. Under his direction, Czech and German artists carved in Prague, especially in the triforium of the cathedral, some masterly portraits in stone which are remarkable for their realism, reproducing every detail of the individual portrayed. Under this new artistic inspiration many Gothic Madonnas were sculptured in Bohemia. The realistic presentation of Our Lady and the Child recalls Parler's influence, but the richness of the draperies and the delicacy of the execution are almost an anticipation of the Renaissance. The Bohemian Madonnas are among the outstanding creations of European sculpture of this period and exerted considerable influence in Germany and in Austria.

The greatest achievements were in painting. Czech Gothic painting started rather late. French influence is visible in the illuminations made around 1320, e.g., the "Passional of Cunigunda." Italian influences enriched these traditions, and soon Czech painters and illuminators achieved such a degree of perfection that their works should be regarded as the best products of this kind in fourteenth century Europe. The greatest master of this Gothic and Italian technique was the anonymous artist who created the cycle of the Passion which is preserved in the monastery of Vyšší Brod. His disciples worked not only in Bohemia but also in Austria. They and other Czech artists painted a number of Madonnas which show considerable originality, providing a sort of transformation of Byzantine-Italian icons. The painter Theodorich produced some remarkably realistic portraits.[30]

The most celebrated illuminator was the master who decorated the breviary of Bishop John of Neumarkt (Středa). He shows great originality, and his work is up to the highest standard of illumination produced in medieval Europe. Fresco painting also reached its peak at the beginning of the second half of the fourteenth century. Artists of great skill, especially the royal painter Theodorich, worked in the castle of Karlův Týn (Karlstein), founded by Charles IV for the custody of the imperial insignia, in the church of Emmaus, and elsewhere.

The greatest painter of this period was the anonymous master who decorated the panels of the altar of the Augustinian church in Třeboň. He still worked in the Gothic tradition but used a new technique, which excelled particularly in individualizing the persons represented. His influence was remarkable, not only in Bohemia in his time and in the fifteenth century, but also in Austria, Franconia, Silesia, and Poland. These traditions were continued in Bohemia under Wenceslas IV, who was himself a great bibliophile. Laurin of Klatov became particularly famous for his illumination of a missal, called of Hasenburg, finished in 1409, in the reign of Wenceslas.

Gothic art penetrated early, also, into the north of Hungary, into the present-day Slovakia. The main propagators of this style were the German colonists, who were attracted by the silver and gold mines opened in this area. The Gothic style prevailed in Slovakia until the first half of the sixteenth century. The influence of the Bohemian school of Peter Parler is evident in Bratislava in the funeral chapel in the church of the Franciscans, constructed in the closing years of the fourteenth century. The Augustinian church in Nové Mesto is an imitation of the Karlov church in Prague.

Influences of the Parler school, coming, however, probably from Vienna, can be discovered also in the most monumental construction in Slovakia, the cathedral of Košice. New features, introduced by the Parler school, can be traced also in other Gothic churches in Slovakia.

The best of all the native architects was the master Stephen in the second half of the fifteenth century, the builder of the cathedral of Košice and of other monuments. Many castles and town houses were also rebuilt in the Gothic style.

Very few examples of stone sculpture have survived in Slovakia. The best are the works of Stephen's school in Košice. More plastic art works have survived in wood, mostly altars. In this respect, the most productive period was the second half of the fifteenth century, the center being again in Košice, where a German master worked whose school produced some remarkable works. The influence of the Polish school, formed around the German master Veit Stoss (Stwosz) in Cracow, can be traced in Bardejov and in Levoča, where his disciple Paul worked.

In painting, the Italian influence is visible, introduced by the masters called in by the members of the Anjou dynasty. After 1400 Czech influence can be traced in certain illuminations. In addition to Czech influences, Silesian and Austrian influences are evident in painting produced in northern Hungary. Some are monumental masterpieces, the richest being the altar of Košice with forty-eight panels. In the rich mining cities, some remarkable altar paintings were produced by prominent masters.[31]

Culturally, Poland also made great progress from the eleventh century onward, especially after the definite re-establishment of the national kingdom in the fourteenth century. Geographical conditions, in the way of its great distance from the cultured West, and political division precluded Polish cultural achievements up to the beginning of the sixteenth century from being as spectacular as those of the Czechs. Again, the clergy led this advance in Poland although the education of native priests to succeed foreign missionaries was slow and progress in Christian practice rather laborious after the first outburst of enthusiasm during the reign of Bolesław the Great.

This slow progress of Western ideas in Poland is illustrated by the fact that the Church reforms of Gregory VII were only accepted in Poland in the early thirteenth century, much later than in Bohemia.

From the earliest times the Poles entertained vivid cultural relations with the West, especially with France. Even their first historian is believed to have been a Frenchman or a Walloon, an anonymous priest called Gallus.[32] His Latin chronicle, written in Poland between 1110 and 1135, is the most important source for early Polish history. His work was continued by a bishop of Cracow, Vincent Kadłubek. The work of the latter, although often tendentious and founded on legend, was particularly popular. He was educated in Paris and died in 1223 as a Cistercian, two details which illustrate the general situation among the more educated clergy in Poland at that period. Other chroniclers were Bogufal, bishop of Poznań; Martin called the Pole, although he seems to have been a Czech living in Silesia; and John of Czarnków (died 1389). The latter was a contemporary of Casimir III, but, unfortunately, he has little to say about the great king's reign, being more interested in that of Louis of Hungary, whom he disliked. In 1347 Little Poland also obtained its first legal statute voted by the diet of Wiślica.[33]

New religious orders introduced into Poland, the Premonstratensians, Cistercians, Franciscans, and Dominicans, became in Poland, as in Bohemia, new and important links with the cultured West. Interest in Christian missions was increasing in pagan Prussia and in Lithuania. A Polish Franciscan, Benedict, accompanied Plano Carpini on his mission to Mongolia (1245-1247). He wrote a description of their journey to the court of the khan Batu, adding some interesting details to Carpini's account.

As in Bohemia, religious writings in Latin testified to the definitive integration of Poland into the framework of Western, Latin culture. There are some antiphons in verse in honor of SS. Gregory and Adalbert, a verse psalmody, a history of St. Adalbert, songs on St. Stanislas, epitaphs, hymns, prayers, and sermons. The number of such compositions is far from remarkable, and they cannot be compared with similar productions in Bohemia in the thirteenth and fourteenth centuries.

Profane Latin writings in verse are more numerous. There are short compositions commemorating Polish military encounters with their enemies or deaths of ecclesiastics, saints, and princes; some short epic songs, some of them already preserved in Gallus' chronicle; epigrams; and inscriptions. Among didactic poems Cato's distichs should be mentioned. Again, such poetic productions are more numerous in the fifteenth century.[34]

The foundation of the University of Prague contributed considerably to the spread of Western culture in Poland, for many Polish youths obtained their education there. The foundation of a university, or rather a law school—but it had also two chairs for medicine and one for liberal arts—in Cracow in 1364, with three chairs for canon and five for Roman law, gave a fresh impetus to the progress of learning in Poland. Casimir modeled his foundation not on Paris, but rather on Bologna and Padua, a circumstance which testifies to closer relations between Poland and Italy. However, despite a promising start, the high school had a short life, but it was reconstituted in 1400. This foundation brought the Poles into greater prominence in contemporary Europe.

The Church has been seen to exercise a considerable influence on the Polish nation from the beginning of its history, and churchmen were mostly responsible for the resuscitation of the Polish kingdom. One of the consequences of this situation was that Polish cultural life became more latinized than that of any other European nation. This does not mean, however, that cultural progress was fostered only by the clergy. Knowledge of Latin was more widespread than elsewhere, and intellectuals used this language as the vehicle of their ideas. As a consequence, national literature developed much later in Poland than in Bohemia, and the formation of a Polish literary language was very slow. Only recently has it been acknowledged how profound were Czech influences on the development of the Polish literary language and on Polish national literature.[35] Some Bohemianisms seem to have survived in the oldest Polish religious song *Bogurodzica dziewica* in honor of Our Lady. Bohemianisms can be detected even in some Latin works written in Poland, which contain explanations in Polish, and in chronicles and documents.[36] The near kinship of the two Slavic languages was fully felt by the Poles.

Among the earliest examples of old Polish writings are translations of religious works from the Latin. Typical examples of this kind are the "Sermons of the Holy Cross (Sw. Krzyż) and of Gniezno." [37] The Psalter of St. Florian originated in the monastery called *Mons Mariae* in Kladsko (Glatz), founded by the Archbishop of Prague, Ernest of Pardubice, about 1350. It is written in three languages, Latin, Polish, and German.[38] The Polish translation was evidently made with the help of a Czech Psalter, as is shown by its numerous Bohemianisms. It might have been written for the Maiden-King Jadwiga. Translations of some prayers and prayer books also date from the same period, for example, that of Wenceslas (*Modlitwy Waclawa*). Some short forms of oath in Polish from the end of the fourteenth century onward are also preserved.

Czech works must have circulated in Poland and were copied there, as many Polonisms in the Czech manuscripts show, for example, a copy of Czech prayers in verse and prose, a manuscript of Cracow University, or the song on St. Dorothy. The Polish legend of St. Alexius kept, at least, the epic form of Czech legends.

The Polish religious lyric also appeared only at the end of the fourteenth century and found its model in Czech religious songs. At least six Polish songs celebrating Christ's Resurrection are known which have been translated from the Czech. Two Czech carols were also adapted in Polish, and also a song on the Holy Ghost. Three other songs from the Czech Marian cycle were adapted to the Polish, as was also the invocation of St. Dorothy.[39]

The profane lyric only began to be cultivated in Poland from the fifteenth century on, and there again, Czech influence is marked. Czech linguistic and literary influences penetrated into Poland mainly through Silesia, where Czech elements were most numerous in all respects. Already in the thirteenth century notices in Czech are found in official documents. Because of its relations with Bohemia, Silesia was the most cultured Polish region during the thirteenth and fourteenth century.

In the fine arts also, Poland only reached the highest level of her achievement in the sixteenth century. Previously she was content to follow the evolution of art in western Europe, accepting patterns and incentives from her neighbors, Germany and Bohemia, but also from France and Italy. The style of church architecture—rotundas with apses —developed in Bohemia during the Přemyslide period found its way into Poland, and especially to Cracow. The religious orders brought with them to Poland the artistic traditions, both Romanesque and Gothic, which they had known in their homelands. The architecture imported by the Cistercians developed in Poland during the thirteenth century. This combination of Romanesque elements with ogival arches was also adopted for the construction of Franciscan and Dominican churches. The most interesting examples of this architecture are the abbeys of Sulejów, Wachock, and Mogila and the Dominican church in Sandomierz, which also reveals some Lombard elements in architecture and decoration.

The Gothic style spread over Poland during the fourteenth and fifteenth centuries. In the South, especially in the region of Cracow, French Gothic predominated. German Gothic penetrated into the West and North of Poland. In general, German colonists contributed considerably to the development of Gothic art in the cities which they founded. The Teutonic Knights, whose grand masters were often great builders, adopted that special style of Gothic architecture which had developed in northeastern Germany in the rich cities of the Hanseatic League. Some of the prominent buildings which the Knights constructed, such as the church of Our Lady in Danzig (1345-1503) and the palace of the grand masters at Marienburg (1276-1335), a most imposing structure in brick, had a great influence upon building in northeastern Poland. Czech Gothic art, represented by the disciples of Peter Parler, also found its way into Poland. But the late Gothic style only flourished in Poland in the fifteenth century.

The most ancient sculptural monuments in Poland are the decorations of Romanesque churches, especially the bronze gate of the cathedral in Gniezno (1129-1137) and the door of that of Plock. Gothic sculptured monuments date from the fourteenth and fifteenth centuries. The most prominent are those of the princes of the Piast dynasty, which are preserved in Wrocław (Breslau), Opole, Kresoborz, Lubusz, and Cracow. From the middle of the fourteenth century on, wood carving developed considerably in Poland. Some good specimens of carved wooden altar decorations are still extant.

Among the best specimens of pictorial art are the miniatures and designs in the codex containing the life of St. Hedwig, which are the work of Nicholas Pruzia (1353). The Bohemian art of illumination, which was a blend of French and Italian traditions with Czech original contributions, only reached Poland in the fifteenth century.

As already shown, the Slovaks, although sharing the cultural evolution of Hungary, were influenced by incentives coming from Czech and Polish lands. The lands of the Slovenes, under German princes, were in the sphere of German culture and had to wait until the sixteenth century for the formation of the Slovene literary language and first Slovene literary works.

The cultural life of the Bulgarians and Serbians developed in a quite different manner. Both peoples were able to build on the basis of their Byzantine inheritance. In Bulgaria, during the Second Empire, literature continued to develop along the same lines that it did during the reigns of Symeon the Great and Samuel.[40] There was a considerable reproduction of the old literary works, as is shown by the great number of manuscripts, mostly emanating from Macedonia, of works originally produced in the eleventh, twelfth, and thirteenth centuries. Numerous *sborniks* (anthologies) are mostly miscellanies containing theological, apocryphal, and legendary lore, a sure sign that the literary products of earlier years retained their popularity.

For the history of Bogomilism, great importance attaches to the *Synodik* of Tsar Boril,[41] published in 1211, containing the records of the council which he convoked in Trnovo to combat this heresy. Among original works are legends concerning some new national saints, especially those of St. John of Rila and Tsar Peter. Legends concerning Russian and Serbian saints also appear in Bulgarian collections of lives of the saints. In 1371, the Serbian monk, Isaiah, translated the works of Dionysius the Pseudo-Areopagite and thus brought to his countrymen's attention the Neoplatonic philosophy which inspired this work. The translation was also intended for the Bulgarians.

Other Greek mystic writers also found translators into Bulgarian, namely, Symeon Neos Theologos, Nicetas Stethatos, Gregory Sinaites, and others. Two theological works were also translated, the *Hexameron* of Severianos of Gabala and the *Panoplia* of Euthymius Zigabenus, which was one of the principal theological books of the Byzantines.

The works of Greek mystics were widely read in old and new translations and in the original. The Greek mystical movement of the Hesychastes found numerous adherents in Bulgaria. One of them was the most prominent reformer of the period, Theodosius of Trnovo, who lived during the reign of Tsar John Alexander (1331-1371), a great lover of learning and scholarship. Theodosius' disciple, the monk Dionysius, was a celebrated translator of John Chrysostom's works. Another disciple, Euthymius, who was elected patriarch in 1375, founded a literary school of Bulgarian, Serbian, and Russian writers. His works, mostly biographies of national saints and letters to prominent ecclesiastical dignitaries, constitute an important source for the history of the fourteenth century.

He also attempted a revision of Old Slavonic biblical and liturgical texts.

Joasaph, the metropolitan of Bdyn and most probably one of Euthymius' disciples, composed a life of St. Philothea of Trnovo. Two other disciples of Euthymius—Cyprian, who died in 1406 as metropolitan of Kiev, and Gregory Camblak of Trnovo—became founders of literary activity in Russia. The latter composed, among other works, twenty-four homilies and a panegyric on Euthymius and Cyprian. His biography of the Serbian king, Stephen Uroš II, deserves to be mentioned. The biography of St. Romil attributed to him was actually written by a hermit named Gregory. A third Bulgarian scholar from this circle, Constantine the Philosopher, found refuge in Serbia after the collapse of Bulgaria and became a promoter of literary activity there.

Some original historical works must have been composed during this period since allusions may be found to their existence, but unfortunately none of them have been preserved to our day. All that is extant is a brief note on the foundation of the Bulgarian patriarchate and a *Spomenik*—a list enumerating the deceased tsars, together with the names of their wives, patriarchs, bishops, and prominent boyars. From the beginning of the thirteenth century there exists a *Synopsis of Peoples and Languages* giving details of different tongues and alphabets.

The only important remnant of old Bulgarian historiography, the catalogue of old Bulgarian *khagans*, was preserved in a voluminous historical compilation composed on the initiative of Tsar John Alexander, and is known in two versions. The first goes back to the year 963; the second to 1204. This *Chronograf*, or *Letopis*, is compiled from the works of Malalas and George the Monk, the legend of Alexander, and from some apocryphal writings. It became very popular in Russia.

Tsar John Alexander was also responsible for having the Greek chronicle of Constantine Manasses translated into Slavonic. This translation is very well done and contains numerous interpolations inserted by the translator, most of them taken from Byzantine sources. The work contains a version of the legend of Troy, which seems to have been translated from a Latin Western source and is written in the Bulgarian idiom of the fourteenth century.

Secular literature was enriched during this period by a translation of the romance *Stefanit and Ichnilat*, an extract from the Indian *Panchatantra*. The Persian rendering of this story, considerably modified, passed into all medieval European literatures. A Greek translation was made in the eleventh century, and it was rendered into Old Slavonic, most probably in Serbia, in the following century, whence it reached Bulgaria.

Bulgarian literary output during this period did not achieve the same reputation as the works produced in the Golden Age during the tenth century, but the literary activity of the Second Bulgarian Empire was, nevertheless, quite remarkable.

The intellectual evolution of medieval Serbia was naturally influenced by the Slavonic centers which existed in Bulgaria, for it was from these sources that the Serbians obtained their Slavonic liturgical books and the Holy Writ in Slavonic. These Slavonic books from Bulgaria were copied in Serbia and slightly adapted to the Serbian vernacular. The Serbians were as fond as the Bulgarians of apocryphal literature, and as a result of this, Serbian manuscripts are found to contain most of the apocryphas known in Bulgaria and Russia, namely, the *Narratives of Adam,* the *Book of Enoch,* the *Narratives of Abraham,* the legends concerning Solomon, the *Apocalypse of Baruch,* the *Gospel of St. Thomas,* the *Gospel of Nicodemus,* the *Gospel of St. James, Abgar's Epistles, Acts of the Apostles,* the *Questions of the Apostle Bartholomew,* and the *Questions of John the Theologian.* The apocryphas which seemed to have been most popular in Serbia were the *Descent of the Virgin into Hell,* the *Discussion of the Patriarch Methodius* on the end of the world, the *Paralipomena of Jeremiah,* and the *Vision of Isaiah.*

Romances which were popular in Bulgaria were also introduced into Serbia. In the Serbian *Aleksandrida,* however, the hero is transformed into a Christian knight. The story of Troy as preserved in the translation of Manasses made in Bulgaria [42] seems to have been translated from a Latin original in Bosnia or Dalmatia, and first in a Glagolitic text. The Serbians were familiar with the stories of Tristram and Buovo d'Autona and the letter of Prester John on a Christian kingdom in India. There is evidence that legends about Charlemagne had penetrated from the West into Dalmatia and Serbia, while there is also reason to claim that the Western legend of Arthur was known in medieval Serbia. This is another illustration of the way in which Eastern and Western elements were fused in Serbia. The Serbians also read the legends of *Barlaam and Josaphat* and the tales of *Stefanit and Ichnilat.* The story of *Solomon and Kitovras* seems to have reached Bulgaria from Serbia.

The Serbian version of the *Physiologus,* with its descriptions of real and fabulous animals, which was so popular in medieval Europe, is preserved in some manuscripts dating from the fifteenth century and is very different from the Greek and Syriac originals of the same work.

Original works in medieval Serbian literature are mostly biographies of Serbian rulers and archbishops. The first were the lives of Stephen Nemanja, or St. Symeon, written by his sons, King Stephen Prvovenčani and St. Sava.[43] These works are very attractive in their simple and fresh sincerity and illustrate very clearly how deeply Christian ideas had penetrated the minds of thirteenth century Serbians.

St. Sava also wrote two *Typiks*—statute books—for the monasteries of Studenica and Chilandari. Chilandari in fact became an important cultural center during the whole history of medieval Serbia. From Byzantine material St. Sava compiled a new Old Slavonic *Nomocanon* (called *Krmčija Knjiga*), which became the classical work of Slavonic Orthodox canonical writing.[44] The Greek canonical collection of Matthew Blastares was also translated into Serbian in the fourteenth century.[45]

Sava's disciple, the monk Domentijan, continued the tradition begun by his master and wrote two original works, biographies of St. Sava and St. Symeon. The first of these was revised in the fourteenth century by Theodosius. From the same period also dates a collection of *Carostavnik* (chronicle of the tsars), also called *Rodoslov* (genealogy), attributed to the Archbishop Danilo and containing biographies of the kings Radoslav, Vladislav, Uroš, Dragutin, Milutin, Stephen Uroš III, and Queen Helena and also of the Serbian archbishops.[46] Another life of Uroš III was written, as mentioned above, by Gregory Camblak of Bulgaria. The Bulgarian Constantine the Philosopher, who took refuge at the Serbian court, wrote a *Life of the Despot Stephen Lazarević* (1432), which is one of the best pieces of original composition in Old Serbian literature.[47]

There are in existence about thirty chronicles dating from different periods, the oldest from 1371-1390 and the most recent from 1526.[48] Their literary value is small, but they constitute historical sources which should not be neglected. The best of them are the *Chronicle of Peć*, which ends with the year 1391; that of Koporin, written by Deacon Damian in 1453, and that of Karlovci (Karlowitz), dating from 1503.

There also existed a number of popular books dealing with such subjects as the interpretation of dreams and remedies for use in sickness, which are of little literary value.

Two important Serbian juridical documents deserve special mention. The first, written in 1288 in a city of the coast of Croatia called Novi, bears the title *The Law of Vinodol* and is most valuable for the student of Croatian and Serbian history.[49] The other, *The Code of Stephen Dušan*, which has already been mentioned several times, is a faithful mirror of the high standard of civilization achieved by the Serbians during this most brilliant period of their history.[50]

After the occupation of Bulgaria and Serbia by the Turks, literary activity in both countries came to an abrupt end. In both countries, wandering minstrels with their national songs kept old traditions alive, and it is only in recent times that their repertoire has received the attention it deserves. Their popular songs formed a link with the old poetic traditions. They revived the interest of the masses in Serbian romances and kept the embers glowing of memories of the great days of the Serbian and Bulgarian nations.

Bulgarian art developed during the Second Empire under the influence of the Byzantine cultural renaissance. Bulgarian architecture of this period lacks the grandiose magnificence which characterized some of the edifices constructed especially by Symeon the Great. The oriental features which were a mark of many Bulgarian monuments of the period of the First Empire were later replaced by Byzantine features. The old basilican form is abandoned, and churches are built in the form of a cross inscribed in a square and surmounted by a dome. The churches are of smaller proportions, and stress is laid mainly upon decoration, both interior and exterior. As in Byzantium, besides different kinds of stone, red bricks were used and interspaced between the stones. The decorative effect of this technique is rather remarkable.

Trnovo was, of course, the main center of Bulgarian art during this period. The church of St. Demetrius (1186), that of the Forty Martyrs, dating from the first half of the thirteenth century, and that of St. Peter and St. Paul were the principal buildings constructed after the pattern mentioned above. The mosaic-like exterior decoration achieved by the new device was brought nearest to perfection in the church of St. John in Mesembria, dating from the fourteenth century.

The same kind of architecture was used in the building of the churches in Ochrida, which are claimed by both Bulgarian and Serbian art. There are four which deserve special mention—St. Clement's (built in 1295), St. John's (fourteenth century), Constantine and Helena (thirteenth and fourteenth centuries), and that of the monastery of St. Naum (fourteenth century).

Churches were also richly decorated with frescoes. It can be surmised that it was Byzantine artists, refugees in Bulgaria after Constantinople had been occupied by the Latins in 1204, who gave the necessary impetus to the remarkable activity in Bulgaria at this period. But Bulgarian artists also participated, and a Bulgarian school of painting was founded which flourished in the thirteenth and fourteenth centuries. The most beautiful frescoes, truly a gem of Bulgarian art, were those executed in 1259 in the small church of Boiana, near Sofia. Several motifs of the frescoes, as well as their execution, betray a Byzantine origin, but the Byzantine artist who worked upon them gave proof of a surprising originality, especially in the numerous representations of Christ. In their presentation of actual personalities they display a discreet realism. The pictures of Tsar Constantine and his wife and that of the founder are true portraits in spite of a certain ceremonial stiffness.

The painters of the fourteenth and fifteenth centuries give evidence of a predilection for motifs relating to Christian antiquity, which they tried to interpret in their own individualistic manner. During the fifteenth century, moreover, the influence of the Italian Renaissance on Bulgarian art was especially marked.

Miniature painting developed also under Byzantine influence and reached a very high level of quality in the fourteenth century. The miniatures of the splendid manuscript of the translation of the Chronicle of Manasses, written between 1356 and 1362 and now preserved in the Vatican, are particularly important. When the painter was depicting scenes from Bulgarian history which had been added by the translator, he had to abandon his Byzantine model and seek inspiration from his own individual talent. The other prominent work of this kind is a gospel, written for Tsar John Alexander in 1356 and now in the British Museum.

The monastery of Rila is in possession of some masterpieces of Bulgarian woodcarving. Icons were numerous, and some of the silver cases decorating them are remarkable, the best specimens being those of St. Clement's in Ochrida. Gold and silver jewelry which has been preserved often shows Bulgarian individual elements on a Byzantine base.

The evolution of art in medieval Serbia is again characterized by the mingling of Byzantine and Western influences. Monuments of art, mostly churches and monasteries, are particularly numerous. The Nemanjas made liberal use of their great economic resources, and almost every ruler had an ambition to build a church for his own burial.

Three different periods can be distinguished in the evolution of Serbian art, especially architecture. Under the kings of Dioclea and the first Nemanjas, the emphasis is upon Western patterns. On the Serbian coast in the first stage of Serbian history, that pre-Romanesque style of architecture dominated which is found in Croatia and is characteristic of the whole of the Adriatic seaboard. The bas-reliefs which adorn some of these structures have the same typical features that are found in the rest of Europe in the early medieval period. Besides a number of small vaulted churches of irregular plan, the Latin basilicas of St. Sergius and St. Bacchus on Bojana and that of the Archangel Michael near Cattaro deserve to be mentioned.

These old traditions, enriched by the new Romanesque style and by Byzantine influence, were followed by the architects who worked under the first Nemanjas. The church of Studenica, covered with marble slabs, was built in the old form of a domed basilica; the monastery of St. George near Novi Pazar and that of Morača are the best specimens of this type. But soon new Byzantine forms—churches in the form of a cross with one or more cupolas—and Byzantine technique—the use of stones and bricks of various colors—penetrated into Rascia. Serbian architects quickly mastered the innovations, and combining them with Western Romanesque and Gothic patterns, they created some remarkable structures. The church of Žiča, the church of Queen Helen in Gradac near Rascia, and that of Sopoćani (1272-1276) are typical examples of this mixture of styles which characterizes the architectural school of Rascia. The church of Dečani (1327-1335) is another jewel of this architecture, the most original and the most attractive, a real masterpiece of Serbian art.

In the following period, the Byzantine style predominated. The center of artistic activity was now Macedonia. The form of the cross is the basis, and more cupolas are added. The church of Chilandari monastery was rebuilt in this style. The most perfect specimens of this architecture are the churches of Staro Nagoričino (1312-1313) and of Gračanica in Serbia (about 1321), each with five cupolas and each showing again a remarkable originality on the part of the Serbian architects. The church of Lesnovo (1341) and that of Markov Manastir also deserve to be mentioned.

The third period of this architectural evolution coincides with the last years of Serbian independence. As the valley of the Morava was, at that time, the center of the Serbian state, the monuments of this Serbian national school are scattered throughout it. The artists of this school followed the patterns of the first Nemanjas—the basilica form and also the form of an elongated cross, which was typical of the Serbo-Byzantine school. Following the example of Mount Athos, they added two lateral apses to their structures. The most important monuments of this school are the church of Ravanica, built by the Knez Lazar himself, and the churches of Kruševac, Kalenić, Ljubostinja, and Manasija, the last two forming the most harmonious products of this school.

Another characteristic of Serbian art is the extensive use of decorative sculpture on the exterior of churches. Naturally, in the first period, Romanesque decorative motifs as used in Dalmatia and Italy preponderate. The richest plastic ornamentation, inspired by Western motifs, is to be seen in Dečani. The Serbo-Byzantine school, of course, adopted Byzantine ones, but there are also to be observed motifs and methods which were native to the Caucasus region. These are more frequently used by the artists of the school of Morava. Besides Byzantine influences, one can also notice a slight influence of Islamic art.

Great originality was displayed by Serbian artists in the frescoes with which they decorated the churches. Serbian paintings of the thirteenth century continued the Byzantine traditions already introduced into Serbia in the twelfth century (Nerezi); Mileševo and Sopoćani present the best examples and betray the strong influence exerted by early Byzantine art, which had found its clearest expression in splendid mosaics. This is made evident not only by the monumental nature of the pictures but also by the use of a yellow background instead of the customary blue, in imitation of the golden background of the mosaics. On the other hand, figures are presented in an original fashion and with very realistic endeavors to express emotion. In these traits, we can often discover parallels to Italian art of the first half of the thirteenth century. These compositions, indeed, make a profound impression by reason of their monumental and decorative character and by their fresh, clear colors.

In the fourteenth century, Serbian painting came under the influence of the Byzantine renaissance of the late thirteenth century (especially Nagoričino). The modeling of the figures became quite remarkable. The sharp gradation of light and shade and the adroit disposition of the figures, which look less monumental but are more numerous, produce a most impressive effect of life and movement. Another kind of painting, best represented in Markov Manastir, lays less emphasis on the modeling of the figures but excels in giving the impression of life and movement and proves to be very decorative. In the churches of the Morava valley, the style of Nagoričino and Gračanica prevails, with more stress on the ornamental side.

A beginning has only recently been made with the study of Serbian icons and miniatures. Italian influences are marked in the miniatures of the Gospel of Miroslav (end of the twelfth century), while the Gospel of Prizren betrays more originality, reflecting rather oriental influences. One of the best examples of this form of art is the Psalter of Munich (end of the fourteenth century). Serbian miniatures are, in general, less finely designed, but they show more life and are realistic. They include a large number of portraits of Serbian kings and nobles. The realism displayed in their execution is surprising, and they certainly equal in quality Byzantine portraits of the same period.

It is greatly to be deplored that such a rich and promising artistic tradition should have been so suddenly interrupted by the catastrophe which befell Serbia in the fifteenth century. Under Turkish domination, these traditions were kept alive as far as possible, but progress was halted.[51] Only those Serbian émigrés who found refuge in Hungary were able to continue their creative work, and several churches and monasteries which were built there in the seventeenth and eighteenth centuries are their memorials. Yet the last period even witnessed a kind of artistic renaissance, the centers of which were Novi Sad and Belgrade. It was a movement which formed a link uniting the modern Serbian artistic revival with the glorious past.

NOTES

1. Cf. F. Dvornik, *The Slavs*, pp. 147 ff., 225 ff.
2. *Ibid.*, pp. 325 ff.
3. *Ibid.*, pp. 312 ff.
4. The study of this kind of literature has hitherto been neglected by Czech literary historians. Most of the Latin poetry of Czech origin was published by G. M. Dreves, who had started his important collection of medieval hymns in 1886 with a volume entitled *Cantiones Bohemicae*. He found over three hundred compositions which can be regarded with certainty as of Bohemian origin. They are scattered in the forty-nine volumes of his *Analecta hymnica* (Leipzig, 1886-1906). The first Czech specialist who drew attention to this literature was Z. Nejedlý in his history of Czech chant in the pre-Hussite period (*Dějiny předhusitského zpěvu v Čechách* (Prague, 1904)). Cf. the reprint of the late J. Vilikovský's study "Latinská duchovní lyrika v Čechách" in his *Písemnictví českého středověku* (Prague, 1948).
5. For comparison with Western literature of this kind see A. Wilmart, *Auteurs spirituels et textes dévots au Moyen Age* (Paris, 1932).
6. Cf. J. Vilikovský, *op. cit.*, pp. 26-40 with bibliography in Czech.
7. On the oldest Czech religious hymns see R. Jakobson, *Nejstarší české písně duchovní* (Prague, 1929), pp. 37 ff.
8. Cf. F. Spina, "Über das alttschechische Ostrower Lied" *Archiv für slavische Philologie*, vol. 37 (1920), pp. 406 ff. In spite of Spina's doubts it seems more likely that the song is a Czech adaptation of an unknown Latin song. Indications on editions of medieval Czech literary productions and ample bibliographical notices will be found in J. Jakubec's history of Czech literature *Dějiny literatury české* (Prague, 1929), vol. I, pp. 56-314. The more recent work by J. Vlček, *Dějiny české literatury* (Prague, 1951), vol. I does not give bibliographical indications. Cf. also V. Flajšhans, *Písemnictví české slovem i obrazem* (Prague, 1901), pp. 28-141. Editions of many early Czech literary works with commentaries cited in this chapter have been published by the Polish Slavic philologist A. Brückner in his *Böhmische Studien, Abhandlungen und Texte* (see Bibl.). The recent work *Příspěvky k dějinám starší české literatury*, ed. by J. Hrabák (Prague, 1959), not available to me, contains eleven studies on Czech medieval literature.
9. The text with bibliographical notices in F. Spina, *Die altčechische Katharinenlegende der Stockholm—Brünner Handschrift* (Prague, 1913). New edition with Czech commentary by J. Vilikovský, *Legenda o svaté Kateřině* (Prague, 1946).
10. Cf. J. Vilikovský, *Písemmictví, op. cit.*, pp. 141-60.
11. The poem must have contained over eight thousand verses, of which only about a half are preserved.
12. Most of these compositions were published by H. Kunstmann (see Bibl.), with bibliographical indications.
13. The first collection of Czech lyric poetry was published by J. Fejfalík under the title *Altčechische Leiche, Lieder und Sprüche des XIV und XV. Jahrhunderts* (see Bibl.). A more recent edition by J. Vilikovský, *Staročeská lyrika* (Prague, 1940). A thorough study of this literary genre was made by V. Černý, *Staročeská milostná lyrika* (Prague, 1948). See the clear and sug-

gestive review of these works by O. Odložilík of Pennsylvania University in *Speculum,* 26 (1951), pp. 743-50.

14. V. Černý has shown (*op. cit.,* pp. 186-234) that, contrary to previous notions, the contacts which Guillaume de Machaut and Eustache Deschamp had with Prague could not have exercised any influence on the spread of new literary ideas from France to Bohemia.

15. Cf. Z. Nejedlý, *Dějiny, op. cit.,* pp. 126-36.

16. Another aspect of this literature, the songs of the vagrant students, was also known in Bohemia. The satiric "Song of the Gay Paupers" is composed in this spirit.

17. This is particularly illustrated by the Czech-Latin dictionary composed by Master Klaret and his collaborators about the year 1360. It contains about seven thousand words, some of them newly formed. Cf. V. Flajšhans, *Klaret a jeho družina* (2 vols., Prague, 1926, 1928). Two Latin-Czech dictionaries were also compiled at this period.

18. This tendentious opinion dominates especially the work of B. Bretholz, *Geschichte Böhmens und Mährens* (Liberec, 1921). The first volume of this work has a subtitle which reveals its tendency: *Das Vorwalten des Deutschtums bis 1419.* In his critique published in the Czech Historical Reviews (*Český Časopis Historický*), 27 (1921), pp. 247 ff., J. Pekař repudiated sharply this tendentious opinion. On the cultural role of Germans in Bohemia cf. K. Krofta (see Bibl.).

19. See above, Chapter II, p. 31.

20. See above, Chapter V, p. 113.

21. Beneš is regarded by many historians as of German origin. There is, however, no ground for this suspicion.

22. On Charles's role in the intellectual movement in Bohemia see the comprehensive study by S. H. Thomson "Learning at the Court of Charles IV," *Speculum,* 25 (1950), pp. 1-20.

23. In chapter II of his book *The Emperor Charles IV* (New York, 1935), B. Jarret gave an abridged translation of Charles's biography.

24. The "Mirror" was published by S. Steinherz (see Bibl.). The editor's surmise that the work was written by Charles IV himself is not warranted. In this connection it should also be mentioned that Charles IV was the author of the coronation ceremonial of Czech kings. The Latin original, modeled on the French coronation ceremonial, was already translated into Czech during the reign of Charles IV. Cf. above, Chapter IV, pp. 126, 147.

25. He composed a kind of diplomatic protocol called *Summa cancellariae Caroli IV,* which also contained forms of letters in German, and a *Summa cancellariae officii olomucensis.* The first was published by F. Tadra (Prague, 1895). See also his study "Cancellaria Iohannis Noviforensis," *AÖG,* 68 (1886), pp. 1-157. John's works have been published by J. Klapper and P. Piur in K. Burdach's *Vom Mittelalter zur Reformation,* vol. VI, 1, 2, 4, vol. VII (1931, 1932, 1935, 1937).

26. Another representative of this movement was the Augustinian Nicolas of Laun (Louny). See the recent study on him by J. Hemmerle, "Nikolaus von Laun" in *Studien zur Geschichte der Karls-Universität zu Prag.,* ed. by R. Schreiber (Freilassing-Salzburg, 1957), pp. 81-129.

27. Matthias' chief work is the Latin treatise *Regulae veteris et novi testamenti.* It was published by V. Kybal in five volumes (vol. I-IV in Innsbruck, 1908-1913, vol. V, ed. by O. Odložilík) (Prague, 1926). There is a Czech monograph on Matthias written by V. Kybal (*M. Matěj z Janova,* Prague, 1905).

28. The first two rectors of the important foundation of the "Brethren of the Common Life" in Zwolle, Gerard Skadde and Lubert Bernier van den Busch, had also studied in Prague. For details, see the study by E. Winter, "Die europäische Bedeutung des Frühhumanismus in Böhmen," in *Zeitschrift für Deutsche Geistesgeschichte*, vol. I (1935), pp. 232-42. On the Dutch *devotio moderna* see the book by A. Hyma, *The Christian Renaissance: A History of the "Devotio moderna"* (Grand Rapids, Mich., 1924).

29. The history of early humanism in Bohemia and that of the Bohemian *devotio moderna* deserve a special study. So far, only E. Winter (*Tausend Jahre Geisteskampf im Sudetenraum*, Prague, 1938, pp. 57-98, 118 ff.) has sketched the main features of this movement. Czech historians have concentrated their attention on John Hus and saw in the representatives of these movements only his forerunners. This view is quite incorrect. K. Burdach (*Vom Mittelalter zur Reformation*, Prague, 1912-1937) collected much valuable material for the study of early humanism in Bohemia, but a great deal still remains to be done before this interesting movement can be fully appreciated. The works of John of Jenštein, preserved in a Codex in the Vatican library (Vat. Lat. 1122), must first to be edited and studied. The sixth centenary of the foundation of the University of Prague, celebrated in 1948, should have been a stimulant for studies of this period, but, unfortunately, events in Bohemia both immediately before this year and subsequently did not favor such an undertaking. B. Červinka's study, *Příspěvky k životopisu Jana z Jenštejna* (Prague, 1936), gives important contributions to Jenštein's biography.

30. There is a monograph devoted to him written by A. Friedl, *Magister Theodoricus* (Prague, 1956). The same author has written a monograph on the illuminations of a codex, preserved in the Vatican library, produced by Czech artists; see *Kodex Jana z Jenštejna* (Prague, 1931). The standard work on medieval Czech art, *Dějepis výtvarného umění v Čechách*, vol. 1 (Prague, 1923-31), was edited by Z. Wirth with the collaboration of outstanding Czech art historians. It supersedes the work in Czech of J. Braniš (1892-93), devoted to the same period, and B. Grueber's book (see Bibl.). Cf. also the recent publication on Gothic mural painting in Czech lands *Gotická nástěnná malba* (Prague, 1958), in course of publication.

31. On the history of art in Slovakia see the work by V. Wagner, *Dejiny vytvarného umenia na Slovensku* (Trnava, 1930).

32. A Czech historian has recently put forward the hypothesis that the author of the first Polish chronicle might have been the Archbishop of Gneizno, James of Žnin, who was of Czech origin, a scion of the Czech dynasty of the Slavníks like St. Adalbert, bishop of Prague (F. M. Bartoš, "Nejstarší polský kronikář a jeho český původ," *Věstník* of the Czech Academy, 61 (1952), No. 1. Cf. the monograph by M. Plezia, *Kronika Galla* (Cracow, 1947).

33. It was translated for the first time into Polish in 1449. A second translation dates from 1460, a third from 1503. Cf. R. Hube, *Prawo polskie XIV wieku* (Warsaw, 1881), pp. 27-98.

34. See the account given by W. Bruchnalski "Poezya Polska średniowieczna" in *Encyklopedya Polska*, Dzieje literatury pięknej. (Warszawa, 1918), part I, pp. 54-90. Cf. A. Brückner, *Średniowieczna poezya lacińska* (Cracow, 1892), which deals mostly with Latin poetry from the fifteenth century on.

35. See for details the short study by R. Jakobson, "Polska literatura średniowieczna a Czesi," *Kultura* (Paris, 1953).

36. On the Polish glosses in Latin documents see J. Łoś, *Poczatki piśmiennictwa polskiego* (Lwów, 1922), pp. 3-98. The first phrase in Polish can be

read in the Latin foundation document of the monastery in Henryków (*Kniha Henrykowska*), written around the turn of the thirteenth to the fourteenth century.

37. See W. Nehring, *Kazania gnieźnienskie* (Cracow, 1897) and A Brückner, "Kazania Świętokrzyski," *Prace Filologiczne*, 2 (1888), pp. 697-740, separate edition (Warsaw, 1891). On the relations between the medieval Polish and Czech sermons cf. B. Vydra, *Polská středověká literatura kazatelská a její vztahy ke kazatelské literatuře české* (Prague, 1928) (unobtainable in U. S.). On medieval Polish sermons in general see A. Brückner, *Kazania średniowieczne*, Cracow Academy. *Rozprawy* of the Philol. Section, 24 (1895), 25 (1896).

38. See bibliographical data on the Psalter in Łoś, *op. cit.*, pp. 40 ff.

39. Blessed Ladyslaw of Gielniow (ca. 1470-1505) is said to have composed some Polish songs.

40. For details see F. Dvornik, *The Slavs*, pp. 177 ff.

41. The best edition is that in the *Bulgarski Stariny*, vol. VIII (Sofia, 1928). On this document cf. D. Obolensky: *The Bogomils*, pp. 234-49.

42. On the problems concerning this translation see A. Wesselofsky, *Die altslavische Erzählung vom Trojanischen Kriege* (see Bibl.).

43. On St Sava see the studies by Serbian scholars in *Svetosavski Zbornik* (Belgrade, Serbian Academy, 1939).

44. A new edition of Sava's works was made by V. Ćorović, *Spisi Sv. Save* in *Zbornik za istoriju, jezik i književnost,* published by the Serbian Academy (Belgrade, 1928).

45. Ed. by St. Novaković, *ibid.* (Belgrade, 1907).

46. Published by G. Daničić, *Životi kraljeva i arhiepiskopa srpskih* (Belgrade, 1866). The Serbian translation is by L. Mirković (Belgrade, 1935-38). On Croatian and Slovenian literature, see Chapter XVI.

47. Ed. by V. Jagić in the *Glasnik* of the Serbian Academy, 42 (1875).

48. Published by L. Stojanović in *Zbornik za istoriju, jezik i književnost,* Serbian Academy (Belgrade, 1927). See also V. Jagić, *Ein Beitrag* (see Bibl.).

49. Ed. by M. Kostrenović in *Rad* of the Yougoslav Academy, 227 (1923), see above pp. 139, 174.

50. See the edition by S. Novaković *Zakonik Stefana Dušana*, Belgrade, 1898. For details, see C. Jireček, *Das Gesetzbuch des Serbischen Caren Stephan Dušan* (see Bibl.). Most recent critical edition by N. Radojčić, *Zakonik Cara Stefana Dušana* (Beograd, 1960). Cf. above Chapter VI, pp. 144, 148, 149.

51. Only the Dalmatian cities, which were under Venetian supremacy, were able to participate to the fullest extent in the evolution of Italian art and architecture during the period from the fifteenth to the eighteenth century. The Dalmatian school of art of the fifteenth century produced some remarkable works. See, for bibliography and more details, D. Westphal: *Malo poznata slikarska djela XIV do XVIII stoljeca u Dalmaciji* (Lesser known Dalmatian paintings from the XIV to the XVIII Centuries) (Zagreb, 1937). Cf. also the studies by M. Abramić ("Sur quelques bas-reliefs byzantins en Dalmatie") and by L. Karaman ("Notes sur l'art byzantin et les Slaves catholiques de Dalmatie") published in *L'Art Byzantin chez les Slaves* (Paris, vol. V, part two, pp. 317-80.

Chapter VIII

THE CZECH REFORMATION

AND ITS AFTERMATH

Wenceslas IV's character—His first conflict with the archbishop—The higher nobility opposes Wenceslas—Growing unpopularity of Wenceslas' regime in Germany—Wenceslas' change in Church policy brings about his downfall in Germany—New political unrest in Bohemia—Growing decadence in Bohemian ecclesiastical life—The Czech reformist movement—John Hus's reformist activity—Wycliffe's teaching and its influence on the Czech reformists—Conflict between German and Czech masters over Wycliffe—New change in Wenceslas' ecclesiastical policy and its consequences on the organization of the university—John Hus and the abuses in the preaching of indulgences—His exile—King Sigismund, John Hus, and the Council of Constance—Hus's trial and tragic death. A fatal mistake—John Hus's teaching—Stormy echoes of Hus's death in Bohemia, growth of the "Utraquists"—The moderates and the radicals—New storm and Wenceslas' death—Czech opposition to Sigismund, John Žižka, leader of the opposition—Proclamation of the Four Articles—Hussite wars—The defeat of the radical wing and the acceptance of the Four Articles by the Council of Basel—Causes of the rise of radical movements in Bohemia—The Utraquists and Sigismund's successor. King George's conflict with the Papacy—A radical reformer, Peter Chelčický—Rise of the Bohemian Brethren

Charles IV's death was tragically premature. His eldest son, Wenceslas, was only seventeen years old when he succeeded his father. Charles had done all he could to secure the two crowns of Bohemia and of Germany to his beloved son, whom he had initiated into royal and imperial business from his early youth. Wenceslas was well educated and had inherited many good qualities from his father. He lacked, however, one thing, the serenity and firmness of character which his father had acquired from the bitter experiences of his youth. Wenceslas' youth had been excessively easy, with a loving father providing for everything. In the first years of his reign Wenceslas followed his father's example and, surrounded by his father's experienced councilors, displayed some of the good qualities of his father. But his predilection for hunting and amusements soon led him to neglect his royal duties, while he showed his sympathies for townsmen and the lower nobility by appointing men of low birth to high court dignities. This was resented by the higher nobility, which had occupied all high offices in the land and at court under Charles. Wenceslas' innovations testified to his progressive mind and opened a new chapter in the government of the realm, but they alienated from him the higher nobility, which was very powerful. Charles's great success had lain in winning these circles for collaboration with the crown.

In another respect also, Wenceslas abandoned his father's tradition. Good relations between Church and crown were soon disturbed by clashes between Wenceslas and Archbishop John of Jenštein. The new archbishop, a severe ascetic, did not always follow the example of his great and wise predecessors, Ernest of Pardubice and John Očko. He was determined to defend all the rights and privileges of the Church as he saw them and was supported in this unbending attitude by some of his advisers. On the other hand, Wenceslas' new councilors added fuel to the fire so that, despite short reconciliations, the feud between king and archbishop continued.

The tension reached its breaking point in 1393. Wenceslas intended to found a new bishopric and to endow it with the property of the Abbey of Kladruby. The archbishop, however, opposed the foundation, and on the death of the abbot, he appointed a successor without consulting the king, thus ruining his plan. This led to the imprisonment of the archbishop's advisers. John of Nepomuk, the archbishop's vicar general, was tortured and paid with his life for defending the archbishop's case. His body was then thrown into the Vltava river from Charles's bridge. John of Nepomuk was regarded as a martyr; he was canonized in 1729 and became a popular patron saint of Bohemia. The archbishop looked in vain for the support of Pope Boniface IX because the latter needed the king's help. Discouraged, the archbishop abdicated and spent the last years of his life in Rome.

It must be said that Wenceslas, although popular with the common people, failed to handle the internal situation with the delicacy and firmness required. Rumors spread in Prague that he was indulging too much in drink and was neglecting his duties through laziness. All this encouraged the nobility to take bold action. A confederation of the leading noble families of Bohemia, called "League of the Lords," was organized and led by Henry, lord of Rosenberg, and Wenceslas' own cousin Jošt (Jodocus, Jobst), margrave of Moravia.[1] The king's brother Sigismund played a double game, sympathizing with the league. Thus the peace and concord in the Luxemburg dynasty, which Charles had so warmly recommended to his kinsmen, was dangerously shaken. When Wenceslas refused the demand of the league to appoint only members of the higher nobility to state offices and to rule according to their advice, they took him prisoner and appointed the Margrave Jošt as *starosta* endowed with dictatorial powers.

This time Wenceslas was saved by his brother John, duke of Zhořelec (Görlitz) in Lusatia. John appeared in Prague and won the support of the townspeople. Further help came from Jošt's brother Procopius and from some German princes. The burghers of the royal towns also started to mobilize their forces. So the league was forced to free the king, but he was unable to win a victory over his powerful adversaries. The domestic war went on, and Wenceslas was compelled to ask Sigismund and even Jošt for mediation. The compromise concluded between the king and the league was very favorable to the lords. Henry of Rosenberg became burgrave, and Jošt practically reigned in Prague. Wenceslas fought back, however, as soon as he was able to do so, and he soon banished Jošt from Bohemia.

These events in Bohemia prevented Wenceslas from devoting more time to the situation in Germany. There the main difficulties which rendered a successful government impossible arose from the rivalry between the towns and the nobility. German towns were different from Italian city republics. German territorial lords were anxious to acquire complete sovereignty (*Landeshoheit*) for their lands, and disliked the free towns in the middle of them which tempted peasants to abandon the soil and to live under the protection of the burghers. Wenceslas needed money to pay the huge sums which Charles had promised the Electors for the election of his son. Fearing they might be pledged to the lords as security for this payment, the towns started to found leagues to defend their freedom. The king made some attempts to enforce a general peace (*Landfriede*), but when the Bavarian cities were defeated by the lords in 1388, the town leagues were all dissolved. However, the *Landfriede* concluded at the Reichstag in Cheb (Eger) (1389) assured them equal participation in the land courts with the nobles. The Reichstag of Eger was perhaps the most memorable event in Wenceslas' career as German king.

His enemies in Germany were, however, still numerous, and the lack of energy manifested by Wenceslas in ruling his homeland encouraged them to accuse him of neglecting his royal duties in Germany. Wenceslas hastened to Germany and at the Diet of Nürnberg (1398) tried in vain to disarm his enemies, who were already planning to elect Rupert, the Elector of the Palatinate, as a new king. Wenceslas' change in his ecclesiastical policy brought about the decision against him.

So far Wenceslas, following the advice of his late father, had been a faithful supporter of Pope Urban VI and his successor Boniface IX against the antipope Clement VII, who resided in Avignon. Wenceslas' fidelity to the Roman Pope had radical and far-reaching consequences for his international policy. He abandoned the alliance with France, which supported the Avignon pope, and made approaches to Richard II of England, whom he requested to accept Urban VI as the true pope. Richard not only agreed to this, but concluded a treaty which was to be sealed with his marriage to Wenceslas' sister Anne. The marriage took place in 1382, and Wenceslas was fortunate enough to receive from his brother-in-law a huge sum of money as a subsidy.

During his stay in Germany, after the Diet of Nürnberg, Wenceslas changed his policy and went to France in order to work for the healing of the scandalous schism in the Church. He was half won for an agreement with the French king, Charles VI, which would invite both popes to abdicate, after which a general council would elect a new pope whom both France and Germany would accept. This, of course, displeased Boniface in Rome, so that he sided with Wenceslas' enemies in Germany. With his consent the three ecclesiastical Electors then deposed Wenceslas, electing in his stead the Elector of the Palatinate, Rupert (1400). The most serious accusation launched against Wenceslas was that of having conferred the title of Duke of Milan on Gian Galeazzo de Visconti in return for a huge sum of money, an act which was interpreted as an attempt to dismember the Empire.[2]

But this was not the end of Wenceslas' troubles. Encouraged by his opponents in Germany, the Bohemian lords of the league had renewed the civil warfare in 1399. Although Wenceslas succeeded in detaching his cousin Jošt from the league by conferring Lusatia on him, he had to give in and appoint a council composed of the principal members of the league. However, Wenceslas was determined to fight back and trusted for assistance to his brother Sigismund of Hungary, whom he had freed from similar treatment by the Hungarian nobles. Wenceslas invited Sigismund to Prague, offering him co-regency in Bohemia and inviting him to accompany him on his Roman expedition since he had finally decided to seek coronation as emperor. Sigismund, however, deceived his brother most shamefully, imprisoned him, and appointed Bishop John of Litomyšl as regent of Bohemia (1402).

A revolt by royal towns and the king's adherents broke out. Sigismund was prevented from dealing with it by a revolt in Hungary. Before he could return to Bohemia, Wenceslas had succeeded in escaping from Vienna, where Sigismund had left him in the custody of his ally, the Austrian duke, and hastened to Prague. Sigismund's action had outraged even Wenceslas' enemies, and they decided to cease all hostilities against the king, who was at last able to resume full sovereignty over his lands.

In spite of the agreement of 1403 between the king and his former adversaries, the struggle for power in the state continued between the higher nobility and the lower Estates, who had always been faithful to the king. Wenceslas had shown a stubborn determination during the prolonged struggle. It must be said that he defended his supporters in all situations, repaying fidelity with fidelity. The higher nobility failed to win, but Wenceslas lost most of his personal prestige. The royal dignity was also considerably diminished when it became apparent that powerful men were able to imprison the king and, at least temporarily, to usurp the supreme power in the land.[3]

The struggles for supremacy which had brought so much unrest into the political life of Bohemia were complicated by different currents appearing, at the same time, in its religious life. Charles IV was not only a wise ruler who appreciated the importance of good relations between Church and state, but also a pious Christian mindful of his duty to support the Church materially. He added to the numerous ecclesiastical institutions already existing in the kingdom and was most generous in his endowments. He regarded this as good policy because Church lands were under the control of the crown. Charles's example was followed by his nobles, and soon the burghers also began to endow old and new ecclesiastical foundations. The same was happening, of course, in all European countries, but it seems that in Bohemia the Church was particularly rich at the beginning of the fifteenth century. This is illustrated by the unequal distribution of arable land and forests among the different classes.[4] One-sixth of the lands belonged to the crown, two-sixths were the property of the higher and lower nobility and of free peasants, but the rest was the property of bishops, chapters, town and country clergy, and religious communities.

In view of this situation, an ecclesiastical office was regarded as the safest and best living, and many noble families vied to secure for their sons, often only children, one or more higher ecclesiastical dignities. The fiscal policy introduced by Pope John XXII made this possible through financial arrangements of different kinds with the Curia. Many of the offices were also given to laymen for services rendered to the king, and often also to foreigners who did not even reside in the country.

All this led to a decline of morals among the clergy. Rich endowments fostered worldliness and luxury. Soon, however, there were insufficient benefices for the constantly growing number of priests. Many of them were hired as curates by rich prebendaries to perform priestly services which they themselves, not being ordained, could not perform. Many, however, unable to secure even such a modest post, wandered from one parish to another seeking work and were forced to accept occupations which degraded their priestly dignity. This unequal distribution of wealth in the Church created much bitterness among the more unfortunate lower clergy, who were also critical of the great sums of money which had to be sent to the Curia. This situation deteriorated rapidly during Wenceslas' reign because the king was less piously disposed than his father and did not provide the Church with new endowments.

The decline of the moral level of the clergy, living as they were in comfort, had already started under Charles IV. The emperor was well aware of the conditions of clerical life and gave his support to two enthusiastic reformers, the Austrian Konrad of Waldhauser and the Czech Milič of Kroměříž. Both found their most dangerous opponents in the Franciscans, who were mostly settled in the German cities and, jealous of the reformists' success among the faithful, disliked the criticism that they had abandoned the profession of poverty so dearly cherished by their founder. Milič held some exalted views about the imminent coming of the Antichrist because of the general corruption of morals, and so he was accused of heresy and died at Avignon (1374), where he went to defend his views.[5]

The disciples of Milič were particularly numerous, and in spite of persecutions by his enemies, they continued their reformist work in Bohemia. Archbishop Ernest of Pardubice and John Očko of Vlašim also tried to arrest the moral corruption of the clergy by organizing synods to which they invited reformist preachers. This was continued by Archbishop John of Jenštein. All other members of the Czech *devotio moderna* —Master Adalbert Ranconis (Vojtěch Raňků), a well known personality in Paris and Oxford; Master Matthew of Janov; the nobleman Thomas Štítný—were active in the reformist movement and propagated their ideas by preaching or writing. The activity of the reformists was eagerly followed by many devotees and found a particularly favorable echo among the burghers and the lower classes of the cities. The movement grew, especially when a rich merchant called Kříž founded a special chapel, called the Bethlehem, for reformist preaching in Czech. The call for reform became a mighty current permeating religious and public

life in the capital when a young priest, John Hus, of the younger generation of the reformists, was appointed preacher at the new center in
succession to his teacher, Stephen of Kolín.[6]

John Hus was born in Husinec in southern Bohemia in 1371. As he confessed, he also wanted to become a priest in order to enjoy a more comfortable life. He studied at the University of Prague, sharing the miseries
of poor students. He became a bachelor of arts in 1393 and in 1396 obtained the degree of master of arts. From 1398 he lectured at the faculty
of arts, and in 1400 he was ordained priest. In 1401 he became dean of
the faculty of philosophy; it is likely, though not sure, that in 1402 he
functioned as rector of the university for half a year, in accordance with
the custom of that time. At the same time he had started his career as
a preacher at the church of St. Michael in the Old Town. He was so successful that in 1402 he was appointed preacher at the new foundation of
Bethlehem. Probably, at that time Hus had experienced an inner change.
As he confessed many times, "the understanding of the Holy Writ had
opened his eyes," and thenceforward he took his priestly office very
seriously, devoting all his powers to the salvation of souls.[7]

He must have been a very talented orator because his success was outstanding. It was, however, not only his oratory which attracted the faithful to his sermons, but also his exemplary priestly life. Hus was wholly
devoted to his vocation, satisfied with his modest salary as a preacher, and
chaste, intent only on the spiritual progress of his hearers and the extirpation of the abuses which were "soiling the immaculate dress of the
Church."

Not only the burghers and the populace listened to his vehement criticism of the decline of morals, both generally and among the clergy in
particular, but the ecclesiastical authorities also seemed to favor his
activity. The new Archbishop Zbyněk of Hasenburg (Házmburk), who
was enthroned in 1403, approved his reformist zeal and urged him to
denounce to the ecclesiastical authorities, either orally or in writing, any
abuses in Church administration of which he should become aware. Hus
became a member of a commission appointed by the archbishop to examine the miracle of the bleeding wafers in Wilsnack, and on his advice
the archbishop declared the "miracle" to be false and forbade all pilgrimages to the place. Twice, in 1405 and in 1407, Hus was invited by
the archbishop to preach on Church reforms at synods of the clergy.
King Wenceslas also seemed to approve of his activity as a reformer,
probably under the influence of Queen Sophia, who appears to have been
one of Hus's admirers.[8]

Hus's activity also encountered, of course, severe opposition on the
part of rich prebendaries, who accused him of exaggerating the abuses

and degrading the priestly dignity in the eyes of the simple people. In spite of that, Hus would have ended his career as a zealous leader of the Czech *devotio moderna* if he had not fallen under the spell of another famous reformer, who in his criticism of Church disorders went on further to attack even Church doctrine—John Wycliffe.

Czech members of the faculty of philosophy were interested in the philosophical writings of the famous Englishman and preferred his realism, teaching that universals have a more "real" existence than things, to nominalism with its teaching that universals are mere names. This they accepted the more readily because nominalism was the official philosophy of the German professors at the university, who were always in the majority, dominating the three "nations" and thus enjoying a permanent position of majority against the single Czech "nation," which possessed only one vote. Hus also read Wycliffe's philosophical works, but he was more attracted by the Englishman's reformist ideas and by the boldness with which he attacked ecclesiastical abuses, aggravated by the outbreak of Western schism. In his sincere zeal for Church reform Wycliffe, however, went too far, demanding the absolute poverty of the Church, whose wealth should be taken over by the state. Exaggerating Augustine's ideas on predestination, he regarded the Church as an invisible society composed of souls predestined for salvation. Of course, such a society, whose head is only Christ, does not need the Papacy, which has been instituted by Antichrist. Wycliffe rejected all religious practices which gave occasion to the abuses which he criticized—veneration of saints and relics, celibacy, hierarchy, monachism—and declared the Bible to be the sole source of faith. Many of his ideas were later accepted by the reformers of the sixteenth century. Although his doctrines encountered strong opposition in England, he died peacefully in his parish of Lutterworth in 1384. Only after his death were the twenty-four articles, extracted from his writings, condemned by a London synod.

Wycliffe's works were made known in Bohemia about 1398 through the intermediary of Czech students at Oxford. Contact between England and Bohemia was, of course, very close, thanks to the marriage of Anne, the sister of Wenceslas IV, with Richard II, king of England.[9] Jerome of Prague, a younger friend of John Hus, seems to have imported into Bohemia Wycliffe's most daring theological treatises. They were eagerly read and studied by Czech professors. Among the most enthusiastic followers of Wycliffe's teaching in Bohemia were the masters Stanislas of Znojmo, Stephen of Páleč, and Jakoubek (Jacobellus) of Stříbro (Mies). Hus certainly made long verbal quotations from Wycliffe's writings in all his works, both Latin and Czech, but he was far from accepting all the

English reformer's ideas. For example, Wycliffe's doctrine of remanence, namely, that after the consecration of the wafer and wine the substance of both still remained in the Eucharist, was never accepted by Hus, although it was accepted by some of his more radical friends. Hus was more attracted by Wycliffe's zeal for reform in the Church and in the life of the priests and accepted only ideas which were congenial to him, although they could not, even in Hus's formulation, be construed to correspond to the teaching of the Church.[10]

The first attack against the propagation of Wycliffe's doctrines by Czech professors was made by the University of Prague in 1403 under the lead of the German members of the university. Since they dominated the three "nations," the university rejected, by three votes to one, the twenty-four articles from Wycliffe's works, which had already been condemned by the London synod, and added to them twenty-one more. A ban was laid on the teaching and propagation of those articles. Stanislas of Znojmo then published a treatise in defense, especially of Wycliffe's sacramental doctrine; but when he was accused by the University of Cracow, he decided to recant.

The accusations, however, did not cease and were also directed against the archbishop and the king, who were said to be slow in combating the heresy. For the first time also, Hus's name was mentioned, together with that of his friends. On the invitation of the Roman Pope, the archbishop, acting as chancellor of the university, convoked the assembly of the Czech "nation" and asked its members to condemn the forty-five articles censured in 1403. The resolution, accepted by the Czech "nation," watered down the condemnation, forbidding the teaching of the said articles only in any significance likely to give rise to scandal or heresy. Some other measures were taken, and Stanislas of Znojmo and Stephen of Páleč were asked to come to Rome. They were arrested on the way and only released after repeated interventions by the king, when they returned home. The archbishop also suspended some suspect preachers. Hus protested against this measure most violently and lost the archbishop's confidence.

The situation was soon aggravated by new international complications. In order to bring the scandalous schism to an end, most of the cardinals abandoned the rival popes—Gregory XII in Rome and Benedict XIII in in Avignon—and convoked a council at Pisa to elect a new pope. As already mentioned, the Roman Pope was a supporter of the German king Rupert and had even confirmed the deposition of Wenceslas IV by the Electors. In order to win the support of Wenceslas, the cardinals promised to recognize him as the legitimate king of Germany if he ceased obedience to the Roman Pope and accepted the pope whom the Council would elect. Wenceslas, who had never abandoned hope that he would triumph over Rupert, accepted the proposal eagerly. However, he encountered rigid opposition from the archbishop and the German masters of the university. In order to be able officially to proclaim the neutrality of his country in the strife of the two popes, Wenceslas needed at least a favorable declaration from the university, and this only the Czech "nation" was ready to grant. So, on the advice of Nicholas of Lobkovic, his chief councilor, Wenceslas decided to change the constitution of the university and, allegedly on the pattern of the statutes of the University of Paris, gave to the Czech "nation" three votes and to the other "nations" only one vote. This was proclaimed in the famous decree of Kutná Hora on January 18, 1409, which caused a great upheaval among the German masters and students. When the king had rejected all possible compromise and had simply confirmed a Czech rector and dean, the German masters and students quitted Prague. In all they numbered about one thousand, although it may have been as high as three to five thousand if servants and dependents are included. Some of them went to Leipzig, where a new university was founded by them. Others went to the universities of Heidelberg, Vienna, Cologne, and Erfurt, spreading everywhere the rumor that Bohemia was full of heretics.

The University of Prague thus lost its international character and ceased to be the center of learning in the Empire. Of course, the growing number of universities in Germany had pointed to such an outcome in the near future. In spite of the loss of its international character, the Prague university would have been able to maintain its relations with other centers of learning. But since its professors favored teachings elsewhere regarded as heretical, Charles's foundation became more and more narrowly national and isolated from the rest of the learned world.

Wenceslas obtained his vote from the university and recognized as Pope Alexander V, whom the Council of Pisa had elected. However, Alexander V did not find universal recognition, and for some time Christendom enjoyed the scandalous contest of three popes fighting for recognition. The Archbishop of Prague supported Wenceslas only when he had threatened to confiscate all the property of the reluctant clergy.

Hus and his friends, who had helped to bring about this situation, soon saw that their position had deteriorated considerably. New accusations were launched against Hus, who had now become the leader of the Wycliffites. He was elected the first rector of the university after the departure of the Germans and had the university and the Czech people behind him. The archbishop invited him to appear before the Czech inquisitor and denounced him to the Curia. The Pope ordered energetic measures to be taken to stop the spread of Wycliffe's teaching, and allowed preaching only in parish churches (1410). This measure, promulgated by the archbishop, was directed against Hus's preaching in the chapel of Bethlehem. Hus disregarded the archbishop's order and appealed from the archbishop's decision to the new Pope John XXIII.

The archbishop was, however, determined to break the party of Wycliffites, as Hus and his followers were called. Wycliffe's teaching was condemned once more, and about two hundred manuscripts containing the English reformer's writings on both philosophy and theology were publicly burned in the courtyard of the episcopal palace. This hasty act was sharply condemned by the university. In spite of the excitement which this incident had caused, Zbyněk excommunicated Hus and his followers for disobedience. Hus protested and appealed to John XXIII, the new Pope. He continued to preach and to teach at the university and was supported by the majority of the populace. The king and queen and some prominent burghers sent petitions to Rome in his favor, while Hus also sent his friends to Rome as his representatives.

The negotiations were fruitless. In March 1411 Hus's excommunication was confirmed, and his intercessors, the councilors, were threatened with a similar sentence. The king became irritated by the imputation that his lands harbored heresy. When the archbishop placed Prague under an interdict, against which the king was determined to use force, a new and sharper conflict was only avoided by the sudden death of Zbyněk on his way to Hungary to seek protection from King Sigismund.

There was still some hope that the conflict would find a peaceful solution because the new archbishop, the king's German physician Albík of Uničov, was more pacifically minded than his predecessor. Even in Rome the situation looked more hopeful for Hus, when a new incident ruined all hopes and brought the conflict to a climax. John XXIII excommunicated Ladislas, king of Naples, who had refused to recognize him and menaced the Pope with his military forces. The Pope declared a crusade against Naples, and indulgences were promised to all who should contribute, according to their means, to this enterprise.

The papal bulls were solemnly promulgated in Prague by a special legate. Hus immediately attacked the bulls and the manner in which the preachers were recommending the sale of the indulgences to the people for money. He introduced the question of indulgences before the forum of the university. There, however, he encountered staunch opponents in his former friends Stanislas of Znojmo and Stephen Páleč, who had abandoned the party of the Wycliffites, and in other masters of the theological faculty. Riots broke out which threatened to ruin the sales of indulgences. The king, who supported John XXIII, forbade opposition to the indulgence preachers, threatening with the death penalty anybody who interfered with their activities. Three youths who made a demonstration against the preacher were arrested and executed.

This was a hasty act which added fresh fuel to the fires. The populace rioted, and the bodies of the unfortunate young men were brought to Bethlehem chapel and buried by Hus, who proclaimed them to be holy martyrs. Excitement grew in Prague and throughout Bohemia, and the king tried in vain to bring about a reconciliation between Hus's friends and the party of the theologians. Thinking that time might help to heal the wounds, he advised Hus to leave Prague for some time. His opponents were also ordered to leave.

Hus's situation had, of course, deteriorated in Rome because of his opposition to the indulgences, although the Pope had meanwhile been reconciled with Ladislas of Naples and there was no need for a crusade. In the summer of 1412, Hus was excommunicated anew because of his failure to appear before the Curia. In order to avoid the reproach of utter disobedience, Hus appealed to Christ as the supreme judge, hoping that the king's and the archbishop's intervention would ease the sentence. This was, however, a vain hope. Hus had lost the king's support because of his undiplomatic attitude during the controversy over the indulgences. In order to avoid the laying of an interdict on Prague because of his stay there, he quitted the city for some time, leaving his friends to seek a reconciliation with the king and the appeasement of his opponents. The appeasement was not effected, and the angry king also ordered Hus's main opponents to leave Prague.

Hus retired to the castle of Kozí Hrádek in southern Bohemia, which belonged to one of his supporters, and later to the castle of Krakovec near Prague. There he devoted himself to writing his Czech and Latin works, including his major work *De ecclesia*, and to preaching to the peasantry. From time to time he also appeared in Prague and preached. The memory of his stay in southern Bohemia certainly helped to propagate the Hussite movement in that part of the country after his death.

A new phase began in Hus's affairs when King Sigismund won the consent of Pope John XXIII to the convocation of a general council at Constance. Sigismund acted in his new function as king of Germany. In 1410 the antiking Rupert died, and the German Electors duly divided their votes between two members of the Luxemburg family—Sigismund, king of Hungary, and his cousin Jošt. The latter died soon after, and Sigismund came to an understanding with his brother Wenceslas by which the latter resigned the dignity of King of Germany and reserved for himself that of Roman emperor, which he had, however, never obtained.

The council was expected not only to end the schism by deposing the two opponents of John XXIII, who had himself promised to resign, but also to end the controversy about Hus and the Wycliffite movement in Bohemia. Sigismund was ready to grant Hus a safe conduct to Constance and back, and the latter accepted the idea, hoping rather naively that he would be able to defend his teaching in public hearings in the presence of the conciliar fathers. He was accompanied by some trusted friends of the Czech nobility. The cordial reception which he received in German towns on his way, especially in Nürnberg, gave Hus the false impression that all would be well in Constance also, and there he made his first mistake. Instead of going to Speyer to meet Sigismund, he decided to send one of his noble friends to bring him the safe conduct promised by Sigismund, and himself to go straight to Constance. Had he appeared there in the company of Sigismund, he would have spared himself many troubles. On arriving at Constance and receiving a friendly reception from the populace, Hus made another mistake. Although still excommunicated, he continued to say Mass and to preach to circles of friends. At the instigation of his main accusers—John Železný (of Iron), bishop of Litomyšl; Michael de Causis; and Stephen Páleč—Hus was incarcerated in the Dominican monastery. With the help of his friends he was, however, able to write letters and to prepare his defense.

When Sigismund appeared on Christmas Eve 1414 in Constance and learned of Hus's imprisonment, he was furious; but the council, determined to show its superiority not only toward the Pope but also toward the Roman king, refused to release Hus, and Sigismund sacrificed him to the achievement of good understanding with the fathers. Hus's lot worsened when John XXIII, after his flight from Constance, disowned his resignation. Hus was placed under the surveillance of the bishop of Constance and imprisoned in chains in the cold dungeons of Gottlieben castle, where soon even John XXIII, captured on his flight, was interned.

In the meantime a special commission examined Hus's writings, pointing out dubious and erroneous views. First, Wycliffe's doctrines were again condemned, and then Hus was granted three hearings. He was not always tactful in his remarks and was disillusioned in his naive expectation that he would be allowed to expound his views and be convinced of errors only by quotations from Holy Writ. There was much confusion in the accusations launched against him, and he constantly protested that he was unjustly accused of errors. One of his theses, however, was sufficient—in the eyes of his adversaries—to condemn him as an exponent of views subversive of Church and society, namely, his view that no pope or bishop in mortal sin was true bishop or pope. When he applied the same principle to civil authority also, Sigismund, who heard him, replied calmly, "John Hus, everybody is a sinner." [11]

One cannot avoid the impression that the fathers of the council, then without a pope, were anxious to show their solicitude for the pure Catholic faith and needed the condemnation of some heretical doctrines. This might be the reason why the trial of Hus was speeded up so much.

In spite of that, however, there is much evidence to show that many fathers of the council would have preferred to obtain a recantation from Hus rather than to condemn him. Various forms of recantation were proposed to him, but he refused even the mildest one, prepared by the Cardinal of Ostia, declaring that he could not perjure himself by renouncing doctrines which he did not hold or denying truths in which he believed, and appealed to the judgment of Christ. Finally he was condemned as a heretic, and Sigismund, forgetful of his safe conduct, ordered him to be burned at the stake (July 6, 1415).[12]

It was a great mistake. Sigismund should have sent him back to Wenceslas, who would doubtless have found a milder solution. The petition of many Bohemian nobles to the council in favor of Hus should have shown Sigismund that he would incur strong opposition in that kingdom, which he hoped to inherit after the death of his childless brother.

It is difficult to make a final judgment on Hus. If he did err, he was induced into error through his sincere desire for Church reform. His zeal led him to overstep the mark. There was in him a mystical desire to suffer and to die for his convictions, and he gave expression to it several times in the years preceding his death. He seems to have been excessively proud of his own moral conduct, and the admiration and devotion of his faithful followers made him blind to the consequences to which some of his exaggerated views and teachings could lead. The most dangerous of Hus's views were his theses on the Church and on papal authority, as they were interpreted by his opponents. Among the thirty articles taken from Hus's writings and regarded as heretical, thirteen were concerned with the authority of the Pope.

In this respect Hus had only adapted some of Wycliffe's teachings on the Church as the community of the faithful predestined to salvation. In the early stages of his controversy with the antireformists, Hus interpreted this doctrine in a way which could be reconciled with official Catholic doctrine. As the supreme head of the Church on earth, however, he regarded not the Pope, whose predestination to salvation was unsure, but Christ. These ideas were mainly inspired by the sad situation in the Church, with two or three popes who were doing little for its reform and for that of the clergy. Hus's ideas represented, however, a very dangerous challenge to the Pope's authority and to his legislative power.

It is questionable how far Hus believed all the theses extracted from his works, often regardless of the context, in face of his frequent protests that he was being unjustly accused. Medieval theologians often went very far in expounding their views and in academic discussions.[13]

Hus is often regarded as a precursor of Luther. There are some points in his teaching which recall doctrines later expounded by the Protestants: the stress laid on the authority of the Bible, the preaching of the Word of God, the limitation of priestly authority, and others. These similarities are, however, only superficial. At bottom Hus was a medieval Catholic priest with all the marks of his time.[14] It was never his intention to found a new Church, and he always regarded himself as a faithful son of the Church. He wanted to die a devout Catholic and was most relieved and consoled at being allotted a confessor, who gave him an unconditional absolution for his sins. There are so many alleged aggravating circumstances in his conduct, so many questionable actions on the part of his adversaries, that it is best to leave the final judgment on John Hus to Christ, whom he had loved and to whom he had appealed.

The tragic death of John Hus at the stake aroused a wave of indignation in Bohemia. Peter of Mladeňovice, who described Hus's trial and tragic fate, had overheard Sigismund's exhortation to the leaders of the council not to let Hus return alive to Bohemia, and therefore the outburst of resentment turned especially against the perfidious king. The Czech Diet sent a strongly worded letter of protest to the council, in which it defended the memory of Hus "of pure morals and unsullied fame." A league was formed for the defense of free preaching and in defiance of the interdict which was reimposed on Prague. The university was recognized as the supreme tribunal in doctrinal matters in Bohemia. Altogether 452 noblemen, led by Čeněk of Wartenberg, signed the declaration of the league. The Catholic League, headed by Bishop John of Litomyšl, had little success.

The execution of Jerome of Prague, Hus's friend, in May 1416, after his condemnation by the council, added fuel to the fire of revolt which had started in Prague.[15] Moreover, the council summoned the members of the league to appear before its tribunal. The summons and the interdict were disregarded, and soon most of the churches in Prague were in the hands of Hussite priests. The most distinctive feature of the new religious body was the dispensation of Holy Communion to the laity in both kinds. This was not Hus's idea, nor is it yet clear how this idea had reached Bohemia, but it was Jakoubek (Jacobellus) of Stříbro, the radical follower of Hus who suggested the introduction of this practice to Hus. The latter was never enthusiastic about this innovation, and even when he finally agreed to it in a letter written from Constance, he regarded it only as useful for the increase of piety, but never as necessary for salvation, as some of his more radical followers taught. So it happened that Hus's followers were soon called by the Catholics Utraquists because they received Holy Communion in both kinds (*sub utraque specie*).[16]

The large number of Czech noblemen who had so frankly declared their pro-Hussite sentiments is noteworthy. It is clear that the appeal of Hus and his friends to secular authority for help in the reform of the Church had been readily answered in Bohemia. The Hussite reformers were not satisfied with the vague appeals for individual reform to which their predecessors had generally limited themselves. This is characteristic of the Hussite movement. Of course, social and economic causes contributed to this development. The lower nobility were often in difficulties because their small holdings were surrounded by the latifundia of rich ecclesiastical institutions and by the more extensive properties of the higher nobility and could not compete with their products. They therefore listened the more eagerly to the voices of the reformers, condemning Church property. They hoped thus to add some of the ecclesiastical lands to their poor holdings. This explains also why the Hussite armies found so many able warriors among the lesser nobility.

When all the heresies which were attributed to John Hus are considered, it is surprising how mild were the doctrinal "errors" which were openly taught by the Hussites after their leader's death. This is illustrated by the attempts on the part of the moderate Hussites and of Wenceslas to come to terms with the Church in 1415. The archbishop was willing, but the council reimposed the interdict on Prague, which he had lifted. Thereupon the rector of the university, John Cardinal, made further concessions to the archbishop with regard to his authority and to Church property, insisting only on utraquism, but the council was adamant and suspended the university. Only then, in 1417, was the program drafted by the Hussite League in 1415 put fully into practice, and it was decided that Hussitism should be established everywhere.

The conservatives were not alone in invoking the succession to Hus. There was also in Prague a core of radical reformists, whose preaching went much further than that of Hus. It centered around two Germans, Nicholas and Peter, who had been expelled from Dresden because of their heretical teaching. They were welcomed in Prague and began teaching at the "Black Rose." Their doctrine was not so much Wycliffite as Waldensian. In their radicalism they rejected purgatory, prayers for the dead, the worship of saints, capital punishment, and the possession of property, demanding the absolute poverty of the Church and the right to preach God's word to anybody, even to women. These were all teachings which were popular among the Waldensians.

The two Germans exercised a great influence on Hus's younger friend Jakoubek (Jacobellus) of Stříbro, who was also a great admirer of Matthew of Janov. He followed Nicholas and Peter in many respects, rejecting all unnecessary learning, preaching simplicity in Church decoration, and turning against the veneration of the saints, their statues, and relics, but with less radicalism than his German friends. Another radical was the priest John of Želiv, who exercised great influence on the populace of Prague. These radical ideas were also propagated in some parts of Bohemia and Moravia by wandering preachers and found especially ready acceptance in southern Bohemia, where there were still some remnants of the Waldensians who had been identified there in the thirteenth and fourteenth centuries. A new and important center of this radicalism arose at Ustí. It was called Tábor and soon became a refuge of radical Hussites.

This radicalism was not approved by the conservative wing of the Hussites or by the university. The radicals were several times admonished to restrain themselves. A kind of agreement between the conservatives and the radicals led by Jakoubek was reached at the synod held in Prague in September 1418. The religious principles of the Utraquists were laid down for the first time, in twenty-three articles. These paid due attention to Jakoubek's radical teaching but eliminated all Waldensian doctrines. The main Catholic principles were, however, proclaimed to be valid, but in such a manner that the radicals were not bound to introduce Catholic practices to which they objected.[17]

The Catholics were, in the meantime, encouraged by events in Constance. Sigismund had at last achieved his aims. A new Pope, Martin V, was elected and recognized by all Western Christianity. However, Church reform, the second end for which the council had been convoked, was not realized. Anxious to curtail the power of the council, which claimed to be superior to the Pope, Martin V dissolved it. However, he confirmed all conciliar decrees against Wycliffe and Hus and encouraged Sigismund to take drastic measures against the heretics in Bohemia.

This gave more courage to the Czech Catholics and provoked an incident which was to become fatal. Wenceslas, alarmed at the fact that his realm was regarded as heretical, issued a decree giving only three churches in Prague to the Utraquists. The latter held a mass meeting of protest; and when a procession of Utraquists with a demagogue priest John of Želiv, carrying a monstrance, passed the town hall of the New City, stones were thrown at it from the hall windows. The enraged populace invaded the hall and threw all the councilors from the window into the street, where they were massacred. When Wenceslas learned of this incident, he had a stroke and died (August 16, 1419).

It was a great misfortune for Bohemia that at one of the most critical points in its history it should have had such a weak king at its head. His councilors, chosen among favorites and upstarts, spoiled the position by their unfitness, while the moody character of the king made firm administration an impossibility. It is doubtful whether Wenceslas was aware of the seriousness of the situation, which had been deteriorating for so many years.

His heir Sigismund had some clear ideas, but he was thriftless and even more devoid of character than his brother. His ambition drove him to embark on many great projects, but he lacked the stability of character to realize them. At the time of Wenceslas' death, Sigismund's chances of winning over the Czechs were very scant. Perhaps if he had been able to enter Bohemia with a strong army soon after his brother's demise, he might have imposed his rule before the opposition could become organized. But at that moment he was trying to save something of Hungary's ambitions in the Balkans. There was no firm government in Prague during the regency of Queen Sophia and then of Čeněk of Wartenberg. Catholics and Hussites fought each other in the cities.

The Czech nobility did not at first question Sigismund's right to the succession, but they demanded from him the sanctioning of Utraquism, the abolition of simony, reform of the clergy and their exclusion from lay offices, the freedom of the university, and the honoring of Hus's and Jerome's memory, besides other conditions of a political nature. Sigismund gave evasive answers to the delegates of the Diet, and his former behavior made it clear that he was far from willing to subscribe to the demands of the Utraquists.

The opposition to Sigismund's rule in Bohemia came from the more radical elements of the Hussites, whose center was at Tábor. Fortunately for them, they found at the decisive hour a good statesman, Nicholas of Hus, and, even more important, an excellent general in the person of John Žižka of Trocnov.[18] The latter belonged to the lesser nobility of southern Bohemia. He held a post at the queen's court and was very religious and a great admirer of John Hus. After having received from the university a positive answer to his question concerning the permissibility of using arms against violence and persecution, Žižka started to prepare for resistance to Sigismund. He first concentrated his small forces in Plzeň (Pilsen), but was outnumbered there by the followers of the king. He therefore abandoned his plan and chose Tábor, which he fortified, as his center. It soon swarmed with radical Hussites. The royalists wanted to destroy this dangerous center of resistance in the bud and attacked Žižka at Sudoměř.

There Žižka showed his military talent for the first time by adopting a new formation of mobile wagons which could be used as a moving fortress and which protected the warriors on their travels. His new tactic proved annihilating for the enemy.

In the meantime Sigismund had shown his real sentiments toward the Hussites by burning a citizen of Prague for his Hussite tenets and summoning the whole of Christendom to a crusade against heretical Bohemia. The crusading armies began to move against Prague in June 1420. The common danger brought the conservative and radical Hussites together, and again Žižka's military talent won a crushing victory over the crusaders on a hill near Prague which still bears his name. Sigismund, crowned in haste as king of Bohemia at the cathedral of St. Guy, had to make a precipitate retreat.

This cooperation between the two factions led to the publication of the Four Articles of Prague, the famous charter of the Hussite faith. The first article proclaimed that the Word of God should be freely preached by priests in the kingdom. The second stressed the dispensation of Holy Communion in both kinds. The third attacked the earthly possessions of priests and monks, who were urged to live model lives. The fourth demanded that all mortal sins, especially those committed publicly, should be punished by competent authorities. In this way a kind of unity was achieved between the two groups, whose teachings were so different.

This unity was sealed by a new victory in the same year on the Vyšehrad when Sigismund tried to relieve the garrison besieged in the fortress. He was forced to make an ignominious retreat. Unfortunately, for the first time iconoclastic tendencies were manifested by the victorious Taborites. The royal castle, Charles IV's pride, was destroyed, the church robbed of its decorations and vestments, and the residences of the canons destroyed. The surrender of Kutná Hora in April 1421 crowned the victory of the Hussite army.

Its cause was further strengthened by the acceptance of the Four Articles by Conrad of Vechta, archbishop of Prague, who was, moreover, a German. In this mood the Bohemian Diet met at Čáslav,[19] deposed Sigismund, and appointed a commission of regency of twenty members. The Four Articles were formally proclaimed to be the creed of Bohemia.

The Hussites then offered the Czech throne to Vitold, brother of the Polish king Władysław, and the king's nephew Korybut was sent to Bohemia. But Sigismund adroitly upset these plans by making peace with Vitold and Władysław, thus depriving the Czechs of Polish and Lithuanian support. Sigismund's crusading armies, however, suffered one crushing defeat after the other, first at Žatec (Saaz) in the autumn of 1421, then at Nebovidy and at Německý Brod in January 1422.

Not even the dissensions among the radical Taborites weakened the military strength of the Hussites. Some extremists who had denied the real presence of Christ in the Eucharist were burnt as heretics, and the sect of the Adamites, who preached that everything, even women, should be shared in common, was exterminated (1421) by Žižka, who, with his immediate followers, had never adopted the views of the extreme Taborites on the Eucharist or the veneration of saints.

But not even the death of the blind Žižka (October 11, 1424), at a moment when the hero had achieved a new reconciliation with Prague and the moderate Utraquists, dismayed the Taborites, great though the loss was. The more intimate followers of Žižka separated from the main group and called themselves "Orphans" (*Sirotci*), but the command of the Hussite armies soon passed into the able hands of a priest Procopius Holý.

A new army of German crusaders was massacred by the Hussites at Ústí (Aussig) in April 1427, and another crusading expedition met a shameful defeat at Tachov in August of the same year.

In the next year Procopius invaded Silesia and forced its dukes to accept his terms. When new negotiations with Sigismund had again broken down, Procopius' armies invaded Germany. Thuringia and Saxony knew the horrors of war, and the Hussite propaganda aroused dangerous reactions among the German masses. The demand arose for the convocation of a new council, voiced by the Hussites in a special manifesto addressed to the princes and people of Germany (1430).

Before convoking a Council, Martin V proclaimed a new crusade. In August 1431 the largest crusading army yet invaded Bohemia, but the "warriors of God" won their greatest victory over the invaders at Domažlice. Cardinal Cesarini accompanied the crusaders as papal legate and barely escaped, leaving behind him his cardinal's robes together with the papal bull. Only now was he convinced that the sole means to reduce the Hussite danger was to give them a hearing at a general council. In spite of the opposition of the new Pope, Eugenius IV, the council was convoked at Basel in 1431, and delegates were sent to Bohemia to invite the Hussites to attend the meetings with a promise of a safe conduct for their delegates. Among the Czech delegates were Procopius; John of Rokycany, a most prominent Utraquist priest; and the English Wycliffite, Peter Payne, who had found a new home in Bohemia. The Hussite delegation arrived at Basel in January 1433. The basis of discussion was the Four Articles of 1420, and the negotiations were continued in Prague.

In the meantime dissensions started to appear among the Hussites. The Taborites and the Orphans became increasingly hostile to the continuance of negotiations, fearing that reconciliation with the council would lead to the acceptance of papalism, while the moderates were in favor of reconciliation. They were tired of long and devastating wars and looked with mistrust at the growth of radicalism and the lack of discipline among the Taborites and Orphans. The lords, who had enriched themselves from the confiscation of ecclesiastical lands, wanted peace in order to restore the disrupted economy. When the Taborites attacked the Catholic center at Plzeň, the Utraquists made an alliance with the Catholic minority, and their forces almost annihilated the army of the radical Hussites in the battle of Lipany (May 30, 1434). Procopius, who had broken away from the moderates, and his lieutenant Prokůpek perished on the battlefield with most of the leaders of the radical wing.

So it became possible to continue negotiations, and the Bohemian delegation secured the acceptance by the conciliar fathers of the Four Articles, called "Compacts" in their watered-down form.[20] There followed the recognition of Sigismund as king of Bohemia and the tacit acceptance of John of Rokycany as the new archbishop of Prague.

Peaceful conditions were enjoyed again by the Czechs. The results were hardly worth the sacrifices borne by the nation over so many years. The only evident concession grudgingly made by the council, but not yet approved by the Pope, was the use of the chalice for the laity. On the other hand, however, the Czechs soon found themselves isolated in the society of the high Middle Ages, a position which was to prove a great handicap in the near future.

One may wonder why such a violent revolution against the medieval spiritual order should have started in Bohemia rather than in another country. John XXII's fiscal policy had permeated Church institutions everywhere, not only in Bohemia, and had contributed everywhere to the decadence of the clergy. That the outburst should have proved so violent in Bohemia was due primarily to religious reasons. Under the reign of Charles IV Bohemia was the center of the Empire, and all the spiritual currents of Europe converged upon Prague and its university, the only one in the Empire. The Czech intellectuals saw Cola di Rienzo, Petrarch, and many other leaders of contemporary European thought. Hitherto, Hus, the central figure of the Czech Reformation, has been the main subject of study, and his reformist work has been exalted. His activity, however, would never have reached such proportions without the basis laid by the numerous members of the Czech *devotio moderna*. In these circles the desire for reform was absolutely sincere and stemmed purely from religious motives. As has been seen, Milič of Kroměříž even went to Rome to lay a concrete plan of reform for the whole Church before the Pope.

Social and economic causes contributed considerably to the violence of the Bohemian outburst. In this field, however, the Czechs were not alone in protesting so vehemently against the medieval social order. The second half of the fourteenth century was a crucial period throughout Europe, thanks to the transition from the old agrarian economy previously predominant to the new monetary economy. Nor was the transition effected without violent eruptions. Cola di Rienzo started the movement in Italy; Etienne Marcel followed, inciting the artisans of Paris against the nobility; while Guillaume Caillet at the same time led the French peasantry against the lords. England suffered more than France, the situation being aggravated by the losses undergone in the war with France. This also explains the origin and spread of Wycliffe's teachings among the people. The ferocity of the Peasants' Revolt of 1381 led by Wat Tyler and John Ball and the humiliation it brought upon Richard II are well known. In Paris, in 1411, the Bastille was taken for the first time by a revolutionary mob led by Caboche, a forerunner of the French Revolution. In Germany, the continuous wars between the city leagues and the nobility filled the country with unrest and disorder.

Moreover, after the discovery of the silver mines, Bohemia was the richest land in Central Europe. The uneven distribution of wealth already mentioned was bound to lead to an outburst somewhere. This was complicated by a national problem. The wealth was mostly concentrated in the cities, whose burghers were in great majority Germans. In order to get a clear idea of the growing animosity between the Czech majority and the German minority, which was in possession of wealth and exercised an influence disproportionate to its numbers, the Czech rhymed chronicle of Dalimil, written in the fourteenth century and avidly read and copied during the Hussite period, should be read. The same sentiments are expressed in the Latin treatise *Theutonicis bonum dictamen.*

In order to explain the introduction of the vernacular into the liturgy the Cyrillomethodian tradition must be recalled. This had never completely disappeared although the Slavonic liturgy was suppressed at the end of the eleventh century. The canonization of Procopius, the founder of the Slavonic Abbey of Sázava in 1204, considerably revived this tradition, which can also be traced in new legends on SS. Cyril and Methodius, St. Procopius, and St. Wenceslas. Charles IV must have been aware of this when he asked the Pope for permission to found several monasteries with a Slavonic liturgy. Only one was permitted, that of Emmaus, and its monks joined the Utraquists when it came to the point. Jakoubek, in 1417, quoted the concession given to Emmaus when he commanded the introduction of the national language into the liturgy. This should all be taken into account in order to explain the violence of the Czech revolution against the medieval religious and social order.

Sigismund did not long enjoy his recognition as king of Bohemia. He died in the following year (1437), and his son-in-law, Albert of Austria, king of Hungary, was elected king; but he died in 1439, after having secured his throne against the King of Poland, whose son was elected by Albert's opponents. Albert's own infant son, Ladislas Posthumus (1439-1457), was accepted as the legitimate king; but the Emperor Frederick III of Austria, who was acting as his guardian, kept him outside the borders of Bohemia. Fortunately for that country, however, an energetic young nobleman, George of Poděbrady, put an end to the state of anarchy when he seized Prague in 1448. He became the leader of the Utraquists but devoted all his energy to achieving a reconciliation with the Catholics. Elected administrator of the kingdom, he crushed the radical Hussites when he captured their stronghold of Tábor in 1452. He also succeeded in bringing the young king to Prague. A new era of collaboration between a young Catholic king and the Hussite leader seemed to have opened; but once again fate intervened when Ladislas suddenly died.

When George of Poděbrady was elected king (1458-1471), he continued his policy of reconciliation. His hope that the Four Articles, called Compacts, which had been approved by the Council of Basel, would also be acceptable to the Pope did not materialize. Pius II rejected them in 1462, and his successor Paul II excommunicated George and deprived him of his kingdom. George, however, defended his rights energetically against some dissident nobles and against the Hungarian king Matthias Corvinus (1458-1490). The latter posed as the champion of the Pope's decision and invaded the country with the hope of making himself king of Bohemia with the help of his Catholic supporters within the country. He had some success in Moravia and Silesia, but George fought back with the utmost valor. In order to secure the help of Poland, he made a great personal sacrifice in renouncing his favorite plan that one of his sons should succeed him and found a new Czech national dynasty. He offered the Bohemian succession to Vladislav, son of the Polish king Casimir IV. Unfortunately, he could not enjoy the fruits of his final victories over the rebel nobles and the Hungarian king, for he died of dropsy at the age of fifty-one.[21]

George of Poděbrady was one of the best of the Czech kings. He tried hard to bring his country out of the isolation into which the Hussite wars had carried it. He saw clearly that with the decay of the imperial idea and the loss of prestige suffered by the Papacy during the schism, there was no central power in Europe which was likely to have enough authority and wield sufficient power to keep the Christian princes at peace and to help in solving European political problems. He therefore proposed the formation of a union of princes, headed by the King of France. The main role of the union was to be leadership in the wars against the Turks and the preservation of peace in Europe. This project, a kind of union of nations, was of course premature, but it certainly deserves to be mentioned as an interesting attempt at realizing in the fifteenth century an idea which has been the preoccupation of so many statesmen in the twentieth.

Judged in the light of subsequent events, the stubborn opposition of the popes to the Four Articles was a mistake. The Articles could quite easily have been reconciled with Catholic doctrine. The two main points on which the Utraquists insisted were a national liturgy and Holy Communion under both species. Another mistake was Rome's refusal to consecrate the Utraquist John of Rokycany, who was elected archbishop of Prague. The Utraquists were at heart Catholics; and if they had been given the support they asked for, they would very likely have been able to prevent the spread of a new reformist movement, that of the so-called Bohemian or Moravian Brethren, which was a continuation of the radical Hussite wing.

The spiritual father of this movement was the greatest and most original religious thinker of this period, Peter Chelčický (about 1390-1460). Although the scholarly education of this simple squire in South Bohemia was rather poor—he had a very inadequate knowledge of Latin—his literary activity was remarkable in all respects. He was inspired by the Czech reformers, Thomas Štítný, Matthew of Janov, and John Hus. He had also tried to penetrate the doctrines of Waldes (Peter Waldo) and Wycliffe, but in his treatment of their teaching, Chelčický showed great originality. He scrutinized it in the light of the Bible and of his own stubborn intellect and came to conclusions far beyond those of any other medieval religious thinker. He expounded these conclusions in numerous dogmatic and polemical treatises, many of them since lost, but his main literary and theological achievements are his *Postilla* and his *Síť Víry* (Net of Faith).[22]

According to the main idea expounded in his writings, only the first Christians had realized truly the precepts of Christ contained in the gospels. Everything subsequently added to the teaching and the conduct of the primitive Church is an invention of the Antichrist. Therefore, a true Christian should faithfully follow God's precepts derived from the Bible as his own intellect understands them, trying to renew the simple and primitive Church of the apostolic age. He should reject all Church tradition, the complicated development of the liturgy, and Church hierarchy because all these are tenets of the Roman Church, which is paying homage to the devil. But this is not all—a true Christian should also reject the political organization of the state and all privileges of kings, of the mighty, and of the clergy. He should not submit to laws or use the tribunals, and above all, he should reject any use of force and wars. In this respect Chelčický differs sharply from the Taborites, who had defended their faith with the sword.

Chelčický's writings preach a kind of Christian nihilism, in the most forceful and suggestive way. But the radical thinker escaped the practical consequences of his teaching, which could disrupt all social and religious order, by insisting that the most important precept of the Bible was not to resist evil. In this he was several centuries ahead of the Russian thinker, Tolstoj. Therefore, Chelčický urged the passive acceptance of all the injustices which were befalling the peasants and which he condemned so mercilessly.

A group of devout and enthusiastic listeners to Rokycana's sermons on the ideals of the first Christians, preached at Our Lady of Týn, soon came into touch with Chelčický and started to read his books. They found a leader in brother Gregory (died 1474), a monk of the Slavonic monastery of Emmaus in Prague and Rokycana's nephew. So it happened that Rokycana himself became, albeit unwillingly, in some way responsible for the start of this interesting movement.

In their enthusiasm to realize the ideals of the first Christians, Gregory and his followers, calling themselves the Unity of Brethren, accepted almost all the tenets of Chelčický's beliefs under the impression that they reflected the conduct of the first Christians. They also made practical deductions from these. Because they rejected the secular power with all its "pagan practices and rights," a brother was not allowed, during the first phase of the Unity's existence, to hold a secular office or to serve in the army. The Brethren were organized in a body in the winter of 1457-1458, when Rokycana obtained from King George permission for them to settle on the royal estate of Kunvald and there to practice their religion. The Brethren were soon joined by the "Brethren of Chelčice," intimate followers of the religious thinker, and by the remnants of the Taborites and Waldensians.[23]

This focused the attention of the Utraquist clergy on the Unity, and the Brethren were soon accused of heretical tenets. Rokycana had to intervene, and he admonished Brother Gregory and his followers to abandon their heretical beliefs. The king, anxious to show his zeal for the orthodox faith and so to obtain the confirmation of the Compacts by the Pope, started to persecute the Brethren in 1461. In 1467 the Brethren, breaking definitively with the Utraquists, founded their own organization, directed by three elected priests who were consecrated by a Waldensian bishop. A new persecution started, which lasted down to the end of King George's reign. Toward the end of the fifteenth century Brother Lukáš (Luke) succeeded in reconciling the different trends in the Unity and completed its organization as an independent Church. The strict discipline professed at the beginning of the Unity was abandoned, and candidates who could not give up their worldly occupations were admitted to the Unity, whose membership grew considerably.

This desire to reintroduce into the Church the practices of primitive Christianity is a very characteristic trait of the Czech Reformation. It led the Czech reformers to a rapprochement with the Christian East, where, so they believed, primitive Christian life still prevailed. The Utraquists initiated negotiations about 1452 for a union with the Church of Constantinople. A letter sent in 1452 "to the priests and princes of Bohemia" by the Church of Constantinople also expressed this hope of union with the Czech Utraquists. It was answered in the same year by the Utraquist Consistory of Prague. The fall of Constantinople in 1453 of course put an end to these negotiations.

The same desire to find a Church in which primitive Christian traditions were still alive prompted the Bohemian Brethren to send emissaries to Eastern lands in search of such a Church or community. The results of these expeditions are unknown. One of the emissaries, Martin Kabátník, left a vivid description of his journey, "From Bohemia to Jerusalem and Egypt." His description of Cairo and of Egypt is particularly lengthy and interesting, but of his religious experiences he says very little, having probably related them to his Church orally.

The teaching of the Bohemian Brethren, based on Chelčický's ideas, was much more radical and revolutionary than that of the Utraquists. So it happened, that it was not the Utraquist Church, as is sometimes believed, but that of the Unity of Brethren which became the precursor of the Protestant Reformation, or rather of its most severe and doctrinally most radical branch, Calvinism. As a consequence of Rome's opposition to Utraquism, which was at heart Catholic, when Luther's doctrines began to penetrate the Czech lands, most of the Utraquists, although Catholics at heart, embraced Lutheranism.[24]

NOTES

1. Charles IV's brother John Henry, margrave of Moravia, died three years before the emperor. Jošt succeeded his father as margrave, and John Henry's other son, Procopius, inherited lands in Moravia, while the third son became bishop of Litomyšl and afterward patriarch of Aquileia.

2. The best work on Wenceslas' reign in Germany is still that written by Th. Lindner (see Bibl.).

3. A complete indication of sources and bibliography concerning the reign of Wenceslas IV is to be found in F. M. Bartoš's work, *Čechy v době Husově, 1378-1415* (Prague, 1947), pp. 450-58 (Bohemia in Hus's time). On pp. 459-74, the author gives all known details on Wenceslas' councilors. R. Holinka wrote a monograph on the ecclesiastical policy of John of Jenštein during the pontificate of Urban VI (Cirkevni politika Jana z Jenštejna za pontifikátu Urbana VI, Prague, 1933).

4. The estimate given by J. V. Šimák in *Hus a doba před nim* ("Hus and the time before him") (Prague, 1915), p. 29, is here followed.

5. Already in 1367 Milič went to Rome to defend himself against accusations launched against him by his enemies. In 1368 he presented a memorandum to Pope Urban V setting out his ideas on the urgency of Church reform, to be initiated by the convocation of a general council. The most recent Czech monograph on Milič was written by O. Odložilík (*Jan Milič z Kroměříže*, Prague, 1924).

6. A critical study on the activity of this ardent reformer and Czech patriot was published by O. Odložilík (*Štěpán z Kolína*, Prague, 1924, Husitský archiv, vol. 1). For more bibliographical data on him see *ibidem*, p. 46.

7. The five hundredth anniversary of Hus was commemorated by two standard works: V. Novotný and V. Kybal, *M. Jan Hus, život a učení* (Prague, 1919-1931 a complete bibliography will be found there) and J. Sedlák, *Mistr Jan Hus* (Prague, 1915). The most important works on Hus in English are: Count Franz von Lützow, *The Life and Times of Master John Hus* (London, 1909); O. Odložilík, *Wiclif and Bohemia* (Prague, 1937); M. Spinka, *John Hus and the Czech Reform* (Chicago, 1941), K. Krofta's study on Hus in the *Cambridge Medieval History*, vol. VIII (1936). An important contribution to the study of Hus in English was also made by Mandell Creighton, *History of the Papacy during the Period of the Reformation*, Vol. I (London, 1882). Cf. also the older publications by E. Gullet, A. H. Wratislaw, E. Denis, and H. B. Workman. Cf. also D. S. Schaff and the popular book on Hus by J. Herben (see Bibl.).

8. She is said to have been escorted to Hus's sermons by a member of the royal staff, the nobleman John Žižka, who was to become the military leader of the Hussites.

9. For details see O. Odložilík, "Wycliffe's Influence upon Central and Eastern Europe," *Slavonic Review*, 7 (1929), pp. 637-48, and his short study *Wyclif and Bohemia*. Cf. also R. R. Betts, "English and Czech Influences on the Hussite Movement," *Transactions of the Royal Historical Society*, 21 (1939). Wycliffe's influence penetrated as far as Dalmatia, as was shown by M. Brandt in his book on Wycliffe's heresy and the social upheaval in Split (Spalato) at the end of the fourteenth century, *Wyclifova hereza i socijalni pokret u Splitu krajem XIV st.* (Zagreb, 1955).

10. Long quotations from Wycliffe's writings are copied, especially in Hus's work *De ecclesia*. J. Loserth (*Hus und Wiklif*, 2nd ed., Berlin, 1925), declared it a plagiarism of Wycliffe's writings. His criticism is, however, excessively severe and unjust because it disregards medieval methods in this respect.

11. It should be stressed, however, that Hus did not deny to those in mortal sin the right to execute the functions of their offices. Most of the accusations against Hus were taken from his treatise "On the Church" (*De ecclesia*), which

his Czech adversaries had brought to Constance. In Hus's previous writings not enough material could be found for his condemnation. The French scholars Peter d'Ailly and Gerson were the most prominent examiners.

12. A scathing criticism of the conduct of the council toward Hus can be read in Dom Leclercq's translation of Hefele's history of the councils: *Histoire des Conciles*, vol. VII (Paris, 1916), pp. 329-37: "Huss etait-il coupable? Devant le supplice qu'on lui infligea et l'attitude qu'il observa, un grand nombre ont été troublés et ont eu peine à admettre que celui-là fût digne d'un pareil traitement qui le subissait avec cette résignation. . . ."

13. V. Novotný and V. Kybal in their standard work on John Hus have tried to rehabilitate him in many respects. V. Kybal came to the conclusion that Hus's teaching could be reconciled in most, if not in all, instances with Catholic doctrine if examined in the light of contemporary theological discussions and if the extraordinary circumstances in which Hus and other reformers had to think and write were taken into account. This presentation does not coincide with the examination of Hus's doctrine previously made by two Catholic specialists: A. Lenz (*Učení M. Jana Husi*, Prague, 1875) and Sedlák (*M. Jan Hus*, Prague, 1915). Kybal's argument deserves more profound study. It shows, at least, that scholars, when speaking of Hus's heretical teaching, should do so with more reserve. Cf. also P. de Voogt study (see Bibl.).

14. On Luther's attitude to John Hus and on the place which Hussitism had in the first stage of the Reformation, interesting data has been collected by A. Kraus in his Czech work on Hussitism in contemporary literature (*Husitství v literatuře prvních dvou století svých*, Prague, 1917), part one, ch. VIII, pp. 150 ff. It should be pointed out that Hus's work *De ecclesia* was printed in 1520 on Luther's initiative. It was also translated into English by D. S. Schaff (New York, 1915) in commemoration of the fifth centenary of Hus's death. New edition by S. H. Thomson (Boulder, Colo., 1956).

15. Jerome, more a humanist than a reformer, was a friend of Poggio Bracciolini, who has described Jerome's character and expressed his admiration for the courage and dignity with which his friend died at the stake.

16. This was in some ways a logical consequence of the curtailment of the privileges of the clergy, who had hitherto alone enjoyed this right.

17. The history of the Hussite factions from 1415 to 1418 is very complicated. It was recently analyzed in a thorough study by H. Kaminsky, "Hussite Radicalism and the Origins of Tábor 1415-1418," *Medievalia et Humanistica*, 10 (1956), pp. 102-30. This work also gives a more complete bibliography on Hussitism.

18. Nicholas, who played a prominent role during the first stage of the struggle, soon died as the result of an accident. There is an exhaustive biography and study of Žižka by F. G. Heymann, *John Žižka and the Hussite Revolution* (Princeton, 1955). This gives a very detailed bibliography on the hero and on the Hussite wars (pp. 499-507). The author is not biased by Czech national tradition, and his judgment of Žižka as a man and a soldier is fairly balanced. Cf. the very precise and clear review of this book by O. Odložilík of the University of Pennsylvania in *Speculum*, 31 (1956), pp. 381-84. On p. 383 the reviewer gives a succinct account of the opinions voiced on Žižka by three prominent Czech historians—F. Palacký, V. V. Tomek and J. Pekař (*Žižka a jeho doba*, 2nd ed., 3 vols., Prague, 1933). Cf. also R. Urbánek, "Jan Žižka" in *Slavonic Review*, No. 8 (1924). The social and revolutionary aspect of

Hussitism was studied by two Czech historians of the new regime, J. Macek, *Husitské revoluční hnutí* (Prague, 1952), 2 vols., G. Graus, *Městská chudina v době předhusitské* (Prague, 1949).

19. For more details, see the study by F. G. Heymann, "The National Assembly of Čáslav," *Medievalia et Humanistica*, 7 (1952), pp. 32-55.

20. This is the content of the "Compactata": I. The Holy Sacrament is to be given freely in both kinds to all Christians in Bohemia and Moravia and to those elsewhere who adhere to the faith of those countries. II. All mortal sins shall be punished and extirpated by those whose office it is to do so. III. The Word of the Lord is to be freely and truthfully preached by the priests of the Lord and by worthy deacons. IV. The priest in the time of the law of grace shall claim ownership of no worldly possessions.

21. The age of George of Poděbrady has been studied most thoroughly by the Czech historian R. Urbánek in his work *Věk poděbradský*, published in V. Novotný's Czech history (Part III, vols. 1, 2, 3, 1915-1930). Non-Slavic historians will welcome the bibliographical notices given by O. Odložilík and H. Markgraf (see Bibl.).

22. On Chelčický's numerous writings and their edition, see Jan Jakubec, *Dějiny, op. cit.*, pp. 463-500. A German translation of his "Net of Faith" was made by C. Voge, *Petr Cheltschizki, Das Netz des Glaubens* (Dachau, 1924).

23. The main source for the history of the Brethren is their Acts or Archives preserved at Herrenhut in thirteen volumes. They are partly published by J. Bidlo, *Akty Jednoty bratrské* (Prameny dějin moravských, Prague, 1915 ff.). The main works on the Unity are: A. Gindely, *Geschichte der böhmischen Brüder* (Prague, 1857, 1858), J. Goll, *Quellen und Untersuchungen der böhmischen Brüder* (Prague, 1878, 1882), new edition by K. Krofta (Jar. Goll, *Chelčický a Jednota XV století*, Prague, 1916), J. Th. Müller, *Geschichte der böhmischen Brüder* (Herrenhut, 1922-1931, 3 vols.), a new Czech edition of Müller's work by F. M. Bartoš, *Dějiny Jednoty bratrské* (Prague, 1923). Recently R. Říčan, *Jednota bratrská* (Prague, 1956).

24. See below, Chapter XVI, pp. 396 ff.

Chapter IX

THE RUSSIAN PRINCIPALITIES,

THE RISE OF LITHUANIA AND MOSCOW,

THE JAGIELLONIAN FEDERATION

The German military orders and the North Russian principalities—Galicia, Volhynia, and the Latin West—Lithuania and the Russian principalities— Early history of Moscow—Dmitrij Donskoj—Jagiello of Lithuania, Moscow and Poland—Vitold's chances of assembling the Russian lands around Vilna—Lithuania and Poland—Vitold's religious plans—Grand Prince Basil I and the Byzantine emperor—Vitold's short-lived success

Certain external factors which had so often intervened in the affairs of Poland during the thirteenth and fourteenth centuries also had a powerful impact on the history of her eastern neighbors, the Russians. The expansion of the tribes along the Baltic coast in the direction of the lands claimed by the Russians had already started during the Kievan period. Jaroslav the Wise (1019-1054) had to take energetic measures, such as the foundation of Dorpat (Jurjev), to arrest the progress of the Baltic Lithuanians and Letts and of the Finnic Estonians into the Russian hinterland. But an even greater menace arose for the Russian principalities of the North.

At the beginning of the thirteenth century the Knights of the Sword (Fratres militiae Christi), also called Sword Bearers, founded in 1202 for missionary work among the northern pagans, settled at the mouth of the Dvina. From the city of Riga (founded in 1198), an important center of German missionary enterprise, they started to expand toward the Russian principality of Polock. In the course of many encounters between the Slavs and the Knights, Dorpat was lost, and for some time even Pskov and Izborsk had to recognize the supremacy of the order.

When the Livonian Knights of the Sword were united in 1237 with the

Teutonic Order, already firmly established in Prussia, a strong German center was formed in the North which spelled danger not only to the native pagan population, but also to the Orthodox Slavs beyond. Moreover, another Germanic nation, the Swedes, had begun to expand into Finland and were casting envious eyes on Novgorod.

The German conquest of a great part of the Baltic coast, in the eleventh and twelfth centuries, also had serious economic consequences for Novgorod. The new German cities of Lübeck, Stralsund, Wismar, Rostock, Greifswald, and Lüneburg—the so-called Wendish members of the powerful commercial Hanseatic League—took over from the Russians the flourishing trade with the Baltic lands, England, and the rest of western Europe. New cities founded on the Baltic—Reval, Narva, Abo, Viborg—also became serious competitors of Novgorod and Pskov. All these developments were taking place at a most fateful moment, when the Tatar hordes were engulfing Russian lands. No help came from the West, which was blind to the new Asiatic danger, but instead a new pressure from the North added to the general confusion in Russia.

There are some indications that the Russians resented this hostile intervention by the West. The anti-Western mentality, which was nonexistent in the Kievan period, started to manifest itself at the beginning of the thirteenth century.[1]

The first great conflict between the Russians and the West opened in 1240, the year which marks the final conquest of Russia by the Mongols. Thanks to the energetic Alexander, prince of Novgorod and (after 1252) of Vladimir, the Swedish advance was stopped on the river Neva, whence the hero of the battle obtained the title Nevskij. Two years later Alexander routed the Teutonic Knights in a battle on Lake Peipus, so that at least Novgorod and Pskov were saved.

There was one other principality besides Novgorod which was spared by virtue of its geographical position from the worst effects of Tatar domination and which was also exposed to Western influences—this was the principality of Galicia-Volhynia. This territory, of little importance during the tenth and eleventh centuries, began to acquire significance in the second half of the twelfth century when considerable numbers of refugees from the inroads of the Cumans into the neighboring southern principalities sought greater security there. Galicia and Volhynia were first united by Prince Roman (1199-1205), son of Mstislav II of Kiev. He had, however, to defend his ambitious political projects against powerful and jealous western neighbors, the Poles and the Hungarians. He died suddenly when fighting the Poles, after having extended his supremacy over Kiev.

After Roman's death, Andrew II, king of Hungary, invited by Roman's widow, declared himself protector of her two young sons Daniel and Vasilko. The Hungarians were already in possession of the province known today as Subcarpathian Russia, inhabited by a Slavic population of the same tongue as that of Galicia-Volhynia. They were eager to extend their domination over the Slavic lands beyond the Carpathian Mountains. Profiting by the occasion, Andrew II occupied the capital, Halicz, and assumed the title of "King of Galicia and Voldimiria" (Lodomiria = Volhynia), a title which the kings of Hungary retained until 1918, like that of "King of Serbia, Bosnia, and Bulgaria." Andrew's son Koloman was then crowned king of Galicia. Andrew's ally and father-in-law, Leszko of Cracow, occupied Przemysl and Brest, leaving the rest of Galicia to the Hungarians and part of Volhynia to Roman's sons. Quarrels between the Hungarians and the Poles resulted in the conquest of Galicia by Mstislav, another member of the Rurik dynasty.

The whole of Galicia and Volhynia were again united by Roman's sons Daniel and Vasilko, who not only succeeded in obtaining control over the whole of Volhynia but also expelled from Galicia Prince Rostislav,[2] the son-in-law of the Hungarian king (1245). Nevertheless, because of the Tatar danger, Daniel tried to be on good terms with Poland and Hungary and also turned for help to the Papacy. Innocent IV (1243-1254) promised to organize a crusade against the Tatars. Daniel offered to become a Roman Catholic and was crowned king of Galicia in 1253 with a crown sent by the Pope. When he saw, however, that the Pope was unable to keep his promise and that no help was forthcoming from the Latins, Daniel gave way to the opposition which his attempt at reunion had provoked at home, and renounced his alliance with the Papacy. In his struggle against the Tatars and in his attempts to liberate Kiev, Daniel could count only on his own forces. He did not succeed in his bold attempts and died in 1264.

After his death and that of his brother, Galicia-Volhynia soon became the object of the plots and ambitions of greedy neighbors, Poland, Hungary, and Lithuania, who waited only for the opportunity to divide the principality among themselves. On the other hand, Daniel's sons did not conceal their ambition to extend their authority over Hungarian, Polish, and Lithuanian territory. This was especially the case with Leo, the most energetic of them and founder of the city of Lwów. After the extinction of Roman's dynasty the nobles elected as king Bolesław-George, a Polish prince and a relative of the previous rulers. The jealous neighbors profited by the discontent aroused by the rule of the new prince, a Catholic, among his Orthodox subjects. Bolesław-George was poisoned (1340) by supporters of the Lithuanian candidature. The intervention of Casimir III, king of Poland, acting in collaboration with the Hungarian king, with whom he had concluded a secret treaty (1339), foiled the Lithuanian chances of obtaining the whole of the territory. From 1349 to 1772, the year of the first partition of Poland, Galicia formed a part of the Polish kingdom, while Volhynia was incorporated into Lithuania.

The impact of Lithuania on Russian and Polish historical evolution is intimately connected with the establishment of German military power on the Baltic. Under pressure from the Teutonic Knights, the Lithuanians, hitherto divided into many tribes, succeeded in achieving a certain degree of unity, and since their way to the north and west was barred by the Knights and their German colonists, they started to expand toward the south.

This expansion into Russian territory was promoted by the first known Lithuanian prince, Mendovg (Mindaugas, c. 1240-1263). He succeeded in becoming master of the so-called Black Russia on the upper Niemen and its affluents with the cities of Nowogródek, Grodno, Volkovysk, and Slonim, and also of the principality of Polock, which was much subdivided. Mendovg established his residence in Nowogródek. In order to protect himself against the Teutonic Knights who were preparing a crusade against him, he became a Christian and obtained, like Daniel of Galicia, a crown from Pope Innocent IV (1251). But when Mendovg had strengthened his power, he abandoned the God of the Germans and relapsed into paganism. He was, however, sufficiently intelligent to appreciate the new political organization which he found in the Russian lands, and this also helped him to strengthen his authority in his native Lithuania.

This policy of expansion among the eastern Slavs was followed by his successors during the fourteenth century. Gedymin (1316-1341), who became the real founder of the new Lithuanian power, extended his sway over the principalities of Minsk, Turov, Pinsk, Vitebsk, and the whole middle Dnieper region. He transferred his residence to Vilna, which became the center of the new Lithuanian state. His son Olgerd (Algirdas) (1341-1377) tried in vain, with the help of his brother Keistut, to get rid of the German menace. Olgerd was, however, more successful in his expansion in the South and penetrated into the region of Černigovsk-Seversk on the Desna. He lost Galicia to the Poles but succeeded in keeping Volhynia. He penetrated from there into Podolia and, after defeating the Tatars (1368), conquered the rest of the Kievan principality. He succeeded in extending his sway from Podolia toward the shores of the Black Sea. The princes of Smolensk, and for some time even Pskov, recognized his supremacy. His influence reached the principality of Tver' and only stopped near the walls of Moscow.

This enormous expansion was achieved not only by force of arms but also because the Russian princes greeted the Lithuanians as their liberators from the Tatar yoke. The alliance with Lithuania also strengthened their resistance against the pressure of the Teutonic Knights in the North. So it happened that in the years 1238 to 1386 almost all southern and western Russia was brought together in one mighty political unit. The Lithuanian princes resuscitated to some extent the Russia of Oleg, Vladimir, and Jaroslav the Wise. Only its center was no longer Kiev but Vilna (Wilno).

It was an interesting development, the more so as the Lithuanian rulers left untouched the political, religious, and administrative organization in most of the Russian principalities which recognized their supremacy. Only some western Russian lands became a part of Lithuania proper, but in the principalities of Polock, Vitebsk, Smolensk, Kiev, Volhynia, Podolia, and Černigovsk–Seversk, Russian princes of the Rurik dynasty continued to rule as before, only recognizing the supremacy of the Lithuanian princes, to whom they rendered tribute and military help.

The Lithuanians were still pagans and eagerly accepted the superior civilization which they found in the new countries. Many of the Lithuanian nobles joined the Orthodox Church, married into the Russian nobility, and adopted Russian customs. Soon Old Slavonic in its West Russian version became the official language of the Lithuanian court and was used in administrative, legislative, and judicial procedure. Specifically Russian titles and offices, which had developed during the Kievan period in both urban and territorial administration, also appeared in purely Lithuanian territories, and the Lithuanian nobility called themselves boyars like their Russian colleagues. The old Russian legislation, as it had developed in Kiev, was also adopted by the Lithuanians and later became the basis of the first Lithuanian Statute, published in 1529. Even Vilna, the capital of the new state, was for the most part Russian.

If this situation, which characterized the evolution of Lithuania in the fourteenth century, had continued during the next century, Lithuania and southern and western Russia would have witnessed a phenomenon similar to that which happened in Kiev in the tenth and eleventh centuries, when they were governed by a Scandinavian ruling class. The Lithuanian dynasty and people were on the way to unite the whole of Russia and to coalesce with the native population into one political and national unit.

Olgerd seems also to have aimed at extending his sovereignty over the eastern Russian principalities which were still under the Mongol yoke. History was to show that the Russian territories would finally be gathered not around Vilna, the residence of the Lithuanian dukes, but around Moscow and its princes, who in Olgerd's time were slowly assuming the leadership of the eastern Russian principalities.[3]

The rise of Moscow is a fascinating story.[4] The city is mentioned for the first time in history in 1147 as a relay post of the princes of Rostov and Suzdal', but as a city—*gorod*—it appears only in 1156. At that time the first wooden foundations of the Kremlin were built. Until halfway through the thirteenth century Moscow remained an insignificant border city and fortress on the northern boundary of the principality of Suzdal'-Vladimir. Its real history only started about the year 1263, when the hero of the battle of the Neva, Alexander, prince of Novgorod and Vladimir, follow-ing the custom of the Rurik dynasty, left the city with its lands to his youngest son, Daniel (1263-1303). As the youngest son, Daniel had to be content with the smallest part of his father's principality. Its only ad-vantage was that it was well populated. It was situated at the focal point of important river communications, and its distance from the center of Mongol power afforded a certain protection against their devastating expeditions. Peasants looking for safety against such invasions preferred to settle on the lands of the small new principality.

Daniel enlarged his territory by adding to it the principality of Pere-jaslavl', which he inherited from his nephew, while his son George (1303-1325) added some further conquests from the principalities of Rjazan' and Smolensk. George was the first to dispute the grand princely title which was held by Michael of Tver', the senior of the family. Although defeated by Michael, George had more success when he invoked the help of the Mongols. But he had to pay with his life and was assassinated at the Khan's residence by Michael's son Dmitrij in 1325. The murderous feud with the house of Tver' was continued by George's brother Ivan (1325-1341), who again secured victory with the help of the Mongols. Alexander of Tver' and his son were executed by the Khan, as had been the fate of Dmitrij and his father Michael. Ivan of Moscow obtained the grand princely title and forced the principalities of Tver', Rjazan', and Suzdal' to recognize his supremacy.

Thanks to the economic prosperity of his state, Ivan tripled its extent by purchasing lands and cities from other principalities. The impoverished princes of Uglič, Beloozero, and Galič, probably unable to pay the Tatar tribute, were forced to sell out to Ivan. The Muscovite thus extended his possessions and authority considerably toward the north.

Attracted by Ivan's liberality, numerous boyars quitted the service of their princes and entered that of the grand prince. Ivan knew how to secure their fidelity by granting them important privileges. He also ran-somed thousands of Russian prisoners from the Mongols and settled them on his territory, a practice which was particularly beneficial to the grand prince. For his skill in financial and economic matters, Ivan was called Kalita (money bag). Thanks to the rich presents which he lavished upon the Khan and his courtiers and thanks to his unscrupulous and abject subservience to the Mongol overlords, Ivan Kalita obtained for himself and his successors from the Khan Uzbek, who used to show him particular favor, the great privilege of collecting the tribute which the Russian subject princes had to pay to the Mongols.[5] This privilege implied a great relief for the Russians because the visits of Mongol tax collectors often proved very tiresome. The prestige of the grand princes of Moscow grew considerably, thanks to this display of favor on the part of the Tatar khans, while it gave them also new possibilities of gathering Russian territory around their principality.

The princes of Moscow were indebted for the growth of their power not only to the favor shown to them by the khans, but also, and even more, to the support of the Russian Church. About the middle of the fourteenth century Kalita registered another great success by conquering Vladimir, capital of the principality of Suzdal'. This was the residence of the Metropolitan of Kiev, who had left the ruined city in 1299. The Metropolitan Peter, a native Russian, used to visit Kalita in the Kremlin and died there in 1326. His successor, the Greek Theognostos, fixed his residence finally in Moscow. It was an event of immense importance for the Grand Principality of Moscow when it became the spiritual heir of Kiev, the center of the Russian Orthodox Church. The metropolitan of the Russian Church was the only symbol of the unity of all Russia, divided as it was into numerous principalities, several of them under Polish and Lithuanian sovereignty. By the same stroke of luck, Moscow thus became the symbol of this unity. Ivan Kalita realized all this and was clever enough to exploit his opportunity. He started to call himself "Grand Duke of Vladimir and of all Russia."

A new danger loomed ahead when Kalita's successor Simeon (1341-1353) succumbed to an epidemic of plague, together with his two sons and his brother Andrew. His surviving brother and successor, Ivan II the Meek (Krotkij) (1353-1359) was a less able ruler. Fortunately, the new Metropolitan Alexei (Alexis), himself a descendant of a boyar family (the Pleščely), had the necessary qualities of statesmanship and was able to take the affairs of the grand principality into firm hands. When Ivan II died suddenly, leaving only a minor son Dmitrij, Moscow seemed to be close to ruin. The foundations laid by Ivan I Kalita proved, however, to be solid. The boyars, who had profited greatly from the prosperity of the principality, became stout supporters of the young Dmitrij (Demetrius), realizing that it was in their own interest to have a single ruler governing a prosperous state

Although the grand princely title was temporarily lost to Suzdal' from 1359 to 1363, the boyars did not leave the service of the young prince of Moscow. During the minority of Dmitrij the Metropolitan Alexei showed the qualities of an able diplomat and a brilliant administrator. He succeeded in frustrating the plan of Olgerd of Lithuania to have his own metropolitan for his Orthodox subjects. Olgerd first supported the monk Theodoret, who had been ordained by the Bulgarian Patriarch of Trnovo as Metropolitan of Kiev. Refusing to recognize the authority of Alexei, who had been ordained by the Patriarch Philotheos (1354-1355) of Constantinople as "Metropolitan of Kiev and of all Russia," Olgerd obtained from the patriarch the consecration of Roman, a kinsman of his wife, as Metropolitan of Kiev. Both metropolitans claimed to exercise authority over all Russian lands. The synod of 1356 convoked by the Patriarch Kallistos I (1355-1363) divided and delimited their jurisdiction, giving to Roman the title of "Metropolitan of Lithuania" and confirming to Alexei his title of "Metropolitan of Kiev and of all Russia." Roman continued to exercise his jurisdiction over Russian lands, but Alexei succeeded in arresting his activity and secured from the patriarch the suppression of the Lithuanian metropolitan see after Roman's death in 1361. Alexei, residing in Moscow, was again metropolitan of all Orthodox Russians both inside and outside Lithuania.

Aided by the Muscovite boyars, Alexei, who was in high esteem at the Khan's court, worked for the return of the grand princely dignity to Ivan Kalita's grandson. He succeeded at last, and in 1363 the young Dmitrij obtained, in face of the disputes of his rivals, a *jarlyk* (Tatar official decree) in Saray, the residence of the Khan, confirming his grand princely title.

With the help of his numerous boyars, the young Dmitrij succeeded in occupying Vladimir and defeating his rival of Suzdal'. Peace was confirmed by his marriage with the daughter of the Grand Prince of Suzdal'. Although Dmitrij allowed his father-in-law to keep the grand princely title, he acted henceforward as the sole grand prince of all Russia. He intervened in the disputes among the princes of Rostov, and with the help of the Metropolitan Alexei and of Sergius, abbot of the Holy Trinity Monastery, one of the most popular Russian ascetics and saints, Dmitrij forced the brother of the Suzdalian grand prince to give back Nižnij Novgorod to the legitimate heir. For the second time ecclesiastical sanctions were used to enforce the political decision of the Grand Prince of Moscow.[6]

It was at that moment that Dmitrij had to face the attempt of the Lithuanian grand duke Olgerd to unite all Russia around Vilna. The Lithuanian menace was the more serious as Olgerd was in alliance with his father-in-law, Michael of Tver', another pretender to the dignity of grand prince. Three times the Lithuanians with their ally invaded Moscow's territory, but each time without success. The leadership of the Muscovite grand prince in eastern Russia was for the first time demonstrated to contemporaries when, in 1375, Dmitrij appeared before Tver', accompanied by the contingents of nineteen East Russian princes and reinforced by units from Novgorod. Michael of Tver' had to capitulate. He was allowed to keep the title of grand prince which he had obtained from the Khan, but only as "younger brother of the Grand Prince of Moscow." Dmitrij's position was already so strong that he could overlook the pretensions to the glittering title of the princes of Suzdal', Tver', or Rjazan', all of whom were forced to recognize his supremacy. It was more important for him to weaken Tver' by detaching a part of the principality from the prince's immediate obedience and to obtain from him the promise of military support against Moscow's foes, even if they should be Lithuanians or Tatars.

Soon afterwards Moscow's leadership was demonstrated in a more telling way. The Empire of the Golden Horde was again immersed in a crisis. The numerous plundering expeditions of undisciplined Tatar bands into Russian territories forced the East Russian princes to retaliation. Russian warriors under Dmitrij's leadership dared to go as far as Kazan'. Dmitrij was particularly successful against the Tatars in 1378 on the Oka River. Mamai, the mighty "khan maker" who himself became khan, prepared a great expedition against Moscow and its allies. The Khan concluded an alliance with the Lithuanians, led by Olgerd's son Jagailo (Jagiello), and invaded Russia with a huge army. In the hour of danger Dmitrij made an appeal to the national and religious sentiments of the Russians. Before he marched with his 150,000 men, collected from all the eastern principalities with the exception of Rjazan' and Novgorod, Dmitrij went to the monastery of the Holy Trinity in order to obtain the blessing of the most venerable Russian religious hero, the Abbot St. Sergius. The battle of the Kulikovo meadow (1380) on the Don is one of the most memorable events in the history of Muscovy.[7] It was the first Russian victory over their oppressors and made a most profound impression on all contemporary Russians, earning for Dmitrij the title Donskoj. It was, however, not a decisive victory, and Dmitrij had to submit to the Tatars again two years afterward when Mamai's murderer and successor, the mighty Tocktamyš, succeeded in penetrating as far as Moscow, which was taken and destroyed. The grand prince had again to promise obedience and to pay tribute, but he had proved that the Tatars could be defeated and that their power could be broken by a common effort of all Russians under able leadership. The memorable battle won a new prestige for Moscow, and national feeling, which seemed barely existent during the period of oppression, started to assert itself, with the blessing of the Church. These sentiments found expression in the contemporary recitals and poems, the "Disaster of Mamai" and the "Zadonščina."

Before dying, Dmitrij Donskoj made another important innovation in Muscovite political traditions. Although the principle of primogeniture in the succession to the grand princely title had already been tacitly established in Moscow, the old order of succession, with the division of the patrimony into *udĕls* among the surviving children, was still in use. In his testament Dmitrij also left *udĕls* to his sons, but he reserved the most important and greatest *udĕl*, with the grand princely dignity, to his eldest son. Thus, the monarchic principle, which was slowly being accepted in Moscow, was considerably strengthened. It was another important step toward the autocracy of the grand princes which was to develop during the following generations.

Dmitrij Donskoj was well aware of the advantages to be derived from a friendly Lithuania. After showing his strength to Olgerd, he engineered the marriage of his brother Vladimir with Olgerd's daughter, probably in 1371, and was anxious to enjoy good relations with some Lithuanian princes.

After Olgerd's death in 1377, Dmitrij came forward with a very bold plan, the details of which were only recently made known, which illustrates his statesmanship.

An arrangement was concluded by Dmitrij with Olgerd's widow and her son Jagailo, better known as Jagiello (1377-1434), in virute of which the latter was to marry Dmitrij's daughter. The correspondence concerning this agreement is lost. In the Muscovite grand princely archives there was recently discovered a copy made in 1626 of a document revealing not only the existence of such an arrangement but also its main stipulations.

The surviving copy of this interesting document reads as follows: "Letter of the Grand Prince Dmitrij Ivanovič and of the Grand Duchess Uljanič Olgerd's (widow), concerning the marriage of the Grand Duke Jagailo (son) of Olgerd that he should marry the daughter of the Grand Prince Dmitrij Ivanovič and that the Grand Prince Dmitrij Ivanovič should give him his daughter in marriage and that he, the Grand Duke Jagailo, should be subject to them (*byti v'ich volĕ*) and that he should be baptized in the Orthodox faith and that he should proclaim his Christianity to all men." [8]

If this project had materialized, the evolution of Russia and of eastern Europe would have followed quite different channels. It would probably have accelerated the union of all the Russian lands in one mighty state and the liberation of the rest of Russia from the Tatar yoke, prevented the spread of the bitter antagonism of the eastern Russians against the Latins, and given the Poles, the nearest and most cultured Western nation, a better opportunity to act as friendly transmitters of Western culture to the Orthodox Russians.

Dmitrij's plans failed, however, to achieve realization. The Lithuanians were attracted not only by the possibilities opening before them in Russian lands, but also by Poland, which was able to offer its pagan neighbors a culture superior to that available in the Russian principalities.

As the Lithuanian grand duke stood at the crossroads, facing a choice between Russia and Orthodoxy or Poland and Roman Catholicism, a new situation had developed in Poland which induced the Poles to use all their diplomatic abilities to win over Jagiello.

The increasing danger arising from the Teutonic Order had cost the Poles Pomerania with Danzig. The great Polish king Casimir III had to accept this situation, and his Hungarian successor Louis of Anjou did little to improve it. After his death, according to an arrangement made with the Polish nobility, his ten-year-old daughter Jadwiga was crowned "King of Poland" (1384). The Polish nobility, anxious to find an effective ally against the Germans, persuaded the young queen, who was already betrothed to William of Austria, to marry Jagiello of Lithuania. This marriage (1386) not only ended Polish-Lithuanian rivalry for Galicia and Volhynia, but led to a personal union between the two countries. Jagiello turned his back on Moscow, and instead of embracing Orthodoxy, he promised—in the agreement of Krewo, 1386—to become a Roman Catholic, to convert his whole nation to the Roman faith, to place Lithuanian forces at Poland's disposal, and to unite his territories with Poland.[9]

Jagiello's decision was influenced by the fact that the Teutonic Order menaced not only Poland but also Lithuania. He had himself had bitter experience with the order. His ascension to supreme power in Lithuania after the death of his father Olgerd was not obtained without bloodshed. In order to prevent his uncle Kiejstut from assuming the grand ducal dignity after Olgerd's death, Jagiello had to conclude a secret treaty with the Teutonic Order, sacrificing the Lithuanian province of Samogitia and acknowledging the order's supremacy.

He had succeeded in outwitting Kiejstut, who died in a Lithuanian prison, and in imprisoning his other rival, his cousin Vitold (Vitautas). But the latter escaped from captivity and found refuge with the order. When Vitold promised the order further territorial concessions and declared his willingness not only to be baptized but to become the order's vassal, the grand master turned against Jagiello and started to help Vitold to regain his patrimony. Only a reconciliation between the two cousins, initiated by Jagiello himself (1384), saved Lithuania from becoming the order's vassal. It was probably this experience with the order which stimulated Jagiello's decision to reject Moscow's proposal and to accept Poland's offer. This arrangement was a very serious blow to the order's political plans, but it diverted the Lithuanians from the path followed some centuries earlier by the Scandinavian Varangians. The Lithuanian dynasty became Roman Catholic, and the people had to follow the example of Jagiello, who took the baptismal name of Władysław.

It was to be expected that the antagonism between Moscow and Lithuania would become more bitter as a result of this development. Moscow seemed, from now on, entitled to pose not only as the political center of all Russia, but also as the sole protector of Russian Orthodoxy against latinism.

Such a development, however, did not materialize immediately on Jagiello's conversion to Roman Catholicism and the conclusion of a Polish-Lithuanian union. Despite all this, the idea of collaboration between Moscow and Lithuania still had numerous adherents in East Russia. On the Lithuanian side Olgerd's idea of gathering the Russian principalities around Vilna found a new protagonist in Jagiello's cousin Vitold.[10]

After his reconciliation with Jagiello, Vitold (1384-1430) obtained from his cousin as his appanage the important Russian territories of Brest, Drohiczyn, Mielnik, Bielsk, Šaraš, Kamienice, Volkovisk, and Grodno. On Jagiello's advice Vitold embraced Orthodox Christianity, a circumstance which considerably increased his popularity among his Orthodox subjects. This seemed to indicate that Vitold intended to devote his talents to further penetration into Russian lands.

The conclusion of the Polish-Lithuanian union of Krewo (1386), however, changed Vitold's plans. He had to accept the union, and in order to demonstrate the unanimity of the dynasty, he let himself be baptized, with his cousin, according to the Roman rite, retaining, however, the name of Alexander, which he had chosen when becoming an Orthodox Christian. But Vitold never liked the union with Poland, and although Jagiello had appointed his brother Skirgiello as his representative in Lithuania, Vitold soon came forward with pretensions to the grand ducal title. It quickly became apparent that he was determined to weaken the union as much as possible and to secure independence for Lithuania and its Russian principalities. He was encouraged in these plans by the son of Dmitrij Donskoj, Basil I (Vasilij), who, after escaping from being held as a hostage of the Tatars, visited Vitold in Łuck and asked for his daughter in marriage.

Soon Vitold attempted to obtain his ends with the help of the Teutonic Order and of Basil I, who had become grand prince of Moscow (1389-1425) after the death of Dmitrij and had concluded the marriage with Vitold's daughter. Jagiello was forced to enter into new negotiations with his ambitious cousin. In the treaty of Ostrów (1392) Vitold was given back the patrimony of his father and became the real master of Lithuania proper. Skirgiello moved his residence from Troki to Kiev.

All this seemed to indicate that a new era of cooperation between Moscow and Lithuania was opening. In reality, however, Basil I turned toward the East rather than the West in his policy of expansion. He annexed Nižnij Novgorod and Murom and extended his influence over some colonial possessions of Novgorod in the Northeast. A new Tatar menace, however, arrested this expansion. The revolt of Tocktamyš against the great Khan Tamerlane (Timur-Lenk) once more weakened the Khanate of the Golden Horde. Defeated by the great conqueror, Tochtamyš fled to Vitold. Once more a mighty Tatar army, led by the formidable Tamerlane, stood on the frontier of Muscovy. The invasion was averted, according to the pious belief of contemporaries, through the intercession of the Blessed Virgin. On the day when the most venerated icon of Our Lady, which had been moved from Kiev to Vladimir by Andrew Bogoljubskij, was brought to Moscow, on the orders of the metropolitan, Tamerlane left Russia. The popularity of the famous icon, of course, increased considerably among the faithful, and also that of the young grand prince.

This threat, though fortunately averted, was a reminder to East Russia that the Tatar danger, although diminishing, was still there. Therefore, the expedition against the Tatars, which Vitold was organizing in 1399, despite the warning of Jagiello and Jadwiga, in order to install his protégé Tocktamyš as khan, seems to have been greeted in Muscovy with sympathetic approval. Many wished success to the Lithuanian grand duke, hoping that a Tatar defeat would inaugurate the complete liberation of Russia from Tatar suzerainty. These hopes were, however, vain. Vitold's army suffered a resounding defeat on the river Vorskla. Instead of achieving liberation from the Tatars, a new Tatar invasion devastated Russian lands and reached the walls of Moscow's Kremlin. Basil I had again to promise tribute and to recognize Tatar sovereignty.[11]

Moscow would not have gained much if Vitold had succeeded. His ultimate aim was the conquest of Muscovy with the help of his Tatar ally, whom he hoped to install as khan. Basil's submission to the Tatars prevented any repetition of Vitold's attempt, even when the Lithuanian saw the son of his unfortunate ally seated on the throne of the khan.

The defeat on the Vorskla River shattered Vitold's hopes of dominating the whole of eastern Europe, and he was forced to reconsider his lukewarm attitude toward the Polish-Lithuanian union. In 1401 Vitold's and Jagiello's vassals confirmed at Vilna and at Radom the agreement concluded by the two cousins. A permanent defensive alliance was stressed in the document, and the relationship of Vitold to the King of Poland was newly defined. Jagiello remained king of Poland and grand-duke of Lithuania, but in the latter country he associated Vitold with his power and granted to him the grand ducal title and authority for life. The local princes still existing in Lithuania and in its Russian provinces—though Vitold had replaced most of them by governors—had to render homage to Vitold, but the whole country was regarded as a fief of the Polish crown. Vitold thus succeeded in obtaining a new legal guarantee of the autonomy of his country, but he had once more to acknowledge its dependence on Poland.

The complications with the Teutonic Order sealed the new agreement. The defection of Jagiello's youngest brother Svidrigello (Svidrigailo) to the order was remedied through reconciliation, but Samogitia, whose inhabitants had revolted against the order, could not be recovered. The treaty of 1404 restored to Poland only the Dobrzyń province in return for a very large sum of money.

After this interruption Vitold resumed his plans of eastward expansion into Russia. In 1404 he annexed to his grand duchy the principality of Smolensk, which had loosened its former intimate relationship with Lithuania. When, however, Vitold showed his intentions of annexing Novgorod and Pskov, Moscow intervened, and Vitold had to fight his own son-in-law. The peace treaty signed in 1407 gave Smolensk to Lithuania, but Vitold had to abandon his plans against Novgorod and Pskov. The Ugra River formed the frontier between the two countries.

New complications with Svidrigello and the Teutonic Order arrested momentarily any further Lithuanian progress toward the East. The order was even able to win over to its side King Wenceslas of Bohemia and King Sigismund of Hungary. The joint action of Jagiello and Vitold was this time, however, crowned with complete success. At the bloody battle between Tannenberg and Grunwald (1410) the army of the order was utterly defeated, and the grand master and most of its other leaders lost their lives on the battlefield. The order never completely recovered from this blow.

Unfortunately, the victory was not fully exploited by the Poles and Lithuanians. Besides a war indemnity, the only gain was the recovery of Samogitia by Vitold, but only for his lifetime. When new danger threatened both countries from the order, which had refused to accept Sigismund's mediation, Poland and Lithuania were induced to conclude a new convention which should demonstrate more clearly the union between them. The convention of Horodło, signed in 1413, stressed once more the autonomy of Lithuania, which was to have its grand dukes even after Vitold's death. This stipulation certainly satisfied Vitold's ambitions.

On the other hand, however, the new convention stipulated that Lithuania should be increasingly westernized and assimilated to Polish political institutions. New local offices modeled on the Polish example were introduced, an advisory character was given to the grand-ducal council, and the foundations were laid for the development of a parliamentary system. However, only Catholic nobles were admitted to enjoy these privileges. Moreover, Polish aristocratic traditions were introduced when forty-seven Lithuanian noble families were adopted by Polish aristocratic clans and given permission to use the coats of arms of the Polish clans which had adopted them.

It was again principally the danger emanating from the order which induced Vitold to agree to such changes in Lithuania. The disputes with the order continued and were the subject of many discussions, even at the Council of Constance. Sigismund's arbitration in 1420 was rejected by the Poles as being excessively favorable to the order, and they exercised constant diplomatic pressure on the Roman king in order to induce him to modify his favorable attitude toward the order. One form of Polish pressure lay in the candidature of Sigismund Korybut, Jagiello's nephew, to the Bohemian throne, which was favored by the moderate Hussites.[12] Finally King Sigismund gave in, afraid of the support given by Vitold to Sigismund Korybut, and reconciled himself with Jagiello in Košice (Kassa, Kaschau) in 1423.

Vitold must have appreciated that the growing differences in religion and social organization between Lithuania and the Russian principalities under his sovereignty formed the main obstacle to the realization of his all-Russian plans. Therefore, although himself formally a Roman Catholic, he continued to manifest open sympathy for the Orthodox Church in his realm. In spite of that he was bound to forfeit the sympathies of his Orthodox boyars. The outbreak of open hostilities with Basil I therefore resulted, for the first time in Lithuanian and Muscovite history, in a kind of exodus of his Russian boyars toward Moscow. In order to impress his Russian subjects, Vitold, accompanied by his cousin the King of Poland, made a military demonstration in his eastern provinces, after the battle of Tannenberg-Grunwald.

In order to break the religious attraction exercised by Moscow on his lands, Vitold decided to follow the example of Olgerd and to set up an independent metropolitan for his Russian subjects. He induced his Orthodox bishops to elect, in 1415, the Bulgarian Gregory Camblak as metropolitan of Kiev. The Metropolitan Photius of Moscow protested, and the Patriarch of Constantinople, who had refused all Vitold's requests for an independent metropolitan, excommunicated Gregory. This plan may have originated in Jagiello's and Vitold's western policy. They hoped that the presence of the new metropolitan of Kiev and of all Russia at the Council of Constance (1415) would provide incontrovertible evidence that there was no reason why the Teutonic Order should be allowed to continue its activity in Prussia: not only had all pagans in those parts been converted, but the Poles and Lithuanians were also bringing back to Rome the Russian schismatics. The whole plan misfired. The learned Bulgarian refused to back their political plans and turned down the proposals of the council for reunion. After his death (1419), the Muscovite metropolitan continued to exercise his jurisdiction over the Lithuanian Orthodox.

It should be stressed that in this whole affair the Byzantine emperor and patriarch had constantly taken the side of Moscow. They not only repaid in this way the rich subsidies they were obtaining from Moscow in their desperate struggle against the Turks, but also demonstrated the firm solidarity of all the Orthodox. In 1414, the Emperor Manuel II (1391-1425) married his son to Basil's daughter. He sought by this gesture to ensure Moscow's financial help for his disappearing empire. The union with the imperial house of Constantinople, however, served to increase considerably the prestige of the Muscovite dynasty among the Russian princes.[18]

At this stage an incident deserves mention which threatened at the beginning of Basil's reign to jeopardize the good relations between Byzantium and Moscow. In order to lend more emphasis to his growing political position, the Grand Prince Basil ordered the Greek emperor's name to be omitted from the liturgy. The Patriarch Anthony intervened and sent him in 1393 a long letter in which he took pains to explain the position of the basileus in the Christian commonwealth. He cannot, so he argued, be lowered to the level of other rulers since he helped the Church from the beginning in fighting heresies, convoked the Holy Synods which defined the true doctrine, gave us the holy canons, and upheld the discipline of the Church. The basileus is not the ruler of the Romans only, but of all Christians, and his name is mentioned in the holy liturgy by every patriarch and bishop. He is so exalted that even the Latins, now that they are severed from the Orthodox Church, venerate him as they did before the separation; all the more reason then for the Orthodox to honor him. That his power is now limited by reason of hardships suffered at the hands of the infidel Turks is no reason why Christians should relax in their allegiance.[14]

This interesting document shows that Byzantine ideas on the role of the emperor had not altered from the fourth to the fourteenth century and that the Russians shared them throughout the four centuries of their national existence. Basil I's initiative betrays, however, a tendency on the part of the grand princes to make their prominent position felt everywhere, even in Constantinople. Nevertheless, Basil I accepted the patriarch's explanation, and the intimate relationship between Byzantium and Moscow was demonstrated during the Lithuanian attempt to limit the jurisdiction of the Metropolitan of Moscow over Lithuanian territory. The incident, although for the time being without consequences, indicated, however, the direction in which the grand princes of Moscow would guide their religious policy in the future.

In spite of this, Vitold enjoyed, toward the end of his life, an unexpected opportunity to realize his old all-Russian plans. His son-in-law Basil I of Moscow had before his death recommended his family and his successor Basil II to the protection of Vitold. Basil I died in 1425, and the old grand duke devoted his last years to triumphal expeditions through East Russian principalities, reassembling Russian lands under his protection. One after the other the princes promised obedience and brought tribute and presents. The reports which Vitold gave to the Grand Master of the Teutonic Order concerning his victorious expeditions show how dear to him had been his dream of reuniting the Russian lands. The princes of Rjazan', Perejaslavl', Pronsk, Novosělsk, Odojev, Vorotynsk, Tver', and Smolensk promised obedience, and their territories surrounded Moscow, which was under his sponsorship. In 1428 even Pskov recognized him, but the proud Republic of Novgorod resisted and remained hostile even after its defeat.

But all was in vain, and Vitold lacked the time to consolidate his successes. He died in 1430 still toying with the idea of assuming the royal title, which had been suggested by the Roman king Sigismund at the assembly of Łuck.

Vitold's successor Svidrigello, although quite popular among the Russians in spite of his Catholicism—even Novgorod accepted his protectorship (1432)—was unable to retain Vitold's inheritance. Old rivalries between Poland and Lithuania concerning Podolia and Volhynia broke out, and once more Svidrigello appealed to the Teutonic Knights for help. Deposed and replaced by Sigismund, Vitold's brother and Jagiello's cousin, he maintained himself for some time in the southern Russian provinces. There was a moment, during this struggle, when it seemed that the Russian provinces under Lithuanian sway would form an autonomous unit and that the Jagiellonian commonwealth would disintegrate into three parts—Poland, Lithuania, and southwest Russia.

In order to maintain his position in the South Russian lands, Svidrigello entered into negotiations with Pope Eugenius IV, and also with the Council of Basel (1434), promising to work for the union of his Orthodox subjects with Rome. He spoiled his own chances by his alliance with the order and by his maltreatment of his own allies among the Russian nobles. In 1435, he even put the Metropolitan Gerasim (Harasim) to death, accusing him of rebellion, although he had been his candidate for the rank of Metropolitan of Kiev and of all Russia, securing in 1431 the consecration of his candidate by the Patriarch of Constantinople, thus eliminating the candidate proposed by Moscow.

Svidrigello was finally defeated by Sigismund in 1435.[15] Jagiello himself died May 31, 1434. All this gave East Russia the necessary respite to recover its independence. After the first critical years of his reign in Moscow, Basil II was able to resume the task of gathering the Russian lands around him,[16] and the last chance for Lithuania vanished.

NOTES

1. In 1212, Vladimir Toropeckij, the prince of Pskov, was deposed, according to the Fourth Novgorod Chronicle (*PSRL*, vol. 4), because he married his daughter to the brother of the German bishop, Albert of Riga, founder of the Livonian Knights of the Sword. In 1233, the Dominicans were expelled from Kiev. A strong echo of this animosity can be noticed also in modern Russian historiography. L. P. Šaskol'skij attributes the organization of the anti-Russian "crusade" of 1240-1242 to the Papacy, "Papskaja kurija—glavnyj organizator krestonosnoj agressii 1240-1242 g. protiv Rusi," *Istoričeskie zapiski*, 37 (1951), pp. 169-88. Cf. also V. T. Pašuto in his popular work on Alexander Nevskij, *Aleksandr Nevskij i bor'ba russkago naroda za nezavisimost' v 13 v.* (Moscow, 1952). On the German expansion in the Baltic, cf. also Chapter I, pp. 13-15.

2. On Rostislav's political ambitions among the southern Slavs, see above, pp. 104, 119. On Polish, Lithuanian, and Hungarian attempts at annexing Galicia and Volhynia, see also Chapter IV, p. 77.

3. On the history and political organization of the Lithuanian-Russian commonwealth, see M. K. Ljubavskij, *Očerk istorii litovsko-russkago gosudarstva* (Moscow, 2nd ed., 1915), *idem, Oblastnoe dělenie i městnoe upravlenie litovsko-russkago gosudarstva* (Moscow, 1893). V. T. Pašuto's studies on the origin of the Lithuanian state, published in *Voprosy istorii*, vol. 8 (1947), pp. 74 ff., in *Izvestija Akademii Nauk SSSR*, serija istorii, vol. 9 (1952), pp. 29 ff., and in *Vestnik istorii* (1958), pp. 40-62, were criticized in *JGO*, N.F. 4 (1956), pp. 159-65, by M. Hellmann ("Zu den Anfängen des litauischen Reiches") and by G. Stökl, *ibid.*, vol. 6 (1958), p. 482. The critics agree with Pašuto's thesis that the progress of the Lithuanians into Slavic principalities was facilitated by the willingness of the retinues of the princes, after their subjection to the Tatars, to offer their services to the Lithuanian princes, the only ones who could resist the Tatars. This explains also why the rule of the Lithuanians was accepted without protest by the Slavic population. On the beginnings of Lithuanian rule, see also H. Paszkiewicz, *The Origin of Russia* (London, 1954), pp. 185-232. Cf. also Hellmann's study in *Saeculum* (see Bibl.). On the relations between the Jagiellonians and Moscow in the thirteenth and fourteenth centuries, see also H. Paszkiewicz, *Jagiellonowie a Moskwa, Litwa a Moskwa w XIII i XIV wieku* (Warsaw, 1933).

4. On the early history of Moscow, cf. the recent publication by the SSSR Academy, *Istorija Moskvy*, vol. 1 (1952), where also summary indications on Russian bibliography will be found. The history of Moscow by I. E. Zabelin (*Istorija goroda Moskvy*, Moscow, 1905) is now superseded for the early period by M. N. Tikhomirov's *Drevnjaja Moskva* (Moscow, 1947).

5. Cf. Chapter XV, p. 368.

6. On the Russian principalities of the North during the Tatar period, the work by A. V. Ekzempljarskij (*Velikie i udelnye knjazja severnoj Rusi v tatarskij period*, 2 vols., St. Petersburg, 1889-91) is still often quoted. See also vol. 3 of the *Očerki istorii SSSR* (Moscow, 1953), edited by B. O. Grekov, L. V. Čerepnin, V. T. Pašuto.

7. The memory of it is proudly recalled also by present-day Russia, as illustrated by the historical novel by Sergej Borodin, a Stalin Prize novel for 1942. It was translated into English by Eden and Cedar Paul (*Dmitri Donskoi*, London, New York, 1944).

8. Published by L. Čerepnin in his study, "Dogovornye i dukhovnye gramoty Dmitrija Donskogo," *Istoričeskie Zapiski*, vol. 24 (1947), pp. 225-66 (the passage, pp. 247-50). Cf. the mention of the document by O. Halecki, "Imperialism in Slavic and East European History," *The American Slavic and East European Review*, 11 (1951), p. 6. It is not quite clearly established whether the initiative for a Polish-Lithuanian rapprochement came from the Poles or from the Lithuanians. H. Paszkiewicz (*Origin of Russia*, pp. 233-54) brought forth some new arguments which support the thesis that the initiative came from the Lithuanians. Anyhow, the decision between the two powers was not easy for Jagiello. Only the acceptance of Latin Christianity could make the "missionary" activity of the Teutonic Order, then Jagiello's most dangerous adversary, come to a stop. On the other hand, such a decision meant the abandonment of the ambitious plan of gathering all Russian principalities around Vilna.

9. These are the standard works on the Polish-Lithuanian commonwealth in Polish: L. Kolankowski, *Dzieje Wielkiego księstwa Litewskiego za Jagiellonów* (Warsaw, 1930), vol. I, 1377-1499; O. Halecki, *Dzieje unji Jagiellońskiej*, 2 vols. (Cracow, 1919-1920); St. Kutrzeba, *Unija Polski z Litwą* (Cracow, 1914); H. Paskiewicz, *Jagiellonovie a Moskva*, vol. I: *Litwa a Moskva w 13 i-14 w.* (Warsaw, 1933). On Vitold see the monograph by J. Pfitzner, *Groszfürst Witold von Litauen als Staatsmann* (see Bibl.). *Ibid.* pp. 9-12 the author reviews Polish, Russian, and German studies on Vitold. A most complete indication of sources and bibliography concerning this period and the Polish-Lithuanian union will be found *ibid.*, pp. 225-39. On Lithuania and Russia in the fifteenth century see H. Jablonowski (see Bibl.), with detailed bibliography.

11. For details see especially G. Vernadsky, *The Mongols and Russia* (New Haven, 1953), pp. 263-82. On Tamerlane see H. Lamb, *Tamerlane the Earth Shaker* (New York, 1928). Cf. also the general survey on the Mongol period in Russia by A. Nasonov, *Mongoly i Rus* (Moscow, 1940).

12. See above, Ch. VIII, p. 201.

13. Detailed information on the religious policy of Lithuania and Moscow, with references to Slavic and other sources and works, will be found in A. Ammann's book *Abriss der Ostslavischen Kirchengeschichte* (Vienna, 1950), pp. 73-129.

14. I. Miklosich, I. Müller, *Acta et diplomata graeca* (see Bibl.) vol. II, pp. 188. "Therefore, my son, it is not loyal to say that we have the Church with-

out a Basileus, because it is impossible for Christians to have a Church and no Basileus. The Basileia and the Church have so much in common that they cannot be separated. Christians can only repudiate emperors who are heretics, fight the Church, or introduce doctrines irreconciliable with the teaching of the Apostles and the Fathers. But the great and holy autocrator, by the grace of God, is an Orthodox and a believer, a champion of the Church, its protector and avenger, so that it is impossible for bishops not to mention him in the liturgy. Of whom then do the Fathers, the councils, and the canons speak? Always and everywhere they speak loudly of the one legitimate Basileus, whose laws, edicts, and charters are in force all the world over and who alone, and nobody else, is everywhere mentioned in the liturgy by the Christians."

15. The struggle of Svidrigello and his popularity among the southwest Russian princes is described in detail by M. Hruševsv́kyj in his *Istorija Ukraini-Rusi* (New York, 1955), vol. IV, pp. 177-242. The monograph by A. Lewicki, *Powstanie Świdrygiełły*, published in the historical series of the *Rozpravy* of the Polish Academy (Cracow, 1892), is complemented by O. Halecki's study on the last years of Svidrigello (*Ostatnie lata Świdrygiełły i sprawa wołyńska za Kazimierza Jagiełłończyka*, Cracow, 1915). Lewicki's affirmation (*op. cit.*, p. 58) that the Teutonic Order played a role in the conclusion of Svidrigello's pact with Moscow in 1408 is disproved by K. Forstreuter in *Preussen und Russland* (see Bibl.), p. 49. On Svidrigello's attempts to bring about the union of his Orthodox subjects with Rome see A. M. Amann, *Ostlawische Kirchengeschichte* (see Bibl.), pp. 127-219. On the role of the Teutonic Order in this affair during the Council of Basle (1431-1435) as Svidrigello's ally cf. K. Forstreuter, *op. cit.*, pp. 51 ff. Svidrigello's unionist policy naturally turned Jagiello and Sigismund against the idea of union, and this mistrust continued in Poland for some time, even after the Council of Florence (1439). On the other hand, it would appear that his unionist policy alienated Svidrigello's supporters in his Slavic provinces. On Svidrigello's attempts at union see O. Halecki, *From Florence to Brest* (Rome, 1958), pp. 39 ff.

16. Cf. below, Chapter XII, pp. 259 ff.

Chapter X

THE JAGIELLONIAN
DYNASTIC COMMONWEALTH
AND THE TURKISH DANGER

Jagiello's son Władysław, king of Poland, elected king of Hungary—Sigismund of Hungary and the last days of Serbia—Władysław, the "hero of Varna"—The conquest of Serbia, Bosnia, Hercegovina, Zeta, and Albania by Mohammed II—Matthias Corvinus and Vladislav the Jagiellonian, king of Bohemia and Hungary—King Casimir IV of Poland and Lithuania—Turkish progress toward the southern frontier of Poland—John Albrecht's disastrous expedition toward the Black Sea ports—Alexander's success in the Crimea—Sigismund I of Poland and the Habsburgs—King Louis the Jagiellonian's tragic death at Mohács—Habsburgs replace Jagiellonians in Bohemia and Hungary—The Habsburgs, the last Jagiellonians and the Turks

The Polish-Lithuanian union had the natural consequence of greatly enhancing in eastern Europe the prestige of the dynasty which had effected it. The Jagiellonians became the most important dynasty after the Habsburgs, and the eyes of Poland's neighbors were directed toward Cracow and Vilna whenever a political crisis arose or a new ruler had to be selected. The first such case occurred in Hungary in 1440, after the death of Albert II of Habsburg, who had succeeded Sigismund in 1437. Władysław VI, king of Poland (1434-1444), the son and successor of Jagiello, was elected king of Hungary. The election was a serious defeat for the Habsburg dynasty, which was only able to retain the throne of Bohemia for Albert's posthumous son Ladislas.

It was the growing Turkish danger which had induced the Hungarian magnates to seek for help in Poland. The disastrous defeat of the Serbians on the Kosovo Polje was the first warning signal to Hungary that it might be the next victim of the advancing Turks.

Hungary had always manifested a lively interest in the Balkan lands, especially in Serbia and Bosnia. When Lazar's son Stephen Lazarević (1389-1427) became, after Kosovo, a Turkish vassal for the remnant of Serbia, Hungary, under Sigismund, was alarmed by the turn of events and vainly claimed sovereignty over Lazar's lands. Hungary's alarm grew when Bayazid occupied the rest of Bulgaria in 1393. A short-lived military success against the Turks in 1395 encouraged Sigismund to organize a crusade in 1396. But all his claims and hopes were crushed when his army was annihilated by the Turks at Nicopolis in the same year.[1] The situation of the Serbian ruler was, however, relieved by the Mongol invasion of Asia Minor and the defeat of Bayazid's army by Tamerlane near Ankara in 1402.[2] Even Byzantium now came forward and showed interest in expiring Serbia. In 1402, Stephen Lazarević received from the Emperor John Palaeologus the title of Despot, which was at that time the highest distinction the shrinking Byzantine Empire was able to award. This was a dying gleam of Byzantine glory in the twilight of its waning years, but the Serbian prince gloried in it and paid belated homage to the emperor as head of Orthodox Christendom.

Under Stephen and his nephew and successor, George Branković (1427-1456), who became despot in 1429, Serbia became a more compact territory, for the lands of the Knez Lazar and of the Branković and Balša families, whose representatives had behaved as independent rulers, were reunited under one rule. Thus Serbia almost regained the extent of the kingdom under the Nemanjas in the thirteenth century. The Despotate of Serbia naturally paid tribute to the Turks, but it was also a vassal of Hungary, and in recognition of this fact King Sigismund conferred on the Despot Stephen numerous important possessions in Hungary.

Sigismund is often and rightly blamed for not having concentrated his Hungarian and German forces for a decisive struggle with the Turks. If he had directed the armies of the crusaders against the Turks instead of against the Hussites, he would have had a fair chance of arresting definitively the progress of the Turks and of helping the Balkan peoples to liberate themselves from the Turkish yoke. In his time Turkish expansion was only in its beginnings, and their power far from its peak.[3]

That this opportunity was missed by Sigismund is all the more regrettable in that the Ottoman power was undergoing a serious crisis as a result of its defeat by the Mongol invaders of Asia Minor at Ankara. The Turkish Empire was only saved by Mohammed I the Restorer (1413-1421), who began the war against the Venetians, and Murad II (1421-1451). Sigismund failed to exploit this opportunity, and after his death in

1437 the Turks took advantage of the situation to attack the Serbians and put an end to the independence of the Serbian despotate in 1439. This new catastrophe was a stern warning to the Hungarians that the Turkish danger was approaching their own lands.

The election of Władysław to the Hungarian throne happened at the very moment when Sigismund, grand duke of Lithuania, the son of Keistut, had been assassinated by his rebellion subjects. The king, invited by the Lithuanians to rule over the grand duchy, sent his brother Casimir there as viceroy, but he was soon proclaimed grand duke by the Lithuanian nobles and, under their influence, ruled without much regard for Poland.

Władysław was anxious to carry out the promised expedition against the Turks as soon as possible. Unfortunately, new troubles in Hungary spoiled his plans. The widowed Queen Elizabeth claimed the Hungarian throne for her infant son Ladislas, who had been recognized as successor to his father in Bohemia. The queen was supported by the Emperor Frederick III, by the German cities in Hungary, and by the Czech Hussite detachment led by John Jiskra. The latter had occupied the northern part of Hungary, modern Slovakia, in the name of the infant king and had cut Hungary off from Poland. Defeated by Władysław's general John Hunyadi, the queen only came to terms in 1442.

All this delayed Władysław's expedition considerably. Encouraged by the papal legate Cesarini, the king and Hunyadi invaded the Balkans in 1443 and met with a great success. Hunyadi took Niš and advanced to Sofia.

Sultan Murad II asked for peace, promising to restore Serbia to George Branković. It is generally believed that a peace treaty was concluded and sworn by Władysław in Szeged. Not only was Serbia freed, but Wallachia also was abandoned to Hungary. The king, however, was persuaded, so it is said, by the legate, Cardinal Cesarini, not to keep the peace treaty but to continue the crusade against the Turks, on the grounds that a Christian was not bound to keep a treaty concluded with an infidel. He was punished for this perjury when his army was cut to pieces at the battle of Varna in 1444, and the king and the legate lost their lives on the battlefield.

This traditional evaluation of the events of 1444 is to some extent, however, in need of reassessment. The king can be definitely blamed only for having accepted the sultan's offer to start peace negotiations, which were conducted in Adrianople, the sultan's residence, and for having promised to ratify the conditions agreed upon. Murad II, anxious to transfer his army to Asia Minor, where a new danger was threatening him, agreed to the conditions mentioned above and accepted the treaty, which was to be ratified by the Hungarian king in Szeged. There is no doubt that George Branković had concluded the truce, but the king, on the advice of the legate, seems to have refused to ratify the treaty, already sworn by Murad, preferring to continue the crusade. In fact, the chances of success seemed good despite the absence of the Serbian contingent. The Venetian fleet was expected to prevent the sultan from bringing his main army from Asia Minor to Europe, and the king's small army seemed capable of defeating the Turks and helping the Byzantine emperor in his distress.[4]

Unfortunately, the king could not initiate his campaign as soon as was planned. This delay and the circumstance that the Christian fleet was unable to prevent the transport of Murad's army across the Straits to the European shore proved fatal to the expedition and to the king. John Hunyadi, voivode of Transylvania, who had participated in the negotiations and had accompanied the king, was, however, able to save himself and the major part of his army.

Hunyadi once more invaded Serbia in 1445 and met the army of Murad II at the Kosovo Polje. The Christian army, however, suffered a severe defeat on the same battlefield where not long previously the fate of independent Serbia had been decided.

When Mohammed II the Conqueror (1451-1481) came to power, the fate of the last remnants of the Byzantine Empire was soon sealed. In 1453 Constantinople fell. Alarmed by the Turkish progress, Hunyadi made repeated raids into the territory conquered by the Turks. Mohammed, however, advanced as far as Belgrade, which he besieged.[5] The last glorious deed of the Hungarian hero was his relief, with the help of a Serb contingent, of the heroic defenders of that city in 1456. After Hunyadi's death, however, nobody was able to stop the Turkish advance.

George Branković, already attacked in 1454, had to ask for peace and became the sultan's vassal. George died in 1456, and his successors were mediocre rulers who, struggling among themselves, were unable to save Serbia. In 1459, after the occupation of the new Serbian residential fortress of Smederevo (Semendria), the conquest of the whole of Serbia was terminated. This was the end of medieval Serbia. Only the conferment by the Hungarian kings up to the beginning of the sixteenth century of the dignity of Despot on members of the Branković family, and on other Slavic nobles who had settled in Hungary after the conquest of Serbia, recalled this last stage of Serbian medieval history.

After the conquest of Serbia, Mohammed II turned against Bosnia. This country had been plunged into anarchy after the death of its greatest ruler, Tvrtko I (1391). From Sigismund onward, Hungary claimed suzerainty over Bosnia, but most of the magnates behaved as independent princes respecting the authority neither of the Bosnian kings nor of their Hungarian suzerains.[6] The southern part of Bosnia (Hum) was almost independent from 1440 and was called Hercegovina after Stephen Vukčić, its ruler, who had taken the title of *herzeg* (duke). At first, from 1414 on, the Turks contented themselves with incursions into Bosnia. Only in 1463 did Mohammed II make the decisive attack. He encountered little opposition. The feudal lords recognized Turkish sovereignty and, in order to save their lands, accepted the faith of the Prophet. The Bogomils also embraced the religion of the Turks in great numbers. The last Bosnian king, Stefan Tomašević, was captured and executed. Hercegovina fought for its freedom for some time, but in 1466 the Ottoman Turks became complete masters even of that country.

In the meantime the Turks were also breaking the resistance of Albania. There the leader and inspirer of resistance was Scanderbeg (George Castriota), an adroit strategist, well acquainted with Turkish manners because he had been educated as a hostage at the sultan's court. He had achieved great military fame during the Turkish campaigns against the Mongols in Asia Minor, but for reasons which are not yet clear, he escaped in 1443 and rallied the Albanian tribes around him. In his struggle against the Turks he was supported first by Alfonso, king of Aragon and Naples, and from 1458, by Venice. He harassed the Turks with some success by his attacks and, entrenched in his fortress of Kroia, resisted the Turkish onslaughts vigorously. However, when he died in 1467, his country's resistance was soon broken, and Albania became a part of the Ottoman Empire.[7]

The longest resistance was encountered by the Turks in Zeta, later called Montenegro. This country was governed by the valiant family of the Crnojević, who led a defense which was facilitated by the mountainous character of the country. Only in 1479 were the Turks able to impose their overlordship on the country. The Crnojević resisted, however, even after that, supported by the Venetians. Only in 1499 was this part of the Balkans completely subdued.[8]

These events were an indirect consequence of the disaster suffered by the Hungarian king at Varna in 1444. Hungary was the only Christian nation which was able to intervene in the Balkan peninsula and was directly interested in its fate. Unfortunately, the political situation in Hungary was not always favorable for such intervention.

After Władysław's death, the Hungarian crown was offered to Ladislas Posthumus, king of Bohemia, the son of the Emperor Albert II, who preferred to reside in Buda rather than in Prague, where he felt ill at ease amid his Utraquist subjects. After his death (1457), the son of the heroic

John Hunyadi, Matthias Corvinus (1458-1490) became king of Hungary. Unfortunately, like Sigismund, Matthias was attracted by the prospect of conquests in the more cultured Bohemia and Austria rather than in the Balkans. If he had been able to concentrate on the war with the Turks, he would have stopped their advance in the Balkans for a long time, thanks to his reorganization of Hungarian military power. The financial reforms which he introduced helped him to establish a standing army, with Czech and other mercenaries, which commanded the respect of the Turks. In 1479 he won a resounding victory over the Turkish army, which had invaded Transylvania, and in 1480 he reconquered part of Bosnia. He erected two military banates there, that of Jajce and that of Srebernik, but was not able to exploit the troubles which broke out in Turkey after the death of Mohammed II in 1481.

Matthias's policy of expansion in the West led him into conflict with George of Poděbrady, king of Bohemia, and, after his death, with the Jagiellonians, when Vladislav, eldest son of Casimir of Poland, was elected king of Bohemia. The compromise of Olomouc (1478) left to Matthias Moravia, Silesia, and Lusatia, the provinces of the Czech crown which he had conquered. But when after Matthias's death (1490), the magnates elected Vladislas king of Hungary also, the conquered Czech provinces were reunited with Bohemia.

Vladislas had first to defeat his own brother John Albrecht, who had also competed for the Hungarian crown. Unfortunately, Vladislas was a weakling, completely in the hands of the magnates, who had elected him for this reason in order to increase their own influence. So most of the gains realized by Matthias in internal and international policy were lost during the new reign. The standing army which the valiant Matthias had created was disbanded, and thus vanished an important factor which could have held the Turks at bay.

Fortunately, Sultan Bayazid II (1481-1512) was not an aggressive ruler, and his successor Selim I (1512-1520) had to deal with new troubles in the East. So it happened that the peace treaty with Hungary was renewed by the Turks every third year as it expired. The opportunities of intervention in the Balkans were, however, missed, and all Hungary achieved in Dalmatia was the conclusion of a treaty with Venice.

The Polish Jagiellonians could not intervene directly in southern Europe. After Władysław's tragic death at Varna, the Polish throne stayed unoccupied for two years because of rumors, readily believed, that the king was not dead but only a captive of the Turks. In 1446, the Bishop of Cracow, Oleśnicki, who occupied a leading position in Poland, obtained general support for the election of the dead king's brother Casimir, grand duke of Lithuania. Casimir accepted, but resisted Oleśnicki's efforts to bring Lithuania into a closer union with Poland. Crowned king of Poland in 1447,[9] he defended the principle of equality between the two realms and terminated the territorial dispute between them, leaving Podolia to Poland and Volhynia to Lithuania.

Meanwhile the Turkish danger was approaching Poland's frontiers in the South, on the boundaries of Podolia. The two Rumanian principalities of Moldavia and Wallachia were the nearest neighbors of Hungary and Poland and, of course, most endangered by the advance of the Turks. Wallachia had already concluded a kind of alliance with Poland in 1390, but Polish influence there was only spasmodic because it was separated from Poland by Moldavia. The prince of Moldavia became a Polish vassal as early as 1387, under Jagiello, and this relationship between the two countries persisted through the fifteenth century. The most valiant Moldavian prince was Stephen the Great (1457-1503). He was able to preserve the independence of his country although it was attacked several times by the Turks, who had overrun Wallachia at the time of the fall of Constantinople.[10]

More serious was the Turkish conquest of Caffa, the Genoese colony in the Crimea, which was a very important commercial center. Endangered by the Turkish advance toward the Crimea, Caffa appealed to Poland for protection. But Poland could not help, and in 1475 Caffa fell to the Turks.[11] The establishment of the Turks in the Crimea had an ominous significance for the Polish-Lithuanian commonwealth. The Tatar Khanate of the Crimea, governed by the Gireys dynasty, had been, hitherto, an ally of Poland-Lithuania. After the conquest of Caffa, the Khan Mengli changed sides and became a vassal of the Turks and the ally of Moscow. Through frequent invasions of the Russian lands under Lithuanian suzerainty, he cut Lithuania off from the Black Sea.

The Turkish advance did not stop there. In 1484 Bayazid II attacked Moldavia and conquered the two important Black Sea ports of Kilia and Akkerman. This serious loss induced Stephen the Great to approach Poland for help and to pay homage to Casimir. The latter, however, did not dare to enter into direct conflict with the Turks. But with the help of a Polish military detachment Stephen was able to drive the Turks from Moldavia. The combined military forces were, however, insufficient to free the Voivode Stephen from the tribute which he had to pay the Turks and to reconquer the Black Sea ports. Further Polish intervention was frustrated by an attack on the part of the Golden Horde, instigated by the Khan of the Crimea and the Turks.

New complications on the southern frontier materialized under the reign of Casimir's successor John Albrecht (Jan Olbracht) (1492-1501). The new king was very popular with the Polish knighthood and the burghers, but although desirous of strengthening the royal power, he was forced to make new concessions to the higher nobility in order to obtain the means necessary for his enterprises. He did not forget Polish interests in the south, and the Venetians made great efforts to persuade him to continue the Turkish war. But, seeing that he needed some more time to prepare his plans, he accepted Bayazid II's offer and, in 1494, concluded a truce to last until 1497.

Plans for the reconquest of the Black Sea ports and of Caffa were discussed at the meeting of all Jagiellonians held in Levoča in Upper Hungary in 1494. It was decided to take the necessary measures to strengthen the authority of Vladislav in Hungary, but during the discussions of the campaign against the Turks it appeared that Poland and Hungary disagreed concerning the position of Moldavia. Hungary regarded the latter as its vassal, a circumstance which had made Stephen of Moldavia suspicious of Poland.

John Albrecht made preparations for an expedition to the Black Sea coast, which he realized in 1497. The Lithuanians, led by their Grand Duke Alexander, prepared their own expedition. Unfortunately, the whole enterprise ended in disaster. It is still not clear what induced Stephen of Moldavia to manifest hostility toward the Poles as soon as they touched Moldavian soil. Instead of fighting the Turks, the Polish army besieged without success Stephen's capital of Suczawa. When a truce was concluded through the diplomatic intervention of Vladislav of Hungary and the Polish army was retreating through the province of Bukovina, it was attacked by Stephen's forces and suffered a serious defeat. It was saved by the help sent by the Grand Duke Alexander, but the whole expedition of Polish and Lithuanian forces ended in failure. The Turks retaliated by twice invading Poland and devastating the country as far as Lwów, Sambor, Sanok, and Przeworsk. John Albrecht had to conclude a defensive alliance with Hungary and reconcile himself with Stephen of Moldavia. He refused to take part in the crusade which was destined to help the Venetians in their war with the Turks (1499), and started negotiations for a truce which was concluded in 1500.

John Albrecht was succeeded by his brother Alexander (1501-1506), previously grand duke of Lithuania. He could do little to ameliorate the situation in the south. He was deeply engaged in conflicts with Moscow, which had been aggravated by his profound westernization and polonization of the Russian lands under Lithuanian suzerainty. He defended the rights of the crown valiantly against the ambitions of the nobles, but with little success. Thanks to the intervention of Vladislav of Hungary, a compromise was concluded between Poland and Moldavia. Bogdan, the son and successor of Stephen, ceded the province of Pokucie to Poland

and married a Jagiellonian princess (1505). This success was followed in 1506 by the defeat of Mengli-Girey, khan of the Crimea, by the Lithuanians, and the Khan was forced to abandon his alliance with Moscow.

The reign of Sigismund I, called the Old (1506-1548), marked the zenith of Poland's cultural development and was deeply influenced by the Renaissance.[12] Peaceful conditions on Poland's southern border were soon disturbed. Bogdan profited by the change on the Polish throne to reoccupy the ceded province of Pokucie (1508). Expelled by Polish mercenaries, he again invaded the disputed land in 1509. Thanks to the mediation of Hungary, whose sovereignty over Moldavia had been recognized by Poland in 1507, peace was concluded in 1510. New complications in Turkey, where Selim revolted against his father Bayazid and was determined to conquer Moldavia, and in the Crimea, where Mengli-Girey concluded an alliance with Moscow, demanded caution on the southern boundary. The incursions of the Tatars were stopped by the offer of a financial subsidy to the Khan, and the new Turkish sultan Selim I (1512) renewed the truce with Poland.

Complications with the Grand Master of the Teutonic Order, who was supported by the Emperor Maximilian I, and the danger threatening Poland-Lithuania from Moscow induced Sigismund I to enter into negotiations with the Habsburgs. A treaty between the Jagiellonians and the Habsburgs was concluded in 1515 in Vienna and was sealed by the marriages of Louis Jagiello of Hungary and Bohemia with Maximilian's granddaughter Mary, and of Ferdinand, one of the emperor's grandsons, with Louis' sister Anne.

Fortunately, Sultan Selim I, busy in Egypt and Armenia, did not accept Moscow's offer of an alliance against Poland and renewed his armistice with her. But under the reign of his son Suleiman the Magnificent (1520-1566), the Turkish danger appeared in all its magnitude. In a new attempt at the conquest of Europe the Turks invaded Hungary, then ruled by the Jagiellonian Louis II (1516-1526), son of Vladislav. Like his father, Louis had also been accepted as king of Bohemia. In 1521 Belgrade was taken by the Turks, and the way into Hungary lay open.

In the meantime, however, Hungary's power of resistance had been undermined by misrule and social unrest due to the exploitation of the peasantry by the nobility, whose influence on public affairs had increased considerably during the weak reign of Vladislav. In the face of the new danger the young king appealed to the Bohemian Diet and to Poland for help. Only a small detachment of troops could be sent by Sigismund of Poland, and the Czech contingents arrived too late. The young king dared to face the Turkish forces at Mohács (1526), but his small army was completely annihilated and Louis himself lost his life.[13]

At the same time, the southern border of Poland was also in flames. The Turks, with their Crimean puppet Seadet Girey, invaded and devastated the Russian provinces under Polish and Lithuanian rule. These incursions induced the king to strengthen the defenses of the southern frontier. For the first time the old idea of maintaining a standing army of mercenaries on the southeastern frontier was put into practice, thanks to the energy of the Polish grand hetman John Tarnowski. The incursions into Polish territories were stopped, and soon the Lithuanian hetman Ostrogski secured the Lithuanian borderlands similarly.

In this connection, the Cossacks first entered into Lithuanian history. They were settlers of very heterogenous origin, mostly Poles and Russians, fugitive peasants and nobles who had settled in the borderlands between Poland-Lithuania and the Tatar khanate, which began at that time to be called Ukraine. They organized themselves into military associations for the protection of their property. The Lithuanian Diet conceived the idea (1524) of enrolling them into the Lithuanian army for the protection of the frontiers. In 1533 a flotilla on the Lower Dnieper was also created in order to ensure security in these regions. However, the Polish attempt at the reconquest of the Black Sea port of Oczakov was frustrated by Suleiman and his puppet khan of the Crimea. Moreover, the defeat at Mohács had opened a threat to Polish security on the Hungarian border.

Sigismund would perhaps have had some chance of being elected king of Bohemia and Hungary if he had announced his candidature immediately when he received the news of the Mohács disaster. He did so too late and without real conviction, and this gave their chance to the Habsburgs, who claimed both crowns by virtue of the treaty of 1515 and the marital ties which had sealed it. The election of Ferdinand I of Austria (1526-1564), husband of the Jagiellonian princess Anne and brother of the Emperor Charles V (1519-1556), was effected after long bargaining in Bohemia. In Hungary, however, a double election took place, one party of the nobles voting for John Zápolya. Civil war followed between the two candidates. This was a great disaster for Hungary and for Central Europe. A divided Hungary was unable to resist the invaders, and the Turkish tide engulfed the Hungarian plains. The greater part of Croatia was conquered. Dalmatia, occupied by Venice after the disintegration of the Bosnian kingdom, was also invaded. Ragusa only saved its independence by virtue of its important commercial relations with the Turks. The peace treaty of 1540, however, gave the Dalmatian coastal cities to Venice.

In Hungary both rivals appealed to Sigismund of Poland for support. The king was in a difficult situation. Zápolya was his brother-in-law, and the Polish gentry favored him. Ferdinand invoked the Vienna agreement, and despite the hostility of the majority of the Polish gentry to the Habsburgs, he also found some support among the Polish nobility. All Sigismund could do in such circumstances was to endeavor to stop the civil war and reconcile the two contestants. This was in vain, and Zápolya, twice defeated by Ferdinand, fled to Poland and was saved by the sultan, with whom he had concluded an alliance through the mediation of his Polish supporters. With the sultan's help Zápolya was able to conquer Buda and to advance as far as Vienna.

Suleiman made another expedition against Vienna in 1532, and Sigismund, impressed by the progress of the Turks, concluded a peace treaty with the sultan in 1533. Fearing new hostile action by the sultan, Ferdinand and Zápolya agreed in 1538 to partition Hungary. Zápolya received Transylvania with Buda and the central part of Hungary, but it was stipulated that after his death all that remained of Hungary should come under the sovereignty of the Habsburgs.

New troubles with Moldavia complicated the situation on Poland's southern boundary. The new Voivode of Moldavia, Peter Rareş, although a Hungarian vassal, profited by the struggle for the Hungarian throne to assume an aggressive attitude against Poland. He occupied the Moldavian province of Pokucie, ceded to Poland, but was defeated by Sigismund's hetman Tarnowski, who recovered the disputed province (1531). Further incursions by Rareş into Poland were stopped by a new advance of the Turks in this region, who replaced him as Voivode by Stefan and became undisputed sovereign of Moldavia.

On the other hand, events in Hungary gave the sultan new pretexts for intervention. Poland's attitude toward the two rulers of divided Hungary was rather equivocal. In 1538 Sigismund gave his final consent to the marriage of his son Sigismund August with the Habsburg archduchess Elizabeth. In spite of that the Polish queen Bona, of the Italian family of the Sforzas, was more favorable to Zápolya and persuaded the king to give their daughter Isabella in marriage to him. The latter, counting on Polish and Turkish help, forgot the agreement concluded with Ferdinand in 1538. When Zápolya died in 1540, the Hungarian nationalist aristocracy proclaimed his baby son John Sigismund king of Hungary. The Polish king asked the sultan to support his grandson, while at the same time he gave assurances to Ferdinand that he would maintain his neutral attitude in Hungarian affairs in return for the recognition of Bona's claims to the Duchy of Milan.

Ferdinand's campaign against Buda led to a Turkish invasion of Hungary (1541). Ferdinand's army was defeated, and Buda added to the

Turkish possessions in Hungary. John Sigismund was given Transylvania with lands to the east of the river Tisza under Turkish suzerainty. Another invasion by the Turks in 1543 extended their possessions further. The fear of renewed Turkish progress induced Bona to give her consent to Isabella's renunciation of the Hungarian throne in return for concessions which Ferdinand promised her in Silesia (1544).

Polish nationalists, with Queen Bona, continued their hostile attitude toward the Habsburgs and even proposed the conclusion of an anti-Habsburg alliance with Turkey and France. The pro-Habsburg party demanded instead a war against Turkey. Promises by the Habsburgs to Bona concerning her claims to the Duchy of Milan averted the conclusion of an anti-Habsburg coalition, and Sigismund August married the Archduchess Elizabeth (1543), who, however, died two years later.

It was in the interests of the Habsburgs to provoke a conflict between Poland and Turkey. Poland needed free access to the Black Sea, and in 1545 the port of Oczakov, which she coveted, was seized by the Polish army. A war was, however, averted because the queen induced the Diet to vote an indemnity to Turkey for the damage and loss.[14]

During the first years of the reign of Sigismund August (1548-1572) the Habsburgs continued to fan anti-Turkish feeling in Poland. The young king did not hide his dislike for the turbulent Polish gentry and only gave his confidence to some of them whom he had himself raised to the rank of magnates. The most influential among these were the Radziwills, who occupied the first place in Lithuania. In order to enhance his prestige inside the kingdom, Sigismund August considered it advantageous to strengthen his ties with the Habsburgs.

In 1549 he concluded an entente with Ferdinand I, king of Bohemia and Hungary, and with the Emperor Charles V. This implied the abandonment of the interests of Zápolya's son and of Sigismund August's sister Isabella in Hungary.

Poland's conclusion of a pact with the Habsburgs was, of course, received with displeasure in Turkey. But because the sultan was then at war with Persia, he failed to take any hostile action against Poland. The anti-Turkish agitation in Poland, fomented by the Habsburgs and their partisans, had some success. Some adventurers among the Polish nobility undertook an expedition in 1552 against Moldavia, which was under Turkish domination. Nevertheless, the sultan confirmed the Polish-Turkish peace treaty in 1553. Further incursions of this kind, undertaken between 1560 and 1562 and in 1572, failed to bring about the rupture of friendly relations between Poland and Turkey. The sultan did not want to push Poland into the arms of the Habsburgs. On the other hand, Sigismund August, heavily engaged in his wars with Muscovy,[15] did not desire any complications with Turkey. Twice, in 1565 and in 1569, the possibility of a Polish-Turkish alliance against Moscow was discussed, but failed to materialize.

The Habsburgs were thus left alone in their struggle with the Turks in Hungary. Ferdinand I was in constant warfare with Suleiman's forces in Hungary from 1551 to 1562, without decisive result. After succeeding his brother Charles on the imperial throne (1556), Ferdinand made peace with John Sigismund Zápolya, abandoning to him his claims to Transylvania. The Turks continued to hold Hungary proper, and Ferdinand was induced to pay tribute for the western part, which was left to him.

Ferdinand's successor Maximilian II (1564-1576) limited himself to raids into the Turkish part of Hungary, and Suleiman organized a new expedition against him in 1566. This was his thirteenth campaign against the West. It proved to be his last; he died during the unsuccessful siege of Sziget, which was defended heroically by the Croatian Count Zrinski. This was the end of the Turkish offensive. Maximilian II failed, however, to profit by this success, and concluded in 1568 an eight years' peace with Selim II, the Sot (1566-1574), without trying to profit by the reign of this intelligent but incompetent ruler. Not even the great naval victory won by Spain and Venice over the Turks at Lepanto (1571) roused Maximilian to action, although the victors were eager to continue the war against the Turks. The absence of action from the Habsburgs and Jagiellonians gave some respite to the Turks, whose empire's strength was rapidly declining. The death of Sigismund II August (1572) marked the end of the Jagiellonian dynasty, and the throne of Poland was once more open to competition.

The heavy engagements which Poland had contracted toward Lithuania against the growing Muscovite power were the main reason why the Jagiellonian commonwealth was not able to contribute more effectively toward combating the Turkish danger, although Jagiellonian kings were for some time in occupation of the thrones of Poland-Lithuania, Bohemia, and Hungary.

The other reason was the weakness of the Polish kings due to the decline of royal authority and the growth of the influence of the nobility both economically and politically. The king depended completely on the good will of the gentry and the nobles, who made decisions about taxes and levies in their Diets. Queen Bona, Sigismund I's wife, realized this all too well, and one of her main preoccupations was the creation of a private fortune for the dynasty, following, in this respect, the example set by the German kings of the thirteenth and fourteenth centuries. She also tried to introduce many other economic and political reforms which would have strengthened the royal authority, but was unable to win the democratic gentry and the egoistic magnates to her ideas: so it happened that the role which the Jagiellonians seemed predestined to play against the Turkish danger ended in disappointments for which they can hardly be blamed.

NOTES

1. For details see S. A. Atiya, *The Crusade of Nicopolis* (London, 1934). Cf. also J. Dąbrowski, *Władysław I Jagiellończyk na Węgrzech* (Warsaw, 1922).

2. Stephen, with his army, participated in the battle near Ankara as in all previous Turkish expeditions against Bulgaria, Rumania, and Sigismund. His policy, like that of other Serbian magnates, was to save what was left of Serbian national existence at the price of alliance with the Osmanlis. Before his death Stephen approached Sigismund and recognized Hungarian suzerainty.

3. For details see G. Beckmann, *Der Kampf Kaiser Sigismunds* (see Bibl.).

4. For details see O. Halecki, *The Crusade of Varna* (see Bibl.). On pp. 82-93 the author has republished some documents concerning the treaty which have hitherto been differently interpreted. Some new light on the whole affair is thrown by the letters of Cyriacus of Ancona, which are the main arguments used by the author for the revision of Władysław's attitude. Halecki's interpretation, although impressive, is not quite convincing. How can such an early origin of the tradition accusing Władysław of perjury be explained? Even if the king should be freed from the accusation of perjury because he had not ratified the treaty already sworn by Murad, his attitude must have appeared deliberately deceitful to many. When he gave Murad the assurance that he intended to ratify the treaty, he wished to induce him to withdraw his army to Asia, intending to continue the war and to expel the Turks from Europe. On the reaction which this victory had on Turkey cf. L. Fekete "Das Fethnāme über die Schlacht bei Varna," *Byzantinoslavica*, 14 (1953), pp. 258-70. Cf. also G. Ostrogorsky's remark in his *History of the Byzantine State*, p. 503.

5. Useful bibliographical notes in Slavic, Hungarian, and Rumanian on the Turkish advance toward the Danube after the fall of Constantinople are given by J. Macůrek in his study "Tureckaja opaznost i srednjaja Evropa nakanune i vo vremja padenja Konstantinopolja" (*Byzantinoslavica*, vol. 14, 1953), pp. 130-57.

6. Tvrtko's successors were as follows: Dabiša (1391-1395); Dabiša's widow, Helen (1395-1398); Tvrtko's son Stephen Ostoja (1398-1404); Tvrtko II (1404-1408); Stephen Ostoja (1408-1418); his son, Stephen Ostojić (1418-1421); Tvrtko II (1421-1443); Ostoja's son, Stephen Thomas (1444-1461); his son, Stephen Tomašević (1461-1463). Their reigns were all filled with strife with the magnates, with Hungary, and with the Turks. See the fullest account in V. Klaić, *Geschichte Bosniens* (Leipzig, 1889), pp. 248-439. Cf. also P. W. Vlajić, *Untergang des bosnischen Königreiches* (Sarajevo, 1926). Recently O. O. Mandić, *Bosna i Hercegovina* (Chicago, 1960).

7. For details see A. Gegaj, *L'Albanie et l'invasion turque* (see Bibl.).

8. See for details S. Gopčević, *Geschichte von Montenegro und Albanien* (Gotha, 1914), pp. 79-124. The cultural level in Montenegro at this period must have been quite high, thanks to the connections with Venice. The

Grnojević founded in Cetinja the first printing office in the Balkans. All known Serbian incunabula—liturgical books—were printed there.

9. The Polish historian F. Papée devoted a special study to the reign of Casimir IV and to his son John Albrecht: *Studia i szkice z czasów Kozimierza Jagillonczyka* (Warsaw, 1907); *Jan Olbracht* (Cracow, 1936).

10. See for details R. Rosetti, *Stephen the Great* (see Bibl.), pp. 87-103.

11. There is a good monograph on Caffa in Polish by M. Małowist, *Kaffa—kolonia genueńska na Krymie i problem wschodni w latach 1453-1475* (Warsaw, 1947), with useful bibliographical notices (pp. 347-52) and with a résumé in French (pp. i-xxxi).

12. See below, Chapter XIII, pp. 299 ff.

13. On the Czech participation in the defense of Central Europe against the Ottoman Turks see the study by J. V. Polišenský "Bohemia, the Turk and the Christian Commonwealth" (see Bibl.), with Czech bibliographical references.

14. On the attempt made by Poland and the Habsburgs to gain access to the Black Sea at the end of the sixteenth century see the monograph by J. Macůrek, *Zápas Polska a Habsburků o přístup k Černému moři na sklonku 16. století* (Prague, 1931). See below, Chapter XVII, pp. 448 ff., 463.

15. See Chapter XI, pp. 252 ff., Chapter XII, p. 275.

Chapter XI

POLAND-LITHUANIA AND THE BALTIC

Unrest in Prussia after the Polish victory at Grunwald—The Prussian Union, Poland regains sovereignty over Prussia and Pomerania—Albert of Brandenburg and the secularization of Ducal Prussia—Polish-Lithuanian progress in Livonia—Repercussions of Livonian affairs on Poland-Lithuania: the Union of Lublin, 1569—Poland's passive policy in Prussia

From the outset the Polish-Lithuanian federation was faced with problems, not only on its southern and western frontiers but also in the North, where it had been cut off from the Baltic by the Teutonic Order. The defeat inflicted on the order at Grunwald-Tannenberg in 1410 was achieved thanks to the intimate collaboration of the Polish and Lithuanian rulers, Jagiello and Vitold. But that victory was not properly exploited by the Poles and Lithuanians, and the Treaty of Toruń (1411) was very unfavorable to the victors.[1] Only the province of Samogitia (Żmudź) was ceded by the order to Lithuania, and that only for Vitold's lifetime. Numerous matters remained in dispute, including that of the payment of a considerable indemnity to Poland.

It was to be regretted that the victors' slow advance into Prussia after the victory gave a new respite to the order. The quick surrender of Prussian barons and cities to the advancing Poles after Grunwald showed clearly that the new state on the Baltic was not as strong as it appeared, and that it was past its zenith.

There were several reasons for this. First of all, despite the progress of German colonization in the conquered lands, many national differences continued to exist in the Teutonic state. The nobility of Chełmno had retained its Polish character and mentality. The Pomeranian nobles shared certain common interests with the Poles of Chełmno, and these differed from those of the German cities on the coast. The German and Prussian nobility in the western regions had different interests again, but all alike resented the monopolization of power in the state by the order, whose members, mostly recruited from Germany, were regarded by the native aristocracy as aliens. The native elements had no voice in the highly centralized state. The privileges which the Polish nobility had acquired in Poland naturally attracted the Prussian nobles, while important economic causes were leading the prosperous towns into opposition to the order, which was their dangerous competitor.

This spirit of revolt against the Knights grew in proportion to the decline in their religious spirit during the fourteenth century, when the raison d'être for the order, the enforcement of Christianity on the pagans, disappeared after the conversion of the Lithuanians. In spite of the iron rule of the Knights, opposition manifested itself in the outbreak of riots in Danzig in 1361 which were marked by the voicing of slogans favorable to Poland. In 1378 the Pomeranian nobility petitioned for the reduction of taxes, and the so-called Lizard League (*Eidechsen Bund*) among the nobles of Chełmno seems also to have been a demonstration of opposition against the order.

All these potentialities were neglected by Poland after the victory of Grunwald. But the Knights did not forget what had happened and took especial vengeance upon the town of Danzig and on the nobles of Chełmno. In spite of the temporary recovery of the order after 1410, the emancipatory ambitions of the Estates and the desire of the cities for freedom remained strong. The defeat had depleted the ranks of the order, and the Knights never recovered completely from this terrific blow. They tried hard, however, to regain their old position, and received some support from the German and Hungarian king Sigismund, who was jealous of Poland and particularly resented her retention of Galicia, which was coveted by Hungary. The king's policy was, however, vacillating, and so the two contending parties appealed to a higher tribunal for a solution of their differences. The Papacy rather favored the order but lacked the power to impose its will. The Poles brought their complaints before the forum of the Council of Constance in 1415 and developed vigorous propaganda against the order among the other Christian nations. Paul, the rector of the University of Cracow, proclaimed certain principles there which appeared revolutionary to most of his contemporaries. He defended the pagans' right to existence and declared the practice of forcible conversion to be unchristian. He also denied the emperor's right to distribute the territory of the pagans to the order. Sigismund's decision in 1420 in new disputes rather favored the order. This induced the Poles and Lithuanians to initiate a new campaign, which ended in 1422 by securing the possession of Samogitia for Lithuania. New conflicts arose from 1431 to 1435. In 1435 the order concluded an alliance with Svidrigello, but its Livonian branch, which had invaded Lithuania, suffered a serious defeat. The peace concluded by the two parties had to be guaranteed also, on the victors' demand, by the Prussian Estates, and the order had to promise not to have recourse to either the Pope or the emperor. The stipulations of the peace treaty were fiercely attacked by the branch of the order in Germany, and this conflict weakened its internal cohesion considerably. It provided new evidence of the diminution of the order's prestige.

The principal blow against the order was, however, launched by the Estates and towns of Prussia. Profiting by the decline of the order's power and fearful of the consequences of the anarchy which was noticeable among the ranks of the Knights, the nobles of Chełmno formed the so-called Prussian Union, which aimed at extending the privileges of the Estates. The order refused any further extension of rights and was supported in this refusal by the emperor and the Pope, who were averse to seeing it further weakened. So the members of the union turned their eyes toward Poland and revolted against the order in 1454, invoking the protection of the Polish king Casimir IV (1447-1492). The king proclaimed the "incorporation" of Prussia under the crown of Poland in the same year, guaranteeing and increasing the privileges of the members of the union.

This, of course, resulted in a military conflict between Poland and the order. But this time it lacked any character of a national war, such as had been enjoyed by that which ended at Grunwald. The Poles were supported by the Prussian Union headed by the German city of Danzig, which placed all its wealth at the disposal of the Polish king. Although reinforcements from Germany were vainly awaited and the proclamation of an interdict against the union proved of no avail, the order defended its territory with great vigor. It had at its disposal not only the knights and monks, but also seasoned mercenary troops. The Poles relied on their general militia, but its arms and tactics were outmoded so that it was no match for the experienced forces of the order. Consequently the war lasted for thirteen years.[2] Only when the Poles, with the financial help of Danzig, hired mercenary troops—many of whom were Czechs familiar with the new tactics—did their chances improve, and the order had to acknowledge defeat.

The Treaty of Toruń in 1466 was much more favorable to Poland-Lithuania than the first treaty concluded there in 1411. The victors, however, did not seize this opportunity to liquidate the order completely. The Polish nobles failed to see that it was in Poland's interest to remove the order altogether from the Baltic lands. They also feared that in such an eventuality, the Pope and the emperor would intervene in favor of the Knights. So it came about that the order saved its existence in Prussia, although it lost most of its lands. Pomerania with Danzig, the district of

Chełmno, the northwestern borders of Prussia with the cities of Malborg (Marienburg) and Elbing, together with the lands of the Bishop of Warmia (Ermland) became Polish and were later called "Royal Prussia." East Prussia with Königsberg remained under the sovereignty of the order but as a fief of the Polish crown. The grand master was given the title of Prince-Senator of Poland and had to pay homage to the king and to render assistance to his feudal lord in the event of war. It was also stipulated in the treaty that in future Poles should be admitted as member of the order, although it should continue to retain its German character.

The Peace of Toruń brought great advantages to Poland. Lands for which the Poles had been fighting for almost two centuries were recovered for the mother country, and the Vistula again became a Polish river. Access was gained to the Baltic and remained open to Poland until almost the last quarter of the eighteenth century. The king rewarded the Prussian cities with grants of local autonomy and many privileges. The reconquered territory was not incorporated directly into Poland, but received an autonomous status in administration, legislation, and judicial matters. This autonomous status was represented by the Prussian Diet, composed of representatives of the nobility, the clergy, the cities, and the newly installed administrative hierarchy.[3]

The order signed the Treaty of 1466, but its members had no intention of fulfilling the conditions. Unfortunately, the Poles overestimated the weakness of the order and paid insufficient attention to its changing mood, as a result of which Polish nationals remained excluded from membership. With the help of the Hungarian king Matthias Corvinus (1458-1490), the order attempted to change the conditions of the peace treaty, and its grand master, Martin Truchsess, refused to pay the homage due to the King of Poland. In 1478 he even made a bold attempt to recover the lost territories. King Casimir IV suppressed this revolt after he had been reconciled with the Hungarian king by the Treaty of Olomouc,[4] and the grand master was forced in 1479 to humble himself before the Polish sovereign. For the rest of the fifteenth century the order loyally fulfilled the obligations of the treaty.

The order continued, however, to maintain its relations with the Empire and found comfort in the fact that neither the emperor nor the Papacy had recognized the Treaty of Toruń. The order's ties with Germany were strengthened when Frederick of Saxe-Meissen was elected grand master in 1498. He effected some reorganization of the institutions of the order on the lines of a German principality. As a prince of the Empire he refused fealty to Poland unless the conditions of the peace treaty were changed. Only in 1501 did King John Albrecht (1492-1501) dare to demand that the grand master take the oath of allegiance. He died, however, before he could achieve his aim, and his successor, Alexander (1501-1506), heavily engaged in war with Russia, could not do anything to enforce the demand of his predecessor.

After Frederick's death Albert of Hohenzollern, son of the Margrave of Brandenburg-Ansbach and of Sophia Jagiello, daughter of Casimir IV, was elected grand master (1511).[5] He continued to refuse the oath of allegiance to his uncle, King Sigismund I (1506-1548), and found an ally in the Emperor Maximilian I. The latter was hostile to the Jagiellonian dynasty because it occupied the thrones of Bohemia and Hungary, which the Habsburgs coveted. Emboldened by the support of the Habsburgs, Albert demanded not only release from his obligations, but also the restitution of some territories on the right bank of the Vistula. He worked to form an anti-Polish league, to include Muscovite Russia, whose principal aim would be the partition of Poland.

King Sigismund put an abrupt end to this planning by concluding a treaty of mutual assistance at Vienna in 1515 with the Habsburgs. This was sealed by the marriage of Louis Jagiello, heir of Hungary, with Maximilian's granddaughter and of Ferdinand, one of the Emperor's grandsons, with Louis' sister Anne. In spite of that, the Prussian problem remained unsolved, and Albert continued his military preparations.

War was declared by Albert in 1519 after Maximilian's death. No decisive results were achieved, and through the mediation of Louis of Hungary and the Emperor Charles V an armistice was concluded at Toruń in 1521. The immediate effect of this conflict was to weaken the order yet further. The master of the German branch assumed the rank of a German prince in 1521, and his example was followed in 1530 by the master of the Livonian branch.

Albert contemplated a similar step. But when staying in Germany, he came into touch with Luther, whose teaching impressed him deeply. Albert accepted Luther's suggestion of transforming the territory of the order into a secular duchy. Of course such a plan, which would make Albert a prince of the Empire, could not count on the support of the emperor, who was the leader of the Catholic party in Germany. There was only one way out of this dilemma for Albert—to abandon his anti-Polish attitude and enter into feudal relations with Poland. The idea was also favorably received in Prussia, where Luther's teaching had quickly gained considerable support. So in 1525 Albert approached King Sigismund I with his project.

Albert's idea was received at the Polish court with mixed feelings. The fact that by becoming a Lutheran prince, Albert had to break completely not only with the Papacy, which had hitherto protected the order, but also with the emperor and the Empire, proved decisive in securing the agreement of the Poles to Albert's proposals and to the secularization of the order. A peace treaty was concluded at Cracow in 1525, and on the market place there Albert paid homage to Sigismund and swore allegiance as a Polish vassal.

The solution of the Prussian question left Poland and Lithuania to face another Baltic problem. To the north of Prussia and Lithuania lay the territories of Livonia (Livland) with Courland and Estland—the modern republics of Latvia and Estonia.[6] Since the thirteenth century these territories had been heavily settled by German colonists who had come at the invitation of the Knights of the Sword, who were akin to the Teutonic Order, with whom they were united in 1237. After the secularization of the Teutonic Order in Prussia the Livonian branch continued to exist independently. Another powerful political factor in Livonia was the Archbishop of Riga, who disputed the overlordship of the country with the order.

Livonia was coveted by the mighty ruler of Muscovy, Ivan IV the Terrible, who was determined to obtain an outlet on the Baltic for his growing empire. William, archbishop of Riga, the brother of Duke Albert of Prussia, together with some influential members of the order, represented the Polono-Lithuanian party, while the master of the order, Heinrich von Gallen, with his followers sought a friendly agreement with Moscow.

Sigismund August saw clearly that it was in the interests of Poland-Lithuania to unite Livonia with his realm and thus to protect Lithuania from a Muscovite attack on its northeastern flank. He found an ally in Albert of Prussia, and already in 1552 the king and the duke discussed the possibility of secularizing the archbishopric and the order, in whose territories Protestant ideas had spread. Livonia should then be united with Poland-Lithuania in the same way that Prussia had been.

When however, the master of the order concluded an agreement with Moscow in 1554, war broke out between the archbishop and the master. The archbishop was defeated and made prisoner, but thanks to the intervention of the Emperor Ferdinand, Gallen's successor recognized the king's overlordship, and William of Riga regained his freedom. When Ivan IV invaded Livonia in 1558,[7] a pro-Polish party in the order elected a new master, Gotthard von Kettler. The latter, foreseeing a prolonged struggle with Moscow, sought a defensive agreement for Livonia not only with Lithuania but also with Poland. But the old Lithuanian spirit of particularism reappeared, and the agreement was signed in 1559 by Lithuania alone.

It soon became evident that the Lithuanian forces alone were insufficient for the defense of Livonia, being also heavily engaged on the southern frontier of Lithuania. Other powers then sought to exploit the Livonian siuation. Denmark occupied the island of Oesel, and the Swedes landed in Estonia (Estland) and took possession of Reval (Tallinn) in 1561. These complications speeded the march of events. The master and the archbishop agreed to the secularization of their religious foundations. Gotthard von Kettler became duke of Courland as a vassal of the Polish king, and the remainder of Latvia with Riga submitted directly to Sigismund August.

It was hardly to be expected that the Emperor Ferdinand I (1556-1564) would tolerate the new situation because Livonia was regarded as an imperial fief. Sigismund August averted the emperor's intervention and the possibility of his making an alliance with Moscow, thanks to his own allies in Germany. The most powerful of these was the Elector of Brandenburg, a member of the other branch of the Hohenzollern family. In order to gain his alliance, Sigismund August extended the right of succession to the Duchy of Prussia in 1561 from Albert, his brothers, and their descendants, to include the Elector of Brandenburg and his offspring. This was a heavy price because Poland was forfeiting the possibility of incorporating Prussia directly on the expected extinction of Albert's progeny.

In the same year the Muscovites again invaded Livonia, and the war lasted until 1570. At first Poland was allied with Denmark against Sweden and Moscow, but this alliance was reversed when the Russians appeared to threaten the Swedish possessions in Finland. Poland-Lithuania was obliged to create a kind of navy of freebooters, but Danzig and the Hanseatic cities soon began to protest against the curtailment of their trade with the Baltic and with Russia. At the Peace Congress of Stettin in 1570 an attempt was made to coordinate the interests of Poland, Denmark, Sweden, the Emperor Maximilian II (1564-1576), and the Hanse. But the emperor defended his claims to sovereignty over Livonia, and Poland's claims were rejected, the Hanseatic League especially opposing her insistence on closing the river Narva to navigation as this would impede its resumed trade with Russia.

The extension of Polish interests along a large new section of the Baltic coast brought Poland into more intimate contact with England. Several embassies were exchanged between the two courts. The Polish embassy of 1555 revealed clearly the main object of Polish preoccupations. Its leader, the humanist Kryski, asked Queen Mary Tudor to confirm the rights and commercial liberties which the Hanseatic League had hitherto enjoyed in London. This plea was made at the request of the Prussian cities in the league, which were now under Polish supremacy.

Livonian developments also had a considerable effect on the internal evolution of Poland-Lithuania. At the outset of his reign Sigismund Au-

gust did not hide his mistrust of the gentry, who were clamoring in the
Diets for constitutional reforms and for a closer union between Poland,
Lithuania, and Prussia. However, a rapprochement was brought about as
a result of the more intimate contact deriving from the king's need for the
gentry's help in the Livonian war. So it came about that in 1562 and
1563, at least a part of the reforms was carried into effect. The Diet of
Piótrków enacted the return to the crown of all properties which had
been appropriated since 1504 by the magnates without the consent of the
Diets. The king, on the other hand, promised to devote one quarter of
such revenues to the creation of a standing army.

The demands for a more intimate union of Royal Prussia with the
Polish crown proved vain, however. Neither the king nor the magnates
paid sufficient attention to such propositions, and the Prussian nobles
and cities defended their privileges stubbornly, refusing to create a common diet with the rest of the realm. Meanwhile the concession made by
the king in permitting the Brandenburg line of the Hohenzollerns to succeed to Ducal Prussia put an end to all hopes of tightening the bonds
uniting the duchy with Poland.

Only the efforts for a more intimate union between Poland and Lithuania led to a positive result, after protracted negotiations punctuated
by new crises. The king did not desire to lose the firm Jagiellonian dynastic basis in Lithuania through a more intimate union with Poland
since only a member of the Jagiellonian dynasty could be chosen as
grand duke. Consequently, in order to preserve their union with Lithuania, the Poles were bound in a crisis to elect a Jagiellonian as king of
Poland.

In Lithuania opposition to closer union was strongest among the magnates, of whom the Radziwills were the most powerful. They even cherished the hope that in the event of Sigismund August's death without
issue, one of their family would be elected grand duke. Moreover, particularism was still strongly entrenched in Lithuania, where the union
with Poland was tolerated as a necessity. Even during the discussions
on union, this spirit constantly appeared whenever the Lithuanians were
able to register a military success against Moscow.

The war with Muscovy was, however, too heavy a burden for Lithuania, and it became increasingly evident that without the military help
of Poland, Lithuania could not resist Ivan IV's armies. The struggles in
Livonia demonstrated this very clearly. Soon the Lithuanian gentry
joined their Polish confreres in their efforts for a more intimate union between the two states. The Lithuanian gentry were jealous of the privileges
enjoyed by their Polish counterparts and sought to emulate them. It was
soon clear that as a first step the Lithuanian Diet must achieve equality
in composition and rights with that of Poland as a prelude to a more

intimate union. In 1565 this equality was realized by a royal proclamation. Not only was the Lithuanian Diet reorganized on the Polish model, but dietines were also created, and juridical and administrative reforms on the Polish pattern were introduced into Lithuania.

The two Diets began their negotiations early in 1569 at Lublin. But the old spirit of Lithuanian separatism manifested itself once more. During the first phase of the negotiations on the conditions of union, the members of the Lithuanian Diet left the city, secretly hoping thus to adjourn the negotiations. However the king and the members of the Polish Diet continued to work on their plan of union, which provided for one common diet but would preserve the peculiar political status of Lithuania. Lithuania was to keep its separate offices and its own army. Moreover, the king and the Polish Diet incorporated into the crown of Poland three Ruthenian provinces hitherto under Lithuania—Podlasie, Volhynia, and Braclav.[8] Kiev also became a part of the Kingdom of Poland. This aggrandizement of Poland was motivated by the desire for full Polish participation in the Lithuano-Russian conflict and in the defense of southern Lithuania against the Tatars, which could only be achieved if Poland had a common frontier with both.

The weakened financial and military situation of Lithuania forced its nobility, assembled at Vilna, to accept the Union of Lublin despite the opposition of the Radziwills. The Lithuanians demanded only that besides a common diet, separate diets should continue to exist in both countries for the discussion of local affairs. Thus the union between the two countries was represented by a common king and a common diet, to whom he owed his election, which would assemble at Warsaw near the Lithuanian border. After his election there should be only one ceremony of coronation at Cracow. The common diet was to make decisions on the conduct of foreign affairs.[9]

The conclusion of the Union of Lublin certainly marks an important phase in the history of eastern Europe. Praised by Polish historians as an extension of Western civilization far into the East, it is decried by others as an act of violence against the Lithuanians. But the contemporary Ruthenian nobility in Volhynia and Kiev, anxious to secure liberties similar to those of the Polish aristocracy, did not see the matter in this light, while the rest of the population of course did not count. One thing is certain, however: from 1569 the hostility of Muscovy against Poland increased considerably, and once Russia had overcome the internal difficulties consequent to the extinction of the Rurik dynasty, this inveterate enmity to Poland was to prove fatal both to her and to Lithuania.

On the other hand, however, the Poles were not able to bring about a closer union of Prussia with the Polish crown. Sigismund August missed the best opportunity when Albert was succeeded as duke of Prussia by his mentally defective only son Albert Frederick, who was unable personally to assume the reins of government. This offered a possibility for the King of Poland to nominate a Pole as regent of Ducal Prussia, as the pro-Polish Prussian Estates expected. Sigismund and his senate, however, lacked any clear policy concerning Prussia and did not realize that it was vital for Poland to bring the whole Baltic coast under her control. The opportunity was missed, and the actual government was assumed by the Prussian ducal council. On the other hand, Sigismund's decision to bring Royal Prussia into closer union with the crown and to curtail its autonomy resulted in unrest which was only quieted with difficulty.

Under the new Polish king Stephen Bathory (1576-1586) a dangerous attempt was made under the leadership of Danzig to detach the Pomeranian coastal region from Poland.[10] The king was forced to go to war against Danzig, whose burghers had placed themselves under the protection of the King of Denmark. The courageous and energetic Stephen Bathory, however, found very little understanding among the Polish aristocracy for his Prussian policy. The war with Danzig began in 1576 but ended the next year with the Peace of Malborg. Danzig returned to Polish obedience, paid an indemnity, and was granted a full amnesty. By 1585 the city had regained most of the privileges which had been curtailed under Sigismund II.

Heavy engagements on the Russian front, however, made it impossible for Stephen Bathory to concentrate his attention on Ducal Prussia. He renounced all plans for a closer union of Prussia with Poland and entrusted the guardianship of Albert Frederick and the administration of Prussia to George Frederick of Brandenburg-Ansbach, giving him the title of Prussian Duke. Thus the succession in Ducal Prussia was extended to another branch of the Hohenzollern family.

Another opportunity was missed by Stephen Bathory in 1582, when the Prussian Estates, dissatisfied with the regency of George Frederick, organized strong opposition to him and appealed to the Polish king for intervention. The king and his chancellor Zamoyski, instead of choosing a Pole for the regency, sided with the Hohenzollern in his struggle against the rebellious Estates. The latter again appealed vainly to the Polish king in 1585 and 1597. In this way George Frederick was able, thanks to the support of Poland itself, to strengthen the ties between Ducal Prussia and Brandenburg.

Sigismund III (1587-1632), of the Swedish House of Vasa, continued to follow his predecessor's passive attitude towards Ducal Prussia. When George Frederick of Hohenzollern died in 1603, Sigismund III, instead of appointing a Polish regent, entrusted the administration of Prussia to Joachim Frederick, Elector of Brandenburg, and after his death in 1609 to his son and successor John Sigismund. The Polish aristocracy had no more understanding for Polish national interests in Prussia than their king, who was more interested in his claims to the Swedish throne, and so the Diet sanctioned his policy in 1611. The Elector, after paying homage to the Polish king, obtained a further extension of the succession to Prussia. Only after the extinction of the whole dynasty of Brandenburg should Ducal Prussia revert to the Polish crown. The Elector promised to maintain a navy for the protection of Prussian commerce in the Baltic, to pay three hundred thousand guldens yearly to Poland, and to assist his feudal lord in the event of war.

When the mentally defective Albert Frederick died in 1618, the Elector of Brandenburg became duke of Prussia. Although the feudal relationship of Prussia to Poland continued, the bonds between the Polish crown and Ducal Prussia were naturally loosened. Polish influence in Prussia continued to diminish until in 1657 Prussia came under the independent sovereignty of the Elector of Brandenburg, who ceased to be a Polish vassal. His independent sovereignty was also to prove fatal to the liberties and privileges of the Prussian Estates.

Of course the Poles of the sixteenth and seventeenth centuries could not foresee the consequences of their passive policy toward Prussia. Their kings, engaged in conflicts with Muscovy, Sweden, and Denmark, doubtless regarded their arrangements with the Hohenzollerns as advantageous in the circumstances then prevailing. Nevertheless, the lack of a firm and stable policy in Prussia helped the Hohenzollerns to build up their own powerful authoritarian state and to increase their influence in Germany. For this neglect Poland was to pay heavily in the eighteenth century, when it was Prussia which initiated the partition of Poland.

NOTES

1. See Chapter IX, p. 225. Cf. the monograph by C. Krollmann, *Die Schlacht bei Tannenberg, ihre Ursachen und Folgen* (Königsberg, 1910).
2. K. Gorski made a study of the repercussions of this war in the lands on the Baltic, *Pomorze w dobie wojny trzynastoletniej* (Poznań, 1932).
3. On the first forty years of Royal Prussia's history see K. Gorski, "Pierwize czterdziestolecie Prus Królewskich, 1466-1506," *Rocznik Gdański,* 11 (1937). See also his more general study on the Teutonic Order, *Państwo krzyżackie w Prusach* (Gdańsk-Bydgoszcz, 1946).
4. Cf. above, Chapter X, p. 237.
5. On Albert's policy toward Poland see the monograph by E. Joachim (see Bibl.). On Prussian attempts to conclude an alliance with Russia see K. Forstreuter, *Preussen und Russland* (see Bibl.), pp. 75-100. Cf. also Chapter XII, p. 272.

6. For the medieval history of Livonia, the second volume of Th. Schiemann, *Russland, Polen und Livland* (Berlin, 1887) is still useful. See also M. Hellmann, *Das Lettenland im Mittelalter* (Münster, 1954) and W. Kirchner, *The Rise of the Baltic Question* (Newark, 1954). See also Chapter I, pp. 13, 14.

7. For more details see Chapter XII, p. 275.

8. The Polish point of view on this incorporation is expounded by O. Halecki in his study *Przyłączenie Podlasia, Wołynia i Kijovczczyzny do Korony w roku 1569*, published by the Polish Academy (Cracow, 1915). Cf. Chapter XVIII, pp. 476, 487.

9. Several important studies on the juridical relationship between Poland and Lithuania were published by prominent Polish historians in the symposium *Polska i Litwa w dziejowym stosunku* (Warsaw, 1914). Cf. also O. Balzer, *Tradycija dziejowa unii polsko-litewskiej* (Lwów, 1919) and his study *Stosunek Litwy do Polski*, published in vol. III of his posthumous works (Lwów, 1937) with a résumé in French. A short review of the history of the union was given by O. Halecki, "L'évolution historique de l'Union polonolithuanienne" in *Le Monde Slave*, 2 (1926). Cf. also his bibliographical review of Polish works on Poland and Lithuania published in *Pamiatky VI zjezdu histor. polskich* (1935), under the title "Przegląd badań nad dziejami Litwy 1385-1569."

10. For details cf. the study by K. Lepszy, "Stefan Batory a Gdańsk" in *Rocznik Gdański*, 6 (1932).

Chapter XII

THE GROWTH OF MUSCOVY AND ITS RELATIONS WITH POLAND-LITHUANIA

Basil II's struggle for the Muscovite throne and his new Tatar policy—Lithuania and Basil's agglomeration of East Russian lands—Basil II and the Council of Florence—Moscow, Poland-Lithuania, and Byzantium—Ivan III, the great reassembler—Ivan III, Casimir of Poland-Lithuania, and the Tatars—Ivan III, the Byzantine princess Zoe-Sophia, the Pope, and the Turks—Basil III continues Ivan's policy of agglomeration—Ivan IV's victories over Kazan' and Astrakhan' and Russian expansion in the Khanate of Sibir'—Ivan IV's progress in the Baltic lands—Ivan's candidacy for the Polish throne and reverses in the Baltic—Ivan IV and the nobility —Ivan IV and the European diplomatic scene—Fedor I, the Russian patriarchate, and the extinction of the Rurik dynasty

While Poland and Lithuania were increasingly attracted toward the West and had to take their share in the struggle of central and southern Europe against the Turks, Moscow gained the necessary time to overcome its internal crisis and to continue the regrouping of the eastern Russian principalities around Moscow. Basil I's son, Basil II (1425-1462), succeeded as ruler of Moscow according to the new system of primogeniture, which had slowly been introduced into the political life of the principality. This principle seems to have already been so widely accepted at that time in Moscow that when Basil II's uncle George (Jurij) contested the young prince's rights, he did not dare to invoke the obsolete principle of succession by the oldest member of the dynasty. George appealed instead to the stipulations of Dmitrij Donskoj's testament, which he wrongly interpreted to his own advantage. Dmitrij had indeed mentioned George as successor to Basil I, but only in the event of the latter's dying without issue.

The Khan, called in to arbitrate in the contest, decided in favor of

Basil II. When George resorted to arms and chased the young grand prince from Moscow, the Muscovite boyars and people rose in defense of Basil II's rights and forced George to abandon his claim. When George, who had again succeeded in chasing Basil II from Moscow, died suddenly, his eldest son Basil Kosoj claimed the succession to his father by right of primogeniture. He was defeated and lost his appanage, his eyesight, and his life.

Fortunately for Basil II the power of the Golden Horde, centered at Saray on the Volga, was slowly disintegrating. Many groups of Tatar warriors detached themselves from their political center, and their leaders established independent hordes. Other groups were roaming the no man's land of the steppes as *Kazaks*—free warriors. Basil II succeeded in defeating one of these hordes which was attacking Rjazan' (1443-44). A curious incident which happened in 1445 proved the inauguration of a new period in relations between the Muscovites and the Tatars. When Ulug-Mahmed, the leader of another horde, occupied the New Lower Castle (Novyj Nižovyj Gorod) near Gorodec [1] and attacked Murom, Basil II tried to chase the horde away from Russian lands, but was defeated and taken prisoner.

Curiously enough, Basil was able during his imprisonment to befriend many Tatar nobles, including the two sons of Ulug-Mahmed—Jakub and Kasim. After having promised a substantial ransom, Basil was set free and returned to Moscow accompanied by numerous Tatar princes, who were sent to supervise the collection of the ransom.[2]

When, however, Ulug-Mahmed was assassinated by his eldest son Mahmudek, who established himself as Kazan', Basil II succeeded in winning over most of the Tatar princes who had come with him, together with the money they had collected. They were joined by others who did not agree with Mahmudek, but were attracted by the promises of the grand prince. So it happened that Basil won a number of loyal Tatar vassals, of whom he could make use not only for his domestic policy, but also in his fight with other Tatar hordes.

This, of course, provoked some criticism on the part of the native boyars. So Kosoj's brother Dmitrij Šemjaka profited by Basil's absence from Moscow during his pilgrimage to the Holy Trinity monastery to occupy the capital, take Basil prisoner, and blind him.

Basil II, freed on the insistence of Iona, bishop of Rjazan', and established by Šemjaka in Vologda, was reinstated on the throne by his Russian and Tatar supporters. Kasim and Jakub, who had taken refuge in the Čerkasy region on the middle Dnieper after the tragic death of their father, went to Basil's help and joined forces with his supporters. Šemjaka was forced to abandon Moscow and to free Basil's family, but was allowed to keep his patrimony.

In spite of his defeat, Šemjaka continued his fight for the grand princely throne. Basil II then appealed to the judgment of the Russian Church. The prelates took a very firm position and sent an urgent letter to Šemjaka asking him to cease his opposition. The document is of great importance because it shows how firmly the ideas of monarchy, primogeniture, and Muscovite hegemony were embedded in the minds of contemporaries.

In their letter the bishops compared the insurrection of Šemjaka's father against the grand prince with the sin of Adam, whom Satan had induced to revolt against God. Šemjaka's behavior is compared to that of Cain against his innocent brother Abel, or of the cursed Svjatopolk, who had martyred the great saints Boris and Gleb.

The prince was threatened with excommunication by the Russian Church, and this sentence was actually implemented when he persisted in his policy. Šemjaka was finally defeated and poisoned by a Muscovite agent in Novgorod, where he had taken refuge (1453). This incident testifies again to the immense service rendered by the Church to the princes of Moscow in their striving for ascendancy and how the attitude of the higher clergy favored the growth of the monarchic idea in East Russia.

The Tatar contingents in Basil's service rendered Moscow a signal service by helping the Russians to repulse the attacks of the Tatar hordes of Kazan', of Saraj, and of the Dnieper in 1449 and 1451. In order to silence the protests of Russian boyars against the grant of Russian cities as appanages (*kormlenie*) to Tatar princes, and in order to secure Moscow's frontiers against the attacks of the hordes of Kazan' and Saraj, Basil II settled the Tatars with Prince Kasim in Gorodec-on-the-Oka, and thus founded a new Tatar khanate—the Tsardom of Kasimov, loyal to Muscovy. It was a signal success indicating that the era of Mongol domination over Russia was coming to an end.

It was fortunate for Moscow that while these events were taking place, the Lithuanian danger had evaporated for many years. Vitold's plan to strengthen the autonomous status of Lithuania by giving its grand dukes the royal title was resumed for some time by his successor, Jagiello's brother Svidrigello. But it all came to nought in the fratricidal struggles between Svidrigello and Vitold's brother Sigismund.[3] Under the Grand Duke Sigismund, and more especially after 1440 under his successor, Jagiello's son Casimir, Lithuania was increasingly assimilated with Poland. This tendency grew when Casimir became king of Poland.

In these circumstances, the princes of Tver' and Rjazan', who had joined Vitold's Lithuanian commonwealth in 1427, saw greater opportunities in the struggles for the Muscovite throne and abandoned their idea of union with Lithuania. Basil II won his victory over Šemjaka with the help of Tver', and the good relationship between Moscow and Tver' was strengthened by the marriage of Basil's eldest son Ivan with Mary, the daughter of Boris of Tver'.

Thanks to these circumstances, Basil II, the least capable of Moscow's grand princes, became one of the most successful "reassemblers of the Russian lands." Under different pretexts he got rid of princes who had shown sympathy with his opponents, and annexed Možajsk, Borovsk, and Serpukhov. He installed a Muscovite governor in Rjazan', nominally on behalf of the young prince whom his dying father had recommended to Basil's protection. Then he attacked Novgorod because the city-republic had shown too little sympathy in his struggle for his inheritance. Novgorod lost Ustjug and Vjatka and had to pay huge sums of money to the Muscovite. While its *veče* lost the right of legislation, the city had to surrender its seal and was deprived of the right of asylum.

Moreover, religious questions soon raised new complications for Lithuania in its Russian provinces and provided Basil II with the opportunity to proclaim the Grand Prince of Moscow sole protector of the Orthodox faith. The occasion for this was the union between Byzantium and the Roman Church, concluded at the Council of Florence (1439). The Russian metropolitan Isidor (Sidor) attended the council with the reluctant permission of the grand prince. Isidor was a prelate who had been chosen as metropolitan by the patriarch against the wishes of the Muscovites, who had proposed Jonas (Iona) of Rjazan' for the dignity. Basil II manifested his true sentiments by warning Isidor before his departure not to come to any agreement with the Latins. The metropolitan, however, accepted the Union of Florence, was made a cardinal and papal legate, and on his return to Moscow started to preach in favor of reunion with Rome.

It is interesting to read the account in the *Second Sophia Chronicle* [4] and in the *Voskresenkij Chronicle* [5] of Isidor's journey to Ferrara and of the council itself as seen by a contemporary Orthodox Russian, together with the description of the astonishment of the grand prince and the Muscovites when they heard about the reunion concluded with the Latin "heretics." Isidor caused a Latin cross to be carried in front of him and even kissed this heretical symbol in Dorpat (Jurjev) at the start of his journey, while "seduced by the devil," he mentioned in the liturgy the name of the Pope. But the Most Christian Tsar of All Russia, to whom God the Lord had given to understand and discuss everything most wisely, was not deluded by all this. When he heard all these horrible things— the metropolitan had even read in public a letter from the Pope to the Orthodox prince—Basil II refused the blessing of the heretical metropolitan, urged him to do penance in a monastery, deprived him of his dignity, and, finally, let him go "to his Pope." [6]

The initiative of the grand prince was applauded by all the bishops and the entire Russian Orthodox Church.[7] Boris of Tver', whom Isidor had hoped to win over, cast him into prison, and he did not even meet with any success in Lithuania. It is characteristic of the Russian attitude that even when Šemjaka succeeded in occupying Moscow (1446) and deprived his cousin Basil II of his eyesight, he failed to show any interest in the fate of the Metropolitan Isidor, although his own revolt against the grand prince was sharply blamed by the Russian hierarchy. On the contrary, Šemjaka even speeded up further developments. As he refused to make peace definitively with Basil II, who was again victorious and had recovered his grand princely dignity, as long as there was no metropolitan in Russia, Basil convoked a synod (1448) and let the bishops place Jonas, bishop of Rjazan' on the metropolitan throne. The Patriarch of Constantinople was completely ignored in the election and installation of a metropolitan of Kiev and all Russia.

Thanks to events in Poland and Lithuania, the new metropolitan was also able to extend his jurisdiction over the Orthodox in the Polish-Lithuanian commonwealth. Casimir, king of Poland, found a dangerous adversary in Lithuania in Michael, the son of Sigismund. He was, therefore, anxious to be on good terms with Basil II and confirmed the friendly relations between the two realms by a treaty signed in 1449. As a result Jonas obtained official confirmation in 1451 of his jurisdiction in Lithuania and, later, also in Polish Galicia. When in 1452 Bishop Daniel, who had been consecrated by Isidor, accepted Jonas as his metropolitan, the victory of Moscow was complete.

It should be stressed that Basil II did not intend to break completely with Byzantium. His first reaction was to write to the Emperor of Constantinople, John VIII (1425-1448), complaining about Isidor and asking permission to elect a new metropolitan in Russia, without the intervention of the patriarch. The letter is preserved, and its first draft should be dated 1441. It was, however, not sent because in the meantime the grand prince had learned that both the emperor and the patriarch of Constantinople had also accepted the union with the Latins. It may have been sent two years afterward to the new Patriarch Gregory Mammas, because the *Second Sophia Chronicle* contains a copy of the letter with the new date.

Little information is available about the reaction which this letter aroused in Constantinople, if it ever got there. The true sentiments of the grand prince concerning a complete break with Byzantium are reflected, however, in a letter which he sent in 1451 to the Emperor Constantine

XI (1449-1453), informing him that the Russian bishops had elected a new metropolitan, Jonas of Rjazan'. The letter is extremely deferential, and the grand prince takes great pains to explain his own and his bishop's initiative. The journey to Constantinople being so full of dangers because of the Tatars and the Turks, and with disunity ravaging the Church, the grand prince and the Russian hierarchy felt constrained to take such an initiative. The emperor is asked not to misinterpret this initiative. No offense was intended toward the emperor or the patriarch, but circumstances forced the Russian action. The grand prince also expressed his desire to explain his initiative to the patriarch, but he did not know if there was a patriarch in Constantinople in 1451.[8]

This letter is an important document as evidence of the sentiments of fifteenth century Russians toward the Emperor and the Patriarch of Constantinople. It shows also that the separation from Constantinople was not as sudden as it would appear and that the Russians would probably have continued to recognize the Emperor of Constantinople as the head of Eastern Christendom even though their metropolitans might have been chosen without reference to the patriarch—if the Turks had not put a sudden end to the Byzantine Empire in 1453.

This event and the evolution of the Polish-Lithuanian commonwealth had a profound influence on the future status of the East Russian Church. King Casimir of Poland changed his attitude toward Jonas, the metropolitan if Kiev and all Russia, and asked Rome to ordain a new metropolitan of Kiev in succession to Isidor. In 1459, Isidor's disciple Gregory appeared in Lithuania and was recognized as metropolitan of Kiev. There was a danger that the new metropolitan would be accepted in Tver' and Novgorod, while the King of Poland even requested the Grand Prince of Moscow to accept him. The request was naturally rejected, but as Gregory boasted that he had been consecrated by the Patriarch of Constantinople, Gregory Mammas (1443-1450), it seemed necessary to strengthen the position of Jonas.

A synod of the Russian Church was convoked in 1459, at which the bishops repudiated Gregory and declared Jonas and his successors to be the rightful metropolitans of Kiev and all Russia. This decision consummated the separation of the Russian Church from Constantinople and proclaimed its independence. Although the bishops of Lithuania, supported by King Casimir, remained faithful to Gregory, Jonas succeeded, at least, in preventing the defection of Tver' and Novgorod to his rival. From that time on, however, western and southern Russia remained ecclesiastically separate from East Russia. After Jonas' death, his successor abandoned the old title and called himself Metropolitan of Moscow.

The proclamation of Moscow's ecclesiastical independence was a fateful step which had serious consequences for the further evolution of Rus-

sia and of Orthodoxy in general. The Russian Church lost the support of
the distant, but influential, Patriarch of Constantinople and was forced
increasingly into dependence on the Grand Prince of Moscow. From
that time on the new metropolitan was to be elected by the bishops but
confirmed by the grand prince. The synod of 1459 specifically recognized
this right of the Muscovite ruler, whose prestige was naturally enhanced
by this prerogative.

On the other hand, Constantinople's "apostasy" from orthodoxy in
accepting the Union of Florence made the Russian Church more self-
conscious as the sole upholder of the true Orthodox faith. The fall of
Constantinople was regarded by Jonas and his contemporaries as God's
punishment for this "apostasy" and convinced the Russians that their attitude toward the union with the "heretical" Latins enjoyed divine approval.
The definitive victory of Basil II over Šemjaka and the death of the latter
were interpreted as God's reward for the grand prince's uncompromising
attitude in matters of faith. All this confirmed the Russian Church in its
suspicious attitude toward all influences penetrating East Russia, whether
from the Latin West or the Greek East, and made its spiritual isolation
more complete. The grand prince was soon regarded as the intrepid
champion of Orthodoxy, assuming in some way the role of the Emperor
of Constantinople, while the political animosity between Poland-Lithuania and Moscow added new fuel to anti-Latin sentiments. So the final
stage of Moscow's political and religious leadership, which was reached
under Ivan III, Basil III, and Ivan IV, was prepared. All this was to
nourish the doctrine of the "Third Rome," which has so powerfully affected Russian thought: the first was Rome, which was corrupted; the
second Byzantium, which betrayed Orthodoxy; the third is Moscow; a
fourth there cannot be.[9]

Ivan III (1462-1505) was the grand prince who not only consolidated
the foundations on which the State of Moscow was built,[10] but also
definitely ensured its dominant position in East Russia and made its growing power known to the courts of contemporary Europe. Basil II, anxious
to secure his son's succession, had associated Ivan from his infancy with
the direction of political and military affairs. His father's misfortunes had
hardened Ivan's character and determined him to take all precautions
against a repetition of similar events. He was full of physical energy, conscious of the sublime position which the grand prince occupied in the
state, and resolved to preserve and strengthen his autocratic powers. He
had some statesman-like talents, was patient and astute in negotiations,
and preferred to attain his aims without recourse to war.

In East Russia four princes still enjoyed a shadow of independence,
those of Jaroslavl', Rostov, Tver', and Rjazan'. There also existed five

appanages, of which four had been given by Basil II to Ivan's brothers and the fifth, that of Vereja, was in the possession of Prince Michael, son of Andrew. Novgorod, although its rights and possessions had been diminished, was still powerful and determined to defend the remnant of its independence. The city-republic of Pskov was more loyal to the grand prince.

Ivan III concentrated his attention first on the liquidation of his potential adversaries inside East Russia. In 1463 the Prince of Jaroslavl' submitted to Moscow, followed in 1474 by the Prince of Rostov. In 1465 the independence of the principality of Vereja was liquidated with astute ruthlessness. Ivan proceeded with similar methods against his brothers. When his brother George died in 1472, he simply occupied his appanage, thus breaking with the ancient custom that in such cases the appanage should be divided among all surviving brothers. He inherited the appanage of his youngest brother, but Boris of Volokolamsk and Andrew of Uglič [11] concluded an alliance and revolted against Ivan. A new Tatar invasion forced Ivan to make peace with his brothers, but in 1491, forgetting his promises which he had confirmed by oath, Ivan treacherously arrested Andrew and his sons and let them die in prison. Not even the intercession by the metropolitan in their favor moved the grand prince. This time he openly confessed that he sought to obviate any danger for himself or his successors from any other member of the dynasty. Boris was left in peace as he was no longer dangerous. Before Ivan's death, half of Boris' principality was bequeathed to the grand prince by his nephew.

The struggle for Novgorod lasted longer. [12] Within the city-republic the grand prince was supported by a pro-Moscow party, which had numerous adherents among the poorer classes of citizens. At the beginning of Ivan's reign, however, a strong pro-Lithuanian party dominated the policy of the republic. As a result, the brother of the Kievan prince was called to Novgorod to act as reigning prince and protector of the city. The Muscovite party, however, increased its strength when Theophilus, Moscow's candidate, was made archbishop of Novgorod.

Impressed by the defeat of the Teutonic Order in 1466 and its final submission to Poland, Novgorod concluded a formal agreement with King Casimir. When Ivan heard this news, he lost no time in invading the republic (1471) before the Polish king could do anything to protect his new ally. The Novgorodians were defeated and had to pay a huge sum of money to the victor, to cede important parts of their territory, and to renounce their alliance with Poland-Lithuania. From that time on, Ivan III acted as supreme judge in Novgorod. When a new revolt broke out in the city in 1477, the grand prince marched once more against the city and forced it to capitulate. Ivan III defined his suzerainty over Novgorod in unmistakable terms, swept away the last vestiges of its democratic and autonomous institutions, and in order to symbolize the city's new status, took with him the bell which had formerly called the citizens to the *veče* —the city assembly.

It was hard for the Novgorodians to reconcile themselves to the loss of their ancient rights. In order to prevent a repetition of previous events, Ivan III occupied the city, made a blood bath among those who were planning a new revolt, and deported a hundred aristocratic families from the city. New attempts at revolt provoked further cruel measures. Over seven thousand citizens and merchants were forcibly exchanged for merchants and nobles from Moscow and other cities. This last measure, completed in 1488, finally broke the independent spirit of the city and brought about its economic decline. The Hanseatic factory was closed in 1494.[13] Novgorod and its huge colonial territory were definitively incorporated into the Muscovite state.

In his campaign against Novgorod, Ivan III was supported by Prince Michael of Tver'.[14] The latter realized too late that by helping Ivan to reduce Novgorod he not only had contributed to the growth of Moscow's power, but had also deprived himself of a valuable ally. The ideas of independence and the pretensions to hegemony in East Russia which had formerly been so strong in Tver' manifested themselves again in the second half of the fifteenth century. They are reflected in the *Chronicle of Tver'*, written in 1455.[15] The chronicler presents Tver' as the focus of events in East Russia and attacks Moscow, arguing that its grand prince had no right to pose as the protector of Orthodoxy. This role should be ascribed to the Grand Prince of Tver'. It claimed that the end of Byzantium had in no way changed the situation in the Orthodox Church, as the Patriarch of Constantinople still resided in that city. Therefore the patriarch, and not the Metropolitan of Moscow, was the true head of Orthodoxy.

It was too late for Tver' to claim such a prominent place in East Russia. Many boyars were quitting the service of the Grand Prince of Tver' seeing that they had better prospects in that of Moscow. Alarmed by the increasing strength of Moscow, to which he had himself contributed, Michael made an alliance with King Casimir. The resulting war between Michael and Ivan manifested the weakness of Tver' and the hopelessness of Michael's situation. His boyars were deserting him in masses, and the city was defenseless. No help came from Poland-Lithuania, and in 1485 Tver' was annexed to Moscow while its unfortunate last prince took refuge in Lithuania.

The princes of Rjazan' did not follow Michael of Tver' and remained faithful vassals of Moscow. Ivan III inherited the city of Rjazan' from one of his nephews and acted as sovereign in the rest of the principality. This satisfied Ivan, and he left the incorporation of the whole principality into Muscovy to his successor. Thus with the exception of Seversk, still under Lithuania, almost the whole of northern and northeastern Russia was united under Moscow.

For future expansion eastward, particular importance should be attached to the new territorial acquisitions beyond the region of Perm. In order to stop the incursions of Mongol tribes into Moscow's territory, Prince Theodor (Fedor) Kurbskij penetrated through the middle Urals into Siberia in 1483 as far as the rivers Irtyš and Ob, and in 1499 this success was substantially extended.

For the first time Moscow could think of expansion into the southern and western Russian principalities which had been incorporated into Lithuania. Casimir, the ruler of Poland and Lithuania, was unable to stop Moscow's drive. He was preoccupied for many years with the war against the Teutonic Order, until the Peace of Toruń in 1466 gave Poland direct sovereignty over Danzig, Pomerania, Chełmno, and West Prussia, with suzerainty over East Prussia, which the order retained as a vassal state.

In view of the earlier menace of the order to Novgorod and Pskov, it was not surprising that Novgorod now looked for support to Poland-Lithuania. But despite his enhanced prestige Casimir had to neglect the northeastern frontiers of Lithuania for the sake of Jagiellonian dynastic ambitions in Hungary and Bohemia.

On the death of George of Poděbrady, king of Bohemia, in 1471, Casimir supported the candidature of his own son Vladislav to the Bohemian throne against the claims of King Matthias Corvinus of Hungary. The resulting war held Polish forces engaged while Ivan III crushed Novgorod. Matthias fostered the resistance of the Teutonic Order, and it was only after Casimir agreed in 1478 to abandon Moravia, Silesia, and Lusatia to Matthias, while Vladislav kept Bohemia, that the grand master was induced to pay homage to the Polish king. On the death of Matthias in 1492 Vladislav reunited the Czech lands and also gained the crown of Hungary.[16]

The House of Habsburg regarded with jealous eyes the expansion of the Jagiellos in Central Europe. The Emperor Frederick III (1440-1493) and his son Maximilian I (1493-1519) claimed the crowns of Bohemia and Hungary for themselves.[17] All this explains why the Novgorodians and the Prince of Tver' waited in vain for help from Poland, while Ivan III was able to win an ally in the emperor against Poland.

All that Casimir attempted in order to help Novgorod was the conclusion of an alliance with the Khan of the Golden Horde [18] against Ivan. But again his calculations proved wrong, for the Golden Horde only enjoyed a shadow of its earlier power. From the beginning of the fifteenth century on, its empire began to disintegrate. It finally split into three main khanates, Kazan', the Golden Horde, and the Crimea. This disintegration of the Mongol empire led numerous **Tatar** nobles with their retinues to enter the service of Moscow. Ivan III, continuing his father's policy, welcomed them, and Tatar detachments played an important role in his campaigns. He was astute enough to use the services of Tatar nobles in the diplomatic relations which he initiated with the eastern neighbors of the Golden Horde. This enabled him to isolate Khan Ahmad, who still nourished plans for forcing Moscow back into its former vassalage. His rivalry with the Khan of the Crimea, however, prevented him from achieving his aim.

With the help of another Tatar prince, Kasim, whom Basil II had won over, Ivan made a bold attempt to obtain control over the Khanate of Kazan'. He succeeded in forcing its Khan to accept formal Muscovite suzerainty. In 1474 Ivan III won a great success by concluding an alliance with Mengli Geray, Khan of the Crimea, whose father had been Casimir's ally. The situation had changed, and the Khan promised support to Ivan in the event of a Polish attack. This alliance remained valuable for Ivan even after 1475, when the Turks conquered the Crimea and made Mengli Geray their vassal.

Thus Ivan III was in a strong position in 1480, when Ahmad, the Khan of the Golden Horde, advanced with his army against Moscow as Casimir's ally. The armies met on the frontiers of Lithuania and Muscovy, but neither dared to start the fighting. Ivan, not sure of himself, hesitated, and the Khan waited for the Lithuanian troops, which failed to appear. A daring raid by Ivan's Tatar vassals into the steppes near Saray forced the Khan to retreat. The suzerainty of the Golden Horde over Russia, which had been almost a dead letter for the last decades, thus came to a definite end in 1480.

With the help of his Crimean ally, Ivan III succeeded in installing as khan of Kazan' Mehmed-Amin, who swore allegiance to Moscow (1487). Soon afterward the Muscovites and the Crimeans moved against the remnant of the Golden Horde. Ahmad's sons lost their lives in fighting against the Crimea, and in 1502 the Golden Horde, completely dismembered, ceased to exist. Thus Ivan's eastern policy had registered an unexpected success while Poland and Lithuania lost their eastern ally, for the Khanate of Astrakhan', founded on the ruins of the Golden Horde, was too weak to be dangerous to Moscow.

The growing prestige of Moscow created a strong impression among many princes in southern and western Russia. Religious and political differences were undermining the loyalty of the Russian population to Casimir, who had united in his own lands the administration of both Poland and Lithuania. Catholic propaganda among the Orthodox population began to increase under Casimir, and the enemies of union with the Latins looked toward the Grand Prince of Moscow as the protector of Orthodoxy. Casimir was forced to make some concessions to his Orthodox subjects. In 1432 he admitted Orthodox nobles to state offices, and in 1440 Prince Alexander, a relative of Basil III, was appointed governor of Kiev. In spite of that, many South Russian princes quitted the service of Casimir and with their *votčiny*, boyars, and servants passed over to that of Moscow. Separatist sentiments manifested themselves increasingly among the Lithuanian and South and West Russian nobility. When Casimir refused their request that one of his sons should become duke of Lithuania, a revolt broke out under the leadership of Prince Michael, who had been for a short time prince of Novgorod and whom Casimir had refused to establish in Kiev. There may well have been some connections between the ringleaders of the conspiracy and Moscow. Michael was executed by Casimir, but many South Russian nobles joined Muscovy. Ivan III seems to have avenged Michael's execution by letting his allies, the Crimean Tatars, attack Kiev (1482). The Khan sent Ivan the sacred vessels which his warriors looted from the Kievan churches.

Ivan III, who was seeking to suppress in his own realm the old privilege of the boyars of choosing freely the service of a prince, defended this right in the case of Lithuanian princes who came over to Moscow. Casimir, too heavily engaged in Central Europe and hampered in his actions by the caprices of the aristocratic Polish Diet, was unable to stop these defections. The situation became even more difficult for Poland when the personal union between Lithuania and Poland was dissolved after Casimir's death in 1492. The Lithuanians elected his son Alexander as grand duke, and the Polish Diet offered the Polish crown to his other son John Albrecht (Olbracht) (1492-1501). Ivan profited by this occasion to make an open attack. Unable to resist, the Lithuanians proposed a marriage between Ivan's daughter Helen and their Duke Alexander. The latter had to cede to Ivan (1494) the territories of those princes who had joined Moscow and the city of Vjazma.

Unfortunately for Alexander, the zeal of his ecclesiastical advisers spoiled everything and gave Moscow a new opportunity to pose as the defender of Orthodoxy. Under the influence of Catholic zealots, Alexander attempted to restore the Union of Florence and started to remove the Muscovite boyars from Helen's retinue. The exodus of Orthodox boyars —or the change of obedience according to the old Russian custom—started again and led to a new war with Lithuania in 1500. Ivan III posed as the defender of Orthodoxy and complained that his daughter was denied the exercise of her religion as promised in the marriage agreement, a pretension which does not seem to have been fully warranted. The Poles were saved by the army of their vassal the Grand Master of the Teutonic

Order, but in the peace treaty concluded in 1503, Alexander, now also king of Poland (1501-1506), had to cede to Ivan all the territories belonging to the princes who had joined Moscow. Ivan's possessions in the West had grown considerably, as the territory which he had acquired comprised nineteen cities and seventy counties. It included the principalities of Černigov and Briansk and parts of the principalities of Smolensk and Vitebsk.

In his struggle with Lithuania Ivan made it clear for the first time that he regarded as the main duty of Moscow's grand princes the unification under Moscow of all principalities which had once belonged to the Kievan state. When signing the treaty of 1494, Ivan III gave himself the title "Ruler of All Russia," much to the displeasure of the Poles and Lithuanians, who saw clearly its implications.[19]

The Tatar and Lithuanian problems were the main preoccupations of Ivan, and he had no understanding for other international questions which engrossed the minds of the statesmen of contemporary Europe. The Turkish expansion in the Danube basin provided a growing danger for Central Europe and Christianity, and the Papacy exhorted Christian rulers unceasingly to organize crusades to stem the Turkish progress, free the Balkan Christians, and reconquer Constantinople. The discovery of a mighty Christian state in the East, beyond the borders of Poland and Lithuania, suggested the idea to Pope Paul II of winning its ruler for the pious enterprise of liberating the Balkan and Greek Christians from the Turkish yoke. In Rome under papal protection was living Zoe Palaeologus, daughter of Thomas, the last Greek despot of Mistra, and niece of the last Byzantine emperor, Constantine XI. Thomas, who had taken refuge in Rome after the conquest of his lands by the Turks, recommended his daughter to the Pope's protection. Ivan III had been a widower since 1467 and was looking for a new bride. So the niece of the Byzantine emperor seemed to be most qualified to become grand princess, the more so as such a union would enhance the prestige of Moscow, not only in Russia but also in western Europe. As Zoe had been educated in the spirit of the Union of Florence, the Pope hoped through her to win Ivan for Church union. The negotiations, started by the learned Greek Cardinal Bessarion, were happily concluded, and Zoe, who changed her name to Sophia, became Ivan's wife.

She was accompanied to Moscow by a papal legate, Italian architects, and some Greeks. The Pope's expectations were, however, completely disappointed. There was no sympathy in Muscovy for reunion, as was illustrated by an incident before Sophia had reached Moscow. When he learned that the papal legate had caused the Latin cross to be carried in front of the matrimonial cortege, Philip, the metropolitan of Moscow, declared openly that he would leave the city if the cursed Latin symbol were permitted to be carried through its gate. So the legate had to dispense with the cross, and Ivan himself had only polite answers to the legate's exhortations to join the union. Sophia herself assuaged the fears of the metropolitan, for although educated as a Catholic, she preferred in Russia to be the wife of the protector of Orthodoxy.

Ivan made the most of his marriage in order to enhance his prestige. He made important changes in court ceremonial according to the Byzantine model and the observances of West European courts. He assumed the coat of arms of the Byzantine emperors—the double eagle, which remained on the Russian escutcheon until 1917, when it was displaced by the sickle and hammer. He let himself be praised as the protector of the Orthodox faith, but he was not at all interested in the Byzantine political heritage and still less in a war with Turkey. His ally, the Crimean Khan, was a Turkish vassal, and the Turks were more dangerous to his Lithuanian and Polish enemies. Moreover, he was protected from any Turkish attack by the Moldavian prince, Stephen the Great, whose daughter had married Ivan's son Dmitrij. In his diplomatic relations with the West, Ivan realistically concentrated his interest on Poland-Lithuania and the defense of his approaches to the Baltic Sea. This was the main aim of his negotiations with the Habsburgs and with Denmark. An alliance was concluded with the latter state as a means of protection against Sweden, which began to evince a growing interest in the Baltic lands.

Ivan's son Basil III (1505-1533) remained faithful to the realistic policy of his father. He consummated his father's plans for the unification of all East Russia under Moscow by annexing Pskov (1510) and Rjazan' (1517). Although the Khan of the Crimea had renounced his alliance with Ivan's successor and had started to make devastating inroads into Russian territory, Basil III did not change his attitude toward Turkey, under whose suzerainty the Crimea stood. In 1519 the Grand Master of the Teutonic Order informed Basil III through his envoy that the Pope was planning to form an anti-Turkish league and would invite the grand prince to adhere to it and, of course, also to the union of the Churches. The Pope was ready in this event to crown him as "the Christian, most noble, and invincible Tsar of all Russia." The grand master added to the message an expression of his hope that Basil "would fight for his Constantinopolitan inheritance." The grand prince, however, did not deign to give an answer to this invitation.

The efforts of the Habsburgs to arouse Basil's interest in the projected anti-Turkish league were equally vain. Their envoy, Sigismund von Herberstein,[20] went twice to Moscow, on behalf of the emperors Maximilian and Charles V, but all his eloquence was wasted. Moscow stubbornly refused in its foreign policy to look beyond South and West Russia, still under Lithuania and Poland.

At first Basil III hoped to annex these provinces with the help of his sister Helen, after the death of her husband Alexander. However, Sigismund, the brother of the latter, assumed rule over Poland and Lithuania (1506-1548), and so Basil had to have recourse to arms. He was aided in his attack by Michael Glinskij, a disgruntled magnate of Tatar extraction who had defected to Moscow and was active in the formation of an anti-Polish alliance between Moscow, the Teutonic Order, and the emperor. The war lasted years; and although Poland was supported by the Crimean Khan and the alliance planned by Glinskij failed to materialize, Basil III was able to keep Smolensk,[21] which he had annexed in 1514, when he concluded an armistice with the Polish king in 1522.

Troubles which had developed in the East in the vassal Khanate of Kazan' induced Basil III to terminate his Polish campaign. The Russian vassal in Kazan' was suddenly displaced by a brother of the Crimean Khan (1521), and both khans marched against Moscow, which was once more in great danger of being taken by the Tatars. The danger was averted, but Basil saw that he must pay more attention to the Crimean menace. He established a line of defense on the bank of the river Oka and then led his armies three times against Kazan'. In 1531 he succeeded in taking the city and in establishing a khan of his own choice there. Although less successful than his father, Basil III followed the main lines of his foreign policy.

Basil III owed his success to his father's statesman-like reorganization of the political and social life of Muscovy.[22] During the minority of Basil's son Ivan IV (1533-1584), the solid qualities of the foundations for Moscow's growth, as laid by Ivan III, were amply proved. When Basil III died, Ivan was only three years old, and his mother Helen assumed the regency. There was a danger that Muscovy would follow the path which had led Poland to the brink of ruin. The boyars started to claim increased rights in the government of the state. The boyar families of Šujskij and Belskij fought for the regency. When Ivan was eight years old, he lost his mother, who is said to have been poisoned by the boyars. The Šujskij neglected the education of the boy and did not hide their intention of replacing the Rurik dynasty on the Muscovite throne by one of their own princes.

In spite of that, the wheels of government set in motion by Ivan III continued to turn, and it was again the Russian Church which saved the Rurik dynasty and the autocratic regime.

Two metropolitans, Daniel and Joasaph, were promoted by the Šujskij and deposed when they showed their determination to block the boyars' plans. In 1542, however, Macarius, one of the most energetic and most famous of Muscovite prelates, became metropolitan and, after a five years' struggle, succeeded in 1547 in having Ivan IV proclaimed of age. The intelligent priest Sylvester was appointed as Ivan's guardian down to the year 1553.

The government of the young ruler [23] continued to develop the military-manorial system which had been introduced by Ivan III and which had contributed considerably to reinforce the military strength of Muscovy. In 1550 a special life guard regiment of a thousand sons of boyars was founded. Its members were given lands near the capital and had to be at the disposal of the tsar at all times. Modernization of the army also went on with the help of foreign specialists. The young ruler is said to have had 150 cannons at his disposal when he started his military campaign against Kazan'.

The Khanate of Kazan' continued to block Russian progress toward the middle Volga, and Ivan's predecessors had made several attempts to obtain possession of it. The campaign, prepared by Ivan's government, was regarded as a kind of crusade against the infidels. In 1552 Ivan's army, thanks to the use of a new technique in the beleaguering of cities, succeeded in storming the stronghold and occupying the whole khanate. New lands were thus opened to Russian colonists. In the following years Ivan's army fought its way down the course of the Volga River, and in 1556 the Khanate of Astrakhan' too was in Russian hands. Thus the waterway of the Volga and free access to the Caspian Sea were opened to Russian commerce. The Caucasus was reached, and a fortress erected on the river Terek.

It was a great victory. Ivan IV was compared with the greatest Russian heroes—Alexander Nevskij, Dmitrij Donskoj, and St. Vladimir. The Moslem world was impressed and forced on the defensive. Moscow, hitherto in constant fear of attacks emanating from the interior of Asia, went over to the offensive. This was crowned by the conquest of the Khanate of Sibir', which was brought to a happy end by the private enterprise of the Stroganov family, with the tsar's blessing. The Stroganovs, wealthy pioneers and merchants in those parts, hired a detachment of Cossacks led by their hetman T. Ermak, and in 1582 the first important phase in the conquest of Siberia was brought to an end. It was crowned by the foundation of Tobol'sk in 1587.[24]

Ivan IV was also a pioneer in other sectors of Russian evolution. From the outset of his reign he saw how important it would be for Moscow to have free access to the Baltic, to renew the old commercial traditions of Novgorod, and to trade directly with the countries of western Europe without the mediation of the German Hanse. He also realized that free access to the Baltic would facilitate for Moscow closer political relations with the Western powers and so help his growing state to obtain more of the badly needed specialists from the West.

So far, only England had succeeded in opening direct commercial intercourse with Russia, via the White Sea and the port of Arkhangelsk, thus cutting out the Hanseatic League.[25]

The English merchant venturers were seeking a direct route to Central Asia and profited by the Russian conquest of Kazan' and Astrakhan', where they were granted the right to trade duty free. The port of Arkhangel (Arkhangelsk), however, had the disadvantage that it could only be used during the short summer season.

Ivan IV therefore cast his eyes toward the Baltic and determined to conquer the whole of Livonia with the parts of Narva, Reval, and Riga. To his mind the conquest of this land was a part of the Muscovite program of reassemblement of Russian lands around Moscow. Had not Dorpat (Yurjev) been founded by Prince Jaroslav of Kiev, and was not this region a part of the patrimony of the House of Rurik?

After exhaustive military preparations Ivan IV started his Baltic campaign in 1558. The moment seemed very propitious for Moscow. The Livonian Order, which controlled the country, was in a state of decadence, and the rivalry between the grand master of the order and the Archbishop of Riga had reduced the military forces of both. All this helped the Muscovites to realize a signal success in the first years of the war. The Livonian fortresses could not withstand Ivan's artillery. Narva was taken, Dorpat had to surrender, and Reval was beleaguered.[26]

The capture of Narva was very important for Ivan, and he did all he could to win the sympathies of its burghers. His goal, however, was the conquest of Reval and Riga. Russian victories speeded up the disintegration of the order, culminating in the secularization of its lands and of the archbishopric of Riga. This, however, gave Livonia's neighbors the opportunity to intervene. Estonia with Reval recognized Swedish sovereignty, Livonia that of Poland-Lithuania, while Denmark occupied the island of Oesel. Instead of a disorganized order, Moscow now had to face powerful and determined neighbors.

This resulted in some reverses for the Russian army in the conquered territory, Lithuania being the most dangerous enemy. Ivan IV then decided to attack Lithuania in its most vulnerable spot. Assuming the command of his army, the tsar marched against Lithuania and, in 1563, won a signal victory which allowed him to occupy the important city of Polock and a great part of Lithuanian territory as far as Vilna. New complications, however, started to develop for Moscow when in 1569 Lithuania had to accept union with Poland, so that Moscow had to face the combined forces of both nations.

In order to strengthen his position in Livonia, Ivan IV decided to stop the assimilation of the conquered country to Russian ways of living and to give it an autonomous status. Livonia was made into a kingdom, and Ivan's ally the Danish prince Magnus was proclaimed king under Muscovite suzerainty. In spite of some successful fighting in Livonia, Magnus was, however, unable to take Reval, which was supported by the Swedes.

After the extinction of the Jagiellonian dynasty in 1572, there suddenly appeared the possibility of a union between Poland, Lithuania, and Muscovy. A great part of the Polish nobility was favorable to the election of Ivan IV as king of Poland-Lithuania. The Archbishop of Gniezno, Uchański, himself supported Ivan's candidature, declaring that Poland and Russia, two Slavic nations, should have one ruler.

However, French, Turkish, and Swedish diplomacy and the Habsburgs opposed the realization of such a bold plan. Finally, Ivan IV spoiled all his chances by his attitude and his conditions. He insisted on having Livonia as a part of Muscovy, asked for the cession of a great part of the Rusisan lands under Lithuania, especially of Kiev, and demanded that he be elected king separately by Poland and Lithuania and be crowned king by an Orthodox metropolitan. Moreover, he never showed any favor to the Polish nobility, who were the decisive factor in Poland. There was also the deep-seated difference in religion and in cultural orientation. So Ivan's candidacy to the Polish-Lithuanian throne ended in complete failure.

Ivan resumed his offensive in Livonia in 1575. Confident of final success, he felt able to relegate Magnus to the background and in 1577 launched his greatest campaign for the conquest of the whole of Livonia. He occupied the whole country with the exception of Riga, Treyden, and Dünamünde. This campaign exhausted all the financial and military resources of Moscow; and when the new Polish king, the energetic Stephen Bathory (1575-1586), struck at the Muscovite possessions, the tsar lacked the necessary means to stop the Polish-Lithuanian armies. Polock fell to the Poles; Magnus, who had joined them, attacked the region of Dorpat; and the Swedes made progress in the Gulf of Finland. In 1580 Velikie Luki was lost, and in the next year Bathory attacked Pskov, whose garrison and citizens defended themselves heroically. The Swedes took Narva, and news reached Ivan of fresh troubles in Kazan' and Astrakhan'.

Depressed and humiliated by these reverses, Ivan turned toward Rome, appealing to the Pope for intervention. The Pope, hoping to achieve his favorite aim, the union of the Russian Church with Rome, sent the Jesuit Possevino to Russia. Through his mediation a truce was concluded in 1582, followed by the conclusion of peace with Poland-Lithuania and

Sweden. Ivan had to renounce all his conquests in Livonia and in Lithuania, while the Swedes kept Estonia with the port of Narva.

The prolonged Baltic wars proved very onerous for the Muscovite state. Ivan was not only obliged to speed up the military manorial organization introduced by his grandfather in order to increase his military power, but also had to extend military service to the boyars, who had hitherto held their hereditary estates (*votčiny*) exempt from military service. These measures and Ivan's personal character alienated many of his boyars from him, and some left his service and joined the Lithuanians. The most prominent among these was Andrew Kurbskij, with whom Ivan carried on a voluminous correspondence. These defections increased Ivan's dislike for the aristocratic classes and induced him to introduce a new institution, the so-called *opričnina*, which was directed against the old nobility. Their estates were confiscated and given to the *opričniki*.[27] The whole reorganization of Russian social life was carried out with great ruthlessness, and all these upheavals, of course, did not facilitate the realization of Ivan's dreams of expansion.

There was, however, also a democratic trait in his autocratic and merciless behavior. It manifested itself in some of his proclamations and, especially, in 1564, when Ivan IV quitted Moscow with his family, announcing his abdication of the throne because he could no longer tolerate the intrigues of the boyars, for whose deeds he declared the Russian people to be in no way responsible. He returned to Moscow at the request of the city's burghers and continued his social reforms with the sanction of the people, given to him at the Assembly of 1566—regarded by Russian historians as the first real Zemskij Sobor—to which he invited also merchants and traders.

In spite of the social unrest caused by the tsar's autocratic and antiboyar policy, the Muscovite state had made great progress in many respects under Ivan IV. An immense new empire in the East was added to the already vast domains of Muscovy, the ring of isolation from the West was broken, foreign traders and diplomats appeared at the tsar's court and in the cities, and for the first time Muscovite envoys were received at many courts of western Europe.

The object of several diplomatic missions sent to Moscow by the West was to win the mighty new Christian power for an anti-Turkish alliance. Therefore, the popes and the emperors—Frederick III and Maximilian—stressed the Byzantine heritage which had fallen into the hands of Moscow, and hoped that the mighty Christian ruler would free the Orthodox Christians in the Balkans from the Turkish yoke. They conjured up before the eyes of Ivan the vision of the ruler of Moscow conquering Constantinople and receiving in this center of Eastern Christianity the homage not only of his Orthodox subjects, but also of the representatives of Western Christianity—the Pope and the emperor—who were willing to greet him as a true emperor, successor of the rulers of Byzantium.

But Ivan IV was not impressed by the idea which inspired the popes, namely that the whole of Christendom should be ruled by two emperors, the western and the eastern. He did not underestimate the power of the Turks, under whose sovereignty the khans of the Crimea had placed their lands. In his foreign policy Ivan IV remained faithful to the cautious and realistic program which had become a dynastic tradition. Instead of organizing hazardous expeditions against the Crimea and the Turks, he concentrated his gaze on the shores of the Baltic Sea and on the vast plains beyond the Volga and the Ural Mountains, where Russian forces were encountering least resistance. The promise of the imperial title on the part of the westerners meant nothing to him. He assumed this title as belonging to him by the grace of God, who had given complete sovereignty to him and to his ancestor. He accepted the homage of the Patriarch of Constantinople when the latter recognized his title of Tsar in 1561, but refused the patriarch's offer to come to Moscow and to perform a new coronation, being satisfied with the coronation performed by the Metropolitan of Moscow in 1547. He even refused to accept the blessing which the patriarch had sent him through the intermediary of a Greek metropolitan, under the pretext that, when traversing Lithuania, the Greek had kissed Latin crosses.

This attitude of Ivan IV is very enlightening. It reveals his intention to bring the recent evolution in Muscovite history to a crowning culmination and to make not Constantinople but Moscow the center of Orthodoxy. Even in this respect he was following in the steps of a dynastic tradition already revealed by his forefather Basil I, who gave the bold order to omit the name of the Byzantine emperor in liturgical prayers.

This last phase in the evolution of Moscow was only reached under Fedor (Theodor) I, his son (1584-1598), thanks to a clever maneuver by Boris Godunov, the regent. After the death of Fedor's uncle Nikita Romanov, Boris ruled in the name of his brother-in-law, a weak character, incapable of holding the reins of government. Profiting by the visit of the Patriarch of Constantinople to Moscow in search of subsidies—Boris succeeded in obtaining the transformation of the Metropolis of Moscow into a patriarchate (1589). Four new metropolitan sees were founded in Novgorod, Kazan', Rostov, and Krutica. The patriarch adopted as a special distinction the white mitre, which, according to the native legend, had been sent from Rome to Constantinople and had from there reached Russia. Ivan IV's dream was realized, but only in part. The Eastern patriarchs, who convened a council in 1590 and 1593 in Constantinople in order to confirm the new foundation, accorded to the Patriarch of Moscow only the fifth place among the eastern patriarchates, after Constantinople, Alexandria, Antioch, and Jerusalem.

Boris Godunov proved to be a good administrator and an able ruler. He succeeded in checking the attempts of the old nobility to regain their former influence in the government, secured the southern frontier against Tatar attacks by constructing a chain of fortified places, and continued the successful penetration of Siberia.

This hopeful evolution was, unfortunately, interrupted by the death of the tsar, who left no heirs. As Ivan IV had killed his eldest son in an attack of insane rage and as his youngest son Dmitrij had died in a tragic accident in 1591, the Rurik dynasty, which had started its successful career in Moscow under Daniel and Ivan Kalita, was extinct.

NOTES

1. G. Vernadsky in his book *The Mongols and Russia* (see Bibl.), p. 316, rightly argues that the Khan's attack could not have been directed against Nižnij-Novgorod at the confluence of the Oka and Volga rivers, as is generally believed.

2. B. Spuler, *Die Goldene Horde* (see Bibl.), p. 165, thinks that Ulug Mahmed, when releasing Basil II, missed his best opportunity of completely subjugating Moscow. G. Vernadsky (*The Mongols and Russia*, p. 319), however, states that the Khan had weighed all his chances well, and realizing that Moscow's power was increasing, he correctly calculated that this was the best decision to make. Of course, he did not foresee the possible reaction of his son Mahmudek.

3. Cf. Chapter IX, pp. 228, 229.

4. PSRL, vol. VI, pp. 151-63.

5. *Ibid.*, vol. VIII, pp. 100-109.

6. In one passage of the *Stepennaja Kniga* (*ibid.*, vol. XXI, 2, p. 462) Basil's initiative is stressed even more. "All were silent," says the compiler, presenting the bishops and boyars as asleep and neglecting thier duties. "There was found only one (man) zealous for God and His true law"—Basil II. This passage seems to reflect the further evolution of the idea of the tsar as autocrator, as it was manifested under Ivan IV, during whose reign the *Stepennaja Kniga* was written. In another passage (*ibid.*, pp. 506-12) the abridged version of the *Voskresenskij Chronicle* is given.

7. For more details see M. Cherniavsky, "The Reception of the Council of Florence in Moscow," *Church History*, 24 (1955), pp. 347-59. This also gives a good analysis of Russian sources dealing with the events. A detailed review of the literature concerning the Union of Florence and its aftermath in Russia is given by Hruševs'kyj in his *Istorija Ukrainy Rusi*, vol. 5, pp. 508-618, 657-61. The Western point of view on the union and its consequences in the Russian Church is given by A. Ziegler, *Die Union des Konzils von Florenz* (see Bibl.).

On Poland and the union see O. Halecki, *From Florence to Brest* (Rome, 1958), pp. 33-140.

8. This letter and other documents concerning Russian ecclesiastical affairs of this time are published in the first volume of the *Pamjatniki drevne-russkago kanoničeskago prava* (St. Petersburg, 1908, Russk. Ist. Bibl. vol. VI).

9. For more details see below, Chapter XV, pp. 374, 387.

10. On Ivan III's reform of Muscovite administration and military and social organization, see below, Chapter XV. On Russian foreign policy in the second half of the fifteenth century see the monograph by K. V. Bazilevič, *Vnešnjaja politika russk. centr. gosudarstva. Vtoraja polovina XV veka* (Moscow, 1952). A short but useful survey of Ivan III's and Ivan IV's policy toward the West (Poland, Lithuania and Livonia) will be found in Herta v. Ramm-Helmsing's study *Die Moskauer Westpolitik Ivans* (see Bibl.), pp. 61-69.

11. There exists a short monograph of little historical value on Uglič and its princes by L. F. Solovev, *Kratkaja istorija goroda Ugliča* (St. Petersburg, 1895). On Andrew, see *ibid.*, p. 24.

12. A comprehensive history of old Novgorod has not yet been written. Besides general works on Russian history, the following studies give more details on Novgorod: S. Solovev, *Ob otnošeniakh Novgoroda k velikim knjazjam* (Moscow, 1846); G. E. Kočin, *O dogovorakh Novgoroda s knjazjami* (Leningrad, 1939), published in Učenye Zapiski of the Pedagogical Institute, vol. 19; N. I. Kostomarov, *Severnorusskija narodopravstva vo vremena udelno-večevago uklada*, vol. II, Novgorod and Pskov (St. Petersburg, 1863). On the growth of Muscovy in this period, see especially A. E. Presnjakov, *Obrazovanie velikorusskago gosudarstva: Očerki po istorii XIII-XV stoletij* (Petrograd, 1918). Important documents on the fourteenth and fifteenth centuries were published under the editorship of S. N. Valk, *Gramoty Velikogo Novgoroda i Pskova* (Moscow, 1949) by the Academy of Sciences of the USSR, Leningrad division of the Institute of History. A complete bibliography of source material concerning Novgorod's history is to be found *ibid.*, pp. 338-44. The most recent publication on Novgorod in the sixteenth century, with important bibliographical indications, is by A. P. Pronštejn, *Velikij Novgorod v XVI veke* (Khar'kov, 1957). There he also discusses the controversy concerning the conclusion of the treaty of 1471 by Novgorod with Casimir of Poland. Recently A. A. Zimin, "O khronologii dogovornykh gramot velikogo Novgoroda s knjazjami XIII-XV vv.," *Problemy istočnikovedenija*, vol. 5 (1956), pp. 300-27, accepted this thesis that the treaty was only a project put forward by the Novgorodians and that its realization was frustrated by Ivan III, whose invasion was already on the move when the project was discussed.

13. Cf. P. Johansen, "Novgorod und die Hanse," *Städtewesen und Bürgertum als geschichtl. Kräfte*, Gedächtnisschrift F. Röhrig (Lübeck, 1953), pp. 121-248. Cf. also N. A. Kazakov's studies on the same subject in *Istoričeskie zapiski*, 28 (1948), pp. 111-31, and *ibid.*, 47 (1954), pp. 259-90. Cf. also M. P. Lesnikov' study, *ibid.*, 39 (1952), pp. 259-79.

14. An exhaustive history of the principality of Tver' is still one of the desiderata of Russian history. So far only V. S. Borzakovskij has dealt with the history of Tver' (*Istorija Tverskago knjažestva*, Petersburg, 1876). Some valuable additional notes on the reign of Boris were given by I. Vinogradov in his study *Novyja dannyja po istorii Tverskago knjažestva: Knjaženie Borisa Alexandroviča (1425-1461)* (Tver', 1908), not available in the United States. The older history of Tver' especially needs more thorough examination.

15. Polnoe sobranije, vol. XV. On chronicles written in Tver' cf. A. N. Nasonov, "*Letopisnye pamjatniky Tverskago knjažestva.*" Izvestija Ak. nauk SSSR, otd. gumanit. nauk, VII serija (Leningrad, 1930), nos. 9, 10. Idem, "*Letopisnye svody Tverskago knjažestva*, Doklady Ak. nauk SSSR, serija B. (November-December) (Leningrad, 1926).

A similar mentality is mirrored in the "Praise of the Pious Grand Prince Boris of Tver'," written shortly after 1453 and ascribed generally to the monk Thomas (Foma) of Tver', published by N. Lichačev in *Pamiatniki drevnei pis'menosti*, vol. 168 (Moscow, 1908), pp. 1-15. Cf. however, W. Philipp, "Ein Anonymus der Tver Publizistik im 15. Jahrhundert" in *Festschrift für Dmytro Čyževskyj* published by the Ost-Europa Institut der freien Universität Berlin, slavistische Veröffentlichungen, vol. 6 (Berlin, 1954), pp. 230-48. W. Philipp shows that the attribution of this panegyric to Foma cannot be maintained. The "Praise" is an anonymous work.

16. For details see above, Chapter X, p. 237.

17. See below, Chapter XVII, pp. 437 ff., for more details.

18. The classical work on the Golden Horde is still that written by B. Spuler, *Die Goldene Horde* (see Bibl.). For this period see pp. 109 ff. For an exhaustive bibliography see pp. 456-516.

19. It was this growing self-consciousness of Muscovy, nourished by so many successful operations, which awakened a pro-Muscovite spirit in the Russian part of the Lithuanian state. The religious question only served to encourage this development. It should be stressed that such a tendency hardly existed in this part of Lithuania before the last quarter of the fifteenth century. For details see H. Jablonowski, *Westrussland* (see Bibl.), pp. 113-32, where a complete bibliography on this period in Slavic languages will be found.

20. His *Rerum Muscovitarum commentarii* (Vienna, 1549), which appeared in several editions in Latin, German, and Italian, provides a very important historical source on Muscovy at this period. It was the first description of the new state, which was still virtually unknown in western Europe.

21. For more details and for Basil's negotiations with the Habsburgs, see Chapter XVII, pp. 439 ff. The history of Smolensk down to the beginning of the fourteenth century was studied by P. V. Golubovskij, *Istorija Smolenskoj zemli do načala XV st.* (Kiev, 1895). This is a serious study on Smolensk's development under Lithuanian sovereignty. On pp. 87-170 the author deals with Smolensk's industry and commerce and publishes its commercial code, dating from the thirteenth century.

22. See Chapter XV, pp. 379 ff.

23. The monograph by S. F. Platonov, *Ivan Groznij* (Petrograd, 1923) is regarded by many as the most balanced description of Ivan's reign. The Russian academician R. Wipper (*Ivan Grozny*, translated by J. Fineberg, Moscow, 1947) however, depicted Ivan in a way which is in many respects original. On Ivan's social reforms see Chapter XV.

24. On the Russian conquest and colonization of Siberia in the sixteenth and seventeenth centuries see S. Bachrušin, *Očerki po istorii kolonizatsii Sibiri v XVI i XVII vv.* (Moscow, 1928). A good review of Russia's eastward expansion from the beginning down to modern times—comparable to that of the United States westward—was given by Vernadsky, *The Expansion of Russia* (see Bibl.), pp. 391-425, where a more complete bibliography is listed. Cf. also the works of F. A. Golder, and Juri Semjonov (see Bibl.). An extensive literature on Siberia's early history will be found in G. V. Lantzeff's book *Siberia in the*

Seventeenth Century (see Bibl.), pp. 215-30. A history of Siberia was written by V. K. Andrejevič (*Istorija Sibiri*, 5 vols., St. Petersburg, 1887-1889) replacing those written by the first historian of Siberia, G. F. Müller in 1750 and by J. E. Fischer in 1774. There is an English translation of one of G. F. Müller's works under the title, *Conquest of Siberia* (see Bibl.). Cf. also N. N. Firsov, *Čtenija po istorii Sibiri* (2 vols., Moscow, 1920-1921).

25. For details and bibliography see Inna Lubimenko, *Les relations* (see Bibl.).

26. See also, Chapter XI, pp. 252, 258, and Schiemann's work quoted there (vol. II, pp. 229 ff.). On Prussia and Ivan IV see K. Forstreuter, *Preussen und Russland* (see Bibl.), pp. 101 ff.

27. For details see Chapter XV, pp. 384, 385.

Chapter XIII

THE RENAISSANCE AND THE SLAVS. SLAVIC CULTURAL ACHIEVEMENTS IN THE FIFTEENTH AND SIXTEENTH CENTURIES

I. *The Renaissance in Italy, the Low Countries, France, and Germany; its influence on the Slavs—Czech literary activity reflecting the religious struggles of the fifteenth century, Hus and Hussite literary production—The Utraquists and the Romanists—Survival of humanism in Moravia, new humanistic influences from Italy—Czech humanists—German humanism and its influence on the Unity of Brethren —The Renaissance, Czech historiography and belles lettres—Renaissance in Czech art—*
II. *First Polish contacts with Western humanism—Polish kings and humanists—The "golden age," Polish writings on statesmanship—Polish national literature—Nicholas Rey—John Kochanowski, the great Polish poet—Kochanowski's contemporaries and epigoni—The Renaissance in Polish art—Polish cultural influences in Lithuania, West and South Russia; first literary productions in Belo-Russian and Ukrainian—Reaction of the Orthodox against the union, Orthodox polemic literature—*
III. *East Russian literature of the thirteenth and fourteenth centuries echoes national calamity—Growth of Muscovy and opposition to it reflected in fifteenth century literature, South Slavic literary influence—First Russian heresies and polemic literature—Maxim the Greek —The Muscovite ideology of unification mirrored in literary activity— The Italian Renaissance and East Russian art—Icon painting, a Russian national art—*

283

IV. *Dalmatian and Ragusan humanists—First Croatian lyrics and play-writers—The golden period of Ragusan poetry—Character of Dalmatian literary production—The Italian Renaissance in Dalmatian art*

I

The fifteenth century witnessed the final stage in an evolution which had begun already in the eleventh century. It was a movement which led the Western nations to the emancipation of their thought from old ways, to an individual conception of their conscience and of the law. This evolution went through several stages, beginning with the break away from feudal legal customs by the burghers of the rising Italian city-states. This new class of medieval society had to turn to the principles of Roman law, kept alive in Byzantium, for a solid basis on which to organize the life of its cities. The introduction of the study of Roman jurisprudence at the University of Bologna opened the way for the discovery of the cultural heritage of the classical age, and the spread of the new teaching introduced the notion of individuality in private and public law.

The other important stage was the discovery of Greek philosophy by the West, with the help of the Arabs and Jews. The introduction of Aristotelianism at the University of Paris opened a new chapter in the history of theological speculation, with which the names of St. Thomas Aquinas and his followers are so brilliantly associated. Inspired by the same classical tradition, Roger Bacon introduced the experimental method into England.

The new notions of individual emancipation penetrated increasingly among the intellectuals and conflicted with the old feudal methods, provoking in almost all countries dangerous social, political, and religious crises. The prosperity of the free commercial enterprise of the cities created the era of early Western capitalism, a fact which also had important consequences in the political field. Western monarchism came into being and found its legal basis in Aristotle's teaching that government should be in the hands of the best man.

The humanists, admirers of Latin and Greek antiquity, discovered the literary and artistic treasures of the classical age, which provided new incentives for Western writers and artists. It was again Italy which contributed most to the propagation of the new ideas. Dante, Petrarch, and Boccaccio demonstrated new methods in literature, Brunelleschi and Donatello in art. Florence took the place of Constantinople in the cultivation of Hellenic civilization. The Medici princes collected Greek manuscripts and welcomed Byzantine scholars, refugees from their enslaved country. Their example was followed by other princes and cities and by the popes. The era of the Renaissance was born, characterized by the struggle for self-emancipation, toward the reassertion of the rights of individual thinking and acting. It was an era of intellectual and artistic revival, inspired by the examples found in the literary and artistic works of the classics. These seemed to express so well the ideals of emancipation and reassertion of human personality and individuality for which medieval man had been struggling.

The Italian Renaissance can boast of splendid achievements in scholarship, literature, and art. The names of Giovanni Villani, the first chronicler who wrote in Italian with scholarly method, of the annalist Poggio, of Ariosto with his *Orlando Furioso*, of Donatello, Leonardo da Vinci, Michelangelo, Tizian, Raphael, and Galileo, were known to all the intellectuals of contemporary Europe. The Italian Renaissance, however, went furthest in its emancipation from traditional beliefs and ways of life and in its cult of the pagan heroes of antiquity. It also produced Machiavelli, who expounded in *Il Principe* a new notion of the state, liberated from all moral rules. It produced also Pomponazzi, founder of the rationalist school of Padua.

Another important center of the Renaissance, differing in many respects from Italy, grew up in the other capitalist center, in the Low Countries. The humanists of the Low Countries did not go as far as the Italians in their emphasis on human individuality and on emancipation from medieval beliefs and methods. They adapted the new critical methods to the study of the Bible and limited themselves to proposing religious and social reforms within the Christian framework. This is characteristic of the greatest of Dutch humanists and philosophers, Erasmus of Rotterdam. He was not only the author of the satiric *Encomium Moriae* ("Praise of Folly"), but also a critical editor of the New Testament. He was a friend of St. Thomas More, the prominent English humanist. The latter, with Colet and Latimer, worked for a reform of the Church in England without adopting the extreme views of some Italian humanists.

In Germany the movement spread mainly among the cities of the Rhine and South Germany. Reuchlin and Melanchthon, Dürer and Holbein were its best representatives.

The French Renaissance developed under the influence of the Italian and Dutch movements. Flemish influence was at first strong in French Renaissance painting, but after the arrival of Leonardo da Vinci at Fontainebleau, Italian influence in art become more pronounced. In the adoption of Italian Renaissance art, the French, however, only abandoned gradually their traditional Gothic art. A similar phenomenon can be observed in England. The greatest achievements in the science of law were reached in France by Guillaume Budé and Jean Bodin, during the sixteenth century.

Italian and Dutch influences can also be noticed in the work of the greatest French writers of this period, Ronsard, Rabelais, Montaigne, and Calvin. Rabelais followed Erasmus but was also influenced by the rationalism of Pomponazzi. Montaigne's *Essays* made him a precursor of Voltaire. Calvin sought to realize the ideals of the Renaissance within the framework of Christianity, but his religious passion led him too far and he became the most radical of the reformers.

Calvin's writings are regarded as being among the classics of French prose. In this respect the French Renaissance achieved remarkable results. The idiom of the center of France was made the official language of the kingdom by Francis I. Thanks to the leading writers of this period, the language developed rapidly, and French literature of the sixteenth century gave a foretaste of classical French literature, thus inaugurating the era of modern development.

It was to be expected that such a lively movement, bringing so many new notions which appealed to human longing for progress in knowledge and for free expression of man's individual thinking, should also influence the cultural progress of the Slavic nations in the fifteenth and sixteenth centuries. The use of the Latin language by scholars naturally promoted these influences, and the elegance of the classical Latin in which many of the humanists communicated their ideas invited the intellectuals in many Slavic nations to vie with them in their literary production. The cultivation of their native languages by many prominent writers of the Renaissance could only encourage the development of literary works in Slavic languages.

There are, however, two observations which must be borne in mind when studying the influence of the Western Renaissance on the Slavic nations. The origin and spread of the Renaissance was intimately connected with economic conditions. The prosperity which the new commercial intercourse of the Western maritime nations with the East and with the New World had brought to western Europe in its train was a great stimulant for the progress of the new movement. On the other hand, however, central Germany, impoverished by the loss of its international commerce, was hardly touched by the Renaissance. The Slavs thus obtained the new incentives mainly from Italy, Holland, and France.

The Czechs were geographically nearer to the centers of the Renaissance than were the Poles and the Russians. The promising humanistic movement which had such encouraging results in Bohemia was, however, stopped by the Czech Reformation. So it was natural that literary activity in Bohemia at the beginning of the fifteenth century should reflect strongly the religious struggles which had started in the fourteenth century and continued in the following period.[1]

Among the foremost writers of this period is, of course, John Hus. Because of his religious teachings Hus is a controversial figure among the Czechs. All are, however, unanimous in praising his merits for the growth of Czech national consciousness and for the evolution of the Czech literary language. In this respect the Czechs had not to wait for the incentives of the Renaissance. Hus wrote his first Czech works in the years between 1406 and 1410, but he composed his most important Czech writings only during the last three years of his life, from 1412 to 1415. He wrote in the language in which he had preached, choosing the dialect of Prague for his orthographic reforms, which he expounded in his Latin work on Bohemian orthography. He greatly contributed to the modernization of the literary language and of Czech orthography. Under the influence of the Church Slavonic spelling applied by the Czech monks of the Emmaus monastery, he endeavored to render each speech sound by a single letter, and his reform with its broad use of diacritic signs underlies the modern alphabets of Czechs, Slovaks, Croats, Slovenes, a large number of other new national alphabetic patterns, and even the international system of phonetic transcription.

Hus's letters, in Czech and in Latin, make a strong appeal to modern readers. They are written in a most lively language and best reveal the individual character of the Czech reformer. Many of them were written in Constance and are most moving.

The most prominent of his other writings in Czech are the two which he addressed to his lady listeners in Prague. These are a series of expositions of the faith (*Výklad*) and the *Dcerka* ("The Little Daughter"). His *Postilla* was written in 1413 and is very important for the insight it gives into Hus's teaching and thinking. The Czech treatise *On Simony* manifests his zeal for Church reform.

Among his numerous Latin writings, the commentary upon the work of Peter Lombardus, *Super IV sententiarum,* is the best example of Hus's philosophical teaching.[2] His treatise on the Church, *De ecclesia,* is based on Wycliffe's composition of the same name.

It should also be stressed that Hus played an important role in the history of Czech religious music. The singing of hymns formed an important part of the services held by Hus in his chapel. He himself composed several hymns for his congregation. His example was followed by his disciples, and so it happened that the singing of hymns and songs played a prominent part in the history of the Hussites[3] and became one of the most characteristic features of Hussite literature.

The singing of religious songs was also an integral part of the Hussite liturgy. The more conservative Hussites in Prague, led by John of Příbram, kept the old Latin liturgical order, but John of Želiv, the leader of the radical elements there, even began to say the Mass in Czech. From this center new Czech religious chants originated, and these were also sung by the partisans of Jacobellus, who represented the central group of the Hussites in Prague. The Taborites, who generally reduced the liturgy to its essentials—reading from Holy Writ, chant, the Lord's Prayer, consecration, and communion—also favored the use of religious singing.

The *Cantionale of Jistebník*, which was composed about 1420, gives a clear picture of this type of literature in the Hussite period. It was a kind of handbook of religious chant and of the liturgy used by the radical party of John of Želiv in Prague and by the Taborites. Latin liturgical songs are to be found with older Czech compositions in new editions. In addition, the collection contains new songs for the Mass, songs for Sundays and festivals, prayers in verse, and also war songs. Many of the compositions reveal the reformist spirit of John Hus and of his followers. Most of them are anonymous. In most of the new songs dogmatic theology and polemic spirit prevail over true religious feeling, and they reveal little lyric sentiment.

A special place among the new songs should be given to war songs. The most popular of these was the song of Taborite origin—some used to attribute it to Žižka himself—"All ye warriors of God" (*Ktož jsú boží bojovníci*), which has a dignified and powerful melody.[4] It was sung by the Hussite warriors before an encounter with the enemy. Hussite victories were celebrated in verse, while other songs were composed in honor of Hus and Jerome of Prague.

Satiric compositions in verse are also numerous. They were directed by the Catholics against Wycliffe and the Hussites and by the latter against the Catholics. Their tunes served to propagate among the populace the ideas they contained. Several disputations in verse were also composed at this period and sung by the people.

Two verse compositions of a historical nature have survived. The first deals with the origins of Hussitism, the second, only partly preserved, was a rhymed Czech chronicle. Two similar verse compositions celebrate Žižka's extermination of the Taborite extremists.

The more radical Jacobellus wrote a Czech commentary to the Apocalypse and Czech sermons on the Epistles which were read at Sunday services. He also translated Wycliffe's *Dialogue between Truth and Untruth on the Poverty of the Clergy*.

Even the warrior Žižka has a place in Hussite literature. He is the author of the *Military Regulations*, which he composed with his officers and published in 1423. Some of his letters, which are preserved, disclose Žižka's profound religious sentiments.

Among the conservative Hussites, John of Příbram deserves to be mentioned. He was a stubborn adversary of the English Master Peter Payne, called Magister Engliš, with his Wycliffite teaching. His most important

Czech treatises are those *Of the Great Torment of the Holy Church* and the *Lives of the Priests of Tábor*.

Peter of Mladeňovice also belonged to the moderate party. His *Relatio de magistri Joannis Hus causa*, of which he also published a short version in Czech, opens the series of Hussite historiography. The most important source for the period between 1414 and 1431 is the *Chronicon* compiled by Laurence (Vavřinec) of Březová, of which a Czech version is preserved. He also celebrated the victory at Domažlice in Latin verses. He edited a Latin *World Chronicle*, which only goes on to the seventh century. His translation of the *Travels of Sir John Mandeville* and his book on the *Explanation of Dreams* were both very popular. The collection of contemporary documentary evidence called *Ancient Bohemian Chronicles* deserves especial mention. The account of events goes from 1378 to the end of the fifteenth century. For the events after 1400 this anonymous collection becomes an important historical source. The anti-German spirit of the Hussites is mirrored in other compilations.

The radical reformers were not favorable to the study of science. Only medical science found any favor. The German, Albík, archbishop of Prague, was the author of some Latin treatises in which he recommended a new method, dieting. Christian of Prachatice published a Latin herbarium and a general medical book in Czech. Some other medical works, popular at that time in western Europe, were translated into Czech during the fifteenth century.

Interesting documentary evidence on the religious ideas of the Taborites and on their polemics with their adversaries is to be found in the *Chronicon sacerdotum Taboriensium*. It was written in two parts by Nicholas of Pelhřimov, called Biskupec (died about 1459), who directed the religious and secular administration of the Taborites as head of their priests. The chronicle also gives an account of the negotiations at the Council of Basel.

The main representative of the conservative Utraquists was John of Rokycany, archbishop-elect of Prague (died 1471). His sincere attempts at a reconciliation with the Catholics were unsuccessful. He was often attacked by his adversaries—a derogatory Czech song against him is extant—but he defended the orthodoxy of the Utraquists courageously in both Latin and Czech writings. His patriotic and religious spirit found expression in eloquent sermons which sometimes recall the oratory of John Hus. Many of them are preserved in his *Postilla*, written in the spirit of the Czech reformers and in a lively language which reveals the influence of Hus's literary tradition.

The persecution launched against the Brethren forced them to defend their doctrines in writing. They did this in the form of anonymous letters addressed to Rokycana, to King George of Poděbrady, and to their adversaries. Brother Gregory was the main author of these apologies. He also composed some other writings in which he dealt with religious and social questions discussed by the Brethren.

Rokycana's successor Wenceslas Koranda (1425-1519), a sworn adversary of the Brethren, was a prominent member of the embassy sent by King George to Pope Pius II in 1462, requesting the Pope to confirm the Compacts. Although Catholic nobles were among the members of the embassy, the Pope refused confirmation. All this is described in Koranda's account, which also contains his apology for the Compacts and the Pope's somewhat ungracious answer. In other writings, Koranda attacked the teaching of the Brethren and the adversaries of Utraquism. These were collected by himself in Czech and in Latin in his *Manuale.*

In his efforts to obtain the confirmation of the Compacts and to bring Bohemia out of the political isolation into which the accusation of heresy had brought her, George also used the services of foreign diplomats. One of them was the German Gregory of Heimburg (died 1472), who defended George in his letters and in his *Apology.*[5] Another was Antony Marini of Grenoble (de Gratianopoli), who had been very useful to the king on diplomatic missions to Rome, France, Poland, and Hungary. On the invitation of the king, Marini wrote a politico-economic treatise, of which, unfortunately, only the least interesting part is preserved.

Two other descriptions of embassies sent to France are preserved. One is the diary of a junior member of the embassy in 1469, Jaroslav, and the other the description of an embassy led by Leo of Rožmitál to France, Spain, and Portugal in 1465-1467, composed by Šašek.[6]

Another prominent defender of George of Poděbrady and of Utraquism was the nobleman Ctibor Tovačovský of Cimburg. He set out his ideas in an allegorical dialogue entitled *Truth's Quarrel with Falsehood.* More important is his legal work, generally called the "Book of Tovačov" (*Kniha Tovačovská*), in which the author described in detail the legal customs of Moravia.

Some satiric songs reflect the tense atmosphere surrounding relations between the Utraquists and the Romanists. A few poetic descriptions of warlike events are also preserved, especially the song on the battle of Varna (1444), which is wrongly presented as a victory of the Christians.

Although some of the early Italian humanists were already known and appreciated in Bohemian intellectual circles under Charles IV and Wenceslas IV,[7] the full force of the Renaissance was only felt in Bohemia at the end of the fifteenth century after the religious struggles had subsided. The officials of Sigismund's imperial chancery were mostly Italians, and they communicated their humanist enthusiasm to their Czech colleagues and friends. The Austrian and German humanists, Jerome Balbus and Conrad Celtes, also found admirers and imitators among Czechs.

Moreover, the tradition initiated by the early humanists did not die out. Even during Bohemia's internal struggles it persisted in Moravia, where the Hussite movement was less strong, in the canonries of the Augustinians, and at the court of the bishops of Olomouc.

This explains why the principal representatives of Czech humanism were mostly Catholics. The main inspirer of the first Czech humanists was Aeneas Sylvius Piccolomini, later Pope Pius II, who was secretary to the chancery of the Emperor Frederick III. He had already met many Czech intellectuals at the Council of Basel and influenced profoundly his Czech colleagues in the chancery. He entertained a lively correspondence with them after they had returned to their own country. Official business brought Aeneas Sylvius to Bohemia—he visited Tábor twice—and he conceived the idea in 1458 of writing in his elegant Latin a history of Bohemia, based on his own experiences and on the material translated for him from Czech documents by his friends. Of course, the Hussite movement was sharply condemned by this devout Catholic, so that he is often accused of anti-Czech bias. But his work made Bohemia and the foremost representatives of the Hussite movement—his characterization of Žižka is particularly suggestive—known in the whole contemporary world of learning. The first Czech translation of his history appeared in 1510.

Of course, humanism only affected a highly educated elite of noblemen who had received a classical training abroad. During the religious disputes the University of Prague had lost its scholarly character and become a battleground of confessional controversies. Humanistic tendencies only penetrated university circles late and very slowly. The first representatives of Czech humanism were mostly admirers of Cicero's eloquent Latin, of Martial's satire, and of Horace's and Virgil's poetry. In their literary productions they imitated their classical masters and neo-Latin poets and writers. They seldom gave expression to their own individual feeling. However, they followed their masters in their tolerant attitude toward the religious opinion of other men. This was a new and welcome trend in the Czech atmosphere, which was still filled with religious fanaticism.

Although writing in Latin, the Czech humanists were not alien to the patriotic feeling which characterizes the movement. This is particularly evident in the work of John Pflug of Rabstein (died 1473), a Catholic prelate who used his humanistic training and diplomatic skill in his *Dialogus* to defend King George against the opposition of the nobles. John of Rabstein can, however, be regarded as the continuer not only of the humanist tradition, but also of the Czech *devotio moderna*. His *Dialogus* is written in this spirit. There he condemns sharply the persecution of individuals because of their faith.

The Czech humanists were also interested in Platonic philosophy. Unfortunately, the main philosophical work of this type, the *Microcosmos* of John Šlechta of Všehrdy, is lost. The Moravian humanist Augustin of Olomouc (Kasebrot) is the author of an important critical work, the *Dialogus in defensionem poeticae.*

The most eminent representative of Czech humanism is Bohuslav Hasistein of Lobkovice (1460-1510). He was initiated into classical lore during his studies in Italy and became profoundly penetrated by the spirit of humanism. Renouncing a political career, he settled down on his estate and devoted his life to the study of the classics and to Latin composition. He carried on a lively correspondence with prominent humanists abroad, and his numerous letters show that he had mastered the stylistic art of Cicero and Seneca. He was a born poet of high qualities, and in his odes he often depicted in Horace's and Virgil's manner the charm and beauty of his Bohemian homeland. He is rightly counted among the best neo-Latin poets.

Czech humanists soon began to write also in their native tongue, translating classical and neo-Latin works into Czech. They showed here a preference for the practical aspects of Roman culture, namely, legal science and rhetoric. The same practical sense induced them to choose didactic and satiric poetry for their studies and to pay little attention to the lyric and to drama. Erasmus of Rotterdam attracted the humanists more than anybody else. Printing was introduced into Bohemia from Nürnberg, reaching Pilsen in 1468 and Prague soon after. This encouraged the translation and printing of the works of Petrarch, Poggio, Boccaccio, and even Lucian of Samosata.

A few names of such writers deserve mention: Gregory Hrubý of Jelení; [8] Wenceslas Písecký, one of the first Czech humanists to study the Greek classics; and Nicolas Konáč of Hodištkov, the translator of Lucian and Boccaccio and author of a satirical work on the vices of the different classes of society.

The most monumental work of Czech humanism was written by the patriotic jurist Victor Kornel of Všehrdy (about 1460-1520). He did not study abroad, but became so closely acquainted with humanistic lore in Bohemia that he was praised as a prominent humanist even by Bohuslav Hasistein. He used his knowledge of Roman law and his critical sense, sharpened by his humanistic knowledge, in his appreciation of Czech custom law in his *Knihy devatery* ("Nine Books"). It is a very remarkable achievement in Czech legal science. His example was followed by Paul

Christian of Koldín (1530-1589), whose *City Laws of the Bohemian Kingdom* were also accepted in Moravia, and partly in Silesia, remaining in use until 1812.

It was a pity that the hostile attitude of university circles toward humanism forced Sigismund Gelenius (1497-1554), the foremost Czech humanist, to become a "corrector" at the famous printing house of Frobenius in Basel. A friend of Erasmus and Melanchthon, he had pursued his studies at Italian universities but could not obtain a post in the university of his native land. He excelled at Basel as one of the greatest philologists of the sixteenth century and one of the first critical editors of Latin and Greek classical works.

When humanism began to triumph at Prague University, in the third decade of the sixteenth century, it was not in Padua and Bologna that Czech humanists sought their inspiration, but in Wittenberg, the center of Luther's teaching. This last period of Czech humanism, profoundly impregnated by the teaching of the great German reformers, is more prosaic and less attractive. The Italian vivacity and love of beauty which had previously inspired Czech humanists had to give way in Bohemia to the German genius, more pedantic and thorough but less interested in the joys of life. A consequence of this was the spread of Protestant ideas in Bohemia and a germanization of Czech intellectual life.

The humanism of Wittenberg was, however, more acceptable to the intellectuals of the Unity of Czech Brethren. It soon penetrated their ranks, generally inspired by the gentle spirit of Melanchthon's new Protestant piety. As a consequence the majority of the Brethren arrived at a positive attitude toward learning. This new tendency vanquished the conservative minority, thanks to the organizing talents of Bishop Lucas of Prague, and paved the way for the acceptance of Brethren who could not abandon their high positions in worldly affairs or in scholarship. The Brethren started to found schools, to send their disciples to German universities, and to use the rhetorical and didactic art acquired through the study of the classics in their polemics with Catholics, Utraquists, and Lutherans.

One of Melanchthon's disciples was the most prominent writer of the Unity, Bishop John Blahoslav (1523-1571). He studied not only in Wittenberg, but also in Basel, and visited other important centers of learning. He represented the Unity in meetings with Catholics, Utraquists, and Lutherans, at home and abroad, defending, like Lucas of Prague, its independent position. Under his direction the victory of the intellectual party in the Unity over the conservative minority became definitive, and the cultural level of the Brethren reached a new peak.

Blahoslav was familiar with all branches of humanism, but he possessed above all excellent philological talent. This he manifested in his main works *On Music* and *Czech Grammar* and in his translation of the New Testament (1564). Contrary to the general opinion he did not translate this directly from the original. He was not as familiar with Greek as with Latin, but besides Latin translations, he also made use of the Greek original. His philological talent helped him to give the Czech literary language a new, lively, and elegant form, which became the basis for the new translation of the whole Bible by a committee of the Brethren. This was published in 1588 at Kralice, in Moravia. It was also made from the Latin with assistance from the original languages, and the language of the translation became classical for almost three hundred years.

Blahoslav also wrote a masterly book on *The Origins and Rules of the Unity of Brethren*. His *Cantionale* (1561), published for the use of the Brethren, contains 735 songs, composed or adapted by him, mostly in the spirit and style of the Psalms. In historiography the Brethren were particularly active, often using this literary genre for the defense of their creed against Catholics and Lutherans. John Černý initiated this genre and was followed by many others. Their works give quite a clear picture of the history of the Unity of Brethren.[9]

In general, Czech historiography of this period profited little from the new humanistic spirit. Only in the Latin history written by John Skála of Dubravia and in the Czech chronicle by Kuthen are timid attempts at the imitation of classical examples to be found. In his *Czech Chronicle* (1537), Bohuslav Bílejovský tried to show that Utraquism was an ancient Czech custom introduced by St. Methodius. The *Chronicle of Prague*, written by Bartoš Písař, shows more historical sense and gives a pretty clear picture of the first years of Ferdinand I's reign. This work is a valuable historical source, as are also the *Memorials* of Sixt of Ottersdorf, which describe the unsuccessful rising of the Czech nobility in 1546 against the same Habsburg ruler. Translations of early Christian chronicles and light literary compilations of little historical value proved more popular. This was especially the case with the chronicle of the Catholic writer Wenceslas Hájek of Libočany, which was full of fabulous stories presented in a pleasant and entertaining way.

Czech humanists were little attracted by the philosophical aspect of the Renaissance. Its moralizing content, however, appealed more to the similar tendency which they had inherited from the Czech reformers. This explains why the work of the English philosopher Walter Burley *De vita et moribus philosophorum et poetarum* aroused the interest of three Czech humanists. The last of these was Nicholas Konáč of Hodištkov (died 1546), a Utraquist nobleman and printer. He composed or translated several works of this kind, the best of his literary productions being an allegorical complaint of Virtue or Justice on the decadence of morals. The Utraquist priest John Češka (died 1551), an admirer of Petrarch, composed a treatise similar to that of Burley. Other anonymous compositions of this kind, still rooted in the medieval spirit, reflect satirically the *joie de vivre* which already characterized the Renaissance period. They are preserved in the *Collection of Neuburg*.

Czech belles lettres of this period produced little which could bear comparison with such products in the West. Humanistic influences are discernible in this type of Czech literature, with its imitations of Boccaccio and other famous writers of the Italian Renaissance. Most of the translations and adaptations, however, were made not from Italian originals, but from German translations.

More interest and originality attaches to some descriptions written in this period of journeys in foreign countries. They improve on the similar compositions by King George's ambassadors described above. John Hasistein of Lobkovice (1450-1517), brother of the famous humanist Bohuslav, described vividly his pilgrimage to the Holy Land via Venice, Rhodes, and Cyprus. In Odalrich Prefát's description of a similar voyage made in 1546, interesting observations on Cyprus shortly before it fell to the Turks are to be found. Christopher Harant of Polžice included in his report on a similar pilgrimage much of his humanistic learning. The description of the embassy to Constantinople in 1591 and the imprisonment of its members in Turkey, written by a junior member of the embassy, Wenceslas Vratislav of Mitrovice, also proved very popular.

The main representatives of the scientific world in Prague—Kepler, Tycho Brahe, and Tadaeus Hájek—wrote their mathematical and astronomical works in Latin. Hájek and other scientists used Czech only in writings for popular use—astronomical calendars and herbariums.

In the last decades of the sixteenth century Czech literature found an enthusiastic promoter and organizer in Daniel Adam of Veleslavín (1546-1599), a former professor at Prague University and a famous publisher. His publishing house issued a great number of chronicles, religious and geographical books, and translations of all sorts, such as appealed to the taste of the sixteenth century public. In his choice of publications he had several collaborators. He showed some talent in his historical compilations, but his main contribution to Czech literature and linguistics lay in his lexicographical works. Veleslavín's Czech was regarded as classical, and he himself was praised by literary historians as a writer of genius. More recent researches, however, are more critical concerning Veleslavín's merits for Czech literary history. His Latin-influenced Czech syntax and style does not attain the purity of language used by the translators of the Bible of Kralice. The multiplicity and variety of literary productions published by Veleslavín's care or by himself is so impressive that, so far, literary historians have characterized the second half of the sixteenth century as the golden age of Czech literature. This judgment seems, however, exaggerated. The multiplicity and variety of literary works cannot supplant the lack of originality and of art which characterizes most of these literary products.

Some influences of Renaissance architecture were already visible in the Vladislav Hall in Prague's royal castle at the end of the fifteenth century, but they dominate Czech art only in the sixteenth century. Gothic features, however, continued to be preferred by Czech builders, especially in church architecture. Monuments in pure Renaissance style were built in Bohemia by foreign architects. John Spatius and Paolo della Stella built the Belvedere in the royal castle, others the summer residence called *Hvězda* (Aster) and some buildings in the royal castle.

The Bohemian nobility imitated the example of the Habsburg kings and invited foreign architects to erect palaces for them in Prague and in the country. The best of those in Prague is the palace now known as that of the Schwarzenbergs. The country was soon full of Renaissance palaces and other buildings, the most characteristic of them being the constructions in southeastern and southern Bohemia on the property of the mighty nobles of Rosenberg. There the leading artist was Baltazar Majo da Vomio, who was aided by others of his compatriots. The burghers of many Bohemian cities also employed Italian artists for constructions in the new style. Plzeň, Pardubice, Prachatice, Litoměřice are particularly rich in Renaissance monuments.

A similar activity also started in Moravia thanks to the generosity of the higher nobility, especially the nobles of Boskovice, Žerotín, and Pernštýn. There too, burghers followed the examples of the nobility. The plastic decoration of the new buildings was also generally the work of Italian artists. The last echoes of late Gothic art were soon silenced by purely Renaissance motifs. In certain places, however, where the German element predominated, German and especially Saxon influence showed itself side by side with the Italian. Italian artists also introduced into Bohemia and Moravia the painting of frescoes and stucco work. This technique became very popular, and all new buildings were decorated at least with simple sgraffito. Renaissance painting found its best centers in Prague and Kutná Hora. The incentives came mostly from Germany, and the influence of Cranach and Dürer was very profound.

The lands inhabited by the Slovaks came into touch with the Renaissance earlier than the Czech lands. The marriage of King Matthias Corvinus with a princess of Aragon brought numerous Italian artists to Hungary in the second half of the fifteenth century. Many of these worked in the north of the country, although Gothic elements still survived there in all artistic activity. Besides Italian influences, German Renaissance motifs from Austria also penetrated Slovakia. The Turkish advance into the interior of Hungary, however, stopped this promising development. But in the numerous works of fortification against the Turkish danger, in cities, castles, and churches, the new technical advances of the Renaissance were employed. This is, of course, a characteristic feature of the cities of Slovakia, which was almost the only part of Hungary not occupied by the Turks. It should be noticed that the parts of modern Slovakia most profoundly penetrated by the Reformation, especially the region of Spiš and eastern Slovakia, remained faithful to the Renaissance style longer than the western part of the country, where the Counter Reformation and its new baroque style soon became victorious.

II

The influence of the Renaissance was particularly remarkable in Poland.[10] Unlike Bohemia, that country had not been tormented in the fourteenth and fifteenth centuries by religious struggles. The predominance of the Roman Catholic clergy caused the whole intellectual and political life of Poland in the early period of its history to become almost completely latinized. It was therefore natural that the first Polish humanists should be members of the clergy, who wrote exclusively in Latin. This also explains why early Polish humanism was not as secular and "pagan" as Italian humanism.

Although cultural influences in Poland in the early stages of Polish history came mainly from the West—France, Belgium, and Italy—German examples found more imitation in the twelfth and thirteenth centuries. The struggle with the Teutonic Order, supported by Germany, however, induced the Poles to turn again toward the West, especially Italy, for cultural inspiration.

The first humanistic impulses generally penetrated Poland through Bohemia and Hungary. The University of Cracow, reconstituted in 1400, eagerly accepted these incentives and gave a fresh impetus to the progress of learning in Poland. This foundation brought the Poles enhanced prominence and prestige in contemporary Europe. This fact manifested itself especially at the Council of Constance (1414-1418). The head of the Polish delegation, Nicholas Trąba, archbishop of Gniezno, was one of the candidates for the papacy, while Andrew Laskarz, bishop-elect of Poznań, a learned and zealous promotor of the idea of conciliar supremacy over the Pope and of Church reform, played a prominent role in the discussions. The rector of Cracow University, Paulus Vladimir of Brudzeń, wrote a treatise on the authority of the Pope and the emperor with regard to the conversion of the infidels, which attracted the attention of the fathers because of the boldness of his ideas. At the Council of Basel, Dean Nicholas Lasocki came into contact with Italian humanists, among whom was Guarino Guarini, and became its most energetic propagator among Polish youth.

The influence of humanistic ideas from Bohemia and Hungary and the incentives which contact with contemporary humanists gave to the Polish representatives at Constance and Basel produced remarkable results. The eminent Polish statesman, Cardinal Zbigniew Oleśnicki, and Gregory of Sanok, archbishop of Lwów, were the first Polish humanists. Humanistic studies, especially Livy's historical works, inspired Oleśnicki's protégé, Canon John Długosz (1415-1480), who became archbishop of Lwów, to write a history of Poland (*Annales seu cronica inclyti regni Poloniae*) which is the best Polish work of its kind. It is an achievement which supersedes all writings of this kind in contemporary Europe. Długosz' work was imitated and continued by others, and it dominated Polish historiography down to the eighteenth century.

The University of Cracow contributed considerably during the fifteenth and early sixteenth centuries to the spread of learning in Poland. It was outstanding in mathematics, astronomy, and philosophy before it degenerated. Nicholas Copernicus (died 1543), who made Poland famous by the publication of his epoch-making astronomical works, was educated at the University of Cracow.

The first literary centers of the pre-Renaissance period were formed in Poland by foreign humanists, the Italian Philip Callimachus Buonacorsi (died 1496) and the German Conrad Celtes (died in 1509). Gregory of Sanok took the political refugee Callimachus under his protection. Callimachus, who had first stayed in Hungary—he wrote a Latin history of Hungary and of the Turkish wars, was appointed by King Casimir to be tutor to his sons. Celtes founded the first literary society, called Societas Vistulana, in Cracow. He was generally supported by the German burghers of Cracow, but met with less sympathy among the Poles than did his Italian colleague. Other humanists came from Switzerland, and of these the most prominent was the younger Rudolph Agricola. Through the Swiss humanists the Poles also first came into contact with Erasmus of Rotterdam, with whom they later came into correspondence.

The worldly spirit of the Renaissance becomes apparent, at this early stage of Polish humanism, in the work of John Ostroróg on the organization of the state. In his *Monumentum* Ostroróg manifested strong national and anticlerical tendencies, defending the rights of the nobility in the organization of the state. He set down some original ideas about the state and was the precursor of political and social conceptions which did not become generally current until much later.

Casimir's sons, John Albrecht, Alexander I, and Sigismund I, who succeeded each other on the throne and were educated by Długosz and Callimachus, were all zealous promoters of the Renaissance. The reign of Sigismund I (1506-1548) is particularly important for the promotion of humanistic civilization in Poland. He himself was a typical Renaissance prince, entertaining foreign and native humanists at his brilliant court. The influence of the Italian Renaissance in Poland reached its peak after 1518 when the king married the Italian princess Bona Sforza. She brought her own entourage to Poland, including artists and ladies in waiting, many of whom later married Polish nobles. Her court became the center of Polish humanistic society, seeking inspiration in the newly discovered works of classical writers and of prominent figures of the Italian Renaissance. Bona also introduced into Polish politicial life the principles of Renaissance statesmanship, aiming at the strengthening of the royal power and at the limitation of the influence of the nobility in state affairs. *The Advices of Callimachus,* a theoretical discussion of political problems, attributed to Buonacorsi and reflecting some ideas propagated by Machiavelli, clearly illustrates this struggle between the Renaissance statesmanship aiming at absolutism, propagated by Bona, and the egoistic policy of the Polish nobility, which bitterly opposed the political ideas of the Renaissance although they willingly accepted its other inspirations.

Sigismund I was also a generous patron of the new trends in the fine arts, and his example was followed by Polish magnates. His chancellor Christopher Szydlowiecki gathered many humanistic writers and scholars at his residence. Even more outstanding in Polish humanism was the Vice-Chancellor Peter Tomicki, bishop of Cracow. He not only introduced Renaissance culture into the university, where he promoted the teaching of Roman law, but he also greatly encouraged linguistic studies. Stanislas Gorski, who published Tomicki's important diplomatic and private correspondence, which is one of the main sources for the study of the Polish Renaissance, was another prominent humanist. Archbishop Andrew Krzycki was celebrated as a Latin poet, and the Bishop of Poznań, John Lubrański, founded in that city a humanistic college which propagated the new movement in Great Poland. The noble family of Łaski also contributed greatly to the spread of the new trend. One of its members, John, was in close contact with Erasmus and other humanists in Basel, the center of the Swiss Renaissance. He later became the leader of the Polish Protestants. Two other Latin poets should be mentioned, the diplomat John Dantiscus, from Danzig, and the particularly talented Clement Janicius, a peasant's son, whom his noble patron had sent to Italy.

These men, aided by other less prominent humanists, prepared the way for the great efflorescence in learning, art, and literature in Poland during its "golden age," from the middle of the sixteenth century to the beginning of the seventeenth, during the reigns of Sigismund II August (1548-1572) and Stephen Bathory (1576-1586). Most of the prominent writers of this period still wrote in Latin. A prominent place in Polish political literature was held by Frycz Modrzewski (1503-1572), one of the greatest Polish thinkers of this period. In two treatises he advocated the equality of all Poles before the law, protesting against discrimination between nobles, burghers, and peasants. His greatest work, *De republica emendanda*, deals with the problems of government and statesmanship. In five books he treated of public morals, laws, war, the Church, and education. He advocated a strong central government, sound finances, and a well-organized army, protesting against the selfish policy of the nobles and the exploitation of the peasants. His ideas on Church doctrine reflect his sympathies for the Reformation. He asked for a reform of the religious life and of the clergy, for the abolition of celibacy, for the introduction of the vernacular into the liturgy, and for the distribution of Church property. He was attacked on account of such ideas by the leaders of the Catholics, but he continued to work for Church reform, recommending tolerance in religious affairs.[11] Laurence Goślicki also made an interesting contribution to political literature in the spirit of the Renaissance period. Stanislas Iłowski wrote the first Polish treatise on historical theories. Bishop Martin Kromer, the last of Długosz's disciples, analyzed Poland's customs and constitution.

During the reign of Stephen Bathory, the most prominent protagonist of humanism was his chancellor John Zamoyski (died in 1605). He was so great an admirer of the Roman republic and its institutions that he wished to transform Poland into a kind of republic, with an elected king, based upon absolute liberty and equality. Unfortunately, in accordance with the spirit of the age, he restricted liberty and equality to the gentry alone.

It is interesting to note how many Polish intellectuals of the sixteenth century were interested in political theory. In reviving some Roman republican ideas and combining them with humanistic individualism, Polish statesmen created a constitution without a parallel in Europe's history.

Zamoyski also cherished the idea of making Cracow a kind of international center of humanistic studies. A new college to replace in some way the university, at that time stagnant and decaying in its scholasticism, was planned for Cracow. But the foreign scholars who were invited to settle in Cracow failed to arrive. Therefore, in 1594, Zamoyski founded a new university in his own town of Zamość, where humanistic studies were assiduously cultivated. In doing this, he was following the example of

King Stephen Bathory, who founded a university at Vilna in 1579, of which the Jesuit Peter Skarga was made the head.

The penetration of Poland by humanistic studies and ideas opened the way for Polish national literature. Up to this time original compositions in Polish were few.[12] This dearth forced many Poles to read Czech literature so that Polish libraries still possess numerous Czech manuscripts, and as late as 1519, the Czech version of the *Chronicle of Troy* was copied in Poland. All this indicates that the Polish literary language evolved rather laboriously, with the help of many Czech words, as is evidenced by the frequency of Bohemianisms in Polish. Many original compositions in Polish are lost, but their number increased during the fifteenth century. Religious songs were more numerous and were collected in the first Polish *cantionale,* which, however, survives only fragmentarily. The most famous composer of Church songs was Władysław of Gielniow. His best composition is a song on Christ's Passion. He is regarded as the author of a collection of songs called *Christ's Psalter,* but it is possible that this collection is only an adaptation of a similar Czech work.

The best Polish song of the fifteenth century is a hymn on the Holy Ghost. From this period there are preserved also some "Polish legends in verse," especially the legend of St. Alexius.

Only a few secular poems have survived, although their number must have been much larger. Most of them, love songs and others, were probably composed by the students of Cracow University. A song about the murder of a gentleman in Cracow in 1461 and one on the battle at Grunwald were particularly popular.

There were also some didactic poems; the longest appears to be on the manners to be observed at meals, composed by a certain Słota, probably a student of Cracow. The destruction of the city of Sandomierz by the Tatars was also described in verse. The most successful moralizing song is the "Disputation of Master Polycarpus with Death." "The Complaint of a Dying Man" is an adaptation of a Czech song. A "Satire on Peasants" is full of humor. There was more originality in the *Memoirs of a Janissary,* written by Constantine, a native of Bosnia. It is, however, not sure if the text of this interesting literary monument was written originally in Old Slavonic or in Polish. A Polish version was already known at the beginning of the sixteenth century. It was very popular and often copied. It was also translated into Czech and, because of its contents, remains a curiosity in contemporary European literature.

The beginnings of Polish literary activity are thus rather modest when compared with Czech achievements. In contrast to Bohemia, the example of some Renaissance writers and of the Reformation, with its demand for

religious propaganda in the vernacular, promoted considerably the spread
of native Polish literature. In a short time it achieved such an astonish-
ingly high standard that the golden age of Polish literary production coincides with that of Polish humanistic culture.

The first poet of importance who initiated the Polish golden age was a
follower of the Reformation, Nicholas Rey (1505-1569).[13] He did not get
his education abroad, a fact which illustrates how deeply the ideas of the
Italian Renaissance had penetrated Polish society in the sixteenth century. He was the first to show that literature can be cultivated successfully
in the vernacular, and contributed most to the victory of the vernacular
over Latin in Polish literature. He wrote in the lively and picturesque
tongue spoken by the contemporary Polish nobility, and although lacking
in broader education, he was able, thanks to his talents, to express his
ideas with ease, with a good sense of rhythm and rhyme and in a truly
realistic way. He started his career as a poet with a satire which is regarded as the best Polish satire of the whole sixteenth century. In the
imaginary discourse between a noble, a priest, and a peasant, Rey gives
a very lively picture of contemporary Polish society with all its vices. He
blamed principally the gentry and the clergy, reproaching them with the
exploitation of the peasants. In his presentation he showed a remarkable
talent, although the frame of the picture lacks a true artistic touch.

Rey gave vent to his religious feeling and sympathy with the Reformation in his paraphrases of the Psalms, in the composition of religious songs,
and in his *Postylla,* which gives a general explanation of the Gospels with
a pronounced moral tendency.

He tried his talent also in dramatic composition. His *Life of Joseph* is a
Polish adaptation of a work written in Latin by the Dutch Cornelius
Crocus. Another composition of this kind was inspired by the *Mercator*
of a German Lutheran pamphleteer, Thomas Naogeorgus. It expresses
again Rey's antipapal convictions.

Rey's long didactic poem *Wizerunek* ("The Portrait") has a broader
basis. In it the poet describes the life of a young man who wanders
through the world visiting all classical philosophers in search of truth. Rey
was here inspired by the Italian humanist Palingenius and his *Zodiacus
vitae,* but included in his narrative many original sketches, anecdotes, and
satires which often give an insight into the life of the Polish gentry of his
time.

Rey's *Zwierzyniec* ("Bestiary") is a collection of epigrams giving anec-
dotic stories from the life of personalities of the Greek and Latin classical
age, but also of contemporary personalities and of himself. Rey appears
here again as a sharp observer of his time and as an uncompromising
critic of the less attractive aspects of Polish society.

The greatest and best of Rey's works, written in prose, is his *Zwierciadło* ("The Mirror"), in which the author gathered the treasures of his lifetime's experience and philosophy. In the main part of this collection Rey describes how a nobleman should live. His description again gives an interesting picture of contemporary life in Poland. This work was very popular because of its lively style, healthy humor, and sharp satiric criticism.

Rey's works are important for anybody anxious to study the life of Polish society in the sixteenth century and the ideas current at that time. It was Rey who created a Polish prose style characterized by its raciness and liveliness. He also laid a solid basis for the further development of Polish poetry.

When creating the Polish literary language, Rey had also sometimes to use a Czech expression, so that his work shows many Bohemianisms. This seems to have been a general habit at this time. His contemporary Lucas Górnicki, for example, confessed quite openly in his *Polish Gentleman* that when it is impossible to find an adequate Polish expression, a Pole employs a Czech word; but he condemns this practice. John Malecki also emphasizes in 1547 in the course of his *Apology* that it is impossible to make a good Polish translation of the Gospel without the help of a Czech translation.

On the foundations laid by Rey, John Kochanowski (1530-1584) created some masterpieces of Polish poetry which are still read and admired by the Poles and which have been matched only by Mickiewicz. Unlike Rey, Kochanowski obtained a thorough education outside Poland, in Italy, and he also visited France. An admirer of the Latin lyrics of Propertius, Tibullus, Catullus, and Horace, Kochanowski started to compose elegant erotic elegies in Padua. His Latin poems showed his extraordinary talent and superseded all that his Polish colleagues had so far achieved. During his stay in Paris Kochanowski met the celebrated French poet Pierre de Ronsard. Perhaps the famous defense of the French tongue by Joachim du Bellay impressed Kochanowski, and he decided to write in Polish. His first hymn composed in Polish in Paris, "What do you want from us, O Lord, for all your generous gifts," made Kochanowski's name renowned in his country. It is one of his best poems. On his return to Poland, Kochanowski spent some time at the courts of certain magnates and of King Sigismund August, but renouncing public life, he settled on his small estate in Czernolas, where he composed his Polish and Latin poetic works.

In his "Songs," composed at different stages of his life, Kochanowski has shown how much he was influenced by Horace and how well he had mastered his prototype's technique. Besides love songs, the collection contains patriotic, religious, and other poems, all with a rich rhythm and a sonorous melody of verse.

Like Rey, Kochanowski composed a verse paraphrase of the Psalms which became very popular. His profound religious sentiment is also echoed in his *Treny* ("Threnodies"), in which he laments the death of his little daughter Ursula. They are regarded by Polish literary historians as the greatest Polish poetic creation before Mickiewicz.

His *Szachy* ("Chess") is an original adaptation of a composition by the Italian poet Marco Vido. Two political satiric poems, *Satyr* and *Zgoda*, deplore the vices of Polish society and invite the quarreling religious and political factions to peaceful collaboration. An epic poem of some interest is Kochanowski's description of the homage which Duke Albert of Prussia paid in 1525 to King Sigismund August. Kochanowski's only dramatic composition, *The Dismissal of Greek Envoys*, was inspired by Homer's *Iliad* and seems also to have a patriotic background. It was intended to present to Polish youth, on the eve of war with Russia, the example of Greek courage and fighting spirit.

Kochanowski's *Fraszki* ("Trifles") is a collection of short anecdotes, epigrams, and humorous poems which illustrate the poet's life in its different phases. They were very popular among his contemporaries.

Kochanowski is one of the most outstanding authors in the history of Polish literature. He created modern Polish poetry and perfected the Polish poetic language. He brought Polish poetry into intimate relationship with Western Renaissance poetry, although retaining its national character. His masterpieces are not only treasures of Polish culture, but are also among the best products of the European Renaissance.

Kochanowski's contemporary was the gifted lyric poet Nicholas Szarzyński. His best productions are his sonnets and his reflections on the Psalms. These give expression to his profound religious sentiment. Less talented was Sebastian Klonowicz (died 1602). His best poetic composition in Latin, *Roxolania*, is interesting for the study of South Russian (Ukrainian) folklore of the period. He was a burgher and gave vent to his antiaristocratic sentiments in his *Victoria deorum*. One of his best Polish compositions (*Flis*) describes a voyage on the Vistula from Warsaw to Gdańsk (Danzig). In his *Judas' Money Bag* he gives a picturesque description of the life of Polish society with all its vices. In all his poems Klonowicz defended the lower strata of Polish society, protesting courageously against the abuses of the mighty.

Encouraged by the example of Rey and Kochanowski, other writers tried to enrich Polish literature in their spirit. The first historical work in Polish was written by Martin Bielski, whose work was continued by his son Joachim. Bielski also composed some satirico-didactic dialogues echoing his patriotic and moral sentiments. Bartoš Paprocki, known also in Czech literature because of his work on the heraldry of the Czech nobility, is also the author of some Polish satiric compositions. Another contemporary, Matthew Stryjkowski, wrote a chronicle with some passages in verse in which he described events drawn from Polish and Lithuanian history.

One of the masters of Polish prose was the Jesuit Peter Skarga (1536-1612). He was one of the leading figures of the Catholic Counter-Reformation in Poland. Besides numerous polemic and dogmatic pamphlets, Skarga wrote a work on the union of the Orthodox with Rome. His *Lives of Saints* were most widely read and still circulate in Poland in a new edition. His *Sermons Delivered before the Diets* is his most important work, not only because of the perfect oratory and pure language but also because of its content. They were not pronounced at the Diets, but were addressed to the Polish nobles whose egoistic policy was bringing the state to the verge of ruin. He foresees in a prophetic vein the end of Polish independence if the State continues to be administered in the same chaotic and disastrous way. Unfortunately, his warnings were only a voice calling in the wilderness, and his prophecy was disastrously fulfilled.

The new artistic forms of the Renaissance also made a profound impression on the Poles. The German Veit Stoss, who was the most famous sculptor in Poland in the fifteenth century, left the country in 1496. His last two works of art in Poland are the sarcophagus of Casimir Jagiello and that of his friend Callimachus in Cracow. In the latter some Renaissance motifs are already noticeable. Stoss's greatest work of art in Poland is, of course, the famous altar of Our Lady in Cracow. Also, as early as the end of the fifteenth century some Italian models appeared in manuscript illuminations made in Cracow. The flourishing period of Renaissance art starts at the very beginning of the sixteenth century, thanks to the initiative of Sigismund I, and was introduced by Italian artists. The first to work in Poland were the Florentines Franciscus Italus and Luca Berecci. The main work of Franciscus was the reconstruction of the royal palace on Wawel Hill in Cracow. There the first attempts are also apparent at blending it with the late Gothic style, in which Poland's artists were well trained, a blending which became a characteristic feature of the Polish Renaissance. The palace and the Chapel of Sigismund on the Wawel, the work of Berecci, are real gems of Italian art in Poland. A period of feverish building of churches, city halls, and country mansions started in both Gothic and Renaissance styles. An interesting example of Polish traditionalism is the church of St. Anne in Wilno (Vilna), constructed in flamboyant Gothic in brick and showing the influence of northeast German Gothic.

New models coming from Flanders, Bohemia, Germany, and Italy were grafted on to the late Gothic motifs. This blending also triumphed in the art of illumination. The best examples of this kind are the *Liber pontificalis* of Erasmus Ciołek, bishop of Płock, and the prayer book of King Sigismund and Queen Bona Sforza. The first is now in the British Museum, the second in the Bodleian Library. The artists are often anonymous, but the master of illumination and decoration at this period was a Pole, the monk Stanislas of Mogiła. Many German and Italian artists worked on the decoration of the royal palace, among them a brother of the famous Albrecht Dürer.

Among the most gifted Polish disciples of the first great Italian master were Gabriel Słoński (1520-1598), who worked mostly in the region of Cracow, John Michałowicz (1530-1578), a talented builder and sculptor, and John Biały (died 1592), his disciple, who added oriental motifs to Italian and Flemish elements.

The Italian Padovano (died 1574) was a master in monumental sculpture. The great ciborium in the Church of Our Lady in Cracow and Tarnowski's monument in Tarnów are his works. The original parapet, which he added to the walls of the Cloth Hall in Cracow, was imitated not only in other Polish cities, but also outside Poland.

Besides Italians, German, French, and Flemish artists also worked for the Polish court, magnates and cities. All important Polish cities—Cracow, Poznań, Płock, Wilno, Lwów, and later also Lublin and Warsaw—boasted monuments of Renaissance art. The most typical was the town of Zamość, founded in 1580 by the Chancellor John Zamoyski. Although built by the Italian architect Bernardo Morano, aided by native craftsmen, it presents a curious blending of Gothic, Polish, and Renaissance elements. Renaissance art remained the lodestar of Polish artists for the whole of the seventeenth century, in spite of the arrival of the baroque style of the Catholic Counter-Reformation.

When Polish achievements during the Renaissance period are compared with those of the Czechs, it must be confessed that although perhaps Czech literary activity during this period was more voluminous than Polish, Polish literary production surpassed Czech in its quality and value. Unfortunately, for the most part, literary and artistic activity in Poland and its use and appreciation were the privilege of one class, the nobles. The burghers could participate in this activity in a very limited manner owing to the hostility of the nobles to the cities and to their potential role in the state. The lower classes were hardly touched by the new cultural wave.

It is not surprising that the high standard achieved by Polish culture during the period of the Renaissance should also have influenced the non-Polish population of the Polish-Lithuanian commonwealth. The Lithuanian upper classes accepted eagerly the cultural incentives transmitted from Italy by the Polish Renaissance. They even came to regard the Lithuanian nation as racially akin to the Italian on the grounds of the slight similarity of the names.

In South Russia—modern Ukraine—the nobles were won over in large numbers to the new trend in civilization, and attracted by the Polish cultural level and by the privileges enjoyed by the Polish nobility, many of them became polonized and abandoned Orthodoxy in favor of Catholicism. The conclusion of the Union of Brest first appeared to be another step toward the assimilation, or at least the westernization, of the Russian population.

At the same time, the linguistic differences between the Polish-Lithuanian and the Eastern Russians became increasingly pronounced. Some differences were already apparent at the end of the Kievan period, and they developed considerably in the following centuries when the two groups were politically separated. Under these circumstances there gradually developed, on the basis of popular idioms, the West Russian (Belo-Russian) and South Russian (Ukrainian) languages, into which Polish words penetrated. Belo-Russian and Ukrainian idioms could already be traced in the fourteenth century in local juridical and other acts.

In West Russia the most important documents of this kind are the *Sudebnik* of the Grand Prince Casimir in 1468, the Lithuanian Statute accepted by the Diet in 1530, a parish register called the *Metryka Litewska*, and the Statute of 1566. Local chronicles continued to be produced in Church Slavonic, but were colored with expressions taken from the local dialect. The chronicles are, however, less interesting than similar works written in East Russia and are preserved in a fragmentary way in collections of chronicles of East Russia. The level of civilization in West Russia was higher than in East Russia thanks to the cultural influences emanating from Poland. Smolensk was an important center of learning while it was under Lithuanian rule. It could boast the first Russian school for higher education.

In copies of liturgical books made in West and South Russia, Church Slavonic still dominated, but Western cultural influences even penetrated the religious sphere. This became manifest in the fact that the first religious books in Church Slavonic were printed by the German printer Phiol in Cracow. He was followed by the Belo-Russian Skorina, who had conceived the plan of printing the first Bible in Russian. He started to realize his plan in Prague, basing himself on the texts of the Bible in Church Slavonic and of the Czech Bible of 1506, replacing many words by expressions from the vernacular Belo-Russian. He continued his work in Vilna.[14] Some translations from the Greek Fathers were also made in the Belo-Russian dialect, and some of theological and polemical works.

The editions of liturgical works were accompanied by commentaries and introductions, also in the vernacular.

The intellectuals of West Russia, of course, continued to read and to copy literary works from the Kievan period,[15] which were a common heritage of all Russian linguistic and political groups. The South Russians, soon to be called Ukrainians, regarded this Kievan literature as their own product.[16] Next to the *Tale of Igor'*, the *Chronicle of Galicia and Volhynia*, dealing with events from 1200 to 1292, was the most prominent literary product originated in South Russia before the Tatar occupation. Intellectual life was stifled but not extinguished by this catastrophe. A new language was slowly being evolved under the influence of Polish, and at the end of the fifteenth or beginning of the sixteenth century, a translation of the Song of Solomon appeared in the new language. It was made with the help of a Czech translation. Between 1556 and 1561 the Gospels were translated into Ukrainian by Abbot Gregory.

The art of printing began to spread in Ukraine during the second half of the sixteenth century. Ostrog, the residence of the rich and powerful boyar Constantine (died 1608), became an important cultural center. He founded there the first Orthodox academy and also a printing press. Among the many works which were printed there was the Bible of Ostrog, the first complete Bible printed in Church Slavonic.

Constantine was the most prominent defender of Orthodoxy in the Ukraine and Belo-Russia. He opposed the effort for union with the Catholics which culminated at the Synod of Brest. He was aided in his efforts by Prince Andrew Michael Kurbskij (died 1583), who had fled from Muscovy.[17] During his stay in Lithuania, Kurbskij translated numerous works of the Greek Fathers, especially those of John Chrysostom, John of Damascus, Gregory the Theologian, and Basil the Great, in order to strengthen the Russian peoples in Poland-Luithuania in their struggle for Orthodoxy.

The hopes that the Union of Brest (Breść, 1596) would westernize the Russians in Poland-Lithuania and minimize the differences between Catholic and Orthodox Christians did not materialize, despite the fact that a great number of nobles joined the Latin or Uniate Church.[18] The spread of Polish civilization in the Ukraine and Belo-Russia raised considerably the cultural level of the Russian burghers, and this class took the leadership in the defense of Orthodoxy and of the national life. The old religious confraternities which had existed in the Orthodox parishes were transformed into mighty organizations on the pattern of the guilds and started to found schools and printing presses in order to make the nation more resistant to Polish cultural influences. This activity spread over the whole Ukraine and Belo-Russia, and the cultural level of the Russian population reached unexpected heights. The schools vied with similar Polish institutions, giving their students opportunities to acquire a solid grounding in philosophy, history, and literature, besides Orthodox theology. The most important were the schools of Ostrog, Lwów, and Kiev.

The defense of Orthodoxy against Catholic propaganda provoked the rise of a wealth of polemic literature in Ukrainian. Besides Gerazim Smotryckyj, Stephen Zizanija, Christophor Philarete, and others, the most productive polemist was Ivan Višenśkyj from Mount Athos. In his works he condemned the decay of morals wrought by the spread of Renaissance culture and displayed ardent patriotic sentiments. In imitation of Polish usages, many Ukrainian writers started to compose satiric, epic, and lyric poems, of which only a small part is preserved in print. The example of the Jesuit cultivation of dramatic composition in these schools led to similar productions in Ukrainian schools. This provided the basis for later progress in this literary genre. The most famous of Ukrainian playwriters was Mitrofan Dovhalevśki, professor of poetics at the Academy of Lwów. This academy became a center of Ukrainian and Orthodox culture at the beginning of the seventeenth century under the guidance of the Metropolitan Mohyla, and was also destined to have a great influence over cultural development in Muscovy.[19]

III

Smolensk and Kiev were the most advanced Russian outposts in which some echoes of the Western Renaissance, coming through Poland, had sounded. Eastern Russia, soon to be included in Muscovy, was completely closed to any such influences, and cultural and national life developed there along the lines traced during the Kievan period, in the atmosphere of Byzantine civilization.

The literary products of East Russia from the thirteenth to the seventeenth century naturally reflect the political and cultural development of the nation during this period. The nation lived its own life, in conditions which differed considerably from those in which western Europe was developing, and, therefore, its literary production had little in common with that of the West. Three phases can be distinguished in East Russian literature down to the seventeenth century. That of the thirteenth and fourteenth centuries echoes the oppression suffered by the nation under the Tatar yoke. The fifteenth century is characterized by the rise of Moscow to leadership. This is reflected in Muscovite literary works, but in many provincial works the spirit of opposition provoked by this in other principalities can be detected. Sixteenth century literature is already Muscovite. The writers had to accept existing facts, and provincial literature of the previous period had to be adapted in order to reflect the new politcial situation.

The national disaster prompted Serapion, bishop of Vladimir (1273-1275), to meditate on the reasons which caused the calamity, and in his five sermons, he interpreted it as God's punishment for the sins of the nation. Of course, the catastrophe was also described in the chronicles, the most telling being the account in the Laurentian Chronicle of the Tatars' ravages in northern Russia. The most interesting poetic lament on the downfall is the *Slovo* (*Discourse on the Ruin of the Land of Rus'*), which, though only preserved fragmentarily, has a high poetic value.

The desire to be freed from the Tatar yoke probably prompted the Russians to adapt the legend which came to northern Russia in the thirteenth century in a Serbian translation of a Latin original. This described the existence in India of a legendary Christian kingdom able to give powerful help to other Christians in their struggle with the infidels. The mental depression under which the Russians then suffered seems to explain why the *Legend of the Twelve Dreams of the Emperor Mamer*, with its apocalyptic tendency, became popular. The legend is of Eastern origin like some other legends, among which that of Stephanit and Ichnilat was the most popular. A true picture of the social tension in East Russia on the eve of the Tatar invasion is given in the *Supplication of Daniel the Exile*, where a serf describes the position of the unfree and dependent.

The Life of Alexander Nevskij reflects the more hopeful sentiments provoked by the hero's victories over the Swedes and the Teutonic Knights. It was probably written in Suzdal'. The *Life of Abraham of Smolensk*, written by his disciple Ephrem, testifies to the high cultural level of this city, which boasted a school where, it was said, not only Slavonic but also Greek and Latin were taught. The *Legend of Ševkol* described the burning alive in Tver' of the cruel Tatar deputy, Ševkol. The shrines of Constantinople were described in two works originating in Novgorod. Moscow produced only the *Life of Peter*, on the first metropolitan of Moscow, in which a strong pro-Muscovite tendency is discernible. Rostov-Suzdal' added to the *Life of Leontius*, on a bishop of that city —written earlier—the *Life of Isaiah and Abraham* (of Rostov), a *Rostov Chronicle*, and an adaptation of the *Life of Peter*, on a converted Tatar prince. The separatist anti-Muscovite tendency is strongly expressed in Rostov's literary production.

These separatist tendencies can also be observed in the provincial literature of the fifteenth century. On the other hand, the ascendancy of Moscow is reflected and promoted by compositions originated in Muscovy or by writers favoring the formation of an autocratic power. Another characteristic of this period is the growth of Serbian and Bulgarian influence on literary production in East Russia in defense of Orthodoxy against heretical movements. This kind of literary production was also heavily influenced by the rivalry which existed between the trans-Volgan monasticism, preaching monastic poverty and religious reform, and the Josephites,[20] who defended the right to worldly possessions and recommended intimate collaboration with the secular authorities.

The most stubborn opponent of Moscow's primacy in East Russia was Tver'. The sentiments of independence and of rivalry with Moscow are especially mirrored in the *Chronicles of Tver'*.[21] The monk Thomas, a contributor to the Tver' chronicle, wrote a *Eulogy* of the Grand Prince Boris Alexandrovič. In this he reported imaginary praises of the grand prince by all the prominent personalities present at the Council of Florence, to which Boris had sent a delegation. He also exalts his victory over the Muscovite army and the help given by Boris to Basil II of Moscow.

Interest attaches equally to the *Journey across Three Seas,* in which a merchant of Tver', Afanasij Nikitin, described his travels across Asia to India. The work shows clearly the high cultural and economic level of the principality during the last years of its independence.

Novgorod's desire to retain its independence is expressed in some legendary accounts connected with the name of Archbishop John (1163-1186) which exalt the glorious past of the republic. The end of its independence is bemoaned in legends about the end of Novgorod with postdated prophecies. The *Tale of the White Mitre,* which is said to have been given by Constantine the Great to Pope Silvester and then brought to Constantinople, whence it was sent to Novgorod to be worn by its archbishops, is a curious document. It illustrates the determination of the Novgorodians to retain at least some of their Byzantine inheritance in the ecclesiastical sphere after they had lost their political independence. The *Life of St. Anthony of Rome,* written in Novgorod in the sixteenth century, also reflects the glorious past of the city and its commercial relations with western Europe.

The annexation of Pskov by Basil III (1510) is described and lamented in the *Tale of the Taking of Pskov,* which shows how difficult it was for the citizens to give up their independence and to accept Moscow's overlordship.

In this respect it is interesting to note that the most fervent promoter of Muscovite supremacy over all Russia was a Pskovian, Filofej of the monastery of Eleazar at Pskov. This shows how hopeless were the dreams of independence nourished by the patriots of Tver', Novgorod, and Pskov.

The victory of 1380 over the Tatars had naturally enhanced the prestige of Moscow and of its grand prince, Dmitrij. It left a strong echo in the East Russian chronicles, especially in the fourth Novgorod, in the first St. Sophia, and in the Resurrection Chronicles. It was celebrated, probably by Sofonij, in a poem called *Zadonščina*.²² The author was greatly inspired by the *Tale of Igor'*; he conceived Igor''s defeat as the first stage of Russia's ruin and the battle of 1380 as the triumphal end of this lingering catastrophe. This work shows a stronger Christian sentiment than the *Tale of Igor'* with its scaldic double faith. This Orthodox religious conception is further reinforced in the *Skazanie*, the renowned Muscovite eulogy of Dmitrij's victory, written under the influence both of the *Tale of Igor'* and of the *Zadonščina*.

The tendency to promote Moscow's ascendancy is evident in these works and is even more pronounced in the life of the hero of the battle, Dmitrij. This spirit also penetrates a polemic directed against the Union of Florence, composed in 1461. This prepared the atmosphere in which Filofej was able to launch his teachings on Moscow the Third Rome.²³

The conquest of Constantinople was described by a certain Nestor-Iskander in the *Tale of the Taking of Tsargrad*. His prophecy that one day the conquered city would be liberated by the Christians also points to the rising Muscovite power as the hope of Orthodox Christians. The *Tales of the Babylonian Empire* were invented or adapted in order to establish the right of Russia to the Byzantine heritage. The insignia of imperial rank which were worn by the Byzantine emperors were there described as having been brought from Babylon, and it was claimed that a Russian had participated in their discovery. This legend prepared the ground for other legendary inventions on the Byzantine origin of the insignia used by Muscovite rulers.

The *Legend of Governor Dracula*, a ruler of Wallachia, depicts an autocratic and cruel ruler. Some definitions of autocracy in the legend express ideas similar to those to be found in Ivan IV's letters. The expansion of Muscovy toward the Caucasus is reflected in the *Tale of Queen Dinara of Georgia*.

Among the lives of saints composed in this period, the *Life of Stephen of Perm* is the most interesting. It reveals that at that time the Russian Church had started missionary activity among the pagans. Stephen (died 1396) converted the pagan Zyrjans, invented a special alphabet for them, and translated the Gospel into their language. The author of this life, Epiphanius, also wrote the *Life of Sergius of Radonež*.

There was frequent ecclesiastical contact with Constantinople, where some Russian monks had settled, and with Mount Athos during the fourteenth century. This made the Russians acquainted with new Greek literary works and with the lively literary activity in Bulgaria and Serbia. As a consequence many South Slavic translations and works penetrated into East Russia, and many Byzantine works were translated. This literary activity was quite remarkable.²⁴

The South Slavic literary influence in East Russia grew in importance during the fifteenth century when many Bulgarian and Serbian intellectuals took refuge there. Next to the Metropolitan Cyprian, a Bulgarian, the Serbian Pachomius Logothetes was the most prominent. He rewrote and adapted many lives of Muscovite and Novgorodian saints in the highly oratorical style used by Byzantine hagiographers. The South Slavic refugees, of course, favored the growth of Moscow, hoping that the Muscovite rulers would accept the Byzantine inheritance and liberate the enslaved Balkan peoples. On the basis of an all-Russian digest, called the *Vladimir Polychron*, Pachomius wrote in 1442 a chronograph in which he gave free vent to his sympathies for the unification of all Russia by Muscovy.

A heretical movement had already originated in Pskov and Novgorod by the fourteenth century. This was the Shearer heresy (Strigol'-ničestvo), founded by Karp, a cloth shearer, which repudiated ecclesiastical hierarchy and denied the necessity of prayers for the dead. It can be interpreted as a form of opposition to the wealthy churchmen. More dangerous was the heresy of the Judaizers, which originated in Novgorod in 1470. The heretics not only were opposed to the economic domination of the Church, but also denied, like the Jews, the divinity of Christ and other Orthodox teachings. In some way they can be compared with the Western Reformers. Their leaders were mostly educated men, and they had their own literature.

In opposing the heretics, Gennadius, archbishop of Novgorod, realized that a new edition of the Bible was necessary. In this important enterprise (1489-1499) he utilized not only the Old Slavonic translation from the Greek but also the Latin Bible, the German translation, and the Hebrew original. One of the members of the commission set up by him was also a Slavic Dominican, Benjamin.

The main opponent of the heresies was Joseph, abbot of Volokolamsk. His polemic writings against the heretics are collected in his work *Prosvetitel'* ("Enlightener"). He fought not only the heretics but also the followers of Nil of Sorsk (died 1508), who preached a reform of monasticism and defended the principle of monastic poverty. The polemic between the two religious factions also found a strong echo in Russian hagiography. The trans-Volgan hermits found their heroes in St. Dmitri Prilutskij and Dionysius Glušitskij; the Josephites, in St. Paphnutius of Borov, whose life was written by Joseph's brother Sanin.

Nil's followers found a prominent ally in the sixteenth century in the person of Maxim the Greek (1480-1556),[25] the highly learned monk of Mount Athos, who had been educated in Greece and also in Italy, where he became acquainted with Savonarola. He came to Russia in 1515 at the invitation of Basil III. His first work in Russia was the translation of a commentary to the Psalter. He continued this activity with the translation of a commentary to the Acts of the Apostles and with some translations and copies for the library of the grand prince. Realizing that the Slavonic translations of Greek liturgical books were full of serious mistakes and mistranslations, he corrected them.

Besides this philological activity, Maxim also evinced a very lively interest in Russian religious, social, and political life. He tried in vain to restore the Russian Church to the jurisdiction of the patriarchs of Constantinople, and he would have welcomed the involvement of Moscow in a conflict with Turkey leading to the liberation of the Balkan Christians. He was anxious to raise Russian religious and cultural life to a higher level, and in numerous *Discourses, Missives,* and *Platonic dialogues,* he fought against contemporary social evils, against ignorance and prejudice, and against external pomp in divine worship. Besides numerous sermons and meditations he gave an exposition of Christian doctrine in his *Lucidarius,* and in his *Discourse on the Basiliea* (kingship), which he represented as a desolate widow, Maxim criticized the abuses of the mighty.

Although he criticized some of the Latin doctrines, Maxim manifested a spirit of restraint when speaking of the Latin West—he had spent two years in a Dominican monastery in Florence. He exalted the possibilities of anyone in Florence or Paris of obtaining a thorough education in humanistic science.

In his desire for a sincere reform of Russian religious life, Maxim sided with the trans-Volgan monks and became an intimate friend of their protagonist Vassian Patrikeev. This made him very unpopular among the Josephites, and when one of them, Daniel, became metropolitan (1522-1539), Maxim lost all support in the official Church. He was accused of having gone too far in his correction of holy books, was thrice condemned, and was confined in the monastery of Volokolamsk and later at Tver'. His friend Vassian shared his fate. Only five years before his death, Maxim was released but was refused permission to return to Mount Athos.

Maxim's fate illustrates how far, in the fifteenth and sixteenth centuries, Muscovy was from the spirit of humanism. Maxim could be regarded as an emissary of the humanistic learning and methods which he had acquired in Italy and in France. Although he had not grasped the real meaning of the Italian Renaissance and remained faithful to his Orthodox thinking, even his moderate way of revealing new approaches to old problems was too much for the Muscovites, whose spirits were firmly anchored in the old ways of life and thought.

The Metropolitan Daniel left some discourses and letters dealing with theological and moral matters which give an insight into contemporary Muscovite society. His successor in the metropolitan see, Macarius (1542-1563), was also a convinced Josephite. The movement of trans-Volgan monasticism was liquidated, on his initiative, in 1554 by a council which condemned the leaders of the movement, Prior Artemius and the boyar's son Baškin, and also accused them of sympathies with Protestantism. The monk Theodosius Kosoj was condemned for the same reason, and the Josephite ideology became firmly established in the Muscovite Church.

One of the most outstanding apologists of autocracy in Moscow was Ivan Peresvetov, a nobleman who came to Moscow from Lithuania about 1538. Peresvetov was strongly influenced by Western political ideas, and in his two works, *The Legend of the Emperor Constantine* and *The Legend of Sultan Mahomet,* he exalted the monarchic regime.[26] In his *Petition* to Ivan IV Peresvetov took a firm stand against the boyars. The same sentiments are expressed in similar writings which originated among the petty nobility.

As has already been seen, Ivan the Terrible expressed his own political ideas plainly in his long letters in reply to the missives of his former friend Prince Kurbskij. Kurbskij was not alone in advocating the need for the participation of the boyars in the government. Such ideas were also spread by the anonymous author of a pamphlet presenting a fictitious dialogue between two wonder-workers of Barlaam monastery.

The unification of all East Russia under Moscow found a strong echo in literature. It is first reflected in the compilation of new Muscovite chronicles, which used the material gathered in provincial chronicles and were based on the two all-Russian compilations, the *Vladimir Polychron* and Pachomius' *Chronograph. The Resurrection Chronicle* brought events down to 1541; its adaptation, the *Nikonian Chronicle,* went down to 1558; and the *Lwów Chronicle* went to 1560. The compilers present the Muscovite rulers as legitimate lords of all Russian lands and solemnly glorify their autocratic regime. The same guiding ideas are expressed in the huge, profusely illustrated *Illuminated Nikonian Compilation,* going down to 1560, which, however, was not completed.

The political unification was accompanied by religious unification, and this found expression in an immense enterprise by the Metropolitan Macarius, the composition of the Grand *Četji Minei,* founded on the translated Greek reading of the lives of the saints for every day of the year. Many lives of Russian saints were added or rewritten according to the decisions of the councils of 1547 and 1549, which had revised the catalogue of Russian saints. Holy books and patriotic literature were added to the lives so that the twelve huge volumes of the monument represent Russian religious scholarship at a time when Moscow was exalted by ecclesiastical writers as the sole bulwark of Orthodoxy, replacing Constantinople, the second Rome.

This glorification of Muscovite achievements found another, no less solemn expression in the composition of the tsarist genealogy (in 1563), called *Stepennaja Kniga* ("Book of Degrees"). In highly flowery style the deeds of Russian rulers of past generations are described, and their full accord with the Church is praised.

Three other compositions give a good insight into the religious and private life of Muscovy in the sixteenth century. The *Domostroj* ("House Order") gives a detailed description of how a God-fearing man should order his house, the *Stoglav* ("Book of Hundred Chapters") contains the decisions of the Council of 1551 regulating ecclesiastical life, and the *Azbukovnik* ("ABC of Knowledge") is a kind of encyclopedic dictionary of the knowledge which a right-thinking man should possess. These three documents form a worthy epilogue to the political and ecclesiastical centralization of the Russian nation, which produced, under the guidance of Muscovite princes and of the metropolitans of all Russia, a uniform and well-ordered frame in which the national life should develop.

It was the art of printing which helped to consolidate the unification of all East Russia under Muscovy and to render uniform the political, religious, and social thinking of the nation. Although the first printing press was established in Moscow in 1563 and the first book, the Acts of the Apostles, was printed in the next year, the new art could be definitely established in Moscow only later and was mostly used for producing books of ecclesiastical content.[27]

Although Muscovy's cultural life and literary productions were virtually untouched by the new trend which had transformed West European civilization, the Italian Renaissance had considerable direct influence in Russian art, especially in architecture. The Mongol period had disastrous consequences for Russian art. In the first decades of the Mongol domination Russia was deprived of almost all of its craftsmen and artists, who were conscripted by the victors and sent to the Khan's court to work for the embellishment of the Khan's residence and to provide jewelry for the Khan's harem and courtiers. Only Novgorod and Pskov were able to preserve most of their artistic traditions and inheritance from the Kievan period.

Novgorod architecture was characterized in the second half of the fourteenth century by a special style which developed on the basis of the cruciform churches with a cupola from the previous period, but which limited the structure to a single apse and had four steep gables. The churches of the Transfiguration and of SS. Peter and Paul represented this new style. Soon, however, Novgorod architects returned to the traditional forms of eastern Russian churches with a cupola and the traditional three apses.

The architecture of Pskov kept the traditional three apses and four piers. The church of St. Basil, dating from 1413, was the most characteristic structure of this style. The construction of open belfries adjoining the churches, which originated in Pskov, was later imitated in many churches in Russia.

In Moscow the traditions of Suzdal'-Vladimir architecture were not forgotten during the Mongol period. What is left of the first known churches in Moscow, that constructed by Prince Daniel in 1272 in the Daniel monastery and the *Spas-na-Boru* built by Ivan Kalita in 1330, indicates this. They are even more clearly visible in the two churches erected in Zvenigorod, the Assumption (1399) and Our Lady's Nativity (1404), in Sergievskaja Lavra (1422), and in the cathedral of Alexandrovo. This type of architecture was more developed in the church of Our Lady's Nativity in Ferapontov monastery (1500).

The Russian native architects were more daring in the Mongol period in their wooden architecture. Improving on the Byzantine and Kievan models with considerable success, the national craftsmen made remarkable progress while the architects created new types of quadrangular, octagonal, and cruciform wooden churches and raised their cupolas to lofty heights. The desire to imitate some of the characteristic features of the wooden architecture but to retain the principal characteristics of the Vladimir style originated new architectural forms in Russia.

They were initiated by Ivan III. Not having competent builders in Moscow for the construction of the Cathedral of the Assumption (Uspenskij sobor), Ivan III, whose new wife Sophia had brought Italian manners and artists to Moscow, invited the architect Aristotele di Fioravante di Ridolfo, from Bologna, to build the church (1475-1479). He taught the Russian craftsmen the new methods of construction, though he had to adapt his plans to the traditional style of Vladimir.

Builders called from Pskov profited by this when building the church of the Annunciation in Moscow (1484-1489). The basis was again the style of Vladimir, but the builders had already tried to carry out in stone some of the bolder features of the wooden architecture. It showed considerable progress in the new direction of Russian style.

Italian architects, Marco Ruffo, Pietro Antonio Solario, and Aloisio da Carezano, started to rebuild the Kremlin, but even here the new Renaissance forms were combined with traditional Russian art (the Granovitaja Palata). Aloisio da Carezano also added new chapels and the Renaissance arcading of the gallery to the church of the Annunciation, which had been damaged by fire in 1547.

Another example of a combination of the traditional Muscovite style with new Renaissance features is the cathedral of the Archangel in the Kremlin, constructed in 1509 by the Milanese architect Alevisio Nuovo.

The new architectural forms added to the Vladimir style by Italian architects had some influence on the new Muscovite style, but the tendency to imitate the bold forms of wooden architecture were increasingly manifested in the work of native builders, who quickly mastered the foreign technique. The first half of the sixteenth century saw arise a number of such buildings, for example, at Djakovo, Ostrov, Kolomenskoe, and elsewhere, but the most daring achievement of this kind was accomplished by the native builders Postnik and Barma in the construction of St. Basil's church (1550-1560) on the Red Square. Here the new Muscovite architecture reached its final efflorescence.

In the Kievan period the centers of decorative art were Kiev and Novgorod. Under the tuition of Greek masters native artists started to decorate the churches with frescoes and founded famous schools of icon painting, which became a Russian national art. During the Mongol period only Novgorod was able to continue this art. New incentives came to Russia even during this period from the third Greek renaissance of the Palaeologi. Contact with the West in matters of art was maintained in the fourteenth and fifteenth centuries through Venice, also through Serbian and Bulgarian channels, and lastly through the Italo-Cretan school, renowned for its Byzantine icons of a Western Renaissance character.

These contacts brought about a revival of Russian painting during the Muscovite period from the fifteenth to the seventeenth century. The Greek Theophanes and his collaborators, with their frescoes and their "illusionism," represent it at its best, in the churches of Moscow and Novgorod. The most famous Russian icon painter was Rublev (died 1430), whose method was declared by the Council of 1551 to be exemplary for icon painters. Daniel Černy followed Rublev's tradition, and Dionysius' frescoes at Theraponton monastery (1500-1501) have been compared with the work of Giotto. Dionysius inaugurated a new style in icon painting of a more narrative nature, and his son Theodore continued his school.

New schools sprang up besides those of Novgorod and Pskov; that of Moscow inherited the excellent traditions of the school of Suzdal', while that of the Stroganov family produced some accomplished miniaturists. The art of icon painting, which represents a remarkable contribution of

Russia to the history of art, flourished down to the second half of the seventeenth century.

The Italian Renaissance also seems to have influenced the Russian art of enameling. Its period of florescence started in the reign of Ivan IV. The fine filigree technique characterizing Russian enamels seems to have been brought to Russia from Mount Athos. The best enamels were produced during the sixteenth and seventeenth centuries, and their style is a curious fusion of different elements, Byzantine, Oriental, Italian, and German, with some original Muscovite features.

IV

Nearest to the West and most exposed to the influence of Italian humanism and of the Renaissance were the Croats and the Serbians. The Serbian kingdom perished, and the national life of the Croats was endangered by constant struggle with the advancing Turks. But Dalmatia was saved, at least for some time, from their occupation and found some relief under Venetian sovereignty. Even more fortunate was Dubrovnik (Ragusa) on the Adriatic, which had become a city-republic, first under the protection of Venice (1205-1358), then under that of the kings of Hungary. Even when the republic had to acknowledge the supremacy of the Turkish sultans, after the battle of Mohács (1526), it was able to retain its autonomous status and continued to flourish, thanks to its busy commercial interchange with Italy and the Ottoman Empire. Its population was already mostly Slavic by the second half of the fourteenth century, and from the fifteenth century on, the Slavic documents of its chancellery were written not in Cyrillic but in Latin letters.

It was natural that Italian humanism should find easy access to Ragusa and the Dalmatian cities. Most young men of wealth studied at Italian universities, and many of them occupied chairs at universities in Italy, Hungary, and Germany. One of them, George Dragišić, a Bosnian who became professor of metaphysics and theology at Pisa, was regarded as one of the best theologians and philologists of his time.

The first Dalmatian humanists wrote their compositions in prose and poetry in Latin. The diplomat Vuk Bobaljović was the first, followed by the first poet laureate of Dubrovnik, Peter Menčetić, a great admirer of Petrarch. The best known of them was I. Crijević, a member of the humanistic circle in Rome. The city of Šibenik also had its humanist, G. Šišgorić, and Trogir its diplomat and historian Coriolan Cipiko.

Under the influence of the Italian lyric and native songs the Croatian lyric developed, and there were soon produced many prominent examples, for instance, Šiško Menčetić' cultured erotic poetry and Abbot

Držić' spiritual and national lyrics. A. Čubranović became famous through his original composition *Jeđupka* ("Egyptian," "Gypsy"). The Benedictine monk Mavro Vetranić composed lyric and epic poems with profound religious sentiment and national feeling. In *The Hermit* he outlined his solitary life on an island, and in his epic composition *Putnik* ("Pilgrim") he described the conversion of a sinner. Many of his lyrical poems are inspired by the Psalms. Influenced by the liturgical compositions popular in Dalmatia, he composed some religious dramas. The greatest influence on the development of South Slavic dramatical production was his *Abraham's Altar,* which was later adapted and put on the stage by Marin Držić.

The latter (died 1567) is the main representative of Ragusan dramatic literature in the sixteenth century. He wrote some dramas with religious subjects and introduced into South Slavic literature the Italian *dramma pastorale,* with which he had become acquainted in Siena. Tasso and Quarini were the most popular representatives of this kind of dramatic art. Three of Držić' pastoral dramas are preserved and are regarded as most interesting products of this literary genre. Into South Slavic dramatic composition Držić also introduced comedies, which were composed in Italy in imitation of Plautus' production. The best of his dramas is his *Novela od Stanca,* a comedy describing the adventures of a naive peasant in the city, which is still popular.

Latin and Greek classical lyrics inspired some poets in Dubrovnik who belonged to the intellectual circle around a highly intelligent and wealthy lady Fiora Zuzzeri (Cveta Zuzorić). Even in this respect the South Slavic poets followed the example of their Italian colleagues. In his lyrical poetry Dinko Ranjina followed Tibullus, Propertius, Ovid, and the Alexandrine poets Theocritus, Moschus, and others. He also translated many classical poems. Dinko Zlatarić generally followed Petrarch in his love poems and his satiric, didactic, and epigrammatic poems. Both had several imitators and followers.

The golden period of Ragusan (Dubrovnik) poetry came during the end of the sixteenth and the first half of the seventeenth centuries. The greatest poet of Ragusan literary history was Ivan Gundulić (1588-1638). His poem *The Prodigal Son* is regarded as the best religious lyrical composition of Ragusa. His best dramatic work is *Dubravka,* and his epic *Osman* is regarded as the masterpiece of the Ragusan period. Gundulić celebrates there the Polish victory over the Turks at Chocim in 1621 and describes the assassination of the Sultan Osman. The poet not only exalts the heroes of the struggle with the Turks, but also prophetically anticipates the liberation of all southern Slavs. He was inspired by Torquato Tasso's *Gerusalemme liberata.*

The other prominent poet of this period was J. Palmotić (1606-1657). For his dramatic compositions Palmotić chose subjects not from the classics or from Tasso and Ariosto, but from the history of Ragusa. The best known of such dramas is *Pavlimir,* describing the foundation of Ragusa. He also composed a religious epic *Kristijade.* A prominent lyricist of the period was Ivan Bunić Vučičević. He favored religious subjects (*Spiritual Songs, Magdalene the Penitent*) but also wrote some love songs and eclogues.

He was the last of the circle of great poets of Dubrovnik. There were, of course, a number of epigoni who imitated their great predecessors. The most prominent among these was Ignatius Đorđić, who was inspired by Ovid. In his paraphrase in verses of the Psalter, one of his best works, he seems to have followed the example of the Polish poet Kochanowski.

The writers and poets of the other Dalmatian cities composed their works in less favorable circumstances than their Ragusan confreres. The danger arising from the Turkish threat to overrun the rest of Dalmatia often induced them to exhort their compatriots and Christian Europe to unite in order to avert the menace. This is particularly true of Marko Marulić (1450-1524) of Split (Spalato), the representative of the religious renaissance in Dalmatia. His Latin treatise on how to choose a good and happy life (*De bene beateque vivendi institutione*) made him well known in contemporary Europe. It went through twenty editions and was translated into Italian (twelve editions), into German (six editions), into French, into Portuguese, and partly into Czech. Among other similar works in which Marulić propagated the reform of Christian life, his *Evangelistarium* was also well known.

He also addressed a long letter to Pope Hadrian VI, asking him to unite all Christian nations for the fight against the Turks, and the same idea is also expressed in his long Croatian epic on *Judith.* The suffering of the Croats under the Turkish yoke is vividly described in his *Molitva* ("Prayer").

Hannibal Lučić (died 1553) best drama *Robinja,* the first original Croatian drama, also has the Turkish domination as its background. He recounts there the fate of a noble Croatian girl who became a Turkish prisoner. In his love songs Lučić followed Petrarch's pattern.

His countryman Peter Hektorović (died 1572), a native of the island of Hvar, became famous with his idyllic epic *Ribanje* ("fishing"), in which he described the life of the fishermen. Even there an echo of the Turkish menace is heard because the author included in his work three epics on the popular hero, Marko.[28]

The most vivid and touching description of the sufferings of the Christian population under the Turks was given by Peter Zoranić from Nin, near Zadar, in his pastoral romance *Planine,* written in prose and in verse. The poetic works of his compatriot George Baraković are also permeated with profound national sentiment. B. Karnarutić, also from Zadar, sang of the death of the Croatian hero Nicholas Zrinski and the capture of Szeged by the Turks.

Literary activity in Ragusa (Dubrovnik) and in Dalmatia started to degenerate in the second half of the seventeenth century. In 1668 Ragusa was almost destroyed by an earthquake, and the city never completely recovered from the catastrophe. This also had an influence on literary production in the city-republic and in Dalmatia. It was a happy chance for the Croats and the Serbians that in Ragusa they found a secure haven for their culture and literature during the most difficult period of their history. When Croatian and Serbian cultural life was reborn after the liberation from the Turks, it was possible to build upon the firm foundations which had been laid by the Ragusan literary school.

It was natural that Dalmatia should also be influenced by Italian art; Venice was, of course, the main intermediary. Venetian Gothic, already permeated with Renaissance motifs, penetrated into Dalmatian cities as early as the beginning of the fifteenth century. Dalmatia produced many artists in this period, but a great number of them stayed in Italy, where they had gone to study. One of them, George da Sebenico, continued, from 1441 on, the construction of Šibenik (Sebenico) cathedral in the Venetian gothic style. He was only attracted by the pure Renaissance style later, and in 1464 he reconstructed in this new style the palace of the rectors in Ragusa. He also produced some sculpture in Šibenik and Split (Spalato).

His pupil, the Slavic Andrew Alexius of Durazzo, terminated the baptistry in Trau and joined Nicolo Fiorentino in the decoration of the chapel of St. John Orsini in the same city. Ragusa, however, closed its doors to any Venetian influence, in politics or in art.[29]

NOTES

1. See details on Czech literature of this period with bibliographical indications on authors and editions of their works in Vlček's *Dějiny české literatury,* quoted in Chapter VII, p. 179. General indications also in *Československá vlastivěda* (Prague, 1929), vol. 8, devoted to Czech literature.

2. Cf. R. R. Betts' paper *The Influence of Realist Philosophy on John Hus* (see Bibl. to Chapter VIII).

3. It is the great merit of Z. Nejedlý to have shown this in his important work, *Dějiny husitského Zpěvu* ("History of the Hussite Song," Prague, 1913).

4. The last words "kill, slay, spare no one," which are usually quoted in order to illustrate the bloodthirsty character of the Taborites, only appeared in 1530 in a printed copy of the song. The synods of the Taborites forbade the killing of prisoners.

5. Published by F. Palacký in FRA, vol. XX (1860): Gregorius Heimburg, *Apologia pro Georgio Poděbrad, rege Bohemiae, 1467.*

6. A new edition of 1957 by M. Letts (see Bibl.).

7. See Chapter VII, pp. 161 ff.

8. Gregory Hrubý was particularly interested in political science. He translated Agapetus' Byzantine treatise on kingship and Bohuslav of Lobkovice's last Latin letter to Peter of Rosenberg on the duties of a governor. His best translation is that of Erasmus' *Encomium moriae.*

9. There is a good monograph with bibliographical data on the historiography of the Unity by K. Krofta, *O bratrském dějepisectví* (Prague, 1946).

10. See the recent general study of the Polish Renaissance and humanism published by S. Zempicki, *Renesans i humanism w Polsce* (Warsaw, 1951). On Polish literature in the Renaissance, see the works quoted in Chapter VII, fn. 34. See also the five volumes on the Polish Renaissance published by the Polish Academy, *Odrozdzenie w Polsce* (1953-56), dealing with Polish history (vol. 1); science (vol. 2); language (vol. 3); literature (vol. 4); art (vol. 5); and the symposium on Polish sculpture, *Sztuka polska czasów nowożytnych,* vol. 1, *1450-1650* (Warsaw, 1953).

11. He was attacked by another political writer, Stanislas Orzechowski (1513-1566), who defended, in his work *Quincunx,* the privileges of the Polish gentry and its "golden liberty," which proved so ruinous for the state.

12. See above, Chapter VII, pp. 167 ff.

13. There is a recent study on Rey and on literary problems of the Polish Renaissance by J. Krzyżanowski, *Mikolaj Rej i Staś Gąska* (Warsaw, 1958).

14. On Skorina's Bible translation, see the study by A. V. Florovskij in Russian in the Czech *Sborník filologický,* 12 (1940-46), pp. 153-259. The author rejects the opinion that Skorina was influenced by Protestantism. The Czech translation was used by Skorina freely, especially the book on Tobias, which is a Belo-Russian adaptation of the Czech text. Czech and Polish translations were used also by the editors of the Bible of Ostrog and of the Bible of 1751.

15. On Kievan literary output, see F. Dvornik, *The Slavs,* pp. 225-50.

16. On the history of Ukrainian literature, see the recent publication by the Ukrainian Academy, O. I. Bileckyj, *Istorija ukrajins'koji literatury* (Kiev, 1954), vol. 1, pp. 1-123 (the early period to the eighteenth century). See also the works of D. Čiževsky, *Ukrajins'kyj literaturnyj barok,* vols. I-III (Prague, 1941-44), *Istorija ukrajinśkorji literatury,* vol. II, *Renesans ta reformcija. Barok* (Prague, 1942), and *Istorija ukrajins'koji literatury* (New York, 1956).

17. On Kurbskij, see p. 377. His works were published by N. G. Ustajalov, *Sočinenija knjazja Kurbskago* (St. Petersburg, 1883) and in *RIB,* vol. 31 (1914). See Bibl. for the translation into English of his correspondence by J. L. I. Fennell (1955) in Chapter XV.

18. A good history of the Orthodox Church in Poland, from the Polish point of view, was written by K. Chodynicki, *Kościół prawosławny a Rzeczpospolita Polska, 1370-1632* (Warsaw, 1934). Cf. also on the role of the Jesuits in the Union of Brest, J. Tretiak, *Piotr Skarga w dziejach i literaturze Unii Brzeskiej* (Cracow, 1912). See also below, Chapter XVIII, pp. 511 ff.

19. See below, pp. 551 ff.

20. See below, pp. 377, 378.

21. Cf. above, pp. 267, 280, 281.

22. Besides the Russian editions analyzed by N. Gudzij, *op. cit.*, pp. 245 ff., there is also the edition and study by a Czech scholar, J. Frček, published in Prague in 1948 by the Slavic Institute.

23. Cf. Chapter XV, p. 374.

24. On this activity, see A. I. Sobolevskij, *Perevodnaja literatura moskovskoj Rusi 14-17 vv.* (St. Petersburg, 1903), pp. 1-37.

25. The standard work in Russian on Maxim is that by V. S. Ikonnikov, *Maksim "Grek" i ego vremja*, 2nd ed. (Kiev, 1915). An exhaustive bibliography will be found in E. Denissoff's work, *Maxime le Grec et l'Occident* (Louvain, 1943). Maxim's works were published in three volumes by the Theological Academy of Kazan' between 1859 and 1862.

26. Similar ideas are reflected in another apology of Moscow's right to leadership, the *Kazan' Chronicle*, exalting Ivan IV's great deed, the capture of Kazan' in 1552. This event probably also inspired an unknown author to compose, on the basis of an older account (bylina), a *Legend of the Kiev Bogatyrs*, exalting the heroism of Russian boyars fighting the Tatars. On Peresvetov, see the study by W. Philip (see Bibl., Chapter XV).

27. On Russian literature of this period, see N. K. Gudzij, *History of Early Russian Literature* (see Bibl.), pp. 182 ff. See also D. Čyževskyj, *History of Russian Literature* (Gravenshage, 1960). On Russian art, see the standard work, *Istorija russkago iskusstva*, ed. I. Grabar (Moscow, 1910-14), 6 vols., and the new edition by the USSR Academy (Moscow, 1953-57), 5 vols. Cf. also S. V. Bezsonov, *Istorija russkoj arkhitektury* (Moscow, 1956), and N. M. Černyšev, *Iskusstvo freski v drevnej Rusi* (Moscow, 1954). See also Bibl. to this Chapter.

28. On Marko, see above, p. 114. On the history of Serbian and Croatian literature, see Vodnik, B., *Povijest hrvatske književnosti* (Zagreb, 1913), with V. Jagić's history of Croatian writings in the Glagolitic alphabet. Cf. also P. Popović, *Pregled srpske kniževnosti* (Beograd, 2nd ed., 1913) and A. Gavrilović, *Istorija srpske i hrvatske književnosti* (Belgrade, 1927); M. Kombol, *Povijest hrvatske književnosti do narodnog preporoda* (Zagreb, 1945); and S. Ježić, *Hrvatska književnost od početka do danas 1100-1941* (Zagreb, 1944). See Chapter XVI, pp. 420 ff. on Slovene and Croatian literature during the Reformation.

29. On the school of art in Dubrovnik, see J. Tadić, *Gradja o slikarskoj školi u Dubrovniku 13-16 v.* (Belgrade, 1952), vol. 1 (1284-1499); vol. 2 (1500-1601). The book contains also documentation on foreign relations of Dubrovnik, especially with the Ottomans.

Chapter XIV

THE SOCIAL AND POLITICAL DEVELOPMENT OF THE WESTERN AND SOUTHERN SLAVS FROM THE FIFTEENTH TO THE SEVENTEENTH CENTURY

Social and economic changes in western Europe—The monarchic idea and Western parliamentarianism—Codification of Western law and maritime expansion—Germany loses international trade routes—New grain markets spur the German agrarian economy—Decline of royal authority in Bohemia under the Jagiellonian kings—Bohemian Diets, the magnates, the knights, the burghers—Problems of the peasantry and the Hussites—Introduction of serfdom in Bohemia—Czech jurisprudence—Decline of royal power in Poland, origin of Polish Diets—The nobles control the government—Decline of Polish cities—Exploitation of the Polish peasantry by the nobles—Attempts at Polish legal codification—Lithuania's status before the union with Poland—Lithuanian sentiments of independence despite the Union—Slow assimilation of Polish institutions—The grand ducal council, origin of the Lithuanian Diets—The union and Lithuanian statutes—Growing Polish influence in the Russian lands—Catholics, Uniats, and Orthodox—Increasing differentiation between South, West, and East Russia: Ukrainians, Belo-Russians, and Great Russians—Growth of the influence of the magnates in Hungary and the Slovaks—The political and national life of the Croats; the Venetians and Dalmatia—The Republic of Dubrovnik—Social and political organization of the Ottoman Empire and its application to Serbians and Bulgarians—Slavic elements in the Turkish army and administration—Deep

*changes in the social life of the Serbians and Bulgarians—The Church,
the Serbian patriarchate—Decadence of Turkish political life and oppression of the Christian population—Attempts at insurrection, hayduks,
uskoks—Serbians and Bulgarians during the Turkish wars, the Catholics
in Bulgaria—Migration of Serbians to Hungary*

The social and economic transformation of western Europe during the
fourteenth century, which has already been described, was also bound
to affect profoundly the development of its political institutions. The
birth of capitalism presaged the end of the feudal era. Capitalism, the
introduction of a money economy, and the extension of maritime navigation gave an international character to the revival and florescence of
trade. Its centers were the cities of Italy, Flanders, France, and England.

However, the new development had to pass through many critical
phases. The government of the patrician class in the cities, which had replaced the nobility, was opposed by the organizations of the artisans and
by the laboring proletariat, which claimed a part in the government. This
revolutionary movement, which had started in Flanders and in Florence,
spread to France and England and even had its effects in Bohemia, but
it was arrested with the help of royal armies.

One of the most important consequences of this new growth of capitalism and urbanism was the suppression of serfdom and the replacement of feudal land tenure by tenant farming. This change was brought
about by the increased value of land and the necessity to produce for
the growing cities more foodstuffs at steadily rising prices. King Louis
IX of France freed all his serfs as early as 1315.

Even this development, however, could not ensue without a crisis. The
peasants, freed, but devoid of resources and exposed to exploitation by
the nobles, revolted in Flanders, France, and England, but could not
arrest the evolution. The consequence of this was the end of the patriarchal relationship between peasants and nobles which had characterized the medieval world. Only one hope remained to the peasants, the
protection of the king, and so they turned their eyes to him.

This profound social and economic transformation resulted in the
growth of royal authority. With the end of feudal bonds the nobility lost
its character of a governing class. It also lost its military role because of
the new developments in warfare. The enhanced importance of infantry
against attacking cavalry was proved by the English and the Swiss, while
the invention of artillery further reduced the value of cavalry and of fortified castles. The nobles thus lost not only their military role but also their
former social position and became mere landowners.

The role of the nobility in the administration of the kingdom was also increasingly curtailed. The king had at his disposal legal specialists and capable administrators. The nobles could not vie with this new class of professional lay intellectuals, which was becoming the main support of the king. In elevating his faithful civil servants to a higher social status, the king was creating a new class of nobility, *noblesse de robe,* representing the elite of royal servants. It was this new class of nobles which helped the old nobility to survive the ruin of the feudal regime, from which it had itself emerged, and to maintain its privileged position for the future.

The natural consequence of this development was the strengthening of the monarchic idea with the help of the jurists. They sought inspiration in the statutes of Roman law, whose study flourished in Western universities. This, however, did not stop the further strengthening of the parliamentary regime, which had already originated in the feudal era. The feudal monarchs were forced to request the necessary financial resources from their vassals—the nobles, the clergy, and the cities. The growing national sentiment demanded the continuation of this collaboration with the representatives of the nation even in the new era. So it came about that the Estates-general in the monarchies of the Iberian peninsula, France, England, and the Low Countries maintained their privilege of voting and approving taxes and of sharing with the king the responsibility of government.

The troubles of the Hundred Years' War between France and England did not weaken parliamentary institutions. In England Parliament was divided into the House of Lords and the House of Commons, the latter gaining more importance with time. An attempt was even made to introduce a general parliamentary representation in France and in England. Unfortunately, Charles VIII (1483-1498) abandoned his project of 1484 for a kind of universal suffrage, and from that time on, the French monarchy, secure in the support of its own bureaucratic institutions, leaned increasingly toward an absolutism which ultimately provoked the Revolution of 1789. A similar attempt at reform in England by Henry VII (1485-1509), who had extended representation in Parliament to the delegates of all landowners of a certain magnitude, was not more effective as the king avoided as far as possible summoning Parliament. Here too, the tendency toward absolutism provoked a revolutionary reaction which beheaded King Charles I and established a republican regime under Cromwell.

Thanks to the revival of the study of Roman law, the Western monarchies were able to strengthen their regime by giving their subjects a solid legal system. The "Book of Laws" (*Las Siete Partidas*), initiated by Alfonso X the Wise (1252-1284) to codify Spanish laws and approved by the Cortes, was the best European code of this time and is directly inspired by the Code of Justinian. In France, Charles VIII (1483-1498) initiated the codification of French customary law; this was partially realized during the reign of Louis XII (1498-1515) and was continued and completed during those of Francis I (1515-1547) and Henry II (1547-1559). Important reforms in the judicial field were introduced in England by Henry VII (1485-1509), who created a supreme court of justice and reformed legal procedure according to the principles of Roman law. A codification of customary law in a monarchic spirit was effected in Portugal under Alfonso V (1438-1481).

These new developments were accompanied by unexpected progress in seafaring. Hitherto the main commercial shipping routes had been in the Mediterranean Sea, around the French coast, in the North Sea, and in the Baltic. When, during the Hundred Years' War, access to the North Sea was temporarily blocked, the Portuguese turned southward, discovered Madeira and the Azores, and established themselves on the West African coast while seeking a new route to India via the Cape of Good Hope. The Kingdom of Aragon successfully disputed supremacy in the Mediterranean with Venice and Genoa and took Tunisia under its protection. After the dynastic unity of Spain had been effected under Ferdinand II of Aragon (1479-1516) and Isabella of Castile (1474-1504), a new discovery of enormous significance was made when Christopher Columbus landed in the New World (1492). Soon afterward England started its maritime expansion. In 1497 and 1498 the Genoese John Cabot, then an English admiral, reached Labrador and Nova Scotia. All these events augured a new era, during which western Europe would dominate the evolution of world history.

This new development in western Europe had a very unfavorable influence on the economic and political evolution of Germany and Central Europe. It has been seen how the German cities on the Danube, the Rhine, and the Baltic profited greatly in the fourteenth century from the commercial activity which spread from Italy to Bruges on the North Sea and to Lübeck on the Baltic. The discovery of silver and gold in Bohemia and Hungary provided the precious metals necessary to finance these growing international commercial transactions. These gave rise to the unsuccessful plans of Charles IV to divert the transcontinental channels of trade through Prague and to make the Vltava and the Elbe the connecting links between Venice and the North Sea.

This prosperity of the German cities continued through the fifteenth century. The growth of industry and commerce in the cities on the North Sea, with their constantly increasing need for foodstuffs, even gave a new incentive to the trade of the Hanse league. The agrarian economies of the Teutonic Order and of Brandenburg profited greatly by this opportunity.

This situation changed, however, in the sixteenth century. The discovery of a direct route to the Far East and of the New World in the West permitted Lisbon to assume the role of Venice in international commerce and to become the distributing center for this merchandise to the rest of western Europe. The gold and silver introduced from the New World in unprecedented quantities provided a solid monetary basis for these transactions and soon made the impoverished mines of Central Europe unremunerative. As a consequence of this new situation the continental trade route through Germany lost its international character, and capital took refuge in the cities on the Atlantic and North Sea coast. The Dutch took over the commercial traffic of the North Sea, which had been hitherto a monopoly of the Hanse, so that the league was left with only the limited trade of the Baltic.

Naturally, under such conditions political development in Germany could not follow the same pattern as in western Europe. Germany, deprived of the capital which international commerce had previously helped her to earn, went back to the medieval urban economy. There was no incentive for a concentration of power in the hands of a monarch, as in the West, and the feudal regime continued to flourish in Germany. The cultural ties with the West were also weakened, although not completely broken. Only the western areas—the Rhineland, the Palatinate, Baden, and Württemberg—were slightly attracted and influenced by the economy of the Low Countries and France. Germany could not participate in the colonial and economic expansion of the West. The leading role was played first by Portugal and Spain, enriched by the treasures of the New World, then by Holland and France, and finally by England.

The new economic prosperity of the West, however, influenced the German economy in one way. The growing and flourishing industrial cities on the coast needed more and more agricultural products, and the Dutch capitalists took the grain trade into their own hands. This gave a new incentive to the economy of the Baltic principalities, Holstein, Mecklenburg, Pomerania, Brandenburg, Prussia, and Livonia. The opening of profitable new markets for grain necessitated an increase in production. Of course, the German peasant-colonists who had replaced the native Slavic and Prussian populations of these lands could not compete with their feudal masters, who possessed most of the arable land and had acquired political jurisdiction over their subjects. As the nobles had no liquid capital in order to hire more workers for the intensification of production, the only course open to them was to force their subjects to cultivate their lands. Thus, in contrast to what had happened in the West, where the serfs were freed, the free colonists in eastern Germany lost their freedom and were reduced to serfdom. Of course, this use of enforced serf labor enhanced considerably the power of the nobility and made the formation of a centralized monarchic regime on the Western model impossible in Germany. Insofar as there was any penetration of the new political ideas into Germany, they were only applied inside the different principalities and strengthened the authoritarian regime of the princes in their own domains.

The principality which profited most from the new situation was Brandenburg. The prince-elector was able gradually to concentrate absolute government in his own hands, with the help of the landed nobility. By confirming their social privileges the Elector also obtained the close collaboration of his nobles in military matters. He had no need to hire mercenaries, for which he lacked the means, since his nobles provided the officers and recruited the soldiers from their own serfs. So it happened that the new situation in the West had helped to create in Germany a centralized principality with an absolute ruler who could count on an army which was recruited among his own subjects and was therefore much more reliable than the costly mercenary armies. All this was bound in due course to have repercussions further east, in Prussia and in Poland, because the eyes of the Electors of Brandenburg were turning more and more toward those lands where further expansion of their power seemed possible.

It was, of course, natural that this new evolution in the West and in Germany should also influence the economic, social, and political situation in the Slavic states. In the sixteenth and seventeenth centuries only two Slavic states were bound to be affected by this changed situation, Bohemia and Poland-Lithuania. Russia was to develop on different lines and was only slightly influenced by the changes in the West and in Germany. The Slovenes shared the fate of the Austrian lands, now firmly in the hands of the Habsburgs; the Slovaks had been incorporated into Hungary like the Croats, who were trying desperately to save the remnants of their national independence; the Serbians and the Bulgarians had been submerged in the Ottoman Empire. Only one free outlet remained to the southern Slavs—the Republic of Dubrovnik (Ragusa), a vassal of the Ottoman Empire, but becoming an important emporium on the Adriatic Sea and endeavoring to find a place in the flourishing Western economy.

The Kingdom of Bohemia was naturally most exposed to social, economic, and political influences deriving from the new developments in Germany and the West. The Hussite wars had, moreover, diminished the prosperity which the country had enjoyed under Charles IV and Wenceslas IV. It was to be expected that after the final victory over the radical Hussites, the nobility, enriched by the confiscation of Church lands, would continue with renewed vigor to increase its influence in the government of the kingdom to the detriment of the royal power, weakened by the wars and the interregnum. The valiant national King George of Poděbrady succeeded, however, largely by dint of his personal prestige, in reestablishing that of the monarchy. But the internal religious strife between Catholics and Utraquists and the warlike complications with Hungary prevented him from consolidating the royal power as he had wished.

However, his successor Vladislav the Jagiellonian was a weakling, unable to continue George's efforts. He even lost what his predecessors had gained. The nobility consented to his election only on the understanding that he would confirm and augment their privileges. The capitulations signed in 1571 precluded the fifteen-year-old king from making any bold attempt to strengthen the monarchic regime in Bohemia. The confirmation of all rights, privileges, and customs of the country meant that no modification in the constitution and no major change in administration could be introduced by the king without the consent of the Diet, which was dominated by the higher nobility. It was characteristic that the young king was asked to promise to respect these *pacta conventa* three times— at the moment when he crossed the frontiers of his new realm, before entering Prague, and before his solemn coronation.

Thus, contrary to developments in France and England, the feudal conception of the royal power continued to prevail in Bohemia, and a further deterioration was suffered during the reign of the Jagiellonian kings.

The Diet's constitutional position and the diminution of royal authority were illustrated by the fact that the decisions of the Diets obtained legal value only when they were incorporated into the *Tabulae terrae* ("tables of the country") in the presence of the envoys (*relatores*) of the Diet and of the king. The Tables could be opened for consultation only in the presence of delegates chosen by the Diet.

During the first years of Vladislav's reign most of the royal domains which were under direct royal administration were alienated in favor of the nobles or of creditors, and in 1500 the king even renounced his right to reclaim his lands after the death of their tenants. From that time on the king was completely dependent financially on votes made reluctantly by the Diets for specific purposes. Soon even the supervision of the expenditure of those sums was claimed by the Diet.

This, of course, precluded any possibility of the king's establishing a standing army of mercenaries such as was being set up in the West. He had no troops at his disposal and could only call on the general militia in the event of invasion or when the Diet gave its assent. The king also lost control over the administration of the country. The two captains administering each district had to be chosen, one from the magnates and the other from the knights, and in 1497 these two orders distributed the main offices of the Kingdom of Bohemia among their members. The magnates reserved for themselves the highly important offices of supreme burgrave of Prague, grand master of the court of Bohemia, grand chancellor, and two of the burgraviates of Karlův Týn (Karlstein), where the coronation insignia and the archives of Bohemia were kept. The knights obtained the offices of grand clerk, vice-chamberlain of Bohemia, and the third burgraviate of Karlův Týn. Only the office of master of the finances could be entrusted at the king's discretion to a member of the third Estate, that of the burghers. A similar compromise between the magnates and the knights was concluded in Moravia in 1523.[1] Thus, the administration of the kingdom was taken over completely by the nobles. The king could make the appointments only after consultation with other grand dignitaries, who were, of course, members of the Diet. The latter contested the king's right to depose them. The grand council, which should have been an advisory body for the king, was composed of high functionaries who could be regarded simply as delegates of the Diet.

Soon the administration of the lands which still belonged directly to the crown also came under the surveillance and authority of the Diet. The royal officers were gradually being transformed into officers of the land. Under Vladislav the judiciary also came under the control of the Diet. The supreme tribunal was composed of a fixed number of magnates and knights, who could not be removed by the king. Its members were recruited by a kind of co-optation or were chosen on the advice of the grand council. The supreme tribunal enjoyed the prerogative of interpreting the competence of the laws, and its decisions were final. It also exercised a political function, being to some degree a permanent committee of the Diet charged with surveillance of the activity of the sovereign.

The Diets were composed in Bohemia of three Estates—the magnates, the knights, and the representatives of the cities. After the Hussite wars the higher clergy was excluded from the Bohemian Diet, while in Moravia it formed one Estate with the representatives of the burghers. The Diets were convoked by the king, and in Moravia also by the supreme captain of the land. For practical reasons local Diets of administrative circles soon came to be convoked and sent their delegates to the national Diet. In Silesia each principality had its own Diet, and common interests were discussed and decided in the Diets of the princes (*Fürstentag*). The custom of convoking local Diets, however, did not develop as well in Bohemia and Moravia as in Poland or Hungary, and it was discontinued when the Habsburgs had succeeded the Jagiellonians.

The dominant element in the Diets and in the kingdom were the magnates, who concentrated in their hands the most important national offices. They were not numerous. In fifteenth century Bohemia there were only about fifty families of magnates, of which about twelve were the most powerful. Their number grew to about seventy in the seventeenth century. In Moravia there existed only about fifteen families of the old nobility. However, they possessed most of the land and were, therefore, able to establish a quasi-oligarchic regime during the reign of the Jagiellonians.

The magnates even tried to dispute the participation of the knights in the government. However, when the knights started to side with the burghers, the magnates were forced to make some concessions to them. It is to be regretted that this coalition of the knights with the burghers did not materialize. Bohemia would then have witnessed a development similar to that in England, where the gentry and the commons formed the lower chamber in the English Parliament. A similar regroupment of forces would have been equally propitious to Bohemia and would have exercised a healthy control over the rule of the magnates.

Soon the two noble Estates started a vigorous common offensive against the third Estate of the burghers. They pretended that the vote of the third Estate was not necessary to promulgate new laws, and refused to present to the delegates of the burghers the articles concerning the municipalities. The cities protested vehemently, but, unfortunately, King Vladislav did not see that his interest lay in supporting the cities. He sided with the nobles and gave the office of vice-chamberlain, whose incumbent generally appointed the councilors in the city administration, to the knights. Other attacks on the autonomy of the cities followed, and the magnates tried to break the resistance of the burghers by various reprisals which harmed the economy of the cities and limited their commerce. A kind of civil war between the nobles and the cities broke out and lasted for about thirty years. The king, a weakling, was unable to stop the strife. At last, in 1517, after long negotiations, the so-called accord of St. Wenceslas was concluded. The burghers surrendered their monopoly of beer brewing, accepted in some cases the competence of the supreme court in city affairs, and reconciled themselves to the fact that the vice-chamberlain should be a noble. In return they were guaranteed their position in the Diet and recovered their freedom to hold markets and their internal autonomy.

It should be stressed that when Bohemia had achieved a high degree of economic prosperity during the reigns of Charles IV and Wenceslas

IV, a development can be discerned in the status of the peasantry there similar to that which led to the abolition of serfdom in the West. According to the feudal conception the peasant was not the proprietor of his land but was only granted it for cultivation under certain conditions by the feudal lord to whom it belonged. In the earlier period, according to Czech custom, he had to deliver a certain quantity of agricultural products to his lord and work for a certain period on the lord's land. German colonists were granted certain privileges, especially the right to be tried by their own judges according to their own law. Soon old Czech settlers also won some of these privileges, so that there was not much difference between the "old Czech" custom and the "new German" custom.

During the fourteenth century the obligations of the peasants toward their lords were gradually converted into rents which were paid twice a year. The duty of the *corvée* could also be redeemed by monetary payment. The greater abundance of capital also induced many lords to grant the lands which they cultivated with the help of the *corvée* to peasants for cultivation, in return for the payment of a rent. So it happened that in many districts the *corvée* had disappeared.

As the prosperity of the peasantry grew, whole villages and settlements purchased exemption from the jurisdiction of their lords, at least in minor matters, and were given their own burgomasters as judges in the first instance or were allowed to live under the laws of the neighboring cities.

In general, it was in England and Bohemia that the problems of the peasantry underwent the most lively discussion during the fourteenth and fifteenth centuries. All Czech preachers and reformers of this period paid special attention to the social position of the peasants. They insisted not only that the peasant's person should be free, but also that the land which he cultivated should be heritable without limitation by his wife or descendants, both male and female, and that he should be allowed to dispose of it testamentarily. Not only did John Hus claim this right for the peasants, but also Archbishop John of Jenštein.

The latter granted this right to all peasants on his estates, and his example was followed, not only by other churchmen but also by many lords who supported the reformers.

John Hus, although accepting the traditional medieval division of society into three classes—the clergy, lords, and laborers—declared that the peasant should own his land. But the more radical Peter Chelčický preached the equality of all men and attacked the ruling class bitterly for exploiting the laborers. Similar ideas were spread by the radical Hussite party of the Taborites, who sounded like an anticipation of the great French Revolution.

The level headed John Žižka, however, saw that the defense of the new faith could not be successful without the help of the nobles and the cities.

He therefore brought his followers back to the recognition of the old medieval order of three classes, while stressing their unity and equality in the acceptance of a common faith. He won his victories not only with the help of the common people, but also with that of the lesser nobility and of cities.

The victory of the magnates, nobles, and cities over the radical wing of the Taborites ended the dreams of the radical social reformers. The prosperity of Charles IV's reign had vanished, and the magnates and nobles had only the labor of peasants to replace the capital which had disappeared with the changed economic situation. The instability of the country after the wars induced George of Poděbrady to concede the claims of the nobles and to publish several edicts limiting the migration of the peasants. The law promulgated in 1487, accentuated by other prescriptions in the following years, is regarded as closing the old order definitively and opening a new era in which serfdom was gradually reintroduced in the kingdom. This situation became more and more aggravated during the sixteenth century. The peasants were increasingly tied to the land given to them for exploitation and could not change their status without the permission of their lords.

In spite of this considerable deterioration in the status of labor, the situation of the peasants in the Czech lands was not as bad as it was, at this period, in Poland and Hungary. They even retained a kind of limited village autonomy, under the direction, of course, of burgomasters nominated by their feudal lords. The servage and the *corvée* only became a really heavy burden in the first half of the seventeenth century.

This political and social organization of Bohemia and Moravia is reflected and analyzed in contemporary writings on jurisprudence. At the beginning of the fifteenth century, Andrew of Dubá described juridical procedure in Bohemia and its organization, together with the legislation of the Bohemian lands. As mentioned in the previous chapter, Victorin Kornel of Všehrdy wrote, in nine books, *On Legislation, Justice and the Tables of the Land of Bohemia.* The first edition of this important work was finished in 1499; the second was published in 1508. Moravian jurisprudence and judicial procedure are described in the *Book of Tovačovský*, compiled between 1481 and 1490 by Ctibor Tovačovský of Cimburk, and in *The Book of Drnov*, which is a new edition of the *Book of Tovačovský* made from 1523 to 1527 by Ctibor of Drnovice. The revival of the study of Roman law stimulated interest in jurisprudence in Bohemia, but its principles did not influence the adaptation of the customary laws.

George of Poděbrady was prevented by circumstance from realizing his plan for the codification of Czech legislation according to the example of other legislators in the West. Only under Vladislav, at the instigation of the Diet, was a codification of Bohemian legislation elaborated, adopted by the Diet, and published in 1500. This work cannot be compared with similar codifications effected in the West. The feudal spirit of the period permeates this work. The predominance of the two orders of magnates and knights is stressed, to the detriment of the burghers and peasants. There is no trace of monarchic principles, but rather a sanctioning of the oligarchic regime of the nobles. Only when the Habsburgs had succeeded the Jagiellonians in Bohemia were attempts initiated to strengthen the monarchic tradition and reduce the influence of the magnates in the government. This was, however, connected with religious problems in Bohemia and with the political struggles of the nation with the new dynasty, which deserve special treatment.[2]

The limitations placed on the royal power in Poland by the nobility as a result of the changes on the throne after the extinction of the Piast dynasty have already been noted.[3] The privileges granted to the nobility by Louis of Anjou and Jagiello became the basis for the continuous growth of the nobility's influence on the government at the expense of the royal power. Moreover, Jagiello, a foreigner, was bound to rule with the help of representatives of the magnates. So it happened that the government fell into the hands of the royal council, composed of magnates, mostly from Little Poland; bishops; the highest officials—the chancellor, the vice-chancellor, the director of finances, and the marshal; and voivodes and castellans who were the heads of the provincial officials. The jurisdiction of this council grew and was extended over administrative and political affairs. The meetings of the royal council became increasingly frequent, especially during the last years of Jagiello's reign. The dominant figure in the council was Bishop Oleśnicki.

On the other side, even the lower gentry succeeded in obtaining more and more privileges which guaranteed the freedom of their persons and the security of their property. The most important of these privileges were enshrined in the Statutes of Nieszawa (1454), which introduced the parliamentary system in Poland. The meetings of provincial officials, which had been convoked in earlier periods to facilitate administration, developed in the fifteenth century into local dietines of all the nobles of the provinces. The statutes of 1454 sanctioned this new institution, giving the dietines the right to elect the provincial officials and stipulating that no mobilization of the general militia could be proclaimed without the consent of the dietines. Moreover, all nobles were exempted from paying duty for their products in the local markets. This privilege was extended in 1496, and nobles were dispensed from the payment of duty for exports or imports.

John Albrecht (1492-1501), one of the best Polish kings, a disciple of the humanist Callimachus, gave a further impulse to the development of Polish parliamentarianism. He favored the lower nobility and tried to rule with the help of their dietines. He also convoked Diets of Great and Little Poland, composed of representatives of the dietines, and finally also general Diets, composed of the representatives of the dietines and of the royal council, which was now called the Senate. The two chambers, however, deliberated separately.

At the beginning of the reign of Alexander I (1501-1506) the Senate made a bold attempt to concentrate all power in the kingdom in the hands of its members. The weak king yielded and issued the so-called Privilege of Mielnik in 1501, but the lower nobility reclaimed its share in the government. Finally, the Diet of Radom (1505) proclaimed a new constitution *Nihil novi,* which definitely sanctioned parliamentary institutions and transformed the Diet into a legislative body. The Senate—composed of magnates, high officials, and the higher clergy—which had hitherto possessed only a consultative voice, was also given a deliberative vote in legislative matters. In practice this vote was extended to all matters subject to the Diet and also included executive powers. From that time on, the king became more and more dependent on his higher officials, a fact which curtailed the royal power disastrously.

Unfortunately, the Constitution of Radom did not cancel the privilege of 1454 giving legislative powers to the dietines. The Diet, although a legislative body, was only the assembly of delegates of the dietines, which continued as independent legislative organs. The dangers inherent in this situation only became manifest toward the end of the sixteenth century when the nobility became increasingly conscious of the importance of its vote in the dietines. The dietines became a dominant factor in Poland during the seventeenth century, when political morality sank particularly low and the nobility was anxious to secure its privileges and material advantages without regard to the interests of the kingdom. The magnates were always able to secure votes for their proposals by exerting pressure on the poorer nobles, who depended on their protection and material support.

Another defect of Polish parliamentarianism was the principle that all decisions in the dietines and in the Diets had to be reached unanimously. During the sixteenth century this principle was practiced with moderation, the minority yielding to the majority and the protests of a few members being overlooked. In the seventeenth century the minority refused to yield, so that the activities of dietines and Diets were often completely blocked. After 1652, however, the practice that the vote of a single deputy could prevent corporate decisions of the assemblies became general. From that time on the principle of *liberum veto* was regarded as the greatest privilege of any member of the nobility, and this practice made the normal functioning of the Polish parliamentary system almost impossible.[4]

The decline of the royal power in Poland was also illustrated by the fact that all high officials, although originally officials of the court, became officials of the crown of Poland. Finally the Diet of Piotrków in 1504 declared the remaining dignitaries of the royal court to be deputies for the dignitaries of the crown. This was particularly the case with the royal treasurer (*thesaurarius regni*), who had to function instead of the treasurer of the crown when the latter was absent.

Soon, the royal income also, as distinct from the public income, came under the surveillance of the Diet. The king could not even dispose of the properties which were regarded as royal estates for the sustenance of the royal court without the consent of the Diet. The remaining royal properties were regarded as belonging to the state in order to provide for the salaries of the officials of the crown. The kings could dispose freely only of their private incomes.

The supreme command of the armies, a royal prerogative, was also restricted by the introduction at the end of the fifteenth century of the new military office of the hetman, who functioned as a minister of war. When, under Sigismund I (1506-1548), another post of "hetman of the camp" was created, the first hetman was called "grand hetman" (*hetman wielki*). As commander-in-chief of the army, he was almost more powerful than the king, and sometimes his authority also became dangerous to the Estates. Like the treasurer of the crown, he also was excluded from the Senate.

The supreme dignitaries—the grand marshal, the grand chancellor, the vice-chancellor, the grand treasurer, and the marshal of the court—were called ministers and had to take an oath of fidelity to the king and to the crown. They were responsible not only to the king, but also to the Diet. The king could only admonish them if they were lax in the execution of their duties.

The authority of the king became more and more illusory when the elective system was firmly established. The nobility forced the king on his election to sign special *pacta conventa*, which further diminished the royal authority and guaranteed all the privileges of the nobility. When Henry of Valois was elected in 1573, the nobles bound the king to finance the army and navy in case of war from his own private income. In the famous "articles of Henry" (*articuli Henriciani*), the right of the nobility to refuse obedience to Henry if the king would not fulfill all the conditions of the *pacta conventa* was also stressed. In these circumstances it was no wonder that Henry did not feel at home in Poland.

The right of refusing obedience to the king was further defined later, and at the beginning of the seventeenth century the cases in which obedience should be denied were specified. The archbishop of Gniezno, the senators, and then the Diet were first to admonish the king, and if he refused to revoke his ordinance, obedience should be denied him.

During the sixteenth century the magnates also succeeded in dominating the higher clerical positions with their rich incomes. Some of the financial privileges of the clergy were curtailed. In 1496 the Diet voted a law, sanctioned by Pope Julius II in 1505, reserving all higher ecclesiastical dignities to the members of the nobility. Only five canonries in the Polish chapters were reserved for commoners, graduates of universities. During the sixteenth century the Diets gradually extended this aristocratic privilege to all monasteries also. Only members of the nobility could become abbots.

The burghers, although admitted to the assemblies during the fifteenth century, were excluded from the Polish Diet. The cities, mostly founded by German colonists and enjoying an autonomous status under the Law of Magdeburg, had played an important role in Poland during the fourteenth century. Casimir the Great and Louis of Anjou favored them, hoping to find in their burghers a counterpoise to the magnates and nobles. Cracow was a member of the Hanseatic League, and its burghers, enriched by their commercial operations, often played the role of bankers to the court. The cities profited greatly from the commerce between East and West and between Poland, Hungary, and the Black Sea.

An important role was played in these commercial activities, especially in the transactions with the East, by the Armenians. In the eleventh century, after the invasion of the Seljuk Turks had ruined their kingdom, the Armenians migrated in large numbers to Trebizond in Asia Minor, to Moldavia, and to the Crimea, and on the invitation of the Grand Prince Dmitrij of Galicia, many of them settled in that country (in 1062). When Galicia came under Polish suzerainty, Casimir confirmed to the Armenians, most of whom were settled in Lwów, the autonomous status granted them by Dmitrij. He also confirmed their own bishopric in 1367, which later became an archbishopric and continued to exist down to our own days.[5] The Armenians lived mostly in the cities of Galicia, but also spread to other Polish cities.

This situation, however, changed in the fifteenth century. The Ottoman conquest of the Danubian lands, of the Genoese colony of Caffa in the Crimea, and of the seaports on the Black Sea stopped the commercial traffic between East and West. The city of Lwów was particularly affected by this loss. All the commercial activity which still remained was concentrated in the Baltic cities, especially Gdańsk (Danzig). Commercial transactions in the interior also suffered a setback. This took place at the time when the magnates and the lower nobility were increasing their privileges and when Polish parliamentarianism was being born. Thus it happened that the burghers were not recognized as an Estate, and their representatives were not admitted to the Diets. Only two representatives of Cracow were entitled to be present at the debates, and they had no right to vote. King John Albrecht and Alexander I tried in vain to remedy this situation, and so the Polish kings lost forever the opportunity of finding in the burghers allies against the nobles.

On the other hand, when the nobles had succeeded in reducing the royal authority to a cipher and had secured control over political and social life in Poland, the cities were deprived of any support they might have expected from the kings and were completely at the mercy of the nobility. The freedom from customs duties accorded to the nobles for the import and export of goods was another blow which undermined the commercial activity of the cities. Soon the nobility began to intervene directly in the economic life of the cities. The guilds of artisans lost their right to fix sale prices for their products. The Diets gave this right to their representatives in different counties or to the *starostas,* who often had no idea of the cost of production and fixed arbitrary prices; all this ruined the formerly flourishing organization of the artisans. The burghers were also forbidden to own land, and the nobles to exercise any occupation of a burgher. Soon the cities lost their administrative autonomy and came under the control of the voivodes and the *starostas.* All this contributed to the final ruin of the cities. At the end of the fifteenth and the beginning of the sixteenth centuries, the number of burghers in the cities had diminished considerably. Although during the sixteenth century all burghers were completely polonized, the cities—contrary to what had happened in Bohemia—did not play any marked role in Poland and in Polish national life before the nineteenth century.

The economic transformation in the West soon had a ruinous effect on the situation of the Polish peasantry. King Casimir had already been forced to protect the peasants from exploitation by their lords. He particularly favored the extension of the "German law," given to the German colonists with a limited administrative autonomy, to villages with a native Polish population. When, however, in the fifteenth and sixteenth centuries the export of agricultural products to the West through the port of Gdańsk (Danzig) had reached unprecedented proportions and the prices of grain and meat had increased, the Polish nobles extended their arable land, forming extensive domains. For the cultivation of these new arable lands they needed the work of their peasants. Soon the Diets began gradually to limit the personal freedom of the peasants, and in 1532 the peasants were completely attached to the glebe and only allowed to change their residence with the permission of their lords. The autonomous status of the villages was also gradually limited and disappeared completely after 1518. The lords obtained unlimited jurisdiction over their peasants, and the remnants of the formerly independent burgomasters became mere executives of the orders of the lords. Only the peasants settled on lands belonging to the king or to the Church retained the right of appeal to a higher instance.

Naturally, the *corvée* was introduced and was definitely regulated in 1520. Nominally the peasant was bound to work on his lord's lands at least one day in the week, but in reality, in most cases the *corvée* was extended to several days in a week, especially on the estates of the magnates.

After Casimir's statutes,[6] another attempt at the codification of Polish law was made in 1488. But only the statutes of three Diets, those of Warta, Nieszawa, and Korczyn, were added to the Statutes of Casimir in this code. Therefore, the Diet of Radom entrusted John Łaski with the task of reassembling all the ancient laws, privileges, and statutes of the Polish kingdom. This codification was terminated in 1506, and the whole collection was called the Statute of Łaski. Some texts of German law are to be found in this code, besides documents of Polish law. The decisions of Polish Diets, published gradually, completed the Statute of Łaski.

In 1523 there was published also a handbook of Polish juridical procedure, called *Formula processus*, which was adopted by the whole land. Another similar handbook, embracing Polish public and private law and called *Correctura of Taszycki* after the principal of its six compilers, was, however, rejected by the Diet in 1534.

Mazovia, which was only united with Poland in 1526, had its own customs and laws. Their codification was completed in 1540 and called *Statuta ducatus Mazoviae*. These special statutes were in force in Mazovia even after its reunion with Poland. But, from 1576 on, the Polish code began to be adopted in Mazovia also; it was completed by some special dispositions which differed from those of Polish law and were valid only in the Dukedom of Mazovia.[7]

Prior to the dynastic union in 1385, the political organization of Lithuania was quite different from that of Poland. Lithuania was less homogeneous and less centralized than Poland. Its center was Lithuania proper, to which some neighboring Russian principalities had been annexed—Polesie, Black Russia (Grodno-Novogrodek), and parts of Belo-Russia on the rivers Berezina, middle Dnieper, and upper Pripet. This territory was divided into the two palatinates of Vilna and of Troki, having its own central administration and judicial system and its own Lithuanian law, based on the old Russian customs from the Kievan period. This part of the state was the most populous, and most of the old Lithuanian nobility owned lands there.

The immediate neighbors of Lithuania proper were some appanages of Russian princes—Pinsk, Kleč, Horodec, Kobrin. The Lithuanian province of Samogitia and the other former Russian principalities—Polock, Vitebsk, Smolensk, Kiev, Volhynia, Podlasie, and Podolia—retained the local laws and privileges which they had enjoyed before coming under Lithuanian supremacy.

Every new grand duke of Lithuania confirmed these privileges and promised not to submit the native population of the Russian provinces to the jurisdiction of any foreign, i.e., Lithuanian, court. Because of this particular aspect of the relations between Lithuania proper and the former Russian principalities, some specialists call the Lithuanian-Russian state a federal state.[8]

The Russian administration, legislation, and offices established in the Kievan period were also introduced by the Lithuanian rulers into Lithuania proper, the Old Slavonic language in its West Russian form became the official language of the whole of Lithuania,[9] and at the end of the fourteenth century nine-tenths of the population of Lithuania spoke Russian.

This process of the russification of Lithuania was, of course, slowed down as a result of the Union of Krewo, concluded in 1386. Such a situation, however, revealed that it would not be easy to make this union a reality. Although according to the Krewo agreements Lithuania-Russia was to be incorporated in Poland, the opposition of the Lithuanian nobility prevented not only incorporation but even a real union with Poland.[10] Jagiello had to give way to the Lithuanians and appoint his cousin Vitold grand duke. The latter extended Lithuanian domination to the coast of the Black Sea and even cherished the idea of transforming the grand duchy into a kingdom. He strengthened the grand ducal power considerably by abolishing all appanages and replacing the princes by governors, although he left the extent and the privileges of the former principalities untouched.

But even the new union proclaimed at Vilna in 1401 by Vitold and Jagiello did not change the status of Lithuania. The Union of Horodło in 1413 confirmed Lithuania's right to have its own grand duke, who should be appointed by the Polish king with the consent of Polish senators and Lithuanian boyars. Sigismund was, however, proclaimed grand duke by the boyars, and a new union of 1432-1434 confirmed him in the dignity. In spite of these unions, renewed in 1439-1440, 1499, and 1501, the Lithuanians regarded their state as equal to Poland and independent although the grand ducal dignity was reserved to a Polish king, or to his son, of the Jagiellonian dynasty.

In spite of this sentiment of independence in Lithuania, Polish customs, political institutions, and language penetrated Lithuania increasingly. The Lithuanian magnates were more attracted by the Catholic faith and Western culture, represented by the Poles, than by the old Kievan civilization and the Orthodox Christianity to which many of them had previously adhered. In the fifteenth and sixteenth centuries Lithuanian cities followed the example of the Polish burghers in accepting the Law of Magdeburg, while feudal institutions were introduced under influences emanating from the state of the Teutonic Order and from Poland, binding the population to military service in return for lands granted to them by the sovereign.

The first important step in this process of assimilation was made at the Union of Horodło in 1413. This enabled Polish social institutions to take firm root in Lithuania proper. Forty-seven Polish noble families adopted an equal number of Lithuanian boyars and granted them the use of their own coats of arms. This privilege was granted only to Catholic boyars, but the latter were allowed, in 1434, to grant the use of their escutchons to Orthodox boyars also, with the consent of the Polish nobles. This privilege was of importance because it opened the way for the new nobles to important offices of state and dignities, granted them complete freedom in handling their property, and brought them closer to the status of the Polish nobility, which was coming to enjoy an exceptionally privileged position.

The complete assimilation of the boyars in the former Russian principalities was, however, not easy. There were many classes of nobles and boyars in the former Kievan principalities, and social life had retained a more democratic and patriarchal form. The princes still enjoyed their dominating position in the former principalities, but there were many differences in the position of the boyars. Some of them were also princes, but under the supremacy of the more powerful princes; some were independent boyars; and others were boyars dependent on princes or on other boyars.

It was natural that the Lithuanian and Russian princes, mostly descendants of the dynasties of Gedymin and of Rurik, should be the first to profit by the privileges granted in 1413 and 1434. Thus they were able to retain most of the important offices in the land, in the grand ducal council, and later in the Diets. They formed the dominant class, exercising great influence in the social and economic life of the state. Some of these families are well known in Lithuanian and Polish history, for example, the princes of Ostrog, the Czartoryskis, Glinskis, Sapiehas, and Radziwills.

The members of the higher nobility also laid hands on the new offices which were introduced on the Polish model into the Lithuanian-Russian state during the fifteenth and sixteenth centuries. Such were the offices of the marshal; of the chancellor, who was minister of the interior and of foreign affairs, with the registrar as head of his chancery and in charge of diplomatic correspondence; of the vice-chancellor; of the chief accountant (*podskarbnik*); of the grand hetman, who was supreme commander and became minister of war only before the conclusion of the Union of Lublin; and of the hetman of the camp.

After the disappearance of the appanages, the old Kievan administration was gradually assimilated to the Polish model. The old Russian functions were replaced by those of *palatini, starostas,* voivodes and castellans. The judicial system was also adapted to the Polish system, so that at the time of the conclusion of the Union of Lublin in 1569, there was not much difference between the administrative and judicial systems in force in Lithuania and in Poland.

The composition and functions of the old council of the grand duke, which originally resembled the Muscovite duma, were also gradually changed in accordance with the Polish example. It was originally composed of the princes related to the reigning grand duke and of the boyars charged with the government of the provinces. The number of councilors grew to include the four Roman Catholic bishops, all princes occupying high offices in the state or at court, and also some other princes. The council was originally a consultative and advisory body, but its importance grew, under Polish influence, and it became a central administrative, judicial, and legislative organ. In 1492 the council obtained a most important privilege, which was to transform Lithuania into an aristocratic and oligarchic monarchy. According to this decree, which was confirmed in 1506 and derived its inspiration from similar Polish decrees, no decision of the grand duke could be promulgated without the participation and consent of the council. This privilege guaranteed to the princes a position superior to that of the ordinary boyars.

The Russian lands had their own assemblies both before and after their incorporation in Lithuania. Their *sejms,* or *sojms,* were originally assemblies of the grand dukes and princes holding appanages, or assemblies of the council of the princes. There were also Diets of different provinces which were called *večes* (later *zbor*), following the usage in Kievan principalities.[11] These *večes,* however, included not only the nobles, but representatives of all the Estates. They functioned down to the second half of the sixteenth century. At that period, again under Polish influence, the nobility started to exclude all other Estates from the *večes.* In this way dietines were introduced into Lithuania-Russia, and during the sixteenth century Diets were also convoked by the grand dukes in Grodno, Minsk, or Vilna. The council became the senate, and the boyars formed the lower chamber. From 1544 on, the boyars obtained increasing privileges which made their position more analogous to that of the Polish nobles. But it was only in 1563 that Sigismund II (1548-1572) granted to Orthodox boyars complete equality with Catholics, thus enabling them to occupy high offices of state and to be members of the council.

The great nobles, however, opposed the complete equalization of the Lithuanian nobility on the Polish model. So, while the boyars realized that they could only achieve this equality if Lithuania were united with Poland, the higher nobility, defending its privileged position, opposed the idea of union. A more serious step toward this goal could only be undertaken after the death of the leader of the princes, Nicholas Radziwill, called the Black, in 1565. As mentioned before,[12] the disastrous wars with Moscow forced the Lithuanians to envisage the idea of union with more favor. In the same year the Diet of Vilna voted a new statute for Lithuania, dividing the country into provinces (*powiat*), comprising six palatinates, on the Polish model, with the full Polish administrative system, and extending the privileges of the lesser nobility.

The Union of Lublin was signed by the Lithuanians in July 1569.[13] But although the two states were united with a common ruler, the Polish king, and a common Diet, and the state was later called *Rzeczpospolita polska* (Polish Republic), a true union could not be achieved. None of the three nations—Poles, Lithuanians, and Russians—which had concluded it was satisfied with the union. The old Lithuanian sentiment of independence soon manifested itself. The Lithuanian Diets continued to function, and in 1588 a new statute was promulgated introducing several institutions which were not in accord with the spirit of the union. The Union of Lublin is not even mentioned in the statute, and the Grand Duchy of Lithuania is still regarded as an individual political unit.

This statute also concluded the codification of Lithuanian legislation. The first attempt at such a codification was made by Casimir IV (1440-1492) in 1468. Casimir's *Sudebnik* was superseded by the so-called First Statute of Lithuania, approved in 1528-1529 by the Diet of Vilna. This was followed in 1566 by a new edition, called the Second Statute. All three editions of the statute are based on the old Russian law which was effective in the Russian principalities. Of course, in each edition the influence of Polish law became more evident. It is interesting to notice that although in the Polish codification the influence of Roman law is hardly traceable, in the Second (1566) and Third (1588) Lithuanian Statutes the influence of Roman, as of German, law can easily be discerned. This statute was written in Russian and also became an important source for the codification of Muscovite law, the famous *Uloženie* of Tsar Alexis.[14]

In spite of this Lithuanian particularism Polish influences continued to penetrate not only into Lithuania proper, but also into the former South and West Russian principalities. As the privileged position of the nobility grew stronger, so that of the peasants deteriorated, as it had in Poland. Some old Russian noble families in Lithuania proper were soon polonized, and the use of the Polish language in Lithuanian Diets and dietines increased steadily. In 1696 it was decided that all official documents in the administration and judicial procedure of the grand duchy should be composed in Polish.

The westernization of old Russian institutions and the polonization of cultural life was, of course, most effective in Galicia, which had been under Polish supremacy since the time of Casimir III the Great (1333-1370).

Although Casimir left the autonomous status of the country untouched and promised to respect its religious and national traditions, Polish influences were bound to be felt in Galicia to an increasing degree. The kings granted lands in this fertile country to Polish nobles, and their numbers soon increased to such an extent that they occupied the chief offices of state. This fostered the spread of the Western feudal system in Galicia, and Latin gradually replaced Old Slavonic in official documents. This evolution reached a climax in the fifteenth century when Latin became the official language of the Galician Diets and courts. In 1433 the Roman Catholic nobility in Galicia obtained the same privileges as the Polish nobility, and two years later the country was divided into three administrative provinces. This was practically the end of the autonomous status of Galicia. In the sixteenth century the Polish language began slowly to replace Latin in official use.

The westernization of Galicia also became apparent in religion. Roman Catholicism naturally spread with the influx of Polish noble families and with the growth of the Polish element in the new cities. Catholic monastic orders had already found a sympathetic reception during the reign of Galician princes. The number of Catholic monasteries increased with the growth of the Catholic population owing to the steady influx of colonists, and in 1375 a Roman Catholic archbishopric was founded for Galicia and the Catholic hierarchy was reorganized.

The Orthodox Church was, of course, left its freedom in spite of some high-handed action on the part of the kings. In 1303 an unsuccessful attempt was made to secure the independence of the Galician Orthodox Church from the Kievan metropolis. The Patriarch and the Emperor of Constantinople had to yield, however, in 1370 and permit the establishment of a Galician Orthodox metropolitan in face of the alternative that the Orthodox bishops would be placed under Rome.[15]

A similar situation developed in the former Kievan principalities which were attached to Poland in 1569 by the Union of Lublin. Although they were granted an equal status with the Polish lands and an autonomous regime, the Polish language nevertheless came to replace Latin and South Russian (Ukrainian) in most official acts by the end of the sixteenth century. The situation worsened for the South Russian element when the Polish kings began to grant vast territories in South Russian lands to Polish nobles, profiting by the stipulation of the Union of Lublin which opened the former Lithuanian state to the Poles. With the Polish nobles, Polish peasants also started to settle in considerable numbers in the principality of Kiev, in Volhynia, and Podolia.

The main obstacle to a more profound assimilation of the Russian lands by Poland lay in the religious differences between the two nations. The West and South Russians, who were soon to be called Belo-Russians and Ukrainians, were Orthodox, and their faith formed an important link uniting them with the eastern Russians under Moscow. Profiting by the apparent decadence of the Orthodox Church in these territories, Polish ecclesiastical circles, supported by the government and by some Ukrainian prelates, worked for the union of the Orthodox in the Polish commonwealth with the Roman Catholics. After prolonged negotiations the union was proclaimed in 1596 at Brest Litovsk and at first encountered widespread acceptance among the Orthodox hierarchy.

At the same time Polish Roman Catholic institutions were favored by the ruling class. Latin bishoprics were founded in Kiev and other towns, and Latin orders founded monasteries, convents, and schools among the Orthodox population. All this was interpreted by the Russian population as an attempt to Latinize both the Uniats and the Orthodox.

In reality, many South Russian noble families were polonized and became Roman Catholics, but a reaction soon set in among the middle classes. National feeling rose higher and also reached Galicia, the part of the old Kievan Russia which had been longest exposed to Polish influences. The haughty treatment of the Uniats by the Latin hierarchy and the exclusion of the Uniat bishops from the Senate spoiled Polish chances of promoting a more solid union of the two nations.[16] The Orthodox nobility defended the rights of its Church courageously in the Polish parliament, and the Orthodox middle classes stiffened in their opposition to the Catholics. The leaders of the Orthodox West and South Russians in Poland and Lithuania turned increasingly toward the Orthodox tsar of Moscow as the protector of Orthodoxy. All this prepared the ground for the popular insurrection against Poland which was finally to lead to the separation of southern Russia from the Rzeczpospolita and its union with Moscow.

This development in the southern and western Russian lands was, on the other hand, of incalculable importance for the further history of the whole of Russia.

The split between the East, South, and West Russian lands was becoming more and more apparent. Westernization was bringing many cultural advantages to the West and South Russians, but it separated them increasingly from their Eastern brethren, who lived under very different conditions. The century-long symbiosis of the South and West Russians with Lithuania and Poland certainly helped to accentuate the linguistic differentiation between the Russian East, West, and South, which became more evident in the sixteenth and seventeenth centuries. It is legitimate to affirm that without this long separation of South Russia and West Russia from East Russia and their long symbiosis with the Lithuanians and Poles, which left such deep marks on their political and cultural life, there would most probably not have been a Ukrainian (South Russian) or a Belo-Russian (West Russian) nation.

On the other hand, the steady westernization going on in the Russian lands under Polish and Lithuanian rule was causing many Russians to become increasingly suspicious and hostile toward everything coming from western Europe. The higher civilization of which the West boasted, and which it offered with the condescension of a "nouveau riche" to its poorer neighbors, the Orthodox Russians, created in the East Russian mind a kind of inferiority complex, which led it to cling all the more passionately to the inherited forms of Orthodox Christianity as if it were the only true realization of Christ's doctrine, the only true religion, to which the rest of the world was to be converted.

Political and social development in Hungary was similar to that in Poland. During his long reign from 1387 to 1437, Sigismund was more interested in the affairs of the Empire and of Bohemia than of Hungary. So the kingdom was slowly transformed from the strong monarchic form renovated by the Angevin kings into a state with an aristocratic regime. Sigismund had to confirm all the privileges granted to the nobility by his predecessors. He also had to promise to convoke each year a Diet composed not only of the magnates and the higher clergy, but also of representatives of the lower nobility elected in the dietines of the counties (comitats) into which the country was divided. The principal cities were also represented, but received only one vote together.

The royal offices in the provinces became offices of the land as in Bohemia and Poland, and the nobility with its dietines soon brought all administrative and judicial power in the counties into its own hands. The nobility claimed more and more privileges and slowly transferred the burden of military costs and service on to its subjects. The high offices, of which that of the palatine was still the most important, were all in the hands of the magnates. The situation of the peasants worsened, and although Sigismund confirmed their right of free movement in 1405, the nobility was constantly denying it and attaching the peasants more and more closely to the glebe. The maltreatment of the peasantry provoked some insurgent movements, which were, however, mercilessly suppressed by the nobility.

The election of Albert of Austria, king of Bohemia, to the Hungarian throne in 1437 gave the nobility a new opportunity to demand further privileges and to diminish the royal authority. The king had to transform the office of the palatine into an office of the country and give the nobility the right to participate in the election of the palatine. He also had to promise to guarantee the defense of the kingdom out of his own resources.

In the struggle for the Hungarian throne of Albert's widow Elizabeth, who defended the rights of her posthumous son Ladislas against the election of the Jagiellonian Władysław, the greater part of modern Slovakia was occupied by Czech troops under the command of the Utraquist John Jiskra of Brandýs, who championed the rights of Ladislas. Elizabeth was also supported by some influential Croatian magnates, especially the Frankopani, and by George Branković, the Serbian despot, who had been granted large estates in southern Hungary. The struggle for the throne, of course, again increased the influence of the magnates in the kingdom.

This was illustrated by the fact that after the tragic death of Władysław at Varna (1444), and during the minority of Ladislas Posthumus, the government of the whole country came into the hands of a few magnates. Although elected by the Diet (1445) as governors, they regarded the parts of the state entrusted to them as their fiefs, not caring at all for the interests of the kingdom.

The dismemberment of the kingdom was prevented by the election as governor of John Hunyadi,[17] who defended the country not only against the Turkish invaders but also against the usurpations of the magnates. During the reign of his son Matthias (1458-1490) the royal power acquired a new prestige. The energetic king made a bold attempt to transform Hungary into an absolute monarchy. He reformed the office of the palatine, transforming the supreme officer into a representative of the king and regent during an interregnum, strengthened the royal authority in the administration and in judicial procedure, and even made an attempt to codify Hungarian law in a monarchic spirit.

All his reforms were, however, rejected by the magnates after his death, and the new king Vladislav II (1490-1516) had to promise never to introduce reforms "as did King Matthias." The reign of this weakling was filled with the struggles of the lesser nobility with the magnates for the government. The lesser nobility succeeded in securing more influence in the Diets and in the royal council. This was transformed from an advisory organ into a supreme constitutional factor, which formed a kind of committee of the Diet, as in Poland. The lesser nobility also won more rights in the counties and obtained the right to elect the vice-župan, who became an officer of the county. Magnates and prelates were also subjected to the judges of the counties.

In 1514, after the defeat of a new insurrection of the peasantry, the nobility obtained the suppression of the last vestiges of freedom for the peasants. They were made subject to the administrative and judicial authority of their lords and were bound to carry out the *corvée* and to pay their lords for the land they cultivated. All these privileges were codified in the *Opus tripartitum*, composed by Werboczy and presented to the Diet in the same year. The royal power was further curtailed in that the king was bound to reign with the help of the "nation"—the higher and lesser nobility. The "nation" was declared to be a part of the ideal unity symbolized by the holy crown of St. Stephen. It obtained the confirmation of all its privileges and also the right of resisting the king if he should try to curtail these.

Although the *Opus tripartitum* was not approved by the king and was not favored by the magnates, it was used as an official lawbook in Hungary down to the year 1848. The misrule of the nobility continued during the reign of Louis II (1516-1526) and brought about the catastrophe of Mohács, followed by the occupation of Hungary by the Turks.

The Slovak nobility shared with its Magyar colleagues in the growth of the influence of the privileged classes in the land. National bias does not yet seem to have made its appearance in Hungary, and the Slavic tongue was not only spoken freely in the kingdom but, under the Jagiellonians, was even used in the Hungarian Diet. It was during the fifteenth century that the cultural relationship of the Slovaks and the Czechs was at its closest.

This was due to the influence of the University of Prague and to the Czech troops defending Upper Hungary during the minority of King Ladislas Posthumus against John Hunyadi, who had been elected administrator of the kingdom by the Hungarian nobility.[18]

The political and national life of the Croats suffered greatly under the impact of the Turkish advance. The Venetians had coveted Dalmatia for generations, ever since they had captured Zara in 1203 with the help of the crusaders. Success came at last in 1420, when almost the whole of Dalmatia fell into Venetian hands, and the conquest was consolidated in 1444. In order to assert the fact that the kings of Hungary and Croatia had not renounced their rights in Dalmatia, Vladislav II (1490-1516) took the title of "King of Dalmatia, Croatia, and Slavonia," but otherwise nothing was achieved for the reconquest of the lost province.

The Turkish advance after the battle of Mohács (1526) further diminished the territory of the former Croatian national kingdom. The whole of southern Croatia became Turkish, and the Venetians lost eight cities. The peace of 1540 guaranteed to the Venetians only the possession of the Dalmatian maritime towns, the interior becoming a Turkish province governed by a sanjakbeg in the city of Clissa. This led to a mass migration of the Slavic population from Turkish Dalmatia into the cities, which thus lost their Latin character.

In order to strengthen the defense of what was left of Croatia, Ferdinand I (1527-1564) erected a military zone near the Turkish frontier which was later divided into two parts, the *krajina* of Slavonia and the *krajina* of Croatia. The military zone was exempt from the jurisdiction of the ban and Diet of Croatia and was governed by generals appointed by the emperor. This curtailment of Croat sovereignty over a part of the kindom's territory was but poorly recompensed by the union of what was left of Slavonia and Croatia under one ban and one Diet.

The Venetians did not exploit their naval victory at Lepanto (1571), in which a Dalmatian squadron participated, to extend their possessions in Dalmatia. Free Croatia suffered yet further losses, and when Rudolf II (1576-1612) concluded peace with the Turks in 1606, only the western part of the country remained in his hands.

Dissatisfaction with the policy of the Habsburgs, which aimed at depriving Hungary and Crotia of their autonomous status and transforming them into Austrian provinces, manifested itself increasingly in Croatia under Ferdinand III (1637-1657) after the peace of Westphalia (1648). Finally, angered by the refusal of Leopold I (1658-1705) to exploit the victory won over the Turks in 1664, the Croatian nobility decided to end the Habsburg regime in Croatia. Their leaders, Peter Zrinski and Krsto Frankopan, started negotiations with France, Venice, Poland, and Turkey, but the plot was discovered and both leaders were decapitated in 1671.

The Venetians were also successful in their new conflict with the Turks (1645-1664), but it was only after the defeat of the Turks at Vienna (1683) that a great part of Hungary and Croatia could be freed. The peace of Karlovci (Karlstadt, Karlowitz) in 1699 restored the whole of Dalmatia to Venice, including the coast of Hercegovina. But the Emperor Leopold I added the conquered lands in Slavonia and Croatia to the military frontier zone, much to the disappointment of the Croats, who saw in this a new curtailment of their autonomy and of the rights of their kingdom.

The Republic of Dubrovnik (Ragusa) had severed its relationship with Hungary after 1526 and ceased paying tribute to the Emperor Ferdinand I as king of Hungary. A new relationship with Hungary was initiated after the victory of the imperial army over the Turks in 1664 in the hope that Leopold I would continue his campaign and liberate Bosnia and Hercegovina. In that event Dubrovnik could have freed itself from vassalage to the sultans. In this, however, the Ragusans were as disappointed as the Croats by the emperor's failure to exploit his victory and by his conclusion of peace with the Turks.

Although as a vassal of the sultans the Republic had to render useful services in order to preserve its independence, the Ragusans sympathized with the Christians in their conflicts with Turkey. So although recognized as neutrals even by the Christian allies, the Ragusans secretly sent them a squadron of transport ships before the battle of Lepanto.

The territory of the Republic of Dubrovnik obtained a new guarantee of its independence by the treaty of Karlovci. This was important for the city-republic because it was coveted by Venice. Profiting by the disastrous situation of Dubrovnik after the earthquake of 1667 had ruined the city and buried a large part of the inhabitants inthe ruins, the Venetians attempted to occupy the port of Gruž (Gravosa).

In spite of this terrible catastrophe the courage of its new leader, the patrician Nicholas Bona, enabled the city to rise afresh from the ruins. Its prosperity was not as remarkable as in the fourteenth and fifteenth centuries. It could not vie with Spain, Portugal, Holland, and England, whose merchant fleets dominated the oceans,[19] but its trading vessels still plied busily in the Mediterranean and were often seen in Istanbul, Greece, Egypt, Tunisia, and Morocco.

Dubrovnik gained a new prosperity in the eighteenth century, and its commerce flourished especially during the Napoleonic wars. One of the most prominent mathematicians, astronomers and philosophers of the eighteenth century—Ruder Bošković (1711-1787)—was a native of Dubrovnik. The republic's independence was, however, ended in 1808, when Napoleon incorporated it in the Illyrian Province under General Marmont, whom the emperor created duke of Ragusa. In 1814, it became an Austrian possession.

The political and social position of the Serbians and Bulgarians under the Turkish domination was determined primarily by the political and social organization of the Ottoman Empire. There was very little in the Ottoman national life which was comparable with that of the western states or of the Balkan states prior to their conquest by the Turks. The Ottoman state was founded on the absolute power of the ruler, the sultan. This was a principle which was unanimously recognized by all his subjects. His absolute power was only limited by the prescriptions of the Islamic religion, which also provided a firm framework in which the moral obligations and the rights and duties of the sultan and of his subjects were definitively regulated. In spite of that, the Ottomans showed respect for the rights of foreigners and left them intact provided they did not contradict the Islamic prescriptions.[20]

Moreover, the Ottoman Empire was a strong military state and differed, in this respect, from western political units. The military spirit permeated everything, even the administrative system. The Turks did not have any noble class as it had developed in the West. The sultan could promote anybody to any high office, and hereditary succession to a dignity or office was rather exceptional.

Another special feature of the state organization in the Ottoman Empire was that it opened the administrative offices of state to subjects of non-Turkish race who had accepted the faith of Islam. So it often happened that almost the whole administrative apparatus was in the hands of renegades from the subject Christian nations. Only theological and judicial careers seem to have been closed to the renegades.

A special feature of this practice was the formation of the corps of Janissaries, the kernel of the Ottoman army and the bodyguard of the sultan. This consisted of young Christian boys, who were educated in the Islamic religion and in a strict military discipline. It was a form of blood tax (*devşirme*).

Another characteristic feature of the Ottoman state organization was its administrative system. The conquered lands were divided into administrative units called *sanjaks* (originally meaning a "flag," later a "regiment") under a *sanjakbeg*. A number of sanjaks formed a *vilayet* under a *beglerbeg* (governor). The begs and beglerbegs were both military commanders and civil administrators completely dependent on the sultan, who could transfer and depose them at will. Only the judges were, in principle, independent of the begs.

Only one thing could bear comparison with Western feudalism—the *spahilik,* or special Turkish agrarian system. The Ottomans were most probably inspired in this respect by the military organization introduced into Asia Minor by Byzantium in order to strengthen the imperial army. Every Turk was bound to perform military service. But as it was impossible to pay the whole standing army directly from the sultan's treasury, as was the case with the Janissaries, all conquered land was divided into smaller or larger units, which were granted to the *spahis,* the Turkish cavalry soldiers. These were paid by the tribute in money and natural products levied on the Christian peasants.

In spite of the similarity of this system to Western feudal practice, the spahis did not form a Turkish nobility in the Western sense of the word.

They were not the proprietors of the land granted to them, and although it was usually granted afresh to their sons, the land was not originally heritable in the family. The spahis could be transferred into another sanjak or deprived of their tenure if they were not able to do military service or if they acted contrary to the pleasure of the sultan. According to the extent of their grants (*timar* or *ziâmet*) they had to appear when summoned, either alone or with one or several soldiers. They were also charged with policing the peasants on their lands, but had no judicial jurisdiction over them. Similar fiefs appertained to certain offices, but the largest formed the sultan's private property.

The Christian subjects, mostly peasants, who were called *raja*, had also to pay a head tax to the state. Sometimes they were obliged to work on the construction of bridges or roads, but the *corvée* only appeared at a later period and was regarded as illegally enforced. The lands of the peasants were granted to them by the sultan—regarded as the representative of God, who was the master and rightful owner of the universe—by a hereditary lease. The peasant could, however, sell, exchange, sublet, or donate his land with the permission of the spahi, which could be obtained for a small payment. The peasant could even call his spahi before the tribunal of a judge (*kadi*) if he thought that he was being maltreated by his master. The peasants elected their own burgomasters (*knes*), who directed the affairs of the villagers.

There also existed, especially in Bulgaria, some privileged villages whose inhabitants were dispensed from taxes in return for special services which were expected from them, for example, the guarding of important passes, bridges, or fords; mining; and other obligations.

There were also auxiliary troops recruited from the Christian Slavic population (*vojniki*). After the occupation of Hungary by the Turks, many Serbians, although Christians, served with the *martoloses,* or mercenaries, who garrisoned its conquered cities. They were particularly numerous about the middle of the sixteenth century.

As the Janissaries were mostly recruited from the Slavic lands, the Slavic tongue became the second language in these elite troops. Most of the renegades who served in the administration of the Empire were also of Slavic origin. Some of them reached very high positions at the court. So it came about that the Slavic language, especially Serbian, was often used in the Turkish diplomatic service, and many diplomatic documents were composed in Slavic and written in Cyrillic letters.

When all this is borne in mind, one is forced to conclude that the material situation of the Christian population in the Ottoman Empire was not as bad as might be thought, at least during the first period of Turkish rule. For all that, the Serbians and the Bulgarians experienced deep changes in their social and national life during the Turkish occupation of their countries. The first important change was a complete leveling of their social hierarchy. The Ottoman Turks, who were so anxious not to allow any politically influential aristocracy to arise in their own ranks, although Turkish dynasts did in fact exist, could not tolerate among their subject peoples the further existence of their former leading families. All members of the reigning and noble families were exterminated. Only in Bosnia could the old nobility survive because the Bogomil sectarians accepted the faith of the Prophet. In Albania the nobility also managed to survive, for the same reason. The Serbians and the Bulgarians became nations of peasants, the more so as in the cities which flourish under Ottoman rule, the Turks predominated and commerce was mostly in the hands of non-Slavic, often foreign elements, Italians, Ragusans, Jews, and Levantines.

Without their political leaders the Slavs were completely isolated from the rest of the world, unaware of the social and cultural progress which the Western world was making. Left without the possibility of raising their cultural level, they clung to their old religious and national traditions, sometimes reviving ancient customs, which were almost forgotten. They were also nations of small farmers, as all the large estates had been confiscated and the Ottoman agrarian policy did not favor large landholdings among its Christian subjects.

Deprived of their political leaders, the Balkan Slavs could look only to their Churches for moral support and guidance. Fortunately, as the Ottomans had founded all their own political and juridical life on the principles of their religion, they were ready to accord to the Churches of their raja the main directive role in their social and juridical life. The priests were regarded as natural leaders of the faithful, and their intermediary role between the state and its Christian subjects was readily acknowledged. The bishops and priests acted as judges of their faithful, and canon law was regarded as the lawbook of the Christians.

So it happened that the Ottoman Empire granted to the Church more influence over the life of the faithful than it had ever enjoyed before. The position of the Church, however, underwent two unfortunate setbacks. First, the churches lost almost all their possessions, which were generally given as endowments to the mosques. The priests were also touched by the leveling of the non-Moslem population. The priests had to take up an occupation in order to live, and most of them cultivated the land like their parishioners. This brought them nearer to their people, but on the other hand, most of their time had to be devoted to nonsacerdotal occupations. Moreover, the education of the clergy suffered heavily.

There were no schools for the laity or even for the clergy, who had to learn the essentials for the celebration of the liturgy from their fathers or from other priests. Of course, the religious instruction of the people was almost nonexistent, only the traditional forms of worship being strictly observed.[21]

The Serbians were fortunate in having their patriarchate re-established. This was due to a Serbian renegade Mehmed Pasha Sokolović (1508-1579), the son of a Serbian priest, who had attained to the highest office at the sultan's court, that of grand vizier. He seems to have kept in touch with his family, and his elder brother Makarij, abbot of the Chilandari monastery at Mount Athos, appears to have visited him several times in Istanbul. Probably at the request of Makarij, supported by the grand vizier, Suleiman the Magnificent re-established in 1557 the Serbian patriarchate, which had been suppressed in 1459. Makarij became the first patriarch and set up his see at Peć (Ipek).[22] All territories inhabited by the Serbians became subject to the patriarchate, which became an important national institution.

The re-establishment of the patriarchate was the more fortunate as the situation of the Christian population of the Ottoman Empire soon afterward deteriorated considerably. Mehmed Sokolović, who had given faithful service to three sultans as grand vizier—Suleiman the Magnificent (1520-1560), Selim II (1566-1574), and Murad III (1574-1595)—and had succeeded for many years in stopping abuses from creeping into the Ottoman administration, was murdered in 1579. This opened the way for corruption and misrule throughout the political, social, and juridical life of the Empire. Offices became venal, available to the highest bidders; the strict discipline which had characterized Ottoman political life and was the basis of its military strength was sapped by the luxurious life of the ruling class; the authority of the sultan gradually lost ground.

Naturally it was the raja who suffered most under these conditions. They were exploited by the spahis, by the begs and beglerbegs; they could not pay the high taxes and could not find justice in the Ottoman courts. Slowly the peasants became virtual serfs attached to the glebe.

Exasperated by especially cruel acts of maltreatment, many of the peasants left their villages and sought freedom in the mountains. Some of them organized bands and attacked isolated groups of Turks, avenging the injustices done to them and to their compatriots. These *hayduks* were not a real danger for the Turkish military power, although corruption had undermined even the strength of the Janissaries, but they were precursors of the liberation of the Balkan population from the Turkish yoke. So it came about that the idea of liberation was born in the mountains among the courageous fugitives and was nursed by the epic songs cultivated among the mountaineers, which recalled the glorious past of the Serbian kings and heroes in the wars with the Turks. This spirit had never died in Montenegro, which was best situated to defy the Turks since it bordered on the territories of the Venetians, who were almost constantly at war with the Turks. It can be said that the idea of liberation originated in the mountains of Montenegro and was nourished by the stubborn resistance of its mountaineers to Turkish rule.

This situation also forced numerous Serbians to leave the territory occupied by the Turks and to establish themselves in Venetian or Austrian territories. Both governments welcomed them and used their organized bands, called *Uskoks*, in their campaigns against the Turks. The uskoks, however, were not disciplined soldiers, and they continued their invasions of Turkish territory even when their protectors were at peace with the sultans and thus often created a dangerous situation.

When the great Turkish wars began at the very end of the sixteenth century, the Christian powers sought to exploit the revolutionary mood of Turkey's Christian subjects for their own military purposes. Naturally, the Church was the only power which could be of assistance in inducing the Christians to help the Austrian armies and to facilitate their victory by timely insurrection.

The Bulgarian Church continued to be subordinated to the Archbishop of Ochrida. But its bishops also took a very active part in the *pourparlers* with the Emperor Rudolf II (1576 1612), with Sigismund Bathory (1581-1602) of Transylvania, and with Michael of Wallachia, which resulted in the insurrection of 1598 when Michael invaded Bulgaria. The promising campaign ended in disaster, and many families of Bulgarian insurgents had to abandon their homes with the retreating Rumanians and were settled in Wallachia. The Metropolitan of Trnovo, Dionysij, also had to take refuge abroad.

During this Austro-Turkish war, insurrection also flared up several times among the Serbians. The Serbians of the Banat revolted in 1594, in the next year Albania and Montenegro were in revolt, in 1596 great unrest arose near the frontier of Bosnia with Venetian territory, in 1603 the Serbians in western Bosnia were on the warpath, and in the next year Montenegro was again in flames. All these insurrections were provoked by false hopes of Austrian victory over the Turks. New persecutions followed each insurrection.[23]

The Treaty of Zsitva-Torok in 1606 demonstrated at least that the power of the Ottomans was declining. When in the Treaty of Vienna (1615) Austria obtained consular jurisdiction in Istanbul over its subjects, the Roman Catholics in the Ottoman Empire increased their activity, proselytizing among the Orthodox Slavs. The Roman Catholic population in Istanbul, which consisted mostly of foreign traders and was served by Italian priests, seems to have grown considerably. It possessed, under Murad III (1574-1595), about seventy places of worship in the city. Some prominent members of the Catholic colony were even quite influential at the sultan's court. During the Bulgarian insurrection the religious and patriotic spirit of the Bulgarian Catholics revived. They were mostly descendants of German miners and other colonists, and their center was Čiprovec, formerly a flourishing mining city. Franciscan missionaries from Bosnia were soon so successful in Bulgaria that their leader Solinat was made bishop of Sofia in 1601. Catholic propaganda had such good results in Bulgaria that in the middle of the seventeenth century two Catholic metropolitan sees were erected, Sofia and Marcianopolis, with bishoprics in Nicopolis, Skoplje, and Ochrida.[24]

One of the Catholic archbishops of Sofia, Peter Parčević (1656-1674), a native of Čiprovec, soon became a national leader and inspirer of the fight for freedom from the Turkish yoke. Already in 1630 and 1632 representatives of the Balkan Slavs tried to incite Ferdinand II of Austria and Sigismund III of Poland to make war against the Turks. The opening of the Venetian-Turkish war (1645-1664) gave them new hope. The voivode of Wallachia Meteir showed anti-Turkish intentions and was offered the rule over a reconquered Bulgaria. Peter Parčević, who had studied in Rome and had an excellent knowledge of the West, was entrusted with a mission to the Polish king Władysław in 1648, but the latter's death stopped all preparations for an insurrection. In 1650 Parčević was again on his way to Poland, Vienna, and Venice and continued his negotiations as archbishop. The appearance of the grand vizier Mohammed Kiuprili, who reorganized, to a certain extent, the Turkish army, and the success of the Turkish armies in Poland, where they were only stopped thanks to the intervention of King John Sobieski,[25] again spoiled Parčević' hope. He died in Rome, broken by his failure to incite the Western powers to a common fight for the liberation of the Balkan Slavs.

New hope awakened after the defeat of the Turks at Vienna (1683). The victorious Austrian armies conquered Belgrade (1688) and invaded Bosnia. Insurrection spread all over the Balkans. In Bulgaria Čiprovec was again the center of a revolt, which spread when the imperial army neared the frontier of Bulgaria. Unfortunately, the insurgent army was defeated by the Hungarian renegade Tököly who fought on the side of the Turks. The insurgents' fortified city of Čiprovec was taken and completely destroyed. The remnants of the population of the district migrated into Wallachia. Only a fraction of the insurgents was able to join the imperial army. This disaster also put an end to Catholic propaganda in Bulgaria and to the prospect of Catholic leadership in the Bulgarian fight for freedom. From that time on the Bulgarians lost interest in

Austrian help and started to look toward Russia, which, under the first Romanovs, was embarking on the conquest of Turkish lands in the Ukraine and the Crimea.[26]

The insurrection of the Serbians, which reached its peak when the imperial army had penetrated as far as Macedonia (1690), did not fare better than that of the Bulgarians. When the imperial armies were forced to leave Serbia, Bulgaria, and Transylvania, a great number of Serbians, with their families, led by the Patriarch Arsenij Crnojević, followed the imperial army and settled in the region of Srem and Slavonia.[27] Emperor Leopold I published a diploma in the same year confirming an autonomous regime for the refugees. The Treaty of Karlovci (1699) granted to Austria the whole of Hungary with the exception of the Banat of Temesvár, besides Transylvania, Slavonia, and Croatia, but Serbia proper remained Turkish. So the refugees had to stay in the lands granted to them. The successors of Arsenij had to abandon the patriarchal title although they entertained relations with the Serbian Patriarchate of Peć. The Serbians continued to enjoy their autonomous status in Hungary, and although they formed an alien group in the Western environment, they started to develop a lively cultural activity, building schools under Western influence and laying the first basis for the modern literature of Serbia. Karlovci, the see of their metropolitan, became their religious and political center, where the definite liberation of the Serbians was prepared. After the suppression of the Serbian patriarchate (1766), Karlovci inherited its role in the religious leadership of the Serbian nation.[28]

NOTES

1. The magnates obtained the office of supreme captain of Moravia, which gave the real mastery of the country, and those of chamberlain and of grand judge. The knights had to content themselves with the offices of judge, vice-chamberlain, and clerk of Moravia.

2. See below, Chapter XVII, pp. 451 ff.

3. Chapter VI, pp. 128 ff.

4. For the evolution of this practice consult L. Konopczyński, *Le Liberum Veto* (see Bibl.), pp. 153-278.

5. In the course of centuries many of the Armenians of Galicia accepted union with Rome, and in the seventeenth century their archbishop, Nikol Torosović, officially recognized the supremacy of the Pope. On the Armenians in Poland see Gromnicki, *Ormianie w Polsce: ich historja, prawa i przywileje* ("The Armenians in Poland: Their History, Rights and Privileges") (Warsaw, 1889), and Cz. Lechicki, *Kościół ormiański w Polsce: Zarys historyczny* ("The Armenian Church in Poland: Its Historical Survey") (Lwów, 1928). Cf. also Völker, *Kirchengeschichte Polens* (Berlin, Leipzig, 1930) p. 68.

6. See Chapter VI, pp. 130 ff.

7. The sources of Polish law are very varied and numerous—chronicles, ecclesiastical documents, formularies, diplomatic and judicial documents, archives of the crown, decisions of the dietines and Diets. Succinct and useful indications on the various editions of these documents will be found in K. Kadlec, *Introduction a l'étude comparative* (see Bibl.), pp. 272-81. Most of the critical editions were made by the Academy of Cracow, which published also the ninth volume of the *Volumina legum* (1889), started in 1732 by J. Zaluski and S. Konarski, completing the second edition of St. Petersburg (1859-61). A collection of Lithuanian legal documents was published by I. I. Jakovkin, *Zakonodatel'nye akty velikogo knjažestva litovskogo* (Moscow, 1936). On the history and organization of the Lithuanian-Russian Diet, see M. K. Ljubavskij, *Litovsko-russkij sejm'*, Čtenija v imper. obščestve istorii i drevn. ross. pri Mosk. univ. (Moscow, 1900-01), and I. I. Lappo, *Velikoe knjažestvo litovskoe* (Jur'ev, 1911). Cf. also G. Vernadski (see Bibl.), pp. 170 ff.

8. Such is also the opinion of the Russian historian of the Lithuanian-Russian state, M. K. Ljubavskij in his work *Očerk Istorii litovsko-russkago gosudarstva do ljublinskoj unii* ("Outline of the History of the Lithuanian-Russian State to the Union of Lublin") (Moscow, 1910) 2nd ed., 1915.

9. Cf. Chapter IX, p. 216.

10. Polish and Ukrainian historians are still debating about the meaning of the document agreed at Krewo. A review of this controversy and bibliographical notes on it will be found in G. Rohde's work, *Die Ostgrenze Polens* (see Bibl.), vol. I, pp. 316-25.

11. On the organization of Kievan Russia see F. Dvornik, *The Slavs*, pp. 218-23.

12. See Chapter XII, p. 275.

13. See Chapter XI, pp. 254 ff.

14. See below, Chapter XIX, pp. 494-496.

15. See below, p. 473.

16. For documentary evidence concerning the treatment of the Uniat Church in Poland by the Latin hierarchy, see E. Schmurlo, *Le Saint-Siège et l'Orient Orthodoxe Russe* (see Bibl.). Cf. Chapter XVIII, pp. 474, 487.

17. It seems now established that Hunyadi was of Rumanian origin. His son, King Matthias, had a Serbian princess as mother, and his first wife was the daughter of the Bohemian king, George of Poděbrady. It is characteristic for the position of the different nationalities of Hungary that none of the king's letters which have been preserved was written in Magyar, but several were written in Czech.

18. John Jiskra of Brandýs, the commander of the Czech troops, surrendered in 1462, after Ladislas' death, to King Matthias Corvinus, the son of John Hunyadi, and, with most of his troops, entered the service of the new king, to whom he remained faithful until his death.

19. There is evidence that in the earlier period Ragusa also traded with America and India, from whose markets it was driven by its mighty western competitors. Cf. the study by C. Mijatović, published in the *Glasnik* of the Serbian Learned Society in vol. 33 (1872), p. 226.

20. The latest detailed outline of the social and political organization of the Ottoman Empire will be found in H. A. R. Gibb, H. Bowen, *Islamic Society and the West* (see Bibl.). Cf. *ibidem*, p. 41, on the influence of Byzantine political institutions on the Turks.

21. A short but clear outline of the social conditions of the Balkan Christians under the Turks is given by M. Braun, *Die Slaven auf dem Balkan* (see Bibl.), pp. 126-43, 163-200. More recent Serbian publications on the subject are reviewed in *Dix années d'historiographie jougoslave* (1945-1955) (Belgrade, 1955), pp. 256 ff.

22. A useful bibliography on the patriarchate and on the Serbian Church will be found in L. Hadrovics, *Le peuple serbe* (see Bibl.), pp. 158-62.

23. An older bibliography in Slavic languages on these insurrections will be found in A. Hajek's, *Bulgarien unter der Türkenherrschaft* (see Bibl.), pp. 22-64, 317-21 and in St. Stanojević's, *Istorija srpskoga naroda* (3rd ed., Belgrade, 1926), pp. 239-314. Recent literature in Serbian is listed in *Dix années d'historiographie jougoslave*, pp. 268-74.

24. A complete bibliography on the Catholic movement in Bulgaria in the seventeenth century will be found in I. Dujčev's *Sofijskata katoliška archiepiskopia prez' XVII vjek'* (Sofia, 1939), pp. 182-84. A long résumé in Italian is on pp. 199-201.

25. Cf. below, Chapter XVIII, pp. 480 ff.

26. See below, Chapter XIX, pp. 502 ff.

27. A recent evaluation of Crnojević and the Great Serbian migration has been written by R. L. Veselinović, *Arsenije III Crnojević u istoriji i kniževnosti* ("Arsenij III Crnojević in History and Literature"), published by the Serbian Academy in 1949.

28. For details see A. Ivić, *Istorija Srba u Vojvodini od najstarijih vremena do osnivanja potisko-pomoriške granice 1702* ("History of the Serbs in Hungary from the Oldest Times to the Establishment of the Military Frontier on Tisza-Maros") (Novi Sad, 1929).

Chapter XV

THE GROWTH OF MUSCOVITE AUTOCRACY:
SOCIAL AND POLITICAL CHANGES
IN EAST RUSSIA

Democratic features in the Kievan state—Autocratic tendencies in the principality of Suzdaľ-Vladimir—Disappearance of the city assemblies (večes)—Introduction of the hereditary principle in Muscovy—Triumph of autocracy—Moscow and the Mongol khans—Byzantine political ideas in Kievan literature—The idealogical basis of Muscovite autocracy—The Russian Church favors monarchy—Religious unity leads to political unity —The Grand Prince of Moscow protector of Orthodoxy, a new wave of Byzantine political ideas reaches Muscovy—Moscow the Third Rome— Mongol influences on the growth of Muscovite autocracy—Muscovite princes refuse to be the heirs of Byzantium. Differences between Byzantine and Muscovite autocracy—The Church and the tsars—Muscovite army reorganized on the Mongol pattern—Administration of Muscovy; Mongol influences in jurisprudence, Byzantine in codification—Social changes in Muscovy—Manorial system (pomestie) with military service introduced by Ivan III—Cities and peasantry in Muscovy—Ivan IV and the higher nobility—Ivan's antiaristocratic measures—The opričnina, *regime of terror—Ivan's conception of autocracy*

In the political transformation of East Russia from the fourteenth century on, one feature seems at first sight to recall the developments in contemporary western Europe, namely, the establishment of a strong monarchy in the Muscovite state. It would, however, be a mistake to attribute the rise of a monarchic system in East Russia to a similarity of circumstances to those in western Europe. Moreover, the Muscovite political structure showed early certain strong autocratic tendencies which

362

were only to be observed much later and to a lesser degree in western European states.

The origins and growth of the autocratic regime in the Muscovite state is still one of the most debated problems of Russian history. In comparing the growth of the monarchies in western Europe and in East Russia, the different origins and causes from which they sprang should never be forgotten. Moreover, the Muscovite monarchy was not preceded by an era of feudalism, as had happened in the West, but by the democratic regime with patriarchal features which characterized the State of Kiev.

There were in the political organization of the Kievan state many special characteristics which had little in common with a monarchic system and which seemed to preclude the possibility of a strong monarchy arising among the Russians. The state was regarded as the common patrimony of the Rurik dynasty, and so, logically, it should be divided among all members of the reigning family. This system naturally led to the creation of as many states or *votčiny* (hereditary patrimonies) as there were branches of the Rurik family, and made it extremely difficult to maintain the unity of the Kievan state. The right of succession by seniority, which gave the oldest member of the dynasty supreme authority and introduced a rotating system of succession in the principalities, was established by the founders of the state in order to reconcile its two fundamental principles—the sharing of the common patrimony between the members of the dynasty and the unity of the state. The danger of a division of the Kievan realm into several independent states was thus to a certain degree averted, but the grand prince, the head of the dynasty, could never pretend to become a monarch. He was bound to collaborate with other princes in the administration of the state and in foreign relations.

There was a further principle in the Kievan political system which discouraged the development of a strong monarchy. In each principality the throne was hereditary in the dynasty, but it was the *veče*, the assembly of the people, which approved the succession or decided between contending candidates. The prince was confirmed or elected for life—only in Novgorod and Pskov was the duration of the mandate indeterminate—but the *veče* also had the right, in certain cases, to depose the prince. There was no coronation ceremony as in the West, and at the enthronement of the princes the people played a prominent role.

There should be a "union" (*odinačestvo*) between the confirmed or elected prince and his subjects. Therefore the new princes were wont to conclude special agreements (*rjady*) with their subjects fixing their reciprocal rights and duties.

The *veče*s were another obstacle to the formation of an absolutist regime. All free men enjoyed the right to participate in the assemblies convoked by the princes, generally in public places in the cities. These had to decide on important questions concerning administration and legislation, sometimes also in important judicial affairs. It was also in the interest of the prince to have popular support on urgent military matters.

The origins and roles of the Russian nobility also differed considerably from those of the Western nations. The class of nobles developed slowly from the military companions of the princes, originally Scandinavians, who formed their retinue (*družina*) and lived with them. Only in the twelfth century did the members of the retinue become permanent settlers on estates given to them by the princes for their services, and only then could this foreign element, together with prominent native landholders, form a single class, whose members were designed by the Bulgarian word "boyars." They occupied different functions in the administration and were bound to military service, but they enjoyed a dangerous privilege—the right to quit the service of their prince, at any time, and freely to join the service of any other prince, even with their hereditary properties (*votčiny*).

The boyars were also members of the prince's council, called *duma*. There is, however, again a marked difference between the composition of the Kievan duma and that of similar institutions in the West. The prince himself chose his councilors not only among his boyars, but also among the clergy and the elders of the cities who represented the population. In general, the duma was composed only of a limited number of councilors. Its composition changed when the princes visited different places in their principalities because on these occasions they used to consult boyars settled on the lands visited or employed in their administration, besides the local clergy and elders. The members of the duma gave advice in all matters concerning the activity of the princes—foreign relations, internal problems, and judicial, legislative, and military matters.

All this shows that the system of Estates which characterized the composition of medieval society in the West had never developed in Kiev. Besides the boyars and the burghers—merchants and artisans—there existed a class of free peasants. When the rich landowners succeeded in controlling the best part of the lands, they handed over their estates for cultivation to peasants under special agreements which seem to presuppose the freedom of movement of the peasants. This, however, only happened during the Muscovite period.

These were the main obstacles to the formation of a strong monarchic and absolutist regime in Russia. The intervention of fate was necessary to produce an atmosphere in which these obstacles could be removed.

The prosperity of the Kievan state was based on the lively commercial intercourse of the Black Sea coast and Byzantium with inland Russia and the countries of Central and western Europe. Cities and their burghers were the main factors in the economic and political life of the state, and the rich merchants dominated their *večes*. The decline of international commerce as a result of the Cuman occupation of present-day southern Russia, which cut the Kievans off from the sea routes, naturally also diminished the importance of the *večes*, but it was not easy to curtail their firmly established privileges.

This was only possible in the new cities founded by the princes in freshly colonized lands. Such a policy was followed conscientiously by the rulers of the new principality of Suzdal'-Vladimir, established in the triangle formed by the Volga in the north and by the Oka in the southeast. Cities such as Rostov and Suzdal', founded by colonists from Novgorod, had, of course, their *večes* and watched jealously over the preservation of their prerogatives. But in disregard of the old institution of *večes*,[1] the princes of Suzdal' established their own functionaries in the cities founded by them. The most energetic among these princes was Andrew Bogoljubskij. Hampered by the *veče* of Suzdal', he transferred his residence to the new city of Vladimir.[2] But he paid with his life (1175) for this intransigent and despotic policy, which was still too alien to the Russians of his time.[3]

In spite of strong opposition, Andrew's brother and successor, Vsevolod, continued to impose his authority on the boyars and the cities. So it happened that during the second half of the twelfth century a strong regime with autocratic features appeared, for the first time, among the Russian people. The Suzdalian princes also made a definite break with the old Kievan system by which the succession to the principalities rotated according to seniority. Instead they regarded their territory as a property over which they ruled as absolute sovereigns. The numerous colonists whom they brought into their territory depended on them for the distribution of land and for security and willingly accepted the new order. Thus the Suzdalian princes sowed the seed from which the autocratic regime of the Muscovite state later arose.

It is true that the regime introduced by Andrew and Vsevolod did not last. The old Russian custom of dividing the territory among the heirs was reintroduced, and the principality lost its unity. One important innovation, however, remained. The heirs regarded their inheritance, their *votčina*, as their private property. This new principle could easily be extended. A more ambitious prince would naturally be inclined to regard not only the part of the principality which he himself inherited, but the whole principality (*volost*) as his private property inherited from his father. This provided favorable ground for the growth of the idea of a hereditary monarchy in the territory where Moscow was to rise. The princes of Suzdal'-Vladimir also transferred the grand princely title from

Kiev to the territory, and from that time on, the struggle for possession of this title, symbolizing sovereignty over the whole Russian nation, continued in this territory among the descendants of Vsevolod, the princes of Tver' and Moscow. These were, with Jaroslavl' and Nižnij Novgorod, new foundations on the vast lands of the Suzdal' principality.

Thus the Suzdal' princes were the first to make a successful attack on the powerful influence of the *veće*s in Russian political life. Although the *veće*s had in some cases survived the Mongol onslaught, their influence diminished steadily during the second half of the Mongol period. Important economic and social changes contributed to this development. The growing decay of commerce considerably diminished the importance if the cities in the political life of the principalities, and the rich merchants, who used to wield marked influence in the *veće*s, disappeared.[4]

On the other hand, the princes had to obtain confirmation of their dignity from the khans of the Golden Horde. They had to appear personally before the khan in order to obtain his decree of confirmation, called *jarlyk*. The khan's will being the main source of their sovereignty, they could thus neglect the voice of the *veće*. So it happened that during the second half of the Mongol period in Russian history, the bells which had formerly convoked the citizens to the city assemblies became silent. Only in Novgorod, Pskov, and, for some time, in Vjazma did the *veće*s continue to exist and to play their important constitutional role. With the decline of the *veće*s an essential democratic element in Russian political life disappeared, and one of the most difficult obstacles to the establishment of an autocratic monarchy was removed. There remained only the privileged boyars and the Mongol khans to set limits to the power of the princes. Such were the political conditions in East Russia when Moscow began to rise to prominence.[5]

But another custom persisted from the Kievan period which could greatly endanger the growth and prosperity of the new principality of Moscow—the traditional division of the patrimony among all the heirs. As already mentioned, Ivan Kalita divided his principality among his three sons, his wife, and his daughters. However, he made a timid attempt at securing the principality's unity by stipulating in his last will that his three sons should rule together in Moscow under the leadership of the eldest, Simeon (1341-1353).

Fate helped Moscow. Simeon, his sons, and his brother Andrew all succumbed to an epidemic, and the only surviving scion of the dynasty, Ivan II (1353-1359), became sole ruler of Moscow. It was a lucky accident that the patrimony did not have to be divided among its many heirs. At the same time the principle of primogeniture, the transmission of the principality from father to oldest son, began to be accepted as a rule. The steadfastness with which the boyars and the Metropolitan Alexis defended the rights of the nine-year-old nephew of Ivan I, Dmitrij Donskoj, shows clearly how firmly this monarchic principle was established in Moscow.

Dmitrij also introduced a new custom by abstaining from dividing his domain between his children and by leaving the major portion to his eldest son, Basil I. The final victory won by Basil II in the fratricidal struggles for the heritage of Basil I [6] marked the definite abandonment of the old Russian order of succession to the rank of grand prince and the triumph of the custom of "father and grandfather," as it was called by contemporaries. Thus one of the main principles of a monarchic regime was firmly established in Moscow. Another principle was proclaimed by Basil II in a treaty with the Grand Prince of Tver'—that of divine right. This was finally defined by Ivan III in 1488 in his reply to the offer of a royal title made by the envoy of Emperor Frederick III. Ivan III declared that he was, by God's grace, hereditary sovereign of his state,[7] having obtained the investiture from God himself, as did all his ancestors, and that he did not need any other investiture.

Under Ivan III the liberation of Muscovite Russia from the Mongol yoke was definitively achieved in 1480. Thus was removed forever the main limitation on the authority of the Muscovite grand princes, and Ivan III was fully entitled to regard himself as a monarch, responsible for his acts only to God.

It was no wonder that Ivan III started to use the title of Tsar in his diplomatic contacts and that he came to behave as a real autocrat, *samoderžavec*, responsible to no one on earth for his actions. He still discussed his projects with the boyars, but once the decision was made, he enforced complete submission, punishing any disobedience severely and even with torture. This autocratic attitude reached a new peak under Basil III. He made his decisions without consulting the boyars in the duma, refused any intervention or advice on the part of the metropolitan, and broke without scruple any kind of opposition to his domestic or foreign policy. Baron Herberstein's account of his embassy to the grand prince gives a contemporary description of the autocratic regime exercised by Basil III. It contains the following passage on the Muscovite autocracy:

> The prince exercises his authority over all people—laymen and ecclesiastics—and disposes, according to his will and pleasure, over individuals and their possessions. None of his counselors has enough authority to oppose him or to dare to express any opinion contrary to

his. They confess publicly that the prince's will is the will of God and that the prince's acts are done according to God's will. Therefore they call him God's chamberlain and steward. They say also that he is the fulfiller of God's will. Therefore, if someone asks for something on behalf of a prisoner, or otherwise for something of importance, the prince answers: "If it pleases God, he will again be free." It also happens that, when someone poses an important or doubtful question, he generally receives the answer, "This is known only to God and to our prince."

There remained, however, one last element in the political structure inherited by Muscovy from the Kievan period which might become dangerous to the full exercise of the grand prince's autocracy—the privileges enjoyed by the class of the boyars. The grand princes could deal with this problem only when other limitations on their autocracy had been removed. The privilege of the boyars of changing the service of princes at will was most burdensome for the princes, who tried from Dmitrij Donskoj on to curtail it by a variety of means. They especially refused to conclude agreements with the boyars or with other princes which assured the boyars of their freedom. Often when such agreements were concluded, they were broken by the princes under different pretexts. The exercise of this right of the boyars was branded as a sin against their lord, a criminal act which deserved punishment.

In spite of many such attempts, the grand princes prior to Ivan IV did not dare to abolish this privilege. Ivan III, who used every means to prevent the use of this right in Muscovy, claimed it on behalf of the princes and boyars who wished to leave the service of the Lithuanian grand duke and join Muscovy. Thanks to all these operations the privilege, although not denied in theory, was in practice transformed under Ivan III into a lifelong obligation to serve the prince. It was only Ivan IV who made a frontal attack on the privileges of the boyars when he destroyed this old class by brutal means and created a new class, that of the *opričniki*. Never again did the old boyars succeed in recovering their rights. The absolutist autocratic regime had triumphed.

These are the main phases in the development of Muscovite absolutism. There were, of course, many other secondary causes. Platonov attributes the rapid growth of the principality of Moscow in large degree to the short sightedness of the khans, who had failed to discern in time that Moscow was becoming potentially their most dangerous adversary. There is some truth in this statement. When the dealings of Prince George (Iurij) and his brother Ivan Kalita with the Khan are studied in more detail, it becomes clear how much the favor of the Khan Uzbeg profited them, both in the expansion of their power and in their struggle with Tver' for the title of Grand Prince of Vladimir. George even became the brother-in-law of the Khan. From the beginning, the Muscovite princes followed a policy of peace and subservience to the khans. It is, however, an exaggeration to believe that the khans were not aware of the danger of giving too much power to the Muscovite princes. When Uzbeg decided to abolish the system of direct collection of taxes in East Russia by Tatar collectors, he did not, as is often thought, entrust the collection to the Muscovite prince only, but to the princes of Tver', Rjazan', and Nižnij Novgorod also, and he instituted special commissioners to supervise all four major principalities. All four princes were granted the title of Grand Prince.

Of course, the Grand Principality of Vladimir was the largest, comprising fifteen tax districts, called *t'ma*. Rjazan' was the smallest with only two tax districts; Tver' and Nižnij Novgorod were each divided into five districts. This, naturally, enhanced the importance of the Muscovite rulers, who were granted the title of Grand Prince of Vladimir. Moreover, in 1392, the Khan Tokhtamyš permitted Basil I of Moscow to occupy the Grand Principality of Nižnij Novgorod. This opened the way for Moscow to extend its suzerainty over other principalities.

The princes of Moscow were indebted for the growth of their power and the development of their autocratic monarchy not only to the favor of the khans, but also, to an even greater extent, to the support of the Russian Church. Although it sounds strange, it must be admitted that the ideological basis for the growth of Russian monarchy was prepared by the ecclesiastical writers of the Kievan period. It must not be forgotten that Russian churchmen were instructed by Byzantine missionaries and by Byzantine literary works translated into Old Slavonic.

It is now recognized that Byzantine political philosophy did not know any other political system than monarchy and favored only autocratic government. Because the Kievan political system presented so many democratic features, it has been thought that Byzantine political ideas never influenced it and that they were even unknown to the Kievans.

It is true that early Russian literature produced none of those treatises on kingship or on relations between rulers and the Church which are so numerous in medieval West European literatures. In spite of that, the people and rulers of the Kievan state had good opportunities of becoming acquainted with the main principles of Byzantine political philosophy and of being influenced by it.[8]

From the eleventh century on, the Russian clergy, the rulers, and their boyars possessed Slavonic translations of Byzantine collections of canon law—the *Synagogué* of John Scholasticus and the *Nomocanon* of Fourteen

Titles, together with the translation of two Byzantine law handbooks, the *Ecloga* and the *Procheiron*. These important writings contained many novels of the Emperor Justinian, conciliar canons, imperial addresses to the conciliar fathers, and other documents giving expression to Byzantine ideas on rulership. These writings were supplemented by translations of the Greek Fathers, of Byzantine chronicles, and of collections of sayings attributed to Greek philosophers and Fathers, some of them impregnated with the spirit of Greek, Hellenistic, and Byzantine political thought. The most important of these collections was the Greek *Melissa* ("Bee"), translated into Slavonic in Kiev in the twelfth century and containing a long chapter on power and kingship.

In these writings the Russian intellectuals could find all the basic ideas of Byzantine political thought: the divine origin of the imperium and the sacerdotium, the necessity for intimate collaboration between these two main factors in human society, the ruler's duty to establish harmony between the spiritual and temporal powers, and his right, or rather duty, to watch over the Church because he was the representative of God on earth. Some of these ideas are also interspersed in the original works of certain Kievan authors,[9] evidently derived from Byzantine writings.

It is natural, therefore, that some features of the medieval Russian political structure should have been fashioned according to the Byzantine pattern. This is helpful toward an understanding of the relationship between the Russian princes and the Byzantine emperors. The Russians accepted the dominating idea of Byzantine political theory, namely, that the Emperor of Constantinople was the representative of God on earth and that he was the supreme legislator for Christians, the supreme authority on earth to which every Christian had to submit in matters concerning the Christian commonwealth. This prominent position of the Byzantine emperor was also acknowledged in Muscovy down to the first half of the fifteenth century. There is nothing in this relationship between the Russian princes and the emperor which could be compared to vassalage as it was known in western feudal states.

The relations between Church and state in Kievan and Muscovite Russia were also modeled on the Byzantine pattern. The preservation of a harmonious relationship between the sacerdotium and the imperium was one of the leading principles of Byzantine political philosophy and was expressed particularly clearly by the Emperor Justinian in Novel Six.[10] This principle became the guiding star for the political and religious evolution of Russia through many centuries. This explains why the Russian hierarchy made the maintenance of good relations with the ruling princes its first task. It was not so much out of subservience, as has so often been said, but because this was a principle inherited from the

Mother Church of Byzantium. In transferring the prerogatives of the Byzantine emperor over the Church to their own princes, the Russian clergy willingly accepted their care and legislation in ecclesiastical matters.[11]

It was thus natural that the Russian Church, following the Byzantine example, rather favored the government of one man. This silent predilection for monarchy and autocracy lay like a substratum even in Kievan political speculation. It helped the Suzdalian princes in their first attempt at establishing an autocratic regime in their principality,[12] and it also helped the Muscovite princes in the establishment of their monarchic autocracy.

When all this is borne in mind, it can be understood why the metropolitans transferred their see from Kiev to Vladimir and then to Moscow when its princes began to aspire to hegemony over the Russian lands.[13] The efforts of the Metropolitan Alexis to secure the rule in Moscow and the title of Grand Prince for the young Dmitrij Donskoj are better understood, as is also the attitude of St. Sergius of Radonež, with whose blessing Dmitrij rode against the huge Tatar army of Mamai. His victory at Kulikovo became a symbol of Russian national awakening, with the blessing of the Church and under the leadership of Moscow.

The idea of the unity of indivisibility of the Russian Church, embodied in the Metropolitan of Kiev, was another important factor which prepared the way for Moscow's hegemony over the whole of Russia. This idea was defended with stubborness by the emperors and patriarchs of Constantinople, who appointed, or at least confirmed, the metropolitans. The attempts to create another metropolitan see in Russia were long opposed by Byzantium, and only the threat to place the Orthodox subjects of the Lithuanian commonwealth and Galicia under Rome induced the Byzantines to yield reluctantly to Olgerd and to Casimir.[14] The Church of Constantinople thereby rendered a signal service to Russia, and particularly to Moscow, at a critical period.

So it happened that the principle of the religious unity of all Russia became a guiding star for Moscow in the political field. The importance of this principle was already appreciated by Ivan Kalita, who started to call himself Grand Prince of Vladimir and of all Russia when the metropolitan fixed his residence in Moscow. This principle guided Basil II, Ivan III, Basil III, and Ivan IV in the merciless annexation of independent principalities in the "reassemblement of Russian lands," in the victorious struggle with Tver' and with the republics of Novgorod and Pskov, and also in their defense against Lithuania, which wanted to realize the same ideal of the reassemblement of the Russian lands around Vilna. The union of Lithuania with Poland and its acceptance of Roman Catholicism transformed this political rivalry into a religious struggle, the defense of Russian Orthodoxy against the "heretical" West. Unfortunately, this political and religious animosity built a wall of mistrust around Muscovite Russia and made its isolation from the West, which had deepened during the Mongol period, almost impenetrable.

In these circumstances there occurred some events which proved fatal for the evolution of Muscovite Russia and which greatly influenced the further development of Muscovite autocracy. When Basil II rejected the union accepted by the Greeks at the Council of Florence (1439) and severed relations with Constantinople, which was accused of shamefully betraying the Orthodox faith, he adopted the language of the Byzantine emperors and declared himself the protector of the true Orthodox faith. The capture of Constantinople by the Turks in 1453, regarded by the Muscovites as God's punishment for Byzantium's "apostasy" from Orthodoxy, consolidated the position of the Muscovite prince in the eyes of the Russian Orthodox.

Moreover, the marriage of Ivan III with Zoe-Sophia Palaeologus, the niece of the last Byzantine emperor, Constantine XI, gave in the eyes of many a kind of juridical sanction to the idea of Muscovite Russia as the political and religious heir of Byzantium.

The Russian churchmen, following the tradition of their Kievan predecessors, contributed considerably in their own interest to the development of this new ideology. If Moscow succeeded Constantinople, then the Metropolitan of Moscow could regard himself as autonomous and as the depositary and interpreter of the true Orthodox faith, which the new heir of Byzantium had to defend. So it happened that in the fifteenth century a new wave of Byzantine political ideas reached Russia and enriched the Byzantine ideological substratum which survived from the Kievan period.

So, for example, in 1492 the Metropolitan Zosimus called [15] the grand prince, in Byzantine fashion, "the sovereign and autocrat of all Russia, new Tsar Constantine of the new city of Constantinople-Moscow." The learned Gennadius, archbishop of Novgorod, also contributed to this development. He linked up the new "Tsar" of Moscow with the Byzantine emperor and was probably looking for more material in Byzantine writings for the propagation of these ideas because in one of his letters he asked for a copy of Photius' letter to Boris-Michael of Bulgaria, which was a kind of treatise on Byzantine political ideas.

Joseph Sanin, abbot of Volokolamsk, one of the most prominent churchmen of this period, is even more systematic in his exposition. He speaks in Byzantine fashion of the heavenly monarchy reflected on earth by the imperial monarchy, and improves on the Byzantine doctrine as follows: "By his nature, the tsar is like other men, but by his dignity he is equal to the Highest God. He is not merely God's servant, but His representative, watching over the purity of the faith and over the safety of the Church. For this reason, God gave him the sword." There is also a touch of the sun symbolism, so common in Hellenistic writings on kingship, when Joseph describes the tsar as surrounded by a divine halo of light. Though subject to law, especially canon law, his power is unlimited, and everybody, even the Church, must obey him. Joseph also believed in the ruler's priestly character, and he gave the tsar a *svjatitel'skij čin.* The Church is above the temporal state, but in view of the tsar's eminence, she is subject to him, and he also enjoys the right to appoint and to supervise the bishops.

Joseph's doctrine was further developed by his disciple, the Metropolitan Daniel, who was appointed by Basil III without any synodal procedure. Daniel combined the ideas of the spiritual and temporal powers and gave both to the divinely appointed tsar. He also emulated his master by adjudging to the tsar the right to persecute heretics and enemies of the Church.

Joseph was a disciple of Pafnutij, abbot of the monastery of Borovsk, who was renowned for his fidelity to Moscow and its rulers. Pafnutij trained a new generation of Russian clergy imbued with the same spirit and promoting the idea of the divinely founded monarchy of Moscow.

It is thus evident that Muscovite churchmen were inspired by Byzantine ideas in their support of tsarist autocracy. In reality, Byzantine political literature was in great vogue in Russia at this period. For instance, the Greek treatise on kingship written in the sixth century by the deacon Agapetus, is preserved in manuscript in an Old Slavonic translation dating from the fifteenth or sixteenth century.[16] The instruction on rulership ascribed to Basil I and addressed to his son Leo VI was also translated at this period. The writings of another Byzantine political theorist, Simeon of Salonika, are also preserved in a Russian translation of the seventeenth century. A Greek treatise on kingship is to be found in a Russian *Sbornik* copied in the fifteenth century, though no Russian translation of it has so far been discovered. It also seems that Patriarch Photius' letter to Boris of Bulgaria on kingship and the treatise on kingship by Theophylact of Bulgaria, dating from the twelfth century, were previously unknown in Russia and must have been translated at this time. All this indicates that the study of Byzantine political literature was particularly intense at the time of Russia's political transformation in the fifteenth and sixteenth centuries.

In this atmosphere was born the idea of Moscow as the Third Rome. The author of the Chronograph of 1512, based on the Bulgarian translation of the Greek chronicle of Manasses, seems to have been inspired by this idea. At the end of his work, after describing the fall of Constantinople, he exclaims: "God will rekindle the spark in the ashes, he will burn the empire of the Ismaelites as a thorny bush, he will let the light of the faith radiate again and send an Orthodox tsar." Unfortunately, all the pious kingdoms have been destroyed by the Turks, but "our Russian land . . . grows, is young, and is elevated, O gracious Christ. Let it grow, be young, and spread to the end of time."

The visions described in the Fourth Book of Ezra (IV Ezra 12:23), which was only translated into Church Slavonic at this time, and the prophecies by Daniel (Daniel 7:19) on the last kingdoms helped further to develop this idea, which was definitely formulated by the Monk Philotheus (Filofej) of Pskov in his letters to Michael G. Misjur'-Munechin and to the tsars Basil III and Ivan IV. In his missive to Basil III he addressed the tsar as "the only basileus of all Christians. All Christian rulership comes under thy basileia." And he explains how the Russian basileia, or tsardom, succeeded the Roman and the Byzantine basileia; that the Roman Empire was to last until the end of the world; and that the Muscovite tsardom, as its heir, was to be the last empire, and after it the eternal kingdom of God, ruled by Christ, would take its place. A new era was opening, the era of the third and last Rome. In his missive to Ivan IV he interpreted the Apocalypse of St. John (12:1-11), in a similar sense.[17]

In spite of this effort on the part of the Muscovite clergy to byzantinize Moscow's new political regime, the new autocrats failed to adopt all the ideas suggested by their intellectuals, and showed little enthusiasm for their new Byzantine inheritance. Before this wave of Byzantine political ideas swept over Muscovite Russia, the grand princes had often to experience the effectiveness of another autocracy, that of the Mongol khans. Under Jengis Khan the Mongols had become masters of all the lands from China to the Black Sea and the Dnieper. They had also inherited the political systems previously dominant in those parts and had developed them further into a despotic and merciless autocracy.

Of course, the influence which the Mongols exercised on Muscovite Russia must not be exaggerated. There was almost no intermingling between the Russian and Mongol peoples. The Mongols did not settle on the land of the peoples they had subjugated, nor was there much intercourse between the masters and the subjugated masses. Russian colonists only reached Mongol lands in the sixteenth century on the middle and lower Volga, after the destruction of the khanates of Kazan' and Astrakhan' by Ivan IV. But even then, religious and cultural differences precluded a more intimate intercourse between the two races. To a certain degree, however, there was a tatarization of the Russian nobility. Many Russian princes married Tatar brides, and in the period when Tatar power was declining, especially from the reign of Basil II onward, numerous Tatar noble families entered the service of the grand princes and were Russianized. In the seventeenth century there were in Muscovy 156 noble families of Tatar origin.[18] This influx of boyars habituated to an absolutist regime may well have helped the Muscovite princes in their autocratic policy. But there was also a considerable influx of nobles from Poland-Lithuania and western Europe,[19] who had not lived under an autocratic regime.

Although there cannot thus have been any direct ideological borrowing from the Mongols, there can be no doubt that their political and social system, with its autocratic absolutism, exercised a profound influence on East Russian development. It seems unthinkable that a regime whose efficiency was so patent to the Russian princes during their visits to the Khan's court should not have induced the Muscovite princes to imitate at home the example of their suzerains. The fact that after the collapse of the Tatar Empire the Muscovite rulers regarded themselves as successors to the khans is certainly very significant in this respect, as are also the undeniable Mongol influences in the development of the Russian administrative, military organization, financial, fiscal, and legal systems.

This also explains why the Muscovite princes were not at all impressed by the suggestions—mentioned above—made to Ivan III and Basil III by Pope Paul II, Emperor Maximilian I, and the Grand master of the Teutonic Order that they should regard themselves as the heirs of Byzantium. They were interested in only one ancestral heritage, the Russian principalities which were under Poland-Lithuania. The fight for this heritage always held first place in their minds, while the Turks figured primarily as the enemies of their rivals.[20] There are also some other important aspects of Muscovite autocracy, as it developed before and under Ivan IV, which differ considerably from Byzantine political theory and show that the Russian clergy was not as successful as is sometimes assumed in its attempts to byzantinize the Russian autocracy. These are even strong indications that Russian ecclesiastical theorists of this period did not understand the full significance of the Byzantine ideas on kingship. The idea propagated by them, that Moscow had become the Third Rome, seems, at least at that early period of Muscovite autocracy, to imply not so much that Moscow had become the heir of Byzantium, as that it had replaced Byzantium, which had become unfaithful to its mission and was therefore punished by God.

The Byzantine emperor was regarded as the head of all Orthodox Christians. This idea seems to be implied also in some declarations of the ecclesiastical theorists responsible for the byantinization of the Muscovite autocracy. Circumstances, however, prevented the Muscovite grand princes from accepting the full implications of the Byzantine interpretation of the emperor's position. The Greeks had apostatized from Orthodoxy when they accepted the Union of Florence. True Orthodoxy was now preserved only in Muscovy, and the grand prince was its protector. The idea that he should become the head and protector of all Orthodoxy, including Greeks and Balkan Slavs, did not enter into the mind of the rulers of Muscovy.

The Byzantine conception of the sublime position of the emperor was also alien to Muscovite autocrats. When the diplomatic correspondence of Ivan III is studied, it is surprising to see that he is only anxious to prove to the western rulers that he is their equal.[21] This is particularly clear from the answers given by Ivan III and his diplomatic agent, Theodore (Fedor) Kuricyn, to the ambassader of the Emperor Frederick III in 1488 and 1489. Ivan III does not even use the title of Tsar as a counterpart to that of Emperor. All he wants to prove is that he is an independent sovereign, who has received his sovereignty from God, as did his ancestors. When he says that his ancestors enjoyed good relations with the Roman emperors who resided in Constantinople, he seems to want to imply that the Muscovite rulers were equal in dignity to the emperors of Constantinople. This is, of course, contradictory to the Byzantine theory that the Byzantine emperor was the full sovereign, the representative of God on earth, and that all other Christian rulers were in one way or another, as it were, his vassals or dependents, sons or brothers.[22]

This tendency to show that the Muscovite rulers inherited their sovereign rights from their ancestors and were equal to other western rulers is even more pronounced in the political literature which was in great vogue under Ivan IV. The legend of Vladimir Monomakh (1113-1125), according to which this Kievan prince obtained the coronation insignia from the Emperor Constantine Monomakh (1042-1054), was invented in order to prove the glorious ancestry of the Muscovite princes and the ancient origin of their suzerainty. Here again the author of this legend presents the Russian soverign as the equal of the Byzantine emperor. But even the Byzantine ancestry was not enough for the Muscovite autocrats. The legendary genealogy of the Rurik dynasty goes back as far as the Roman emperor Augustus, who was said to have been the ruler of the whole world and, when he divided his empire, to have given the northeastern part of it to his brother Prus, who was the ancestor of Rurik.

The Muscovite rulers were not even anxious to secure for themselves the title of Tsar. Ivan III placed great stress on the fact that he was the great *Gosudar* of all Russia, using this word as synonymous with the word "suzerain." [23] Only their diplomatic contacts with the western rulers, especially with the German Holy Roman emperors, induced the Russian rulers to seek a title expressing adequately their sovereignty and their position as equals to the rulers of the Holy Roman Empire. When defending against the Polish court his assumption of the title of Tsar, Ivan IV not only makes use of the legendary traditions of Monomakh and Prus, but also stresses the fact that he is ruler of the Tatar khanates of Kazan' the Astrakhan', the rulers of which had the right to be called tsars. Once more his argumentation betrays hardly any indication to show that Ivan IV was fully conscious of a Byzantine heritage. [24]

Ivan IV's definition of his autocracy illustrates the difference between the Muscovite and the Byzantine conceptions of autocracy. He defined as follows the power of the tsar: "The autocratic regime comes from God, and the tsar carries out God's wishes. He wields every power over all things, and it is his duty to provide for the salvation of his people, whom God has entrusted to his care." Any Byzantine political theorist would have agreed with this definition. He would have hesitated, however, if he could have read some passages of Ivan's correspondence with his former chancellor, Prince Kurbskij, who had left his service and fled to Lithuania. Ivan IV stresses in the correspondence several times that the tsar's power was absolute and that the obedience which his subjects owed him had no limits. Even if the tsar should order something unlawful and sinful, they would have to do it because such was the will of God. They must await the judgment of God, who would one day reward them for the injustice suffered on earth. Only in one case should the subjects refuse obedience, and that was if the tsar should order something contrary to the true faith.

The relations between Church and state in Muscovy also show a new development which increased the influence of the rulers in Church affairs. Since churchmen had favored the growth of Muscovite autocracy, there was a possibility that a compromise might be achieved between the tsarist autocracy and the Church on the basis of the old practice of harmony between the temporal and spiritual power, which had become traditional in Russian life. There was an important movement in Muscovy, led by Nil Sorskij and his disciples, which aimed at the reform of Russian monasticism. Its members were interested only in spiritual things and refused favors and rich endowments. In the relations between Church and state they were opposed to an intimate collaboration with secular authorities, contenting themselves with the old practice of harmony between the imperium and the sacerdotium.

Ivan III, needing more lands for his boyars, was in favor of the ideas of the reformists. They were, however, opposed by another Church movement, led by Joseph Sanin, abbot of Volokolamsk, who advocated a more intimate relationship with the secular power in the struggle against the heretical movement of the "Judaizers," who were attacking the official Church and its rich endowments. Intrigues in the grand princely family complicated the situation. Joseph supported Ivan's wife Sophia and her son Basil against Ivan's daughter-in-law Helen and her son Dmitrij. When Sophia had recovered Ivan's favor and had ensured the succession to her son, Joseph and his supporters triumphed. Himself an autocrat in his monastery, Joseph was the most fervent supporter of the tsarist autocracy and taught, moreover, that a bishop should serve not only the Church, but also the state. The triumph of the Josephites was assured when the Metropolitan Daniel, a faithful disciple of Joseph, dissolved, for reasons of state and in spite of the opposition of the reformist party, the marriage of Basil III with the childless Solomonia and blessed his union with the Princess Helen Glinskij, who bore Basil III two sons.

This brought disaster for the reformists. The last of them were hunted down at the instigation of the Josephites. Any hope of a dignified compromise between Church and state vanished. The tsarist autocracy, thanks to the subservience of the Josephites, could also claim the right of direct interference in Church affairs. This helps to explain the extreme views on autocracy uttered by Ivan IV, who obtained his political education from the Metropolitan Macarius, also a convinced Josephite.

Together with the slow transformation of the East Russian political system, important changes were being introduced in the administration of the state and in its social life. Many of these changes followed a Mongol pattern. The most profound transformation of old Kievan institutions in Muscovy under Mongol influence can be seen in the sphere of military organization. In the Kievan state the core of the grand prince's army was his retinue of senior boyars; junior boyars, called "boyars' children," and the city militia, led by the miliarch (*tysjackij*). The rural population was not bound to military service. The Mongols established a system of universal conscription. Because the cities had lost their former importance in the national life, the function of the *tysjackij*, or commander of the city militia, disappeared.

The grand princes retained only their retinue. They added to it service men, bound to military service and called, in Mongol fashion, *dvor* ("court"). Together these represented the grand-princely military strength.[25] The *dvor* was thus distinguished from the boyars, and the old designation of retinue, *družina*, was not used. After the liberation, the grand princes retained their military *dvor*, but they also retained universal conscription and continued to divide their army into five divisions as the Mongols did. The Muscovite army also adopted Mongol tactics and retained Mongol weapons, to which the use of handguns and of cannon was added. The latter were probably introduced from Bohemia, and the handguns from Persia and India through the intermediary of the Volga Bulgars. The reorganization of the Muscovite army according to the Mongol pattern gave the new autocrats a considerable military strength, which contemporary western rulers could not match.

The Muscovite rulers also retained another Mongol institution which was unknown in contemporary western Europe, the mail service which enabled them to control the remote regions under their rule and to obtain regular information from the frontier and from every province of the state. Ivan III extended the mail service, building new roads and erecting new post stations, called *jamas*, in the Mongol fashion. This post service was much admired by Herberstein and rendered great service to Ivan IV in his campaigns.

Changes in the administration of Muscovy also often followed the Mongol pattern. The grand princes retained the Mongol system of taxation, to which the population had become accustomed and which proved highly effective. Court fees formed another source of grand-princely income. Justice was administered in the cities by lieutenants (*namestniki*) and in the rural districts by district chiefs (*volostel'*) appointed by the grand prince and charged respectively with the general administration of the cities and rural districts. These functionaries were allowed to retain a part of the court fees, but instead of salaries they were allowed to "feed themselves" off their districts. This "feeding system" (*kormlenie*) already existed in the Kievan period but only became fully developed in Muscovy. Appointment to such offices was for a short term because of the dangers of abuse to which such a system lent itself.

Besides this administration by state officials, there also existed in Muscovy a manorial administration, to which the domains of the grand princes, of the boyars, and of the Church were subjected. In this respect the Muscovite administrative system was similar to that of western Europe. The center of the grand-princely administration was the court of the grand prince (*dvor*), and the main official of the court was the major-domo (*dvorski, dvorecki*). He was also judge and administrator of the inhabitants of the grand-princely domains. A number of special departments were created for the administration under the direction of special officials (*putniki*), who were, however, directly responsible to the grand prince. Their reward was part of the income derived from the departments.

Other changes under Mongol influence can be detected in jurisprudence. Corporal and capital punishment, unknown in Kiev but practiced by the Mongols, was introduced into Muscovy, also probably torture, which was so widely used in western Europe. Some influences are also seen in penal and trial law, but none in Muscovite court organization, which remained basically the same as in the Kievan state.

Besides Mongol influences, old Byzantine traditions can also be detected in Ivan III's administrative reforms. This is particularly noticeable in the attempt at a codification of the existing Russian law. In 1497 the grand prince published a code called *Sudebnik,* compiled by his secretary Vladimir Gusev and others. It is based on the Kievan code *Russkaja Pravda* and other collections of Russian local law and customs. Besides procedural questions, it also contains the penal and civil law. This interest in legal questions shows that Muscovite lawyers had not forgotten the old legal principles which were kept alive in Kiev by the translation of Byzantine canon and civil law.

This *Sudebnik* was replaced under Tsar Ivan IV in 1550 by another code called *Sudebnik of the Tsar.* It completes and enlarges the code of Ivan III. The second *Sudebnik* has an important pendant in canon law called the *Stoglav,* a collection of a hundred chapters of ecclesiastical legal customs. It was initiated by Ivan IV, who convoked a council of the Russian Church in 1551 and submitted to the assembly questions on different ecclesiastical problems. The answers given by the prelates form the contents of the *Stoglav.*

The social changes effected in Muscovy during and after the Mongol period were also significant. To the ranks of the boyars was added a new class, that of the princes of the dynasties of Rurik or Gedymin, whose appanages and territories were annexed or were in danger of annexation by Muscovy and who preferred to renounce their sovereign rights, with or without compensation, in favor of the grand prince and to enter his services. Some Tatar princes, often called tsars or tsareviči because they belonged to the dynasties which had reigned over Kazan' or Sibir', also became the Muscovite tsar's vassals. Although they were superior in rank to the boyars, they did not enjoy the right of leaving the grand prince's service at will. This class of princes started to grow in the fourteenth century and was fully developed by the middle of the sixteenth century.

The vassal princes were given posts in the administration and military service similar to those held by boyars. Although less free politically than the latter, they occupied a higher place in the social scale than the boyars and were very anxious to maintain this position. The tsars had to establish a genealogical directory of all princely and boyar families, with detailed indications of functions which their ancestors had occupied, and they had to choose their councilors and high functionaries according to this complicated order of precedence called the *mestničestvo*. No prince or boyar would have accepted a lower position than that which he thought befitted his social rank. The tsar also had to select new members for his boyar duma from the highest class of princes or boyars. Soon the name boyar acquired a new significance—a member of the first rank of the duma, prince or boyar. The members of second rank were called *okol'ničie*—men of the tsar's entourage.

There were two lower classes of Muscovite gentry, the free servitors (*slugi volnye*) and the service-bound servitors. The latter were under the jurisdiction of the major-domo and were therefore called *slugi pod dvorskim*. They were often scions of impoverished boyar families, originally called the boyar sons. Both categories of grand-princely servitors were generally given small patrimonial estates. The free servitors generally occupied positions as junior officers in the army. The service-bound servitors served in the grand prince's personal army (*dvor*); others were employed in the management of the grand prince's domains or performed different functions at the court. Many of them had served at the courts of princes before the latter were forced by circumstances to enter the service of the grand prince. The grand princes welcomed them as they needed more and more reliable personnel to garrison fortified cities and the newly annexed provinces, where the servitors provided a reliable element which could be easily mobilized in case of emergency. Only a few of the boyar sons and of the *dvorjane* were able to ascend into the higher grade of the gentry and become *okol'ničie* or even members of the boyar duma.

The practice of endowing the *dvorjane* with an estate for their sustenance appears to have become the basis for another important social institution introduced by Ivan III—the *pomestie*.[26] After the conquest of Novgorod in 1478, Ivan III confiscated and dismembered the patrimonies of the vanquished Novgorod boyars and distributed their lands among the middle grade and junior officers of his army. The dispossessed boyars were given lands in the region of Moscow. The new squires were called *pomeščiki*. They had, in general, no other means of existence, and they retained their *pomestie* only as long as they rendered faithful and effective military service. Through the creation of military fiefs Ivan III not only broke the power of the old nobility in the conquered territory, but created at the same time a most reliable corps bound to support the centralized Muscovite government. The sons of the *pomeščiki* had to enter military service at the age of fifteen years and obtained more land only if the territory given to their fathers was too small for their sustenance.

Ivan III thus created a new military class based on a new type of economy, the manorial system. It became the solid basis for Muscovite military organization during the three following centuries. Nowhere in Europe was the manorial system as successful as in Muscovy. The introduction of this system, which was perfected in the sixteenth century, permitted the government to establish fiscal unity and to send these military squires to any part of the country or to any frontier where peace was endangered, while it guaranteed constant administrative and economic control over them. Only the Turkish *timar* system of the *spahis* could be compared with the Muscovite manorial system.[27]

The sixteenth century also saw the rise of the courtiers, the *dvorjane* or *dvorjanstvo*, to new prominence. The tsar created a third rank of duma membership, to which the *dvorjane* could be admitted. The top *dvorjane*, who were thus admitted to the highest council of the tsars, soon came to be regarded as equal to the boyars. This development reached its peak in the eighteenth century, when the term *dvorjanin* meant any nobleman and the term *boyar* ceased to be used.

The cities in Muscovy were never able to regain the importance which they had held in the state in the Kievan period. With the *večes* there disappeared also the last traces of the basic equality of the burghers. The merchants, divided into three classes according to their wealth (*gosti, gosti*-hundred, *sukonniki*), were exempt from taxation, but their services were used in financial administration and in the collection of indirect taxes. The other burghers were divided into middle burghers, occupying a better position in commerce and the artisanate, and junior burghers, who were petty artisans and workers; and all were subject to heavy taxation (*tjaglo*). They lived mostly outside the city proper, in the town settlement, called *posad*.

The peasants acquired a new name during the Mongol period. They were not called *smerdi*, as was the case in the Kievan state, but Christians (*khrist'jane*). This use started probably on Church lands but was extended also to the peasants on the lands of the tsar and of the nobility. The peasants settled on Church lands enjoyed exemption from paying the *tjaglo* during the Mongol period because the Church was exempt from paying taxes. This distinction between the peasants settled on Church lands and those on the lands of the nobility, however, ceased to exist after the liberation from the Mongol yoke. Because the manorial peasants were also bound to manorial duties, the peasants on Church lands, exempt from such duties, paid higher state taxes. Down to the middle of the sixteenth century the peasants were still free to move to another estate, after they had settled their accounts with their present master. The introduction of the *pomestie* system, however, soon posed the problem of supplying labor to the *pomeščiki*, who were the core of the Muscovite military power. This forced the government to limit the right of free movement on the *pomestie* lands. This limitation, introduced in 1581, was a bad omen for the peasantry and inaugurated the introduction of serfdom, which was definitely established in 1649.

The influx of so many princely families into the ranks of the Muscovite boyars represented a certain danger for the autocratic regime of the grand princes. Because the members of this highest noble class were accustomed to governing in their former principalities, it was hard for them to accept without regret their new status as grand-princely servants. Placed in the highest offices, they expected to share their new sovereign in the government of Muscovy. The example of Poland-Lithuania, whence many of them came, was before the eyes of some, and they may well have hoped to transform the Muscovite regime into an aristocratic monarchy. Ivan III and Basil III thought it necessary to take severe measures against some of them who had acted too independently in performing their new duties.

This danger naturally increased during the minority of Ivan IV. His mother Helen Glinskij had to use all her energy to defend the rights of her young son against the encroachment of the higher nobility, anxious to extend their influence in the government. She even had to imprison two brothers of her late husband and her own uncle. After her untimely death—there were rumors that she had been poisoned by the boyars—the intrigues of the higher nobility increased. The young tsar grew up in this poisoned atmosphere, and he could never forget his maltreatment by the Šujskij princes, who had obtained control of the regency. In one of his letters to Kurbskij, Ivan IV recalled with profound bitterness the bad experience of his unfortunate boyhood. He was filled with a profound dislike and hate for the boyars, who had manifested so little respect for the tsar, of whose supreme and autocratic power the young Ivan had so high a conception. This was inculcated in him by his teacher, the Metropolitan Makarij.

In realizing his political program of an absolute regime incarnate in an autocratic tsar appointed by God and sharing his power with nobody, Ivan IV transformed profoundly the social and political situation in Muscovite Russia. He was encouraged in his negative attitude toward the higher nobility by the lower nobility, which was envious of the rich boyars and always ready to support the tsar in his attempts to break the power of the princes. One of the petty nobles, Ivan Peresvetov,[28] encouraged the tsar in his writings to take bold action against the boyars. He was an adventurer who had served first the Polish and Czech kings and became in his writings a fervent propagandist for autocracy. He described impassionedly the abuses of the boyars and the maltreatment of their peasants, declaring that only the firm hand of an autocratic tsar could curb them and protect the people. It seems that many people in Muscovy thought like Peresvetov and were convinced that only an autocratic tsar could protect the poor and lowly against abuses by the mighty.

Ivan IV's first actions, although revealing an antiaristocratic tendency, were moderate. He first of all set up, besides the duma, an intimate council (*izbrannaja rada*) composed of a limited number of nobles of whose reliability he was sure—Kurbskij was the most prominent of them —and of members of lower classes (the priest Sylvester and Adašev, a petty boyar). The young ruler's antiaristocratic tendency was further revealed in his *Sudebnik* and in his introductory speech to the ecclesiastical assembly of 1551. The powers of the boyar-governors were limited and partly transferred to the representatives (*izljublennye starosty*) elected by the cities and districts, and the system of the *kormlenie,* which gave rise to abuses, was abolished. The choice of about one thousand of the lower boyars to whom he gave property near the capital, and whose function was to be ready at any moment to embark on any mission entrusted to them by the tsar, could be interpreted as an enlargement of the *pomestie* system.

More offensive to the higher nobility was the order (*ukaz*) of 1556 which ended the privilege of the boyars of transferring their allegiance to another prince and extended the obligation of military service to the holders of hereditary lands (*votčiny*). It was particularly this "degradation," making them equal to the holders of the *pomestie,* which was resented by the higher nobility. It seems that Prince Kurbskij, in his first letter to Ivan after his defection, had this *ukaz* especially in mind.[29]

All this was, however, surpassed by the violent blow directed against the princes and the old boyar families by the creation of the new class of the *opričniki,* men wholly devoted to the tsar and chosen by him (1565). Ivan IV embarked on this policy with the blessing of the people, who had begged him to return to Moscow and to reign as an autocrat, after his mock resignation. The *opričniki,* chosen among the *dvorjane* and petty nobility, were settled on the hereditary lands of the old boyar families in the central part of Muscovy. The former owners were in part mercilessly exterminated and in part settled in newly annexed territories on the borders of the state. It was a revolutionary measure, sanctioned, in the eyes of the tsar, by the idea of the supreme autocratic powers given to the tsar by God, by virtue of which he was absolutely free to assign to any subject the duties toward the state which he judged fit.

The regime of terror introduced by these brutal changes lasted for about twenty years. Countless thousands of people suffered from the excesses of the *opričniki*, and many were mercilessly massacred.[30] The system of the *opričnina* was gradually extended to other parts of Muscovy. At the end of Ivan's reign almost half of all dominions were included in the *opričnina*, the other half, the *zemština*, which Ivan had first permitted to enjoy a kind of autonomy, being finally subjected to the control of the *opričniki*.

It appears that Ivan's violent actions were inspired by the high conception of autocracy which he always professed. Believing blindly and firmly in this idea, he regarded it as his sacred duty to realize it in all its fullness. His own personal inclination toward cruelty and his desire to avenge the humiliations he had suffered from the boyars in his youth led him to regrettable excesses in the realization of his dream. The example of his predecessors, who had often imitated Mongol methods, gave a certain sanction to his merciless procedure. He is a typical example of the fanatic believer in the truth of an idea whose realization he regards as a sacred duty which justifies all means. Such examples can be found in all times.

Only after Ivan's death could the extent of the harm done to the state by his reforms be appreciated. However, in general, Ivan IV had attained his aim. The power of the old nobility was broken, and a new nobility was created which was absolutely devoted to the autocratic tsar. Although the old nobility tried later to recover its influence, it was never again able to occupy in the state the place which it had enjoyed before Ivan IV.

NOTES

1. This has been shown by two prominent Russian historians, S. M. Soloviev (*Istorija Rossii*, 2nd ed., St. Petersburg, 1896, vol. I, pp. 458 ff., 490 ff.), V. Ključevskij (*Histoire de Russie*, translated by C. Andronikof, Paris, 1956, vol. I, pp. 342 ff.) and not disproved by the objections of A. Presnjakov, *Obrazovanie velikorusskago gosudarstva* (St. Petersburg, 1918), pp. 26-47, and A. N. Nasonov, *"Russkaja Zemlja," i obrazovanie territorii drevne russkogo gosudarstva* (Moscow, 1951), pp. 173-196.

2. When he became Grand Prince of Kiev, he refused to follow the example of his father George Dolgorukij and establish himself in Kiev, still faithful to its democratic system of *veče*, and remained in Vladimir. The center of Russian power was thus transferred from the south to the north.

3. Andrew's tragic end shows that before the creation of the Suzdal' principality, there may have existed in the triangle between the Volga and the Oka a strong class of boyars, who came most probably from Novgorod and who established themselves in some places among the native Finnic population. The rapid cultural growth in the principality in the thirteenth century also indicates that the princes of Suzdal' had built on solid foundations which they

found ready in their territory. In this way, some of the findings of A. N. Presnjakov and A. N. Nasonov can be reconciled with the view of the older school of Russian historians represented by S. Soloviev and V. Ključevskij. On Suzdalian cultural achievements cf. F. Dvornik, *The Slavs*, pp. 252 ff.

4. A. M. Sakharov recently reviewed this development in his study on the political evolution of the northeastern Russian cities after the Mongol onslaught, "O političeskom razvitii severo-vostočnykh russkikh gorodov posle mongolo-tatarskogo našestvija," *Vestnik moskovskogo universiteta*, ist.-fil. serija (1956, 2), pp. 3-18. He came to the conclusion that during the first century of Mongol rule, when the cities had to be self-sufficient, there was a revival in the activities of the *veČes*. This situation, however, did not last because the cities failed to produce a class which would be economically strong enough to direct the policy of the cities. The rich merchants had joined the class of the landowners, and the boyars imposed their own will.

5. On the rise of Moscow see above, Chapter IX, pp. 217 ff.

6. See Chapter XII, pp. 259 ff.

7. This was an idea which Russian churchmen helped to promote. Vassian, bishop of Rostov, wrote to Ivan III after 1480, encouraging him to continue the war with the Tatars: "Tsar and Autocrator beloved by God. . . . The Lord gave into your hands this strong and pious land, to you and to your sons from generation to generation unto eternity."

8. All documentary evidence with bibliography will be found in F. Dvornik: "Byzantine Political Ideas in Kievan Russia," published in *Dumbarton Oaks Papers*, 9-10 (1956), pp. 73-121.

9. Especially in the works of the metropolitans Ilarion and Nicephorus, of Prince Vladimir Monomachus, of bishops Luke Židjata and Cyril of Turov, and of the monk Jakov, and in the Russian Primary Chronicle.

10. This is the most important passage quoted from the Slavonic translation of the Novel: "God's greatest gifts to men coming from above, from his love of mankind, are the priesthood and the tsardom, of which the former serves divine interests while the latter has the control over human interests and watches over them: both spring from the same principle and adorn human life. Hence nothing claims the tsar's care so much as the dignity of the priests, since these continually pray to god for them. . . . If these two institutions fulfill their roles, a kind of harmony will arise which can only prove useful to the human race. . . ."

11. The first evidence lies in Vladimir's first edict regulating relations between the Church and the civil government. Vladimir is said to have published it at the exhortation of the clergy and after "having opened the Greek *Nomocanon*." Vladimir's ordinances supplemented by Jaroslav the Wise can be traced to Byzantine sources. For details see F. Dvornik, *op. cit.*, pp. 97 ff.

12. Andrew's death gave an opportunity for the author of the Laurentian Chronicle to give vent to all his sympathies for the strong monarchy of one man. After comparing the grand price with David and Solomon, he exclaims: "The tsar, in his earthly nature, is similar to any other man, but because of his power he is of great dignity—like God." Never before has the power of a Russian prince been exalted to such a degree as in this eulogy of the first Russian autocrat.

13. Cf. Chapter IX, p. 218. Kiev was left by the metropolitan in 1299. The Metropolitan Peter, a native Russian who had been preferred by the Patriarch of Constantinople to a candidate proposed by the prince of Tver' and resident in Vladimir, looked naturally for support to Moscow, the opponent of Tver'.

Peter died in Moscow in 1326, and his successor, the Greek Theognostus, fixed his residence definitively in that city.

14. For details, see A. M. Ammann, *Ostslavische Kirchengeschichte* (Vienna, 1950), pp. 88-98, 185 ff.

15. In the introduction to a new paschal canon for the beginning of the eighth millenary started in 1492, the year in which the end of the world was vainly expected. According to old belief, the world, created in seven days, would last only seven thousand years. The document is published in the *Pamjatniki* of early Russian canon law, pp. 795-802.

16. On this translation see the thoroughgoing study by I. Ševčenko (see Bibl.).

17. Philotheus' texts were published by V. Malinin in his book, which is important for the study of Muscovite political theories, *Starec Eleazarova monastyrja Filofej i ego poslanija* (Kiev, 1901). The other important study on the growth of Muscovite autocracy is that written by Djakonov, *Vlast' moskovskich gosudarej* (St. Petersburg, 1889). Cf. also V. Valdenberg, *Drevnerusskie učenija o predelakh carskoj vlasti* (Old-Russian Theories on the Limits of Tsarist Power) (Petrograd, 1916). Recently N. S. Čaev devoted a study to the idea of the Third Rome in *Istoričeskie zapiski*, vol. 17 (1945). The most recent bibliography on this problem will be found in D. Stremoouchoff's study *Moscow the Third Rome* (see Bibl.), pp. 84-101. This study and that by R. L. Wolff, *The Three Romes* (see Bibl.), complete the older work by H. Schaeder, *Moskau das dritte Rom*, (see Bibl.), since reprinted, where a complete bibliography in Russian and other languages and the translation of Filofej's letters will be found. It should be noticed that the first Russian patriarch, Job, managed to include in the foundation charter of the patriarchate (1589) Filofej's words on Moscow as the Third Rome.

18. Among them were some well-known families, for example, the Godunovs, Uvarovs, Urusovs, Apraksins, Akhmetovs, Deržavins, Ermolovs, Karamzins, Muratovs, Turgenevs, Khomjakovs, Jusupovs.

19. Cf. G. Vernadsky, *The Mongols and Russia* (see Bibl.), p. 370. There were 229 noble families of German and West European origin and 223 of Polish and Lithuanian origin. In the seventeenth century families of foreign origin seem to have outnumbered the native Russian noble families, of whom 168 were descendants of the Ruriks, 42 "Russian," and 97 of uncertain ancestry. Of course many "Polish" and "Lithuanian" families were probably Russian in origin.

20. Cf. Chapter XII, p. 268. This is illustrated by the answer vouchsafed to the envoy of the Teutonic Order by the boyars. When the envoy expressed his astonishment that the Grand Prince Basil III could not conclude an armistice with the Polish king and fight for the cause of all Christians against their common enemy the Turk, who was in possession of Constantinople—"the inheritance of the tsar of all Russia," the boyars answered him: "The grand prince wants to have his inheritance—the Russian lands" and will fight for it against the King of Poland. See the original text in the *Sbornik imperat. russkago istoričeskago obščestva*, vol. 53, pp. 55-92 (St. Petersburg, 1867-1916).

21. Ivan III was anxious to uphold the dignity of his state in the eyes of the rest of Europe. His ambassadors were instructed to be very punctilious as regards etiquette and never to yield precedence to other ambassadors or officials during audiences and official ceremonies. The behavior of Muscovite ambassadors especially puzzled the Italian diplomats. Muscovy also had a **very**

elaborate ceremonial for the reception, audiences, and entertainment of foreign ambassadors. Many of these customs were inherited from the Mongols and appeared very strange to Western diplomats. Cf. also below, Chapter XVII, pp. 437 ff., on Muscovite diplomacy.

22. A similar tendency can also be discovered in Basil II's letter to the Emperor Constantine Palaeologus, dated 1451-52, in which he announces the election of Jonas to the dignity of Metropolitan of All Russia. Basil II mentions his "ancestor (*praroditel'*) the most blessed saint and equal to the apostles, the Grand Prince Vladimir," and he calls him "the Autocrat of all Russian lands." He uses here the same title which he had given at the beginning of his letter to the emperor.

23. See the documentation in the *Pamjatniki diplomat. snošenij drevnej Rossii s deržavami inostrannymi* (see Bibl.), pp. 10 ff.

24. Most of the documentation concerning the use of the tsarist title by Ivan IV will be found in vol. 59 of the *Sbornik imperat. russkago istoričeskago obščestva* (St. Petersburg, 1867-1916). Cf. also the *Pamjatniki,* quoted above, vol. 1, pp. 604 ff.

25. A new office was also created, again on the Mongol pattern, that of a quartermaster general, called *okol'ničij.* The term was later used to designate a member of the Duma of the second rank.

26. O. P. Backus, in his study, *Die Rechtstellung der litauischen Bojaren* (see Bibl.), thinks that the introduction of the *pomestie* could hardly have been inspired by similar feudal institutions in Lithuania, where in the fifteenth century the military obligations attached to the ownership of property were already disappearing.

27. In spite of some similarities between the Byzantine system of *pronoia* (see above, Chapter XIV, p. 354) and the Turkish *timar* system, there is no direct evidence to prove the influence of these two systems on the introduction and organization of the *pomestie.* Nor can the Russian social and military organization be called feudalism in the sense that it existed in medieval Western Europe, although some scholars (A. Eck, for example) would like to do so. Cf. the study by M. Szeftel, "Aspects of feudalism in Russian History," in *Feudalism in History* (see Bibl.), pp. 167-82. A. Eck gives the most extensive information in non-Slavic literature on social and economic changes in Muscovy (see Bibl.). The Russian specialist N. P. Pavlov-Sil'vanskij in his *Gosudarevy služilye ljudi* (The Sovereign's Serving People) (St. Petersburg, 1898), was too much influenced by Western European feudalism when studying the Muscovite system.

28. For detail and bibliography see W. Philipp's work on Peresvetov quoted in bibliography to this chapter.

29. Ivan's distrust of the nobility increased when he learned that during his illness in 1553, which appeared to be mortal, the boyars failed to support his desire for the succession of his son Dmitrij. He started his fierce campaign against the boyars in 1560, after the death of his beloved wife. He first broke with his counselors, the priest Sylvester and the boyar Adašev, and surrounded himself with men of low social origin.

30. Among the prominent victims was the Metropolitan Philip. His courageous interventions in favor of persecuted boyars and his sharp criticism of the *opričnina* induced the *opričniki* to launch false accusations against him. He was exiled to Tver', where he was strangled in 1569 by one of the *opričniki* acting on the tsar's orders. A monograph of the Saint was written by G. Fedotov (*Sv. Filipp mitrop. Mosk.*) (Paris, 1928).

Chapter XVI

THE REFORMATION AND THE SLAVS

The Renaissance and the decadence of Church life—Reaction of the faithful—Humanists and Church Reform—Luther, Zwingli, Calvin.

I. *The religious situation in the Czech lands—Luther, the Utraquists, and the Czech Brethren—Ferdinand I, the Neo-Utraquists, the Brethren, and the Catholics—Progress of the Reformation during the reign of Maximilian II, the* Confessio Bohemica—*Catholic, Lutheran, Philipist, and Calvinist tendencies—Rudolf's Letter of Majesty, religious freedom—Catholic reaction, revolution of the Protestant Estates—Election of Frederick, collapse at the battle of the White Mountain—Reformation among the Lusatian Sorbs, origin of Sorbian literature—Spread of the Reformation in northern Hungary—Lutheranism among the Slovaks and Germans, Calvinism among the Magyars—Religious freedom and organization of Lutheran and Calvinist Churches in Hungary—Catholic Counter-Reformation and the Slovaks*

II. *Situation in Poland—Prussia as center of Lutheran propaganda—Confederation of Warsaw, spread of Lutheranism and Calvinism—Czech Brethren in Poland—Attempts at formation of a Polish national Church—Anti-Trinitarianism—Catholic reaction, Hosius, and the Jesuits—End of the Reformation in Poland—Influence of the Reformation on Polish cultural life*

III. *Primus Trubar, the Slovene Luther—Reformers as founders of Slovene literature—Catholic Counter-Reformation follows methods of the Protestant reformers—Spread of the Reformation among the Croats—Protestant Croatian literature—Flacius and Vergerius, Croatian reformers—Catholic Counter-Reformation, creation of Serbo-Croatian literary language—Protestant and Catholic Pan-Slavic ideas, Križanić—Protestant propaganda among Orthodox Slavs—Protestantism and the eastern Slavs—Protestantism and Muscovy*

There is one phenomenon in the Western Renaissance which is extremely puzzling. The remarkable cultural and scientific progress made by the western nations was accompanied by a wave of hedonism which led to a sharp moral decadence in all respects, especially in Church life. This is all the more remarkable as Eastern Christendom never underwent such an experience. The Byzantines had no need to rediscover the heritage of classical and Hellenistic culture. Their intellectuals always enjoyed free access to the works of Greek poets, philosophers, and writers; their priests were trained not only in theology, but also in classical philosophy; their artists continued to work according to the traditions inherited from the classical and Hellenistic age. So they were able to produce in any age masterpieces such as the newly discovered early fourteenth century mosaics and frescoes of Kahrije Djami in Istanbul. These clearly reflect Hellenistic qualities in style and technique, while they are tempered and spiritualized by Christian sentiments.

The Christian East had also experienced some crises in the adaptation of its teachings to classical and Hellenistic cultural traditions. By the fourth century already a solution had been found to their use in the interpretation of the new faith. Although devout monks often warned the faithful against the study of the pagan and worldly writings of the ancients, their works continued to form the basis of Byzantine education. Only one Greek scholar was seduced by the pagan classics to such an extent that he became the author of a paganized philosophical system—the fifteenth century scholar Plethon—but he found no disciples in his aberration.

It is difficult to explain why the Renaissance worked such havoc in the moral behavior of so many westerners. It would be unjust to impute the profound changes in fifteenth and sixteenth century western Europe solely to the new spirit of individual freedom discovered in the writings of ancient philosophers, which had been introduced by fugitive scholars from Constantinople. It would be equally erroneous to regard the Renaissance as the cause of the Reformation, which broke up the unity of Western Christianity. As a matter of fact, a decay in morals and in Church discipline occurred several times in the West prior to the Renaissance period. Its origins lay in the bad example given to the faithful by the worldly life of members of the hierarchy who were excessively involved in the snares of the feudal system which had been established in the Germanic kingdoms.

The reformers of the eleventh century, in trying to disentangle the Church from these ties, destroyed unwittingly the whole basis on which the restored Roman Empire had been constructed by Charlemagne and Otto I, and it never recovered from the blow. The idea of universality which this empire represented was realized by the Papacy, the opponent of the Empire, especially under Innocent III at the beginning of the thirteenth century. But the reawakening of national sentiment leading to the creation of national monarchies made serious inroads into the papal system of universal government. The conflict between Philip the Fair of France and Boniface VIII wrought further havoc, and the "Babylonian Captivity" of the Papacy in Avignon, followed by the Great Schism of the West, tore yet further into shreds the universal banner upheld by Rome. The silence which ensued on the many exhortations of the Papacy to a new crusade demonstrated clearly that the political prestige which the bishops of Rome had enjoyed in the Middle Ages had definitely vanished.

The centralized fiscal regime introduced by John XXII, and extended over the whole Church, was becoming more and more unpopular. Although the financial resources accumulated in this way in Rome were used for embellishment of the Eternal City and for promoting art and learning, they contributed also to the worldliness and corruption of the papal court, which was the most splendid in Europe. In the intricacies of European politics of the sixteenth century, the popes behaved like Italian princes, concluding alliances and waging wars for the protection or aggrandizement of their dominions.

The consequences of this decline of the papal idea and of the hierarchic order of the Church were soon reflected in the attitude of the faithful. Confidence in the guidance of the highest ecclesiastical authorities in general religious life, still so strong in the Thirteenth century, was considerably shaken by all these disorders. Most of the richly endowed bishoprics and abbacies of Europe had become mere sinecures for the scions of noble families, who often did not even exercise their religious functions, while the faithful lacked the leadership to which they were accustomed. A dearth of zealous priests in the cities and the country parishes aggravated this situation, and so it was no wonder that the reception of the Eucharist, especially in Germany, and attendance at Mass were diminishing. Piety began to become increasingly individualized and to deviate ever further from participation in collective religious practice, for which the necessary opportunity was often lacking. An increased addiction to magic and to belief in secret satanic forces, which characterized the sixteenth century and which not even the reformers could shake, provided a false manifestation of these tendencies. On the other hand, the spread of devotion to the Suffering Christ, to His infancy and His tomb, to the Blessed Virgin under different titles, and to the saints, a devotion which could be practiced privately at home and in the family, testified to the attempts of the sincere faithful to satisfy their religious needs. The application of the great new invention of the printing press to the propagation of religious literature, both in Latin and in the vernacular, and the awakening interest in the Bible accentuated this trend.

Together with these tendencies, a wave of mysticism pervaded the devout, who were still numerous. This preserved the new spiritual trend from becoming materialistic, but it also accentuated the tendency toward individualization in religious life and its manifestation without the intermediary of the clergy, the official services, and the sacraments. The great mystics of the fourteenth and fifteenth centuries—the Germans Meister Eckhart, Tauler, and Suso; the Flemings Ruysbroek and Groote, whose name is connected with the classical product of the *devotio moderna,* the *Imitation of Christ;* the French "Ecstatict Doctor," Denis of Chartres—all gave a new basis to medieval piety. They led the faithful face to face with God, the majestic absolute Being, in Whose presence the sinner feels to the full his guilt and his impotence.

The Humanists set a course which was diametrically opposed to this. Valla and his pupils, headed by Pomponio Leto, rejected all notions of sinfulness and exalted human nature, erecting the material enjoyment of nature's gifts into the aim of human life. The majority remained faithful to Christian principles, attempting, however, to accommodate to Christian teaching the new notions of the dignity of man and of the free use of his capacities and nature's gift. Most humanists endeavored to alleviate the weight of sin on the conscience of the faithful by insisting that man should enjoy God's gifts and by excusing him on the grounds of his composite nature.

This attitude toward man's nature and toward sin of course reduced the desire for salvation and underrated the role of the Savior as mediator between God and man. Christ came to be regarded more as an example of a perfect man, His divine nature being more or less overlooked. So Christianity came to be envisaged as continuing the work of the wise men of antiquity, and Christ as a helpful example to humanity on the road toward better achievements and happiness. Since Christ's example was portrayed in the Bible, this, together with their philological interests, provided a new incentive for the humanists to read the Sacred Books in their original form and to spread their knowledge among the faithful.

In the comments of the humanists, however, some views can already be discerned which were later to achieve their full significance in the mouths of the reformers. The indifference of the humanists toward man's acts induced them to minimize the importance of good works and devotion. Erasmus of Rotterdam, the leader of this group of humanists, declared that faith alone was the gate leading to Christ. The French humanist Lefevre, who seems to have been nearest to traditional Christian teaching, was even more outspoken. He assured the faithful that man would be saved if he were converted to a perfect faith, regardless of his own efforts and deeds. This, however, did not mean that the humanists rejected the saving grace of good works. But the stress on faith and criticism of the abuse of rites in popular worship contributed somewhat to spreading the more radical teachings of the reformers among intellectuals.

The Christian humanists appreciated fully the sad situation of the Church in their age. They regretted it, depicting the abuses in lively, witty, and daring language,[1] and admonishing the popes to do their duty and to stave off what threatened to disgrace the Church. They did not, however, pretend themselves to become zealous reformers. But their exhortations went unheeded, and the few attempts at reform on the part of the Papacy proved more academic than real. When Louis XII of France sought to force the hand of Julius II, with whom he was at issue, he convoked a council for the reform of the Church at Pisa and then at Milan. The Pope replied by calling a Church assembly at the Lateran, but the theoretical threat of the superiority of a council over the pope was quietly liquidated by Leo X, who concluded a concordat in 1516 with Francis I which was advantageous to both parties. This ended the attempts at reform of the Church from within, much to the disappointment of Erasmus.

A radical change was necessary, but the academic exhortations of the Christian humanists were insufficient to bring this about. A more radical shock was needed to arouse the conscience of the authorities and to spur them to action. This shock proved to be more radical and dangerous than could have been expected, and it was initiated by a single man, a monk and a professor at the University of Wittenberg—Martin Luther (1483-1546). His mystic mind shared the anxieties of so many of his pious contemporaries as to the possibility of salvation in view of the immensity of the Absolute and the sinfulness of human nature. He found an answer in his interpretation of St. Paul's Epistle to the Romans,[2] which he eagerly applied to himself and which had already been in some degree suggested by the Christian humanists. This was a firm and intrepid faith in God and in His promises, which alone ensured man's salvation. A logical consequence of this seemed to Luther to be the rejection of the need for good works and of those ritual and sacramental means, including indulgences, which the Church regarded as helpful on the road to salvation. These means were already compromised in the eyes of many by abuses, and numbers of the faithful had already abandoned the habit of recourse to them. Luther's teaching on the priesthood of all believers rendered the intermediary role of the clergy unnecessary. This was a revolutionary doctrine which threatened the very bases on which religious life had hitherto been constructed, and its consequences shocked even the Christian humanists who had so severely criticized the abuses. Luther's teaching on the corruption of human nature and man's impotence to rise above it defied the thesis of the ancient philosophers and of all humanists on the free will of man, and Erasmus came forward with a glowing defense of man's freedom.

But aided by social disorders, by national sentiment against Roman intervention in German political and religious life, by the avidity of the feudal nobility to aggrandize their lands at the expense of Church property, and finally by a general feeling of the necessity for reforms, Luther won ground after a fierce battle. More than half Germany accepted his doctrines, and they spread into all the northern Germanic nations.

Two Christian humanists went even further than Luther. The Swiss Zwingli, preoccupied by the problem of sin, came to the conclusion that good deeds could only be achieved by the help of divine grace, which is reserved to those who are predestined for salvation. The French divine, Calvin, was a rationalist lawyer opposed to the mystical faith of Luther Calvin envisaged faith as being founded on reason illuminated by Christ's words as contained in Holy Writ. Like the humanists he also thought that man should be free in his thinking, but he did not derive from this any principle of tolerance for the opinions of others. He insisted rather that anyone teaching something which, in his opinion, contradicted the truth contained in the Bible should be punished.

Like Luther, Calvin was preoccupied with the problem of salvation, and like Zwingli he preached that some souls were predestined by God to salvation and others to damnation. Rejecting all the means recommended to the faithful by the Church as aids on the way to salvation, he retained besides the sacrament of baptism only the Eucharist, in which the soul is united with God, not in the transubstantiated species of bread and wine but spiritually in heaven. In contrast to Luther, Calvin preserved the two Catholic principles of universality and individuality. His Church, although national in its organization, was adapted to the autonomous status of the City-Republic of Geneva. It was not subject to political authority like the Lutheran Church, but preserved the spirit of universality with its attempt to dominate the secular power by forming a kind of theocracy under which all the political and private life of the citizen was strictly supervised. This teaching responded better to the humanistic feeling then prevalent in Europe, and thanks to the college founded in Geneva for the training of ministers, it was propagated all over northern Europe, mostly among urban populations.

The response of the Slavic nations to influences emanating from Italy and western Europe during the period of the Renaissance has been shown. It was therefore natural that the new religious movement, which was in many ways linked with the Renaissance, should also spread among the Slavs. This was the more to be expected as most of the Slavic nations lived in close proximity to Germany, which was the hotbed of the new doctrines.

I

Of all the Slavic nations the Czechs seemed best prepared to receive the new doctrines which Martin Luther started to preach in Saxony at the beginning of the sixteenth century.[3] The Utraquists, who constituted the majority of the population of Bohemia, were still without a bishop and claimed in vain recognition by the Pope of the Compacts, accepted at the Council of Basel. At the diet of 1478 they reorganized themselves under the direction of a consistory composed of eight priests and four laymen and aided, in the execution of its jurisdiction, by six noblemen. Deans were established and charged with the supervision of the priests of their districts. The favor which King Vladislav II (Ladislas II) (1471-1516) manifested to the Catholics—refusing to appoint Utraquists to the highest dignities of the kingdom—provoked stormy protests from the Utraquists. But at the diet of 1485 religious freedom for both confessions was decreed, and it was confirmed anew in 1512. The Catholic members of the Estates even promised to support the requests of the Utraquists in Rome for the consecration of a Utraquist bishop.

The renewed requests of the Utraquists, however, found no hearing in Rome, which continued to demand complete submission and the abandonment of their special practices. For some time the Utraquists were able to obtain the collaboration of two Italian bishops, who consented to ordain their priests. One of them, Philip de Novavilla, even resided in Prague and directed the Utraquist Church. After his death (1507), however, the ordination of Utraquist priests became very difficult, and the Church often had to content itself with priests of low moral value who had been disciplined by the Catholics.

The Czech Brethren, the third religious body in Bohemia and Moravia, had resolved the problem of ordination in the most radical way by abandoning the principle of apostolic succession in favor of the appointment of bishops and priests by the congregations. They further democratized the organization of their Church by entrusting its administration to four bishops and ten priests elected by a general synod of the whole Church, to which noblemen and lay protectors were also admitted; this was called the minor council. They retained, however, the celibacy of the clergy and continued to enforce a rigid moral discipline on all members of the Church.

The exemplary life of the Brethren attracted more and more adherents among the nobility and the people, and their success stiffened the opposition of the Catholics and Utraquists to them. The Brethren defended themselves in writings against the accusations. After Vladislav's death the persecution of the Brethren was stopped, and the teachings and practices of the Brethren continued to attract the radical elements among the Utraquists, who were embittered by the continuous negative attitude of Rome to their aspirations. The Utraquists thus appeared split into two factions, the conservatives continuing to hope for a reunion with the Catholics and the radicals hostile to Rome and favoring the union with the Brethren. The position of the Utraquists deteriorated gradually because of the low moral level of their clergy, which contrasted sharply with the exemplary life of the clergy of the Brethren. Having no bishops who could ordain candidates of their own choice, the Utraquists were unable to remedy this sad situation.

It was thus natural that Luther's criticism of some Catholic institutions as needing to be reformed or discarded and his attacks against the Papacy, which showed itself so hostile to the Czech Utraquist Church, found a profound echo among the radical Utraquists. Their interest in Luther's initiative grew when they learned that in his disputation with Dr. Eck in Leipzig in 1519, Luther had declared that Hus's condemnation was unjust and that he had publicly accepted Hus's teaching on the Church. On Luther's initiative Hus's work *De ecclesia* ("On the Church"), was printed in 1520. There is no doubt that Luther's teachings on the Church and on the universal priesthood of all the faithful are a further development of ideas which had been indicated by Hus in his works on the Church.

The spread of Luther's ideas among the more radical Utraquists—some of whose priests had also started to preach against the veneration of images of saints and to abolish some liturgical uses still practiced by their Church—alarmed the conservative Utraquists, who were still in the majority. The synod of 1521 forbade any innovations, declaring that the Utraquist Church should continue to profess the traditional teachings concerning the interpretation of Holy Writ, the seven sacraments, the veneration of saints, and fasting. The administrator of the consistory, fearing a further spread of Luther's teaching, started to negotiate with the Catholic higher clergy and with the king for a possible union with the Roman Church. This attempt was, however, frustrated by the decision of the Diet, impressed by the letter sent by Luther to the Estates of Bohemia in which he urged them to remain faithful to the Hussite spirit and to continue their negative attitude to Rome.[4]

The Czech Brethren were also attracted by Luther's doctrine, which in many respects, especially in its teachings on the Church, the priesthood, and the liturgy, was almost identical with their belief. Their envoys approached the German reformer, and a lively dispute developed between Luther and their leader Lucas on the doctrine of the Eucharist and the sacraments. The Brethren, however, anxious not to be identified with the followers of Luther, maintained their own doctrine on transubstantiation, the sacraments, the celibacy of priests, and the necessity for good works for the salvation of souls. Lucas reacted even more energetically against the doctrine of the Swiss reformer Zwingli on the Eucharist and excluded from the Unity those members who had adhered to Zwingli's teaching. In order to stress their differences with the sect of the Anabaptists,[5] the Brethren abandoned the rebaptism of new adherents.

Luther's teaching continued to spread among the radical Utraquists, who already constituted a strong party called by historians the Neo-Utraquists. Luther advised them, in a letter to the city council of Prague, to ordain their own priests. In the synod convoked in 1524 the majority of the Neo-Utraquists voted for the introduction of some Lutheran practices, but the conservatives soon obtained the direction of municipal affairs and the prominent propagators of Neo-Utraquism were exiled from Prague.

The conservative Utraquists approached the Czech Catholics, and both parties promised to respect the Compacts and not to tolerate the Brethren. Negotiations were inaugurated with the papal legate for a recognition of the orthodoxy of the Utraquist Church and its union with Rome. The determination of Rome again made a reconciliation impossible. The Utraquists refused the legate's condition of complete submission and the abandonment of all practices which were not general in the Roman Church, while they regarded his concession of Communion in both species by the laity as insufficient.

Although Ferdinand I (1526-1564) was most opposed to the spread of the Reformation and was determined to bring about a union of the Utraquists with the Roman Catholics, he unwittingly helped the Neo-Utraquists to gain new ascendancy at the beginning of the reign when he replaced the conservatives in the consistory with radicals. The growing Lutheran influence among the Utraquists manifested itself at their general meeting of 1534, and the king, alarmed by the resolutions forced through by the Neo-Utraquists, who were eager to conclude a union with the Brethren, opposed the implementation of the resolutions, stressing that besides the Catholic faith, only the Utraquists and their Compacts were admissible in the kingdom.

In the meantime, the Czech Brethren continued their friendly relations with the German reformers. In their confession of 1535, published in 1538 with Luther's preface, the Brethren made some serious concessions to Luther and Melanchthon's teaching on the Eucharist and the sacraments. Their leader, Bishop Augusta, also entertained friendly relations with the reformers of Strasbourg, especially Bucer, and with Calvin; he main-

tained, however, the autonomous position of his Church vis-à-vis the reformed Churches and the Utraquists.

The evolution in Germany naturally had its repercussions in Bohemia
among the Neo-Utraquists and the Brethren. The Emperor Charles V
(1519-1556), anxious to bring the evangelical princes into accord with
the Council of Trent, which was inaugurated in 1545, started to negotiate with their League of Schmalkalden. The negotiations remained fruitless, and he was ready to go to war, supported by the Catholic League
led by the Bavarian duke and by Ferdinand of Bohemia. The Bohemian
Estates, favoring the Neo-Utraquists and the Brethren and unwilling to
give Ferdinand their support, organized a Czech League for the defense
for their religious convictions. The defeat of the League of Schmalkalden
and their leader, the Elector of Saxony, at Mühlberg (1547) also reversed
the situation in Bohemia. Not only were four of the leaders of the opposition executed on Ferdinand's orders, but others too were punished by
confiscation of their properties, and the Brethren in Bohemia were subjected to a new persecution.[6] Many of them left their country and settled
in Poland.[7]

Ferdinand, however, did not succeed in inducing the Utraquist Church
to abandon its particular usages and to submit to Rome. The defection of
Maurice, duke of Saxony, from the emperor changed the military balance in Germany, and this gave new hope to the Czech Neo-Utraquists,
who favored the Reformation. The peace of Augsburg (1555) divided
Germany into two portions, Catholic and Protestant, and established the
principle of *cuius regio, eius religio,* giving the territorial sovereigns the
right to dictate their religious conviction to their subjects.

Charles V abdicated in 1556, realizing his failure to reconstitute a
universal empire and to re-establish religious unity in Germany on a
Catholic basis. After succeeding him on the imperial throne, Ferdinand
took up a milder attitude toward the Protestants and the Brethren. The
Neo-Utraquists profited by this new situation and became bolder in the
propagation of Protestant principles. The Brethren became more active,
not only in Moravia but also in Bohemia.

Ferdinand, unable to bring about the union of the Utraquists with
Rome, tried at least to rejuvenate the Catholic Church in his kingdom,
and in 1556 he established the Jesuits in Prague. Their house and college, the Clementinum, a former Dominican friary, became an important
center for the education of priests and Catholic intellectuals and soon
rivaled the university, which was almost completely in the hands of the
Neo-Utraquists.

In 1561 Ferdinand obtained from the Pope the appointment of Anton
Brus of Mohelnice (Möglitz) to the archiepiscopal see of Prague, which
had remained unoccupied for 140 years. Since the Neo-Utraquists were

masters of the consistory and thus able to impose Protestant teaching on the Czech Church, Ferdinand reserved to himself the right of nomination to the Utraquist consistory (1562), appointing conservative Utraquists to the leading functions.

He also continued to work for the realization of a compromise between the Catholics and the Utraquists. He succeeded in 1564 in obtaining from Pius IV the privilege for laymen to receive Holy Communion in both species in Bohemia and neighboring lands. If such a concession had been granted by the Pope a century before, the Czech Utraquists would probably have been satisfied and would have made their peace with Rome. In 1564 it was too late. Not even the conservative Utraquists felt satisfied with this concession, and it encountered general mistrust among the Protestants. On the other hand, the intransigents at the Council of Trent disapproved of it, and the concession was revoked.[8]

The Neo-Utraquists and the Brethren concentrated their hopes for the free exercise of their faith on Ferdinand's son Maximilian II (1564-1576), who was already recognized as the future king of Bohemia in 1549. In his youth Maximilian had shown some sympathies with Lutheranism, maintaining a pro-Lutheran preacher at his court in Vienna and avoiding religious functions of the Catholic Church. However, mainly for political and dynastic reasons, he remained a nominal Catholic, and before his election as king of the Romans (1562), he took the usual oath to protect the Church. Although he remained faithful to his promise, he favored many ideas put forward by the reformers and wished that his Catholic and evangelical subjects might reach a compromise so that religious peace could be preserved.

In the Bohemian kingdom he adopted the religious policy of his father, favoring the conservative Utraquists and moderate Catholics. He induced the Archbishop of Prague to start ordaining Utraquist priests, but this had to be abandoned in face of protests from Rome. He refused the request of the Neo-Utraquists to be granted the right of electing the members of the consistory, and was most annoyed at their request that the Compacts should be discarded from the privileges of the kingdom because they no longer satisfied their religious needs (1567). Maximilian accorded this, but refused to grant the Estates the right of Protestant worship according to the Confession of Augsburg—the right of worship in their castles and on their own lands, a privilege which he had been forced to concede to the Estates of Lower and Upper Austria (1571).

The suppression of the Compacts, which had formed a part of the fundamental law of the kingdom, amounted to de facto recognition of the existence of other religious bodies besides the Catholics and the Utraquists in Bohemia—the Lutherans and the Brethren. Although Maximilian was rather benevolent to the Brethren, he was obliged to regard them as a body which was not officially admitted in the kingdom, and was induced in 1568 by their Catholic and Utraquist foes to close their churches in Bohemia.

The Neo-Utraquists, now much bolder in their Lutheran tendencies, were trying to come to an understanding with the Brethren and to form a Czech Protestant Church. This tendency, favored by Bishop Augusta, who was released from prison, was, however, opposed by the most prominent representative of the Brethren—Blahoslav. The autonomous status of the Unity was thus preserved.

The Neo-Utraquists did not abandon their efforts to form a Czech Protestant Church, and in the *Confessio Bohemica,* which they presented to Maximilian in 1575, they made important concessions to the religious beliefs of the Brethren. The twenty-five articles of this confession were based on the Confession of Augsburg of 1555. The Lutheran conception of justification was fully accepted, but the teaching on the Eucharist resembled more the ideas of Calvin, which at that time were favored on this point by the Brethren. The Protestant Estates also demanded the retention of the consistory as the supreme authority of the Czech Church, but asked that the appointment of its officials should be reserved to them.

The emperor was in a difficult situation. He was exhorted, on the one hand, by his relatives and by the Pope not to make any concessions to the Protestants, and on the other hand, he needed the support of the Estates, now in great majority Protestant, for his Turkish wars and their consent for the election of his son Rudolf to the Bohemian throne. At last a compromise was concluded. The consistory, with members appointed by the king, continued to control the conservative Utraquists, but the Neo-Utraquist three Estates were given the right to elect fifteen defensors, who would rule over them. A superintendent was to be appointed by the defensors for each district for the supervision of its clergy. Full liberty of worship was given orally by Maximilian to the Estates. The Brethren, who did not join the Neo-Utraquists, were, however, again regarded as a sect which should not be allowed to exist. The division of the Utraquists into two sections, one gravitating toward Catholicism and the other, constituting a great majority, openly accepting Lutheran and Calvinist teaching,[9] thus became definite.

Maximilian's successor Rudolf (1576-1612) was a man of considerable knowledge and wide scientific interest and a great lover of art. But he was eccentric, mentally unbalanced, weak, and incapable of making a decision at the right moment. During the first years of his reign the religious situation continued to develop peacefully in his kingdom. The Catholics, who had suffered great losses in the first half of the sixteenth century, began to recover some of their position thanks to the activity of the Jesuits and of other orders, now directed by the Archbishop of Prague and by Marc Kuen and his successor V. Prusinovský as bishops of Olomouc. Although they constituted a minority, especially in Bohemia, the main administrative offices in the kingdom were in the hands of Catholic nobles, whose number had grown as some of them had been converted by the Jesuits and educated in their schools.

The principal aim of the Catholics was to prevent the realization of an independent Church organization for the Neo-Utraquists and to dominate the consistory of the conservative Utraquists, who were favorable to Catholicism. In order to obtain the consecration of their priests, the directors of the Utraquist consistory in 1587 secretly renounced the use of their special practices, except for the use of the cup for the laity, and accepted priests ordained by the archbishop. In 1591 Fabian Rezek, the new administrator of the Utraquists, promised complete obedience to the archbishop and became a Catholic. About fifty Utraquist priests followed this example, and in 1593 the administrator and his clergy were officially received into the Catholic Church in Rome. Returning to Prague, he abdicated his office, and the archbishop became the head of all the Utraquist clergy. But on the protest of some Utraquist city councils, the king had to re-establish the Utraquist consistory and appoint new administrators in order to prevent the Utraquist burghers from embracing Protestantism.

Nevertheless, the Neo-Utraquists gained more and more adherents. They were, however, split into three factions. The main body professed the Bohemian confession presented to Maximilian in 1575. Many, however, especially the German nobles and burghers, favored the Lutheran faith as expressed in the original Confession of Augsburg of 1530 and 1577. Others were "Philipists," accepting Philip Melanchthon's edition of 1540 of the Augsburg confession, which revealed some Calvinist tendencies. The most radical among the Neo-Utraquists were in favor of pure Calvinism and were in frequent contact with Heidelberg, the center of German Calvinism.

The Neo-Utraquists were aware that these differences in teaching weakened their position, and therefore renewed their requests for the erection of their own consistory to act as the supreme authority of the Czech Protestant Church. Some Catholic nobles were ready to support the demand of their Protestant colleagues on condition that they would join them in the suppression of other creeds, especially that of the Brethren. The Protestants, however, refused to be separated from their allies, and so their request was rejected by Rudolf (1584).

At the same time the king renewed the former decrees against the Brethren, which were not, however, enforced. The Brethren were also

going through a religious crisis. They stopped sending their young men
to study at Wittenberg when the purely Lutheran spirit, after 1574, prevailed there over Melanchthon's teaching, which was nearer to that of
the Brethren. The Unity began sending its students and priests to Strasbourg, Basel, and Geneva. The consequence of this was that Calvinist
teaching began increasingly to permeate the Unity. The conservatives
resisted this penetration for a long time, but finally the Calvinist trend,
which was especially strong among the Brethren in Moravia, proved victorious and became more and more pronounced in their confessions and
catechisms.

The Catholics, emboldened by the progress of the Counter-Reformation started by Rudolf's nephew Ferdinand in Styria, and by their own
success in Bohemia, obtained from Rudolf in 1602 the issue of a decree
renewing that of 1508 and threatening with death all who professed a
faith different from that of the Catholics and of the old Utraquists. The
decree was directed primarily against the Brethren, but also menaced all
Neo-Utraquists. The papal nuncio was the main inspirer of this decree.
It remained, naturally, completely ineffective, and at the Diet of 1603,
the leader of the Brethren, Wenceslas Budovec, speaking also in the name
of the Protestants, attacked very strongly the whole religious policy of the
king.

Rudolf was also ill advised in his religious policy in Hungary. When
his army had been able temporarily to liberate the greater part of the
country from the Turks, Rudolf initiated a Counter-Reformation there on
the suggestion of his Catholic advisers. The insurrection of the Hungarians, who penetrated into Moravia, induced the members of the Habsburg dynasty to declare Rudolf's brother Matthias head of the family
because of Rudolf's incapacity and his ill health bordering on insanity.

Matthias, after terminating the Hungarian troubles and concluding a
peace with the Turks (1606), which Rudolf hesitated to ratify, decided to
effect the dethronement of his brother. He was supported by the Estates
of Hungary, Austria, Moravia, and Silesia. Only the Estates of Bohemia
continued to support Rudolf, but their Protestant majority decided to
obtain from him a decree of toleration for their religion. The leader of
the Protestants and Brethren, Wenceslas Budovec, presented to the
king a memorandum of twenty-five points. After protracted negotiations
and seeing that refusal would provoke a revolution, Rudolf rejected the
protests of his Catholic councilors and signed on July 9, 1609, a decree
called the *Letter of Majesty*. This ensured the free exercise of their religion to all professing the *Confessio Bohemica*.

Rudolf gave way to the Protestants only after prolonged hesitation and
tergiversation. In order to give this new turn in religious policy at least

a semblance of continuity with the previous laws of the kingdom, Rudolf insisted that the word "evangelical" confession be replaced by the word "Utraquist." The Estates accepted this substitution the more willingly as this fiction offered the Protestants the possibility of winning over the rest of the conservative Utraquists with their Catholic tendencies. All, even the Brethren, gave communion to the laity in both species.

The Catholic and "Utraquist" Estates completed this important document with an agreement guaranteeing full religious liberty to all in Bohemia, even the peasants, and both parties were given the right to exercise their religious worship freely on crown lands. The conservative Utraquists were allowed to retain their priests who had been ordained by a bishop. This arrangement facilitated the liquidation of the old Utraquist consistory and the erection of a new one in which the Protestant Utraquists should be represented by the administrator and five assessors, and the Brethren by their senior bishop, who was second to the administrator, and two priests. Three professors from the university, the direction of which was given to the Utraquists, were added to the new consistory. The Brethren were also largely represented among the twenty-four defensors elected by the three Estates. However, in spite of the opposition of the old Utraquists and the Lutherans, the Brethren were allowed to keep their own ecclesiastical order and discipline. The newly established "Utraquist" Church was divided into districts directed by archdeans and deans, who were assisted by local consistories.

The Czech national Church thus obtained, at last, a firm basis for its reorganization. The Brethren, who had hitherto only been able to hold their services in private houses in Prague, were given the Bethlehem Chapel, where Hus had preached, for their worship, and another church was given to the Brethren of German extraction. The German Lutherans also obtained their churches. Evangelical worship was soon established in fifty churches in Prague and in five hundred parishes in Bohemia.

Some difficulties, however, soon appeared. Some of the conservative Utraquists, although now under the direction of the new consistory, refused to adopt the Protestant liturgy and continued to observe Catholic customs. Together with the Lutherans they objected to the acceptance of the Brethren into the new Church organiztion. The Protestants continued to be split into three factions, Lutherans, Philipists, and Calvinists, who attracted more and more adherents. In spite of these differences, internal peace among the denominations continued to be preserved. The Brethren, especially in Moravia, developed an increasing tendency toward assimilation with the rest of the Church.

It was to be expected that the Catholics, although in a minority, would not accept the situation without a struggle. They had able leaders in John

Lohelius, archbishop of Prague (1612-1622), and Cardinal Dietrichstein, bishop of Olomouc (1599-1636). They were supported in their efforts to win the country back to Catholicism by high royal officials, especially Martinic and Slavata, whom Matthias had retained in office when he became king of Bohemia (1612-1619) after Rudolf's enforced adbication. The efforts of the Catholics produced considerable results in Moravia, where the number of Catholic parishes grew from 50 in 1560 to 280 in 1619. In Bohemia the Catholic nobles appointed Catholic priests wherever possible and tried to place at least the remaining conservative Utraquist priests in parishes on crown lands and in royal cities.

The most dangerous point of contest was the erection of Protestant churches on Church lands. According to the old Czech custom the Church lands were regarded as royal fiefs given for the use of the Church, and the Protestants therefore extended the rights accorded to them by the *Letter of Majesty* to Church properties. The Catholics contested this and obtained from Matthias in 1616 a declaration which confirmed their interpretation. The Catholics felt encouraged when Matthias' nephew Ferdinand II, who had succeeded in recatholicizing his Duchy of Styria, was recognized in 1617 as the future king of Bohemia. So it happened that in the same year, the archbishop gave orders to destroy the church which the Protestants had built in Hroby (Klostergrab), which was an ecclesiastical property, while the Abbot of Břevnov closed the Protestant church in his city of Brumov (Braunau).

This was interpreted by the Protestants as a breach of their privileges, and when the king refused to consider their complaints, the representations of the Estates decided to break with him. So on May 23, 1618, after a stormy meeting, they threw the king's most trusted councilors, Counts Martinic and Slavata, with the recorder of the land Fabricius, out of the windows of the council chamber.

This was the famous defenestration which is regarded as having inaugurated the Thirty Years' War. It recalls the defenestration of Catholic city councilors in 1419 which had opened the Hussite wars. It was an open revolution. The Estates elected thirty directors, who took over the government of the country. The Jesuits were expelled from Bohemia, and the archbishop and other Catholic dignitaries left the country. It seemed that the whole country would become Protestant.

The Estates, of course, declared the election of Ferdinand II as successor to Matthias invalid, and after Matthias' death (March 29, 1619), they looked round for a new king.

They would perhaps have had a better chance of success against Ferdinand II if they had won John George, Elector of Saxony, for their cause. But the latter, a strict Lutheran, looked askance at the growth of

Calvinism in Bohemia, and the election of Frederick, Elector Palatine, a convinced Calvinist, brought the Saxon Elector on to the side of Ferdinand, who was chosen as emperor by the German Electors. The Calvinistic zeal of Frederick's court preacher, Abraham Scultetus, alienated many Czech Lutherans, who were scandalized at the iconoclastic excesses which he committed in the Prague cathedral, which became a center of the Calvinist cult.

The help which came from the Protestants in the Empire was not as large as was hoped for, and King James of England, although father-in-law to the new Bohemian king, remained neutral in the war against the Habsburgs. The army of the Bohemian Estates was ill prepared and lacked talented generals. With the help of Maximilian of Bavaria, Ferdinand was able first to crush the Protestant Estates of Austria and to march victoriously through Bohemia to Prague. The short battle on the White Mountain near Prague, on November 8, 1620, decided the fate of Bohemia for centuries to come. Frederick, the "Winter King," lost his courage and fled in panic to Silesia with his court. This meant the defeat of the Czech Reformation [10] and the opening of a new chapter in Czech political and religious history.

The remnants of the Sorbs, or Wends, living in Lusatia, which at that time still belonged to the crown of Bohemia, were also engulfed by the Reformation, together with the German population of that land. This was not surprising as the Reformation had started in Saxony, which neighbored on Lusatia. Most of the Sorbs were ecclesiastically subject to the bishopric of Meissen, which had been since 1399 immediately dependent on the Pope. The progress of Lutheranism was, however, slowed down by the efforts of Bishop John VII von Schleinitz (1518-1537). But when John IX von Haugwitz (1555-1581) resigned in order to become a Protestant, Luther's doctrine became dominant in Lusatia.[11]

Thanks to the zealous activity of John Leisentritt (1527-1586), a German from Olomouc in Moravia and dean of the Chapter of Budyšin (Bautzen), who acted from 1560 on as bishop's commissioner in Upper and Lower Lusatia, the Catholic faith survived. He was also active in literature, and his German book of hymns became very popular in Germany. In order to strengthen Catholic propaganda among the Lusatians, he advocated, vainly of course, the celebration of the Mass in the vernacular.

Leisentritt's efforts for the erection of a bishopric for Lusatia remained unsuccessful. The ecclesiastical administration of the Catholics of Lusatia remained in the hands of the dean of the Chapter in Bautzen. When Lusatia was ceded by Ferdinand II to Saxony in 1635, the emperor reserved to himself the protectorate over the remaining Catholic institutions in the land. The surviving Sorbs in Lusatia (about 100,000) are divided; the majority belong to the Lutheran Church, while the rest, especially in Upper Lusatia, are organized in Catholic parishes.

The Reformation also laid the first foundation of Sorbian literature. Hitherto, the few priests who spoke Sorbian seem to have used Czech religious books for religious instruction. The Catholic catechism which is said to have been composed in Sorbian at the end of the fifteenth century has not been preserved, and the first known Sorbian literary monument is the translation of the New Testament into the dialect of Lower Lusatia by Nicholas Jakubic in 1548. This was followed by the translation of the Psalter into the same dialect. In 1574 the translations (by Albin Moller) of Luther's hymnal and small catechism were printed in Budyšin (Bautzen). This catechism was also printed in the Upper Lusatian dialect in 1597.

In the second half of the seventeenth century the Protestant Michael Frencel was particularly active, translating parts of the Gospel and the New Testament into the Upper Lusatian dialect. He was followed by the Jesuit James Ticin, author of a treatise on Sorbian orthography; by the Catholic writer George Swótlik, translator of the Bible and author of the first Sorbian dictionary; and by John Chojnan, author of the first grammar (1650). Unfortunately the first Protestant and Catholic Sorbian writers used different orthographies in their works. This circumstance hampered the evolution of a Sorbian literary language and divided it into two dialects.

It was thought that the Reformation would find a fertile soil among the Slovaks [12] because its preachers found their task facilitated by the existence of numerous Hussite enclaves in northern Hungary. The soldiers of John Jiskra were believed to have been the main propagators of Hussitism when they were holding the country for Ladislas Posthumus, king of Bohemia.[13] This opinion has, however, been disproved by recent research.[14] Luther's teaching found its first adherents among the German burghers of the cities of northern Hungary, who continued to be in touch with the motherland. Some influential followers of Luther could also be found at the court of Louis II in Buda. One of the first missionaries of Lutheranism there was the court preacher John Cordatus, a native of Moravia.

These first echoes of Lutheranism in Hungary were not silenced by the decrees voted by some Hungarian Diets on the initiative of the watchful papal nuncio. More favorable conditions for the spread of the new doctrines appeared after the catastrophe of Mohács (1526). Two archbishops and five bishops perished with the king on the battlefield, and the Papacy neglected for too long a period to fill the vacant sees. This circumstance and the general political chaos during the struggle between the two contestants for the Hungarian throne, Ferdinand I and John Zápolya, aggra-vated by the progress of the Turks, facilitated the spread of the Reforma-tion in the kingdom. In the region inhabited by the Slovaks many Magyar nobles and imperial generals protected the preachers who were spreading Luther's doctrine. The major towns in the Slovak country became centers of Protestantism, and the Reformation spread from the German cities among the Slovak population. Many names of Slovak preachers are known from between 1530 and 1540. Only some mining centers, especially Krem-nica and Banska Bystrica, resisted, for some time at least. Bratislava (Pressburg) was in great majority Protestant about 1550, and the Refor-mation found acceptance in the rest of Hungary and in Transylvania.[15]

For some time chaotic conditions prevailed among the Protestants in Hungary because a variety of theological teachings—pure Lutheranism, Philipism, Zwinglianism, and Calvinism—found acceptance, while Ana-baptists also came from Moravia. The Hungarian Diet of 1548 voted a law which was directed against the Anabaptists and Calvinists. In order to show that their belief was different from that of the censured sects, the five main cities of Slovakia in 1549 presented to the emperor their con-fession, composed by Leonard Stöckel, a disciple of Luther and Melanch-thon. This confession, called *Confessio Pentapolitana*, was based on the Confession of Augsburg, which was also adopted by the seven Slovak mining cities in their *Confessio Heptapolitana*. The Saxon colonists in Transylvania also adopted the Augsburg confession, and their Church was the first dissident religious body in Hungary to obtain official recognition (1552).

The Germans of northern Hungary and Transylvania, with the Slovaks, thus definitely became Lutherans. The Magyars hesitated for some time between Luther and Calvin. The main propagandist of Luther's teaching among them was Matthias Biró. After visiting the centers of the Swiss Reformation, he started, however, to preach Calvin's teachings, and be-came, with Peter Melius, the main organizer of the Magyar Calvinist or Reformed Church. The Magyar Lutherans and Calvinists separated definitely about 1560, and the Synod of Debrecin (1567) gave a solid theological basis to Magyar Calvinism, which became the profession of the majority of the nation.

The Catholics only started to react more vigorously after the laws voted by the Hungarian Diet of 1548. The Catholic Counter-Reformation was inaugurated by Archbishop Nicholas Oláh, who also introduced the cup for the laity in northern Hungary in order to attract the Protestants. His successor Simon Forgách definitely settled the Jesuits in Slovakia. Sup-ported by the royal court, the Catholics succeeded in occupying the most important positions in the administration and in the army, and claimed the return of churches and properties occupied by the Protestants. The Hungarian Diet, where the Protestants then had a majority, protested against the use of military force in the recatholicization of Košice and Levoča, but Rudolf II rejected the protest and, obeying the advice of the Catholic hierarchy, renewed the anti-Protestant decrees of Louis II. The insurrection of Bočkay of Transylvania, who profited by the dissatisfaction of the Protestants with Rudolf's religious policy, changed the situation. Rudolf was forced, in the peace treaty of 1606, to give religious freedom to the Hungarian nobility and cities.[16]

Only then could the Protestants in Hungary effectually organize their Churches. Hitherto, the Protestants had remained subordinate to the jurisdiction of the Catholic hierarchy, to whom they had also to pay the tithe. Their ministers started to organize themselves into larger groups, called *contubernia* or *fraternitates* (brotherhoods), but the seniors of the confraternities whom they had chosen had to be confirmed in their offices by the Catholic hierarchy. Only after 1606 were the Protestants allowed to appoint their own bishops and superintendents. The organization of the Protestant Churches of northern Hungary was completed in 1610 at the Synod of Žilina in modern Slovakia, presided over by the new palatine George Thurzo, who was a militant Protestant—the restoration of this dignity was one of the conditions of the peace treaty of 1606. The ten counties of northern Hungary—modern Slovakia—were divided into three provinces, each of which was to elect its own superintendent or bishop. Special inspectors, elected for each province, had to see that national rights of the German and Magyar minorities in the ten counties were observed. Another synod of 1614 created a similar organization for the counties of northeastern Hungary. The Slovak Protestants entered into a lively intercourse with their Czech coreligionists and accepted the Czech translation of the Bible (the Bible of Kralice [17]), which was used in Protestant worship in Slovakia until modern times. An important contribution to Slovak literature was provided by the *Cithara sanctorum* ("The Harp of the Saints"), a collection of about four hundred religious songs composed by the minister George Tranovský (1636). Besides translations and adaptations of Hussite and Lutheran compositions, it also contains original songs and is still used by Slovak Protestants.

The Catholic Counter-Reformation in Hungary reached its peak under Archbishop Peter Pázmány (1616-1637), a Jesuit. He reorganized the Catholic Church, founded special colleges in Vienna and Rome for the education of Hungarian priests, and transformed the higher school of Trnava into a university (1635). Being himself a scion of an old Hungarian aristocratic family, he concentrated his efforts on the conversion of

Hungarian nobles and succeeded in winning over the great majority of the Hungarian magnates. With their help, Catholic missionaries worked successfully among their subjects. The use of the cup for the laity was also discarded by him. Pázmány's successors continued this activity, and so it happened that the Catholic Church regained the leading position among the Slovaks and Magyars which it had lost in the sixteenth century.

This situation could not be changed even when Bethlen Gábor, the prince of Transylvania, allied himself with some Protestant nobles of northern Hungary and, declaring himself protector of the Hungarian Protestants, invaded the territory of modern Slovakia. He was elected king of Hungary by the Protestant nobles in 1620, and in alliance with the Austrian and Bohemian Protestant Estates, he threatened the position of Ferdinand II. The defeat of the Czech Estates at the White Mountain (1620), however, changed everything, and Bethlen preferred to conclude a peace treaty with the emperor and to renounce his royal title in return for some territorial concessions. He obtained the confirmation of religious liberty from 1608, but the Catholic Counter-Reformation continued to spread and was not even stopped by Bethlen's successor George Rákoczi, who invaded northern Hungary as an ally of France and Sweden. In the peace treaty of Linz (1645), Rákoczy obtained an extension of privileges for the Protestants, but the Catholic Estates were already strong enough to block the effective implementation of some of its stipulations. The decline of Transylvania under Rákoczy's weak successor deprived the Hungarian Protestants of their influential supporters.

II

The history of the Reformation in Poland reveals some features which are peculiar to that country and which cannot be detected in other Slavic lands.[18] There was no Polish Reformation in the fourteenth century as there was in Bohemia, and although the Hussite movement found some echo in Poland, it never exercised a marked influence on the national and religious life of the country. It was natural that the ideas of the German reformers should have found easy access to Poland, as to Bohemia, but the Poles also enjoyed very lively intercourse with the Swiss intellectuals, especially with Basel and the circle around Erasmus. This explains why the influence of the Swiss reformers, Zwingli, Bullinger, and Calvin, was stronger in Poland than in other Slavic countries.

The contact with the German, Swiss, and French Reformation was mainly due to Polish students, who could be found, at the beginning of the sixteenth century, at all the universities in Italy, Switzerland, France, and Germany. The decadence of the University of Cracow forced the sons of the Polish nobility to go abroad for their education. Many of these young nobles enjoyed personal relationships with prominent reformers, especially in Basel, Zürich, Geneva, Wittenberg, and Strasbourg. One of them, S. Górka, was even elected rector of the University of Wittenberg in 1554.

It has been shown how these contacts with learned centers abroad had first helped to introduce humanistic studies into Poland.[19] Although the fervent Polish humanists included many prominent members of the higher clergy, humanism finally had some very unfavorable effects on the Polish Church, as it had in some other countries. The prominent position of scholastic theology in Polish intellectual life was shaken, and the University of Cracow, clinging stubbornly to the old scholastic methods, was unable to adapt the new system to Polish religious thinking. The humanistic ideals of individual independence and liberty of opinion, derived from the classics, also encouraged the Poles to be critical of some ecclesiastical institutions. The secularization of intellectual life and the loosening of moral principles deriving from the Italian Renaissance made all the more regrettable inroads into Polish religious life because they corrupted many of the Polish hierarchy. This resulted in a lowering of the moral standard of the Polish regular and secular clergy. It has indeed been disproved that Queen Bona, wife of Sigismund I (1506-1548), sold ecclesiastical preferments to the highest bidders among the nobility in order to provide the means for her own political and economic plans.[20] Yet the situation among the higher clergy deteriorated, and this naturally facilitated the penetration of reforming ideas into Poland.[21]

There was yet another factor peculiar to Poland which played a great role in the spread of the Reformation in that country—the antagonism between the higher clergy and the nobility. The latter refused to respect certain privileges of the clergy, especially the payment of tithes, and opposed most stubbornly the exercise of ecclesiastical jurisdiction over members of their class. The struggle between the nobility and the higher clergy, although the latter was exclusively composed of scions of noble families, lasted a long time and embittered political life in Poland.[22]

It was natural that Luther's theses should have evoked an especially strong echo among the German population in Poland, especially in Royal Prussia. Gdańsk (Danzig) was the first place where Luther's teaching found a fertile soil. The preaching of some native monks and priests who had joined the German reformists aroused an overwhelming response. The city council, which opposed the spread of the Reformation, was forced to give way to a newly elected council; churches were given over to the reformers; Church property was secularized; monasteries and convents disbanded.

The reaction, however, soon came. The deposed councilors appeared before King Sigismund I (1506-1548) to ask for intervention. The fact that political and social questions were involved led the king to intervene in 1526 against this first attempt at a Reformation in Royal Prussia. Sigismund feared that Danzig might pass from the orbit of Poland to that of Germany, and he was disturbed by what appeared to many to be a revolt of the lower orders against the patriciate. Moreover, he had incurred much criticism in the Catholic world for giving his consent to the secularization of Ducal Prussia. So the old council was reinstated, Catholic worship restored, and fifteen leaders of the reformers condemned to death. Albert, duke of Prussia, only succeeded in saving six ministers from the death penalty.

Soon, however, Albert's residence at Königsberg became a center from which the Reformation penetrated into Poland. Many of the Polish nobility also showed sympathy with the Reformation, although they were not yet ready to break openly with Rome. Pressed by the higher clergy, King Sigismund I published some edicts banning the importation of books written by the reformers and forbidding Polish students to visit Protestant universities. The clergy also made full use of their rights of jurisdiction against suspects and heretics, but the Lutheran doctrines continued to spread, all the more so as the efforts of the Primate John Łaski to reform the Polish Church remained vain.

Sigismund August (1548-1572) seemed favorable to the Reformation. Before he acceded to the throne, he received letters from Melanchthon and Calvin and chose his chaplains among the reforming clergy. The hopes of the Protestants that the young king would embrace the Reformation were, however, foiled by an accident. The majority of his nobles, especially the Protestant nobility led by Andrew Górka, and likewise Albert of Prussia were opposed to the king's marriage with Barbara Radziwill, whom he loved dearly. The higher clergy were favorable, and the Primate of Poland placed the royal crown on her head in Cracow and thus ended all doubts about her worthiness to become queen of Poland. This incident alienated the king from the Protestants, and he promised to remain faithful to the Catholic Church.

In spite of that, Sigismund August was disinclined to use forcible means to stop the spread of the Reformation in his kingdom. He permitted Lutheran worship in Danzig and Royal Prussia (1557) and in Livonia (1561) and could do little when many Polish nobles started to introduce Protestant worship into the churches on their lands. Here again the nobles clashed violently with the higher clergy, who had hailed their Protestant confreres before ecclesiastical tribunals. In several attempts at a compromise the king was forced to water down ecclesiastical privileges to the utmost.

As a result of this strife the Confederation of Warsaw was concluded at the Diet of 1573, after Sigismund August's death in the previous year. This bound the members of the Diet, whatever their religious confession, to live in freedom and not to permit the persecution of anybody on religious grounds. This was to serve as a basis for a declaration of tolerance to which the new king would have to swear to adhere after his election. The confederation was worded in the spirit of the religious peace of Augsburg of 1555, and although its wording was not as clear as that of Augsburg and although it did not specify any profession of faith, it was regarded as the great charter of liberty for Polish Protestants. Henry of Valois was the first king to make, in his oath, a declaration based on the confederation.

So it happened that the Reformation was able to spread more freely in Poland. Luther's doctrines as expressed in the *Confessio Augustana* spread principally among the German population in Royal Prussia and in the cities which still had numerous German burghers. It also penetrated into Great Poland, where a number of nobles introduced it into the churches of their lands.

As already indicated, the Polish nobility only began openly to join the Reformed Church in the later period of its development, when Calvin was the most prominent reformer. His teaching attracted the Polish nobility more than Lutheranism, which was at that time compromised in the eyes of many by fruitless dogmatic strife. Moreover, the contacts between Switzerland and Poland had, in the intellectual field, been more lively than those with Germany. Reforming ideas coming from Switzerland and France appealed more readily to the national sentiments of the Polish nobility than did those coming from Germany. The deductions which could be derived from Calvinist teaching in the sphere of political speculation also appealed to the Polish nobility. Unlike Luther, Calvin did not invest the secular power with control over the Church, and the nobility were completely favorable to the idea of limiting the royal power. In the political sphere Calvinism was conducive rather to republicanism and democracy, which could, of course, only mean government by a bourgeois and aristocratic oligarchy. All this explains why Calvinism found such ready acceptance in Poland and why so many prominent noble families in Great Poland accepted Calvin's doctrine. From there Calvinism penetrated into Lithuania, where its main propagator was Prince Nicolas Radziwill, called the Black, the most influential and wealthy magnate in the country. He was joined in his zeal for Calvinism by a number of other Lithuanian nobles, many of whom had been Orthodox. Calvinism took especially firm root in Little Poland. Besides the magnates, the petty nobility showed great interest in Calvinism, which became almost the national Reformed Church of Poland.[23]

Besides the Lutherans and the Calvinists, known as the Reformed Church, a third religious body found many adherents in Poland, namely the Czech Brethren. Expelled from Bohemia in 1548 after the unsuccessful revolt against Ferdinand I,[24] many of the Czech Brethren migrated into Great Poland, where they found a welcome refuge on the lands of such nobles as Andrew Górka and Stanislas Ostroróg. Many Polish noble families joined them. The affinity of the Czech and Polish nations and of their languages helped the Czech Brethren in propagating their confession in Poland. Their most important communities were in Poznań (Posen) and in Leszno (Lissa), which later became their religious center. In the seventeenth century the famous last bishop of the Czech Brethren, J. Amos Komenský, made its school well known by his introduction of new teaching methods. The Czech Brethren succeeded, even in Poland, in keeping the direction of their Church in the hands of their ecclesiastical leaders. Polish Lutherans and Calvinists were not able to imitate the Brethren in this way because of the overwhelming influence which the nobles, to whom the Reformed Churches owed their existence, exercised in the different communities. Because the kings did not embrace the Reformation, it was not possible to imitate the Church organization in Germany, where each prince as *summus episcopus* was head of the Church in his territories. The coherence of the religious communities could be maintained only by the synodal institution. Both Lutherans and Calvinists tried at several synods to introduce a system which would give their superintendents and higher clergy a prevailing influence in the direction of the communities. But the role of the nobles in the Reformed Churches was too great, and no success attended such efforts to democratize the synodal institution or to diminish the interference of the nobles in religious affairs.

This preponderance of the nobility in the direction of ecclesiastical life was one of the greatest handicaps of the Polish Reformation. Another was the diversity in the Creed which stood in the way of the formation of a Polish national Church. The first who expressed the desire for a national Church was the famous humanist Andrew Frycz Modrzewski.[25] Although he remained a Catholic, Modrzewski sympathized with the Reformation, and, as already mentioned, in his daring work *De republica emendanda* he set out his ideas on a universal Church with freely elected bishops and and a pope, who would, however, possess his prerogatives only by human rights, by the consensus of all the national Churches which would join the universal organization. Such ideas could, of course, never materialize. The Protestants also felt the urgency to remove the differences in teaching between their Churches. The first attempt of this kind was made in 1555 at the diet of Piotrków when the Protestant nobles presented to the king a common confession composed by Stanislas Lutomirski. The confession, however, found little acceptance. The Czech Brethren rejected it and concluded in the same year a religious union with the Calvinists of Little Poland, retaining, however, their own system of worship and Church discipline.

Two prominent Polish reformers, F. Lismanini and John Łaski, called by their brethren of Little Poland, continued to work for a union among the three branches of the Reformed.[26] Łaski, one of the most prominent Polish reformers, well known abroad and acquainted with Calvin and Melanchthon, favored the Helvetian confession of faith but found little support among the Lutherans and the Czech Brethren.

After his death the question of a common confession was debated at several synods of the Reformed Churches, especially in 1570 at the Synod of Sandomierz. There the three Churches reached a compromise in which the Lutheran and Calvinist teachings on the Eucharist, although differing on the essential question of the real presence of Christ under the species of bread and wine, were both stressed, and the three bodies confirmed to each other the orthodoxy of their respective confessions of faith. Although a common confession was not arrived at which could become the basis for a national Reformed Church in Poland and although the different religious practices of the three Churches continued to exist, the compromise of Sandomierz gave to the Polish Reformed Churches a solid basis for friendly collaboration. In the history of the Reformation in general, it represents the first attempt at the realization of a Protestant universal Church, which was the ideal, albeit never realized, of many reformers.

Unity among the Reformed Churches was, however, compromised by the spread of new doctrines attacking the basic Christian teaching on the Trinity. The propagators of anti-Trinitarianism came from Italy. Some of them stayed in Basel, Bern, and Zürich, but fearing the fate of the Spaniard Servetus, who was burned at the stake in Calvin's Geneva for anti-Trinitarianism, they went to Poland to spread their teaching. The first of them, Francesco Stancaro (died 1574), after violent outbursts against the traditional teaching that in the redemption not only Christ's humanity, but also his divinity had participated, reconciled himself at the end of his life with the Protestant Church. But other Italians, namely, Blandrata, Alciati, Ochino, Gentile, were even more outspoken in their denial of the Trinity. They found disciples among Polish and Lithuanian reformed theologians; Peter Gonesius (Goniadzki) was one of the first, and Gregor Pauli became the most zealous anti-Trinitarian. These men continued to spread the anti-Trinitarian doctrines even when their foreign preceptors were banned from Poland by a royal edict of 1564. In the next year Gregor Pauli of Cracow, with his followers, separated himself from the Reformed Church and founded his "Little Church."

The anti-Trinitarians were about to split into several branches because of differences in their beliefs, but the "Little Church" was saved from disintegration by another Italian reformer, Fausto Sozzini (or Socinius) (1539-1604), a nephew of Lelio Sozzini, who was esteemed among the reformers for his writings. Before coming to Poland, Fausto Sozzini already enjoyed some reputation as an acute reformed theologian and a good organizer. Although his teaching on Christ revealed pronounced anti-Trinitarian tendencies, Fausto Sozzini showed a certain restraint in his anti-Trinitarian teaching when he was trying to convince the radically anti-Trinitarian Bishop of Transylvania, F. Dávid, that Christ, although divine only by "adoption" by the Father, should be worshipped by Christians.

In spite of his reputation and good relations with the Polish nobility, Sozzini was at first not welcomed by the Polish anti-Trinitarians. Thanks to his perseverance and theological talents, he finally succeeded in bringing about a kind of uniformity among the different doctrines and also in convincing the anti-Trinitarian Anabaptists that the second baptism of adults was not necessary. His teaching, which included the Protestant doctrine of man's salvation through faith, appealed to many because it seemed to simplify the fundamental doctrines of Christianity. It was clearly summarized in the catechism of Raków (1605), the city which became the intellectual center of the Polish anti-Trinitarians. It was not surprising that the Polish anti-Trinitarians were also called Socinians, although Sozzini was not the founder of their Church.

Socinianism spread in Poland and Lithuania. At the time of its greatest influence it counted over seventy congregations, twenty of which were in Orthodox Volhynia. It found, however, few adherents in Great Poland. During the first half of the seventeenth century Polish anti-Trinitarianism, also called Arianism, flourished. Sozzini's confreres and disciples published numerous religious books and treatises, which were printed in Raków. Simeon Budny,[27] one of the followers of the radical anti-Trinitarian of Greek origin, James Palaeologus, who worked in Transylvania and in Poland, edited a new Polish translation of the Bible with anti-Trinitarian tendencies. The anti-Trinitarian schools, especially those of Lubartów and Raków, were famous. This period of florescence, however, soon came to an end. The anti-Trinitarians were opposed not only by the Catholics, but also by all Protestant denominations in Poland and abroad. Suspected of disloyalty during the Swedish wars,[28] they were banned from Poland by King John II Casimir in 1658. Even before this blow they had lost many of their adherents through the conversion of their nobles to Catholicism. The remnant of the Polish anti-Trinitarians dispersed in

Transylvania, Prussia, Holland, England, and North America. There they contributed to the origin and spread of the Unitarian movement.[29]

The teachings of the anti-Trinitarians compromised all Reformed Churches in the eyes of the Polish Catholic population—although the Lutherans, Calvinists, and Czech Brethren disagreed with it most sincerely—because it attacked the basic principles of Christian doctrine. The disunity among the Reformed Churches also gave the Catholics an effective weapon in their campaign against the spread of the Polish Reformation. Soon the Catholics obtained an able leader in the person of Stanisław Hosius, bishop of Warmia (Ermland), the son of a German immigrant but educated in Poland. Profiting by the chaotic state of dogmatic beliefs among the Reformed, Hosius composed a "Confession of the Catholic Faith." Thanks to its clarity and unity of teaching, this made a great impression in Poland, where it went into many editions, and was also translated into other European languages. Soon also, after Poland had accepted in 1564 the decisions of the Council of Trent, the deplorable situation among the Polish hierarchy was remedied by effective reforms, which had already been anticipated by Hosius and the papal nuncios.

Hosius' activity inaugurated the Polish Counter-Reformation, and this was successfully continued by the Jesuits, who were taken under special royal protection in 1565. The Jesuits soon succeeded, thanks to the modern methods employed in their schools and to their superior education, in winning a great number of noble families back to the Catholic faith. The Polish Reformation owed almost everything to the nobles, and when they or their descendants became Catholics, the Reformed Churches slowly disappeared on their lands and the places of worship occupied by them had to be restored to Catholic worship. The Protestants soon realized that they had neglected the simple faithful and that the Reformation had not penetrated among the Polish masses. Once the material and moral support of the nobles was lacking, the simple faithful lost all interest in the religion which they had perforce followed as being that of their masters.

The Jesuit missionaries did not limit their activities to the conversion of the nobles, but paid attention also to the burghers and peasants, attracting them with their sermons, elaborate liturgical ceremonies, and the superior education which they offered to the sons of both nobles and burghers in their numerous colleges and schools. The Reformed had enjoyed freedom in spreading their doctrines, and there were very few cases of religious persecution in Poland during the Reformation period. The spirit of tolerance was a characteristic feature of Poland at this time, and now this freedom profited the Catholics in their anti-Reformation drive. So it happened that the massive conversion of the nobles back to Catholicism was obtained without the use of pressure. In 1569 the number of

Protestant senators exceeded that of Catholics by fifty-eight to fifty-five. Yet by the end of the seventeenth century the remnants of the Reformed Churches were regarded by the Poles as unwelcomed sectarian minorities. In 1666 the last Protestant representative in the Senate, the castellan of Gdańsk (Danzig), disappeared, and in 1718 the last Protestant member of the Polish Diet.

In the surviving communities the German element, increased from time to time by new German colonists, soon prevailed. The final liquidation of the Polish Reformed Churches was not achieved without methods of force. As the Catholic Counter-Reformation progressed, measures were enacted by kings and Diets limiting the building of churches for the dissidents, ordering the return of places of worship to the Catholics, and penalizing Catholic converts to Protestantism. The situation of the Reformed Churches was weakened by their discord in matters of faith. The compromise of Sandomierz remained rather a dead letter, being especially unpopular among the Lutherans. The suspicions voiced by the Catholics against their loyalty during the Swedish wars (1656) naturally worsened their political situation in the kingdom. Under the reign of John III Sobieski (1674-1696) the pressure relented, but their efforts to obtain a legal status of toleration did not succeed during the last phases of Polish independence. Only in 1768, under the threat of Russian bayonets, was an edict of tolerance enacted for the Polish commonwealth. At that time the once flourishing Polish Reformed Churches possessed only fifty-five communities in Great Poland, of which only seven were Calvinist. In Little Poland there were eight Calvinist and one Lutheran, and in Lithuania thirty Calvinist and five Lutheran communities.

The Czech Brethren were strengthened by refugees from Moravia after the defeat of the dissidents in 1620 and by the prestige of the last bishop of the Czech Brethren, J. A. Komenský. Their center in Leszno (Lissa) survived many catastrophes and still exists with four other communities.

Although the Reformation in Poland failed to achieve lasting results, its influence on the cultural life of the Poles in the sixteenth and seventeenth century was remarkable. The need to provide the faithful with Polish prayer books and to propagate the Reformation induced the reformers to publish their books in the vernacular language. At first, when it was not possible to publish Protestant books in Poland, Königsberg, Duke Albert's residence, became the center where Polish religious publications were printed, often with the financial help of the Prussian duke. John Seklucyan was the main publisher, printer, and bookseller there. From 1555 on, the Protestants also possessed several printing and publishing houses in Poland. Luther's catechism was translated, hymns and songs were composed and printed for liturgical use, and in 1556 the first Polish *Postilla* was published by Seklucyan, to be superseded by the *Postilla* by Nicholas Rey, which was the best Protestant publication in Polish. Not without reason is this Protestant author called the father of Polish literature.[30]

Seklucyan's publication of a Polish New Testament, in which his main collaborator was Melanchthon's disciple S. Murzynowski, was soon superseded by the translation of the whole Bible in 1563. This Bible, called the Bible of Brześć (Brest), after the place where it was printed, or of Radziwill, after the donor of funds for its translation and publication, was one of the best literary achievements of the Polish Reformation. Besides other authors of religious literature, the Polish Calvinists also had several poets, who composed religious songs.[31]

The Protestants also started to introduce new methods into their schools. The building of schools for Protestant youth was one of the main preoccupations of the reformers. In this respect tradition was particularly strong among the Czech Brethren, whose schools survived the mass conversion of the Polish nobility, previously the main supporters of Protestant schools. Among the prominent teachers at Protestant higher institutions were to be found Calvin's French disciples, John Thenaud and Peter Statorius.

The Catholic Counter-Reformation had to follow the same paths in order to be successful in its propaganda. The Jesuit fathers erected schools in all prominent towns and, in 1578, an academy in Wilno, which obtained from Stephen Bathory the same privileges as those enjoyed by the University of Cracow. In order to offset Protestant literary production, the Catholics were also induced to publish religious works in Polish. Besides Peter Skarga, who has a place of honor in Polish literature, many other Jesuits translated and composed religious works. The most prominent of them was James Wujek. His translation of the Bible into Polish (1599) superseded a previous Catholic translation of 1561 and became a "Polish Vulgate." His *Postilla* was destined to replace Rey's work, written in the Protestant spirit.

Other Catholic authors emanated from the circle around Hosius. These included his successor Martin Kromer; a historian and apologist, V. Kuczborski; and the biographer of Cardinal Hosius, Stanislas Reszka. Some Catholic historians, P. Piasecki and S. Starowolski, presented a very biased picture of the Polish Reformation. This literary activity also continued in the seventeenth century. At this period, among the reformers German writers took over the defense of their creeds.

III

The influence of the Reformation among the Slovenes and Croats is intimately connected with the penetration and the development of Luther's teachings in Austria proper. The Slovenes lived mainly in Carinthia, Carniola, and southern Styria, in Gorizia, Gradiska, and Istria. The lands of the Croats had long been united with the Hungarian crown and, insofar as they had escaped Turkish conquest, were also under the rule of the Habsburgs. They were therefore more closely connected with the Austrian lands than previously.

Luther's teachings started to penetrate into Austria soon after 1520. The situation of the Church there was no better than in Poland, a circumstance which greatly facilitated the spread of the Reformation. The movement, however, soon became compromised in the eyes of many sympathizers by the outbreak of a peasant revolt in 1525, which was mercilessly suppressed by Ferdinand I. In spite of that, and in spite of the measures taken by Ferdinand I, many nobles embraced the new doctrines, even in areas under his direct jurisdiction.

For the Slovene lands the conversion to Lutheranism of a Slovene priest, Primož Trubar (Primus Truber) (1508-1586), had the greatest importance. As a poor student he went through the schools of Rijeka (Fiume), Salzburg, Trieste, and Vienna. Thanks to the protection of the Bishop of Trieste, the famous humanist Peter Bonomo, Trubar, already known for his preaching activity in Trieste and Carinthia, was appointed (1542) canon and preacher in Ljubljana (Laibach). Suspected by the Bishop of Ljubljana because of his teaching, Trubar had to leave the parish of St. Bartholomew, which he administered from 1546, and went into hiding (1547) in the residences of Protestant nobles. The next year he took refuge in Germany and became preacher in Rothenburg ob der Tauber, and later parish priest of Kempten and of Urach near Tübingen. In the meantime the Reformation had taken very solid root in Carniola, and in 1560, the Diet invited Trubar to take over the direction and organization of the Protestant Church among the Slavic population. In spite of difficulties raised by the Catholic authorities, Trubar worked, with two interruptions, as superintendent of the Protestant Church in Carniola until 1565, when he was exiled for life from his country by the son of Ferdinand I, the Archduke Charles. Trubar again took refuge in Germany and died as parish priest of Derendingen, near Tübingen, in 1586.

Trubar was influenced in his teaching not only by Luther, but also, like the Poles, by the Swiss reformers K. Pellikan and J. H. Bullinger, whose commentaries on the New Testament provided the basis for his preaching, and by Calvin. Trubar's ambition was to make the teachings of the re-

formers accessible to his compatriots in their own language. It was a difficult task because no books had hitherto been published in Slovene. Trubar followed the example of Luther and used the language of the ordinary
people in his compositions and translations. He was supported in his
enterprise by Duke Christopher of Württemberg, whose father had been
deprived for some years of his duchy by the Habsburgs (1520-1534) and
who was himself their passionate opponent. He was also supported by
Count Hans von Ungnad, former governor of Styria and a talented general, who resigned his post in 1555 after refusing to execute Ferdinand's
anti-Protestant measures, and chose voluntary exile in Germany.

Trubar succeeded in setting up a Slovene press at Urach, near Tübingen, and his *Catechism* was the first book ever published in Slovene
(1551). He continued this activity and translated first some parts of the
New Testament and then, in 1582, the whole of the New Testament into
Slovene. The catechism appeared in several different editions, and in
1566 he translated the Psalter. His Slovene edition of the confessions of
Augsburg, Württemberg, and Saxony, called *Articuli,* and his hymns and
church songs were also important. As superintendent of the Slovene
Protestant Church, Trubar saw the need to compose a new prayer book
for his Church, based on the Church ordinances of Württemberg, Nürnberg, and Mecklenburg.[32] In 1586 he terminated his translation of Luther's
Postilla. Trubar is rightly called the Slovene Luther and the Columbus of
Slovene literature. His writings, the first in Slovene, are still objects of
serious study by Slavic philologists.[33] One of his countrymen, Adam Bohorič, published the first Slovene grammar in 1584 at Wittenberg. So it
happened that the foundations of the Slovene literary language and
writings were laid by the first Slovene reformers.

Trubar's successor in Ljubljana, S. Krel, added to Trubar's writings a
catechism for Slovene schools, some church songs, and the translation of
Spangenberg's *Postilla.* Christopher Spindler (1569) continued to direct
the Protestant Church in Carniola and reorganized the school of Ljubljana with the help of Bohorič in 1575. During this period the general
Diet of "Inner Austria"—Carinthia, Carniola, Styria, and Istria—most of
whose members were Protestants, met at Bruck an der Mur in 1578 and
induced the Archduke Charles to promise respect for the reformed religion in all lands with the exception of places under the archduke's direct
jurisdiction.

The Reformation spread further, and the printing of Protestant writings was accelerated by the foundation of a printing press in Ljubljana
by Hans Mannel (1575). The same printing press was about to print also,
at the request of the Diet of Bruck, the first Slovene translation of the
whole Bible, completed in 1580 by George Dalmatin, when it was closed

by order of the archduke and its founder exiled. The first Slovene Bible was thus printed in Wittenberg (1584). Dalmatin enriched the young Slovene literature with a popular prayer book, church songs, and other writings.

The Slovene candidates for the ministry could obtain a higher education only in Germany, at Tübingen, which continued to be the cultural center for Slovene and "Inner Austrian" Lutherans.[34] The progress of the Reformation in these lands was, however, stopped when Ferdinand II became the ruler of "Inner Austria" in 1590. Determined to speed up the Counter-Reformation, Ferdinand II forbade the preaching of the Reformation and banned Protestant ministers throughout his territories. F. Trubar, the son of the founder of Slovene literature, who was then the superintendent of the church in Carniola, went into hiding for some time with some of his ministers at the residences of Protestant nobles. But as the anti-Protestant decrees were increasingly enforced, Trubar escaped to Württemberg, where he died in exile.

In spite of new measures against Protestant churches and religious practice, the nobility resisted stubbornly all efforts to win them back to Catholicism. Only in 1628, when Ferdinand II gave them the choice between exile and conversion, did a great part of them embrace the Catholic faith, but many members of noble families preferred exile and settled mostly in Nürnberg and Regensburg.

Fortunately for Slovene national life, the Counter-Reformation had to use the same means in its efforts as did the first Slovene reformers. The Jesuits, the main protagonists of the Counter-Reformation, paid special attention to the simple people and preached in Slovene besides cultivating church songs in the vernacular. Instead of the suppressed Protestant school in Ljubljana, they founded their own gymnasium there, which functioned from 1604 on. They did not neglect primary education and gave Slovene youth the opportunity for higher education in Vienna and Graz. Bishop Hren (Chrön) of Ljubljana even found the zeal of the Jesuits in preaching in Slovene rather excessive. In their schools the Jesuits performed different dramatic popular representations in Slovene of Jesus' life, and they also preached sermons in Slovene in Trieste. In their propaganda they used not only Catholic books and publications, namely, the *Evangelistar* by Bishop Hren, but also the writings of Slovene Protestants. The Bible translation by Dalmatin, corrected in the Catholic spirit, was in great esteem among the Slovene counter-reformers, who also used the translations of Protestant Postillas and other writings. So it happened that the cultural inheritance of the Slovene reformers was not lost, but continued as a basis for the further evolution of Slovene literature and culture.

The Slovene reformers, when preparing laboriously their first writings in Slovene, were well aware of their national kinship with the Croats, Serbians, and Bulgarians. Trubar and other Slovene reformers expressed in the introductions to their writings their desire to bring all the South Slavic nations into the Reformed Church. This emphasis on Slavic solidarity in the sixteenth century is rather an interesting phenomenon. Some of the reformers went even further and expressed hopes that through the translation of the Bible and other writings into a Slavic language, even the Turks would become acquainted with Christian teaching and embrace the reformed religion, since the Slavic tongue was in general use among them. In this way, the Turkish danger, which preoccupied everyone including the Slovene reformers, would be averted in a peaceful way.[35]

These were naive hopes, but thanks principally to the first Slovene reformers, Protestantism was also able to take root among the Croats. Trubar prepared the way also for the printing of Protestant books in Croat. Being aware of the fact that the southern Slavs used two alphabets different from the Latin—Cyrillic and Glagolitic[36]—he took great care to equip his printing press to produce Protestant publications for both Croats and Serbians.

The Reformation penetrated into Croatia principally from Austria through Carniola, and only partially from Hungary. For the spread of reformed ideas among the Croats the Slovene printing press in Urach near Tübingen was naturally of the greatest importance. The Croats who at that time still lived in Carinthia and Carniola were the first to be won over by the Protestant propaganda of the Slovene preachers. The first Croatian center of Protestantism was the town of Metlika, where the first Protestant Croatian school had also been founded. The most zealous preacher in this center was Gregory Vlahović, who also propagated among the Croats Slavic Protestant publications printed in Urach. The spread of the new faith in Croatia proper was facilitated by the sympathy with which it was greeted by the Ban Peter Erdödy, the Bishop of Zagreb, Matthew Bruman, and some other Croat nobles.

In the Croatian *Krajina*,[37] or military frontier area, Protestant preachers found a fertile soil, thanks to numerous German soldiers who had embraced the new faith. Protestant congregations were founded in the principal cities of this region. Karlovac, the main city of the *Krajina*, could boast not only a German preacher for the Protestant members of the garrison, but also a Croatian preacher for the natives, besides a Protestant school and a church which existed down to 1645.

The noble family of the Zrinskis favored the spread of the Reformation not only in the *Krajina* but also in the territory between the Drava and Mura rivers, which was outside the Ottoman Empire. George Zrinski, the son of Nicholas the hero of Sziget, openly joined the Protestant Church and erected a printing press on his estate in Nedjelište at a time when the printing press in Ljubljana was beginning to be hampered in its activity by the Catholic Counter-Reformation. The new Slavic printing press produced the works of the Croatian reformer Nicholas Bučić, which are, however, not preserved. In 1586 this printing press was transferred to Varaždin, another important center of Croatian Protestantism. A. Vramec's *Postilla* was printed there (1586). This caused this learned theologian of Zagreb to be accused of sympathy with Protestantism. He is better known as the author of a chronicle, printed in 1578. The printer Mannel (Manlius), exiled from Ljubljana, continued his activity at Varaždin and, from 1587 on, at Eberovo in Hungary, whither this printing press was again transferred. This transfer, however, deprived the Croatian Protestants of a most important instrument in their religious propaganda.

The Reformation penetrated into Slavonia, the country between the Drava and Sava rivers, from Varaždin and Zagreb and also from Hungary. As the Hungarians rather favored Calvinism, so the Croats of Slavonia generally accepted the doctrines of the French reformer. Only the German settlers preferred Lutheranism. The most successful Calvinist preacher in Slavonia was the Slovak Michael Starin. Thanks to his activity the Protestants of Slavonia were already able to organize their first synod in 1551 and formed an autonomous seniorate under the Hungarian superintendent of Baranja. This progress of the Reformation in Slavonia was facilitated by the fact that the province had no Catholic bishopric of its own. It was administered partly by the bishops of Zagreb, whose representatives had difficulty in securing free admission into Slavonia when this country became a Turkish province. Furthermore the Bishop of Pécs, Andrew Dudić, who had jurisdiction over the other part of Slavonia, joined the Reformation together with his clergy.

Istria became familiar with the principles of the Reformation through the intermediary of Venice. It is interesting to stress that the Slavic population of Istria gave Yugoslav Protestantism its most famous representatives, Flacius (Vlasić) Illyricus, Peter Paul Vergerius, Stephen Konzul, and Mathias Grbić (Mathias Garbitius Illyricus).

From Istria Protestant ideas penetrated into the Dalmatian cities, which were then also under Venetian rule. Strong echoes of Protestant propaganda even reached the Republic of Ragusa. In this region, the most important Protestant convert was Markantonio de Dominis (Gospodnetić), bishop of Senj, and from 1602, archbishop of Split (Spalato). Deprived of his dignity by Rome, he transferred his activities to Germany and England, where he joined the Church of England, and although he returned to Catholicism, he did not regain papal favor.

The main desire of the Croatian Protestants was to publish a Croatian translation of the Bible. All prominent Croatian reformers—Peter Paul Vergerius, Flacius, Grbić—were deeply interested in this enterprise, which was realized by Stephen Konzul (Istranin) and Anthony Dalmatin. The Croatian Bible was printed in Glagolitic type at Urach (1562), where a Croatian printing press had been set up beside the Slovene press. An edition in Cyrillic type followed in the next year. During the existence of the Croatian printing press at Urach (1561-1568) several other Protestant writings were published in Croatian translations—a catechism with Flacius' work *De vocabulo fidei*, Melanchthon's *Loci theologici*, the Confession of Augsburg (*Articuli*), an apology for this confession, the *Postilla* of Luther, Melanchthon, and John Brenz. Most of these publications were printed in the three alphabets used in Croatia and Serbia—Glagolitic,[38] Cyrillic, and Latin. The most original of Croatian Protestant publications was *The Discussion between a Papalist and a Lutheran*, published in 1555. The author of this treatise was most probably Peter Paul Vergerius, who used the pseudonym Antony Senjanin, or one of his friends acting under Vergerius' inspiration.

However, the Reformation did not penetrate the Croats as deeply as it did the Slovenes.[39] The Catholic Counter-Reformation started early in Croatia under the aegis of the Bishop of Zagreb, George Drašković (1563-1578), who also acted from 1566 on as ban of Croatia. His successors continued this activity in Slavonia also. With the conversion of the Zrinskis to Catholicism in 1623, the Protestants lost their main supporters. In 1609 the Ban Thomas Erdödy, who had already protested against the attempts of the Hungarians to extend to Croatia the decree of religious liberty issued by King Matthias for Hungary in 1606, succeeded in obtaining from the Croatian Diet a proclamation that only the Catholic faith could be professed in Croatia. This spelled disaster for Protestant ministers. When Slavonia was liberated from the Turks, the Catholic Church regained its former position there also.

The Reformation could spread in Istria and Dalmatia only as long as Venice enjoyed strained relations with the Papacy. When, however, the republic entered upon friendly relations with Rome, the Catholic Counter-Reformation was able to initiate its work of restoration, and during the seventeenth century Protestantism disappeared almost completely from these lands.

Protestantism did not influence Croatian cultural life as much as it did Slovene. Its contributions to Croatian literary activity are rather modest. More lasting for the Protestant movement in general were the achievements of the most prominent Croatian reformer, Matthew Vlasić, or Flacius Illyricus (1520-1575). Flacius studied in Venice, Basel, Tübingen, and Wittenberg. He lectured at the University of Wittenberg, but had to leave there because he opposed violently certain religious ideas of Melanchthon, who seemed more inclined to a compromise with Calvinist teaching. He continued his polemics with Melanchthon in Magdeburg, where he wrote his best known defense of Luther's doctrine, the *Catalogus testium veritatis* (1556). There he commenced work, with many collaborators, on the monumental historical work, the *Centuriae Magdeburgenses* (1559-1574). The thirteen volumes of the *Centuriae* inaugurated a new period in the writing of ecclesiastical history; they were answered from the Catholic side by Cardinal Caesar Baronius' *Annales ecclesiastici* (Rome, 1588-1607, twelve volumes). Flacius continued his defense of the purity of Luther's teachings, but his uncompromising attitude lost him his university posts in Jena and Strasbourg. He died in poverty in Frankfurt's hospital without completing his most outspoken defense of Luther, the *Clavis scripturae sacrae* (1567).

Peter Paul Vergerius also played a remarkable role in the history of Protestantism. Before his conversion to Lutheranism, Vergerius was bishop of Modruš and then of Kopar (Capodistria) (1536), and rendered Rome important services as papal legate in Germany. He won many proselytes for his new faith in Istria and Italy, and his diplomatic services were used by Christopher, duke of Württemberg, on many occasions. On his mission to Poland he also became acquainted with the Czech Brethren, whose confession he published at his own expense in Tübingen. Less prominent than his two Croatian compatriots was Matthew Grbić, a disciple of Luther and Melanchthon, who became professor in Wittenberg and then in Tübingen.

The Catholic Counter-Reformation had, of course, to use the same means for the suppression of Protestantism that the reformers had used to propagate it. Catholic literary production was, however, slow to appear. Only in 1628 did the first Croatian prayer and hymn book appear, composed by the Jesuit Nicholas Krajačević (Sartorius). But the interest manifested by Rome in the suppression of heresies and schism in the Balkans speeded literary production. Even the Glagolitic type which Count Ungnad had transferred to his property in Carinthia and then to Graz, after the suppression of the printing press in Urach, did not escape the attention of the Catholic propagandists. At their suggestion the type was confiscated by Ferdinand II and finally given to the Congregation for the Propagation of the Faith in Rome, which used it for printing Glagolitic books for the Slavic liturgy in Croatia.

On the initiative of the Roman Congregation, the Jesuits and Franciscans began a lively activity among the Croats. The schools and "academies" organized by the Jesuits contributed considerably to the growth of Croatian cultural life. Thanks to their literary activity the Croatian literary language gradually became stabilized.[40] The first Croatian grammar was published in Rome in 1604 by the Jesuit Bartol Kašić (1575-1650), who was also the most prominent writer of the Croatian Counter-Reformation. His most important work was a *Life of Our Lord* (Rome, 1638). He also translated the *Roman Ritual* (1640) and the Bible, though this remained in manuscript. He also wrote lives of several saints. In his linguistic endeavors Kašić was supported by the Italian Jesuit Jacob Mikalja and by another prominent Catholic writer, G. Habdelić, the author of a Croatian dictionary.

Besides the Jesuits, Franciscans were also an important element in the Catholic Counter-Reformation and in missions among those Croats still under Turkish rule. Among them F. Glavinić and Levaković, both well versed in the Old Slavonic language, were charged with re-editing the Glagolitic liturgical books. Levaković was also known as a Church historian and ecclesiastical writer.

Besides the poet I. T. Mrnavić, M. Divković (1563-1631), who adapted in Croat sermons by Bellarmin and I. Herolt and different legends, was a fertile religious writer. He also reproduced old Croatian religious songs in his very popular *Nauk Krstjanski* ("Christian Teaching").

Other Franciscan writers composed their religious writings in a similar pattern; P. Posilović, P. Papić, I. Ančić, I. Bandulavić, N. Krajačević (Sartorius)—known as a propagator of religious songs, B. Milovec, and A. Georgicević continued to write in the idiom of northern Croatia (Kajkavština). I. Belostenec (died 1675), from the Congregation of St. Paul, revealed himself as a good Croatian theologian, especially in his *Ten Discourses on the Eucharist.* The best prose writer from the region of Zagreb was the Jesuit G. Habdelić (1609-1678) (Juraj Habdelis) with his moral and didactic works, the popular *Mirror of Our Lady* and *The First Sin of Our Father Adam.*

The Croatian Counter-Reformation inherited from the Slovene and Croatian Protestant writers yet another idea, the union of all Slavs in one Church. Most of the prominent Croatian counter-reformers were educated in the academies founded for the southern Slavic students in Loreto and Rome. There they were influenced by the unionist atmosphere which at that time prevailed in Rome. Propaganda was naturally centered on the lands of the southern Slavs, especially Bosnia, where Catholics, Orthodox, and Musulmans were intermingled, and Croatian intellectuals were often chosen by Rome for missionary or diplomatic services among the Orthodox.

The most typical representative of this movement among the Croats was George Križanić (1618-1683), who can be regarded as a precursor of the Pan-Slav movement of the nineteenth century. He not only preached the racial unity of the Slavs, but also dreamed of the formation of a common Slavic language. He extended his unionist ideas to Orthodox Russia, trusting for the liberation of the Slavs from the foreign yoke to the tsars, the only Slavic rulers, who, when united with Rome, would realize the political and religious unity of all Slavs.

His *Encycopedia on the Schismatics* remained a torso, but he explained his political and national ideas in his *Politica,* written in exile in Tobol'sk in the linguistic mixture of Old Slavonic, Russian, and Croat which he wanted to promote as the literary language of all Slavs. Although his ideas failed to find a favorable echo among contemporary Croats and Russians, he remains the most prominent political theorist among his contemporaries in Slavic lands.[41]

The interest in the Orthodox Slavic peoples which the Catholic Croatian counter-reformers had shown was, of course, evoked by the general religious policy of the Papacy, but it could also have been stimulated by the knowledge that their Protestant compatriots had been the first to attempt to open the way for the Reformation into Orthodox lands. In this respect the "oecumenical" plans of the small group of Slovenes and Croats centered around Trubar's printing press in Urach near Tübingen, supported by the generous Count Ungnad, have only recently attracted due attention.[42] The correspondence of Ungnad with them and with the protagonists of his enterprise reveals that this small group proceeded according to a well-designed plan and that their sympathizers had established a network of agents for smuggling the books printed in Cyrillic letters among the Orthodox Slavs.

Well aware that they needed the collaboration of some Orthodox in the translation of Protestant literature, Primus and Stephen Conzul engaged two Serbian refugee monks for some time in Urach. But they were very disappointed when the plan to bring to Tübingen a highly intelligent and learned Orthodox Serbian, Demetrius, could not be realized. The latter was first secretary of the voivode of Wallachia and then spent some years at the patriarchate in Byzantium. After having probably become acquainted with the Reformation in Transylvania, he went to Wittenberg in 1559, where he was completely won over to the new faith by Melanchthon. Demetrius was willing to transmit the Greek translation of the *Confessio Augustana* and other writings to the oecumenical patriarch and to work for the Reformation among the Orthodox Slavs, Greeks, and Rumanians.

For a short time he was able to work on this plan when a friend, the Greek prince James Heraklides, became ruler of Moldavia. The latter, in exile in Germany, was won over by Melanchthon to the Reformation.

After serving in Charles V's army, Heraklides invaded Moldavia in 1561, with the help of the imperial resources. It was then ruled by Alexander VI, an ally of the Turks, both of whom James defeated and established himself as ruler. His attempt to introduce the Reformation into the conquered land was the only instance when Protestantism was about to impose its doctrine on an Orthodox land. The attempt miscarried. A revolt of the Orthodox population broke out, and Heraklides was killed in 1563.

The circle of Urach did not miss this opportunity: knowing that the Rumanians used the Slavonic liturgy and Cyrillic letters, they offered to send books in Cyrillic letters to Moldavia. This was the end of Demetrius' activity among the Slavs and the Rumanians, although he seems later to have transmitted to the oecumenical patriarch Melanchthon's profession of faith and Luther's catechism.[43]

Ungnad and his collaborators had conceived their plans on a grandiose size. They even tried to win the Emperor Maximilian II to their ideas, and Ungnad addressed letters to all Protestant princes and cities in Germany. In all these invitations to participate in the realization of their plan, they stressed not only the necessity of propagating the Reformation among the Orthodox Slavs, but also the possibility of making the Turks in this way better acquainted with reformed Christianity and of converting them.

The eastern Orthodox Slavs were also included in this plan. Ungnad's agent in Vienna, J. Frölich, followed closely the Protestant propaganda in Lithuania and among the West Russians and Ukrainians and entered into correspondence with Count Radziwill on the subject of propagating Protestant publications in Slavic, printed in Cyrillic letters, among the Lithuanian Slavs. He also addressed himself to Duke Albert of Prussia, knowing well how interested the duke was in propagating the Reformation in Poland and Lithuania.

Before his Moldavian venture, Demetrius had expressed his desire to go as far as Muscovy to found there a school and to propagate the "true religion" among the Muscovites. Even Flacius Illyricus was interested in Protestant missions among the Ukrainians and Russians. Protestant literature printed in Urach was sent to Bohemia, Poland, and Lithuania, but the degree of success it encountered among the Orthodox intellectuals is quite unknown.

The example given by the South Slavic enthusiasts and their German supporters seems, however, to have stimulated a similar movement on the part of Count Radziwill and other Lithuanian nobles. The printing press of Nieśwież, founded by them, was provided with Cyrillic type, and Symeon Budny published there in Ukrainian a catechism and a short work explaining to the Orthodox the Protestant teaching on justification

(1562). Although himself a Pole, Budny exhorted the nobles, who were abandoning not only their Orthodox faith but also their native language, to continue to use their Russian idiom, confident that this would attract other Orthodox to the Reformation. Budny's writings impressed some Orthodox priests, but they also provoked a polemical reply by Artemij. How seriously Budny was engrossed in his task is also evident from his letter to Zwingli's successor Henry Bullinger in which he asked the Swiss Reformer what Protestants should believe about the Filioque—the Latin doctrine of the procedure of the Holy Ghost from the Father and the Son—which was so sharply condemned by the Orthodox.

Soon afterward, however, Budny adhered to the anti-Trinitarian body and had to defend this doctrine against his own coreligionists. The theological disputes among the reformers, which became more and more passionate, killed this "oecumenical" spirit which had characterized the reforming movement among the southern Slavs and which had also reached the eastern Slavs.

The hopes of the Lithuanian Protestants that their Reformation could also spread into Muscovy were perhaps awakened by the fact that in 1553 a group of Russian monks, headed by Fedosij Kosoj and Ignacij, had fled from Moscow because they were threatened by their ecclesiastical authorities for teaching some doctrines even more advanced than those of the Protestants. Converted Orthodox priests preaching the Reformation in Vitebsk and Polock are mentioned, but very little Protestant propaganda penetrated into Muscovy proper.

The contemporaries of Ivan IV could learn about the Reformation from German and Western artisans and specialists, whom the tsar needed for his military and economic reforms, and from English merchants, who obtained permission to build their own church in Moscow. But the tsar's attitude toward the new teachings is best illustrated by an incident which happened in 1563 in Polock. On conquering the city, Ivan ordered the arrest of the preacher Thomas and, after beating him with his stick, ordered him to be drowned in the icy waters of the Dvina.

A timid attempt at winning Ivan's sympathy for the teaching of the Brethren was made in 1570. A Polish delegation was sent to Moscow for peace negotiations with the tsar, and as the two leaders were members of the Polish branch of the Unity of the Brethren, they asked their priest John Rokyta, of Czech origin, to accompany the delegation as its chaplain. Rokyta accepted the invitation, seeing in it an opportunity to spread the doctrine of the Brethren among his East Slavic confreres.

His hopes were not fulfilled. The tsar received him in solemn audience and, after insulting him and calling him a heretic, asked him ten questions which Rokyta had also to answer in writing. The tsar's reply to his writing was presented to Rokyta in another solemn audience in a written treatise bound in gold brocade, adorned with pearls, and full of injurious words. He ended the audience with the words: "You are not only a heretic, but also a servant of the Antichrist. . . . I forbid you, therefore, to preach your doctrine in our land, and I rather ask our Lord Jesus Christ with fervor to preserve the Russian people from the darkness of your infidelity." Ivan treated Lutheranism in a similar way in his discussion with the German minister Bockhorn, although he praised Luther's Biblical lore. Thus ended the attempts at Protestant propaganda in Muscovy.

NOTES

1. For example, Erasmus wrote in his *Praise of Folly:* "The bishops entrust the care of their sheep to others . . . they supervise only the nets in which they fish for money. The cardinals do no better though they are the successors of the Apostles. But if they only considered the symbolic significance of their shining vestments . . . the race for the purple would soon be over. But who would be more afflicted in spirit than the popes, if they ever pondered on the title of Holy Father? They would have no more use for money, honors, power or splendor; nor for taxes, indulgences, horses or mules . . . They would care only for prayers, fasting, preaching and their studies . . . But now they leave their work, as a rule, to Peter and to Paul—who have plenty of time— and take the glory and the joy for their portion . . . They fortify themselves with the fair speeches which Paul mentions and with anathemas, with pictures of the torments of Hell and with sentences of excommunication, but especially against those who seek to diminish the material patrimony of Peter." (Edition and translation by A. Schmid and H. A. Tanzer, Basel, 1931, p. 29.)
2. Rom. 1:17: "The righteousness of God is revealed through faith for faith; as it is written, 'he who through faith is righteous shall live.' "
3. An extensive history in Czech of the Reformation in the Kingdom of Bohemia has still to be written. F. Hrejsa, in his "History of Christianity in Czechoslovakia" (*Dějiny křesťanství v Českoslov.*), 6 vols. (Prague, 1947-1950), devoted much space to the Czech Reformation, but stopped at the year 1576. A Czech bibliography will also be found there. A short popular outline was written by the same author in 1914 (*Česká reformance*); a more scholarly outline with summary bibliographical notes was published by O. Odložilík in vol. four of the *Československ. Vlastivěda* (1932), pp. 341-490. A useful bibliography of Czech studies on the Reformation, and especially on the Czech Brethren, will be found in R. Říčan's recent "History of the Unity" (*Dějiny Jednoty Bratrské*, Prague, 1957), pp. 444-83. The same author also published in German a history of the Reformation in Bohemia (see Bibl.).
4. The Czech lords were moved by Luther's words on John Hus: "I myself and my followers would continue to defend John Hus, the holy martyr of Christ, even if all Bohemia would deny his teaching."
5. Thomas Münzer, the founder of the Anabaptists in Germany, also

propagated his radical teaching, which was condemned by Luther, in Prague. There he found some adherents who were attracted by his ecstatic and prophetic doctrine, which reminded many of the ideals of the radical Taborites. In his manifesto Münzer also recalled the memory of John Hus. His "New Church," which he established in Germany and in Prague, preached a kind of Christian communism. He allied himself with the rebellious peasants in southern Germany, and after the defeat of the rebels, he was executed with many of his followers (1525). In the same year also, many of his adherents in Prague were burned at the stake. The enemies of the Brethren often identified them with the Anabaptists, who were condemned by Catholics and Protestants alike. A more peaceful group of Anabaptists, led by Balthasar Hubmaier, found a refuge in Moravia after the disaster in Germany. Hubmaier and the other leader of the Moravian Anabaptists, Jacob Hutterer, died at the stake in Austria, but their sect continued to exist in Moravia and also spread into Hungary and Transylvania. In Moravia they enjoyed the protection of some magnates who appreciated them as industrious artisans, especially famous in ceramic production. They existed, organized in common families, in Moravia down to the year 1733, when the majority of them were converted to Catholicism. The remainder of them went first to the Ukraine and then settled in 1874 in South Dakota and Canada, where they still exist, organized in about thirty common families.

6. Their Bishop Augusta, accused unjustly of treacherous negotiations with the Elector of Saxony, was tortured and imprisoned for sixteen years.

7. On the Czech Brethren in Poland see pp. 413-418.

8. In Bohemia the use of the chalice for laymen was definitely forbidden in 1622. In Austria Maximilian II suppressed its use in 1571 when he saw that this concession failed to satisfy the Protestants. The Duke of Bavaria did the same. On its use in Hungary, see below, p. 409.

9. The religious attitude of Maximilian II is still an object of controversy among Church historians. He could never make up his mind between Catholic and Protestant teaching. Although he used to attend Mass, he refused the administration of the last sacraments on his death bed. He seems to have favored a religion basically Catholic, but adapted to some Protestant ideas, especially in worship. In this respect his own religious ideas were not far from those of the Utraquists. On the other hand, he professed respect for the religious beliefs of others and was reluctant to use force in religious matters. This spirit of toleration which inspired Maximilian was rather exceptional among the rulers of his time.

10. Among the numerous Czech publications on the defeat of the Protestant Estates, the work by J. Pekař on its causes and consequences should be recommended, J. Pekař, *Bílá Hora, její příčiny i následky* (Prague, 1921). Cf. also the recent works of two young historians on the policy of England and the Lowlands and the Czech insurrection, and on the participation of the Spaniards at the battle of White Mountain, J. Polišenský, *Anglie a Bílá Hora* (Prague, 1949) and *Nizozemská politika a Bílá Hora* (Prague, 1957); B. Chudoba, *Španělé a Bílá Hora* (Prague, 1945). Cf. also the study by F. Kryštůfek on the spread of Protestantism in Bohemia before the defeat of the Estates, *Protestantství v Čechách až do bitvy Bělohorské* (Prague, 1906).

11. The most prominent Sorb of the first Protestant generation was Caspar Peucers, professor of medicine at the University of Wittenberg and son-in-law of Melanchthon. He served as intermediary between the Czech Brethren and

the university, and in his letters to Blahoslav he stressed the affinity between the Czech and the Sorbian languages, declaring the latter to be his mother tongue. He was inspired by the "oecumenical" spirit, but at the end became a victim of the Lutheran anti-Philipist drive.

12. The most recent history of the Slovak Reformation was written by Kváčala, *Dějiny reformacie na Slovensku, 1517-1711* (Lipt. sv. Mikuláš, 1935).

13. Cf. above, Chapter X, p. 234.

14. Particularly by E. Varsik in his book in Slovak, *Husiti a reformacja na Slovensku do Žilinské dohody* (Bratislava, 1932).

15. In 1556 even the Bishop of Nitra, Francis Thurzo, became a Lutheran.

16. Cf. above, p. 402.

17. Cf. above, Chapter XIII, p. 294.

18. An exhaustive history of the Polish Reformation in Polish does not exist. Wotschke (see Bibl.) used in his history only sources accessible in German and Swiss archives and libraries. Important material relevant to the Polish Reformation was published in the review *Reformacja w Polsce*, edited by Professor S. Kot, the best specialist on these problems, and published by the Towarystwo do badania dziejów Reformacije w Polsce, from 1921 to 1938, with a continuation after 1945. The Polish history by X. Y. Bukowski, *Dzieje reformacyi w Polsce*, 2 vols. (Cracow, 1883, 1886), was superseded by Wotschke's work. For S. Kot's publications see Bibl. N. N. Ljnbovič's book, *Načalo katol. reakcii i upadok reformacii w Pol'šě* (Warsaw, 1890) gives the Orthodox point of view on Catholic Counter Reformation in Poland. B. Stasiewski's short study (see Bibl.) gives a good review of progress made in the research on these problems.

19. See above, Chapter XIII, p. 298. Cf. Chrzanowski, I., Kot, S., *Humanizm i Reformacja w Polsce* (Lwów, Warsaw, 1927), an interesting collection of unpublished documents and treatises written by Polish intellectuals.

20. On Bona, see Chapter X, pp. 242, 244, Chapter XIII, p. 299, Chapter XVII, p. 442. Cf. the most recent study on the queen by W. Pociecha, *Królova Bona*, 2 vols. (Poznań, 1949).

21. In his study, *Opposition to the Pope by the Polish Bishops, 1557-1560,* (see Bibl.), S. Kot has shown that although no Cranmer had appeared among the Polish hierarchy, there were, contrary to what has hitherto been thought, some instances of serious opposition by Polish bishops to Rome. Two of them seem even to have openly sided with the reformers.

22. W. Pociecha devoted a study in Polish to this problem in vol. 2 of the review *Reformacja w Polsce* (1922), pp. 161-84.

23. The Lutherans possessed altogether 110 German and 32 Polish communities in Poland. The Calvinist communities, mostly Polish, were more numerous—80 in Great Poland, 250 in Little Poland, and 191 in Lithuania. For detailed statistics see H. Merczyng, *Zbory i senatorowie protestanccy w dawnej Polsce* (Warsaw, 1902).

24. See above, p. 398.

25. On his literary activity see Chapter XIII, p. 300.

26. On the oecumenical movement among the Polish Protestants see the book by K. E. Y. Jörgensen (see Bibl.). On Mdrzewski, *ibid.*, pp. 175-218; on Łaski, *ibid.*, pp. 15-143; on Sandomierz, pp. 237-80.

27. See the complete bibliography on Budny in S. Kot's study *Szymon Budny* (see Bibl.). He was also a zealous propagator of reformist ideas among the Orthodox of Poland-Lithuania. On the literary activity of the Socinians

see the monograph by I. Szczucki, *Literatura arianska w Polsce XV wieku* (Warsaw, 1958). Cf. the short study by I. I. Poretskij, *Simon Budny* (Minsk, 1961).

28. See Chapter XVIII, p. 477.

29. On the Unitarians in the United States see E. M. Wilbur, *A History of Unitarianism* (see Bibl.).

30. On his literary activity see Chapter XIII, pp. 302, 303.

31. For details see I. Grabowski, *Literatura luterska w Polsce wieku XVI, 1530-1630* (Poznań, 1920).

32. A detailed analysis of it was made by F. Kidrić (see Bibl.).

33. Cf. in this respect especially M. Murko's work, *Die Bedeutung der Reformation und Gegenreformation* (see Bibl.).

34. For details see Th. Elze's study, *Die Universität Tübingen und die Studenten aus Krain* (Tübingen, 1877), which is still the only publication to give a clear picture of the importance of Tübingen for the Reformation among the Slovenes.

35. See for detailed quotations M. Murko, *Die Bedeutung der Reformation* (see Bibl.), pp. 6-24.

36. The Glagolitic alphabet was invented by St. Cyril, Apostle of the Slavs, for the Moravian Slavs in the ninth century. It penetrated into Croatia and is still used by a part of the Croatian clergy of the Roman rite. The Cyrillic alphabet is used by all Orthodox Slavs.

37. On the formation of the *Krajina* see above, Chapter XIV, p. 351.

38. The stress layed by the Croatian Protestant leaders on the printing of their books in Glagolitic letters evoked new suspicions among the Catholic hierarchy against the Slavic liturgy of the Roman rite, still in use in Dalmatia and Croatia, because the liturgical books were written in Glagolitic letters. The Synod of Zagreb of 1634 forbade the use of this liturgy, which, however, survived in Dalmatia down to our days.

39. For more detailed study see F. Bučar's history of Croatian Protestant literature, *Povijest hrvatske protestantske kniževnosti za reformacije* (Zagreb, 1910). A complete bibliography of Protestant Croatian literature was published by F. Bučar and F. Fancev ("Bibiografija hrvatske protestantske kniževnosti za reformacije") in *Starine* of the Yugoslav Academy, vol. 39 (Zagreb, 1938), pp. 79-128.

40. The Croatian Protestants used for their writings the idiom spoken in Istria, on the Dalmatian islands, and in North and middle Dalmatia, which was called the ča-dialect. Kašić, however, was of the opinion that the dialect spoken by the largest group of the South Slavic peoples should become a literary language, so he chose for his writings and grammar the što-dialect of Bosnia and Hercegovina as being the purest dialect spoken by the majority of Croats and by the Serbians. He was guided in this choice by the desire to make Catholic doctrine known in the language familiar not only to the Catholic Croats but also the the Mohammedan Bosnians and to the Orthodox Serbians. The missionary and uniat ideas inspired by the Roman Congregation for the Propagation of the Faith dominated Kašić and the Croatian Jesuits. Bosnia and Hercegovina, where Catholic, Mussulman, and Orthodox Slavs lived together, were therefore in the center of papal interest. The dialect of Dubrovnik, used by its writers, was closely related to that of Bosnia. So it came about that after a long evolution the Croats and Serbians have the same literary language.

41. There exists a Croatian biography of Križanić by V. Jagić, *Život i rad J.*

Križanića (Zagreb, 1917). P. Pierling, in the fourth volume of his *La Russie et le S. Siège* (see Bibl. Ch. XII), treats of this activity in Russia (pp. 1-39). See also below, Chapter XIX, pp. 513-523.

42. It is due to the merit of E. Benz, who collected the results of his research scattered in scholarly reviews in his book *Wittenberg und Byzanz* (see Bibl.), especially on pp. 141-208.

43. On Melanchthon's correspondence with the oecumenical patriarch Joasaph see Benz, *op. cit.*, pp. 63 ff., 94 ff. The Patriarch Cyril Lukaris (1572-1638) was the only Orthodox prelate who became a Calvinist. His doctrine was, however, condemned by the Orthodox synods of Constantinople (1638), Jassy (1642), and Jerusalem (1672).

Chapter XVII

THE HABSBURGS, MUSCOVY,

POLAND-LITHUANIA, AND BOHEMIA

Rise of the Habsburgs—First contacts with Muscovy—Muscovite-Habsburg alliance—Sigismund, Basil III, and the Habsburgs—Congress of Vienna (1515)—The Habsburgs and Muscovy profit by mutual friendship—Maximilian II, Ivan IV, and the Polish interregnum—Stephen Bathory's succession, Rudolf II, Fedor—The Habsburgs, Zamoyski, and Boris Godunov—Zamoyski, the Habsburgs, and the Danubian principalities—Charles V's attempts at imperialism—Philip II's political conceptions and their failure—Leading ideas of Spanish monarchic absolutism—Austrian Habsburgs adopt the Spanish conception—Its application in Bohemia—Ferdinand II's monarchic plans in Germany opposed by Denmark, France, and Sweden—End of the Thirty Years' War, peace of Westphalia (1648), ruin of Bohemia—Literary activity of Czech exiles, Komenský, Žerotín—Czech literature of the Counter-Reformation—Czech patriots, decadence of Czech national life—Czech and Slovak baroque art

The leading dynasty in sixteenth and seventeenth century Europe was undoubtedly the House of Habsburg with its Austrian and Spanish branches. The interventions of the Habsburgs in the history of western Europe and of Germany at this period are well known. Many of these interventions also had fateful consequences for some Slavic nations. Similarly some events which are often overlooked not only had a profound influence on the rise and decline of the Habsburgs, but also throw fresh light on the history of contemporary Europe.

First of all it should be borne in mind that the rise of the House of Habsburg in European history is intimately connected with the fate of a Slavic land, the Kingdom of Bohemia. The foundations of Habsburg fame were built, as was shown in Chapter II, on the ruin of the work and dreams of a valiant Czech king, Přemysl Otakar II. The latter lost in the struggle with Rudolf I, the founder of the House of Habsburg, not only his chance of the imperial throne, but also all those Alpine lands from the borders of Bohemia to the Adriatic which had been the fruits of a life of diplomatic skill and military valor. From that time on, the possession of the crown of Bohemia was the main object of Habsburg diplomacy. Rudolf I's son, the Emperor Albert I (1298-1308), married his son Rudolf to the widow of Wenceslas II of Bohemia, and when the Přemyslide dynasty died out in 1306, Rudolf became king of Bohemia. But his own and his father's deaths prevented the Habsburgs from retaining the kingdom in the posession of their dynasty. The House of Luxemburg came forward and disputed with the Habsburgs not only the Bohemian, but also the imperial crown.[1]

Meanwhile further chances were presenting themselves to the Habsburgs in Poland and Hungary. The last Angevin king of Hungary and Poland, Louis the Great, agreed to give his daughter Jadwiga, who was to inherit the Hungarian throne, in marriage to William, son of Leopold III, duke of Austria. The marriage was formally celebrated in 1378 when the princess was only five years old. When the Hungarian Estates had elected Jadwiga's sister Mary as their "king" in 1382, it was agreed that Jadwiga should succeed her father as "king" of Poland. The chances of the Habsburgs were, however, spoiled by the decision of the Polish Estates to marry their ten-year-old "king" to Jagiello of Lithuania. William of Habsburg tried vainly to defend his right. His attempt to occupy the castle of Wawel in Cracow failed, and he had to return to Vienna. Jadwiga, who was fond of her young husband, had to sacrifice her own sentiments to the interests of her kingdom.[2]

The Habsburgs were more successful in Bohemia. A new chapter in Habsburg history seemed to open in 1437, when Albert II (1437-1439), son-in-law of Sigismund, the last of the Luxemburgs, inherited from the latter the kingdoms of Bohemia and Hungary and also the imperial crown of Germany.[3] From 1438 on, the Habsburgs continued to occupy the imperial throne, with but one short interruption, down to the dissolution of the Holy Roman Empire in 1806. This ensured them great prestige in Central Europe. It was one of the least able Habsburg emperors, Frederick III (1440-1493), who was most confident in the future of the dynasty. He became the architect of their ascent in European history by arranging the marriage of his son Maximilian with Mary, daughter and heiress of Charles the Bold, duke of Burgundy. This marriage gave the Habsburgs possession of the Netherlands, one of the richest countries in Europe.

Frederick's inability to act at the right time, however, spoiled the chances of the Habsburgs in Central Europe. He did nothing to strengthen the position of his ward Ladislas Posthumus, son of Albert II and Elizabeth of Luxemburg, recognized as heir of the Kingdom of Bohemia and Hungary. Ladislas was at first deprived of the crown of Hungary (1440-1444) by Władysław, king of Poland, who was killed at Varna. After Ladislas' premature death in 1457, he was succeeded in Hungary by Matthias Corvinus (1458-1490) and in Bohemia by George of Poděbrady. On the deaths of these two monarchs Bohemia and Hungary were united again under Vladislav (Ladislas) II and his son Louis II of the House of Jagiello.

The position of the Habsburgs in Europe was considerably strengthened by Frederick's son Maximilian I, who was elected king of the Romans in 1486. Maximilian was perhaps the ablest Habsburg ruler and is rightly regarded as the second founder of the house.

His marriage with Mary, heiress of Charles the Bold, duke of Burgundy, secured the flourishing Netherlands for his son Philip the Handsome. The latter's marriage with Joanna the Mad, heiress of Ferdinand of Aragon and Isabella of Castile, was to bring the whole Spanish inheritance in Europe and the New World overseas to Maximilian's grandson Charles (1516). It was truly said, "bella gerant alii, tu felix Austria, nube."

Even before he succeeded as emperor (1493-1519), Maximilian developed a lively diplomatic activity in Central Europe. On the death of Matthias Corvinus in 1490 he became a candidate for the Hungarian crown, but had to give way to the Jagiellonians.

These events initiated the rivalry of the Habsburg and Jagiellonian dynasties for predominance in Central and eastern Europe. Maximilian discerned better than his imperial father the danger which threatened the future of his house from the Jagiellonians. The House of Luxemburg had precluded Habsburg domination of Central Europe for a century, but the concentration of the crowns of Poland, Bohemia, and Hungary in the hands of the House of Jagiello could cause the ruin of the Habsburgs. Maximilian wanted above all to prevent the Jagiellonians from occupying the throne of Hungary, and so, foreseeing conflict, he looked around for allies.

The marriage of Ivan III of Muscovy with Zoe-Sophia, the niece of the last Byzantine emperor, focused the attention of the West on the powerful new ruler who neighbored on Poland-Lithuania. Matthias Corvinus, king of Hungary, had already concluded an alliance with Ivan III against Casimir of Poland-Lithuania. The imperial court obtained its earliest information about Muscovy from Nicholas Poppel, a knight who visited Moscow in 1486. The emperor and his son, learning about the rivalry between Muscovy and Poland-Lithuania, sent Poppel to Moscow on an official mission in 1489 to offer friendship to Ivan III. The Muscovites

were rather mistrustful, and Ivan's ambassador, the Greek George Trachaniot, had first to obtain some information as to the sincerity of intention
of the emperor and his son. Serious negotiations only started in 1490,
when the imperial ambassador Jorg von Thurn reached Moscow with the
returning Greek envoy. Ivan III proposed an alliance against Poland-
Lithuania, promising help to the Habsburgs in their efforts to secure their
"inheritance," the throne of Hungary, and Trachaniot was again dispatched to Germany to negotiate the formal conclusion of the alliance.

In the meantime, however, Matthias of Hungary died (1490), and
Maximilian was fighting in Hungary for the vacant throne. Unfortunately,
Thurn and Trachaniot reached Nürnberg only in March 1491, to find that
Maximilian, after recovering the parts of Austria occupied by Matthias,
had been forced by financial difficulties to abandon his campaign in Hungary, although he had won over some influential lords for his candidacy.
Troubles with France, which disputed his wife's inheritance in the Netherlands and Burgundy, and the refusal of the imperial Diet to grant him
the necessary resources for his struggles forced Maximilian to conclude
peace at Pressburg with the victorious candidate, Vladislav, king of Bohemia. The latter, contesting the Hungarian crown with his brother John
Albrecht,[4] agreed that if he or his children should die without heirs, the
throne of Hungary would be inherited by Maximilian or his heirs. The
agreement was sealed by the marriages of Maximilian's grandson Ferdinand and granddaughter Mary with the daughter and son of Vladislav.
Thus Maximilian had obtained all he could have hoped for in this difficult situation without Russian help. He endeavored to obtain from Ivan
III protection of Prussia and Livonia, which he regarded as parts of the
Empire. But the grand prince, who had learned about the treaty of Pressburg, rejected Maximilian's attempts to extend their pact to Prussia and
Livonia, maintaining, however, the validity of their alliance against Poland-
Lithuania. Maximilian was rather embarrassed by Ivan's attitude. For
him the Russian alliance lost all meaning, and he only approached the
grand prince when Vladislav of Bohemia and Casimir's successor in
Poland-Lithuania, John Albrecht, had concluded an alliance with France,
which was still at war with Maximilian for his wife's inheritance (1500).

Maximilian had yet another card which he could use in his contest
with Poland. The Grand Master of the Teutonic Order disputed the validity of the stipulations of the peace of Toruń, concluded in 1466 after
the defeat of the order, and refused the oath of allegiance to the King of
Poland. The emperor took the side of the order and forbade the Grand
Master to render the homage due to the Polish king, on the grounds that
the lands of the order were parts of the Empire. His approach to Ivan
III, however, had no practical importance in the dispute.[5] Ivan had no
special interest at that time in using the alliance in his diplomacy, and

Maximilian I was too much preoccupied with the affairs of his house in the West. Ivan III and his successor Basil III (1505-1533) were, however, well aware of the importance which a closer relationship with the Habsburgs could have for them in the event of a new conflict with Poland-Lithuania, and continued to hold the door open for any new opportunity.

It was Michael Glinskij, a scion of a converted Tatar noble family and a former favorite of King Alexander, who had drawn the attention of Basil III to Maximilian. Glinski, in the course of a dispute with Sigismund I of Poland, Alexander's successor, changed sides and deserted to Moscow. He hoped that the decision of the Hungarian nobles in 1505 to exclude from the succession any foreign ruler of non-Hungarian origin would awaken in Maximilian the suspicion that his Polish rival was supporting the anti-Habsburg party in Hungary, and would incline him to renew the alliance concluded with Ivan III. Basil III, who was then at issue with Sigismund because of the dowry of his sister Helen, the widow of Alexander,[6] followed this advice. Maximilian, being then involved in struggles for Italy, did not respond to the Muscovite overtures. He was, moreover, disappointed by the grand prince's refusal to return to the Hanse the fortune confiscated by Ivan III in Novgorod.

So Basil III had to open the war with Poland-Lithuania without the help of the Habsburgs. He succeeded in occupying Smolensk, but suffered a resounding defeat on the river Orša (1514). This made him more anxious for an agreement with Maximilian. The latter was also more inclined to a closer relationship when he learned of the marriage of Sigismund with Barbara, the daughter of John Zápolya, the leader of the Hungarian anti-Habsburg party. This time Maximilian took the initiative and dispatched to Moscow George Schnitzenpaumer. He was empowered to renew the friendly relations with the Muscovites and to propose the formation of a coalition with Denmark and the German princes against Poland-Lithuania. Evidently, the emperor wished to exploit the threat of a coalition against Sigismund because his complications with France and in Italy precluded him from inaugurating any action in the East.

Basil III seized this opportunity, and thanks to the diplomatic skill of his advisers, he induced the imperial ambassador to conclude a formal anti-Polish alliance. He expected substantial help from the emperor through an attack on Poland to recover the territories lost by the Teutonic Order.

The emperor was very embarrassed when he discovered the astuteness of the Russian diplomats. He had no intention of initiating immediate warlike action on behalf of the Teutonic Order—any more than had the Electors of Saxony and Brandenburg, who were most interested in the conflict of the order with Poland. In order not to offend the grand prince, Maximilian agreed to the new alliance, but he immediately sent an embassy to Moscow with a new text which watered down considerably the alliance previously concluded. Instead of opening hostilities, as requested by Basil III, he proposed a peace conference of the interested parties at the Reichstag of Lübeck. The grand prince protested and maintained that the text of the alliance concluded in Moscow was binding on the emperor.

Although Maximilian never intended to accept all the consequences resulting from an anti-Polish pact with Muscovy, its conclusion brought him more advantages than he could probably have obtained through warlike intervention. Sigismund learned about the negotiations between the emperor and the grand prince and was well aware of the implications of a common attack against Poland-Lithuania by the emperor, the Teutonic Order, and Muscovy. He therefore used the services of Vladislav of Bohemia to wean the emperor away from Muscovy. Maximilian, still preoccupied in the West, responded favorably, and a meeting between Vladislav of Bohemia and Hungary, Sigismund of Poland, and the emperor was convened in Vienna (1515). The emperor's bargaining position was weakened by the negative results of the *pourparlers* at the Lübeck Reichstag. As the coalition between Denmark and the Electors of Brandenburg and Saxony in support of the order could not be realized, Maximilian was obliged to sacrifice the interests of the Empire and to accept the stipulations of the peace of Toruń (Thorn). All disputes between the order and Poland during the next five years were to be presented to the emperor for arbitration. In return for this unexpected concession—Sigismund was evidently unaware of the negative results of the Reichstag at Lübeck—the Jagiellonians confirmed and extended the stipulations of the Pressburg convention in favor of the Habsburgs. The latter were thus freed from Polish competition for the Hungarian throne and won the possibility of inheriting not only the Hungarian but also the Bohemian crown. In order to satisfy in some degree the obligations resulting from his alliance with Muscovy, Maximilian promised to work for the conclusion of a peace treaty between Sigismund and Basil III.

The ties of friendship concluded between the Jagiellonians and the Habsburgs at the so-called Congress of Vienna (1515) proved of paramount importance for the history of Europe. For the Jagiellonians it meant the surrender of their ambition to become a first-class power in Central Europe in favor of the Habsburgs. Their entanglement with Muscovy forced them to give up the role they could have played in Central and western European history. Because of the shaky position of the royal power in Poland and its shameful dependence on an egoistic nobility, they could not continue their expansion in Central Europe and were forced to seek the support of the Habsburgs. For the Habsburgs, the Congress of Vienna, leading to dynastic connections with the rulers of Bohemia and Hungary, was the decisive step toward achieving the great degree of power they were to exercise in Europe for some centuries.

The convention with the Habsburgs gave Sigismund I a respite in his difficult situation, secured the western boundary of his realm, and isolated Albert of Prussia, who was unwilling to pay him due homage. Moreover, through the intermediary of Maximilian he won the hand of a rich heiress, the Princess Bona of Milan.

For Maximilian the Muscovite alliance had thus lost its true meaning. The grand prince was unpleasantly surprised when he learned from Baron Herberstein, the imperial ambassador, that the emperor offered his services as an intermediary for a peace treaty between Poland-Lithuania and Muscovy. This was not the reaffirmation of an alliance which he expected, and the lofty explanation that the emperor saw it as his duty to work for peaceful relations among Christian rulers because Christendom was menaced by the Turkish advance made no impression on Basil III. Nevertheless, he was shrewd enough not to cut off his meager ties with the Habsburgs. The negotiations between Sigismund I and Basil III were protracted, the main obstacle being the grand prince's categoric refusal to cede Smolensk. He even accepted approaches from Albert of Prussia and concluded an alliance with him promising support if he went to war with Poland, without, however, being ready to execute his promise. Not even the conclusion of an armistice could be realized before the death of Maximilian I in 1519.

The Polish king had an unexpected opportunity to play a decisive role at the subsequent election of the new emperor. Albert of Prussia, dissatisfied with the failure of the Habsburgs to support him against Poland, worked feverishly for the election of Francis I, king of France, and even won over the grand prince to this idea.[7] Sigismund tried to profit by this opportunity and to obtain as many concessions as possible before giving his vote as guardian of Louis, the young king of Bohemia. He was, however, forced by the Estates of Bohemia to vote for Charles of Spain without even obtaining from this Habsburg candidate any firm promise regarding either Albert of Prussia or the claims of his wife Bona on the Duchy of Milan.

Charles V (1519-1556) was not well informed about the negotiations between Muscovy and Maximilian I, but he decided to continue the policy of his grandfather and sent an embassy to Basil III offering his mediation in the peace negotiations between Poland and Muscovy. Sigismund was not pleased by this offer because his military situation had improved, and he mistrusted the possibility of a new alliance between the Muscovites and the Habsburgs. Basil III saw in the reopening of diplomatic relations with the emperor the confirmation of the continued existence of the alliance concluded in 1514. At last, thanks also to the intervention of a papal legate sent by Pope Leo X, who had heard false rumors about the eagerness of the grand prince for union with Rome, an armistice was concluded for five years.

The old rivalry between the Jagiellonians and the Habsburgs, however, broke out again after the extinction of the Hungarian branch of the Jagiellonians in 1526. In spite of agreements concluded with the Habsburgs, Sigismund made a feeble attempt to safeguard the realm for his dynasty, and when the anti-Habsburg opposition had elected John Zápolya as their national king against Ferdinand I, Sigismund rather sympathized with Zápolya. Ferdinand I, also king of Bohemia, was suspicious of Sigismund's attitude, but his brother, the Emperor Charles V, remained loyal to the Polish king and refused Basil III's offer to renew the coalition of 1514. However, the exchange of embassies between Muscovy and the Habsburgs induced Sigismund to renew his friendly policy toward the Habsburgs. He accepted Ferdinand's offer to marry his daughter Elizabeth to Sigismund August, the son of the Polish king, and promised to end his ambiguous policy in the contest between Ferdinand and Zápolya in Hungary.

The pro-Habsburg policy was propagated in Poland by two highly influential officials, the Chancellor Christopher Szydłowiecki and the Vice-chancellor Tomicki. After their deaths, however, Queen Bona, always hostile to the Habsburgs, persuaded Sigismund to give his daughter Isabella in marriage to John Zápolya. She did all she could to secure Polish support for Zápolya's infant son and heir John Sigismund, who was also protected by the sultan. Bona also succeeded in alienating her son from his Habsburg wife. But when Elizabeth died and Sigismund August contracted a "morganatic" marriage with Barbara Radziwill, which provoked fierce opposition on the part of the Polish nobility, he sought support in a rapprochement with the Habsburgs. In 1549, a year after his accession to the throne, he made an agreement with them, which contained, besides a commercial treaty, a political clause obliging the parties not to support their reciprocal enemies.

This was of great importance for Ferdinand in his contest with John Zápolya's son and widow, the latter a Polish princess. In spite of French invitations to break with the Habsburgs, Sigismund August remained loyal to his allies. The fear of a Habsburg-Muscovite alliance kept the Pole faithful to his pro-Habsburg policy.

After Basil III's death, his widow Helen, acting as regent for her infant son Ivan IV, sent an embassy to Ferdinand and Charles V. Later came the pretensions of Ivan IV to his Lithuanian "heritage," his assumption of the title of "tsar," and false rumors that he was inclined toward union

with Rome, which would make the Pope and the emperor more ready
to recognize his royal title. All these reports continued to keep Sigismund
August in good relations with the Habsburgs. These relations were
strengthened by the marriage of the widowed Polish king with Ferdinand's daughter Catherine.

So it happened that friendly relations with Muscovy brought the Habsburgs considerable political advantages. But the grand princes, too, had
profited greatly from their contacts with the Habsburgs. Ivan III and
Basil III were well aware of the enhanced prestige which such relations
gave them. The way was thus opened to western Europe, whence they
could import the cultural and industrial goods which their land needed.
They profited by every opportunity to invite western artists and artisans
to open their workshops in Moscow. Basil III even responded to the
overtures of the Pope by dispatching his learned *djak* Dimitrij Gerasi-
mov to Clement VII (1525). He was anxious to extend his contact with
Italy, whence he sought the best artisans for his primitive industry, although he was not at all interested in union with Rome or in the royal
title, which had been promised to him as a reward. Their friendship with
the Habsburgs thus helped the grand princes to break the isolation from
the rest of Europe into which they had been forced by their hostile and
jealous neighbors.

Even Ivan IV thought it advisable to remain on proper, if not on
friendly, terms with the Habsburgs. His attempt to annex Livonia could
have been interpreted as a hostile act against the Empire because Livonia
was regarded as belonging to the Empire, and the grand master appealed
to the emperor for help. In answering the letter dispatched by the emperor in this affair, the tsar claimed that Livonia was a part of his
"patrimony." He reminded the emperor astutely that the Livonians had
apostasized from the true faith, and complained that Russian churches
and icons had been destroyed by them. Thus he showed that he was
well informed about the religious situation in Livonia and cleverly cited
some excesses of the militant reformers there as a cover for his intervention against the wish of the emperor.

The way in which Ivan treated the imperial courier who brought Ferdinand's letter reveals how much the Muscovite rulers esteemed the signs
of deference on the part of the emperors. Regretting that the emperor did
not address his letter to him as tsar, Ivan IV tried vainly to induce the
courier to give him this title, at least orally, during the audience. During
the negotiations for the prolongation of the armistice, the boyars defended Ivan's right to the title by pointing out that even Maximilian I
had given this title to Ivan III. In reality, the imperial ambassador
Schnitzenpaumer had used this title in the draft of the alliance made
in Moscow in 1514, but without the authorization of the emperor. Never-

theless, this point was exploited by Ivan IV, the Metropolitan Makarij, and even Peter the Great as one of the main arguments that this title was due to the ruler of Muscovy. Although Ferdinand I did not agree to give the imperial title to Ivan IV and although he also objected to the Pope's idea of granting the royal title to the Muscovite, the traditional good relations between the Habsburgs and the Ruriks were not interrupted, and in 1564 the Emperor Maximilian II addressed himself to Ivan IV for help in his war with the Turks. Ivan IV, humiliated by certain reverses of his army due to Polish intervention in Livonia,[8] answered very piously that he would very much like to help if he had not so much trouble with the Polish king, and assured Maximilian that if this obstacle were removed, he would join the emperor like a brother in his war with the infidels. When all lands taken by them had been restored to the Christians, then the tsar and the emperor would divide the earth among themselves in brotherly fashion and reign in peace united in one Church.

The death of the last Jagiellonian king (1572) offered new possibilities to the Habsburgs. Although Sigismund August was Ferdinand I's son-in-law and although it seemed probable that he would leave no heirs, the emperor did nothing to improve the chances of securing the throne of Poland for a member of his house. It is true that the Habsburgs were hated by the Polish *szlachta,* hostile to everything German, but many magnates and the higher clergy favored the election of a Habsburg and invited Ferdinand to prepare the way for action in the near future. It was in vain, and the emperor even worked to secure the return of his daughter to Austria because of her estrangement from her royal husband.

Maximilian II was no more fortunate. His invitation to his brother-in-law to join the anti-Turkish League was not accepted (1571), and the king received only vague answers to his suggestions that the Archduke Ernest might be the best candidate for the succession to the Polish throne. Ernest's candidacy seemed to enjoy good prospects in Lithuania, where it was supported not only by the prominent Lithuanian families, but also by the papal nuncio.

The Muscovite tradition of maintaining good relations with the Habsburgs showed itself once more during the negotiations for the succession in Poland-Lithuania after the extinction of the Jagiellonian dynasty. Maximilian II put forward the candidacy of the Archduke Ernest, but in Lithuania the lesser nobility had much sympathy for Ivan IV. Hoping to obtain a prolongation of an armistice, even the Lithuanian magnates, who favored a Habsburg, tried to make Ivan believe that his election had good prospects, not only in Lithuania but also in Poland. Ivan saw, however, that his conditions would not be accepted, and he therefore recommended to the Lithuanians the election of the Archduke Ernest in place of Henry of Valois, the brother of the French king, Charles IX.

The Habsburg candidacy failed nevertheless and French diplomacy triumphed thanks to the clumsiness of the imperial emissaries in Poland and to the hatred of the *szlachta* for the Habsburgs. This brought Maximilian II and Ivan IV into more intimate relationship. The tsar asked the emperor not to permit the king-elect to traverse Germany—hoping that if Henry could not reach Poland in time, a new election would take place giving Ivan a new chance—and offered to the emperor a renewal of the alliance of 1514. The emperor thanked Ivan IV for his intervention in favor of Ernest, but abstained from any hostile act against the elected king.

During the second Polish interregnum, following on the flight of Henry of Valois to France (1574), the chances of the Habsburgs in Poland brightened. The Polish magnates favored the election of a Habsburg, and the position was even more favorable in Lithuania, where the Habsburgs had won over the most prominent magnate family, the Radziwills. Ferdinand I had already conferred the dignity of a Prince of the Empire on the Black Radziwill, and Maximilian II continued this policy of winning over prominent Lithuanian nobles. The Lithuanian *szlachta* were also, in general, inclined to vote for the Archduke Ernest, on the hope that if a Habsburg were elected, Ivan IV would abstain from attacking Lithuania and Livonia. The Polish *szlachta*, however, maintained their violent opposition to the Habsburgs and rather favored Ivan IV, whose candidacy was also supported by the Primate.[9] Radziwill implored the emperor to make an energetic effort to send Ernest to Lithuania, where his election was assured, thus forcing the Poles to accept him; he also wished him to ask the tsar for support for Ernest.

Maximilian II hesitated at provoking such a fait accompli, but sent an embassy to Ivan IV, asking him to support Ernest's candidacy and promising him the title of Eastern Emperor after the expulsion of the Turks from Constantinople, to be achieved by the alliance of all Christian rulers. In the meantime the tsar had lost many adherents in Poland thanks to his indecision and hesitation in giving the *szlachta* more precise promises. So the *szlachta* chose another candidate, Stephen Bathory of Transylvania. In order to prevent the election of the latter, Ivan IV proposed to the imperial ambassadors a kind of partition of the commonwealth by the election of his son Fedor in Lithuania and of Ernest in Poland. If this were impossible, he was willing to conclude an alliance with the emperor in order to prevent Bathory, a vassal of the sultan, from reigning in Poland.

So a double election took place, the majority of the *szlachta* electing Bathory, and the pro-Habsburg nobility proclaiming Maximilian II the successor of Henry of Valois. The cause of the Habsburgs would not have been completely lost if Maximilian II had been able and willing to take measures more energetic than diplomatic interventions with Bathory and the tsar.

Ivan IV continued to press for the division of Poland-Lithuania between the Habsburgs and the Ruriks and sent a solemn embassy to the Reichstag in Regensburg. This was the first to be sent officially to the representatives of the Empire and made a great impression on contemporary western Europe. Ivan urged the emperor to conclude an alliance and to take sharp measures against Bathory. The Reichstag was, however, not willing to grant the emperor the necessary means for such an enterprise, and the inactivity of the emperor helped Bathory in securing acceptance in Poland and Lithuania, even on the part of the disappointed supporters of the Habsburgs.

Maximilian II's successor Rudolf II (1576-1612) was, like his father, interested only in Livonia, and in his missives to Ivan IV he made only vague promises concerning the conclusion of an alliance. The tsar was left isolated, and unable to stop the victorious progress of Bathory's modernized army, he had to ask the Pope for intervention. The legate Possevino was able to negotiate a peace treaty between Bathory, Sweden, and Ivan, but the long-cherished papal hopes for Russia's reconciliation with Rome and her adhesion to an anti-Turkish league were very astutely dissipated by Ivan, who had again shown his diplomatic shrewdness.

Bathory's success induced Rudolf II to make new approaches to Poland. But these remained fruitless because the emperor refused to break off his relationship with Muscovy. The death of Ivan IV focused Bathory's attention on new possibilities in Muscovy, which was now ruled by Ivan's weak son Fedor. Because of rumors that a Habsburg might succeed Fedor as the ruler of Muscovy, Bathory first tried to win support among the boyars for his own eventual succession and, after securing Sixtus V's consent, made preparations for a conquest of Muscovy. Although Rudolf gave a cool answer to Fedor's overtures after his accession, he protested in Rome against Bathory's plan of conquest with the help of the Pope.

Bathory's sudden death (1586) opened new possibilities for the Habsburgs which the hesitating Rudolf failed to exploit. Among the three candidates of his house, the Archduke Maximilian had shown the greatest ambition and energy, but the political situation in Poland was very confused. The anti-Habsburg party in Poland was won over to Sigismund of Sweden, the nephew of the widowed Queen Anne, the sister of the last Jagiellonian king, while the pro-Habsburg party was weakened by the competition between the archdukes Ernest and Maximilian, and the Lithuanians this time favored the election of Fedor. The negotiations with him were shipwrecked on the religious question, and the Muscovites realized too late that it would have been better to have supported the candidacy of a Habsburg. So it came to another double election, the majority, led by the influential Chancellor Zamoyski, electing Sigismund of Sweden, the pro-Habsburg party the Archduke Maximilian. The latter, badly supported by the emperor, tried to conquer the throne by force, but was defeated and captured by the chancellor.

Although the tsar had promised help to Rudolf in the conflict with Poland and the emperor had sent envoys to Moscow for negotiations, the papal nuncio was able to bring about peaceful negotiations with Zamoyski. The chancellor won a diplomatic victory, promising to release Maximilian only if he would renounce his pretensions to the Polish crown and if the emperor refused any help to the tsar in his conflict with Poland or Sweden. Maximilian refused to make such a solemn renunciation and succeeded in escaping from captivity. He persisted in his claim to the Polish crown and frustrated Sigismund's plan of resigning in favor of the Archduke Ernest by divulging the secret. Thus he created new difficulties for Sigismund, who in his desire to secure friendlier relations between Poland and the Habsburgs had married the Archduchess Anne.

The renewed progress of the Turks in Hungary forced Rudolf to seek a new entente with Poland with a view to the formation of a Christian league against the Turks. Although Maximilian was forced by the circumstances to agree to the convention between his house and Poland and although the Pope's legates intervened, full collaboration between Poland and the Habsburgs was not achieved.

In his difficulties Rudolf addressed himself to Muscovy for subsidies. Although Fedor and his highly influential minister Boris Godunov resented the attitude of the Habsburgs in the affair of the Archduke Maximilian, Fedor sent the emperor a gift of precious furs and accepted the mediation of the emperor's envoy in the conclusion of peace with Sweden.

It appears that Boris Godunov, when elected tsar after Fedor's death (1598-1605), counted on the prestige of friendly relations with the emperor in order to strengthen his position among the jealous boyars. For this reason he sent an embassy to the emperor, offering him help in his war with the Turks, asking for the hand of a Habsburg princess, and offering an alliance against Poland. However, his advances met with rather a cool reception at the imperial court. The imperial embassy sent in 1604 asked only for subsidies for the Turkish war, while it was very evasive on the question of marital ties and brought no offer of an alliance. Boris Godunov refused subsidies unless a new alliance were concluded on the model of that of 1514. His sudden death put an abrupt end to further relations between the Habsburgs and Muscovy. It is quite possible that Boris Godunov would have had a better chance in his conflict with the boyars if the Habsburgs had supported him fully. As before, they could never decide on more energetic action and so lost their chances in Poland and in Muscovy.[10]

The setback to the Habsburgs in Poland at the end of the sixteenth century was principally due to the policy of the Chancellor Zamoyski. This shrewd statesman, who was the dominant figure in Polish public life during the last interregnum and the reign of Sigismund III, was an open enemy of the Habsburgs. It was Zamoyski who wrecked all the efforts of the Papacy and of Rudolf II to form a Christian league against the Turks which would include Poland. In this respect he followed the policy of peaceful relations with the Turks, which had already become a tradition in Poland. Seeing the almost hopeless position of the imperial army in Hungary in face of the Ottomans, he avoided any alliance with the emperor which would lead his country into a bloody entanglement with the Turks.

In order to protect Poland from attack by the Turks or their tributaries, the Crimean Tatars, Zamoyski devoted all his diplomatic talent to building up a block of buffer states in the Danubian region. He therefore frustrated all the efforts of Austrian diplomacy to win over the rulers of Transylvania, Moldavia, or Wallachia for an anti-Turkish alliance. He even intervened militarily in Moldavia in 1595 to depose Prince Rozvan, who had accepted imperial suzerainty. He was replaced by a Polish vassal, Jeremiah Mohyla, who was ordered to remain on friendly terms not only with Poland, but also with the sultan, and to refuse any alliance with the emperor. When Prince Michael of Wallachia, a vassal of the emperor, invaded Moldavia, Zamoyski, acting in accord with the sultan, defeated him and reinstated his protégé Mohyla in Moldavia and the latter's brother Simeon in Wallachia. Zamoyski even tried to persuade the Transylvanians, allies of the emperor, to elect a prince who would accept his policy.

Zamoyski was successful in safeguarding Poland from conflict with the Turks. The latter welcomed his policy as long as they were engaged in a war against the emperor in Hungary. However, the situation changed when Poland, engaged in wars with Sweden and Muscovy, needed peaceful relations on its southern and western boundaries. This made a rapprochement possible, and so in 1613 Poland concluded a pact with the Habsburgs. This contained an obligation of mutual support in foreign and internal affairs. The Habsburgs profited by this stipulation in 1620 when Poland abstained from supporting the revolt of the Czech Protestant Estates.

Thus ended the attempts of the Habsburgs at expansion in the East. They were more fortunate in the West, and it was again Maximilian I who laid the foundations for the amazing rise of his house to become a dominant factor in European history in this period. In his wars with France for the inheritance of his wife, Mary of Burgundy, Maximilian I lost the Duchy of Burgundy but was able to save the Low Countries for his son Philip, whom he married to Joanna, daughter of Ferdinand and Isabella of Spain. This led ultimately to the inheritance of the Spanish throne by Philip's son Charles (1516). Supported by the immense financial resources of the Fuggers, the Augsburg financiers who dominated the banks of Antwerp, the greatest commercial center in contemporary Europe, Charles defeated Francis I of France in the imperial election of 1519. He then began to lay the foundations for a universal empire governed by the House of Habsburg of which he was the head.

It was, however, not Germany which was to be the center of Charles's empire. Germany was a loose conglomeration of quasi-independent principalities and cities, built on old feudal principles, and all the efforts of Frederick III, and especially of Maximilian I, inspired by the example of the Western monarchies, to secure some statutory centralization of power in the hands of the emperor proved unsuccessful.

The Low Countries and Spain, which formed the basis of Charles's power, pointed not to a territorial but to a maritime expansion of his imperialism. A universal hegemony could be ensured only if Charles could add to his mastery of the ocean that also of the Mediterranean basin. He almost succeeded in 1525 when at Pavia he defeated and captured Francis I, his dangerous rival in Italy and in the Mediterranean. His success, however, provoked a reaction on the part of the Papacy, which feared a Spanish encirclement in Italy, and of England, which also aspired to maritime expansion. France saw itself forced to conclude an economic and then a political agreement with the Turks, a fact which definitively buried the principle of the unity of Christendom and of Europe.

The wars with France and with Turkey drained the immense financial resources coming from the Spanish empire in America. The expedition against Tunis in 1535 could not reverse Turkish success on the European continent. Meanwhile all attempts at the introduction of some monarchic system into the feudal chaos of Germany were frustrated. At last, disillusioned and convinced of the fruitlessness of his efforts to restore religious unity in Germany, Charles V abdicated (1556) in Germany in favor of his brother Ferdinand I, and in Spain, Italy, and the Netherlands of his son Philip II (1556-1598).

Thus the Roman Empire of the German nation finally lost the religious unity which had hitherto given it some cohesion, while it also shrank in extent. The Low Countries, which had previously formed a part of the Empire, were de facto detached from it, while Lombardy, for whose possession so many German emperors had battled, also passed into Spanish hands, together with Naples and Sicily.

Leaving Ferdinand I in possession of the Romano-German imperial title, Philip II set out to build up a new Hispanic Empire around the Atlantic Ocean. This comprised Spain, with its colonies in Mexico and Peru, and Portugal, which he inherited in 1580 from his mother Isabella, together with Brazil, the coasts of Africa, and the East Indies. His marriage with Mary Tudor in 1554 offered the momentary prospect of uniting another maritime power, England, with Spain.

It was an immense opportunity, but it was not well exploited and it ended in failure. Even Pope Paul IV disliked Philip's exclusive and autocratic championship of the Catholic Church, purified by the Counter-Reformation, and objected to the methods employed by the Spanish Inquisition to preserve unity and purity in faith in all the lands of the new Empire. The popular association of the Spanish marriage with the Fires of Smithfield alienated many in England, where the death of Mary Tudor (1558) reopened the door to the Reformation, and the destruction of the Spanish Armada (1588) finally shattered all Philip's dreams of a world domination by Spain united with England. The same forceful measures employed in the Low Countries provoked a general revolt which led to the secession of the northern provinces as the independent Dutch Republic, while it prepared the formation of Belgium. The conversion of Henry of Navarre to Catholicism opened the gates of Paris to him and spoiled Philip's hopes of securing the French throne for his daughter Isabella. When Philip died in 1598, Spain, exhausted by continual wars, was financially ruined and in economic chaos. The Spanish maritime hegemony was being challenged by Dutch and English fleets seeking to despoil Spain of her empire and her trade in America and the East Indies.

This was a sad end for the grandiose political conceptions of the Spanish branch of the Habsburgs. Philip II, ignoring the political, economic, and intellectual evolution of Spain, Italy, and the Low Countries in the Renaissance period, sought to build the political unity of his territories on the basis of monarchic absolutism and economic statism. Seeing the disruption brought about in Germany by the Reformation, he made himself the champion of Catholicism, preventing by forcible means the spread of any other religious doctrines in his lands. Philip II ignored the fact that the economic prosperity of the Italian, Flemish, and Spanish cities and banks had been created by the initiative of the burghers and merchants working in an atmosphere of free enterprise. Instead he sought to concentrate all the wealth coming from the New World in the hands of the state, which was subordinated to his absolute will. He did nothing to foster the utilization of those riches in Spanish industry, which remained sterile. His absolutism prevented any collaboration with the representatives of the nation, and the forcible means used to attain unity in faith were often more harmful to the Church than helpful.

In spite of this failure, the idea of monarchic absolutism continued to inspire the government of Philip III (1598-1621) and Philip IV (1621-1665). Instead of sustaining the hegemony of his house by ruinous wars, Philip III preferred to ensure it by dynastic marriages with the Austrian branch of the Habsburgs and with the French Bourbons, the leading Catholic dynasties in Europe. He developed even further the idea of the absolute monarch concentrating all power in his own hands through the divine right invested in him, and surrounded himself with a quasi-sacerdotal ceremonial and a splendid court expressing the almost superhuman position of the monarch. This example was soon imitated by other monarchs. The Spanish Habsburgs continued to regard as the basis of their power the unity of faith sanctioned and reinforced by the Inquisition. They safeguarded the purity of the race over which they reigned by the expulsion of the Moors and the Jews, in spite of the disastrous effects of such a policy on the national commerce and finances. This absolutism being supranational, the power of a sovereign whose autocracy is of divine origin can be extended over nations of varying cultures and tongues, united only by the person of the dynast. All power is concentrated in the hands of the sovereign, who has the right to dispose even of the property of individuals if he thinks that it is in the interests of the faith which he protects or of the race whose purity he intends to safeguard. The absolutist regime of the Spanish Habsburgs developed into an oligarchy exercised by the higher clergy and aristocracy. The centralization of all economic power in the hands of this oligarchy aggravated the economic stagnation which had started under Philip II, and resulted in the enslavement of the peasants and the impoverishment of the middle classes. Cultural atrophy was provoked by the regimentation of spiritual forces by the forcible means of the vigilant Inquisition.

The idea of an absolute monarchy was also adopted by the Austrian branch of the Habsburg dynasty. Charles V's brother Ferdinand I, who had been educated in Spain, was equally determined to make the dynastic interests of his power predominant in Austria and in the kingdoms of Bohemia and Hungary over the national interests of those countries. So he started to centralize power in his hands. In 1527 he created two central organs for all his lands, the Secret Council and the Chamber of the Court, to which a War Council was added in 1556. Although vested only with consultative power, they slowly developed into agencies making decisions for the whole Empire. Ferdinand's plan to form a common parliament for all his lands was thwarted by the Estates of the different dominions, which also objected to the existence of the three centralizing agencies. Profiting by the defeat in Germany of the Protestant League of Schmalkalden (1547), with which the majority of the Czech Estates had sympathized,[11] Ferdinand curtailed the privileges of the cities and modified the constitution of Bohemia to strengthen the royal power (1549).

In order to secure the two crowns for their house, the Habsburgs made several attempts to curtail the electoral powers of the Bohemian and Hungarian Estates over their crowns. They were more successful in Bohemia than in Hungary and succeeded in inducing the Bohemian Estates to elect Maximilian II, Rudolf II, and Ferdinand II during the life of their predecessors. The Polish *szlachta* were well aware of these subtle changes introduced in Bohemia and Hungary, and the fear that a Habsburg king would try to introduce a centralized hereditary monarchy into Poland was, together with the national question, the main reason for the fierce opposition of the *szlachta* to the election of a Habsburg to the Polish throne.

Ferdinand II (1618-1637) was more determined than his predecessors to introduce into his lands a hereditary monarchy by divine right, such as had been developed by his Spanish cousins Philip II and Philip III. He also intended to build his Empire on the solid basis of religious uniformity and had already given proof of his zeal for the Catholic Counter-Reformation as governor of Styria. The victory over the Protestant Estates at the White Mountain (November 8, 1620) and the shameful flight of the Winter King Frederick gave him a welcome opportunity to implement his policy, and he exploited it to the full.

His religious zeal turned first against the Czech Brethren and the Calvinists, whose preachers were expelled. Exploiting the rights of a duly elected ruler against his revolted subjects, generally recognized at that period, and the rights of the victor,[12] he condemned to death forty-five members of all three Estates, the ring leaders of the revolution, and on June 21, 1621, twenty-six of them, Czech and German Lutherans, Calvinists, and Brethren, were publicly executed in front of the Town Hall of Prague. The Jesuits were called back, and the university was entrusted to them. New ordinances against the Protestant preachers were issued in 1622 and in the following years. At last, in 1627, the constitution of Bohemia was radically changed by the publication of a new ordinance. The kingdom was proclaimed hereditary in the Habsburg dynasty, and the coronation of a new, almost absolute king became a superfluous ceremonial. The privileges of the three Estates, to which was added a fourth, the ecclesiastical, with the right of precedence, were considerably curtailed. The Diet lost all control over the bureaucracy and was allowed only to propose new measures, which could be rejected by the court. The office of burgrave of Bohemia was abolished, and the direction of Bohemian affairs was centralized in the Bohemian Chancellery in Vienna, which remained for two centuries the last vestige of former Bohemian independence although it served principally as a mere intermediary between the court and the local offices. In religious matters the new ordinance annulled all privileges granted to the Utraquists and non-Catholics and declared the *Letter of Majesty* of 1609 revoked and the Catholic religion to be the only confession accepted in the kingdom.

The consequence of this drastic measure was a mass emigration of nobles and burghers who had refused to become Catholic. The Czech Brethren migrated to Silesia, Slovakia, and Poland. Leszno in Poland again became an important center with the last bishop of the Brethren, John Amos Komenský. Czech Protestants mostly found refuge in Saxony, in Meissen and Lusatia, and in Prussia. The Calvinists were refused sojourn in Saxony by the Elector, a staunch Lutheran, and mostly dispersed over Holland and England.[13]

As the great majority of the Czech nobility had adhered to the Reformation and had participated in the revolution, the consequence of the mass emigration and of the confiscation policy was an almost complete destruction of the old Bohemian nobility. The old families were replaced by alien nobles, mostly from Germany, Spain, and the Low Countries, who bought up the properties of the émigrés cheap or were granted lands by the emperor. This fact and the loss of many Czech intellectuals and burghers inaugurated the germanization of the Bohemian lands. The German language was put on a footing of equality with Czech in the kingdom, and as the new nobles in the Czech lands used only the tongue of the emperor in their official contacts with the court, the use of the native language naturally declined in public life. This situation was aggravated by the wholesale confiscation of Czech books by the zealous missionaries, who objected to their anti-Catholic bias, and their only partial replacement by Catholic religious literature in the vernacular.[14]

Many of these forcible measures employed by Ferdinand II were understood and regarded as legitimate even by the Protestant princes in Germany, who had accepted the unchristian principle of *cuius regio illius et religio* formulated by the Peace of Augsburg in 1555. Yet even Maximilian of Bavaria found it necessary to protest against the misery and chaos which these measures provoked in Bohemia. Ferdinand II, however, had shown too early his true intentions regarding the reorganization of the Empire. He deprived Frederick of the Palatinate of all sovereign rights and handed over the principality together with the electoral dignity to his ally, Maximilian of Bavaria (1623), the most powerful prince of the Empire. This gave a secure majority among the seven Electors to Catholic princes and was, at the same time, a violation of the basic law of the Empire, which granted such a right only to the College of Electors. The events in Bohemia augured Ferdinand II's intention to introduce other changes in order to realize his monarchic plans in Germany. The Protestant princes were alarmed and found a leader in Christian IV, king of Denmark and duke of Holstein, who was hoping to bring the Baltic principalities of the Empire into a closer relationship with Denmark.

The emperor, however, had at his disposal the two best armies in contemporary Europe, that of Maximilian of Bavaria and that of Albrecht von Waldstein (Wallenstein). The latter was a scion of the Czech lesser nobility who had enriched himself by a wealthy marriage, by buying forfeited estates cheaply, and by various shady manipulations. He had formed a well-organized and equipped army of mercenaries, whom he led with superb generalship to defeat Christian IV in 1629. Ferdinand II, thinking that he had now become the uncontested master of the Empire, promulgated the Act of Restitution reclaiming all ecclesiastical property secularized since 1552. This would mean the restoration of the lands of two archbishoprics, twelve bishoprics, and one hundred and twenty abbeys to Catholic control, thus bringing immense patronage under imperial influence. The specter of an absolute monarchy on the Spanish pattern was opening before the eyes of the bewildered German princes. The application of the principle *cuius regio illius et religio* in the newly restituted lands would have changed the religious situation in Germany, as was being done in Bohemia, and would have meant a severe setback for the Reformation.

There was a further aspect of the new situation which alarmed France. If Ferdinand's plans in Germany were realized, France would be encircled and threatened with engulfment by a Spanish-Austrian Habsburg world empire. Moreover, Habsburg influence had again extended eastward. Poland-Lithuania, involved in King Sigismund III's war with Sweden for the inheritance of the Swedish crown and for Livonia (1620-1629), was obliged to be on good terms with the Habsburgs, so that Sigismund thought it necessary to make a political alliance with them.

Ferdinand II revealed another dangerous plan. The recovery for Catholicism of the archbishopric of Bremen, between the Elbe and Weser estuaries, opened to the emperor a free way to the ocean. Meanwhile the duchies of Mecklenburg and Pomerania were bestowed on Waldstein, who was made a duke and admiral of the high seas and the Baltic and promised domination over the Baltic and the Scandinavian states. This, however, aroused the attention of Gustavus Adolphus of Sweden (1611-1632), who had his own plans for the Baltic Sea. After taking Livonia from Poland, he needed only the possession of Mecklenburg and Pomerania to make the Baltic a Swedish lake. Cardinal Richelieu, the chief minister of Louis XIII (1610-1643), realized this and concluded a treaty with Gustavus Adolphus (1631) providing the Swedes with the necessary finances for the war with the emperor.

Gustavus Adolphus, one of the best generals in Europe, found his task facilitated by the dismissal of Waldstein by the emperor in 1630, and defeated the imperial army at Breitenfeld (1631). The Elector of Saxony joined him in invading Bohemia, and thousands of Czech refugees followed the Saxon army, which occupied Prague, in the hope that the tide of events had turned in their favor. Waldstein, however, was recalled by the emperor and reversed the situation, expelling the Saxons from Bohemia. He was defeated when he met the Swedes at Lützen (1632), but Gustavus Adolphus was killed in battle. This gave Waldstein new opportunities for his ambitious political plans, and he entered into secret negotiations with the enemy, aiming probably at the crown of Bohemia. He was assassinated by Irish and Scots soldiers of fortune in his own army in Cheb (Eger) in 1634.[15]

Ferdinand II lost his most talented general, but a Spanish army sent by Philip IV saved the situation by defeating the Swedes at Nördlingen (1634). Peace was signed between Saxony and the emperor at Prague (1635). Ferdinand revoked the Edict of Restitution and ceded Lusatia to Saxony. So it came about that the price for the unsuccessful attempt at the realization of the Habsburg imperial dream in Germany was paid by the Kingdom of Bohemia, to which Lusatia had hitherto belonged.

This turn of events opened a new possibility for the establishment of Habsburg hegemony in Europe and so induced France to come into the open and declare war on the Habsburgs. France's armies battled with the Spaniards; French finances supported the armies of Sweden and of the German Protestant princes. Meanwhile the Dutch navy started a war of maritime blockade, which finally proved disastrous to Spanish power, ruining its financial resources emanating from the colonies and enriching immensely the rebel Republic.

In spite of these disastrous losses, which were followed by unrest in Catalonia and the loss of Portugal, Philip IV persisted obstinately in the costly war in Germany and Bohemia for the Habsburg continental hegemony. The alliance of George Rakoczy, prince of Transylvania (1645), with the Swedes endangered even the imperial residence in Vienna, and the peril was averted only by a separate peace with Rakoczy, who was threatened by a Turkish invasion. The last two years of the war degenerated into senseless devastation, and in 1648 the war came to end at the Charles's Bridge of Prague, heroically defended by the new generation of Czech students and burghers led by Jesuit fathers.

The Peace of Westphalia concluded between France, with its allies, and Ferdinand III (1637-1657) sealed the end of all attempts at the introduction of a monarchic regime in the Empire. The territorial superiority (*Landeshoheit*) of the states of the Empire was finally recognized, and the Empire's territory was diminished by the separation of Holland and Switzerland and by the surrender of Metz, Toul, Verdun, and most of Alsace to France. Sweden almost realized its dream of domination of the Baltic by the acquisition of the bishoprics of Bremen and Verden, and of western Pomerania. The rest of the latter principality went to the Hohenzollern Elector of Brandenburg, who also held Prussia; this was another landmark in the rise of the Hohenzollerns to become the mightiest dynasty of the Empire.

The Counter-Reformation was brought to a halt by the confirmation of the Peace of Augsburg (1555), to which the Calvinists were also admitted. The Czech émigrés, many of whom had fought in the Swedish armies, trusted vainly that the victors would ensure their return to their country and the free exercise of their religion. The religious situation in Bohemia had also changed profoundly during the last decades, as was manifested by the refusal of the new generation of Prague's youth to join the Swedish armies and to surrender the capital to the enemies of the emperor.

Bohemia paid the heaviest price for the imperial dreams of the Habsburgs. The population had fallen from about 3,000,000 in 1618 to about 800,000 in 1654, and of the 150,000 landed peasant families, only 30,000 were left. The towns had suffered most grievously. Over 550 of them had disappeared, and the once flourishing cities were depopulated and their houses in ruins. The absolute power of the sovereign was definitely established, and the administration continued to be increasingly centralized in Vienna.

This political and economic ruin naturally had disastrous effects on Czech national culture. Among the émigrés were numerous intellectuals, writers, and patrons of Czech literature, and the loss in population also meant a loss of reading public. In 1615 already the Diet of Bohemia complained of the increase in the cities of foreigners who did not know the native language. Their number increased after 1620, the place of Czech magistrates and burghers in the cities, of Czech nobles, and of the Czech clergy being taken by foreigners, mostly Germans.

Many of the Protestant emigrants continued to publish and print Czech books in exile, especially in Saxony, Zittau, and Perno, and smuggled them into Bohemia. The Czech Brethren continued to publish their apologetic and pious works in Leszno, especially those of the bishops John Cyrillus and Paul Fabricius. Adam Hartman was the author of a Czech martyrology and of a history of the persecution of the Brethren. Most of these writings lacked originality and revealed the gloomy mentality of the exiled. The Church history of Paul Skála gave valuable and important information on the progress of the Reformation in Bohemia from 1600 to 1623. Paul Stránský wrote an interesting description of Bohemia, its history, customs, and constitution, trying to attract the attention of Protestant Europe to the plight of the kingdom. Andrew of Habernfeld intended to achieve the same end by his passionate description of the Czech struggle against Ferdinand II, from 1617 on. The literary activity of some Czech refugees in Slovakia was more effective. As already mentioned, the most important achievement was the composition of a hymnal, called *Harp of the Saints*, by George Tranoscius. The activity of Czech refugees in Slovakia had its importance for the national life of the Slovaks, confirming their national and Slavic sentiment. They also had disciples among the native Slovaks, one of them being Daniel Sinapius with his oldest collection of Slovak proverbs.

Only one member of the Czech emigration made a really valuable contribution to the cultural progress of mankind, John Amos Komenský (Comenius), the last bishop of the Czech Brethren (1592-1670). He was born in Moravia, studied in Heidelberg, and after 1627 found refuge in Poland. There, in Leszno, he won his reputation as a pioneer of new methods in education. His first scholarly publications—the *Janua linguarum* ("Great Didactic"),[16] a mixture of a grammar and an encyclopedia of useful knowledge, and the *Orbis pictus*, the first children's picture book, written in Leszno—made him widely known, and he received several invitations from Protestant states anxious to introduce his methods into their educational systems.

He spent nine months in England meeting all the prominent English scholars, giving an incentive for the foundation of a learned body which was later realized in the Royal Society. In England he was approached by the son of John Winthrop, the governor of Massachusetts, who invited him to become master of Harvard College. Only his desire to be nearer to his exiled countrymen and the hope of returning home one day induced Komenský to refuse this invitation. Instead, he went to Holland, where he met Descartes, then to Elbing and to Transylvania, where he worked on the reform of schools as a guest of George Rakoczy. After his return to Leszno, he lost all his manuscripts and library and found a last refuge in Amsterdam. Among his numerous publications *The Labyrinth of the World*, which reminds the reader of Swift's *Gulliver's Travels* and

S. M. DRAGANOV
17966 ORANGE TREE LANE
TUSTIN, CALIF. 92680

Bunyan's *Pilgrim's Progress,* the *Orbis pictus,* and *Pansophia* are best known. Although tinged with mysticism, his works revealed a vast erudition and found a vivid response among his contemporaries. He is rightly regarded as a pioneer of modern pedagogy and as such holds a prominent place in history. He was less successful with his pansophistic theories, and his efforts to bring about a union of Protestant Churches and world peace were frustrated.[17]

Besides Comenius another member of the Unity of Brethren enjoyed a European reputation, took an active part in contemporary political events, and was a prominent Czech writer—Charles of Žerotín. A scion of a most distinguished magnate family, Charles studied in Strasbourg, Basel, and Geneva, was a warm supporter of Henry IV, and fought in his army before the latter's conversion to Catholicism. He was known in England, the Netherlands, and Germany, and played an important role in the Moravian Diet. He did not favor the revolt of the Bohemian Estates and remained faithful to Ferdinand II, but although allowed to stay on his holdings, he went into exile in Wrócław (Breslau) and died in 1636 during a visit to Moravia.

His principal writing, regarded as a jewel of Czech prose, was his *Apology,* in which he explained his restrained attitude in contemporary politics. His numerous letters gave important information on different events and prominent personalities of his age. His comments on Moravian Diets illustrated the happenings in the eventful years from 1599 to 1614.[18]

The propagators of the Counter-Reformation [19] were obliged to replace the religious books which they were confiscating with Catholic literature. There is little originality in these works, the authors generally contenting themselves with translations or adaptations of Latin or German religious works. The Capuchin Francis of Rozdražov, a Pole, wrote a treatise against the chalice and a description of the miracles of St Anthony. Among the Jesuit missionaries the most prolific writer was George Plachý (Ferus). Two ascetic writers, George Constantins and Matthias Šteyer, published a Catholic edition of the Bible, called the *Bible of Saint Wenceslas* (1677-1715). They were aided in this edition by John Bannet, who wrote numerous sermons and commentaries on the Gospel and also translated C. Fischer's economic works. In their edition of the Bible, these three Jesuits followed the translation made by the Czech Brethren.

An enterprise of importance for the spread of Czech literature was the publishing organization called The Heritage of S. Wenceslas, which was founded in 1670 on the initiative of M. Šteyer. It existed down to modern times, and a great number of popular Czech works of a religious nature were published by it and distributed among simple people. Šteyer himself, a fervent Czech patriot, was a very fertile writer, seeking inspiration in baroque homiletic, hagiographic, and religious literature of Italian or German origin. Among original biographical works is the description of the life of A. Chanovský, a zealous and saintly missionary, by John Tanner. It illustrates the methods employed by the Jesuits in the recatholicization of Bohemia.

There were also numerous religious poems and songs. They replaced the similar products of Protestant poets. Although seldom of high poetical value, most of these compositions did differ from the songs of the Reformation, which were often too dogmatic and devoid of individual feeling, by their warm sensuality and imagery, which allowed their authors to express their individuality more freely. The poets imitated the Spanish baroque fashion of alternating earthly eroticism with mystical love. They liked metaphors and allegories, following in this the tradition of humanism and the Renaissance. They imitated the Italian and German baroque composers, who had learned from the Roman classic poets how to charm their readers with pastoral fictions and idyllic scenes. Many of them followed the poetic innovations of the Italian Marino with his play upon words and agglomeration of images often hardly related. The main theme of this poetry was the same as that of Protestant compositions, the antithesis of divine eternity and human vanity.

The Czech composers could hardly vie with their Italian and German prototypes, and this kind of poetry sounds strange to modern ears. The products of Czech baroque poetry were therefore regarded as an eloquent illustration of the depths to which Czech literary production had sunk during this "dark age." Recent research has, however, shown that Czech baroque poetry deserves better treatment from literary historians. A more detailed analysis has found in these products many points which shed more light in this darkness.[20]

One of these poets was Adam Michna, a lyricist of some genuine feeling. He was followed by Felix Kadlinský, who introduced into Czech poetry the pastoral erotic combined with heavenly love in his translation of the famous composition *Trutznachtigal* by the German Jesuit Friedrich von Spee. The best of the Czech baroque poets, however, was Frederick Briedel (1619-1680), a Jesuit missionary whose talent was especially manifested in his carols, eucharistic hymns, and hagiographic poems.[21] His contemporary, John Rosa (1620-1689), a lawyer and philologist, composed a Christmas pastoral which is one of the best Czech baroque productions and which served as a model and incentive to Czech poets of the eighteenth century.

All these authors were sincere Czech patriots anxious to preserve the purity of their native language and troubled by the influx of foreign

words and by the neglect of Czech syntax. Many philological works originated in the seventeenth century, some of them rather poor contributions. John Rosa's research in Czech philology was, however, of great
help to the patriots of the eighteenth century.

Warm national sentiment was also to be found in numerous compositions on Czech history. The Jesuits, although foreigners at the time of
their introduction into Bohemia, soon obtained numerous native recruits,
and many ardent patriots came from their ranks. The most notable of these
was B. Balbín, a scion of the Czech lesser nobility. He started his historical writings with the biography of Archbishop Ernest of Pardubice.
His *Epitome rerum Bohemicarum,* revealing to the learned public the
glorious past of Bohemia, was published in 1677. His *Miscellanea* on Bohemian history, although unfinished, provides important information collected from various historical sources. In defense of the use of the Czech
language Balbín wrote an apology which revealed his warm patriotic
feeling. This *Dissertatio apologetica* remained in manuscript until 1775.
Fortunately Balbín had some followers. His friend Canon Thomas Pešina,
with J. Kruger and John Tanner, collected a great amount of material
from archives of noble families and published them in his *Prodromus
Moravographiae.* His *Mars Moraviae,* describing all hostile attacks on
Moravia in the past, remained unfinished. Interest also attaches to his
history and description of the Cathedral of St Vit (Guy) in Prague.

Balbín's and Pešina's disciple, John Francis Beckovský, a member of
the Czech Order of the Cross, published a new edition of the popular
Czech chronicle of Hájek and collected a quantity of material for a continuation down to 1700, which, however, remained unpublished.

The few patriotic writers of the second half of the seventeenth century
worked feverishly on the salvation of Czech culture and on the preservation of the purity of the Czech language. But their efforts were not adequate to stop the germanization of Czech public life and the slow degeneration of the language. This failure was due not so much to the Counter-
Reformation as to the absolutist centralizing policy of the Habsburgs,[22]
to the fact that the majority of the Czech nobility had been replaced by
foreigners, to the devastation of the Thirty Years' War, and to the loss
of native population, which was replaced in the cities by non-Czech im-
migrants. In spite of that, when toward the end of the eighteenth century
a new generation of Czech patriots had started to work for the national
reawakening, it found inspiration in the works of its predecessors of the
seventeenth century.

This political and economic situation explains also why the art of
Bohemia is represented mostly by foreign artists—Italians and Germans.

Baroque art was not introduced into Bohemia by the Counter-Reformation. Among the first baroque monuments in Prague were the church of the Holy Trinity built by the Protestants (1611-1613) and Matthias' gateway to the castle constructed in 1611. Baroque art became, however, intimately connected with the Counter-Reformation, and its products impressed on the Czech lands the characteristic features which prevailed over the creations of the Gothic and Renaissance periods.

The center of baroque art was naturally Prague, although it had ceased to be a royal residence. Two magnates who enriched themselves during the war, Michna and Waldstein, had their palaces built in Prague by the Italian architects A. Spezza and Y. Marinis. Other Italian architects worked on the embellishment of other aristocratic residences. The Sternbergs called in J. Orsi and D. Canevale, who constructed in Prague a copy of Bramante's House of Our Lady at Loreto.

The Jesuits invited Carlo Loragho to build their church of St Salvator. Other churches were built by the Jesuits, mostly in the style of that of Il Gesù in Rome. Loragho collaborated with others in the construction of the shrine of Svatá Hora and built fortifications at Prague. The castle of the Lobkovic family in Roudnice and the residences of the Černíns and Nostics in Prague were constructed by F. Caratti and other Italian architects.

The arrival in Prague of John B. Mathey (1630-1695) from Dijon marked a new period in Czech baroque. He was more original in his architectural conceptions, and following the Roman baroque tradition, he built some monuments of high artistic value (the archbishop's palace, the palaces of Troja and of the Toscan family, the churches of the Order of the Cross and of Strahov). His tradition was continued by Marc Antonio Canevale and by the native architect I. Bayer (church of S. Ignatius, the castle of Hluboká).

John Santini (died 1723) introduced some innovations inspired by Gothic features (Sedlec, Želiv, Kladruby, Plasy), which are especially visible in the castle of the Kinskýs at Chlumec.

The dominant figures of Czech baroque were the two Dientzenhofers, Christian (died 1722) and Kilian Ignatius (died 1751). Christian started to build the church of St. Nicholas, finished the church of the Holy Trinity in Prague, and worked in Břevnov and Cheb (Eger) and in Kuks for Count Spork. His creations were comparable with the best products of European baroque. Bohemian baroque architecture reached its highest peak in the works of his son Kilian Ignatius. He became acquainted with the style of the famous Guarini in Vienna and built some monuments in Bohemia which surpassed even the works of his father (St. John of Nepomuk, Loreto, St. Charles Borromeo, St. Catherine, St. Nicholas in Prague, churches in Karlsbad, Klatovy). The church of St. Nicholas is regarded as the best baroque church north of the Alps. At the end of his career he introduced French classicism into Bohemia. He found many followers, and his influence dominated Czech architecture during the whole eighteenth century.

Moravian architecture could not boast works produced by the Dientzenhofers. It was more influenced by Viennese architecture. Its best products were the churches at Sv. Kopeček near Olomouc, of Rajhrad, and of Kroměříž (Kremsier). The garden of the archbishop in this city was one of the first baroque gardens in this part of Europe.

Baroque sculpture only started to flourish in Bohemia at the end of the seventeenth century. Its most celebrated representatives were F. M. Brokoff (died 1731) and Braun (1684-1738), a native of the Tyrol. They created the extremely beautiful sculptures decorating the Charles's Bridge at Prague and in other places in Bohemia. They were followed by many other artists, and their influence was marked in many cities in Bohemia boasting columns of the Holy Trinity or of Our Lady in the market places.

Painting also only achieved certain heights at the end of the seventeenth century. It was inaugurated by Abraham and Isaak Godyn of the Low Countries, but could boast three native masters, Charles Škréta (died 1674), who tried to combine naturalism with baroque idealism, Peter Brandl (1668-1735), a pupil of the Austrian M. W. Halbachs (frescoes at Břevnov, Kuks, Jindřichův Hradec), and W. L. Reiner (died 1743), a native of Prague. Baroque architecture favored only decorative painting, and therefore other genres in painting found few prominent representatives. The best of them, John Kupecký (died 1740), a Czech by birth, worked only in Austria and in Germany.[23] Moravian decorative painting was influenced more by Vienna than by Bohemia. The minor arts flourished during the reign of Rudolf II. His collections of art were scattered during the wars, and only in the eighteenth century were the Bohemian minor arts revived.

Baroque architecture penetrated into Slovakia (Bratislava, Trnava) from Vienna. Italian architects predominated. They had been called in by the leader of the Counter-Reformation in Hungary, Cardinal Pázmány, and the Jesuits. The aristocracy followed this example in inviting foreign artists to rebuild and decorate its palaces and castles. No creative genius was found in Slovakia. The baroque art of eastern Slovakia differs in many respects from that of its western part, notably by its mixture of Renaissance features with baroque patterns. Polish influences helped to create interesting conceptions in the construction of wooden churches for the Greek-Catholic Ruthenian population in northern Hungary known as Subcarpathian Russia. There were only a few sculptors and painters, mostly Italians and Austrians, and Gothic and Renaissance features in church decoration survived down to the end of the seventeenth century in eastern Slovakia. In plastic decoration J. R. Donner, who worked also in Bratislava, deserves mention. Košice became an important center in the goldsmith's trade in the second half of the seventeenth century.

At the end of the seventeenth century the idea of an absolute monarchy was realized by the Austrian branch of the Habsburgs, not in Germany but in their "hereditary lands," Austria, Bohemia, and Hungary. Bohemia had to pay the heaviest price for this achievement. The Counter-Reformation accompanied this transformation, and so it happened that the baroque style, so characteristic of the "hereditary lands," became a symbol of the victory of the Counter-Reformation and of Habsburg absolutism.

NOTES

1. Cf. Chapter II, pp. 27-30.
2. Cf. above, Chapter IX, p. 222. The relations between the Habsburgs and Poland-Lithuania have not yet been fully examined by Polish historians. Only O. Halecki has devoted a well-documented study to the relations between the Habsburgs and the Lithuanian nobility in the fifteenth century (see Bibl.). He also gives a valuable bibliography in Polish. The rivalry between Poland and the Habsburgs at the end of the sixteenth century in the Danubian principalities was studied by J. Macůrek in his monograph *Zápas Polska a Habsburků o přístupk Černému moři* (Prague, 1931). This contains a summary in French and a complete bibliography.
3. Cf. above, Chapter VIII, p. 237.
4. Cf. above, pp. 205, 232.
5. A curious incident shows how scant was knowledge of Russian in the West. Maximilian asked the grand prince to send him a letter in Latin because he had nobody at the court who understood Russian. Ivan III failed to oblige, and so the emperor had to send the letter to a bishop in Trieste for translation. The translation was, however, so bad that the main passages remained unintelligible, and the emperor had to send the translation to Moscow for verification.
6. Cf. above, Chapter XII, pp. 270, 273.
7. This was the only Russian intervention in the election of an emperor. The Muscovite court does not seem to have been well informed about contemporary affairs because the letter which Basil III sent to France was addressed to "Charles, King of France."
8. Cf. above, Chapter XII, p. 276.
9. Cf. above, p. 276.
10. The diplomatic relations between Muscovy and the Habsburg emperors have hitherto been more fully analyzed only by H. Übersberger (see Bibl.). The documents preserved in Russian archives deserve more attention from Western historians. They give a clear picture of the origins and growth of Russian diplomacy, based on Byzantine and Mongol traditions, with some characteristic Russian features which were very different from Western patterns. Although

young and inexperienced, the Muscovite foreign service knew well how to exploit relations with the West for propaganda purposes to impress the Russian people, and in astuteness its agents often proved superior to the experienced imperial diplomats. Many of its principles have become a tradition in modern Russian diplomacy. The period from 1604 to 1654 is the object of a recent thorough study by W. Leitsch (see Bibl.). The author used also new material from Austrian and Bavarian archives and analyzed Russian studies dealing with this period.

11. Cf. above, Chapter XVI, p. 398.

12. Although Ferdinand II was under the influence of the Spanish monarchic theory investing the monarch with all legislative power, in the case of Bohemia he seems to have been also guided by the idea that as a duly elected ruler and conqueror of a revolted and defeated land, he was not bound by his oath given before his coronation, engaging him to preserve the old customs of the kingdom and the privileges of the Estates.

13. The contemporary historian Slavata, an adherent of Ferdinand II, estimated that in 1628, 36,000 families had left Bohemia, of which 180 were of noble origin. The specialist on this subject, J. Bílek (*Dějiny konfiskace v Čechách*, Prague, 1893), confirms the correctness of this figure. According to him the value of the confiscated property exceeded 100,000,000 gulden, and 500 of the 936 noble estates were forfeited. Some of the refugees migrated from Holland to New Amsterdam (New York) in the New World. The most prominent of them was F. Herrman, author of the first map of Maryland, where he was granted the estate called by him Bohemia. He is counted among the founders of the State of Maryland. Another was J. Philipps, who was granted a large estate on the Hudson River. He founded one of the oldest churches in New York State in the neighborhood of Sleepy Hollow.

14. For these reasons the defeat of the Bohemian Estates at the White Mountain is regarded by the Czechs as a major national tragedy, although the suppression of the revolt was dictated not by national, but by political and religious reasons. Many German nobles participated in the revolt and were punished with their Czech colleagues. The revolt encountered support among many Protestant princes in Germany. The acceptance of the Reformation by the majority of the Czech Estates produced the consequence that the old national animosity between the Czechs and the Germans, which had reached its peak during the Hussite wars, almost disappeared and was replaced by a sentiment of religious brotherhood. This was also manifested by the election of a German prince, Frederick of the Palatinate, as king of Bohemia. It seems probable that the use of the German language and German influence would have increased in Bohemia even if Frederick had been successful, but it is difficult to estimate how far these influences would have gone because of the existence of a numerous Czech intelligentsia and of the attitude of the Reformation toward the use of the vernacular in public worship.

15. The murder did not take place without the previous knowledge of Ferdinand II, who seems in this case to have exercised the rights of an absolute monarch against a traitor. Such a right was, at that time, adjudged to a sovereign. Ferdinand regarded Waldstein's murder as an execution, carried out on the basis of a secret trial and condemnation. The best work on Waldstein is that by the Czech historian J. Pekař (see Bibl.), who also lists the extensive literature on the subject.

16. It was translated into fifteen languages, including Arabic, Persian, and Turkish.

17. Selections of Komenský's writings were published by UNESCO in 1957, with an introduction by J. Piaget and with indications on editions of Komenský's works and a selected bibliography in non-Slavic languages. On Komensky's stay in Poland see L. Kurdybacha, *Působení J. A. Komenského v Polsku* (Prague, 1960).

18. There is a well-written monograph on Žerotín by O. Odložilík (*Karel Starší ze Žerotína*, Prague, 1936).

19. There is as yet no exhaustive history of the Czech Counter-Reformation. Gindely's book (see Bibl.) stops in 1628. V. Líva devoted several studies to the recatholicization of Prague in *Sborník příspěvků k dějinám Prahy*, vols. 5, 7, 9 (1930, 1933, 1935), with a résumé in French. The conversions, although often forced, proved their sincerity during the Saxon occupation of Prague in 1631-33, when only a few of the converts returned to Protestantism although the victory of the Protestants seemed certain at that time. The recatholicization of the countryside was facilitated by the fact that, in many cases, the peasants had been left cold by the religion of their Protestant masters.

20. Some unknown texts have been published by J. Vašica. His study on Czech literature in the baroque period (*České literární baroko*, Prague, 1938), is most informative in this respect. Cf. Čyževskji's review of Czech discoveries (see Bibl.). See quotations of Czech Baroque poetry with German translations in A. Angyal's book (see Bibl.), pp. 31-79.

21. Even the famous exterminator of non-Catholic literature A. Koniáš (1691-1758) was a skilful composer of religious hymns.

22. Balbín saw this clearly, and his apology is a strong protest against this policy. The government was aware of this and refused permission to print it. When the work was published in 1775, its publisher, the patriot Pelcl, was imprisoned for three days; the censor who allowed the book to be printed lost his post; and all printed copies of the apology were destroyed.

23. The most famous of Czech artists of this period was the etcher W. Hollar (1607-1677), who was brought to London by Thomas, earl of Arundel. Greatly influenced by the art of Dürer, Hollar produced over two thousand plates, including various subjects, and portraits and architectural drawings which ensured him a place of honor in contemporary English art. He was buried at St. Margaret's church, Westminster. On Czech painting of the seventeenth century see J. Neumann, *Malířství v 17. stoleti v Čechách. Barokní realismus* (Prague, 1951).

Chapter XVIII

POLAND, MUSCOVY'S "TIME OF TROUBLES,"

AND THE BIRTH OF THE UKRAINE

Failure of Sigismund III in Sweden and of plans for reform—Boris Godunov, the false Dmitrij, Šujskij—The Poles in Moscow—Losses on the Baltic, origins of the Cossacks, first Polish clash with Turkey—The Cossacks as defenders of Orthodoxy—Chmeľnyćkyj's insurrection, Muscovy and the Ukraine, the pact of Perejaslavľ—Polish reaction, Union of Hadjač, division of Ukraine between Poland and Muscovy—Dorošenko's adventure, Poland threatened by Turkey—King John Sobieski's victories and disappointments—Polish economic and cultural setbacks—Polish baroque literature reflects the nation's cultural and political ideas—Peculiarities of Polish baroque art

The election of a scion of the Swedish Vasa dynasty to the Polish throne was recommended not only by the fact that Sigismund III was a nephew of the last Jagiellonian king, but also by the advantages which a dynastic union with the powerful Scandinavian state could bring to Poland. Sweden had already more than once manifested its interest in the Baltic area, which had become important for international commerce thanks to the need of the flourishing Dutch cities for Polish and Baltic grain and Russian hemp and furs, and to the import of manufactured goods into the Baltic lands and Novgorod. This lucrative commerce was almost completely in the hands of Dutch capitalists. It was hoped that the union of Sweden with Poland would not only prevent possible clashes between the interests of the two states in Livonia, but also win for both a share in the profitable commercial traffic in the Baltic.

If there were any such hopes in Poland, they did not materialize. Sigismund III (1587-1632), a young man of German education, could never feel at home in his new realm. The inheritance of the Swedish throne (1592) attracted him more, but he spoiled his chances in his fatherland by his religious intolerance. Being a zealous Catholic, he planned to suppress the Reformation in Sweden and provoked a revolt on the part of the Protestant majority, led by his uncle Charles. Consequently Livonia became a battlefield between the Swedish and Polish armies (1601-1602). When the victories of the excellent Polish generals J. Chodkiewicz and S. Żółkiewski forced Charles to sue for peace, Sigismund could even have gained Estonia for Poland if he had abandoned his claims to the Swedish throne. Chodkiewicz outmaneuvered Charles, who had been proclaimed king of Sweden in 1605, but Sigismund III failed to secure the necessary Polish national support to exploit the success.

The king realized fully the necessity for constitutional reform in Poland, and following the general tendency in western Europe, he wished to introduce changes which would strengthen the monarchic system. He hoped to achieve his aim with the help of the Habsburgs. His marriage with an Austrian princess was interpreted in this sense by the *szlachta,* which opposed his Swedish and Austrian policy. His proposals for reform, although sound, provoked a revolt (1607), which had to be suppressed by his best general Żółkiewski, who, with Chodkiewicz, Potocki, and the majority of the Senate, had remained faithful to the king. But this ended Sigismund's well-intentioned but badly executed proposals for reform.

Meanwhile another unexpected opportunity was arising for Poland in the East. Muscovy was involved in a new political crisis with the extinction of the Rurik dynasty. The people, rejecting the idea of a regency, proclaimed Boris Godunov, Fedor's able minister, as the new tsar. They remembered Godunov's administrative reforms, his success in the new war with Sweden, which brought Muscovy (1595) to the Baltic Sea, and his general skill in directing Muscovite affairs. In order to strengthen his position, Godunov asked for the convocation of a general assembly, which should elect a new tsar. It was composed of five hundred members—prelates, boyars, officers, and representatives of cities, especially of the capital. The first assembly of this kind had been convoked in 1566 by Ivan IV to decide on peace or war with the Lithuanians. Both Ivan and Boris had the idea of gaining popular support in a weighty decision, and Boris knew that he would have to face the opposition of the old nobility. The assembly, *Zemskij sobor,* elected Boris to the throne, as was expected.

Boris Godunov (1598-1605) was one of the most attractive men to wear the crown of Muscovy. He broke the opposition of the nobles by exiling the most dangerous of them, the Belskijs and the Romanovs, and started to introduce many reforms to enhance Muscovite prestige, learning, and prosperity. His prospects seemed good, but a succession of bad crops, epidemics, and famine provoked unrest among the population, which was exploited by a new pretender to the throne, the false Demetrius or Dmitrij, an impostor whose origin and appearance on the scene is still a puzzle to historians of Russia.[1] Pretending to be the son of Ivan the Terrible and to have miraculously escaped the death prepared for him by Boris as regent, he appeared on the boundary of Poland and Russia with an army of Don Cossacks and of Polish volunteers, although Sigismund III did not support him. His appearance initiated the "Time of Troubles" in Russian history, the *smutnoe vremja* (1604-1613), which threatened to ruin everything which the descendants of Ivan Kalita had built up in Muscovy.

Boris was at first successful and tried to unmask the impostor in the eyes of the people as an unfrocked monk who had passed over to the Latins and had promised to suppress Orthodoxy. But the impostor found popular support, and when Boris died suddenly, even the nobility, led by Basil Šujskij, abandoned Boris' son Theodore and went over to the false Dmitrij (1605). Theodore was murdered, and Dmitrij established himself in Moscow.

Dissatisfied with the new tsar's Polish manners and jealous of the influence of his Polish entourage, the higher nobility turned against the false Dmitrij and killed him. The conspiracy led to a bloodbath in which thousands of Cossacks and Polish supporters of the dead tsar perished. The uprising represented an attempt on the part of the higher nobility to recover its power, and its leader, Basil Šujskij, became tsar (1606-1610).

The lower orders of the population, however, rose against the tsar, and the new uprising, led by a former serf Bolotnikov, menaced the social order. Many nobles, dissatisfied with Šujskij, joined the insurgents. Moscow was besieged and was only saved because the nobles, frightened at the excesses of their new allies, abandoned them. This permitted Šujskij to defeat the rebels and to get rid of their leader Bolotnikov (1607).

But the Time of Troubles was not yet ended. A new false Dmitrij arose in the West, a mysterious man called *vor* (robber) in Russian history, and succeeded in grouping around him many baser elements, Cossack, Lithuanian, and Polish. All Šujskij's enemies joined him.

Seeing that the Polish supporters of the new false Dmitrij, who had married the Polish widow of the first false Dmitrij, were his political opponents, Sigismund III came to terms with Šujskij. But when the latter, being hard pressed, concluded a pact with Poland's enemy Sweden, the king decided to intervene directly in Muscovite affairs. He rejected, however, the sound advice of his able hetman Żółkiewski that he should march straight to Moscow and work for the establishment of a federation of Muscovy with Poland-Lithuania on the basis of full respect for the religious and social situation in Muscovy. Instead, Sigismund, pressed by the Lithuanian nobility, started besieging Smolensk, planning an extension of his territory and the conquest of Muscovy.

For this purpose he made an agreement with some of the *vor's* supporters and succeeded in winning over a great part of his forces. At the same time, promising to guarantee freedom of religion in Muscovy, the Polish king accepted the proposition presented by Filaret Romanov and other boyars that his son Władysław should be proclaimed tsar. When the Muscovite and Swedish army sent to relieve Smolensk was defeated by Żółkiewski, the boyars deposed Šujskij and offered the tsardom to Sigismund's son on condition that he should embrace Orthodoxy and rule only with the help of Russian boyars. After defeating the remnants of the *vor's* supporters, the Polish army entered Moscow.

This seemed to be the apogee of Polish influence in Muscovy and represented a complete turn-round in the relationship between the two Slavic nations. It was, however, of short duration. Sigismund III himself contributed to the ruin of the Polish success by insisting that he should be elected tsar instead of his son and that Smolensk should become a part of Lithuania. He even held prisoner members of the delegation sent by the Muscovite boyars, among them Filaret Romanov, who disagreed with his plans. This fomented anti-Polish sentiments among the boyars and the people who feared that Sigismund intended to introduce Roman Catholicism into Muscovy. A strong national movement started to spread in the North and East, and after the *vor* had been assassinated, even his former supporters, the boyars and the Cossacks, rallied to the new movement which was becoming a religious and political crusade against foreign invaders.

The first unsuccessful attempt to expel the Poles from Moscow was followed by the occupation of Novgorod by the Swedes and of Smolensk by the Poles. Thanks to the initiative of the patriots Minin and Prince Požarskij, however, a new national army was formed. A Polish army coming to the rescue of the Polish garrison entrenched in the Kremlin was defeated, and Moscow was liberated with the help of the Cossacks (1612). At the beginning of the next year Požarskij invited every Russian city to send ten representatives to the national assembly. The Zemskij Sobor, representing all classes of Muscovy with the exception of the unfree peasantry, elected as tsar the young Michael Romanov (1613-1645), Filaret's son. A new dynasty was installed on the throne of Moscow and reigned over Russia until 1917.

Thus Sigismund's dream of extending his rule over Muscovy was dissipated, and his failure evoked sharp criticism from the *szlachta*. Fearing a new uprising, Sigismund concluded a pact with the Habsburgs. The new tsar hastened to manifest the spirit of national revenge permeating

Muscovy when a few months after his election he sent an army against Smolensk, then firmly in Polish hands.

The Poles could only retaliate after Żółkiewski had been able to pacify the southern frontier. As soon as an agreement with the Turks had been concluded, in 1617,[2] Władysław, styling himself tsar, invaded Muscovy. The Polish attempt to storm Moscow failed, however, and it was evident that the Polish pretender had no chance to replace the new tsar. A truce was concluded at Devlino in 1618 which left the Poles in possession of Smolensk and Seversk, but Władysław refused to renounce his pretensions to the Muscovite throne.

Sigismund's ambitious and cherished plans in Sweden and the Baltic also ended in failure. Charles IX's son and successor, Gustavus Adolphus (1594-1632), invaded Livonia in 1617 when the Poles were preoccupied with the Muscovite war. It was a retaliation for Sigismund's unwillingness to renounce his pretensions to the Swedish throne. Swedish attempts at winning the support of the Elector of Brandenburg induced Sigismund to agree to the transfer of the Duchy of Prussia, a Polish fief, to the Hohenzollern Elector George William of Brandenburg, an event which was to become fateful for Poland.[3]

Relying on the tacit support of the Elector, Gustavus II continued the war, captured Riga, and in 1625 became master of all Livonia. He then proceeded to occupy the coastal cities of East Prussia, with the exception of Danzig. In spite of military successes by the able hetman S. Koniecpolski, the agreement signed in 1629 sealed the loss of Livonia for Poland and left Sweden in control of the entire Baltic coast from Finland to Danzig. Sigismund preserved only his title to the Swedish throne.

During Sigismund's reign Poland also witnessed the collapse of Zamoyski's policy of neutrality toward Turkey. The main reason for this new development lay in the depredations in Tatar and Turkish territories by the Cossacks, who were settled on the steppes on the confines of Poland-Lithuania, the Turkish Crimea, and Moldavia.

The origins of the Cossacks (Kozaks) are not yet clear, and many theories have been put forward to explain their rise.[4] The word is undoubtedly derived from the Turko-Tatar language. The Turks designated by this word a free man or independent warrior, the Tatars a vagrant warrior, or people leading a nomadic life in the steppes, marauding and plundering.

From the first half of the fifteenth century numerous reports are extant on Tatar Cossacks, although they are already mentioned at the beginning of the fourteenth century. Many of them were engaged as guards by the Genoese colonies in the Crimea, especially Caffa. There were also Tatar Cossacks on the Don, Oka, and Volga rivers, and their services were often used by the princes of Rjazan' and Moscow. The earliest information concerning the existence of Cossacks on the borders of Lithuania, in the region of the Dnieper, dates from the end of the fifteenth century. Even there the Tatar element seems to have predominated at the beginning, although Slavs also soon appeared in their ranks. Small detachments of Cossacks were employed by the voivodes of Kiev and Čerkasy as border guards in the steppes. Their ranks were enlarged by the so-called *ukhodniki,* adventurers who left their dwellings in the spring in order to seek a living in the steppes by fishing, hunting, and robbing travelers, and who visited the cities in the fall to sell their products or booty before returning to their winter quarters.

The numbers of these steppe adventurers were also swelled by young peasants, who were attracted by the riches of the land and by the unrestricted freedom which they could enjoy there because feudal bonds did not yet extend into the borderland, the *Ukraina.*[5] The population of the Lithuanian Ukraina lived in constant danger from devastating inroads by the Tatar hordes. This circumstance forced them to organize their own defense under the leadership of trusted chiefs. They soon began to repay the Tatars for their devastation in their own coin, making daring incursions into the Crimea. It was Vyšnevećkíj (Wiśniowiecki), one of the aristocrats living in the borderland, who organized the first standing regiment of Cossacks for the defense of the Ukrainian population. He fortified the region of the rapids of the Dnieper, called *Porohy* (thresholds), and laid the foundations for the Cossack center called the *Sič* (fort) of Zaporožie. This community, with a republican constitution and common ownership of property by all members, obtained the leadership of all the Cossacks in the Dnieper region. Višnevećkíj also tried in vain to arouse the interest of Lithuania and of Ivan IV in the defense of the Ukraina and in an offensive against the Tatars.

The numbers of the Cossacks, still small during the first half of the sixteenth century, grew considerably after the conclusion of the Union of Lublin in 1569, when the South Russian (Ruthenian) lands were detached from Lithuania proper and opened up to the Polish nobility, who received grants of land from the king and tried to impose on the natives the same feudal burdens as in Poland. Polish and South Russian peasants, eager to escape those burdens, started to join the Cossacks en masse. The South Russian (Ruthenian) element among them grew increasingly important and finally prevailed.

The rise of the Cossacks provided an opportunity for the Polish commonwealth to build up with their help a strong military force to defend its southern frontiers against the Tatars and Turks. In fact, from 1578 on, the kings started to form a special regiment of Cossacks, enrolled in a register. These "registered Cossacks" obtained considerable privileges in the way of local autonomy and were commanded by a chief hetman appointed by the king. Unfortunately, relatively few of the Cossacks were registered. The majority of them, called self-governing Cossacks, were regarded as fugitives, and vain efforts were made to force them to go back to the serfdom from which they had fled.

In spite of that, the Polish government was often forced to appeal to the unregistered Cossacks also for military help. The fame of Cossack exploits against the Tatars and Turks soon spread over the whole of Europe, and attempts were made to win them over to the anti-Turkish league planned by Pope Clement VIII.

All this made the Cossacks more conscious of their strength, and they were angered that the Polish government was so unfavorable to the Cossack community. Instead of trying to register as many Cossacks as possible, and in this way to strengthen the Polish armed forces, the tendency was rather to reduce the number of registered Cossacks, limit their autonomous status, and fill the leading posts in their regiments with Polish or polonized officers.

These and similar grievances induced the Cossacks to rise against the Polish government. In spite of severe reprisals by the latter, especially after the disastrous defeat of the insurgents at Lubny in 1596, the Cossacks were not reduced. The Zaporožian host kept its independence, and Sigismund III soon had to appeal to it for help in his war with Sweden. The troubles in Muscovy, in which Poland had taken so lively an interest, gave the Cossacks a welcome opportunity to increase their numbers and to prove their skill in fighting and plundering. They soon astonished the whole of contemporary Europe with their daring raids, on their own small ships, against the Turkish coastal cities on the Black Sea. They even appeared before Constantinople and raided the suburbs of the city.

These incursions increased after the Polish withdrawal from Muscovy, and the Turkish government protested vainly in Poland, where King Sigismund was quite unable to control the troublesome hordes. In the meantime the Turks had gained control over Wallachia and Moldavia, replacing the Mohyla dynasties with their own candidates. Prominent Polish families who were related to the Mohylas waged their own private wars in favor of their relatives. Their defeat endangered the internal situation in the Polish lands, but hetman Żółkiewski was able to sign an agreement with the Turks promising to abstain from intervention in the Danubian principalities and to restrain the Cossacks (1617).

The Cossacks, however, disregarded the agreement, and the hetman had to repulse another Turkish inroad. In order to keep the Cossacks under control, the number of registered Cossacks was trebled, but when Żółkiewski, well aware of the Turkish threat, invaded Moldavia in order to reinstate a ruler who was favorable to Poland, the Cossacks failed him and this great Polish hero perished with his little army (1620). A new Polish army, reinforced by forty thousand Cossacks, was, however, able to withstand Turkish attacks, and a peace was concluded (1621) confirming the agreement of 1617.

The strength of the Cossacks reached its zenith during the first decades of the seventeenth century.[6] At that time also an important change took place in the aims of the Cossack movement. The movement had originally a definitely social character, and the Cossacks were little interested in religion. From this time on, however, the Cossacks, incited by emissaries of the Greek Phanar, serving Turkish interests, started to become defenders of the Orthodox religion and of the Ruthenian (Ukrainian) people.

This change is connected with the new religious developments during the reign of Sigismund, the conclusion of the so-called Union of Brest in 1596. This brought about two-thirds of the Orthodox population of Poland-Lithuania, including the Metropolitan of Kiev and the Bishop of Łuck, into union with the Roman Church. It crowned the victory of rejuvenated Polish Catholicism over both the Reformation and Orthodoxy, which was then undergoing a profound moral crisis. It was hoped that this union would lead to the disappearance of the religious differences between the Catholics and the Orthodox in the commonwealth and diminish the attraction which Moscow could exercise over the adherents of the Eastern rite.

These hopes, however, were not fulfilled. A third of the population, with two bishops, remained faithful to Orthodoxy and found a zealous champion in Constantine Ostrogski, one of the most influential magnates in the commonwealth. As a result of the union, the Orthodox Church lost its legal position in the commonwealth, and all its rights and privileges were transferred to the Uniat Church. Adherence to the union was, in many cases, especially in Galicia, enforced by the Polish nobility according to the principle *cuius regio illius et religio*. The Orthodox defended their right of continued existence; they joined the revolutionary movement (*rokosz*) of 1607 and regained their basic rights in 1609. The rivalry between the Orthodox, the Uniats, and the Catholics continued, however, the Orthodox demanding vainly the restoration of an Orthodox metropolitan in Kiev.

The South Russian middle classes were, with a few members of the nobility, the main defenders of the Orthodox faith, and in their difficulties they looked to the Cossacks for help. So about 1616 the free Cossacks of Zaporožie were accepted, with their hetman, the famous Sakhajdačny, as members of the Orthodox confraternity formed in Kiev for the defense of Orthodoxy. Under the protection of the Cossacks, Kiev was again rising slowly from its ruins, and in 1620 the Patriarch of Jerusalem secretly consecrated an Orthodox metropolitan of Kiev and five bishops. The Polish government refused to recognize the new Orthodox hierarchy, and this gave the tsar and the Muscovites a welcome opportunity to pose as protectors of the Ukrainian Orthodox persecuted by the Polish Catholic hierarchy and government.

The situation was aggravated by the fact that the Polish Catholic hierarchy never regarded the Uniat bishops as being completely their equal in dignity and rights and continued to treat the Uniats as inferior to Roman Catholics. The Uniat bishops were not admitted to the Polish Senate and were supervised by the Polish native bishops, and the faithful had to pay the tithe not only to their Uniat priests, but also to the Polish Latin priests. Latin churches and parishes were often endowed at the expense of Uniat ecclesiastical institutions, while nothing was done for the education of the Uniat clergy. So the Uniats had to fight on two fronts for their rights, against the Orthodox and against the Polish Latin clergy, many of whom would have preferred a latinization of the Uniats. The authorities in Rome tried vainly to remedy this sad situation.[7]

In the meantime the Ruthenian Orthodox were strengthening their position by founding schools for the education of their clergy and youth and by establishing a printing press in Kiev which published numerous religious books for the clergy and the faithful. The confraternities in Lwów and Kiev were the most active in this respect. Under the protection of the Cossacks Kiev was again growing in importance, and the famous monastery of the Caves was becoming a prominent religious center for the Orthodox in Poland-Lithuania. The Metropolitan of Kiev, protected by the Cossacks, after waiting in vain for some concession from Sigismund III, addressed himself in 1625 to Moscow, offering the allegiance of the Orthodox Ruthenian population to Moscow in order to escape Polish persecution.

Muscovy had not yet recovered from the consequences of the "Time of Troubles" and did not dare to intervene, although visits of Ruthenian Orthodox monks to Moscow were encouraged. This new development was motivated by the severe measures taken by the Polish government against the Orthodox after the murder in 1623 of Josafat Kuncevič, Uniat bishop of Vitebsk, who was later canonized by Rome. This incident shows at once both the seriousness of the conflict and the stubbornness with which the Orthodox rejected the union. This also became evident in 1629 when another attempt at extending the union was frustrated by the Orthodox zealots supported by the Cossacks. The latter continued their unruly activities in spite of the successful campaign in the Ukraina by Koniecpolski in 1625, and they reversed this situation again in 1629.

A welcome opportunity for the Orthodox to improve their lot was offered at the diets to discuss the election of Sigismund's son Władysław

(1632-1648). The Orthodox party, again supported by the Cossacks, won important concessions from the new king. He granted them the election of a metropolitan in Kiev and of four bishops. Church property in the Ruthenian lands was to be divided between the Orthodox and the Uniats, who had to content themselves with four bishops. The churches and monasteries were also to be divided between them. The Orthodox immediately proceeded to the election of a new metropolitan, Peter Mohyla, abbot of the monastery of the Caves in Kiev and a scion of the dynasty which had ruled in Moldavia. With him a new chapter opened in the evolution of Orthodoxy in the Ukraine, which was also to exercise its influence in Muscovy.[8]

These concessions pacified the Cossacks, and when the new tsar Michael Romanov (1613-1645) invaded Poland-Lithuania in 1633, Władysław was able to retaliate with success thanks to the support of the Cossacks. In the treaty of Poljanov (1634) Władysław renounced his claim to the tsardom of Muscovy but retained the Smolensk region together with some other frontier towns.

In the hope of keeping the unruly Zaporožian host under better control, the Polish government built the fortress of Kudak at the threshold of the Dnieper, and this provoked three successive rebellions by the Cossacks. These failed, however, because the registered Cossacks preferred to side with the government. After the suppression of the revolts in 1638, the number of registered Cossacks was reduced to six thousand and their privileges were considerably curtailed. As a result, the Cossacks were subjected to local administrative authorities, which exploited them, and this provoked complaints and discontent.

King Władysław at first worked without success for a satisfactory settlement of his claim to the Swedish throne and obtained only the withdrawal of the Swedes from the Prussian coast. He then intended to try his chances in the south in order to extend Polish influence over Moldavia and Wallachia. He hoped to succeed with the help of the Cossacks, who were asked to start their incursions against Turkish territory. The plan was, however, abandoned because of the opposition of the Polish nobles.

One of the Cossack officers who were informed of the king's plan was Bogdan Chmel'nyćkyj, who profited by this occasion to organize a new uprising. Besides seeking personal revenge for inexcusable wrongs done to him and his family by a Polish nobleman, Chmel'nyćkyj sought to profit by the dissatisfaction among the Cossacks with the rule of the Polish nobility and to obtain some concessions from the king, relying on his friendly disposition to the Cossacks.

The insurgents routed the Polish army, but Chmel'nyćkyj, now hetman of the Cossacks, refrained from further action, hoping that Władysław's son and successor John Casimir (1648-1668) would grant the Cossacks the privileges which they had expected from his father. Circumstances, however, gave a new character to the insurrection. The news of the hetman's success was greeted with enthusiasm among the Ruthenian Orthodox population, and the revolt spread and became a national struggle of the Ukrainian people against "Polish enslavement" and a religious struggle between Orthodoxy and the Catholic Church. The Ruthenian population turned against Polish nobles and their Jewish agents and expelled them, together with the Jesuits, who were regarded as the most dangerous enemies of Orthodoxy. In this excited atmosphere Chmel'nyćkyj's revolution lost its limited social and economic character and became a struggle for political liberties and independence on the part of the whole of the Ukraine.[9] After defeating the king's new army, Chmel'nyćkyj, seeing that he could not continue to count on help from his ally, the Khan of the Crimea, abandoned the idea of complete independence and concluded the treaty of Zborov (1649) with the king. According to this the Cossacks were to obtain an autonomous territory comprising the former principalities of Kiev, Braclav, and Černigov, a territory whose defense would be entrusted exclusively to the Cossack host, comprising forty thousand registered men commanded by a hetman. Orthodoxy was to be reintroduced into Poland-Lithuania, its metropolitan was to be admitted to the Senate, and the Jesuits and Jews were to be excluded from settling on Ukrainian territory.

Neither the Poles nor the Ukrainians were satisfied with these stipulations. A new treaty, concluded in 1651 after a defeat of the Cossacks, who had been abandoned by their former allies of the Crimea, reduced these conditions considerably. The number of registered Cossacks was halved, and they were allowed to settle only in the principality of Kiev. Religious stipulations were totally omitted. As dissatisfaction grew, Chmel'nyćkyj was forced to look for support outside Poland. He established contact with Rakoczy, duke of Transylvania, with the Khan of the Crimea, and with the Turkish sultan. Finally he addressed himself to the Tsar of Muscovy, invoking the national and religious affinity between the two Slavic nations.

When the Metropolitan of Kiev had appealed to the tsar for help in 1625, Muscovy was not strong enough and did not dare to intervene. This time, however, the Zemskij Sobor convoked by Tsar Alexis decided that the Cossacks should be taken under Muscovy's protection and that war should be declared on Poland. In 1653 the tsar's envoys accepted the oath of allegiance of the hetman and his host, guaranteeing them all the rights and privileges hitherto enjoyed by the Cossacks and the inhabitants of the Ukraine. This pact of Perejaslavl' was then completed in Moscow, where the negotiations were continued (1654).

The text of the pact of Perejaslavl' is not preserved, and Russian and Ukrainian historians differ in their interpretation of its meaning. The former interpret it as a simple incorporation of the Ukraine into Muscovy, while the latter are unwilling to admit that it implied any more than a vassalage, or a personal or real union of two independent states.

There is no doubt that the Cossacks had promised allegiance to the tsar, but on condition that they retain their rights and privileges. There was no unconditional surrender. This is shown by the confirmation of the privileges of the Cossacks, the gentry, and the towns of the Ukraine issued by the tsar after the *pourparlers* of Moscow. The Ukraine obtained a large measure of self-government, although its diplomatic relations with its neighbors were somewhat limited. The hetman was to be elected by the Cossacks, but he had to inform the tsar of his election and to promise him obedience. It therefore seems that Chmel'nyćkyj regarded the tsar as his sovereign, not merely as his ally. This kind of relationship is also illustrated by the stipulations—which were not, however, put into practice—that the authority of the tsar should be represented in the Ukraine by the presence of his voivodes, who would reside in the main cities, and that taxes should be gathered into the treasury of Moscow.[10]

The fact that the stipulations of the pact had never been formulated in a precise way and that the tsars often left the hetmans to act as responsible rulers of the Ukraine explains these different interpretations of the pact.

The military operations which now began resulted in the capture of Smolensk by the tsar's army and in the destruction of Vilna. As the Swedish king, Charles X Gustavus, profited by the occasion to invade West Poland, King John Casimir was in a very difficult situation. The lightning success of the Swedish army brought Poland to the verge of collapse. The hetman Radziwill of Lithuania planned a Swedish-Lithuanian union; Rakoczy, the prince of Transylvania, invaded Poland; and the rest of the country was in the hands of the Swedes and the Russians.

A Polish national reaction started against the Swedish garrisons, while the tsar's and the Cossacks' unwillingness to allow the Swedes to obtain too important a foothold on Polish territory saved Poland this time from a partition among its neighbors which was in the making. A successful Polish offensive started from Lwów, which, with Danzig, had remained faithful to the king.[11] Complications with Denmark forced Charles X to hasten home. The intervention of Austria and the intercession of France speeded up the conclusion of the Treaty of Wehlau in 1660. Poland ceded her suzerainty over East Prussia to Frederick William, Elector of Brandenburg. This was another important step in the rise of modern Prussia.

In the meantime, a new situation started to develop in the Ukraine.

The cultural level among the population of the Ukraine was much higher than that of Muscovy because of the penetration of Polish and western influences among the South Russians. Their language had also developed considerable differentiation from the East Russian language. The Ukrainian aristocracy naturally cherished the ideas of political freedom which they had learned from their Polish colleagues. Therefore they soon began to regard with suspicion the system of absolute monarchy which had developed in Muscovy, the more so as it became clear that the tsar aimed at gradually curtailing Ukrainian autonomy and at assimilating the Ukraine completely with Muscovite Russia.

So it happened that polonophile tendencies appeared among the Ukrainian nobility whereas the lower classes sympathized with Muscovy. A sharp conflict between the two tendencies broke out after the sudden death of the great Ukrainian leader Bogdan Chmel'nyćkyj. He had been anxious to keep the dignity of hetman hereditary in his family and had his young son George elected as his successor before his death. But as his son was a minor and not particularly gifted, the Cossacks elected their chancellor Ivan Vyhovskyj, a well-educated and intelligent Ukrainian aristocrat, as acting hetman on Chmel'nyćkyj's death. The pro-Polish and anti-Muscovite tendency in the Ukraine soon made itself apparent under the new hetman. He opened negotiations with the Khan, with Sweden, and with Poland to ensure an independent position for the Ukraine in the Polish-Lithuanian commonwealth. A secret agreement with Poland, called the Union of Hadjač (Hadziacz in Polish), was concluded in 1658. According to this the Polish Rzeczpospolita was to be transformed into a federation of Poland, Lithuania, and the Ukraine. The three nations were to be united under a common, freely elected king and stand by each other in war. Should Muscovy come to an agreement with Poland, it would be admitted into the federation, whose first military aim would be the conquest of the Crimea.

The Grand Duchy of Rus', as the former principalities of Kiev, Braclav, and Černigov were now called, would have its own senate as supreme legislative authority, the executive power being given to the hetman, who would be chosen by the king from four candidates nominated by the Cossacks. Serfdom would be abolished for the Cossacks, many of whose officers were to be ennobled and given state lands. The Orthodox Church would enjoy equal rights with the Catholic, and interesting plans were drawn up for the cultural progress of the Ukraine.

It seemed at first that the compact would be realized. The Russian army sent against Vyhovskyj was defeated, and the way was open to the hetman for an invasion of Muscovy. He missed his opportunity, fearing that some of his rivals might revolt during his absence. In the meantime, strong protests against the Union of Hadjač were voiced among the common Cossacks, who feared that the ennobled officers and Polish gentry would reduce those who were not among the thirty thousand registered Cossacks to serfdom. The dissatisfaction grew, fostered by Muscovite propaganda. The Cossack masses revolted, compelled Vyhovskyj to resign, and put George Chmel'nyćkyj in his place.

The latter annulled the Union of Hadjač and promised allegiance to the tsar. The new agreement, concluded between the tsar and the Cossacks in 1659, limited considerably the autonomy of the Ukraine and strengthened the tsar's control over the hetman and his country. After a great military success by the Poles against Muscovy in 1660, new chaotic conditions prevailed in the Ukraine, the polonophile and russophile parties among the Cossacks clashing violently. George Chmel'nyćkyj, after having been confirmed in his hetmanship by the Polish king, was defeated by the adherents of Moscow, resigned his post, and entered a monastery.

The final result of all this was that the Ukraine was divided into two parts, the lands to the west of the Dnieper being governed by a hetman appointed by the Polish king, those on the east bank by a hetman chosen by the tsar. This division was accepted by both countries in the peace treaty of Andrušovo (Andruszów) signed in 1667. Even Kiev was to be returned to Poland in two years, a stipulation which was never implemented. Moscow was allowed to keep Smolensk and the Seversk Province.

The hetman Dorošenko endeavored vainly to unite the whole Ukraine, although at first he seemed to have a fair chance of succeeding. The division of the Ukraine between Poland and Muscovy was not popular with the Ukrainian people. Moreover, the pro-Muscovite hetman Brjuchovetc'kyj was suspected by the common Cossacks and the peasants of aiming both to form a new upper class with his officers, like that which existed in Poland and in Muscovy, and to curry favor with the Moscow government in spite of its manifest tendency to curtail Ukrainian liberties. He was forced to change his policy and was finally killed by the disgruntled Cossacks.

Dorošenko was thus able to unite the whole of the Ukraine, but his decision to place the united Ukraine under the sovereignty of the sultan proved unfortunate and alienated many of his supporters. Muscovite diplomacy ably exploited the rising discontent among the Cossacks against Dorošenko, the religious factor again proving very important for the tsar, protector of Orthodoxy. Moscow succeeded in winning over Demian Mnohohrišnyj, Dorošenko's representative on the east bank of the Dnieper. After being elected hetman, Mnohohrišnyj concluded the pact of Głuchów (1669), which gave Moscow the right to keep military governors in the garrisons in the Ukraine. The number of Cossacks was fixed at thirty thousand.

Dorošenko's adventurous initiative threatened to become disastrous for Poland. Sultan Mohammed IV (1648-1687), desiring to make his sovereignty over the Ukraine a reality, invaded Poland. The country was then governed by the feeblest king the Polish *szlachta* had ever placed on the throne, Michael Wiśniowiecki, whose family was believed to be descended from a brother of Jagiello. This fact and the memory of the military deeds of his father led the *szlachta* to prefer him to the French candidate, for whom Louis XIV had won over many magnates with bribes. His election took place after John Casimir, discouraged by the futile attempts at a reform of the Polish constitution, had abdicated and settled in France (1668). The first years of Wiśniowiecki's unhappy reign were filled with intrigues by the disgruntled French party, which wanted to enforce his abdication. The Turkish invasion happened at a time when the unfortunate king was discovering another plot against him. The Turks defeated the small Polish army, occupied the fortress of Kamieniec guarding the route into southeastern Poland, and penetrated as far as Lwów.

Terrified by the success of the Turkish army and unable to mobilize Polish forces in time, the king saw himself constrained to conclude the ignominious peace of Buczacz in 1672. Turkish sovereignty over the Ukraine was recognized, Podolia ceded directly to the sultan, and a high annual tribute promised to the victor.

Disaster was averted by the field hetman John Sobieski, who was among the magnates plotting against their king. He hastened to the front and, thanks to his great military talent and personal courage, won four victories in a few days. So the Diet refused to ratify the treaty, and Sobieski was charged to continue operations. The unhappy king died on the very day that Sobieski won his great victory at Chocim (November 10, 1673).

Elected king the next year, John Sobieski (1674-1696) had to return to the front before his coronation. Although the general levy was a failure, Sobieski, aided by his able lieutenants and with a small army gathered mostly at his own expense, stopped further invasion. Thanks to his superb strategy, he was able to defeat the Turks and to obtain (1676) a treaty which gave back to Poland two-thirds of the Ukraine on the west bank of the Dnieper.

There was another loss to Poland which Sobieski would have liked to make good, that of East Prussia. For this purpose he concluded alliances with France and Sweden. His French policy was especially inspired by his French wife Mary. As long as he followed this line, he supported the anti-Habsburg rebels in Hungary and even harbored the idea of reclaiming Silesia for Poland. But he soon realized that the Diet could hardly be won over for a war which might be interpreted as another attempt to found a basis for a dynastic policy. On the other hand, the Turkish danger was still very real, and in order to avert it he could not expect any help from France.

This and the fact that his pro-French policy had encountered strong opposition among the nobility induced Sobieski to reverse it and to conclude a new treaty with the Emperor Leopold I (1658-1705). This was ratified by the Polish Diet and contained an obligation on the contracting parties to help each other if their capitals were threatened by the Turks. This danger soon arose for Vienna because the ambitious grand vizier Kara Mustafa was preparing a new offensive against the Empire and had recognized Tokolli, the leader of the anti-Habsburg party, as king of Hungary.

Sobieski saw clearly that the conquest of Vienna would open the way for the Turks into the heart of Europe and would endanger Poland from the southwest. So, when he was called on by the emperor and the Pope to help the hard-pressed capital, he did not hesitate to lead his army of thirty thousand men to join the imperial army under Charles of Lorraine. It was Sobieski who prepared the plans for the joint move, and it was the whirling charge of the Polish cavalry, led by its king, which routed the Turks and saved Vienna (September 12, 1683). The gratitude of the Viennese was expressed by the preacher at the thanksgiving service in St Stephen's cathedral who took as the text of his sermon the words of the Gospel: "There was a man sent from God whose name was John" (John 1:6).

The victories of the Polish and Austrian armies at Parkań and Gran in the following months initiated the liberation of the whole of Hungary. The Ottoman power never recovered from the crushing blows delivered by Sobieski, and Europe was saved. So it came about that the Turkish danger, which the Jagiellonian kings had vainly attempted to avert, was definitely arrested by the great service to Poland and to Europe of another national Polish king.

The "Holy League," for whose realization Sobieski had been working for some time, was formed in 1684 to include Poland, Austria, Venice, and the Holy See. The Venetians started an offensive in the Morea in Greece, and the imperial troops took Budapest in 1685. In 1687 the second battle of Mohács was won by Charles of Lorraine, who advanced as far as Belgrade. The Turks were, however, able to stop an imperial advance into Bulgaria, Serbia, and Transylvania, and this failure precipitated a mass flight of the Serbians into southern Hungary.[12] The victory in 1691 by Margrave Louis of Baden was crowned in 1697 by the celebrated battle of Zenta, won by the Austrian hero Eugene of Savoy.

Sobieski did not participate in this drive, preferring to continue the fight in the south where Polish interests were directly involved. Unfor-

tunately, instead of pushing from Podolia toward the Black Sea, he devoted all his efforts to the conquest of Moldavia and Wallachia, where he
had to fight not only the Turks but also the native Christian population,
hostile as before to Polish intervention.

He embarked on this enterprise because of his desire to win a dukedom for his son and thus to open for him the way to the Polish throne.
All his attempts between 1684 and 1691 were, however, in vain and also
alienated the Habsburgs, who desired to extend their influence over the
Danubian principalities. Preoccupied with his Danubian campaigns and
eager to obtain the support of Moscow in his wars with Turkey, Sobieski
concluded an "eternal peace" with the Muscovites in 1686 which confirmed the agreements of 1667 and left Kiev definitely in Muscovite hands.

Sobieski was also aware of the necessity to strengthen the royal power,
and his efforts in this respect would perhaps have succeeded if he had
been able to preserve his military fame intact. The reverses suffered in his
Moldavian campaigns, however, diminished his personal prestige and encouraged the opposition of the magnates to his dynastic and monarchic
plans.

He did not even live to see the victories over the Turks sealed by the
treaty of Karlovci (Karlowitz), concluded in 1699, which restored to his
Austrian ally all Hungary, with the exception of the Banat of Temesvár,
besides Transylvania, Croatia, and Slavonia. Venice obtained Morea and
most of Dalmatia, and Poland Podolia, which Sobieski had tried in vain
to regain.

So it happened that the last years of this hero-king, whose reign had
started with such great promise, ended on a distressing note prophetic of
the tragic end to which the egotism of the gentry was leading Poland.
His military achievements, which Poland could not exploit, only helped
the Habsburgs to consolidate their position in Europe.

There were few in Poland who foresaw the menacing final disaster to
which the aristocratic '"parliamentary" system was slowly leading the
country. Many contemporary foreign observers of the Polish political system who studied its effects on the internal situation of the commonwealth
were, however, aware of the weaknesses and did not spare sharp criticism and foreboding prophecies in their memoirs.[13] Sobieski's victories
enhanced Poland's prestige, but toward the end of his reign severe criticism grew again. Moreover, the economic situation in Poland was not bad
at the beginning of the seventeenth century, thanks to the flourishing export of Polish grain through Danzig to western Europe. Of course, this
benefited only the gentry. The situation of the peasants deteriorated
gradually. Of the Polish cities only Danzig continued to flourish. The

burghers of other cities retained some of their sixteenth century prosperity, but their situation became worse after 1648.

It was the Thirty Years' War beginning in Poland with Chmel'nyćkyj's revolt which ruined the country and caused a situation similar to that created by the other Thirty Years' War in Germany and in Bohemia. The country was devastated, smaller towns were completely ruined, industry and handicrafts declined, and even the gentry endured serious losses. The numerous Jews—who were settled in special quarters in Polish cities, acted as middlemen for the gentry in many business transactions, and often financed the kings and nobles—suffered greatly during the Cossack upheaval.

The economic setback naturally had unfortunate consequences for Polish cultural life. Only very few Poles were able to study and travel abroad, and the Polish centers of higher learning, the academies of Cracow, of Zamość, and the Jesuit Academy of Vilna, could not compare with foreign universities. The excellent schools of the Czech Brethren at Leszno and of the Unitarians at Raków became victims of the religious intolerance which started to appear in Poland. The schools of the Jesuits and Piarists do not seem to have reached the same level in Poland as in other countries. The lowest ebb of Polish civilization could be observed at the end of the seventeenth and in the first half of the eighteenth century.

This situation was reflected in Polish literature. The writers of the first half of the seventeenth century were still under the influence of humanism and the Renaissance. None of them achieved the high level of Kochanowski, although they imitated his style and wrote in his spirit. Among the most notable writers were the brothers Simon and Joseph Zimorowicz, who were of bourgeois descent. Simon was the author of one of the best Polish lyrical works the *Roksolanki;* Joseph, besides his poetical *Sielanki,* also described in prose the siege of Lwów by the Turks in 1672.

W. Kochowski's *Annales* described the reign of John Casimir and Sobieski's expedition to Vienna. W. Potocki was a talented poet, but without a deeper literary education. He was the author of the best old Polish epic celebrating the victory of Chocim (1621). The memoirs of J. Pasek (died 1711) were a good product of old Polish prose and gave an insight into the life of the Polish gentry in the seventeenth century. His work was one of the main sources for Sienkiewicz' historical novels. The Latin compositions of S. Szymonowicz (died 1629) were popular in the West, with his best Polish work, the *Eclogues,* revealing a strong humanistic influence. A true baroque poet was A. Morsztyn, who was influenced by the Italian poet Marino. S. Twardowski wrote some epic poems on contemporary events and two rhymed chronicles.

There were many other writers, whose work often remained in manuscript and became known to literary historians only in modern times. Like Czech baroque literature, the Polish output was also judged severely and regarded as illustrative of the rapid cultural decline. Only recently have the literary products of this period been revalued according to the taste and style of that time and become more appreciated by Polish specialists. When compared with Czech baroque literature they are on a considerably higher plane.

For the history of political ideas some interest attaches to the writings of Polish authors in reply to the criticisms of the Polish constitution by some foreign observers. George Opaliński in his *Monarchia* (1614) presented the Polish system as the best realization of republican ideals and later answered the sharp criticism voiced by the English poet John Barclay in his "Mirror of Souls." He was joined in his defense by Luke Opaliński, who, however, pleaded for a reform of Polish parliamentarism and for the strengthening of the royal power in his *Discussion between a Clergyman and a Nobleman.* This was the best Polish contribution to this kind of literature at that time. S. Starowolski and Andrew Fredro also wrote against Barclay, the Swede H. Conring (1655), and the German T. Lansius (1613), who, with the Irishman B. Connor (1696), were the main contemporary critics of the Polish constitution. Their answers show how difficult it was for the Polish gentry to see the disadvantages of their system for the state. A. Fredro was even a champion of the *liberum veto,* which permitted any member of the gentry to veto any resolution of the Diet. This was the main reason for the political impotence of the Polish state from 1658 on.

Italian influences continued to inspire Polish music, architecture, and the decorative arts. Italian musicians made possible the organization of Warsaw's royal orchestra, which soon came to be regarded as the best in Europe and performed numerous Italian compositions. Besides Italian musicians, Poland could boast good native composers, the best of whom was Nicholas Zielinski, who was influenced by the Venetian school. The concerto style of the Roman school is evident in the compositions of B. Pekiel. A. Jarzębski and M. Mielczewski are also regarded as outstanding Polish baroque composers. Italian operas were performed at the royal court, and many magnates had their own orchestras.[14]

The new baroque style penetrated Poland more slowly than Bohemia. The Poles produced a baroque style blended with traditional native elements analogous to their blend of Gothic elements with the Renaissance style.[15] This Polish Renaissance style with Gothic reminiscences continued to dominate Poland during the first half of the seventeenth century. It continued to inspire the construction of new castles, while new churches preserved Gothic features with Renaissance touches (Kazimierz, Warsaw, Wilno, Lublin district). Similar traditions were to be observed in sculpture. In painting Poland produced at this period an engraver, John Ziarnko, who became famous abroad and can be compared with the Czech Hollar, who was working in London.

The baroque style was principally introduced into Poland by the Jesuits and by some nobles who became acquainted with it in Italy. Poland could not boast any famous native architects, as could Bohemia. Italians predominated in the introduction and spread of the baroque style. Giovanni Trevano renovated the Wawel Castle; C. Tencalla introduced it into Wilno (Vilna). Other Italian architects built new residences for the magnates. Tomasso Dolabella of the Venetian school became court painter to Sigismund III. Other artists included the Dutchman J. Mertens and the German B. Strobel.

The baroque style started to flourish in Poland during the reign of Sobieski, when many palaces and churches destroyed during the Cossack upheaval and the Swedish wars had to be rebuilt and redecorated. Besides J. Belotti two other foreign architects became famous, the Dutchman Tylman, who stressed simplicity in decoration but magnitude in construction, and P. Ferrari, who preferred picturesque and rich designs. In general, Polish baroque differs in many respects from its Italian prototypes. It was influenced by Austria and also by Moravia, where some of the Italian architects had previously been working. This is particularly evident in the twin-towered churches which are characteristic of Poland.

Polish decorative art was also dominated by foreign artists. Besides the Italians Palloni and Del Bene, Claude Callot, the nephew of the famous French painter Jacques Callot, and Francis Desportes also worked in Poland. Among Polish painters only Siemiginowski and Tretko deserve mention.

In spite of the decline of Polish political and economic life, Poland's cultural influence continued to be felt among her eastern neighbors. The growth of Ruthenian culture, which was remarkable in the seventeenth century, owes a great deal to the Polish literature and art of the golden age and also of the baroque period. These influences even reached Muscovy, where an assimilation of Polish ways of life can be observed even after the failure of the Polish expedition to Moscow. Some Polish influences can also be seen in the first attempts at the composition of Russian popular fiction and in other fields.[16]

These cultural influences were most profound in the Rumanian principalities of Moldavia and Wallachia. The origins of Rumanian literature owed a great deal to Polish inspiration. This is illustrated by the fact that the first writer of eminence, Miron Costin of Moldavia, wrote an epic history of his country in Polish and dedicated it to King John

Sobieski. On the other hand, many oriental features began to characterize Polish customs and ways of life. In spite of that, Polish culture remained deeply rooted in the West, and this radiation of Polish culture toward the East shows how great a role Poland would have been able to play in the East as an outpost of Western civilization if it had not been so tragically weakened by the selfishness of its own nobility and its consequently disastrous political system.

NOTES

1. Cf. G. v. Poehl's short study "Quellenkundiges zur Geschichte des ersten falschen Demetrius," ZOG 7 (1933), pp. 73-87. The standard work in Russian on Dmitrij and the "Time of Troubles" is that by S. F. Platonov, *Očerki po istorii smutnogo vremeni v Moskovskom gosudarstve, XVI-XVII vv.* (Moscow, 1937). For the study of this period his evaluation of old Russian chronicles and narrations on the "Time of Troubles" (*Drevnerusskija skazanija i povesti o smutnom vremeni XVII veka kak istoričeskij istočnik*), is important. This was first published 1887-88 in the Žurnal of the Ministry of Education and separately in 1888 in St. Petersburg, and the *Pamjatniki* text, published by him in vol. 13 (1891) of the RIB. Platonov's monograph on Boris Godunov (Petersburg, 1921) (German translation by H. de Witte, Paris, 1929) also deals with Godunov's regency during the reign of Tsar Fedor and with the appearance of the false Dmitrij. K. Waliszewski and P. Pierling's works (see Bibl.) also appeared in Russian in 1911 and 1912. According to Platonov, the pretender was a Muscovite who was initiated into his role by the Muscovite boyars, especially the Romanovs, who were hostile to Boris Godunov. The reports on the death of the real Dmitrij were re-examined by G. Vernadsky (see Bibl.). He has rightly shown that the tsarevich's death was accidental and that Boris Godunov was unjustly accused of his murder. A complete bibliography on this problem is given in his study published in the *Oxford Slav. Papers*. On the spread of this legend see also A. A. Rudakov's study in *Ist oričeskie Zapiski*, 12 (1941), pp. 154-283.

2. Cf. below p. 472.

3. Cf. above p. 257. He became Elector of Brandenburg in 1619.

4. G. Stökl in his book *Die Entstehung des Kosakentums* (Munich, 1953), revises (pp. 17-32) all the theories which had hitherto been put forward on the origin of the Cossacks, theories which were often inspired by national prejudices or social bias. He also gives an exhaustive bibliography in Slavic languages on the problem. Of the Slavic authors the famous historian of the Ukraine, M. Hruševśkyj is most objective in vol. VII of his *Istorija Ukrainy-Rusy*, published in Kiev (1898-1931, ten vols.) and republished in New York (1956-1958). On the further history of the Cossacks and of the Ukraine see vols. VIII-X of his work. Cf. also Javorśkyj, *Istorija Ukrainy* (Charkov, 1928) and D. Dorošenko, *Narys istorii Ukrainy*, 2 vols. (Warsaw, 1932-1933). The social aspect of the Cossack movement is stressed by V. A. Golobuckij in his work *Zaporožskoe kazačestvo* (Kiev, 1957). Still useful is D. N. Bantyš-Kamenskij's history of Little Russia (*Istorija Maloj Rossii*, 3rd edn. St. Petersburg, 1842, reprint, 1903). The same author also collected all documents concerning the

birth of the Ukraine from 1649 to 1687, which were edited by O. M. Bodjanskij in the *Čtenija imp. Obščestva istorii i drevnostej rossijskij* of the Moscow University, vol. 24 (1858).

5. The designation *Ukraina* was used in the fifteen and sixteenth centuries, without distinction, for the whole borderland of Poland-Lithuania and Muscovy. Only in the seventeenth century did this name begin to be used exclusively for the Polish-Lithuanian borderlands. On the designation *Ukraina* and its use before the sixteenth century cf. the Ukrainian publication by S. Seluchin, *Ukraina, nazva našoj zemli z najdavnišikh časiv* (Prague, 1936).

6. They were organized into regiments of at least five hundred men, commanded by a colonel; divided into companies of one hundred men each under captains; and subdivided into squads of ten men under an *ataman*. The orders of the hetman (chief commander) were executed by the adjutant, and a chief ordinance officer supervised the artillery. A secretary (*pysar*) handled all official correspondence. The whole organization was based on the principle of free election by the members. The higher officers formed a council (*staršina*). This discussed with the hetman important problems, which were also decided by the general assembly (*rada*).

7. The Russian historian E. Šmurlo, in his book *Le Saint-Siège et l'Orient orthodoxe Russe 1609-1654* (Prague, 1928), published 451 documents, taken mostly from the registers of the Roman Congregation for the Propagation of the Faith, which throw more light on the plight of the Uniats, on the lack of understanding on the side of the Polish clergy, and on the sincere attempts of the Congregation to save the union and to make of it an instrument of attraction for the Orthodox. Polish historians differ in their views on the conclusion of the union. O. Halecki (see Bibl.) is inclined to overestimate the benefits which the union was supposed to bring to the Polish state in leveling the cultural differences between the two nations in the Polish-Lithuanian commonwealth. K. Lewicki, *Sprawa unii kościoła wschodniego z rzymskim w polityce dawnej Rzeczypospolitej* (Warsaw, 1934), stresses that Polish interests suffered because the union preserved the special character of the Ruthenian nation on Polish lands, and this led to the absorption of some Polish elements. He agrees, however, with K. Chodynicki, *Kościoł prawosławny a Rzeczpospolita Polska* (Warsaw, 1934), the most unbiased Polish historian of the union, and with others, that the conclusion of the union was in the interests of the Polish-Lithuanian commonwealth, but that the use of improper measures toward its realization prevented Poland from reaping the expected benefits from it. On the growth of pro-Muscovite tendencies among the Orthodox after the conclusion of the union, see above, p. 347. In his book *From Florence to Brest*, Halecki used some new documentary evidence illustrating especially l'attitude d'Ostrogski.

8. See below, p. 511.

9. This unfortunate development was the consequence of the annexation of Ruthenian lands by Poland after the Union of Lublin. It may well be questioned whether the situation would have become as dangerous if these territories had remained part of Lithuania. It has been shown by O. P. Backus (see Bibl.) that the humiliation of Lithuania through the enforced conclusion of the union had provoked pro-Muscovite tendencies among the Lithuanian nobility of Slavic stock, tendencies which had hardly existed before the union. These tendencies grew considerably after the conclusion of the Church Union (1596) among the Orthodox population, which felt offended by the harsh treatment meted out to the Orthodox by Polish authorities.

10. Cf. V. A. Mjakotin "Die Vereinigung der Ukraine mit dem Moskauer Staat" ZOG 7 (1933), pp. 321-56. The author gives a survey of Russian and Ukrainian literature on the origins of the Ukraine, pointing out the controversial theories and interpretations of existing sources. A complete bibliography on the subject in Slavic languages down to 1933 will be found there. This is completed by H. Schumann ("Der Hetmanstaat" JGO I, 1936).

11. The heroic resistance of the monastery of Czenstochowa, with its famous shrine, against the Swedes fired the patriotic sentiment of the Poles. This and other incidents of Polish tragedy and glory were described in the novels of H. Sienkiewicz.

12. Cf. above, pp. 357-359.

13. One of the most critical comments on contemporary Poland was written in 1658 by George Križanić, the Croatian Pan-Slav patriot (see p. 426) on his way to Muscovy: "Among the Poles [he calls them Ljachi] there is no order in the state, and the subjects are not afraid either of the king or of the judge. Everybody who is stronger thinks to have the right to oppress the weaker, just as the wolves and the bears are free to capture and to kill cattle. There is no tribunal which would punish them for that. Such abominable depravity is called by the Poles 'aristocratic freedom.' They boast that among all peoples only they are free. In no state can one find such a bestial freedom." This is a very severe judgment by a fellow Slav. It shows also how firmly the monarchic and absolutist system had penetrated the minds of contemporary Europeans, who could only regard the Polish "parliamentary" system, based on the old feudal system, as hopelessly outmoded and dangerous for Poland's neighbors.

14. There is a good monograph on the history of Polish music by Z. Jachimecki (*Muzyka polska w rozwoji historycznym*, Cracow, 1948). On Renaissance and baroque music, vol. I, pp. 88-218. On Polish Baroque poetry and letters, cf. A. A. Angyal (see Bibl. Ch. XVII), pp. 173 ff.

15. See above, p. 305.

16. Cf. below, pp. 514 ff.

Chapter XIX

THE MUSCOVITE STATE UNDER THE FIRST ROMANOVS

The three tsars—Muscovy, Sweden, Poland, Turkey—Expansion in the North and in Siberia—Filaret's reforms—The stipulations of the Uloženie of 1649—Innovations in taxation and administration—The first industries and Western influences—Social unrest—The Sobor (National Assembly) —Challenge to tsarist autocracy, Russian diarchy—Nikon's reform of the liturgy—Break between the patriarch and the tsar—Nikon and the Western theory of the superiority of the spiritual power—Byzantine conception of the tsardom—Byzantinization of the tsarist court?—The Old Believers— Foreigners and Kievan scholarship in Moscow—Muscovite historical writings—New trend in biographical literature—Ukrainian scholars and writers—Ukrainian and Muscovite poetry—Origins of Russian drama—Western romances in Muscovite literature—Muscovite architecture and baroque influences—New trends in Muscovite painting

The election of Michael Romanov to the throne ushered in a new period in Muscovite history. It can be called a period of transition between the traditional Russian ways of life, established under the dynasty of the Ruriks, and the new age, inaugurated by the reforms of the fourth Romanov, Peter the Great. The years from 1613 to 1682 were characterized by the efforts of the first three rulers of the new dynasty to restore the old customs and institutions introduced by the first tsars and disturbed by the upheavals of the Time of Troubles. But although they were seeking inspiration in the past and were anxious to follow old traditions, the first Romanovs could not neglect the new trends in statesmanship, administration, and civilization which they could observe among their western neighbors. Nor could they fail to emulate some of these in the task of rebuilding their own state.

Another striking feature of this period was the fact that the rebuilding of the ruined state was successfully accomplished during the reigns of rulers who were distinguished by an appalling personal mediocrity. It must be admitted that this circumstance had influenced the election of Michael in 1613, together, of course, with the prominent position of his family and its kinship to the Ruriks. This appealed to the conservative members of the Sobor and helped to eliminate the candidacies of foreigners such as Władysław of Poland, or of Swedish or Habsburg princes.

Although the Sobor had a good opportunity to curtail the powers of the elected tsar and to increase its own authority in state affairs, its leading members failed to imitate the example of their Polish confreres, who had never missed such opportunities to extend their privileges. The mediocrity of the sixteen-year-old ruler may have seemed to make such a precaution superfluous, or the idea of autocracy may have been already so deeply rooted in the Muscovite mentality that the more liberal-minded boyars did not dare to take such an initiative. Any explanation necessitates taking into consideration the fact that the position of the old boyar families, compromised by their attitude during the Time of Troubles and by their negotiations with the Poles, was considerably shaken in 1613.

The young tsar's education had been totally ignored, and he was unable to rule alone. He therefore left the direction of affairs in the hands of his ambitious mother, Martha, who had quitted the convent into which she had been forced by Boris Godunov, and of his relations, especially the Saltykovs. Fortunately, in 1619 the tsar's father Filaret returned to Moscow from Polish captivity, was elevated to the patriarchal throne, and took the reins of government firmly into his hands. He ruled brutally after eliminating all other competitors, including his former wife, but the few reforms which he introduced helped to save the situation. For the first time in Russian history a kind of diarchy was introduced, the patriarch assuming the title of *velikij gosudar'*, ordinarily given to the tsar, and ruling in the name of his son. After Filaret's death (1633), the Saltykov family regained its influence at the court.

Michael's son, Alexis (1645-1676), was better educated than his father, and even had some literary ambitions. His crude manners were softened by his great kindness. He was a conservative and a *dévot*, enjoying the company of devout and feeble-minded people, then much venerated by the Russians. Yet Alexis accepted the suggestions of some of his more progressive favorites and introduced certain innovations at court in imitation of Western manners. The government was left, however, in the hands of some favorites, the most prominent among whom were his tutor Boris Morozov, Patriarch Nikon, and Artamon Matvejev. The intrigues of the tsar's relatives, however, often made their position precarious.

Alexis' successor, Fedor (Theodore) (1676-1682), the elder son of his first wife, was fourteen years old when his father died. He was educated by Simeon of Polock, a prominent Kievan scholar, and even made some attempts at writing poetry, but his sickly nature did not allow him to play any role in the government of the state. Prince Basil Golicyn was the most prominent and most able of the favorites who directed affairs for him.

After Fedor's death, the intrigues of the families of Alexis' two wives continued to complicate the government of the regency. Fedor's brother Ivan was feeble-minded, and although he was proclaimed successor to Fedor together with his half brother Peter, their sister Sophia became, with the help of the Miloslavskij family and of the tsarist guard (the *strel'tsy*), the real regent until 1689, when Peter took over the government.

The problems which faced the Muscovite government during this period were enormous and difficult to solve. The danger emanating from Poland-Lithuania was only averted because the Polish Diet refused to provide Władysław with sufficient means for his expedition against Moscow. Smolensk and Seversk, however, remained in Polish hands, and the attempt made in 1632 to regain Smolensk ended disastrously for Muscovy. It was no wonder then that in 1651 Alexis hesitated when the Cossacks offered him the submission of the Ukraine.

The success of the war of 1654-1656, which resulted in the recovery of Smolensk and the occupation of Lithuania, was made possible by the action of the Cossacks and by the Swedish invasion of Poland. Alexis' hopes of gaining the Polish crown were dashed by Charles X of Sweden (1654-1660), who proclaimed himself king of Poland and wished to occupy Lithuania, then in Muscovite hands. This ended the peace between the two countries which had been concluded at Stolbovo in 1617 and which had allowed Muscovy to recover Novgorod after payment of a considerable indemnity. The new conflict, which had started in 1656, ended in 1661 with the Peace of Kardis. Muscovy not only failed to recover the lost territories on the southern shore of the Gulf of Finland, conquered by Boris Godunov and lost in 1617, but also had to cede to Sweden the part of Livonia occupied by Russian troops. Muscovy was once again deprived of access to the Baltic Sea. Charles X could boast that without his permission not one Russian vessel could appear in his sea.

The gains in the south confirmed by the treaty of Andrušovo (1667) were again endangered by the adventures of Dorošenko and by Mohammed IV's invasion of the Ukraine. The common Turkish danger for the first time brought Poland and Muscovy into the same camp. In order to defend Kiev, Alexis' army occupied the residence of Dorošenko, situated on the right bank of the Dnieper, halfway between Kiev and the Black Sea. The adventurous hetman went over to Moscow but had to resign his dignity, and the tsar later appointed him voivod of Vjatka. The Poles lost a large proportion of their part of the Ukraine to the Turks (1676).

In 1677 Russian and Turkish armies clashed for the first time in history at Čyhyryn (Čigirin). The Russian success made a great impression at the court of the sultan. But Moscow did not yet feel strong enough to continue the war against her mighty neighbor. When a new Turkish army appeared in order to install George Chmel'nyćkyj, in the new role of a Turkish vassal, as hetman in their part of the Ukraine, the Muscovites with their Cossacks abandoned Čyhyryn and only retained the lands on the east bank of the Dnieper.

A mass migration of Ukrainians into the Russian part started. They were settled in the area of present-day Khar'kov, called from that time on *Slobodskaja Ukraina,* and were administered by a special governor appointed by the tsar. The armistice concluded between Turkey and Muscovy in 1681 guaranteed to Moscow the possession of this part of the Ukraine.

The first open conflict between Muscovy and Turkey took place under the reign of Fedor III. Golicyn, who continued to direct affairs even during the regency of Sophia, was mainly responsible for the further development of relations between Poland, Turkey, and Muscovy. King John Sobieski was anxious to win over Muscovy for the anti-Turkish league. The regents hesitated, well aware that a Polish-Muscovite alliance would not be welcomed by their Cossacks. The outcome of the Polish-Turkish wars, however, induced the Muscovites to overcome their hesitation, and Sobieski's victory at Vienna made a great impression in Moscow. In 1686 an alliance, called an "eternal peace," was concluded between the two countries. In return for Moscow's promise to assist the Poles in their war with the Turks, and for a substantial monetary subsidy, the Poles abandoned definitely their claims to Kiev and promised to grant complete religious freedom to the Orthodox population in their realm.

Golicyn proved, however, to be a poor military leader. His campaign against the Crimea in 1687, undertaken against the advice of the Cossack hetman, Samojlovyč, was a failure. The unfortunate hetman was blamed for the lack of success and exiled to Siberia. The new hetman, Ivan Mazeppa, accompanied Golicyn on the second expedition in 1689, but both were defeated at Perekop. This failure was one of the main causes of the downfall of Golicyn and Sophia. The Baltic and Black seas remained closed to Muscovy, and it was reserved for the new tsar Peter to open a window for Muscovy in both directions.

More success attended Muscovy's expansion under the first Romanov northward and eastward across the Siberian steppes. The colonization of Siberia made steady progress. Enisejsk was founded in 1618, Jakutsk in 1632, Irkutsk in 1652, and Nerčinsk in 1654. In 1637 the Muscovites reached the shores of the northern Pacific. In 1648 a daring expedition cruised in the Arctic Ocean from the mouth of the Kolyma River to that of the Anadyr.

The occupation of the Amur basin in 1649 brought the Muscovites, for the first time, into direct contact with the Chinese and their Manchu emperors. The first clash in 1652 ended in a Russian victory. The first Muscovite embassy, which reached Peking in 1656, failed, however, to settle the dispute. The Chinese assumed the offensive, and fighting and negotiations went on. Golicyn, busy with his Crimean projects, seemed to have neglected the Far Eastern situation. The peace concluded in 1689 was therefore not favorable to Muscovy, which lost the Amur basin and had to recognize Chinese sovereignty in Mongolia. Russian expansion therefore turned northeastward. In 1697 Kamčatka was occupied, and for the first time the Russians were brought into touch with Japan.

Although the first Romanovs had been unable to realize all their expansionist ambitions, they laid solid foundations for the further aggrandizement of Muscovite territory under Peter the Great and his successors. When the desperate situation of the Muscovite state at the end of the Time of Troubles is considered, this was indeed a remarkable achievement.

The Time of Troubles had naturally also left profound traces in the social, economic, and financial structure of Muscovy. The old order was deeply shaken, the land impoverished, the administration disorganized, the government almost without resources. It was imperative to find the necessary means to enable the government to ensure the defense of the country and to bring some order into the administration. The first reforms, introduced by Filaret, were dictated by these necessities.

In order to replenish the state treasury and to remedy the most shocking abuses on the part of the unscrupulous tax collectors, Filaret ordered the compilation of new land registers and appointed new tax assessors from among the class of tax payers. Indirect taxes, often of a very vexatious character, were introduced, and the state monopoly on inns and public houses, introduced by Ivan IV, was reinforced. Unfortunately, the need to increase the taxable capacity of the subjects led to a deterioration in the situation of the peasantry. The peasants, overburdened by their obligations toward their feudal lords and by contributions to the state treasury, were abandoning their lands, and often their families too, in growing numbers and joining the Cossacks or settling on the borderlands. Many of the holders of *pomestija* and *votčiny* could not fulfill their military obligations, having lost great numbers of the peasants who were cultivating their estates for them. Influenced by the complaints of the gentry, Filaret's government authorized landlords to bring back their fugitive vassals if they had not been settled in their new homes for more than five years, a term later increased to ten. This marked a further step toward the establishment of serfdom. On the other hand, Filaret alleviated the position of merchants and artisans settled in the *posady*, or suburbs established on the outskirts of the cities, which were centers of local government. This was achieved by subjecting their competitors to taxation, namely, men in the tsar's service, *služilye ljudi*, settled there or nearby in the so-called *sloboda*.

In order to improve the administration, Filaret increased the number of central government agencies, called *prikazy*, which had come into being under the first tsars.

Filaret's reforms, although not always successful, were completed under Tsar Alexis and found legal sanction in the *Uloženie*—a code of laws based on Byzantine and Lithuanian law, Russian *sudebniki* (codes of justice), ordinances or *ukazy* of the tsar, and decisions of different *prikazy*—and were approved by the Zemskij Sobor of 1649.

The *Uloženie* is an important document, not only marking a great step in Russian legal history but also illustrating the social, financial, and administrative conditions prevailing in Moscow during the reign of the first Romanovs. The fate of the peasants was definitely sealed. They were forbidden to leave their legal residence, and their obligations to their lords became hereditary. Thus serfdom was sanctioned by law. Moreover, the peasants' communal organization, the *mir*, was henceforward not only made responsible for the punctual payment of the taxes of all individual peasants, but was also charged with the regular division among individual members of the land to be cultivated.

The *Uloženie* gives further details on the slaves and a new class of serfs, which is mentioned for the first time in the *Sudebnik* of 1550—the *zakladčiki*. These were men of different classes, who to evade taxation or to pay off a debt, often fictitiously contracted, together with accrued interest, were prepared to serve their creditor for their lifetime. This practice was forbidden, and different abuses connected with it were regulated, especially the habit of placing the *zakladčiki* near the *posady* where they were engaged in commerce or worked as artisans for the benefit of their masters. The inhabitants of these establishments near the *posady*, called *slobody* (free settlements), were subjected to the same taxation as those of the *posady*, and the formation of new *slobody* was forbidden. Unfortunately, in order to preserve its fiscal interests, the government forbade the inhabitants of the *posady* to change their residence, and thus considerably restricted liberties which were indispensable for the healthy evolution of commerce and industry. This restriction, dictated by fiscal interests, was one of the main reasons why cities of the Muscovite dominions were never able to play a role in the state similar to that of the cities of western Europe.

The government intended to promote the evolution of Russian commerce. But the *Uloženie* deprived all foreign traders of the privileges accorded to them by Ivan IV. They were only allowed to trade in Arkhangel. The English merchants were most affected by this stipulation: their merchandise was thenceforth subject to duties, and their privileged position in Russian trade came to an end.[1] The government encouraged the growth of Russian trade by other ordinances. One of these in 1667 excluded foreigners from all retail trade. Native merchants were also encouraged to trade directly with Asia.

All this failed, however, to have the desired effect. There did not exist in Muscovy any organized class of merchants as in the western European cities. The commercial monopoly held until 1649 by foreign, mostly English, traders did not favor the growth of a native merchant class. The fiscal policy of the government, codified in the *Uloženie,* hampered its growth after 1649.

Again principally for fiscal reasons, the Church had to accept important curtailments of its privileged position. Not only were the peasants forbidden by the *Uloženie* to seek the protection (*zaklad*) of the ecclesiastical landlords, who were free from taxation, but strong measures were taken to prevent the increase of Church property in order not to reduce taxable land. Moreover, the judicial, administrative, and financial affairs of the clergy and of peasants settled on lands belonging to the Church were put under the jurisdiction of a special directorate, the monastic *prikaz.* Exemption was granted only to the patriarch and to the institutions depending directly on him.

One class of the population, the tsar's servants (*služilye ljudi, dvorjane*), were most favored by the new order of the *Uloženie.* They were bound not only to render military service, more or less burdensome, according to the size of the *pomestie* lands granted to them by the tsar, but also to render service in a civil capacity. The differences between this new class of aristocracy and the old noble families holding their hereditary lands, *votčiny,* disappeared increasingly, especially after 1682, when the old institution of *mestničestvo,* binding the tsar never to grant to members of the official hierarchy a post inferior to that occupied by their ancestors, was abolished.

The general tendency of the Code of 1649 and of other measures taken by the first Romanovs was to classify the population of the realm into different groups, each charged with special obligations toward the state, and to forbid the transition from one class to another. The primitive fiscal methods, the growing expenses of the state, and its enormous extension induced the government to take such measures.

In spite of its numerous deficiencies, the *Uloženie* marked a notable step forward in judicial matters. Although many of its dispositions were abrogated, it remained in practice in Russia for two hundred years and was only replaced by a new statute in 1833.

The same financial necessities forced the government to try some new experiments in taxation and in the monetary system. The old *sokha*, the area of arable land which could be furrowed with one plough in a day, had hitherto provided a basis for taxation. But from 1646 to 1678, in order to force the peasants to cultivate more land, the taxation was based on the whole farm, *dvor*. Besides this tax, three other direct taxes were levied—the *jam* for the support of the official postal system, the prisoner's tax for the redemption of Russians in Tatar captivity, and the *streľtsy* tax for the upkeep of the musketeers, who formed the core of a standing army and provided the tsar's guard.

Some attempts at indirect taxation, especially on salt and tobacco, had disastrous effects. The taxes were too high and were applied in an inexpert way. Only the tax on alcohol sold in inns, which were government monopolies, brought in a steady income. Some other manipulations testified to very inexpert direction of financial policy. Such was the putting into circulation of German thalers reminted in Arkhangelsk and the conferment on them of a nominal value equal to twice their real value. Another operation, the replacement of silver coins by copper coins which were supposed to have the same value, led to the first inflation in Russia and the financial ruin of many.

Important changes were made by the first Romanovs in the administration of the state. Administrative innovations, largely introduced by Ivan IV, were further developed. The office of the voivode (governor of a district) had grown in importance during the Time of Troubles. He resided in the citadel of the *gorod* proper, sometimes called also *kremľ*, and not only was responsible for the collection of taxes, but also acted as judge in civil cases and as commander of the district's militia. The office was given to a member of the poorer gentry among the tsar's servants, *služilye ljudi;* but the second officer, the *gubnoj starosta,* who acted as presiding judge in criminal affairs, was elected by the gentry.

The governors and the members of their staff were not paid by the government but had to be provided for by the population of the district. The contributions of the population to the maintenance of the voivodes were to be regulated by *starostas,* elected by the inhabitants of the *posady* and the peasantry of the districts. They had to meet every year for this purpose in the local assembly hall, *zemskaja izba,* of the *posad.* This new kind of democratic institution was, however, not a success. The governors acted as absolute masters, interfered with the elections, and soon became famous in Russian proverbs for their rapacity and corruption.

The growing importance of military operations in the frontier regions of Muscovy induced the government to amalgamate considerable numbers of districts in the west, south, and southeast into bigger territorial units called *razrjady.* These were autonomous military units, each governed by a *razrjad voivode,* to whom all the voivodes of the districts were subordinated. They possessed full military and civil powers in their *razrjady,* or regions, and were also responsible for recruiting and paying their troops. The *razrjady* became the nucleus from which developed an administrative reform of Peter the Great, the division of the state into *gubernii,* or governments, presided over by a governor.[2]

The same military necessities forced the first Romanovs to pay more attention to the reorganization of their army. The nobles in possession of the *pomestie* still provided the core of Muscovy's army, but their military qualities were diminishing steadily. The nobles were more interested in the administration of their *pomestie* and in recovering fugitive peasants than in military service. Many of them became bankrupt and were incapable of fulfilling their military duties. Others evaded their duties by bribing the officials charged with the mobilization, or simply by deserting from the army in spite of the severe penalties incurred for desertion in face of the enemy.

The equipment of the cavalry and infantry was obsolete, and the troops were badly trained. The only military unit capable of fighting effectively was that of the musketeers, the *strel'tsy,* introduced by Ivan IV. All this forced the first Romanovs to follow the example of the last Ruriks and to recruit foreign mercenaries, not only for the defense of the southern frontier, but also in their campaigns against their western neighbors. It was again Filaret who inaugurated the reorganization of the Muscovite army. Foreign officers, mostly Polish, German, and English, were engaged to teach the native troops the secrets of modern warfare and to command them. Some of these were granted estates, *pomestie;* others obtained high salaries. New military units were formed. The new corps of cavalry was entitled *rejtari* in West European fashion. New formations of infantry called *soldaty* were recruited from the *služilye ljudi* of the northwestern districts to operate against the famous Swedish army, while the *draguny,* trained for service both on horseback and on foot, were more fit for operations in the steppes. The new military corps were recruited from the impoverished nobles, from the sons of the *strel'tsy,* from peasants who had lost their possessions, from nonregistered Cossacks, and others.

At the same time, the first attempt at general military service was made. It was stipulated that every hundred farms should supply one cavalryman and one infantryman and that large families should give one or two of their sons who were not needed in agriculture to the tsar's army. The levy of troops from the *pomestie,* according to the old system, decreased gradually. About 1680 the gentry of the *pomestie* were able to supply only thirteen thousand warriors.

Thanks to all these measures, the military power of Muscovy grew considerably. After the annexation of the Ukraine, the tsar was able to mobilize over 200,000 men. Of course, only the *strel'tsy* and the foreign mercenaries constituted a kind of standing army. The rest of the mobilized men were generally allowed to return to their homes when a campaign was concluded. But even here the first Romanovs laid the foundations on which Peter the Great and his successors were to build up the military power of the tsarist standing armies.

A further important improvement was achieved in the equipment of the armies. The old-fashioned arms were gradually replaced by firearms of different calibers. Artillery was brought up to date and expanded. This modernization made the tsarist army definitely superior to the Tatar armies and gave it a fair chance in encounters with the valiant Polish cavalry and infantry. However, it could hardly match the Swedish army, the best trained and disciplined in Europe in the seventeenth century.

At first Muscovy had to purchase its modern military equipment abroad, mostly in Sweden and England. Endeavors were made to settle foreign gunsmiths and other artisans engaged in the production of firearms and munitions in the *sloboda* of Moscow and other cities. However, this did not prove satisfactory; so in order to become more independent in this important military aspect from foreign countries, which were often hostile, the tsars were obliged to encourage industrialization for arms production.

First, exploration was fostered in all corners of the Muscovite dominions in order to ensure that the necessary minerals could be found in the country. Then, in 1632, the Dutchman Andrew Vinius obtained a concession to establish at Tula the first big manufacture of firearms. In Moscow, with the help of foreign technicians, cannon of all calibers began to be made. German specialists helped to establish foundries for the manufacture of church bells.

The survey of minerals resulted in discoveries of rich deposits of iron ore in the basins of the Vaga, Kostroma, and Šeksna rivers. The first important centers of the iron industry were founded in these northern regions by Marselis of Hamburg. Other industrial enterprises, such as the first glassworks, followed. The first attempt at a textile industry was made under Alexis. Other industries were gradually introduced, but on a modest scale. Not even Peter the Great was able to speed up the spread of modern industry as he intended. The Russians clung for a considerable time to primitive forms of industrial production, based on domestic craftsmanship in the hands of family groups.

All this shows, however, that Muscovy under the first Romanovs had started to open its doors to Western influences in many fields. Most of these influences emanated from England and Holland, thanks to the lively commercial intercourse between these two lands and Muscovy since the time of Ivan IV. Common hostility toward Sweden brought about a rapprochement between Muscovy and Denmark, which was a powerful state in the seventeenth century, controlling the entrance to the Baltic.

When anti-Turkish sentiment, always latent in Moscow but stifled by fear of Ottoman military power, began to manifest itself more boldly, Venice opened its gates to Muscovite ambassadors. The first envoys made a very bad impression by their uncouth behavior, but reasons of policy helped the Venetians to overcome their disgust and to find their way to Moscow. About 1670 the Muscovites even proposed an anti-Turkish league—this was symptomatic of their new political initiative.

Diplomatic relations with the German princes became more frequent in the second half of the seventeenth century, when Muscovy was interested in securing the neutrality of the German Electors in its war with Poland. Polish and Turkish affairs also opened the way for Russian ambassadors to Vienna. At the same time Serbian and Bulgarian refugees came to Moscow, and the Orthodox Christians of the Balkans looked increasingly to Moscow to liberate them from the Turks. All this illustrates the changed position and prestige of Muscovy in contemporary Europe.

In spite of the efforts of the government to ameliorate the internal situation, the reigns of the first Romanovs were characterized by continuing popular unrest. Although defeated, the Cossacks, who were not incorporated into the army, continued to cause trouble throughout the first years of Michael's rule. They were often supported by disgruntled elements in the borderlands. The appearance of new pretenders claiming descent from the rulers of the Time of Troubles added to the general disorder.

Many of the new measures taken by the government were unpopular and crude, and the rule of the favorites provoked grievances. The revolt of 1648 was directed against Alexis' favorite and brother-in-law, Boris Morozov, but was at the same time a protest against the salt tax. The suppression of the system of voluntary slavery by the *Uloženie* of 1649 was greeted with lively protests by the voluntary slaves and their masters, a fact which throws a characteristic light on the social and economic situation in Muscovy. The naïve and grievous monetary manipulations added fresh fuel to the general discontent and provoked a popular revolt in 1662, which was brutally suppressed.

The most formidable revolt exploded in the Don basin (1669-1671), and was led by a Don Cossack, Stephen Razin. After having established himself between the Don and the Caspian Sea, Razin led a maritime expedition against the Persian coast on the Caspian and returned with rich booty. Many Don Cossacks—runaway serfs and unruly elements generally —joined him, and with this army he captured Astrakhan' and Tsaritsyn. The movement developed into a social uprising of the peasants and native tribes along the Volga against the landowners.

After these successes Razin threatened Moscow. But his motley army could not withstand the few regiments trained in modern warfare which Moscow was able to send against him. Defeated and abandoned by the Don Cossacks, Razin was seized in his stronghold on the Don and executed in Moscow. The tsar's troops finally ended the uprising by recapturing Astrakhan' at the end of 1671. This victory strengthened Moscow's prestige among the Cossacks, but the deeds of the popular leader continued to be celebrated in epic songs, and he was rated as a hero in the struggle for liberation from serfdom.

It may well arouse surprise that the Muscovite state was able to survive and expand during the reign of such weak rulers and after so many upheavals had shaken its foundations. To a certain degree this was due to the cooperation between the ruler and the nation as represented in the Zemskij Sobor, which elected Michael Romanov and which appeared to become a permanent institution in Muscovy. In some way, Moscow seemed to be returning to the democratic institution of the Kievan *veče*s. In fact from 1613 to 1622 the Zemskij Sobor functioned regularly and was afterward convoked several times by Michael and Alexis to discuss matters of importance. There is, of course, a great difference between the Russian national assembly, the Kievan *veče*s, and the medieval or contemporary parliamentary systems of western Europe. The Zemskij Sobor was composed most probably of the boyar duma broadened by the admission of members of the lower nobility, of the higher clergy, and of representatives of the *dvorjane*, merchants, and other burghers. The duma was a kind of senate and functioned when the assembly was not in session. The members of the "lower house" were nominally elected, but were in fact often nominated by local governments. Complete information on the composition and function of the Sobor is lacking, but it often exercised an influence on the conduct of state affairs by its criticism or cooperation. It was probably the voicing of dissatisfaction with some government measures which contributed to the abandonment of this institution after 1653.

In spite of its short existence, the Zemskij Sobor had a profound influence on the conception of the state. The state ceased to be a simple *votčina*, hereditary property of the ruler, as was the case under the Rurik dynasty. Thanks to this collaboration of the people with the ruler, the consciousness of national and religious unity became stronger, and the conception of the Russian land coalesced increasingly with that of the Russian people.

The members of the national assembly never conceived the idea of limiting the powers of the absolute ruler. The conception of an autocratic government deriving its rights from above was so firmly embedded in Muscovite minds that any other political system was unthinkable. The political program of the first Romanovs consisted simply in the enacting and strengthening of the old Muscovite traditions, and autocracy was one of their main principles, sanctioned by the Church and generally accepted. It was therefore in no way surprising that the innovation of a national assembly enjoyed such a short role in Muscovite political life.

The autocratic power of the tsar seems, however, to have been challenged unexpectedly by two churchmen. At first sight the rule of the Patriarch Filaret could be interpreted in such a way. For the first time in Russian history a kind of theocracy was established, and it functioned successfully during the life of the energetic patriarch. In reality, however, the role played by the patriarch was not interpreted by his contemporaries as marking a revolutionary development in the relations between the tsar and the Church. Filaret was the tsar's father and had himself once been a candidate for the throne. He reigned in the name of his obedient son, like so many other favorites of weak tsars before and after him. Moreover, beside him there still existed the authority of the Sobor. Filaret's successors, the patriarchs Joasaph and Joseph, revealed no inclination to claim any effective share in the government. The traditional harmonious relationship between the temporal and the spiritual power, which had been so firmly established in the Kievan state,[3] was again renewed.

Filaret's example, however, easily invited imitation, the more so as he had considerably augmented the prestige and power of the patriarch. Filaret controlled an immense ecclesiastical territory extending from the White Sea to the Ukrainian frontier and from Brjansk in the west as far as Vjatka, with over forty cities. He obtained confirmation of his direct jurisdiction over all churches, monasteries, and religious foundations in this enormous territory, together with the right to act as judge of its population in all but criminal matters. In order to exercise this almost sovereign jurisdiction, Filaret established his own *prikaz* for administrative, financial, and judicial matters and fixed his own taxes and organized their collection. It can readily be imagined how important the position of the patriarch was when it is recalled that in the nineteenth century sixteen dioceses were established on the territory over which the patriarch had exercised sole and direct jurisdiction in the seventeenth century. This situation provided a ready temptation for an ambitious ecclesiastic to pretend to a more prominent role in the government of Muscovy.

Such a man arose in the person of Nikon, who dared to challenge the deep-rooted Muscovite ideas on the relations between the two powers. Furthermore, his name is also connected with reforms which, though overdue and well intentioned, were badly applied and split the Russian Church asunder in a schism lasting down to modern times.

Nikon [4] the son of a peasant, was born in 1605 and christened Nikita. He obtained some education in a monastery and became a priest in Moscow. Under the emotional stress of his children's death he persuaded his wife to become a nun, and he himself entered a monastery near the White Sea, assuming the name of Nikon. When he visited Moscow in 1646 as abbot of his monastery, his appearance, behavior, and eloquence made such a great impression on the young tsar, that Alexis appointed him abbot of the Moscow monastery which contained the Romanov family tomb. Nikon became an intimate of the tsar, and he soon learned how to maintain and increase his influence over the tsar and his government. In 1648 he was appointed metropolitan of Novgorod, the second greatest city of Muscovy.

Nikon's sojourn in Novgorod was probably the most fruitful in his life. There he manifested a sincere zeal for the spiritual welfare of his flock and introduced preaching and religious instruction. These represented an innovation at a time when Muscovite religious life centered exclusively on attendance at liturgical acts. In the ordering of the liturgy Filaret proved himself a zealous reformer. In order to save time, it had become general to combine the long lessons and prayers with the singing of the choir. In this babel of voices, the words could, of course, not be followed. Nikon forbade this abuse, and on his initiative, the tsar extended this prohibition to other dioceses. Nikon also reorganized the singing of the choirs in Byzantine fashion, and the tsar introduced this reform into his private chapel, whence it spread to other churches. In political affairs Nikon also proved his usefulness, and when an uprising started in Novgorod in 1650, he risked his life to stop it.

When the tsar invited Nikon, in 1652, to occupy the vacant patriarchal throne, he accepted the post only after obtaining a written assurance from the tsar that the government would abstain from intervention in religious affairs. As patriarch, Nikon started to speed up the revision of the liturgical books, which had been widely requested and was made necessary by the numerous textual mistakes caused by the inaccuracy of copyists.

This necessity had already been felt in the time of Ivan IV, and a revision was ordered by the Synod of 1551. The first books were very imperfectly printed in 1564 and 1565.[5] After the Time of Troubles the need for new liturgical books was even greater because many had been destroyed. The clerics charged with the revision were zealous reformers but lacked any philological training and did not know Greek, so that their revision only served to increase the mistakes. Besides mistakes in wording, there were also certain marked peculiarities in Muscovite liturgy, and these were pointed out by the Patriarch of Jerusalem when he visited Moscow in 1649, as differing from the usage of the Greek Church.

Although some of these peculiarities appeared very minor—for example, the number of genuflections, the singing of the Hallelujah twice or three times, the making of the sign of the Cross with two or three fingers—they were of immense importance to liturgically minded Muscovites in the seventeenth century. For them the liturgy was the only form of communion with God, and when performed in erroneous fashion it had no value before God and could not benefit the worshipers. Therefore the more intelligent clerics advocated the revision of the books in accordance with the Greek originals since the Byzantine Church was the Mother Church of Russia and the source of Orthodox Christian tradition.

This movement, however, encountered strong opposition among the traditionalists, who vaunted Muscovite Orthodoxy and could not tolerate the idea that their forefathers had worshiped erroneously. They claimed that Byzantium had forfeited its position of leadership because of its "apostasy" in 1439 in accepting the union with Rome, while it could not be trusted because it was under the yoke of the infidels. Moscow, some of them averred, was the Third Rome and the only guardian of Orthodoxy.

Nikon was in a difficult position. After the annexation of the Ukraine, he felt himself compelled to harmonize the language of the liturgical books used in Muscovy with that of Ukrainian ritual books recently re-edited by Mohyla. He thought that the best way to unify the ecclesiastical and literary language used in Muscovy and in the Ukraine was to adapt the Muscovite liturgical books to the Ukrainian. It was a bold attempt at a linguistic rapprochement between the two idioms and would have helped to bridge the differences between the two nations.

Moreover, Nikon was firmly convinced of the Orthodoxy of the Greek Church and determined to accomplish the revision of the Russian liturgical books by collating them with the Greek originals. He obtained sanc-

tion for the project of revision from a Church assembly in 1654 and sent
a long questionnaire about the points in dispute to the Patriarch of Constantinople. Nikon's envoys, led by Arsenius Suchanov, collected almost
seven hundred Greek manuscripts,[6] of which only seven dealt with liturgical questions. Because there was no Muscovite cleric who knew Greek,
it was necessary to bring specialists from Greece, Arsenius and Dionysius,
and from Kiev, Epifanij Slavineckij. Although their work would not have
satisfied the demands of modern scholarship, it marked an improvement,
and in 1655 the corrected Russian Missal was approved by a new synod,
which was attended by the Patriarch of Antioch and the Serbian Patriarch Gabriel. Other synods approved Nikon's changes in Russian liturgical practice, and all Muscovites were ordered to make the sign of the
Cross with three fingers in the Greek fashion.

The reforms, hastily realized, often on very slight philological foundations, encountered strong opposition. The radical Muscovite nationalists
refused to accept the corrected books with their Ukrainisms. They pretended that the revisers included Kievan scholars who were suspect on
account of their knowledge of Latin and their contact with the Roman
"heretics." The opposition was led by the circle of "correctors," who had
been appointed by the Patriarch Joseph and had been dismissed by Nikon.

The opposition found a very able and very passionate leader in the
Archpriest Avvakum (Habakuk). Born about 1620, Avvakum [7] had in his
youth already given signs of possessing a very independent nature and
almost a passion for suffering for his ideas. Although at the beginning
he was not hostile to the idea of correcting the liturgical books, he was
horrified at the numerous changes ordered by Nikon and rejected them,
proclaiming his desire to live and to die according to the old faith, uncor-
rupted by the Greeks. His numerous followers called themselves "of the
Old Faith"—*staroverci*. They were declared schismatics, *raskol'niki*, and
Nikon started to persecute them mercilessly. Although the tsar had a
profound respect for the zealous archpriest, he could not tolerate his
opposition. Avvakum was imprisoned, beaten, and exiled first to Tobol'sk
and then farther into Siberia, but he underwent all this with patience and
courage, his wife faithfully sharing the persecution with her husband.

In the persecution of those who were opposed to his reforms, Nikon
displayed an unusual ruthlessness. Many of his reforms were enacted
without even the sanction of the synod, and the methods employed by
Nikon in imposing them were most brutal. The tsar and his wife did not
share this animosity against the dissenters. It seems that the independent
attitude of Nikon in this matter contributed greatly to the estrangement
between Alexis and himself, which became apparent in 1658. The immediate cause of the break was trivial. Nikon was offended because the tsar,

who had ceased attending services conducted by Nikon, omitted to invite him to an official banquet. The impetuous patriarch sent one of his subordinates to investigate the reason for this omission. His envoy was badly received by the courtiers, and the tsar did nothing to punish those responsible for this maltreatment. The offended patriarch announced his resignation from office and left Moscow, fully expecting that the tsar would come in person to render him satisfaction and beg him to return to Moscow and resume his post.

But in his zeal Nikon overestimated the importance of his position in Muscovy. His overbearing manners and haughty attitude had won him many enemies at court, and the growing interference of the patriarch in state affairs angered the tsar, who was reaching his maturity. Alexis did not come and beg Nikon to return, and although he was gravely disturbed in his conscience by what had happened, he abstained from any move to heal the breach. Nikon, seeing that he had gone too far, declared that he was not resigning his dignity. Thus he prevented the election of another patriarch, but his attempts to regain his former position at the tsar's court proved vain. Finally the tsar convoked a synod in 1666 and, in order to lend it greater weight, invited the oriental patriarchs. The patriarchs of Antioch and of Alexandria attended, representing also their colleagues of Constantinople and of Jerusalem. The council arraigned Nikon, who behaved in a very arrogant manner, especially toward the eastern patriarchs. As a result, he was deprived not only of the patriarchate, but also of his episcopal dignity and was interned in a monastery.

The declaration of the two eastern patriarchs that it was the duty of a Russian patriarch to obey the tsar in all political matters reveals the true nature of the whole conflict. Nikon had tried to introduce into the Muscovite political system a doctrine which was neither Russian nor Byzantine, that of the superiority of the ecclesiastical over the secular power. Nikon must have become acquainted with this doctrine in Novgorod, which had always been more open to Western influences. Some of his reforms in that city, especially the emphasis on preaching and religious instruction, seem to have been inspired by Roman practices, which had been stressed anew by the Council of Trent. Through Novgorod the Russians had also become acquainted in the fifteenth century with the famous Latin forgery, the *Donatio Constantini*. This pretended that the first Christian emperor, before moving from Rome to Constantinople, had made the popes supreme over all bishops and ceded the entire West to them, together with the privilege of wearing imperial insignia.[8] This forgery had become one of the foundations on which the theory of the superiority of the ecclesiastical power over the secular was erected in the eleventh century. Throughout the Middle Ages there were no doubts

concerning the genuineness of the document. It was also accepted by the
Greeks, who only began to question its reliability in the fifteenth century.
At the very time when this document was being introduced into Russian
canonical literature, two humanists, Laurentius Valla and Nicholas of
Cusa, were proving that it was a gross forgery.

In Muscovy, the *Donatio* was exploited by the Synod of 1503 for the
defense of Church property against Ivan III and by the Metropolitan
Makarij in 1550 against Ivan IV.[9] In Nikon's eyes this document clearly
demonstrated the pre-eminence of the spiritual power, which he was
determined to establish definitively in Muscovy. He inserted the *Donatio*
in the Slavonic collection of canon law and acted in its spirit when he
asked the tsar for an assurance that he would not interfere with ecclesiastical affairs. Before he became patriarch, the influence of the *Donatio*
had already become apparent in Nikon's vehement protests against the
curtailment of ecclesiastical privileges by the *Uloženie,* which he regarded as the Devil's handiwork.

The *Donatio* was referred to profusely by Nikon in his answers to
Paissius, bishop of Gaza. The latter's statements were vouchsafed in
reply to questions presented to him by the boyar Simeon Strešnef concerning Nikon's behavior, and played an important part in the patriarch's
condemnation. There he denies to the tsar any jurisdiction over priests
and any right to convoke councils, to nominate patriarchs and bishops, or
to appropriate Church property. He also gives clear vent to his conviction that spiritual power is superior to secular: "Hast thou not learned
from what has been written above that the highest authority of the
priesthood is not received from kings or tsars, but contrariwise, it is by
the priesthood that rulers are anointed to the Empire? Therefore it is
abundantly plain that priesthood is a very much greater thing than kingship. . . ." [10]

This must evidently have appeared to be something new and strange
to the Muscovite mind and completely alien to the traditional course of
Russian political evolution. Nikon would have been better advised if he
had sought guidance not from a Latin document falsely ascribed to
Constantine the Great, but from a genuine Greek document, namely,
Novel Six in Justinian's code of laws. This stressed the sublimity and importance of kingship and priesthood and declared that the well-being
of the human race depended on the harmony between these two, "God's
greatest gifts to Man, coming from above from His love of Mankind." This
document was included in Russian canon law from the earliest times
and appears to have inspired the metropolitans of Kiev in their relations
with the secular power.[11]

Nikon's attempt to introduce into Muscovy [12] this alien principle of
the superiority of the spiritual power over the temporal was belated

and made at a time which was hardly favorable to its acceptance. In the West the spiritual power was in retreat before Bourbon absolutism, and although seventeenth century Muscovy appeared to be deeply permeated with a religious atmosphere, a process of secularization had already started. It had been inaugurated by the disorders of the Time of Troubles, and the anticlerical measures of the *Uloženie* showed how far it had already spread. These measures were taken on the insistence of the laity represented in the national assembly, and the tsar had to promulgate them in spite of his personal sympathies with the Church. The popular opposition to the liturgical reforms accepted by a synod also showed that although the Russian Church was led no longer, as under Ivan III and Basil III, by the monastic world, but by the hierarchy, the bishops' hold over the faithful was not as strong as might have been expected.

So it happened that the old Byzantine conceptions of kingship and priesthood again came to dominate the relations between Church and state, with the emphasis on the right of the ruler to supervise the Church. This was stressed by Paissius in his answers to the questionnaire and also by the oriental patriarchs in the Synod of 1666-1667, which condemned Nikon. Perhaps in order to please the tsar, the patriarchs laid greater stress on the need for the Church to submit to the head of the State than was expressed in Justinian's Novel Six and in Photius' *Epanagoge*. These were known to the Russian hierarchy because both documents were included in the Russian book of canon law, called *Kormčaja kniga* ("The Pilot's Book"). Some of the Muscovite prelates protested against the wording proposed by the patriarchs, feeling that it did not correspond altogether with Muscovite conceptions. Their fears proved well founded because this definition of the relationship between the two powers became the instrument by which the Russian Church was later degraded into an obedient servant of the state according to conceptions which were neither Russian nor Byzantine.

The lively contact with the Orthodox patriarchates of the East seemed to be bringing Muscovy back not only to Byzantine liturgical traditions, but also to earlier conceptions of tsarist autocracy. Hitherto the tsars had been cool toward suggestions by westerners that they were heirs to the emperors of Constantinople.[13] They did not aspire to the leadership of all Orthodox Christians since they regarded the Greeks as apostates from Orthodoxy.

The moral support of the Greeks in the controversy about the correction of liturgical books, however, brought about a rapprochement on the part of official circles in Muscovy with the Greek and the other three Eastern patriarchs. Byzantium was again honored as the source of Russian faith, and Moscow became increasingly interested in the fate of the

Eastern Orthodox. Not only were their bishops given lavish alms when they visited Muscovy, but Alexis began to take a more lively interest in their exhortations to act as the only Orthodox ruler and to become the protector of all Orthodox peoples. The Patriarch of Jerusalem, Paissius (1608-1644), compared his visits to Moscow with the homage which his predecessors had been wont to render to the emperors of Constantinople. In 1653, during the course of his stay in Moscow, the former oecumenical patriarch Athanasius III exhorted Alexis to conquer Constantinople, his inheritance, to become a new Constantine, and to install an oecumenical patriarch in that city.

Moreover, the Orthodox of the Ukraine appealed to the tsar for help, and refugees from the south converged on Muscovy, the only free Orthodox state, expecting liberation through the agency of the Orthodox tsar. The Serbian patriarch Gabriel attended the Synod of 1655 and was able to expound to the tsar on the sad fate of his flock. Even the Catholic Croats seemed willing to accept the Muscovite tsar as the sovereign of all Slavs. Such was the impression conveyed in Moscow by the learned Croatian priest Križanić, whom Alexis had accepted into his service in 1659. Of course the Croatian priest hoped to win over the tsar to union with Rome.

Nor did Alexis repudiate the Byzantine conception of the tsardom as protector of Orthodoxy. Although he was as yet unable to do more than give moral and financial support to his Greek and Slavic admirers, this broader conception of the Russian tsardom was definitely implanted in Moscow under Alexis. It was to become stronger when, under Fedor, Muscovy had for the first time to face the sultan's army. Thenceforward the idea of the liberation of Orthodox peoples from the Moslem yoke became one of the principles of Russian policy.

A further return to Byzantine tradition was planned under Fedor. The young tsar, well versed in literature, planned with his advisers to introduce old Byzantine dignities and titles into his court. A new list of dignitaries of the Muscovite state was composed soon after 1682 and was intended to replace the old system of *mestničestvo,* which had been abolished. The authors of this project had quite a good knowledge of the composition of the Byzantine imperial court. The addition of Byzantine titles to Muscovite dignitaries whose offices had previously existed showed that it was not imperative for practical reasons, and provided clear evidence of an intention to make the Muscovite court as similar as possible to the Byzantine court, which would thus be resuscitated in Moscow.

The introduction of the proposed reform of ranks not only mentioned the crown which Vladimir Monomakh was supposed to have obtained from the Byzantine emperor, but also praised Fedor's father Alexis as exalted "with Greek glory." This was an evident allusion to the Greco-phile tendencies manifested by Alexis. Moreover, there is some evidence that during the reign of Fedor a plan was conceived to translate the whole code of Justinian into Russian and to make it the basis for Muscovite jurisprudence. Furthermore, in the statute of the Academy, whose foundation was planned by Fedor and his counselors, it was stressed that the tsar desired most ardently to imitate the emperors Constantine, Theodosius, and Justinian.[14] Although the projected institution was intended to give instruction not only in the "Slavic" and Greek languages, but also in Latin and Polish, the tsar was presented as desiring to emulate the example of these Byzantine emperors toward learning. All this is highly interesting and shows that Muscovy was slowly emerging from its isolation and striving to find new inspiration in Byzantium, which had been its first teacher and whose inheritance it began to claim. It is possible that if Fedor's reign had lasted longer, Muscovy would have been able to find a solution for some of its problems on a basis more akin to its character and past. This would perhaps have helped it to find an easier transition to the new age which was coming and to lessen the shock which a brusque westernization of Muscovite institutions and life would inevitably incur.

In spite of these attempts to find new inspiration outside Muscovy, the isolationist spirit continued to dominate the religious and cultural life of the state. The Time of Troubles destroyed many of the achievements of the last Ruriks, and the hostile intervention of Muscovy's neighbors, the Catholic Poles and the Protestant Swedes, made the Muscovites even more suspicious of Western influences. No new cultural impulses could derive from Byzantium, still suspect in the eyes of many as "apostate," despite the rejection of the union by the Greeks. So Muscovy remained isolated, clinging rigidly to the Kievan cultural inheritance on which it had founded its growth after the liberation from the Mongol yoke.

The consequences of this situation became fateful for the Muscovite Church. The impassioned opposition to the correction of the liturgical books revealed the deep stagnation in theological thinking and the lack of religious instruction of the Muscovite clergy. All religious activity was centered around long liturgical services, which became, in the eyes of the uninstructed priests and faithful, almost magic acts. They could have the desired effect on God only when carried out in the prescribed form, without changing a single word. This extreme formalism of Muscovite devotion was in startling contrast with the lively theological speculation in the contemporary West.

The Old Believers did not abandon their opposition after Nikon had been deposed. They were again led by Avvakum, who had been recalled from exile but refused to keep silent despite the exhortations of Alexis.

The Council of 1666-1667 endorsed Nikon's condemnation of the schismatics, and the persecutions were resumed. The monks of the Soloveckij monastery on the White Sea revolted and sustained a long siege by the tsarist army. The monastery was only taken, in 1676, with the help of a monk who betrayed his brethren. Avvakum was again exposed to inhuman hardship and suffering in Siberia, which he described vividly in his *Life*. But nothing could break his fanatical zeal. At last, on the order of Tsar Fedor, he was burned at the stake in 1681. Two noble ladies, Fedosia Morozova and her sister Princess Evdokia Urusova, who had led exemplary lives but had joined the schismatics, were tortured and died in prison.

Avvakum's adherents showed great fanaticism. The changes in the liturgical books were regarded by them as the work of the Antichrist, who was identified first with Nikon and then with the tsars who ordered the persecution; and in their mystical ardor they expected the end of the world. Fleeing from the central provinces, they settled mostly in the North and East, avoiding all contact with the official Church and the state. An epidemic of mass suicide by hunger or burning developed among these fanatics, who thus sought escape from the evil of the world. The most merciless persecution was ordered during the regency of Sophia, but nothing could break the resistance of the Old Believers, and they have survived down to modern times to the great detriment of the Church.[15]

Although attendance at services on Sundays, holidays, and during Lent was made compulsory, and although the whole life of the Muscovites seemed to be dictated by the Church, the moral standards of society were generally low, as can be gathered from all travelers' descriptions of Muscovy at that period.[16] They were all shocked by the general illiteracy and coarseness of manners and by the prevalence of drunkenness and other vices. Moral refinement could only be advanced by improved education and by the acceptance of ideas coming from abroad.

There was some contact with Western civilization in Moscow's foreign quarter, called the German *sloboda*. This was mostly inhabited by Protestant German, English, and Dutch merchants, artisans, and mercenary soldiers because the Catholics were regarded as more dangerous to Orthodoxy than were the Protestants. The Patriarch Filaret was particularly embittered against the Poles, who had kept him in captivity for eight years. He therefore placed Poles and other Catholics on the same level as pagans and Moslems and ordered the rebaptism of Catholic converts.[17]

The foreigners lived their own lives and had their own churches and schools. Although the authorities were anxious to prevent any infection of the Orthodox by their heresies, their ways of life found imitators among the upper classes of Moscow. Reports of Russian envoys to Western powers also helped to spread the desire to introduce some western customs into Muscovy. Tsar Alexis and some of his nobles led in the adoption of Western manners. Alexis manifested a lively interest in theatrical representations and founded the first Muscovite school for ballet and drama in 1673, under the direction of the German pastor Johann Gottfried Gregorij.

These were the first timid contacts with Western civilization. There was, however, another and more acceptable cultural center from which Western customs and learning could penetrate Muscovy—Kiev.[18] The Metropolitan Peter Mohyla founded an academy in Kiev, which was organized on the pattern of the Jesuit institutions of learning. This gave instruction in "Slavic," Greek, Latin, and Polish and became an important center of Orthodox scholarship.[19] In 1640 Mohyla proposed to Tsar Alexis the creation in Moscow of a monastery where the monks of the Kiev community would give instruction in Greek and Slavic letters to the children of the Muscovite nobility. The circle of the correctors, whose members were ultraconservative and influenced the direction of religious affairs, did not trust the Orthodox monks who were in touch with the Latins and had read their books. However, the failure of the Muscovite theologians to convert the Danish prince Waldemar to Orthodoxy, and the tsar's consequent refusal of his daughter's hand, convinced them that better knowledge of Greek and Latin would improve their theological preparedness. So, after an unfortunate experience with a Greek, they had to turn toward Kiev, especially as the tsar had asked Mohyla in 1648 to send him two scholars capable of translating the Bible from Greek into Russian.

Mohyla's successor Silvester Kossov sent to Moscow two members of the Academy, Slavineckij and Satanovskij, who began translating religious works from Greek and Latin. The correctors also accepted the Catechism of Peter Mohyla and printed it in Moscow after some readaptation.

The great event happened in 1649, when the boyar Rtiščev, one of the most influential intimates of the tsar and a friend of the correctors, founded the monastery of St. Andrew near Moscow and invited Kievan monks to settle there. Thus the first theological school in Muscovy came into being. It had only a limited number of students, but its influence on Muscovite scholarship was considerable. More scholars came from Kiev, and Nikon entrusted them with the correction of the liturgical books. The rupture with the Old Believers, who were uncompromising opponents of Western learning, eased the atmosphere, and in 1666 the first official initiative was taken by the government toward the establishment of a higher school. The school, headed by a Kievan scholar, Simeon of

Polock, to whom Alexis had entrusted the education of his own children, proved, however, of short duration. Only in 1682 did Simeon's disciple Medvedev become rector of a school which was modeled on the pattern of the Kievan Academy and which favored Latin instruction. Another school, giving preference to instruction in Greek, was founded in the same year. For some years both institutions, representing the two currents in Muscovite society, were rivals, the one favoring contact with the Latin West, the other with Greece. However in 1687 they merged and became the Slavo-Greco-Latin Academy with the exclusive right of teaching foreign languages and the liberal sciences. Unfortunately, this monopoly was also extended to the supervision of everything regarded as dangerous to Orthodoxy, including especially anything emanating from the Latins. The anti-Latin bias was especially propagated by two Greek monks, the brothers Likhudes. When they were denounced by their own patriarch and removed in 1693, the Academy lost some prestige, but it again became an important institution of learning when the pro-Latin teachers had taken over.

In spite of the low standard of learning, literary activity in Muscovy was quite lively.[20] In literature as in other respects the Muscovites were anxious to follow the traditions established in the past. This was particularly evident in some works describing the Time of Troubles. In 1606 an anonymous monk composed *Another Report* on the Troubles; a *Lament* on the destruction of Muscovy dates from 1612; Timofeev's *Vremennik* was written between 1616 and 1620; Palitsyn described the siege of the Sergius monastery by the Poles. All these authors imitated the pathetic style of the times of Makarius, sometimes contenting themselves with a dry enumeration of events and personalities in the tradition of Russian annalistic literature.[21]

Prince Khvorostinin, who was a great admirer of Western customs and literature, went back to this tradition in his historical *Homilies*, probably in order to rehabilitate himself since he was regarded as a great heretic. Prince Šakhovskoj showed more originality in his *Report* on the murder of Dmitrij, which he attributed to Boris Godunov. The best of all these numerous reports and laments is the *Book of Annals*, or *Chronicle*, by Prince Katy'ov-Rostovskij (died 1640), describing events from 1607 to 1611 with the precision of a historian, while avoiding the extremely rhetorical style which characterized other works of his time. He was able to attain this degree of perfection because he also sought inspiration in Western literature. His style and language were influenced by Guido de Colonna's *Trojan War*, which he had studied in a Russian translation.

However, some other historical works were still written in the manner of the medieval chroniclers at a time when in the rest of Europe critical historical methods were already making important progress. Such were the report on the election of Tsar Michael, a handbook of the Muscovite *prikaz* for foreign affairs composed by Matvejev, and the chronicle on the origin of Moscow and on the Russian people by Kamenevič-Rvovskij. Other works owed their inspiration and liveliness to the popular epics, to which dramatic events offered new topics. These works described the sudden death of Michael Skopin, a hero of the war with Poland—one of the best products of this time—and the defense of Azov, captured by the Don Cossacks, against the attacks of the Turks (1641). The latter is in the form of a letter to Tsar Michael, who is asked to take the city under his protection.

Two writers have left descriptions which give a vivid picture of life in Moscow in the seventeenth century. The first is that of Gregory Kotošikhin, an official of the *prikaz* of foreign affairs who turned traitor and gave a biased description to the Swedish government of life in Muscovy and of the political and economic organization with all its deficiencies. The Croatian missionary Gregory Križanić, who desired a strong Muscovy because it was the only hope for the liberation of the Slavs, pleaded in his *Politika,*[22] written during his Siberian exile, for reforms in Muscovy on Western lines. In this and other works he discussed economic, commercial, military, and industrial questions and suggested methods by which the tsar could strengthen his country. He also composed a grammar of common Slavic language, which he composed by blending and combining Church Slavonic with the vernacular language.

Two biographies give a further insight into the life and work of the two great antagonists, Patriarch Nikon and Avvakum. The *Life of Nikon* was composed by his admirer, the monk Ivan Šušerin. Afraid to discuss more profoundly the reasons for Nikon's fall, he contents himself with following the hagiographic pattern in which the lives of the saints had formerly been written.

Avvakum's biography is quite different. First it introduces a great innovation into Russian literature in that it is an autobiography, written in a lively, even passionate style, reflecting the stubbornness and bitterness of this fateful conflict with the authorities. Avvakum also undertook a revolutionary step in the literary field by abandoning the Old Slavonic literary language and writing in the Russian popular idiom. He thus prepared the way for the formation of the modern Russian literary language.

The break with the traditional hagiographic style can also be observed in two other works. *The Legend of Juliana Lazarevskaja* was written already about 1614 by her son, the boyar Kalistratus Osorin. Although not entirely free from traditional hagiographic elements, the legend is rather a biography of a pious lady who lived in the world, not in a convent, and who was not a heroine of excessive asceticism. *The Legend of the Boyarina Morozova* is also a biography of a lady, who was regarded as a heretic because she was a fervent disciple of Avvakum. A certain affinity with *The Legend of Juliana* can be observed in the Story of Sava, Son of *the Merchant Thomas Grudcyn*, written about 1660 by a monk of the Čudov monastery. The story already has certain characteristics of a novel. The pious author described the exploits of a young man who sold his soul to the Devil, but was in the end delivered from his master through the intercession of the Blessed Virgin. The story seems to be independent of similar tales, such as that of Faustus, circulating in the West, and indicates that a new trend was slowly penetrating Muscovite literature.

This new trend was accelerated in the second half of the seventeenth century by the influx of Kievan scholars and Kievan literature which made Polish and Western culture known to the Muscovites. Thanks to Mohyla's efforts, to his Academy and the lively contact with Polish culture, the Orthodox of the Ukraine attained a high degree of culture, so that their theologians even dared to polemize with the learned Jesuits. Smotrickij, bishop of Polock, himself educated in a Jesuit school, wrote prior to his adhesion to the union a series of theological treatises in defense of Orthodoxy, while Zachariah Kopystenskij composed two learned dogmatic and polemical works, the *Book of the Faith* and the *Palinodia*. At the Academy the Latin and pro-Western tendency won an ascendancy over the conservative Greek trend, and its members also adopted the scholastic method in their polemical works. One of the most productive polemists was the Rector Goľatovskij (died 1668). In his *Key of Knowledge* he recommended to Orthodox preachers the homiletic art developed by the Jesuits, and found enthusiastic followers in Bishop Lazar Baranovič and Abbot Anthony Radivilovskij.

Other devotees of these new scholastic methods initiated a new tradition in Ukrainian historiography by following the example of Polish historians. One of them, Innocent Gizeľ, wrote a synopsis of Ukrainian history. Considerable progress was also made in Kiev in philology, especially by Lavrentij Zizanij, and this superseded all previous attempts made. On the basis of a Greek grammatical treatise translated into Slavonic in Serbia, Meletij Smotrickij published in 1619 the first Slavonic grammar (*Syntagma*). This was also accepted in 1648 in refashioned form in Muscovy and continued in use through the eighteenth century in Ukrainian and Russian schools. Pamva Berynda composed at the same time the first *Lexicon*, in which he distinguished between words current in the Old Slavonic language and expressions then in popular usage in the Ukraine. Thus were the foundations laid for the development and normalization of the Ukrainian and Russian literary languages.

Great innovations were also introduced into Muscovy from Kiev in the art of poetry. Many of the compositions of the Time of Troubles contained passages in rhymed lines of unequal length terminating in verbs. This practice can be observed in East Slavic literary works from a very early period, but it became particularly developed in the seventeenth century. This presyllabic verse, ignoring the measure of lines and using assonances rather than strict rhymes, is perhaps also connected with the Kievan tradition. It has, however, a close correspondence with Russian oral tradition. Many poems, including comic and satiric verse, were composed in Muscovy in the seventeenth century.

This was also the period when the oral tradition penetrated into the literature, and one can notice for the first time traces of Russian folklore in the writings. A special form of ballad developed on this basis. The chaplain to an English embassy in 1619, Richard James, saved copies of some of these beautiful ballads, now preserved in Oxford.[23] Then appeared a transition form between the written and oral tradition. The most remarkable of these compositions was the *Tale of Woe-Misfortune.*

Under Polish influence the Ukrainians abandoned the Latin metric system, by which some admirers of Horace and Seneca had started to write poems, and accepted the syllabic Polish versification with lines of equal length, a caesura in the middle of the line, and paired feminine rhymes.[24] A great number of odes, eulogies, and panegyrics were composed in the Ukraine according to this system. The master of this new poetic art was a Kievan monk, Simeon of Polock (1629-1680). He first wrote verses in White Russian, Polish, and Latin, but when he had settled in Moscow in 1663, he started to write in Great Russian as it was spoken in Muscovy. He introduced to the Muscovite court the genre of eulogistic and panegyric poetry practiced in the baroque age in Poland and the Ukraine. He also composed odes, poems on motifs derived from contemporary Western collections of stories and anecdotes, and satiric compositions in which he ridiculed some of the manners of Muscovite society. His verses were assembled in two large collections, the *Rhythmologion* and the *Flowery Pleasance.* Simeon also gave proof of his deep theological learning in his *Scepter of Government,* a polemical work against the Old Believers. He introduced into Muscovy a new homiletic method which he learned from the Poles. This he employed in numerous sermons, which were published after his death in two large volumes.

Even in this respect Simeon of Polock manifested a marked superiority over the Muscovite theologian Ivan Nasedka, one of the correctors who was the author of an *Exposition on Luther*. Nasedka was also a poet and ended his theological work with presyllabic verses.

Simeon's Muscovite disciple Silvester Medvedev (1641-1691) continued to compose poetry, generally in a panegyric style. Karion Istomin, a less talented poet, continued this kind of poetic art into the eighteenth century and also employed it for pedagogical purposes, an innovation which found some imitators. Poetry in the so-called "syllabo-tonic" verse, making a regular metrical use of word stress, was further developed in the early eighteenth century by Peter Buslaev, by Theophanes Prokopovič, and especially by Antiokh Kantemir, who was the most sophisticated of the three. With Tret'jakovskij and Lomonosov there began a new period of Russian poetry, that of accented verse.

Another important innovation in Muscovite cultural life was the introduction of the drama. Even this new art came to Moscow primarily from Kiev. In order to vie with the Jesuits, who attracted many people through the dramatic performances given in their schools, the Orthodox Ukrainians started to develop similar representations inspired by the Byzantine mystery of the Passion (*Christus patiens*) dating from the eleventh or twelfth century. In this way numerous religious dramatic works originated in Lwów and Kiev. In their composition the influence of similar Polish productions became increasingly noteworthy.

It was again Simeon of Polock who introduced this Polish and Ukrainian custom into Muscovy. Aware of the extreme hostility of conservative ecclesiastical circles to any entertainments of this kind, he started by adapting an old Byzantine liturgical representation of the three Holy Children in the furnace in his *Comedy on Nebuchadnezzar* and went on to other similar subjects. He thus opened the way for such representations in Muscovite schools and found a zealous follower in Dmitrij Rostovskij, also an Ukrainian, who was the author of lives of the saints. His work *Mineji* provided a more lively and more interesting hagiographic edition of the great work of Makarius. Rostovskij also added to this work material which he found in the popular legends by Peter Skarga and in the Acts of the Saints published by the Jesuits. This work was very widely read in Muscovy, and in it Rostovskij found new material for his dramatic compositions.

The best of these school dramas in syllabic verse was *Saint Vladimir*, composed by Theophanes Prokopovič, professor of rhetoric at the Kievan Academy, which was also played in Moscow at the beginning of the eighteenth century. This work represents marked progress toward a realistic representation of historical events adapted to the tastes of contemporary society.

The transition from this school dramatic art, limited to religious and moralizing subjects, to more secular dramas written in prose was slow. It was prepared by J. G. Gregorij, the director of the theatrical school founded by Alexis. He also started with Biblical subjects, for example, Esther, Tobias, Judith, but his successors J. C. Kunst and O. Fürst were able to introduce on to the Moscow stage dramatic works popular in western Europe. These were adapted to the Russian by translators of the *prikaz* for foreign affairs, and soon Molière's and Corneille's comedies were accepted in Moscow.

Further progress was made at the beginning of the eighteenth century thanks to the initiative of the Princess Natal'ja, the younger sister of Tsar Peter, who not only built a theater in her residence, but also herself composed four plays inspired by Rostovskij's *Lives of the Saints*. However, she also introduced into her theater plays of a secular character. The Academy of Moscow and other schools also started to produce plays of a secular nature. Generally they were adaptations of Western romances made in a naïve and clumsy way.

The popular Russian theater developed on this basis and flourished also in Peter the Great's reign. There is some evidence that the well-known Russian play *Tsar Maximian* is an adaptation of the Czech play on St Dorothy, who was martyred by Maximian, which was very popular in Czech lands during the baroque period. In Russia it became a disguised satire on Peter's marriage with the Lutheran German Catherine.

The introduction of Western romances and novels into Muscovy started in the second half of the seventeenth century from Poland through Kiev. Again Simeon of Polock provided the necessary initiative. He succeeded in arousing the interest of the tsar in the Polish collection of such stories translated from a Latin original by the Polish Jesuit Szymon Wysocki, and the tsar entrusted a monk with the task of making a Russian translation under the title of *The Great Mirror*. Soon a similar medieval collection, *The Deeds of the Romans,* was translated from Polish; it was followed by the *Tale of the Seven Wise Men,* an adaptation of an oriental romance popular in the West and also translated from the Polish. Similar Polish satiric and other compositions were adapted and found many readers.

Romances and novels of Czech, Italian, and Serbian origin also found their way to Moscow either directly or through Poland: *The Prince of the Golden Hair, Prince Bruncvik of Bohemia, Bová Korolevič,* the romance of *Melusine,* the *Emperor Otto,* and many others.

It has already been seen how in the first half of the seventeenth century some attempts were made at the composition of an original story in the lives of Juliana Lazarevskaja and Fedosia Morozova, in the *Story of Sava,* and the *Tale of Woe-Misfortune.* Toward the end of this period several works appeared which can be regarded as the first Russian realistic novels. These were *The Story of the Russian Noble Frol Skobelev,* which had no moralizing tendency, and *The Story of the Merchant Karp Sutulov,* which adapted from the Arabian *Thousand and One Nights* the motif of the merchant's wife who outwitted three of her suitors. These compositions were followed by other romances and novels inspired by foreign literature introduced into Muscovy, but reflecting the time of Peter the Great, when the borders were open. Such were *The Story of the Russian Noble Alexander, The Story of the Sailor Vasilij,* and *The Story of the Russian Merchant John.* All these heroes were shown as travelers in foreign lands, full of life and avid for adventure.[25]

In the development of art,[26] in the seventeenth century the same tendencies can be traced as in the general policy of the new dynasty and in Muscovite literary activity. The artists sought inspiration in the works of art produced under the last Ruriks, but could not remain indifferent to the influence of the baroque, which had become an international style and penetrated Muscovy from Poland through the Ukraine.

This was particularly the case in Muscovite architecture. The most characteristic church built by Ivan IV was that of St. Basil, with its pyramidal character recalling the tower-churches of wooden construction, and its rows of corbeled arches called *kokošniki.* This remained most advanced in its type but inspired some architects. The most striking example of a pyramidal church is that of the Assumption in Uglič, north of Moscow, built in 1628. It has a simple façade, and its three apses recall the peculiar features of the Suzdal'-Vladimir style of the thirteenth century, but the apses and the nave are tent roofed, and it is crowned with three pyramids, which give the church a very harmonious aspect. Another example of a pyramidal church is that in Putniki (Moscow) built in 1652. It has four spires intersected by a belfry. The pyramidal spires are purely decorative. The architect made free use of the *kokošniki,* which give the building a very picturesque look. Unfortunately this church was the last built in the truly Russian style because Nikon forbade the erection of tent-roofed churches with pyramidal spires, declaring that this architecture was contrary to the tradition of the Church. Only in the north of Muscovy could this type of architecture survive.

Another architectural type, developed on the pattern of the wooden churches which lacked columns, was that of the so-called columnless churches. The first church of this kind was that of the Virgin of the Don, a brick structure dating from 1593. It was surmounted by one cupola with *kokošniki* and a pyramid. The church of this kind built in Moscow after the Time of Troubles was that of Rubcovo (1626), which became a model for other ecclesiastical structures in the Moscow area. The decoration on its façade already showed some baroque influences. The new official style was already fully developed in the church of the Georgian Virgin. Its cupolas with *kokošniki* rested on lantern-like decorated drums. The churches of St. Nicholas in Stolpy and in Pyži and that of the Ascension in the Potter's Quarter were variations of the same architectural type. The church of the Trinity at Ostankino near Moscow, a typical columnless church, and that of St. Gregory in Moscow (1679) already have baroque windows and decorations. A highly typical example of a structure built in the Russian style, but with marked baroque influences, was the church of St. Nicholas of the Great Cross, which is no longer standing. Another characteristic of this structure was that the *kokošniki* had almost disappeared. This was becoming general after 1670, when the builders started to use iron instead of lead in roof coverings. At the very end of the seventeenth century the baroque style invaded Muscovy from the Ukraine, where, however, it had failed to produce any remarkable works of art.[27] The difficulty of assimilating Western art to the traditional Russian practice is illustrated by the church of the Miraculous Virgin in Dubrovitsky near Moscow, constructed by Basil Golicyn. This building, called by some art historians an architectural monstrosity, was in strong contrast to the church of the Virgin at Fili near Moscow, built in 1693, which revealed a return to the Russian pyramidal tradition.

Outside Moscow, Rostov, Uglič, and Jaroslavl' can all boast churches built in the Russian tradition. The most beautiful of these structures is the church of St. John the Baptist in Jaroslavl' on the Volga, built in 1687. It followed the basic design of the columnless churches, but was much larger and a jewel of Russian polychrome decoration. It was a purely Muscovite creation, without any baroque influence, with fifteen gilded cupolas and a belfry separated from the church, as was often the case in Russia.

Wooden church architecture did not disappear. It was practiced in the Ukraine, under the influence of the baroque, and in Muscovy, especially in the north where it followed old native traditions. The best specimen of this architecture is the church of the Transfiguration in Kiži, dating from the beginning of the eighteenth century. The Old Believers also continued to build their wooden oratories in the old tradition.

The construction of belfries and towers in the old pyramidal style was permitted by Nikon. They were seldom tent shaped, but rose in several stories. Good specimens of this architecture are provided by the decidedly ornamental towers of the Novodeviči monastery and the Sukharev tower, built by Peter the Great and one of Moscow's landmarks. These towers were built in the baroque style.

Civil architecture also followed principles and forms similar to these wooden structures. The most remarkable wooden building was the castle of Kolomenskoe (rebuilt 1667-1681), which disappeared in the eighteenth century. The most prominent building in stone was the Terem Palace in the Kremlin, built in 1635 by Michael Romanov. The sculptures around the doors and windows present a curious mixture of Italian and oriental motifs. But its essential features seem to reproduce those of wooden constructions. The Teremok, constructed on top of the Terem for the tsar's sons, is a reproduction of the attic of Russian wooden houses. The other palace, the *Potěšnyj Dvorets* (Palace of Pleasure), constructed in 1652 by Alexis, reveals baroque decoration. Alexis also called craftsmen and artists, mainly from Poland, for the decoration of the Kremlin palaces.

Similar tendencies to those in architecture can be observed in painting. The traditional method of painting icons, prescribed in the Stoglav's injunctions, continued to be obligatory and was restated in 1658, but on the other hand timid attempts can be perceived at imitating new patterns and techniques, with which some of the artists had been able to become acquainted. In Moscow the government workshops established by Ivan IV in the armory (*Oružejnaja Palata*) continued to work in the first years of the seventeenth century. Boris Godunov, when still regent, decorated his office in the Faceted Palace (*Granovitaja Palata*) with frescoes made by the same technique and expressing the same ideas as those ordered by Ivan IV for the Kremlin palace. The Stroganov masters [28] also continued to develop further the traditions of the Novgorod school, but they retained some relationship with the Moscow school.

After the disruption of both schools during the Time of Troubles, Tsar Michael, desiring to repair the devastation in the cultural field and to satisfy the demand for icons, saw himself forced to reorganize the workshops in Moscow and to gather artists from all sides. Many painters of the former Stroganov school were thus absorbed into the new Moscow school. The most prominent among its painters were Prokopius Čirin and Nicephorus Savin. Their icons revealed a more humanistic spirit and more naturalism, although their authors were still anxious to remain within the strict rules governing icon painting. Here may be detected the first inroads of Western art into traditional icon painting. Besides westernizing tendencies, which were constantly increasing, Eastern, almost Chinese, elements can be detected, especially in the icon of St. Alexis. Icons depicting the Creed and the Lord's Prayer show that the artists liked to abandon simple patterns and to venture into a complicated iconography, betraying a tendency to forget the old rules and to use new techniques.

The most able and most daring of the tsar's painters was Simeon Ušakov (1626-1686). A remarkably good designer, he first made designs for embroideries, banners, coins, and gold and silver instruments, and showed in these earliest Russian prints that he was familiar with Western engraving art. At the same time he painted icons for Moscow churches in a style similar to that of the late Stroganov school. He became bolder and his icon of the Annunciation, framed by twelve scenes from the Akathistos Hymn, created a sensation in Moscow. This had innovations transcending the traditional style in the richness and variety of its architectural motifs, costumes, and furniture. The physiognomies of the persons were lifelike and full of movement, the tsar and the tsaritsa were portrayed as St Alexis and Mary the Egyptian, while unusual scenes depicted, for example, the siege of Constantinople. Christ's image on Veronica's veil (the Vernicle) is rather a painting than an icon and reveals the technique of Dutch painting of the sixteenth century, of which Ušakov might have seen some examples in Moscow's sloboda. His pupils continued to paint in this new style, which was far removed from the usual Muscovite austerity.

How daring even these modest attempts at the imitation of Western technique were can be gathered from the hostile attitude of Patriarch Nikon to Western art. He ordered the confiscation and destruction of icons made in the Western style, mostly imported. His adversary Avvakum also uttered violent criticisms of the westernizing painters.

The prospects seemed better in secular painting. Foreign portraits appeared in Muscovy during the Time of Troubles, and the first Romanov tsars seem to have favored portrait painting. Decorative painters were needed in government service, and several foreign painters were engaged to direct decorative work and to instruct native artists. Unfortunately no prominent Western master ventured as far as Moscow since they found appreciation for their services in western Europe. So the Russian artists of the seventeenth century had to content themselves with the samples of Western style and technique which they found in the illustrated Bible of John Piscator published in 1650. This contained about three hundred engravings and was very popular in Muscovy. The frescoes executed toward the end of the century in some Volga cities, especially in Jaroslavl', show a marked influence of the engraving in Piscator's Bible.

This was promising progress, but the Muscovite artists were unable to go further, finding no more Western incentives at home. Only when they were given the possibility of going abroad and studying Western art could they master the modern techniques.

NOTES

1. On Dutch and English merchants in Russia, see the well-documented study by G. I. Lubimenko, *The Struggle of the Dutch with the English* (see Bibl.).

2. Cf. below, p. 537.

3. Cf. F. Dvornik, *Byzantine Political Ideas in Kievan Russia,* Dumbarton Oaks Papers, vols. 9-10 (1956).

4. A complete Russian bibliography on Nikon is discussed in the most recent book on the patriarch by M. V. Zyzykin, *Patriarch Nikon* (Warsaw, 1931), 2 vols., vol. 1: pp. 295-365. The following works deserve special mention: P. Nihalevskij's studies in *Khristianskie Čtenija,* 1881-1890; N. Kapterev, *Patriarkh Nikon i ego protivniki* (Sergiev Posad, 1913); P. S. Smirnov, *Istorija Russk. raskola,* 2nd ed., St. Petersburg, 1895. Important documents on Nikon are translated by W. Palmer, *The Patriarch and the Tsar* (see Bibl.).

5. A good review of religious books printed in Moscow in the sixteenth and seventeenth centuries will be found in P. Pascal, *La Vie de l'archiprêtre Avvakum,* 2nd ed. (Paris, 1938), pp. 221-226.

6. They included works of Homer, Hesiod, Aeschylus, Plutarch, Thucydides, Demosthenes and Byzantine chronicles, lexika, and grammars—literary treasures which were being collected and studied with great zeal in Western lands. Seventeenth-century Moscow, however, had no understanding for such profane works. On this mission, cf. the interesting notice based on a newly discovered manuscript at Mount Athos by M. Laskaris in *Byzantion,* 20 (1958), pp. 543-45.

7. A complete bibliography on Avvakum and the Old Believers will be found in P. Pascal's study, *Avvakum et les débuts du raskol* (see Bibl.). The most important material on Avvakum and the schism was published in nine volumes by M. Subbotin in Moscow (1874-1890). See Bibl. on translations of Avvakum's *Life.*

8. The false document was first used in Novgorod in 1497 by the Dominican Benjamin, who had composed, at the request of Archbishop Gennadij, the *Slovo kratko* ("A Short Treatise") in defense of Church property. The Latin monk also used other Latin documents favorable to the idea of the superiority of the spiritual power over the temporal. On Benjamin's activity see the study by A. Sedel'nikov in the *Izvestija* of the Division for Russian Language and Literature of the S.S.S.R. Academy, vol. 30 (1925), pp. 205-225.

9. It seems that Makarij, when archbishop of Novgorod, had also introduced the practice of the Palm Sunday procession, during which the governor of the city held the bridle of the horse on which the archbishop rode in imitation of Christ. The *Donatio* mentions that Constantine had thus honored Pope Silvester. From Novgorod this practice was transplanted to Moscow when Makarij became patriarch. The tsars honored their patriarchs in this way on Palm Sunday until the abolition of the patriarchate. The authenticity of the *Donatio* began to be questioned in Moscow during the reign of Peter the Great. Cf. the basic study on the Greek and Slavonic translation of the *Donatio* by A. Pavlov in *Vizant. Vremennik,* 3 (1896), pp. 18-82 ("Podloženaja tsarstvenaja gramota . . .").

10. These important documents have been published in an English translation by W. Palmer in vol. 1 of his work on Nikon (see Bibl.). See the quotation on p. 190. Nikon's answers have been published only fragmentarily and in Russian. The best Russian publication on the relations between Nikon and Alexis is that by V. Kapterev, *Patriarkh Nikon i Car Alexej* (Sergiev Posad, 1909, 1912, 2 vols.).

11. See the translation from the Slavonic text in F. Dvornik, *Byzantine Political Ideas,* p. 83.

12. Nikon's attitude in this matter is often misunderstood. H. T. Florinsky, for example, in his handbook—one of the best in English—*Russia, A History and an Interpretation*, vol. 1 (New York, 1953), p. 290, thinks that the theory of "the supremacy of the Church over the State" is a Byzantine theory; this interpretation is far from the truth.

13. Cf. above, p. 375.

14. See the documentation and bibliography in G. Ostrogorsky's study "Das Projekt" (Bibl.).

15. Because they refused to accept the priests ordained after 1666, the radicals among the Old Believers dispensed with the Mass and the sacraments, contenting themselves with baptism and public confession. They are called *bezpopovtsy* (priestless). The *popovtsy*, recognizing the validity of ordinations after 1666, organized themselves into a special body with priests who had adhered to them. Since 1846 they have had a regular hierarchy established by a bishop from Bosnia, and this was recognized by the state in 1881. The persecution stopped only in the second half of the eighteenth century, but started again under Nicholas I (1825-1855). Official tolerance was, however, granted to them in 1874. Both groups split into sects, which are particularly numerous among the priestless group.

16. A résumé in Russian of reports by foreign visitors on Muscovy in the sixteenth and seventeenth centuries is given by V. Ključevskij: *Skazanija inostrancev o Moskovskom gosudarstve* (Moscow, 1916). The author also gives a full bibliography of editions of their works in Russian.

17. This practice was suspended by the Council of 1666-1667, again on the recommendation of the Greeks.

18. The best and latest Russian publication on Ukrainian influences on religious and cultural life in Muscovy is that by K. V. Kharlampovič, *Malorossijskoe vlijanie na velikorusskuju cerkovnuju žizn'* (Kazan', 1914), vol. I, pp. 1-456 on the seventeenth century. Complete bibliography in Russian. Cf. the excellent survey of the first Western influences on Muscovy during the reigns of Ivan IV, Boris Godunov, and the first Romanovs by S. F. Platonov, *Moskva i Zapad* (Berlin, 1926).

19. The basic, although unfinished, work on Mohyla and his disciples is that by S. T. Golubev: *Piotr Mogila i ego spodvižniki*, 2 vols. (Kiev, 1883, 1897). The same author also published a study on the Academy of Kiev in the seventeenth and eighteenth centuries, *Kievskaja akad. v konce 17. i načale 18. st.* (Kiev, 1901). For a complete Russian bibliography on Mohyla and the influence of the Kievan Academy on Russian theological teaching and thinking see G. Florovskij, *Puti russkago bogoslovija* ("Development of Russian Theology," Paris, 1937). See also his study in *Kyrios* (see Bibl. to Ch. XX).

20. On Russian literature of this period see vol. II, part I of *Istorija Russkoj Literatury* (Moscow, 1948). On editions of works here mentioned see the detailed bibliographical indications in A. Stender-Petersen's *Geschichte der russischen Literatur* (see Bibl.), vol. I, pp. 452-458.

21. See above, p. 486. Platonov's edition and criticism.

22. The latest study on Križanić and his political ideas and views on history was published by B. D. Dacjuk: *Jurij Križanić, očerk političeskikh i istoričeskikh vzgljadov* (Moscow, 1946). Cf. above, pp. 427, 433, 434.

23. On the songs of R. James's manuscript and other historical songs, see the well-documented study by C. Stief (see Bibl.).

24. On the presyllabic and syllabic verse and on the further development of

Russian versification, see B. O. Unbegaun's book (see Bibl.) with complete bibliography. Cf. also R. Jakobson's studies (see Bibl.) on the origin of Slavonic popular verse.

25. Full information on Russian translations during the Muscovite period is given by A. I. Sobolevskij, *Perevodnaja liter. Moskovskoj Rusi XIV-XVII vv.* (St. Petersburg, 1903).

26. The following are the most important works in Russian on seventeenth-century art: I. Grabar, ed. *Istorija russkago iskusstva* (Moscow, 1909 ff.), vols. III-IV (Architecture); vol. VI (Painting); A. I. Uspensky, *Carskie ikonopiscy i živopiscy XVII v.* (Moscow, 1910-1916), 4 vols.; A. I. Nekrasov: *Drevne-russkoe izobrazitel'noe iskusstvo* (Moscow, 1937). See also Nekrasov's work on early Russian architecture (*Očerki po istorii drevnerusskago zodčestva XI-XVII veka* (Moscow, 1936).

27. It is said that Napoleon I admired the baroque church of the Assumption in Pokrovskij, built in 1696-1699, and ordered special measures to prevent its destruction during the War of 1812. Unfortunately, in 1714 Peter the Great stopped all construction outside Petrograd so as to speed up the embellishment of the new capital. Muscovite baroque architecture was therefore arrested before it could fully develop.

28. Cf. above, p. 318.

Chapter XX

IMPERIAL RUSSIA AND THE SLAVIC WORLD

Peter's youth—Azov venture, trip abroad, first reforms—Intervention in Poland, foundation of St. Petersburg, victory at Poltava—Defeat on the Prut stops Peter's progress in the south—Victories on the Baltic, birth of imperial Russia—Alliance with Prussia against Poland—Progress in the Far East, in the north, and on the Caspian Sea—Unfortunate dynastic complications—Conception of centralized state with an absolute ruler transformed through Western ideas—Utilitarian conception of the state in Peter's reforms—Reasons leading Peter to a harmful Church reorganization—Peter's theoretician Theophanes, his political philosophy—The Holy Synod a Protestant consistory?—Slow transformation of the synod into a bureaucratic institution, vain efforts at reform—The tradition of the Ruriks and first Romanovs continued by Peter's successors, Russia fails to save Silesia for Bohemia—The darkest days of the Czech people under Maria Theresa and Joseph II—Prussia and Russia make an end to Polish independence—Catherine II's "Greek scheme" a failure—French Revolution stifles Catherine's interest in new social and political ideas—Paul I's "iron curtain," Alexander I returns to reaction and despotism—The Crimean War, reforms of Alexander II dissatisfy Herzen and Bakunin—Reaction under Alexander III and Nicholas II, Ključevskij's prophecy, revolution of 1917—Imperial Russia, Polish aspirations, the Duchy of Warsaw, the Polish kingdom—National reawakening of the Slavic nationalities in Austria—The revolution of 1848, the All-Slavic idea—Imperial Russia and the liberation of the Rumanians, Greeks, and southern Slavs—The new regime realizing dreams of the Ruriks and of Peter the Great

The short survey of the happenings in Muscovy during the reigns of the first Romanovs shows that the "splendid isolation" of Moscow from the rest of the European world was slowly disappearing. The impact of

Western influences on Russian social and cultural life was becoming irresistible, and the tempo of Muscovite assimilation to the rest of Europe was gradually increasing. The westernization of Muscovy had thus started not only under Peter the Great, as is often believed; it was prepared by the changes introduced by his father Alexis and his brother Fedor.

This tempo needed some acceleration, but the impetuous half brother of Fedor transformed it into a whirlwind which swept away most of Muscovite old traditions and brought into Muscovy a new atmosphere, which, however, appeared too strong to many of his subjects and unhealthy to some good Russian traditions.

In many ways, Peter (1689-1725) [1] was continuing the work of Ivan IV. In reality, the growth and the character of both rulers is similar. They both had lost their fathers when only three years old and had spent their boyhood in the whirl of violence and intrigue originating from the jealousy of rivaling relatives and courtiers, who neglected utterly the interests of the young heirs. The memory of this bitter experience of their boyhood influenced the formation of their character and made them hostile to the old aristocracy. This explains the roughness of their manner and the sudden angry outbursts which led them to cruel and vengeful actions against their real or supposed enemies. Both were denied a systematic education and preferred to live in the countryside, far from court life poisoned by the heinous maneuvers of rival political coteries; both also looked for friends and support among the lower social strata of Muscovy.

Ivan IV supplemented the lack of good teachers by his private study of Russian literature, which enabled him to become one of the most cultured Muscovite literary men of his time. Peter, however, lacked Ivan's interest in the humanities, and his spelling remained poor in his letters and documents. His mother was unable to give him any support in his spiritual growth, and Peter spent his time in manual work and military exercises, choosing his companions from soldiers and adventurers living in the foreign quarter called the *Nemeckaja sloboda*. There he found the Dutchman Timmerman, who taught him the principles of mathematics, the French Swiss Lefort, who became his favorite and induced him to visit foreign countries, the Scots general Patrick Gordon, his able military adviser. The Dutchman Karsten Brandt introduced Peter to the art of shipbuilding and nourished Peter's love of navigation, stressing the importance of the navy for the modern state.

It was Peter's new friends, the foreign officers with their regiments, who stood by Peter in August 1689, when Sophia, who had shown her intention to get rid of Peter and to reign as tsaritsa, was dethroned and her favorites handed over to the victorious party. It was a pity that Basil Golicyn, Sophia's right-hand man, who had done the most for the westernization of Muscovy, had to be exiled and thus could not work for the realization of Peter's reforms. His place was taken by his distant cousin and rival, the Prince Boris Golicyn, who held the reins of the government while Peter continued to play his "games of Mars and Neptune" with his foreign friends, accepting their customs in clothing and behavior, indulging with them in riotous drinking, and organizing displays of crass buffoonery and horseplay. The marriage with Eudoxia Lopukhin, arranged by his mother in 1689, proved unsatisfactory, although she bore him a son, Alexis, and another son who did not survive. Estranged from his wife, who was too conservative for his taste, Peter found a mistress in the *sloboda*.

The war with Turkey [2] interrupted this period of revelry and opened new vistas to the young tsar. Invited by his allies, the Poles, and their allies, the Austrians, and pressed by the raids of the Turkish vassals, the Crimean Tatars, and by the rising of pro-Turkish sympathies among the Cossacks, Peter decided to make a diverting attack against the Turkish fortress of Azov, which had already been in the hands of the Don Cossacks for a short time (1637-1642). The first, and unsuccessful, attack showed him the necessity of having a fleet to cut off the city from supplies by ship. With the help of Austrian engineers, Peter created a large shipyard at Voronež on the Don, and thanks to his new fleet and the military advice of Gordon, Azov was taken in 1696. Soon his new naval station at Taganrog harbored fourteen warships, built and manned mostly by foreign masters and seamen, and in 1699 he had the satisfaction of learning about the distressed astonishment of the Turks when the largest of his ships, carrying his envoy, entered the Golden Horn. For the first time, a Muscovite vessel had appeared in the Black Sea.

The first military and naval venture convinced Peter of the necessity of building a large fleet in order to open the Black Sea for Russia, and of creating an alliance with the Western powers—Austria, England, Denmark, Holland, Venice, and the Papacy—against the Turks and their Tatar allies. He needed specialists in Russia for this new naval plan, and after silencing with rough measures certain elements discontented with his westernizing manners, he went on his first excursion to the West (1697). He reached Amsterdam through Riga, Königsberg, and Hannover, then went to London, and returned through Holland, Vienna, Prague, and Cracow with hundreds of foreign specialists hired to work in Russia. The main goal of this journey was to get thoroughly acquainted with the art of shipbuilding and navigation. The tsar worked himself for several months in Holland and in London in shipyards as a carpenter.

The return was speeded up by news of a new revolt of the conservative elements in Moscow, led by the *strel'tsy*. The revolt was crushed with unprecedented cruelty, this suppression marking also the definite end of old Muscovy with its conservative elements. Peter started the westernization of his land with shaving off the venerable beards of his nobles. This gesture illustrates the rudeness and impatience with which the transformation was made of backward Muscovy into a more modern state with a standing army, a navy and commercial fleet, basic industries, a more effective administration, and sounder finances, favoring education at home and abroad. The essentials of this transformation were put into effect during the three years of feverish activity from 1698 to 1700.

During these years, Peter rightly regarded peaceful conditions on all fronts essential for the success of his reforms. His plan of an anti-Turkish alliance miscarried, only Venice being ready to continue the fight. Austria negotiated her own peace of Karlovci in 1699, securing good conditions for herself, but forgetting to support the interests of her new Russian ally. Only in 1700 was Peter able to conclude his peace with Turkey, securing for himself Azov and Taganrog, the rights of pilgrimage to Jerusalem for his subjects, and the more important right of keeping a resident minister in the sultan's capital.

In the meantime, Muscovy was enabled to reinforce its position in the lands of its western neighbor and former rival, Poland-Lithuania, and to secure an ally for the realization of Peter's dream of opening a window for Moscow on the Baltic Sea. The election of Sobieski's successor to the Polish throne in 1697 resulted in rivalry between the French candidate, the Prince de Conti—chosen by a great majority of the nobles—and Frederick Augustus, Elector of Saxony—elected by a minority. Peter, opposed to a candidate presented by France, an ally of Turkey, used threats to force the Polish nobility to accept Augustus II of Saxony as their legitimate king (1697-1733).

Augustus II was an ambitious man. Neglecting the interests of his kingdom, which needed peace, he concluded an alliance with Denmark and with Peter against Sweden, hoping to recover Livonia. The young king of Sweden, Charles XII (1697-1718), proved, however, a very able general. He first forced a collapse of Denmark and destroyed Peter's army at Narva, but instead of marching against Moscow, he concentrated his forces against Poland. In 1702, most of the country, with Warsaw and Cracow, was in his hands, and in 1704 he chose his own candidate for the Polish throne, Stanislas Leszczyński. Then he turned against Saxony and in 1705 forced Augustus to renounce the Polish throne.

Peter profited from the breathing spell resulting from the Swedish campaign in Poland and worked feverishly on the reorganization of his army—he reconstructed his artillery, most of which had been lost at Narva, erected new ironworks, especially in the Urals, and more powder mills and cloth mills for the army, exacted new taxes, and collected new recruits, effecting much of the above with forced labor. His superhuman efforts soon brought results. His reorganized army and newly created small Baltic navy had some success on the Neva River and Lake Ladoga, which enabled Peter to lay the basis for his "darling" foundation of St. Petersburg (1703). Yurjev (Dorpat) was captured, and Narva stormed (1704). The detachments sent to Poland were, however, unable to stop the Swedish successes, and after securing his position, Charles XII decided to march against Muscovy in order to dethrone Peter.

This was the most perilous moment for the young tsar. The enforcement of the unpopular reforms and the weight of the taxation had provoked discontent everywhere. A revolt had broken out among the Don Cossacks, led by Bulavin; and the hetman of the Ukrainian Cossacks, Ivan Mazeppa (1687-1709), made a last attempt at securing political independence for the Polish and Russian Ukraine with the help of the Swedes. Peter intensified the activity to a feverish point on all fronts. The revolt of Bulavin was suppressed, and Peter's intimate collaborator, Menšikov, of humble origin, dealt quickly with Mazeppa's followers, pacified the Ukraine, and destroyed the headquarters of the Zaporožian Cossacks, who had joined Charles XII. Deprived of the support of the Cossacks, the Swedish king was utterly defeated in the battle of Poltava (1709). Most of his army was captured, and he himself, with Mazeppa, took refuge in Turkey.

This signal victory laid solid foundations for the emergence of imperial Russia. The former alliance against Sweden with Poland and Denmark was revived by the addition of Brandenburg and Hannover, Russia thus appearing on the scene of German politics. The reinstallation of Augustus II on the Polish throne marked a definite reverse in the balance of power in Eastern Europe. Peter was the real master of Poland and kept even Livonia after conquering it, although he promised to hand it over to Augustus II. Even the principality of Courland, although a Polish fief, remained virtually in Peter's hands because he married his niece Anne to the duke and kept his garrison there after the duke's sudden death. Moreover, Peter captured Viborg and occupied Finnish Karelia. Riga was taken, and Estonia conquered. Russia was firmly established on the Baltic, St. Petersburg was secured, and Russian vessels cruised for the first time in the Baltic, which had been so far closed to them. Peter inaugurated in the north a policy which has been faithfully and stubbornly followed by all his successors and renewed by the rulers of the USSR. It was the new Russian army, equipped with modern weapons by the immense labor of its chief commander and by immense sacrifices borne by the whole nation, which had ensured this unexpected triumph.

Peter opened new vistas for the policies of his successors also in the south. The refugee king, with the Khan of the Crimea and France, was inciting the Turks to open hostilities with the victorious Peter. The tsar, seeing that a new conflict with Turkey was approaching, looked for allies among the Christian subjects of the sultan. He tried first to win over the Rumanian principalities, Moldavia and Wallachia, which were under Turkish supremacy. He won over Cantemir, the hospodar of Moldavia, but Brancovan of Wallachia was more hesitant.

At the same time Peter opened the way for the Russian penetration into the Balkans when he issued in 1711 a proclamation to the Balkan Orthodox to rise against the Turks. He had in mind not the Greeks—the relations with their religious leaders, so frequent under Alexis, had subsided in Moscow because of the pro-Turkish sentiments of the Phanariots —but the Serbians and Montenegrins. Like his father, Peter had some relations with their ecclesiastical leaders, who were always eager to throw off the Turkish yoke. Moreover, they were alarmed by the progress of the Austrians and feared Austrian attempts at a forced union with Rome; they therefore appealed to the Orthodox tsar for succor. Peter had even recruited Slavic sailors from the Adriatic coast to serve in his navy, and one of them, Savva of Ragusa, was sent to the Balkans as his political agent. The plan was hastily conceived, and only the Montenegrins under their prince-bishop Daniel responded eagerly to the invitation. The catastrophic defeat suffered by Peter on the Prut River (1711) from the Turks made a sudden end to all such plans. Peter was forced to return Azov and Taganrog to the sultan with his new navy and had to promise to abstain from intervention in Poland and give free passage to Charles XII on his return to Sweden. All of Peter's grandiose projects in the south were thus ruined, but were not forgotten by his successors. He showed the way for Russian expansion toward the Crimea and the Azov and Black seas, and he was the first who appealed to the South Slavs for insurrection and declared his readiness to become their liberator. The idea that the tsars were protectors of all Orthodox Christians, accepted already by his father, was thus revived, and the interest in the development of the Balkans never ceased to influence Russian foreign policy.

Peter turned toward the north, the main object of his interests. Profiting by the absence of Charles XII, he completed the occupation of Livonia, Estonia, and Ingria (Ingermanland), with Kronstadt, which he fortified in order to increase the security of St. Petersburg, and invaded Finland and conquered the whole country, although he determined not to keep it. In the meantime his army operated also in northern Germany, helping his allies to deprive the Swedes of all their possessions there, which they had acquired in the peace of Westphalia. He had endless worries with his allies—Saxony, Poland, Denmark, Prussia, Hannover—who were jealous of each other, letting the Russians do most of the fighting and trying to keep the spoils for themselves. When he gave his niece Catherine in marriage to the Duke of Mecklenburg, the tyrannical and uneducated Karl Leopold—he did so against the advice of his friends and allies—he was suspected of desiring to obtain a permanent foothold in Germany, and George I of Hannover, as king of England, was not pleased with the growing influence of Russia in the Baltic. Peter, anxious to finish the costly war, even visited Paris in 1717, trying to win France, which supported Sweden, over to his cause.

Only after the death of Charles XII was the protracted northern war ended. The allies abandoned Peter and came in 1720 to an agreement with Sweden, according to which Hannover retained Verden and Prussia retained Stettin with western Pomerania and the islands of Wollin and Usedom, after promising Sweden a monetary compensation. Denmark obtained freedom from customs duties in the Sound. Peter, left alone and threatened with the alliance between Sweden and Great Britain, remained intrepid and was rewarded in 1721 by the Swedish capitulation. The Treaty of Nystadt assured him the possession of Livonia, Estonia, Ingria, part of Karelia with Viborg, and a number of Baltic islands. He returned Finland and promised Sweden compensation for the lost territories. Thus Peter had realized the dream of Ivan IV.

Russia was firmly established on the Baltic as a great power and was determined to stay there forever. Peter won definitively a prominent place in European history for his country. The acceptance of the imperial title, proposed by the senate after the triumphal reception of the victorious tsar in Moscow, gave the proper expression to this new status of Russia and marked again the realization of the desire of Ivan IV, who had vainly insisted on the equality of the tsarist and imperial title.[3]

Then Peter turned against Augustus II of Poland, who had fallen out with him and who hoped to be able, with the help of the Emperor Charles VI (1711-1740) and King George I of Britain (1714-1727), to establish in Poland a hereditary monarchy, strengthened with an increase of royal power and backed with a standing army. It was too late. Peter, who still held the principality of Courland as a pawn, concluded a treaty with Frederick William I of Prussia (which had become a kingdom in 1701), who was also interested in weakening Poland. Siding with the discontented Polish nobles opposed to the absolutist policies of Augustus, both allies insisted that the old free elective constitution of Poland with all privileges of the nobility, including the right of veto of any member of the assembly, should be preserved. Poland was to be kept weak and disunited.

Although Augustus himself had already broached, before attacking

Sweden, the idea of ceding some Polish territory to his neighbors and although his Prussian ally was very much in favor of a partition, Peter did not plant any diminution of Polish territory, contenting himself with maintaining Poland under strong Russian influence with all means possible.

He found a good pretext for his interventions in the internal affairs of Poland in the Polish-Russian treaty of 1686, which guaranteed the Orthodox in Poland the free exercise of their religion. On the pretext of defending the Orthodox against the Catholics and the Uniats, Peter installed in Poland a representative charged with dealing with disputes between the three confessions and with complaints of the Orthodox. A particularly welcome opportunity for energetic intervention was offered to Peter in 1724. The excesses of some Protestants against the Jesuit college in Toruń (Thorn) were punished by the execution of a number of Protestants, a rare incident in Poland. This provoked great concern in Europe, and Peter profited from it by renewing his alliance with Prussia, asking for the punishment of the responsible men of the "massacre," and guaranteeing with Prussia the rights of Polish religious minorities. He handed to his successors a weapon which they could use with profit at any time, and he thus prepared the way for the partition of Poland, too hampered by the threat of intervention to realize any reform in its political life.

Although involved so profoundly in promoting Russian interests in the south and in the north, Peter did not neglect the Far East. He abstained from challenging the power of the Chinese Manchu dynasty, which was then at its apogee after the reconquest of Mongolia, but he initiated the conquest of Kamčatka and annexed the Kuril Islands. At his invitation, Behring made his first Arctic expedition and discovered the straits still perpetuating his name. This was the beginning of Russian expansion in Alaska, which continuing southward to stop short of San Francisco. He made also a fruitless attempt at direct commercial connection with India.

There was another way to India and China, through Central Asia and Persia, over which the caravans traveled transporting silk and spices. The English and the Dutch had tried several times to reach this trade route, and Ivan IV had wanted to secure this trade for Muscovite merchants. Peter attempted to reach this route by two ways, from Siberia and from Astrakhan'. The four expeditions from Siberia into the Central Asian steppes (1714-1722) found no gold, as was hoped, but Russian progress was further advanced, Omsk was founded, and closer relations with the Kazaks and Kalmyks were knit.

The attempt at extending Russian supremacy over the khanates of Khiva and Bokhara on the Oxus River, isolated from Muscovy by a desert, did not succeed. Asked by the Khan of Khiva for protection from hostile Bokhara, Peter sent there a large expeditionary force with the aim of subduing both Khanates and exploring the road to India (1716-1717). The Russians found, however, a new, unfriendly khan in Khiva, and after initial success, the expedition was trapped by the native army and almost all of its members were massacred.

When preparing this expedition, Peter dispatched his favorite Volyn'-skij as envoy to the Persian shah. The envoy not only concluded a commercial treaty with Persia, but entered also into closer relations with the Armenians, who played an important role in the silk trade, and with the Georgians and brought important information on the internal weakness of Persia to light.

Volyn'skij was appointed governor of Astrakhan' as observer of the developments on the Caspian coasts and in Persia. Taking as pretexts the outrages committed against Muscovite merchants by some tribes nominally subject to Persia and the deposition of the shah by the revolting Afghans, Peter sailed from Astrakhan', sending his cavalry by land, to the Terek River and occupied Derbent, his first objective, an important commercial and strategic center. He did this fearing that Turkey might profit from the anarchy in Persia to advance toward the Caspian Sea to gain control of the silk trade. His hope of occupying Tiflis with the help of friendly Georgians and Armenians was not fulfilled, and he had to retreat to the Terek. Undismayed by this setback, Peter sent another detachment to occupy the Persian port of Rešt. In 1723 Baku was seized, and a treaty was concluded with the shah according to which Peter was left in possession of the Persian Caspian lands in return for the promise of protection against the shah's enemies. The appearance of the Turks in Georgia prevented Peter from extending his influence in the Caucasus. An agreement was reached in 1724, leaving the coastal lands in Peter's hands and Georgia under Turkish supremacy.

Peter, after his experiences with Turkey, abstained from inciting the two Orthodox nations to insurrection as he had done with the South Slavs, although Armenian and Georgian princes and ecclesiastics had already been in touch with the Orthodox tsars for almost a century. But even here he inaugurated a policy which was to be followed by his successors.

In one vital matter Peter had failed his nation—in not securing an undisputed successorship. His marital relations with his first wife Eudoxia were very short. He forced her to become a nun and married secretly his second mistress Catherine, of obscure Lithuanian origin, at the most perilous time of his career; he solemnized this marriage in 1712. Catherine proved to be the ideal wife for Peter, and his letters to her betray a surprisingly tender side of his character, which one would have hardly expected from a man of his temper. Unfortunately, the second boy which his first wife bore him died soon after his birth—Peter did not even find time to assist at the funeral—and five sons of Catherine died also in infancy, so that only Alexis, his first-born, and three daughters were left.

Peter, however, neglected the education of Alexis, and the son became completely estranged from his father, from whom he differed very much in character. Alexis disliked all his father's reforms and did not hide his intention to suppress them and to rule in the old conservative manner. Peter married him to Charlotte, princess of Brunswick, who bore him a son, Peter. The tsar, fearing the destruction of his reforms, insisted that Alexis, who became more and more identified with the opposition, composed of conservative nobles and clergy, should either resign his right to the succession or retire to a monastery. Alexis, in deadly fear of his father, fled and took refuge in Austria. He was lured back by Peter's emissaries, who promised him pardon, and was deprived of the succession, accused of intrigues against the tsar, and condemned to death. Before the tsar could confirm this sentence, Alexis died in prison.

Peter was aware of the vital problems of the succession, and he issued in 1722 a decree declaring that the sovereign could name during his lifetime whomsoever he wished as his successor. Moreover, he had Catherine crowned as empress in 1724, indicating his probable intention that she should reign during the minority of the only Romanov, Alexis' little son, Peter. However, he neglected to make use of his own decree. In marrying his niece Anne to the Duke of Courland, his son to a German princess, his other niece Catherine to the Duke of Mecklenburg, his daughter Anne to the Duke of Holstein, Peter broke with the two-hundred-year-old tradition that no Muscovite princess should marry a foreigner; this custom became a rule, for all rulers of his dynasty who succeeded him, but one, married German princesses. He introduced, however, a foreign element into the life of the Russian court and into the upbringing of the scions of the dynasty which was bound to have its influence on Russian foreign relations and the mentality of some rulers.

In spite of these uncertainties, the succession to the imperial throne was kept in dynastic lines—although these lines were considerably weakened—in spite of rivalries between the old and new aristocracy. The latter, thanks to Menšikov and Peter's guard regiments, won and proclaimed Peter's wife, Catherine I (1725-1727), tsaritsa although she lacked the qualities of a ruler. Menšikov was the real ruler, as he was also during the short reign of the boy Tsar Peter II (1727-1730).

Anna, duchess of Courland, was also accepted (1730-1740), and met no serious opposition although she preferred to appoint German nobles from the Baltic regions to the highest positions. She was succeeded by

Peter's daughter, Elizabeth (1741-1762), the most able of Peter's immediate successors. Peter III (1762), son of Peter's daughter Anne, was a German prince by his education and sentiment. Fortunately, his wife, Sophia of Anhalt-Zerbst, although a German and a Lutheran, became a Russian by conviction and also Orthodox, and as Catherine II (1762-1796) inaugurated a new period in Russian history, continuing Peter's policies and completing the europeanization of Russia.

The succession of six rulers who could have been regarded by strict criteria as unqualified to rule over Russia shows that the idea of a centralized Russian state, ruled by an absolute monarch inheriting his right as a member of a dynasty, was firmly imbedded in the Russian mentality. Also, it was not disputed by other rulers with whom Russia was in contact because this was at that time the only political system accepted everywhere, with the exception of Poland.

Even in this respect, Peter contributed to the assimilation of old Muscovite political ideas to those of the rest of Europe. He was not a thinker and did not care about political speculation, but his practical mind and secular taste made him receptive to the utilitarian conception of the state which was then generally discussed and accepted in the rest of Europe and with which he had become acquainted during his travels outside Russia.

It should be remembered that the Muscovite conception of the absolute theocratic monarchy, inherited from Byzantium, had experienced some slight changes already during the reign of Peter's father and brother. The incentives to such changes came naturally from Poland, where political speculation was particularly in vogue. The Kievan Ukrainian scholars were the natural transmitters of these ideas. Simeon of Polock, for example, taught that the state and the power of the rulers originated not only from God's will—this is the Byzantine tradition—but also from the natural desire of men to form a society, which cannot exist without a chieftain. The ruler should thus care not only for the spiritual welfare of his subjects, but also for their common material good. Simeon thus depicts his ideal ruler not only in the colors used by the authors of the Byzantine mirrors of princes, but also in traits which recall Aristotle's writings and scholastic and contemporary speculations. Stephen Javorskij was, in his courses given at the Kievan Academy, even more influenced by Aristotle and Latin scholastic writers when he discussed the duty of the ruler to establish his relations with his subjects on the notion of justice.

Other contemporary Western ideas on the ruler and the role of the state, based on natural law, ideas which had been promoted by the humanists and by the reformers, were infiltrating slowly into Muscovy, also through translations of certain contemporary writings made from the Polish language on politics. There existed, for example, a Russian translation of the *Secret of Secrets*, attributed wrongly to Aristotle, which was very popular among the Judaizers, the first heretic movement in Muscovy. *Aristotle's Economics* of the Polish commentator on Aristotle, Sebastian Petricius, and the *Common Points on the Institution of Princes* by the German Lorichius were also translated into Russian in the seventeenth century. Even more influence might have been exercised in Moscow by the translation of the Polish political philosopher Frycz Modrzewski's treatise on the republic, also probably made there in the seventeenth century. There it is said that the power of kings is established for the happiness of the subjects and that the rulers are also subject to the law, which should be equal for all. This treatise revealed to the Russian reader many other principles so far not discussed in Moscow.

We must not forget that Križanić had already tried to reconcile certain ideas on rulership discussed by the scholastics in the West with the Russian theocratic views of the absolute ruler. His polemic with political ideas familiar to the Protestants indicates that such ideas were not unknown in Muscovy in the time of Alexis.[4]

Ordin-Naščokin, a prominent statesman of the reign of Alexis, seems to have been acquainted with some of these new ideas. Although stressing Moscow as the center of Orthodoxy, he identified the absolute ruler's welfare with the welfare of the state. This utilitarian concept can be traced also in other writings.[5]

When we have this in mind, we will find it natural that these new notions on the state were known already to the young Tsar Fedor, educated by Simeon of Polock. This is particularly evident from the introduction to his decree suppressing the rights of rank and of precedence of noble families, the famous *mestničestvo;* there Fedor declared that it was his duty as tsar appointed by God to promote all which advanced the common good, and to abolish all which was harmful to it. Thus he thought it necessary to suppress those rights because they were detrimental to the common good of the state. It is the first time that such reasoning can be read in an official Muscovite document.

In this light, we can better understand Peter's mentality and the motives which directed his reforms. Peter was educated, of course, in the old Muscovite tradition, and many of his documents and other writings stress the old conception of the tsar, protector of Orthodoxy, to whom God had entrusted the rulership and the defense of justice. With this traditional conception is intermingled, however, the new notion which particularly appealed to his practical sense, the interest and good of the state. This notion of common utility became the dominant principle of his reign and inspired all his legislation and administration. The autocratic tradition which he had inherited gave him the undisputed right to realize, even by force, his ordinances given in the interest of the common good of the state, as he conceived it.

These general notions satisfied Peter. He manifested, however, a certain interest even in Western political theorizing when he ordered the translation into Russian of a short treatise on *The Duties of a Citizen According to the Natural Law*, written by the German theorist, Samuel Pufendorff. That was the furthest that Peter ventured in theorizing.[6] He left the rest to Theophanes (Feofan) Prokopovič of the Kievan Academy, whom he had chosen as a willing and intelligent agent for the propagation of his ideas.

Because the winning of the war with Sweden was the uppermost interest of the state, it dictated many of Peter's reforms and speeded up their realization. This necessity gave him no time to follow a comprehensive scheme. Thus not all of his reforms became permanent, as did the creation of a senate (1711), comprising a small group of officials appointed by the tsar, entrusted with the formulation of new legislation, with the supervision of the administration of the whole empire, and with the function of acting as a supreme court of justice. This institution lasted until 1917. The senate was also to act as a council of regency in the absence of the tsar. The many *prikazy* inherited from the past were replaced by nine colleges (1718) handling vital state business, for example, foreign affairs, economic affairs, war, navy, finance, justice. They were an imitation of the German and Swedish system and existed only until the reign of Alexander I, who transformed them into modern ministries. Alexander I also abolished the office of the procurator-general, who was to control the action of the senate and watch over the functioning of the colleges.

Peter's changes in local government were inspired by the tendencies toward autonomy of major districts, which could be observed already in the seventeenth century. In imitation of the Swedish model, the whole land was divided into ten vast governments, later considerably augmented, headed by governors with administrative, judiciary, financial, and military powers. The reform of municipal organization with two guilds led, however, to a government of the moneyed class and had to be replaced by new measures by Catherine the Great.

The utilitarian principle of the welfare of the state directed Peter's reforms of the army and inspired his division of the population into classes, each of which had to serve the state in its own capacity. The nobles were ordered to serve in the army or in the civil service; the recruitment of soldiers was distributed among the groups of the peasantry; promotions in the army were regulated not according to privilege of birth, but according to merit, advancement in the other services being organized according to a table of ranks.

Peter's financial reforms were, however, the least satisfactory. The costly wars forced him to increase direct and indirect taxes, which were rather poorly distributed. The capitation tax was the most burdensome for the peasantry. By entrusting the collection of taxes to the nobility, he sanctioned, although not intentionally, the further universalization of the half-free peasants with the serfs. To ensure the collection of taxes, he ordered that the peasant could not leave his settlement without written permission from his master, and thus introduced passports for traveling in the interior of the country, a custom which became a tradition in Russia.

This utilitarian principle directed also Peter's superhuman efforts in the development of Russian industry, economy, and schooling of young citizens. The naval, engineering, and artillery academies founded by him reveal the practical purpose of his reforms in schooling, but he gave also, on the invitation of Leibniz, the initiative to the creation of an academic institution in St. Petersburg, realized only after his death, which was destined to become the most important center of scholarship in the humanities and in all branches of science. The academy is a characteristic feature of Russian scientific life even today.

Many of Peter's reforms were unpopular among his contemporaries [7] and are still severely criticized among many Russian historians. Their realization was often too precipitate, lacked coordination, and was often effected in a haphazard way. At any rate, there is no doubt that his reforms made of Muscovy the modern Russian state, a full member of European life and an important factor in international politics.

There was, however, one reform which can be regarded as harmful to the Russian evolution as it broke too suddenly with old traditions which had directed Russia in the past and which were regarded as sacred by most of his subjects—the reform of Church organization, which meant the end of the Russian patriarchate and its replacement by a synod under state supervision.

It must be stressed that these interventions in Church life were not dictated by a purely secular spirit. In religious matters Peter remained an Orthodox Christian who accepted the creed of his Church and who observed the usual religious customs. The parodies of religious ceremonies, in which he delighted with his boon companions, reveal, however, his antiritualistic, secular, rationalistic taste. His faithfulness to Orthodoxy was also confirmed by his refusal of attempts at union with Rome, although it was suggested to him also by the French Sorbonne and would have brought him political advantages.

Peter regarded his rulership as a privileged duty which was entrusted to him by God, to whom he would have to give account. Even when it seems established that he was influenced by Western contemporary ideas on rulership, this does not mean that the Western conceptions of it in the eighteenth century led necessarily to a hostile attitude toward the Church. Even Pufendorff, Peter's favorite theorist, taught that religion was necessary for the absolute state because it guaranteed the moral behavior of men and the fulfillment of their duties to the state. Therefore, the state should be vitally interested in religion, and the ruler should watch over the Church's fulfillment of its educational and moral duties. The absolute state, according to Pufendorff, gives to the ruler an unlimited power over all institutions of command, and this means also the supervision over all confessions.

These definitions of the ruler's absolute power fitted well into Peter's conceptions, and they could be reconciled, at least superficially, with the basic principles of Byzantine political ideas, namely, that the ruler is a representative of God and that it is his duty to care not only for the material welfare of his subjects, but also for their eternal salvation, which they could attain only when living in the true faith and fulfilling God's commands according to the Church's teaching.

The combination of these new definitions with old Russian conceptions presaged a more strict supervision of Church activity by the state, but did not exclude the continuity of the institution of the patriarchate. The recent developments, however, had made Peter apprehensive of the danger which could threaten the success of his new policy from the head of the Russian Church. So far, the relations between Church and state in Russia had evolved, in general, in harmonious collaboration, the Church supporting the absolute ruler and accepting his protection and direction. There had been, however, the unfortunate attempt by Nikon at reversing this relationship and at introducing into Muscovy an alien, Western, and Latin principle of the superiority of the ecclesiastical power over the temporal. This attempt was thwarted by Alexis with the consent of the bishops, who were also afraid of the growing power which such a theory would give to the patriarch. Nikon's idea was unfortunately revived, although in a milder form, by the Patriarch Adrian, who, when defining his rights, had again mentioned the theory of the two swords, so often invoked by western Latin canonists. He claimed that the Church had the supervision not only over spiritual, but also over secular matters, and that the patriarch, who was the figure of Christ, was another ruler besides the tsar, even superior to him.

Although Adrian made no practical use of this theory against Peter's intervention in Church life, Peter was naturally suspicious of such tendencies, and the example of Nikon made it clear to him that such theories could become dangerous to his conception of the state and of the ruler's rights if the patriarchal throne were occupied by a strong personality. As all opposition to his reforms was concentrating around the patriarch and his own son Alexis, Peter thought that it would be in the interest of the state to discontinue the institution of the patriarchate. He made a very clear allusion to this danger in his ordinances introducing the organization of the synod.[8]

There was another important reason which induced Peter to this radical change. He was well aware of the backwardness of the clergy and blamed the hierarchy for neglecting the education of the clergy and of the faithful. This neglect of the Church's duty was also harmful to the interest of the state.

Although preferring acts to words, Peter saw that general opinion should be prepared for the planned changes by some theoretical explanations which would show that they were commanded not only by practical, but also by historical reasons which connected them with the old Muscovite traditions. His theoretician was Theophanes Prokopovič, whom Peter had recalled to St. Petersburg in 1718. In his treatise, *The Right of the Monarch's Will,* Theophanes gave a detailed explanation of the new ideas on the state and tried to reconcile them with the traditional Byzantine and Muscovite political ideas: [9] The formation of a state is based on the decision of the people, who make a contract with the chosen chief giving him all executive power, but because God determines the will of the people, the ruler can be regarded as instituted by God. The ruler is an absolute sovereign, not bound by the laws, but all his subjects are bound to obey him, even a bad ruler. His will is God's will.

This kind of deification of the ruler is a derivation from the Byzantine theory of kingship. Such a compromise between the political theories based on natural law and the old theocratic idea can hardly be reconciled with contemporary Western theories, especially those of Grotius and Pufendorff. Only in the later evolution of enlightened absolutism was the theocratic reason stressed again.

When describing the duties of the monarch, Theophanes stresses the necessity of his working for the general good of the people, leaving it to the ruler to determine what this general good is. Here Theophanes speaks like a contemporary Western theorist, putting into the background the main idea of the theocratic theory, namely, that the ruler, as representative of God, should promote the glory of God and the salvation of his subjects together with their secular welfare.

In other treatises and also in the introduction to the *Ecclesiastical Regulation,* Theophanes applies his theories on the ruler's rights to religion and the Church. There he stresses the Byzantine idea that the ruler is the representative of God on earth. Thus the Church cannot be regarded as equal to the state or independent of it. Like every other institution, the Church is also subject to the laws and ordinances of the state. The tsar is the supreme legislator and judge and has supreme right not only in secular, but also in spiritual things. He can be even called bishop because God gave him the supervision over the hierarchy. He can thus also decide religious questions.

Theophanes seems here to draw more fully on Byzantine ideas, probably in opposition to Nikon and his followers, who favored the Western and Latin ideas on the independent position of the Church vis-à-vis the state. He weakens, however, this dependence on the theocratic idea when describing the origin of rulership from natural law. His anti-Roman and antipapal tendency influenced him in his praise of the Eastern conception of the relation between Church and state.

The creation of the Holy Synod [10] as the replacement for the patriarchate was thus inspired by modern Western ideas on the absolute power of the ruler, combined with and camouflaged by Byzantine theocratic conceptions. The institution itself seems to be modeled on the colleges introduced by Peter to facilitate the administration. It was given regulations concerning its internal composition and activity similar to those of the other colleges, the future ministries.

It is true that Leibniz had already suggested to Peter that he complete the reorganization of the state machinery by the creation of an ecclesiastical college. Peter, of course, was interested in the way the Protestant rulers were handling Church affairs in their lands, but Peter's synod cannot be compared to the Protestant consistories. Peter himself presented its creation as a continuation of Russian synods, with the difference that the present synod would be a permanent institution. He wanted to make the synod equal in importance to the senate.

Theophanes, on the other hand, was acquainted with Protestant teaching [11] and ecclesiastical institutions, but he also seems to have been more inspired in his theorizing by secular political Western ideas, which he tried to reconcile with Byzantine theocratic theories. For example, when attributing to the tsar supreme decision in spiritual matters, he certainly went further than the Protestant theoreticians. Such a conclusion could be derived only from the Byzantine conception of kingship.

This screening of the innovation with wordings and conceptions which were familiar and generally accepted in Muscovy explains why the suppression of the patriarchate did not provoke serious opposition. Because of that, it was also easy to obtain the sanctioning of the new institution by other Eastern patriarchs, subventioned financially by the tsar. All this could, however, not hide the fact that the Holy Synod was founded not by a free decision of the Church, but by the will of a secular ruler, and that the Russian Church had in fact lost even the sort of independence which it had before Peter. Such a dependence on the secular power could be tolerated by the Church only in a theocratic regime. The secularization of the idea of the state and of the duties of a ruler was bound to bring the Russian Church more and more into dependence on the state and to transform the synod into a bureaucratic institution, executing orders given in the interest of the state.

One of the reasons leading to this unfortunate development was the lack of well-instructed theologians and canonists among the native Russian hierarchy. Peter's exhortations for the erection of schools for the clergy and the faithful were followed slowly and could not remedy the lack of instruction among the hierarchy. Theophanes' seminary, founded by him in St. Petersburg, was organized on the pattern of the Protestant faculty of theology in Halle, and the instruction was given in the spirit of Theophanes' theories, with the stress on secular science. The high clergy was thus unable to ensure the synod a particular position in the state, or at least to maintain it on the level of the senate and the highest organs of the state.

On the other hand, Western philosophical and political theories were spreading more and more among Russian intellectuals. Golicyn, governor of Kiev, gave initiative to the Russian translation of the main works of such leading Western political thinkers as Grotius, Hobbes, Pufendorff, Locke, and others, and also made a futile attempt at the formation of a new constitution in 1730. His opponent, the first Russian modern historian, Tatiščev, was also well versed in Western political lore. Under Catherine II, the secularization of the idea of the state, of course, progressed even further, and this westernization continued during the nineteenth century.

Against this flood of Western ideas, the Russian clergy was unable to put up a barrier which would stop, or at least slow down, the secularization of the synod and the subordination of the Church to the needs of the state. The first vice-president of the synod, Theodosius (Feodosij) Janovskij, made a bold attempt during the reign of Catherine I to save the freedom of the synod. For his protest against the "tyranny of the state," he was deprived of his office and exiled to a monastery on the White Sea. The newly instituted "supreme secret council" made even more glaring interventions into Church life than had been done so far by the senate.

The hope of many opponents to the innovations of Theophanes and Peter that Peter II would come back to the old traditions in the relationship between Church and state were dashed to the ground by the death of the tsar, and Tsaritsa Anne, in opposition to the policy of her predecessor, speeded up the process of the submission of the Church. The voices of the protesting clergy were forcibly silenced. The Tsaritsa Elizabeth, although more favorable to the Church, did not dare to change the institution of her father.

It was to be feared that Peter III, a Lutheran by education, would treat the synod as the Protestant rulers were treating the consistories of their Churches. His attempt at confiscation of Church properties was sanctioned by Catherine II the Great (1764). The secularization of Russian political thinking reached its peak during her reign, and the Russian Church lost the last vestiges of its independence. The office of the supreme procurator, created by Peter and entrusted to a layman who was to supervise the work of the synod, was transformed, and its titulary became the representative of the state, who was to present to the synod the wishes of the ruler. Later, he obtained the rank of an imperial minister. The title of "head of the Russian Church," which Catherine used unofficially in a letter to Voltaire,[12] was assumed officially by the Tsar Paul I.[13]

Only in the nineteenth century was the Russian clergy able to defend the rights of its Church by historical and theological arguments, as theological scholarship had then reached a high level. The study of the Russian past and the movement of the Slavophiles strengthened the interest in the reforms of Church organization. In 1905 these tendencies seemed to have reached the point of realization. The synod presented a plan of reform and asked for the convocation of a Russian council which would elect a patriarch. Unfortunately, the committee approved by the government and charged with the preparation of the council could not terminate its work, and the convocation of the council was postponed in 1907 for "a more propitious time," which never came.[14]

So it came about that the Russian Church was identified with the autocratic tendencies of the state and that the champions of political and social reform of tsarist Russia regarded the Church as their enemy. The Russian Church paid a heavy price in blood in 1917 for the mistakes of imperial Russia. In permitting the re-establishment of the Russian patriarchate, the new rulers realized the wishes and hopes for which the Russian clergy and faithful have worked and suffered the last two centuries. It was, however, too late.

In spite of the frequent changes on the throne after Peter's death, the expansion of his empire continued during the whole eighteenth century in the directions already foreshadowed by the later Ruriks and the first Romanovs—toward Sweden, Poland, and Turkey. For nearly fifty years, Russia continued to interfere with Sweden's policy of keeping the country weak. In vain Sweden tried twice to hit back at Russia. Finally, in order to make St. Petersburg secure, Alexander I (1801-1825) conquered Finland from Sweden and kept it.

Following a similar policy in Poland, the Tsaritsa Anne opposed the re-election of Stanislas Leszczyński, supported by France, to the Polish throne and together with Prussia imposed the election and recognition of Augustus III of Saxony (1734-1763). Thus, the last possibility was lost for Poland to work out a regeneration of the kingdom under the reign of a national king supported by France.

Poland was once more open to Russian armies when they marched under the Tsaritsa Elizabeth, allied with Austria, against Prussia, which had deprived the Austrian empress, Maria Theresa (1740-1780), of Silesia. Poland, under the disgraceful rule of its Saxon king, did nothing to defend its rights, and did not see the danger for itself in the rise of Prussia under the ambitious Frederick II the Great (1740-1786). This was the only opportunity for imperial Russia to render a great service to two Slavic nations—the Poles and the Czechs—in stopping the rise of Prussia and saving Silesia for the crown of Bohemia. Elizabeth, a great personal enemy of Frederick, almost succeeded in destroying him. The Prussian king was, however, saved by Elizabeth's successor, Peter III, a great admirer of Frederick, who restored all of the conquests of the Russian army to Prussia and withdrew from the alliance with Austria. Russia gained nothing for its victories over the Prussian armies. Again, Bohemia had to pay heavily for the survival of the Habsburg dynasty. After the loss of Lusatia to Saxony, the crown of Bohemia lost almost the whole of Silesia to Prussia. The Polish and Czech population of Silesia, already under strong German influence, was almost completely germanized during the nineteenth century.

While this was occurring, the Czech nation was passing through the blackest period of its existence. Only a few families were left of the old national nobility of Bohemia—sharing the main functions of the civil administration of the kingdom with nobles alien in language, having no feeling for the glorious past of the kingdom, subservient to the court of Vienna. This facilitated the encroachment of the court into the remaining Bohemian rights. The Czech language was driven out as a tool of administration and was regarded as fit only for the lowest strata of the population.

During the first phase of the wars for the Austrian succession, there existed the danger that Bohemia would be united with Bavaria when the Duke Charles Albert, allied with France, stormed Prague and was recognized as king of Bohemia (1741). His reign in Bohemia and in Germany, as Emperor Charles VII, was short-lived. Maria Theresa saved the kingdom for herself, and the imperial dignity went to her husband, Francis of Lorraine.

Although Bohemia bore the brunt of the War of the Austrian Succession and although the events had once more demonstrated the importance of the possession of its key position in Central Europe, Maria Theresa's absolutist and centralistic reforms did not stop at its boundaries. The office of the governor in Prague was abolished, and the Bohemian chancellery was united with the Austrian chancellery, remaining so until 1848. Bohemia became one of the hereditary German dominions, one of the fourteen, later seventeen, provinces of Austria. It was divided into sixteen districts, each with a "gubernium" and officials appointed by Vienna without regard to the Estates. Only Hungary, in whose reconquest from the Turks Bohemian regiments and finances had a major share, was able to save its special position with its "lands of the holy crown of St. Stephen."

Joseph II, coregent from 1765 and emperor from 1780 to 1790, improved on this centralizing regime, taking the last restricted functions from the hands of the Estates in the "hereditary lands" and imposing taxes at his will. For utilitarian reasons, German became the language of the administration and in 1774 was made in Bohemia the language of instruction. The knowledge of Czech declined further and was almost on the way to extinction.

Of course, this development remained unknown or ignored in Russia. Catherine II, although breaking the alliance with Prussia, remained inactive in Austro-Prussian conflicts and manifested lively interest only in the developments in Poland. Supported by a Russophile party of the nobility, led by the Czartoryskis, she imposed the election of her candidate and favorite, Stanislas Poniatowski (1764-1795). Prussia welcomed this development, for it saw in a Saxon-Polish state a potential danger to its own expansion.

At last Polish patriots saw the danger to the independence of their country and tried to introduce some reforms to save the kingdom. Russia and Prussia, however, did not want a strong Poland. The reforms were opposed, and the Polish Diet of 1768 had to yield to the wishes of its powerful neighbors and grant also to all dissident religions in Poland equal rights with the Catholic Church.

This provoked a strong reaction, and anti-Russian patriots formed the so-called "Confederation of Bar," supported by France. Poland was invaded by Russian armies, and the Ukrainian population was incited to insurrection. France, in order to save its influence in Poland, provoked a Turkish attack against Russia. Austria, although apprehensive of the growth of Prussia and Russia, refused active participation, and this left

Catherine II a free hand against Turkey. Russian armies defeated the Turks and advanced beyond the Danube. Catherine seemed to be in a position to bring the whole of Poland under her sway and to realize the dream of Ivan IV, who had wanted to occupy the throne of Poland.

In order to prevent this, Frederick II won over Austria to his plan of the partition of Poland between the three powers. Maria Theresa (1740-1780) would rather have liked to obtain back a part of lost Silesia, but her son Joseph II concluded an agreement with Frederick, and the Austrian troops occupied (1769-1770) the Carpathian cities which had been ceded by Sigismund of Hungary to Poland, with a part of Galicia. The anarchy in Poland, where the confederates had deposed their king, speeded up these developments. Through the first partition (1772), Poland lost a third of its territories to Russia, Prussia, and Austria. So started the outrageous tragedy of Poland, brought about by the egoistic nobility, forgetful of its patriotic duties.

It appeared that this catastrophe would save Poland from the worst. The patriotic party, influenced also by ideas which the French Revolution had evoked, recognized at last the right of the burghers, and the Four Years' Diet elaborated a new constitution, promulgated in 1791, which removed all previous abuses, especially the *liberum veto,* and declared the kingdom a hereditary monarchy with the Saxon dynasty, entrusting the king and his council with the executive power and establishing a diet with two chambers vested with the legislative power. Although this constitution was still a far cry from modern conceptions of a constitution, it was the first attempt made outside France to bring into practice some of the new ideas promoted by thinkers of the Enlightenment and of the French Revolution. Because Prussia and Austria favored it, there was a hope that Poland could be saved.

Catherine II was, however, adamant. With the help of a pro-Russian party of the nobility, she instigated a confederation in defense of the old constitution and invaded Poland. The king tried in vain to save the situation by offering the Polish succession to the Grand Duke Constantine, and so it came to the second partition of Poland (1793), between Russia and Prussia. The insurrection of the patriots under Kościuszko (1794) was suppressed, and the plan to transfer the rule over what was left of Poland to a Habsburg prince proved unworkable. The third partition (1795) of Polish territory among the three neighbors made an end to the Polish state.

Catherine II could thus only in part realize her Polish plans inherited from the Ruriks. Not all the "Russian" lands under Poland and Lithuania were joined with Moscow. When working on the realization of the dream of the Ruriks, Catherine did not forget the timid plans of the first Romanovs and Peter I of progress beyond the Danube and into the Balkan lands. The natural ally for the realization of such plans was Austria. Following the visit of Joseph II (1780) to St. Petersburg, an Austro-Russian treaty was concluded with the aim, apparently extravagant but regarded as realizable by many contemporary statesmen, of ejecting the Turks from Europe. Catherine conceived her "Greek scheme"—the creation of a Dacian dukedom comprising Moldavia, Wallachia, and Bessarabia, the restoration of the Byzantine Empire with her grandson as emperor, and division of the rule over the Balkan lands with Joseph II. Their hopes were, however, not fulfilled. Catherine occupied the Crimea and was further able to push the boundary to the Dnieper River and secure Očakov on the Black Sea. Joseph II stormed Belgrade, but his successor Leopold II (1790-1792), menaced by Prussia, was forced to conclude peace, gaining only a strip of northern Bosnia in exchange for Belgrade. Catherine secured, moreover, the protectorship over the Orthodox Christians in the Turkish Empire, a privilege which gave Russia a pretext for intervention in Turkish affairs, which was to be exploited by the tsars in the nineteenth century.

The second partition of Poland was speeded up by Catherine under the pretext that subversive ideas, inspired by the French Revolution, were spreading in Poland and were endangering the social and political order in the neighboring states. This characterizes the social and political evolution in Russia in the eighteenth century. Catherine flirted, at the beginning of her reign, with the new ideas of the French Enlightenment; entertained correspondence with Voltaire, Montesquieu, and Diderot; and read the works of the French encyclopedists. But although she was regarded by many as "progressive" in social and political principles, she was firmly convinced that absolutism was the only political system which could be followed. She was installed as empress by the nobility and was convinced that the state machinery could be entrusted only to the nobility. In spite of the attempt at the creation of a consultative body elected from all classes of the population—with the exception of the serfs, who formed four-fifths of the population—her legislation did almost nothing for the alleviation of the life of the serfs, little for the burghers, but most for the nobility, which was confirmed in its position as a privileged class.

The insurrection of the discontented Cossacks and peasants led by Pugačev (1773-1774), which was suppressed with some difficulty, induced her to effect a reform of the administration. She divided the twenty "governments" instituted by Peter into fifty-one, entrusting the governor's office with a great degree of civilian, financial, and judicial jurisdiction, which so far had been in the hands of the central colleges introduced by

Peter the Great. This led to a healthy decentralization, but the office of governor remained in the hands of the nobility.

The French Revolution stifled in Catherine all interest in new social and political ideas. All propagators of the "subversion" were persecuted. Novikov, propagator of Freemasonry in Russia, who asked for more freedom for the serfs, was imprisoned. Radiščev, who went even further, describing in vivid colors the enslavement of the peasants by the nobility, was exiled to Siberia. Catherine thus refused to follow the example of her ally, Joseph II, also a believer in enlightened absolutism, who made a bold attempt at the abolition of serfdom. Russia, the most powerful state in Central and eastern Europe at that time, became the staunchest supporter of absolutism and the most ardent opponent of the ideas preached by French revolutionaries.

Paul I (1796-1801) made some changes in Catherine's reforms which gave the impression of an improvement in the situation of the serfs. He did so rather to spite the work of his mother, whom he disliked profoundly. In reality he was even more determined to maintain the Russian autocratic regime. For this reason, he changed the order of succession to the throne established by Peter I, introducing the right of primogeniture and fixing the rank and income of the members of the tsarist dynasty. In order to protect Russia from "subversive" ideas coming from France, he erected a kind of "iron curtain"—forbidding any contact with France, making it almost impossible for his subjects to visit western Europe, introducing censorship, forbidding the imitation of French fashions, and sending all suspects to Siberia or to prison. He provoked only discontent and revolutionary sentiments, of which he became a victim.

Alexander I (1801-1825) went back at the beginning of his reign to the more liberal regime of Catherine and lifted to some extent the iron curtain, but in his projects of liberalizing Russian ways of government, the young tsar stopped midway. The reports on the horrors which accompanied the French Revolution deterred him from introducing more hardy social and political reforms, suggested by his excellent secretary of state, Michael Speranskij. The idea of tsarist autocracy was still too deeply imbedded in Russian minds. Speranskij found a dangerous opponent to his proposed reforms in Karamzin, a contemporary historian who exercised a great influence among the Russian nobility and intelligentsia. Karamzin regarded the autocratic and absolutist regime as the only one possible for Russia and opposed any marked changes in the extant social structure of the Empire.

Then, the Napoleonic wars, which threatened to ruin the Russian Empire, absorbed all the attention of the tsar. The final victory over

Napoleon on Russian and Western battlefields, crowned by the triumphal entry of the Russian army into Paris (1814), appeared to Alexander as a direct intervention of Providence. His conception of autocracy became strongly theocratic, with a touch of mysticism. He regarded himself as chosen by Providence to re-establish in Europe the old order disturbed by the Revolution and by Napoleon. He incorporated these ideas into the proclamation of the Holy Alliance, which he hoped would direct the destiny of Europe according to divine laws and with justice. His intentions were sincere, but in reality the Holy Alliance of the victors over Napoleon became a basis for absolutist policy of the great powers, which used it often to suppress all national movements trying to obtain a just share in government. The astute Austrian minister Metternich knew especially well how to use the Alliance for his purposes.

Metternich's influence also detracted Alexander from all thoughts of adapting the Russian regime to the modern ideas of constitutional government in which he indulged during the Congress of Vienna. So it happened that the last decade of Alexander's reign was characterized by a regime of reaction and despotism. Events have, however, proved that it was impossible to stop the spread of liberal ideas in Russia. Many Russians became acquainted with such liberal ideas during the campaigns in western Europe, and the returning officers of the victorious armies spread the knowledge of Western social and political institutions in Russia. The desire was thus provoked for a modernization and liberalization of Russian ways of life. Secret societies were formed in St. Petersburg and in the south, propagating the idea of a constitutional government. When, after Alexander's death, there was for a short time an uncertainty concerning the succession to the throne, the members of the secret association of St. Petersburg, led by Prince Trubeckoj, started open agitation within the army and provoked the Decembrist revolt (1825).

The catastrophic end of this first Russian revolution stopped the social and political progress of Russia for some decades. Nicholas I (1825-1855), in order to protect the Russian autocracy against any such attempts, introduced a harsh police regime and refused to abolish serfdom, limiting himself to only a few measures to end some crying abuses. Many discontented intellectuals left the country and continued their agitation against the tsar from abroad.

It needed a war to cause the breakdown of Nicholas' policy. His drive against Turkey—the claim to the protectorship of the Christians appeared as a useful weapon—provoked the intervention of England and France, thus causing the so-called Crimean War, which culminated in the heroic but unsuccessful defense of Sevastopol' (1854-1856). The war revealed the deficiencies of the Russian bureaucratic governmental system, and the new ruler, Alexander II (1855-1881), saw himself forced to abolish certain measures introduced by his predecessor against the universities, the press, and writers. The most important of his reforms was the abolition of serfdom. It was hailed even by the émigré revolutionaries, such as Herzen, but at the end his *ukaz* of 1861, revealing a compromising attitude favorable to the conservative aristocratic landholders, disillusioned the advocates of more revolutionary measures. The reform of the government of the districts (1864), erecting a kind of district diet, whose members would be elected by all classes of the population and which was entrusted with the local administration, was the most important concession given by the tsar to the advocates of a constitutional regime. Great improvement was made also in the judiciary system and in municipal administration (1870).

Although the tsar was not willing to go further and grant his people more influence on the government—he revealed himself as even more reactionary after the attempt on his life by a revolutionary in 1866—his reforms contributed considerably to the growth of Russian culture. The standard of education on all levels reached unprecedented heights, scholarship improved, and Russian literary achievement reached its peak during Alexander's reign, as the greatest Russian writers—Dostoevskij, Turgenev, Saltykov-Ščedrin, Gončarov, Nekrasov, L. Tolstoj, and others— were given the necessary freedom to create their immortal works.

Although quite profound, Alexander's reforms did not satisfy the radical elements of the Russian intelligentsia. Under the leadership of Herzen, Bakunin, and other émigrés, revolutionary movements were formed abroad which planned to realize radical and social reforms in Russia by the revolt of the people or by the taking over of the government. The assassination of the tsar (March 13, 1881), planned by the fanatic revolutionaries, did not provoke a revolt which would have led to desired reforms, as had been hoped by the radical parties.

It helped only to promote the reaction which characterized the reign of Alexander III (1881-1894) and the first half of the reign of the last tsar, Nicholas II (1894-1917). The dense atmosphere of Alexander's reign was aggravated by the policy of forceful russification of all the peoples of the Empire and by the repression of the Jews and non-Orthodox religions. It needed a war once more and the subsequent defeat by the Japanese (1905), followed by unrest and the threat of open revolution, to bring about the long-needed change. The constitution introduced by Nicholas II (1905) still reserved for the tsar important prerogatives, but the first two dumas ended without having achieved anything. The political atmosphere was in a whirl, stirred by the agitation of the Marxists led by Lenin, and the government had to curtail the electoral rights of the burghers, workers, and peasants in order to obtain a majority. This was a bad omen. People were stirred by social agitation, and the long-overdue reforms could not satisfy the more radical elements. Finally, the prophetic words of the greatest Russian historian, Ključevskij, who knew so well the history of his people and the needs of Russia, were fulfilled. On learning in 1895 about the tsar's declaration that he was firmly determined to maintain all the principles of autocracy during his reign, Ključevskij is said to have sadly made this comment, "Mind my words, with Nicholas II the Romanov dynasty will end. If he will have a son, he will not reign."

And again a war followed by a revolution was needed to make this a reality. Events have shown that not Bakunin's, but Tkačev's, revolutionary methods were better. Against Bakunin's advocation of the revolution of the masses first, which would bring about the desired radical change in government, Tkačev had recommended the forceful seizure of the government by elite revolutionary groups first, and then the influencing of the masses from above. The inexperienced democratic government, badly backed by the rest of the people, could not withstand the shock, and the dictatorship of the proletariat replaced the tsardom. Cleverly blending them with democratic slogans, the new regime succeeded in securing its stability with the help of certain principles inherited from the tsarist autocracy—centralization of power, a potent and subservient bureaucracy, emphasis on the interests of the state, the merciless use of force, surveillance by secret police, and a mighty, modernized, and well-outfitted army. The awe with which the people were accustomed in tsarist Russia to regard the supreme ruler was transferred, thanks to a clever use of propaganda, to the new leaders.

The autocratic ideas on which the rulership of the greatest, and, during the eighteenth century, the only free, Slavic nation was built proved also to hamper Russia in playing the role of liberator which the other Slavic nations expected of her. The sad fate of Poland brought the Slavic question more forcefully before the eyes of the Russian intelligentsia. In the secret societies, plans were forged for the role among the Slavs of the new Russia which would be formed. The northern, or Petersburg, secret circle wanted to transform Russia in a Slavic federation. Colonel Pestel, the leader of the southern secret circle, advocated an independent Poland, allied with Russia, which, however, should have only one official language—Russian. Others dreamed of a union of all Slavs with Russia.

The minister of foreign affairs of Alexander I, the Pole Adam Czartoryski, proposed in 1804 the union of most of the Slavic nations with Russia. This proposal was meant to counteract the plans of Napoleon, in whose armies were thousands of Polish refugees hoping to reconquer the independence of their country with Napoleon's help. These hopes were about to be realized when Napoleon, after defeating the three powers which had been responsible for the partition of Poland, established the Duchy of Warsaw, comprising the Polish territories which had been occupied by Prussia, minus Danzig, a free city. The Duchy was given a duke from the Saxon house and a constitution, and the province of Cracow was joined to it in 1809, after the peace of Vienna. The hope of winning over Alexander I to his side prevented Napoleon from going further, but his invasion of Russia in 1812 renewed the hope of the patriots that after the Russian defeat Poland would be resuscitated. The heroism of the Polish troops in the Napoleonic campaign could not, however, avert the catastrophe.

Nevertheless, thanks to all this, the Congress of Vienna (1814-1815) had to deal seriously with the Polish problem also. Alexander I asked for the union of all Polish lands with Russia, promising the Poles a large degree of autonomy. This was the old dream of the Ruriks, the realization of which was favored this time also by many Poles, led by Czartoryski. Although Prussia was willing to exchange the Polish province of Poznań with Saxony, England, France, and Austria, afraid of too great an expansion of Russia, opposed the plan, and Alexander had to content himself with the addition of the Duchy of Warsaw to his empire and leave Poznań and Galicia to Prussia and Austria.

This solution was not as tragic as it appeared to some Polish patriots. Alexander became king of this new Congress Poland, for which he approved a liberal constitution. Nicholas I was even crowned king of Poland (1829), and respected the Polish constitution. But this did not satisfy the radical patriots dreaming of the restoration of old Poland, with all lands which belonged to it in 1772. The outbreak of the French and Belgian revolution in 1830 also initiated the Warsaw revolt, which was, however, of short duration. In 1831 the Polish army was defeated, the constitution of 1818 suppressed, and the Polish kingdom divided into provinces which were treated as other Russian provinces.

The French revolutionary atmosphere from 1830 and 1848 filled the whole of Europe. The ideas of freedom, equality, and democracy, revived again by the French revolutionary movements, found a profound echo in the Habsburg empire among the non-Germanic peoples. The first signs of a Czech national revival had already appeared at the end of Joseph II's reign. The principles of the Enlightenment, which he himself professed and with which he covered his absolutism, penetrated too among the Bohemian nobility and the middle classes, which were also influenced by Herder's inspiring philosophy. The first defenses of the Czech language appeared, the Royal Bohemian Society of Science was founded in 1784, and Joseph's successor, his brother Leopold II (1790-1792), founded a chair of the Czech language at the germanized University of Prague. His coronation with the crown of St. Wenceslas revived historical memories. These modest beginnings survived the reactionary reign of Francis II (1792-1835)—from 1806 only Emperor of Austria, the Holy Roman Empire of the German Nation having been given the *coup de grâce* by Napoleon—and the Metternich regime, which continued during the reign of Ferdinand I (1835-1848). The revival was speeded up by the work of five great Czech and Slovak scholars—Joseph Dobrovský, the founder of Slavonic philology; Joseph Jungmann, the author of the first history of Czech literature; John Kollár, a poet of Slavic greatness; Paul Joseph Šafařík, also a Slovak, the founder of Slavic archeology; and Francis Palacký, a political leader and the first great Czech historian.

Thanks to their influence, Czech and Slovak national consciousness grew and found its expression in the great upheaval of 1848, which brought about the abdication of Metternich and the promise of a constitution. The solidarity of all Slavic peoples was proclaimed at the first All-Slavic Congress in Prague, presided over by Palacký. There the Russian revolutionary émigré Bakunin expounded his All-Slavic ideas, making exhortations for a general revolution which would destroy Austria, Prussia, and Russia and lead to a new grouping of Europe and the federation of all free and independent Slavic peoples. Palacký, on the other hand, favored a federalized Austria, refused the invitation to the German Diet of Frankfurt, and was cold to the tsarist leadership of Slavdom. All these plans went to the winds. The Czech revolutionary movement was crushed. The new constitution voted by the Austrian parliament in Kroměříž (Kremsier)—where it had taken refuge from revolutionary Vienna—which instituted a decentralized, federal form of government, was abrogated, and the revolt of Hungary was crushed by Russian troops sent by Nicholas I to help the new emperor, Francis Joseph (1848-1916). So it happened that the tsarist intervention helped the Austrian government to reject the idea of federative government, which would have guaranteed to the Slavic peoples in Austria their political and national liberties. A centralistic and germanizing policy followed, and the Compromise of 1867, which left the peoples of Hungary to Magyar domination and the Slavs of the Austrian dominions to German domination, blocked for many decades the realization of Slavic aspirations for self-government and in reality proved to be the gravestone of the Austro-Hungarian monarchy.

The tsarist autocratic policy also hindered the development of the Ukrainian and Belo-Russian languages and peoples, favoring in administration and education only the use of the Russian language. Only during the first half of the nineteenth century did a renaissance of the Ukrainian and Belo-Russian languages and literatures appear.

Although the tsarist autocracy still pretended to be rooted in theocracy and claimed the protectorship of Orthodoxy, the secularization which had permeated Russian political thinking prevented the tsars from applying these principles in practical politics. When the Orthodox Greeks started their fight for their national liberation, Alexander I refused to help, pretending that he was bound by the principles of the Holy Alliance, directed against any revolutionary movement opposing the legitimate rulers. He limited himself, together with France and England, to diplomatic intervention, trying to reconcile the Greeks with the sultan. Only in 1827, when all diplomatic intervention had failed and European opinion was stirred up by the cruel Turkish suppression of the revolt, did Russia, with the two powers, intervene victoriously, and Alexander forced the sultan to recognize the independence of the Greek kingdom (1830).

The victory over Turkey opened to Russia new possibilities for spreading its influence among the Orthodox Rumanians and the Balkan Slavs. The Rumanian principalities of Moldavia and Wallachia and the Serbian principality became autonomous and were placed under a Russian protectorate. This Russian protectorate over the Christians in Turkey opened to the tsars possibilities of intervention similar to those that had been won by Catherine II in Poland, but the jealousy of the other members of the Holy Alliance led to the Crimean War. The loss of the war by Russia, because of the hostile attitude of ungrateful Austria, deprived Russia of the monopolistic protectorate over the Christians in Turkey and of other advantages previously gained. Only in the Caucasus did the protectorship over Orthodoxy bear lasting fruit through the annexation of Georgia after a victorious war with Persia (1813). This opened to Russia the way to the occupation of the Caucasus and to the spectacular progress toward the borders of India, China, and Japan of the second half of the nineteenth century.

The Pan-Slavic idea did not die, but was kept alive—in Russia by the movement of the Slavophiles and among other Slavic nations by the hope that Russia would help them in their struggle for greater freedom. Russia never forgot Austria's treacherous attitude during the Crimean War. The insurrection in Bosnia and Hercegovina (1875) once more put the question of the liberation of the Orthodox Slavs before the European public. The Pan-Slavic movement in Russia grew and found its expression in the foundation of the Slavonic Welfare Society (1857) and in the Pan-Slavic Congress at Moscow (1867). The claims for the right of intervention in favor of the Orthodox Slavs induced a great number of Russian volunteers to join Bulgarian and Serbian armies, although the government hesitated to take the initiative. Only in 1877, forced by public opinion, did Alexander II order his armies to invade Turkey. In order to restrain Austria from an intervention similar to that of 1856, Alexander had to give concessions which limited considerably Russian influence in the Balkans and ensured for Austria a share in the spoils—the eventual occupation of Bosnia and Hercegovina. From that time on the rivalry between Russia and Austria in the Balkans continued to grow and to poison the political atmosphere in Europe. It prevented Russia from playing the dominant role among the Balkan peoples during the wars of liberation (1912), and was one of the main reasons which led to the First World War in 1914.

Tsarist Russia thus did not succeed in profiting fully from the Pan-Slav idea. It is an irony of history that the regime which succeeded the tsarist autocracy inherited even this idea from tsarist Russia and was able not only to make a reality of the dream of the Ruriks in 1939 and 1945, when it united all "Russian" *votčiny* with Moscow, but also to profit from the Pan-Slav sentiments to extend its sway over all Slavic lands in the name of a new "orthodoxy."

NOTES

1. An adequate biography of Peter is still a desideratum of modern Russian historiography. So far the best work on Peter and his reign is that by Ključevskij, *History of Russia* (see Bibl.), vol. 4, pp. 1-264. This study of Peter has been published separately also, *Peter the Great* (see Bibl.). A French translation of this study has also been published separately, *Pierre le Grand*, translated by H. de Witte (Paris, 1953). Platonov's *Petr Velikij* (Paris, 1927) is less satisfactory. M. M. Bogoslovskij collected material on Peter's reign to 1700 only, *Petr I, materialy dlja biografii*, 5 vols. (Moscow, 1940-1948). On economic progress during Peter's reign, see E. I. Zaozenskaja, *Manufaktura pri Petre I* (Moscow, 1947). On Anglo-Russian relations, the most recent study is that by L. A. Nikiforov, *Russko-anglijskie otnošenija pri Petre I.* (Moscow, 1950). A complete Russian bibliography on Peter will be found in B. Kafengaus' study in *Istoričeskij Žurnal*, 9 (1944) and in M. N. Tikhomirov's *Istočnikovedenie istorii S.S.S.R.* (Moscow, 1940), vol. 1, chapters 16-20. Cf. also the symposium on Peter I, *Petr Velikij, sbornik statej*, ed. A. I. Andreev (Moscow, 1947), and the discussion on Peter's ideology and the "rules" he is supposed to have followed in his government by B. I. Syromajtnikov, *"Regularnoe" gosudarstvo Petra Velikogo i ego ideologija* (Moscow, 1943).

2. The best work on Turko-Russian relations in Peter's time is the short study by B. H. Sumner (see Bibl.), giving a complete bibliography of sources and works.

3. The new title "Emperor of All Russia" was recognized the earliest by

Holland. Sweden agreed to it in 1723, Turkey in 1733, England and Austria in 1742, France and Spain in 1745, and Poland only in 1764.

4. See the most recent Russian study on the political and historical ideas of Križanić by B. D. Dacjuk, quoted above, p. 523.

5. On the manuscript tradition of these and other translations and their editions, see the study of A. Lappo-Danilevskij, "L'idée de l'état et son évolution en Russie depuis les troubles du XVIIe siècle jusqu'aux réformes du XVIIIe," in *Essays in Legal History,* ed. P. Vinogradoff (Oxford, 1913), pp. 356-83.

6. The memoranda sent to him by G. W. Leibniz (1646-1715), the famous German philosopher, also influenced Peter's political thinking and reforms. The preface to his army regulations of 1716 stresses the principle of utility in the reforms for the state, and in the law of 1721, instituting the college for municipal affairs, Peter explained his notions on the "police" state, interpreting the word "police" in a much broader sense. His conception is quite close to the concept of the "Polizeistaat" developed in Prussia by Frederick William I.

7. However, many contemporaries supported Peter, giving him useful suggestions for reforms, especially F. Saltykov, A. Kurbatov, A. Nestorov, and others. On the projects for reforms of some of Peter's contemporaries, see I. Pavlov, *Proekty reform v zapiskakh sovremennikov Petra Velikago* (St. Petersburg, 1897).

8. In his recommendations of the synodal system, F. Prokopovič also stressed that this system prevented any open opposition to the state. He also evidently had the example of Nikon in mind.

9. Theophanes' *Pravda voli monaršej* was published in Moscow in 1722. Two years later a German edition appeared in Berlin. The best analysis of this work, together with indications of Theophanes' Western sources, was written by G. Gurvič, *"Pravda voli monaršej" Feofana Prokopoviča i eja zapadno-evropejskie istočniki* (Yur'jev, 1915).

10. The best study in Russian on the creation of the Synod was written by P. V. Verkhovskoj, *Učreždenie dukhovnoj kollegii i dukhovnyj reglament* (Warsaw, 1916). In the introduction, the author gives the criticisms of Russian historians from 1724 to 1916 on Peter's reform. In the second volume he published some of Theophanes' writings and other documents. R. Stupperich's book (see Bibl.) is the best Western study. Cf. also studies by R. Wittram (see Bibl.).

11. R. Stupperich has shown very clearly in his study, "Feofan Prokopovičs . . ." (see Bibl.), pp. 350-62, that, contrary to certain accusations by Russian theologians, Theophanes "had never left the womb of his Church, had lived in communion with his Church and had defended its teaching." A Russian bibliography on Theophanes' theological teaching will be found in this study.

12. A letter of December 27, 1773, no. 136 in W. F. Reddaway's *Documents of Catherine the Great* (see Bibl.), p. 188, "Comme chef de l'Eglise grecque. . . ."

13. I. Smolitsch, *Stellung d. russ. Kais.* (see Bibl.), p. 149, sees in Paul's words only a declaration that the tsar must be a member of the Orthodox Church. Tsar Paul was a very pious man. Smolitsch's study shows that down to 1917 the position of the tsar to and in the Church was never clearly defined.

14. For the failure of the reform, the Minister Pobedonoscev was most responsible.

LISTS OF RULERS

EMPERORS OF RUSSIA

1682-1725	Peter the Great (emperor from 1721)	1762-1796	Catherine II
		1796-1801	Paul
1725-1727	Catherine I	1801-1825	Alexander I
1727-1730	Peter II	1825-1855	Nicholas I
1730-1740	Anna	1855-1881	Alexander II
1740-1741	Ivan VI	1881-1894	Alexander III
1741-1762	Elizabeth	1894-1917	Nicholas II
1762	Peter III		

RULERS OF POLAND

c. 960- 992	Mieszko I	1290-1296	Przemysl (Przemysław)
992-1025	Boleslav I, Chrobry (the Brave)		
1025-1034	Mieszko II	1300-1305	Wenceslas I
1034-1040	Dynastic struggle	1305-1333	Władisław IV, Łokietek
1038-1058	Casimir I, the Restorer		
1058-1079	Boleslav II, the Bold	1333-1370	Casimir III, the Great
1079-1102	Władisław I	1370-1382	Louis of Anjou
1102-1138	Boleslas III, Wry-mouth	1382-1384	Civil strife
		1384-1399	Jadwiga
1138-1146	Władisław II	1386-1434	Władisław V (Jagiello)
1146-1173	Boleslav IV	1434-1444	Władysław VI (III)
1173-1177	Mieszko III	1444-1447	Interregnum
1177-1194	Casimir II, the Just	1447-1492	Casimir IV
1194-1227	Leszek I, the White (rival Władysław, Spindleshanks)	1492-1501	John Albrecht (Jan Olbracht)
		1501-1506	Alexander I
1227-1279	Boleslav V	1506-1548	Sigismund I
1279-1288	Leszek II, the Black		

For continuation, see the table *Kings of Poland, Grand Dukes of Lithuania.*

GRAND DUKES OF LITHUANIA

c. 1240-1263	Mendovg	1382-1392	Jagiello (second time)
1270-1282	Troiden	?-1430	Vitold
1293-1316	Viten	1430-1435	Svidrigello
1316-1341	Gedymin	1435-1440	Sigismund
1345-1377	Olgerd (Keistut co-ruler)	1440-1492	Casimir IV
		1492-1506	Alexander
1377-1381	Jagiello	1506-1548	Sigismund I
1381-1382	Keistut	1548-1572	Sigismund August

KINGS OF POLAND, GRAND DUKES OF LITHUANIA
(Following the Lublin Union of Poland and Lithuania, 1569)

1548-1572	Sigismund II August	1587-1632	Sigismund III Vasa
1573-1574	Henri de Valois of France	1632-1648	Władysław VII (IV)
1576-1586	Stephen Bathory	1648-1668	John II Casimir

1669-1673	Michael Wiśniowiecki	1736-1763	August III
1674-1696	John III Sobieski	1764-1795	Stanislaw August
1697-1733	August II		Poniatowski
1733-1736	War of the Polish Succession		

BOHEMIA

905- 921	Vratislav I	1306-1307	Rudolf of Habsburg
921- 929	Wenceslas (Václav) (Saint)	1307-1310	Henry of Carinthia
		1310-1346	John of Luxemburg
929- 967	Boleslav I	1346-1378	Charles I (IV of the Empire)
967- 999	Boleslav II		
999-1002	Boleslav III	1378-1419	Wenceslas IV
1002-1003	Vladivoj (Polish prince)	1419-1437	Sigismund
1003-1004	Boleslav Chrobry	1437-1439	Albert of Austria
1004-1034	Jaromir, Oldřich	1440-1457	Ladislas Posthumus
1034-1055	Břetislav I	1458-1471	George of Poděbrady
1055-1061	Spytihněv II	1471-1516	Vladislav II
1061-1092	Vratislav II (king 1085-1092)	1516-1526	Louis II

Rulers of Bohemia and Hungary, 1526-1835

1092-1110	Břetislav II		
1110-1120	Bořivoj II	1526-1564	Ferdinand I
1120-1125	Vladislav I	1564-1576	Maximilian I (II of Empire)
1125-1140	Soběslav I		
1140-1174	Vladislav II (king 1158-1174)	1576-1612	Rudolf II
		1612-1619	Matthias
1174-1180	Soběslav II	1619-1620	Frederick of the Palatinate
1180-1189	Frederick		
1189-1191	Konrad Otto	1619-1637	Ferdinand II
1191-1192	Wenceslas	1637-1657	Ferdinand III
1192-1197	Henry Břetislav	1658-1705	Leopold I
		1705-1711	Joseph I

Kings of Bohemia

		1711-1740	Charles II (VI of Empire)
1197-1230	Přemysl Otakar I		
1230-1253	Wenceslas I	1740-1780	Maria Theresa
1253-1278	Přemysl Otakar II	1741-1743	Charles Albert of Bavaria
1278-1283	Regency of Otto of Brandenburg		
		1780-1790	Joseph II
1283-1305	Wenceslas II	1790-1792	Leopold II
1305-1306	Wenceslas III (last Přemyslide)	1792-1835	Francis I

SLOVAKIA

From c. 906 to 1918 under Hungarian rule. From 907 to 1526 Hungary had the following princes and kings.

		997-1038	Stephen I, king from 1000
907- 947	Zsolt	1038-1046	Peter Orseolo
947- 972	Taksony	1041-1044	Samuel
972- 997	Géza	1047-1061	Andrew I
		1061-1063	Béla I
		1063-1074	Solomon

1074-1077	Géza I		1301-1305	Wenceslas II of
1077-1095	László I (Saint)			Bohemia
1095-1114	Kálmán (Koloman)		1305-1308	Otto of Bavaria
1114-1131	Stephen II		1308-1342	Charles Robert of Anjou
1141-1162	Gésa II		1342-1382	Louis the Great of Anjou
1162-1172	Stephen III (Laszlo II,		1382-1385	Mary of Anjou
	Stephen III)		1385-1386	Charles II of Naples
1172-1196	Béla III		1387-1437	Sigismund of Luxemburg
1196-1204	Emmerich		1437-1439	Albert of Habsburg
1205	László III		1440-1444	Vladislav I (Jagiello)
1205-1235	Andrew II		1445-1457	Ladislas (László) V
1235-1270	Béla IV			Posthumus
1270-1272	Stephen V		1458-1490	Matthias Corvinus
1270-1290	László IV		1490-1516	Vladislas II
1290-1301	Andrew III		1516-1526	Louis II

BULGARIA

Macedonian Empire

976-1014	Samuel
1014-1015	Gabriel Radomir
1015-1018	John Vladislav
1018-1187	Under Byzantine control.

Second Bulgarian Empire

1187-1196	Asen I
1196-1197	Peter
1197-1207	Kalojan
1207-1218	Boril
1218-1241	John Asen II
1241-1246	Koloman Asen
1246-1256	Michael Asen

1257-1277	Constantine Tich
1278-1279	Ivajlo
1279-1280	John Asen III
1280-1292	George I Terter
1292-1298	Smilec
Interregnum	
1300	Čaka
1300-1322	Theodore Svetoslav
1322-1323	George II Terter
1323-1330	Michael Šišman
1330-1331	John Stephen
1331-1371	John Alexander
1371-1393	John Šišman

(1365-1396 in Vidin, John Stracimir)

SERBIA

c. 1167-1196	Stephen Nemanja		1321-1331	Stephen Uroš III
1196-c. 1228	Stephen the First-			Dečanski
	Crowned, king		1331-1355	Stephen Dušan, Car
	from 1217			from 1345
c. 1228-c. 1233	Stephen Radoslav		1355-1371	Car Stephen Uroš
c. 1233-1242	Stephen Vladislav		(1366-1371	King Vukašin)
1242-1276	Stephen Uroš I		1371-1389	Prince Lazar
1276-1282	Stephen Dragutin		1389-1427	Stephen Lazarević,
1282-1321	Stephen Uroš II			Despot from 1402
	Milutin		1427-1456	George Branković
			1456-1458	Lazar Branković

HOLY ROMAN EMPERORS

911- 918	Conrad I (Franconian)
918- 936	Henry I, the Fowler (Saxon)
936- 973	Otto I, the Great (Emperor from 962)
973- 983	Otto II
983-1002	Otto III
1002-1024	Henry II, the Saint (Bavarian)
1024-1039	Conrad II, the Salian (Franconian)
1039-1056	Henry III, the Black
1056-1106	Henry IV. *Rivals:*
1077-1080	Rudolf of Swabia
1081-1093	Hermann of Luxemburg
1093-1101	Conrad of Franconia
1106-1125	Henry V
1125-1137	Lothar II (Saxon)
1138-1152	Conrad III (Swabian)
1152-1190	Frederick I, Barbarossa
1190-1197	Henry VI
1198-1212	Otto IV (Brunswick). *Rival:*
1198-1208	Philip II of Swabia
1212-1250	Frederick II. *Rivals:*
1246-1247	Henry Raspe
1247-1256	William of Holland
1250-1254	Conrad IV
1254-1273	The Great Interregnum. *Competitors*
1257-1273	Richard of Cornwall
1257-1272	Alfonso X of Castile
1273-1291	Rudolf I (Habsburg)
1292-1298	Adolf I (Nassau)
1298-1308	Albert I (Habsburg)
1308-1313	Henry VII (Luxemburg)
1314-1347	Louis IV (Bavaria). *Rival:*
1325-1330	Frederick of Habsburg, co-regent
1347-1378	Charles IV (Luxemburg). *Rival:*
1347-1349	Günther of Schwarzburg
1378-1400	Wenceslas (Luxemburg)
1400-1410	Rupert (Palatinate)
1410-1437	Sigismund (Luxemburg). *Rival:*
1410-1411	Jobst of Moravia
1438-1439	Albert II (Habsburg)
1440-1493	Frederick III
1493-1519	Maximilian I
1519-1556	Charles V
1558-1564	Ferdinand I
1564-1576	Maximilian II
1576 1612	Rudolf II
1612-1619	Matthias
1619-1637	Ferdinand II
1637-1657	Ferdinand III
1658-1705	Leopold I
1705-1711	Joseph I
1711-1740	Charles VI
1742-1745	Charles VII (Bavaria)
1745-1765	Francis I (Lorraine)
1765-1790	Joseph II
1790-1792	Leopold II
1792-1806	Francis II

BYZANTINE EMPIRE

976-1025	Basil II
1025-1028	Constantine VIII
1028-1034	Romanus III Argyrus
1034-1041	Michael IV
1041-1042	Michael V
1042	Zoe and Theodora
1042-1055	Constantine IX Monomach
1055-1056	Theodora (again)
1056-1057	Michael VI
1057-1059	Isaac I Comnenus
1059-1067	Constantine X Ducas
1068-1071	Romanus IV Diogenes
1071-1078	Michael VII Ducas
1078-1081	Nicephorus III Botaneiates
1081-1118	Alexius I Comnenus
1118-1143	John II Comnenus
1143-1180	Manuel I Comnenus
1180-1183	Alexius II Comnenus
1183-1185	Andronicus I Comnenus
1185-1195	Isaac II Angelus
1195-1203	Alexius III Angelus
1203-1204	Isaac II (again) and Alexius IV Angeli

1204	Alexius V Murtzuphlus	1341-1391	John V Palaeologus
1204-1222	Theodore I Lascaris	1347-1354	John VI Cantacuzenus
1222-1254	John III Ducas Vatatzes	1376-1379	Andronicus IV
1254-1258	Theodore II Lascaris		Palaeologus
1258-1261	John IV Lascaris	1390	John VII Palaeologus
1259-1282	Michael VIII Palaeologus	1391-1425	Manuel II Palaeologus
1282-1328	Andronicus II	1425-1448	John VIII Palaeologus
	Palaeologus	1449-1453	Constantine XI
1328-1341	Andronicus III		Palaeologus
	Palaeologus		

OTTOMAN RULERS

1281-1324	Osman I	1640-1648	Ibrahim
1324-1360	Orkhan	1648-1687	Mohammed IV
1360-1389	Murad I	1687-1691	Suleiman II
1389-1402	Bayazid I	1691-1695	Akhmet II
1402-1413	Interregnum	1695-1703	Mustafa II
1413-1421	Mohammed I	1703-1730	Akhmet III
1421-1451	Murad II	1730-1754	Mahmud I
1451-1481	Mohammed II, the	1754-1757	Osman III
	Conqueror	1757-1774	Mustafa III
1481-1512	Bayazid II	1774-1789	Abd-ul-Hamid I
1512-1520	Selim I	1789-1807	Selim III
1520-1566	Suleiman I	1807-1808	Mustafa IV
1566-1574	Selim II	1808-1839	Mahmud II
1574-1595	Murad III	1839-1861	Abd-ul-Mejid I
1595-1603	Mohammed III	1861-1876	Abd-ul-Aziz
1603-1617	Akhmet I	1876-1909	Abd-ul-Hamid II
1617-1618	Mustafa I	1909-1918	Mohammed V
1618-1622	Osman II	1918-1922	Mohammed VI
1622-1623	Mustafa I (second time)	1922-1924	Abd-ul-Mejid II
1623-1640	Murad IV		

BIBLIOGRAPHICAL ABBREVIATIONS

AÖG   *Archiv für österreiche Geschichte* (1848-1865 as *Archiv für Kunde österreichischer Geschichtsquellen*), vols. 1- , Vienna, 1865- .

ASPh   *Archiv für slavische Philologie,* Berlin, 1875-1929.

BZ   *Byzantinische Zeitschrift,* Leipzig, 1892-1943, Munich, 1949- .

CMH   *Cambride Medieval History,* Cambridge, 8 vols., 1911-1936.

CSHB   *Corpus scriptorum historiae Byzantinae,* 50 vols., Bonn, 1828-1897.

FOG   *Forschungen zur osteuropäischen Geschichte,* Berlin, 1954- .

FRA   *Fontes rerum Austriacarum,* Abt. 1, *Scriptores,* 9 vols., Vienna, 1855-1904, Abt. 2, *Diplomataria et acta,* vols. 1- , Vienna, 1849- .

FRB   *Fontes rerum Bohemicarum,* 6 vols., Prague, 1871-1907.

HZ   *Historische Zeitschrift,* Munich, 1859-1943, 1949- .

JGO   *Jahrbücher für Geschichte Osteuropas,* Breslau, 1936-1941, Munich, 1953- .

JKGS   *Jahrbücher für Kultur und Geschichte der Slaven,* Breslau, 1924-1932.

MGH   *Monumenta Germaniae historica, Diplomata, Epistolae, Scriptores.*

MHB   *Monumenta historiae Bohemica,* 5 vols., Prague, 1865-1870.

MPH   *Monumenta Poloniae historica,* vols. 1- , Lwów, 1864-1893, 1946- .

OCA   *Orientalia Christiana analecta,* Rome, 1931- .

OCP   *Orientalia Christiana periodica,* Rome, 1935- .

OSP   *Oxford Slavonic Papers,* Oxford, 1950- .

PL   *Patrologia Latina,* 221 vols., Paris, 1844-1880.

PSRL   *Polnoe sobranie russkikh letopisej,* vols. 1- , St. Petersburg, 1841- .

RES   *Revue des études Slaves,* Paris, 1921- .

RIB   *Russkaja istoričeskaja biblioteka,* 39 vols., St. Petersburg-Leningrad, 1872-1927.

RPThK   *Realenzyklopädie für protestantische Theologie und Kirche,* 24 vols., Leipzig, 1896-1913.

SbAW   *Sitzungsberichte der Akademie der Wissenschaften,* philosophisch-historische Klasse, Vienna, 1848- .

SEER   *Slavonic and East European Review,* London, 1921- .

SF   *Südost deutsche forschungen,* Leipzig, 1936 ff.

SR   *Slavische Rundschau,* Prague, 1929-1940.

SRB   *Scriptores rerum Bohemicarum,* Prague, 3 vols., 1783-1829.

SRP   *Scriptores rerum Polonicarum,* 22 vols., Cracow, 1872-1917.

SRS   *Scriptores rerum Silesicarum,* 17 vols., Breslau, 1835-1902.

WMBH   *Wissenschaftliche Mittheilungen aus Bosnien und der Hercegovina,* Vienna, 1893-1916.

ZOG   *Zeitschrift für osteuropäische Geschichte,* Königsberg.
ZSPh   *Zeitschrift für slavische Philologie,* Leipzig, 1924-1944, Heidelberg, 1947-
ZSSR   *Zeitschrift der Savigny-Stiftung für Rechtsgeschichte,* Germanistische Abteilung, Weimar, 1880-1944, 1947-

BIBLIOGRAPHY

1. General

So far only a few attempts have been made at a comprehensive survey of the history and civilization of all the Slavic peoples. The most exhaustive contribution in this field is the Czech *History of the Slavs* (*Dějiny slovanstva*), written by J. Bidlo (Prague, 1927). The same scholar tried also to solve the problem of the periodization of eastern European history, important for a better comprehension of Slavic history, in his study, *Ce qu'est l'histoire de l'orient européen, quelle en est l'importance et quelles furent ses étapes,* Bulletin d'information de l'Europe orientale, 6 (1934). He was joined in the discussion of this problem by O. Halecki, who summarized his ideas in his work, *The Limits and Divisions of European History* (New York, 1950). His book, *Borderlands of Western Civilization* (New York, 1952), constitutes a very good introduction to the history of the western and eastern Slavs. F. Nowak's book, *Medieval Slavdom and the Rise of Russia* (New York, 1930), is only a very short survey.

The most thorough histories of Slavic literature, with a good bibliography, were written in Czech by J. Máchal, *Slovanské literatury*, 2 vols. (Prague, 1922, 1925) and by F. Wollman, *Slovesnost Slavanů* (Prague, 1928). These superseded the work by A. N. Pypine and W. Spasović, *Histoire des littératures slaves,* translated by E. Denis (Paris, 1881). A German translation of this work also exists. This work, although now superseded, does have the advantage that it is accessible to those readers not knowing Czech. A good introduction to comparative studies of Slavic literatures was given by D. Čiževsky, *Outline of Comparative Slavic Literature* (Boston, 1952), and by R. Jakobson, "Kernel of Comparative Slavic Literature," *Harvard Slavic Studies*, 1 (1953), pp. 1-71. E. Damiani made recently a short survey of the history of Slavic literature, *Storia letteraria dei popoli slavi* (Florence, 1952).

Slavic history and civilization from the beginning to the thirteenth century has been outlined by F. Dvornik, *The Slavs: Their Early History and Civilization* (Boston, 1956). *Slavic Civilization through the Ages* (Cambridge, Mass., 1948) by S. H. Cross is useful as an introduction to Slavic studies. For a general bibliography of the Slavic peoples, the work by R. J. Kerner, *Slavic Europe: A Selected Bibliography in the Western European Languages* (Cambridge, Mass., 1918), is still very useful. A basic bibliography with short outlines is given in L. I. Strakhovsky's *A Handbook of Slavic Studies* (Cambridge, Mass., 1949).

On the historiography of the European East, the excellent work by J. Macůrek, *Dějepisectví evropského východu* (Prague, 1946), although written in Czech, is useful to everyone because of the exhaustive bibliography given at the end, pp. 291-331. German bibliography on eastern and southern Europe from 1939 to 1952 is listed in the publication by W. Philip, I. Smolitsch, and F. Valjavec, "Verzeichnis des deutschsprachigen Schrifttums 1939-1952 zur Geschichte Osteuropas und Südosteuropas," FOG 1 (1954), pp. 251-316. See also Valjavec' *Südosteuropa-Bibliographie* (Munich, 1945 ff.). Smolitsch reveiwed Soviet publications on the same subject in the same revue, from 1939-1952, "Verzeichnis des sovjetrussischen Schrifttums 1939-1952 zur Geschichte Osteuropas und Südosteuropas," 3 (1956), pp. 99-281. G. Hanusch compiled a list of all dissertations on eastern Europe published from 1951-1958, "Osteuropa-Lissertationen," JGO, NF, 3 (1955), 4 (1956), 6 (1958). The *Manuel d'histoire russe* by P. Kovalevsky (Paris, 1948) contains short bibliographical indications on different periods of Russian history. More useful in this respect, especially for American students, is C. Morley's *Guide to Research in Russian History* (Syracuse, 1951). Very important are the studies by G. Stökl which appeared in the JGO on historical works published by Soviet scholars, "Russisches Mittelalter und sovjetrussische Mediaevistic," 3 (1955), pp. 105-22, and "Russische Geschichte von der Entstehung des Kiever Reiches bis zum Ende der Wirren 862-1613," 6 (1958), pp. 201-54, 268-88. H. Holm completed these bibliographical studies with his work, "Achtzig Jahre russischer Geschichtsschreibung ausserhalb Russland," in the same review, 5 (1957), pp. 9-42. This study is more critical than the work by I. I. Gapanovitch, *Introduction à l'histoire de la Russie, Historiographie russe hors de la Russie*, translated and annotated by B. P. Nikitin (Paris, 1946). More recent is A. G. Mazour's work, *Modern Russian Historiography* (2nd ed., Princeton, 1958).

An extensive bibliography of the sources for the history of the South Slavs, together with translations into English of certain passages, is being prepared by J. F. Clarke of the University of Pittsburgh. An extensive bibliography is given concerning Yugoslav historiography in *Dix années d'historiographie yougoslave 1945-1955, Comité national yougoslave des sciences historiques* (Belgrade, 1955). Good bibliographical indications may be located in the work *Historija naroda Jugoslavije*, ed. B. Grafenauer, D. Perović, J. Šidak (Zagreb, 1953), vol. 1. The *Bibliografija Jugoslavije*, published in Belgrade since 1950, gives information on recent Yugoslav publications. A bibliography of early South Slavic and Byzantine history is to be found in D. Angelov and D. Dmitrov, "Bulletin des publications sur les travaux bulgares . . . ," *Byzantinoslavica*, 9 (1948), pp. 355-78, covering those works published in Bulgaria from 1939-1945. Information on earlier Bulgarian bibliography is located in the study by I. Dujčev, "Die bulgarische Geschichtsforschung während des letzten Vierteljahrhunderts (1918-1942)," *Südost-Forschungen*, 7 (1942), pp. 546-69.

For Poland, the work by W. Recke and A. M. Wagner, *Bücherkunde zur Geschichte und Literatur des Königreiches Polen* (Leipzig, 1918), gives indications on sources and basic works to Polish history and literature. L. Finkel's *Bibliografia historyi polskiej* (Warsaw, 1891, 1955), 3 vols.,—continued in *Bibliografia historii Polski* (Warsaw, 1954, in progress)—contains information on the sources and works on Polish history from 1815 to 1916. For the Czechs, the bibliography by Č. Zíbrt, *Bibliografie české historie*, 5 vols. (Prague, 1900-1912) is still important. This work was continued by Josef Kazimour, Josef Klik and S. Jonášová-Hájková, in progress. Cf. also J. Macek, V. Husa, and B. Varsik, *25 ans d'historiographie*. (Prague, 1960)

The *Slovenska bibliografia*, 6 vols. (Ljubljana, 1954), contains bibliography for the years 1945-1952 in Slovene.

The *Revue des études slaves*, published since 1921, contains material on contemporary bibliography for all the Slavic peoples.

2. *Handbooks of the General History of the Slavic Nations in Non-Slavic Languages.*

Antonoff, V. *Bulgarien vom Beginn seines staatlichen Bestehens bis auf unsere Zeit, 679-1917.* (Berlin, 1917)

Braun, M. *Die Slawen auf dem Balkan.* (Leipzig, 1941)

Cambridge History of Poland. 2 vols. (Cambridge, 1941, 1950)

Caro, J. *Geschichte Polens.* vols. 2-5. (Gotha, 1863-88). A continuation of R. Roepell's history.

Doroshenko, D. *History of the Ukraine.* (Edmonton, 1939)

Dyboski, R. *Poland in World Civilization.* (New York, 1950)

Florinsky, M. T. *Russia: A History and an Interpretation.* 2 vols. (New York, 1953)

Forbes, N., et al. *The Balkans: A History of Bulgaria, Serbia, Greece, Rumania and Turkey.* (Oxford, 1915)

Gáldi, L., Makkai, L. *Geschichte der Rumänen.* (Budapest, 1942)

Gitermann, V. *Geschichte Russlands.* vols. 1, 2. (Hamburg, 1949)

Halecki, O. *A History of Poland.* (New York, 1943)

Hanisch, E. *Geschichte Polens.* (Bonn-Leipzig, 1923)

Haumant, E. *La formation de la Yougoslavie.* (Paris, 1930)

Hrushevsky, M. *A History of the Ukraine.* (New York, 1941)

Iorga, N. *Histoire des états balkaniques jusqu'à 1924.* (Paris, 1925)

Karamzin, N. *Geschichte des russischen Reiches.* 3 vols. (St. Petersburg, 1842-44). Cf. R. Bächtold, *Karamzins Weg zur Geschichte.* Basler Beitrage für Geschichtswissenschaft, vol. 23 (1946).

Kirchner, W. *An Outline History of Russia.* 2nd ed. (New York, 1950). Germ. ed. (Stuttgart, 1950)

Ključevskij, V. O. *A History of Russia.* Transl. by C. J. Hogarth. 5 vols. (London, New York, 1911-31). German transl. by Reinhold v. Walter, *Geschichte Russlands.* 4 vols. (Stuttgart, 1924-25)

Krofta, K. *A Short History of Czechoslovakia.* (New York, 1934)

Krupnyćkyj, B. *Geschichte der Ukraine.* (Leipzig, 1939)

Lednicki, W. *Life and Culture of Poland.* (New York, 1944)

Leger, L. *Serbes, Croates et Bulgares.* (Paris, 1913)

Lelevel, J. *Histoire de Pologne.* 2 vols. (Paris, 1844)

Lončar, D. *The Slovenes.* (Cleveland, 1939)

Luetzow, C. F. *Bohemia, An Historical Sketch.* (London, 1910; revised ed., 1939, by H. A. Piehler)

Maurice, C. E. *Bohemia from the Earliest Times to the Fall of National Independence in 1620.* (Story of the Nations.) (London, 1896)

Mazour, A. C. *Russia, Past and Present.* (New York, 1951)

Mirsky, D. *A History of Russian Literature.* (New York, 1949). Important for the modern period.

Mishev, D. *The Bulgarians in the Past.* (Lausanne, 1919)

Pares, B. *A History of Russia.* 2nd ed. (New York, 1937)

Platonov, S. F. *Histoire de la Russie.* (Paris, 1929)

Platonov, S. F. *History of Russia.* Transl. by E. Aronsberg. (New York, 1925)

Polish Encyclopedia. (Geneva, 1926). vol. 1, S. Dobrzycki, History of literature, pp. 27-231; L. Konopczyński, History of Poland to 1815, pp. 481-512.

Prokeš, J. *Histoire tchécoslovaque.* (Paris, 1927)

Ristelhuber, R. *Histoire des peuples balkaniques.* (Paris, 1950)

Rose, W. J. *Poland—Old and New.* (London, 1948)

Schevill, F., and Gewehr, W. M. *A History of the Balkan Peninsula.* (New York, 1933)

Seton-Watson, R. W. *A History of the Czechs and Slovaks.* (London, 1943)

Slatarski (Zlatarski), V. N., and Staneff, N. *Geschichte der Bulgaren.* 2 vols. (Leipzig, 1917-18)

Solovjov, S. *Russische Geschichte.* 13 vols. 3rd ed. (Moscow, 1857-63). Cf. Klaus-Detlev v. Grothusen. "S. M. Solov'evs Stellung in der russischen Historiographie," FOG, 4 (1956), pp. 1-102.

Songeon, G. *Histoire de la Bulgarie des origines à nos jours, 485-1913.* (Paris, 1913)

Stadtmüller, G. *Geschichte Südosteuropas.* (Munich, 1950).

Stählin, K. *Geschichte Russlands.* 4 vols. (Leipzig, Berlin, 1923)

Sumner, B. H. *Survey of Russian History.* (London, 1944)

Temperley, H. *History of Serbia.* (London, 1917)

Thomson, S. H. *Czechoslovakia in European History.* (Princeton, 1953)

Tompkins, S. R. *Russia through the Ages: From the Scythians to the Soviets.* (New York, 1940)

Vernadsky, G. *A History of Russia.* 2nd ed. (New York, 1930)

Vernadsky, G. *Political and Diplomatic History of Russia.* (London, 1937).

Wojciechowski, Z. (ed.), *Poland's Place in Europe.* (Poznań, 1947)

CHAPTER I, *Bibliography*

Artz, F. B. *The Mind of the Middle Ages, 200-1500: A Historical Survey.* (New York, 1953)

Barraclough, G. *Mediaeval Germany, 911-1250.* 2 vols. (*Studies in Mediaeval History,* vols. 1, 2.) (Oxford, 1938)

Bayley, C. C. *Formation of the German College of Electors in the Mid-Thirteenth Century.* (Toronto, 1949)

Bernheim, E. *Mittelalterliche Zeitanschauungen in ihrem Einfluss auf Politik und Geschichtsschreibung.* (Tübingen, 1918)

Bidlo, J. "The Slavs in Medieval History," SEER, 9 (1930-31), pp. 34-55.

Bloch, M. *La société féodale: Evolution de l'humanité,* ed. H. Berr. 2 vols. (Paris, 1939-40)

Boase, T. S. R. *Boniface VIII.* (London, 1933)

Bond, F. *Gothic Architecture in England.* (London, 1905)

Bryce, J. *The Holy Roman Empire.* (London, 1922)

Cambridge Medieval History, vol. 6, *Victory of the Papacy* (Cambridge, 1929): E. F. Jacob, *Innocent III;* A. L. Poole, *Philip of Swabia and Otto IV; Germany in the Reign of Frederick II; The Interregnum in Germany.*

Carsten, F. L. *The Origins of Prussia.* (Oxford, 1954)

Clagett, M., Post, G. and Reynolds, R., eds., *Twelfth Century Europe and the Foundations of Modern Society.* (Madison, 1961)

Dvornik, F. *The Slavs, Their Early History and Civilization.* (Boston, 1956)

Encyclopédie de la Pléiade, Histoire universelle (Paris, 1954), vol. 2: G. Leonard, "L'Italie médiévale," pp. 434-594; R. Folz, "Le monde germanique," pp. 595-693; Fawtier, R., "Les Capétiens directs," pp. 708-873; A. Fichelle, "Le monde slave," pp. 1109-67.

Fliche, A. *"Le Chrétienté médiévale,"* Histoire do monde, ed. E. Cavaignac, vol. 7, 2nd part. (Paris, 1929)

Ganshof, F. L. *Feudalism.* Transl. by P. Grierson. (London, New York, Toronto, 1952). The French original is *Qu'est-ce la féodalité.* 2nd ed. (Brussels, Lausanne, 1947), third ed., 1957.

Gierke, O. F. *Political Theories of the Middle Ages.* Transl. by F. W. Maitland. (Cambridge, 1938)

Haaf, R. ten. *Deutschordenstaat,* see footnote 8.

Haller, J. *Von den Staufern zu den Habsburgern.* 2nd ed. (Berlin, 1943)

Halphen, L. *L'essor de l'Europe (12e-13e siècles).* 3rd ed. (Paris, 1948)

Hampe, K. *Deutsche Kaisergeschichte in der Zeit der Salier und Staufer.* 9th ed. by A. Baethgen. (Leipzig, 1946)

———. *Das Hochmittelalter.* (Berlin, 1932)

Haskins, C. H. *The Renaissance of the Twelfth Century.* (Cambridge, Mass., 1939)

Hassinger, E., *Das Werden des neuzeitichen Europa 1300-1600.* (Braunschweig, 1959)

Hauck, A. *Deutschland und die päpstliche Weltherrschaft.* (Leipzig, 1910)

Hellman, M., Bibl. on Teutonic Order, see footnote 8.

Kantorowicz, E. H. *Kaiser Friedrich der Zweite.* (Berlin, 1928). English trans. by E. O. Lorimer, *Frederick the Second, 1194-1250.* (New York, 1957)

Kauffmann, H. *Die italienische Politik Kaiser Friedrichs I, 1183-1189.* (Greifswald, 1933)

Kempf, F. *Papsttum und Kaisertum bei Innocenz III.* (Rome, 1954)

Kern, F. *Kingship and Law in the Middle Ages.* Transl. by S. B. Chrimes. (*Studies in Medieval History,* ed. G. Barraclough, vol. 4.) (Oxford, 1939)

Knapke, P. J. *Frederick Barbarossa's Conflict with the Papacy: A Problem of Church and State.* (Washington, 1939). Good bibl. Written from the Roman point of view.

Koch, F. *Livland und das Reich bis zum Jahre 1225.* (Quellen und Forschungen zur baltischen Geschichte, vol. 4.) (Posen, 1943)

Lewis, E. K. *Medieval Political Ideas.* 2 vols. (London, 1954)

Lodge, R. *The Close of the Middle Ages, 1273-1494.* (Periods of European History.) (London, 1949)

Luchaire, J. *Innocent III: La papauté et l'empire.* (Paris, 1906)

Mâle, E. *L'art religieux du 13e siècle en France.* (Paris, 1923)

Maschke, E. *Der deutsche Ordenstaat.* (Hamburg, 1935)

Mitteis, H. *Die deutsche Königswahl.* 2nd ed. (Brünn, Munich, Vienna, 1944)

———. *Der Staat des hohen Mittelalters.* 4th ed. (Weimar, 1953)

Otto, E. *Friedrich Barbarossa.* (Potsdam, 1943)

Pagel, K. *Die Hanse.* (Braunschweig, 1952)

Painter, S. *French Chivalry: Chivalric Ideas and Practices in Mediaeval France.* (Baltimore, 1948)

Petit-Dutaillis, C. *La monarchie féodale en France et en Angleterre Xe-XIIIe siècle.* (*Evolution de l'humanité,* ed. H. Berr.) (Paris, 1933)

Pirenne, H. *La civilisation occidentale au moyen âge du XIe au milieu du XVe siècle.* (Paris, 1941)

Pirenne, J. *Les grands courants de l'histoire universelle,* vol. 2, *De l'expansion musulmane au traité de Westphalie.* (Neuchâtel, 1947)

Raby, F. J. E. *A History of Christian-Latin Poetry from the Beginning to the Close of the Middle Ages.* 2nd ed. (Oxford, 1953)

——. *A History of Secular Latin Poetry in the Middle Ages.* (Oxford, 1934)

Schubert, H. v. *Der Kampf des geistlichen und weltlichen Rechts, SBAW,* phil.-hist. Kl. (1927)

Sedgwick, H. D. *Italy in the Thirteenth Century.* 2 vols. (Boston, New York, 1912). Popular.

Sellery, G. C., and Krey, A. C. *Medieval Foundations of Western Civilization.* (New York, 1929)

Stickler, M. "Imperator vicarius Papal. Die Lehren der französisch-deutschen Dekretistenschule des 12. und beginnenden 13. Jhs. über die Beziehungen zwischen Papst und Kaiser," *Mitteilungen des Instituts für österreich. Geschichtsforschung,* 62 (1954), pp. 165-212.

Strayer, J. R., and Munro, D. C. *The Middle Ages, 395-1500.* (New York, London, 1942)

Taylor, H. O. *The Medieval Mind.* 2 vols. (Cambridge, Mass., 4th ed. 1949)

Tellenbach, G. *Church, State and Christian Society at the Time of the Investiture Contest.* Transl. by R. F. Bennett. (*Studies in Medieval History,* ed. G. Barraclough, vol. 3.) (Oxford, 1941)

Thompson, J. W. *Feudal Germany.* (Chicago, 1928). To be used with caution.

Totoraitis, J. *Die Litauer unter dem Könige Mindowe.* (Freiburg, Switzerland, 1905)

Tout, T. F. *The Empire and the Papacy, 918-1273.* (*Periods of European History,* ed. A. Hassal, vol. 2.) 8th ed. (London, 1924, reprint 1954)

Ullmann, W. *The Growth of Papal Government in the Middle Ages.* (London, 1955)

——. *Medieval Papalism: The Political Theories of the Medieval Canonists.* (London, 1949)

Vogel, W., Bibliography on the Hansa, see footnote 9.

Wojciechowski, Z. *Territorial Development of Prussia in Relation to the Polish Homeland* (Toruń, 1936)

CHAPTER II, *Sources*

Chronicles and Memorials of Great Britain and Ireland. vol. 27, 1, W.W. Shirley, *Royal and Other Historical Letters Illustrative of the Reign of Henry III.*

Codex diplomaticus Majoris Poloniae, vols. 1-4 (from 984-1400), ed. J. Zakrzewski. (Posnań, 1877-81)

Codex diplomaticus Poloniae Minoris. 4 vols. (from 1178-1450), ed. F. Piekosiński. (Cracow, 1876-1905)

Codex epistolaris Primislai Ottocari II Bohemiae regis, ed. T. Dolliner. (Vienna, 1803). Contains also the letters of Henry of Isernia.

Emler, J. *FRB,* vol. 2 (*Continuators of Cosmas*); vol. 3 (*Dalimil Chronicle*); vol. 4 (*Zbraslav Chronicle*); vol. 5 (*Pulkava Chronicle*). (Prague, 1873 ff.)

——. *Regesta diplomatica necnon epistolaria regni Bohemiae et Moraviae,* ed. C. J. Erben, J. Emler. 4 vols. (Prague, 1855 ff.)

Friedrich, G. *Codex diplomaticus et epistolaris regni Bohemiae.* 3 vols. (Prague, 1904-42). Vol. 3, from 1231-38, is incomplete.

Hampe, K. *Beiträge zur Geschichte der letzten Staufer: Ungedruckte Briefe aus der Sammlung des Magisters Heinrich von Isernia.* (Leipzig, 1910)

Helbling, S. *Poems,* ed. J. Seemüller. (Halle/Saale, 1886)

Krabbo, H. *Regesten der Markgrafen von Brandenburg aus askanischem Hause.* 11 vols. (Leipzig-Munich-Berlin, 1910-33)

Krammer, M. *Quellen zur Geschichte der deutschen Königswahl und des Kurfürstenkollegs.* 2 vols. (Leipzig, 1925-32)

MGHS, vol. 9 (*Hist. an. 1264-1279, Continuatio Vindobon. 1267-1327, Chron. Salisburg.*); vol. 17 (Eberhardus Altahensis, Henricus de Heimburg), *MGH Const.;* vol. 3 (Letters of Rudolf and Přemysl Ottakar II), *MGH Deutsche Chroniken;* vol. 5 (Otakar of Styria).

MPH, vol. 2 (Chronicon of Kujavia, Mechow, Traski); vol. 3 (Chron. of Little Poland). Cf. also *MGHS,* vol. 19 (An. Cracov. Capituli, An. Polonorum, Mechowienses)

Palacký, F. *Über Formelbücher, zunächst in Bezug auf böhmische Geschichte.* (Abhandlungen der königlichen böhmischen Gesellschaft der Wissenschaften, 5. Folge, vols. 2, 5.) (Prague, 1842)

Seton, W. *Some New Sources from the Life of Blessed Agnes of Bohemia.* (London, 1915). See also the edition of the *Legend of Blessed Agnes* and of the letters of St. Clare by J. K. Vyskočil, *Legenda bl. Anežky.* (Prague, 1932)

CHAPTER II, *Bibliography*

Bachmann, A. *Geschichte Böhmens.* 2 vols. (Gotha, 1899, 1905)

Bretholz, B. *Geschichte Böhmens und Mährens bis zum Aussterben der Premysliden, 1306.* (Munich, Leipzig, 1912)

Emler, J. *Die Kanzlei Přemysl Otakars II. und Wenzels II. und die aus derselben hervorgegangenen Formelbücher* (Abhandlungen der böhmischen Gesellschaft der Wissenschaften.) (Prague, 1878)

Fiedler, J. "Böhmens Herrschaft in Polen," *AÖG,* 14 (1855), pp. 161-88.

Franzel, E. *König Heinrich VII. von Hohenstaufen: Studien zur Geschichte des "Staates" in Deutschland.* (Prague, 1929)

Hessel, A. *Jahrbücher des Deutschen Reichs unter K. Albrecht von Habsburg.* (Munich, 1931)

Hugelmann, K. G. *Die Wahl Konrads IV. zu Wien im Jahre 1237.* (Weimar, 1914)

Jastrow, J., and Winter, G. *Deutsche Geschichte im Zeitalter der Hohenstaufen.* vol. I from 1190-1273. (Stuttgart, 1897, 1901)

Kalousek, J. *Die Behandlung der Geschichte König Přemysl Otakars II, in Prof. O. Lorenz, Deutsche Geschichte im 13. und 14. Jahrhunderte.* (Prague, 1874)

Kempf, J. *Geschichte des deutschen Reiches während des grossen Interregnum 1245-1273.* (Würzburg, 1893)

Köster, A. *Die staat lichen Beziehungen der böhmischen Herzöge und Könige zu den deutschen Kaisern.* (Breslau, 1912)

Krofta, K. "Bohemia to the Extinction of the Přemyslids," *CMH,* 6 (1929), pp. 422-47.

Lewis, F. R. "Ottokar II of Bohemia and the Double Election of 1257," *Speculum,* 12 (1937), pp. 512-15.

Lorenz, O. *Deutsche Geschichte im 13. und 14. Jahrhunderte.* 2 vols. (Vienna, 1863-1867)

——. *Geschichte König Ottokars II. von Böhmen.* (Vienna, 1886). Cf. however the critical remarks by J. Kalousek.

Maschke, E. *Polen und die Berufung des Deutschen Ordens nach Preussen.* (Danzig, 1934)

Neumann, W. *Die deutschen Königswahlen und der päpstliche Machtanspruch während des Interrregnums.* (Berlin, 1920)

Novák, J. B. "Henricus Italicus und Henricus de Isernia," *Mitteilungen des Instituts für österreichische Geschichte,* 20.

Pfeffer, W. *Die böhmische Politik unter Wenzel II.* Dissertation. (Halle, 1901)

Priesack, J. D. *Die Reichspolitik des Erzbischofs Balduin von Trier in den Jahren 1314-1378.* (Göttingen, 1894)

Redlich, O. *Rudolf von Habsburg: Das Deutsche Reich nach dem Untergange des alten Kaisertums.* (Innsbruck, 1903)

Thompson, J. W. "Medieval German Expansion in Bohemia," *SEER,* 4 (1925-26), pp. 605-28.

——. "German Medieval Expansion and the Making of Austria," *SEER,* 2 (1923-24), pp. 263-88.

Vancsa, M. *Geschichte von Nieder- und Oberösterreich.* (Stuttgart, 1927). Cf. A. W. Leeper, *A Hist. of Mediev. Austria.* (Oxford, 1941)

Uhlirz, K. and M. *Handbuch der Geschichte Österreichs und seiner Nachbarländer Böhmen und Ungarn,* I. (Graz, 1907)

Wegener, W. *Böhmen-Mähren und das Reich im Mittelalter; Untersuchungen zur Stellung Böhmens und Mährens im Deutschen Reich des Mittelalters 919-1253.* (Köln-Graz, Böhlan, 1959.) To be used with caution. Cf. the review in the Czech Histor. Review, N. S., 8 (1960) ff. 176-85, by Z. Fiala.

Winkelmann, E. A. *Friedrich II.* 2 vols. (Leipzig, 1889-1897)

Wunderlich, B. *Die neueren Ansichten über die deutsche Königswahl und den Ursprung des Kurfürstenkollegs.* (Berlin, 1913).

CHAPTER III, *Sources*

Acta imperii inedita saeculi XIII et XIV (1198-1400), ed. E. Winkelmann. 2 vols. (Innsbruck, 1880, 1885)

Annales Parmenses maiores, MGH, S XVIII, pp. 664 ff.

Archivum Coronae Regni Bohemiae, ed. V. Hrubý. vol. I (1056-1346), vol. II (1348-1355). (Prague, 1928, 1935)

Chronica aulae regiae, FRB, vol. IV (Prague, 1884), FRA, vol. VIII (Vienna, 1875). Cf. J. Loserth, "Die Königsaler Geschichtsquellen," *AÖG,* 51 (1873), pp. 451-99.

Chronica principum Poloniae, ed. Stenzel, SRS, I, pp. 38 ff. Also *ibidem Chronica Polonorum.*

Chronicon Benessii Minoritae, MHB IV.

"Chronicon de St. Denis." *Grandes chroniques de France,* vol. V (Paris, 1837).

Chronicon Francisci Pragensis, FRB IV.

Chronicon Pulkavae, MHB III, FRB V. (Prague, 1774)

Codex diplomaticus Brandenburgensis, ed. A. F. Riedel. (Berlin, 1838 ff.)

Codex diplomaticus Prussicus, ed. J. Voigt. vols. I-III. (Königsberg, 1836 ff.)

Codex diplomaticus Silesiae, ed. C. Grünhagen and C. Wutke. vols. XVI, XVIII,

XXII, XIX, XXX, containing in this order the years from 1301 to 1342. (Breslau: Verein für Geschichte und Altertum Schlesiens, 1892, 1898, 1903, 1923, 1925)

Codex epistolarius Johannis, regis Bohemiae, ed. Jacobi. (Berlin, 1841)

Dantis Alagherii Epistolae, ed. P. Toynbee. (Oxford, 1920)

Froissart, Jean de. *Chronique,* ed. K. de Lettenhove. (Brussels, 1863)

——. *Les chroniques,* ed. A. Buchon. 3 vols. (Paris, 1837-1838)

Guillaume de Machaut. *Oeuvres,* ed. E. Hopeffner. 3 vols. (Société des anciens textes français, vol. 58.) (Paris, 1908, 1911, 1921)

——. *La prise d'Alexandrie,* ed. by M. Latrie. (Société de l'Orient latin, Série hist. I.) (Geneva, 1877)

Johann von Winterthur. *Chronica,* ed. F. Baethgen, *MGH,* S, Nov. Ser. III. (Berlin, 1924)

Johannes de Thurocz. *Chronica Hungarorum,* ed. Schwandter, *SRH* I, pp. 47 ff.

Lites et res gestae intra Polonos ordinenemque cruciferorum, ed. Count Dzialyński. 2 vols. 2nd ed. (Poznań, 1890)

Marsilius of Padua. *Defensor Pacis,* ed. C. W. Previté-Orton. (Cambridge, 1928)

Monumenta Vaticana res gestas Bohemiae illustrantia, pars I, II, ed. Klicmann. (Prague, 1903, 1907)

Nova Alamaniae, Urkunden, Briefe und andere Quellen, besonders zur deutschen Geschichte des 14. Jahrhunderts vornehmlich aus den Sammlungen des Trierer Notars und Offizials Rudolf Losse, ed. Stengel. 1st half (Berlin, 1921), 2nd half, part 1. (Berlin, 1930)

Regesta diplomatica nec non epistolaria Bohemiae et Moraviae, parts II-IV, from 1253-1346, ed. K. J. Erben and J. Emler. (Prague, 1882, 1890, 1892). vol. V (1346-1355), vol. VI (1355-1358), vol. VII (1358-1363), editors: B. Mendl, M. Linhartová et al. In progress.

Regesta Habsburgica, third part (1330-1340), ed. L. Gross. (Innsbruck, 1924)

Regesta historico-diplomatica Ordinis S. Mariae Theutonicorum 1198-1525, ed. W. Hubatsch. 2 vols. (Göttingen, 1948-50)

Regesta imperii inde ab anno 1314 usque ad a. 1347, Die Urkunden Kaiser Ludwig des Bayern, König Friedrich des Schönen und König Johanns von Böhmen, ed. J. F. Böhmer. (Frankfurt a. M., 1839). Additamentum I, II, III (1841, 1846, 1865). See also *Wittelsbachische Regesten,* Ch. IV.

Summa Gerhardi, Ein Formelbuch aus der Zeit Königs Johanns von Böhmen. *AÖG,* vol. 63, ed. F. Tadra. (Vienna, 1882)

Vita Caroli quarti ab ipso scripta, ed. E. Emler, FRB III.

CHAPTER III, *Bibliography*

Aubin, H., Petry, L., and Schlenger, H. *Geschichte Schlesiens,* vol. 1 (to 1526) (3rd ed., Stuttgart, 1961)

Bock, F. *Reichsidee und Nationalstaaten vom Untergang des alten Reiches bis zur Kündigung des deutsch-englischen Bündnisses im Jahre 1341.* (Munich, 1944)

Boswell, B. "The Teutonic Order," CMH, VII, pp. 248-69. On pp. 858 ff. complete bibl. of sources.

Cazalles, R. *Jean l'Aveugle, Comte de Luxembourg, roi de Bohême.* (Paris, 1947)

Drivok, P. *Ältere Geschichte der deutschen Reichsstadt–Eger und des Reichs-gebites Egerland.* (Leipzig, 1875)

Dumontrel, C. *L'impressa italiana di giovanni di Lussemburgo Re di Boemia.* (Turin, 1952)

Emmelmann, M. *Die Beziehungen des Deutschen Ordens zu König Johann von Böhmen und Karl IV.* Dissertation. (Halle, 1910)

Ficken, E. *Johann von Böhmen, eine Studie zum romantischen Rittertum des 14. Jahrhunderts.* Dissertation. (Göttingen, 1932)

Fournier, P. *Le royaume d'Arles et de Vienne (1138-1378).* (Paris, 1891)

Hecht, F. *Johann von Mähren.* Dissertation. (Halle, 1911)

Heidemann, J. "Heinrich von Kärnten als König von Böhmen," *Forschungen zur deutschen Geschichte,* 9 (1871), pp. 261 ff.

———. *Peter von Aspelt als Kirchenfürst und Staatsmann.* (Berlin, 1875)

Homan, B. *Gli Angiovini di Napoli in Ungheria 1290-1403.* Transl. by L. Zambra and R. Mosca. (Rome, 1938)

Hoschek, T. *Der Abt von Königsaal und die Königin Elisabeth aus Böhmen.* (Prager Studien aus dem Gebiete der wissenschaftlichen Geschichte, Heft V.) (Prague, 1900)

Klages, H. E. "Johann von Luxemburg und seine auf Böhmen gerichtete Heirats-politik (1310-1342)," *Mitteilungen des Vereines für die Geschichte der Deutschen in Böhmen,* 50 (1912).

Klein, W. "Schicksale der Überreste des Königs Johann von Böhmen, Grafen von Luxemburg," *Mitteilungen des Vereines für die Geschichte der Deutschen in Böhmen,* 45 (1907), pp. 368 ff.

Kohn, K. *Johann der Blinde, Graf von Luxemburg und König von Böhmen in seinen Beziehungen zu Frankreich.* (Luxemburg, 1895)

Kraack, E. *Rom oder Avignon? Die römische Frage unter den Päpsten Clement V. und Johann XXII.* (Marburg, 1929)

Krammer, H. *Das Kurfürstenkolleg von seinen Anfängen bis zum Zusam-menschluss im Renser Kurverein des Jahres 1333.* (Quellen und Studien zur Verfassungsgeschichte des deutschen Reiches im Mittelalter und Neuzeit, ed. K. Zeumer, vol. V, Heft I.) (Weimar, 1913)

Landogna, F. "Giovanni di Boemia e Carolo IV di Lussemburgo, signore di Lucca," *Nuova Rivista Storica,* 12 (1928).

Lehleiter, A. *Die Politik Johanns von Böhmen in den Jahren 1330-1334.* (Tübingen, 1908)

Lindner, T. *Deutsche Geschichte unter den Habsburgern und Luxemburgern.* 2 vols. (Stuttgart, 1890-1893)

Maschke, E. *Der Peterspfennig in Polen und dem deutschen Osten.* (Königs-berger histor. Forschungen, vol. 5.) (Leipzig, 1933)

Meltzer, F. *Die Ostraumpolitik König Johanns von Böhmen.* (Beiträge zur mittelalterlichen und neueren Geschichte, vol. 12.) (Jena, 1940)

Mirot, L. "La cession de la ville et du comté de Lucques par Jean de Bohême à Philippe VI de Valois en 1334," *Mélanges de philologie, d'histoire et de littérature offerts à H. Hauvette.* (Paris, 1934)

Moeller, R. *Ludwig der Bayer und die Kurie im Kampf um das Reich.* (Eberings Historische Studien, Heft 116.) (Berlin, 1914)

Mollat, G. *Les papes d'Avignon.* 9th ed. (Paris, 1950)

Mommsen, T. *Italienische Analekten zur Reichsgeschichte des 14. Jahrhunderts,* MGH, Schr., vol. 11 (1952).

Müller, K. *Der Kampf Ludwig des Baiern mit der römischen Kurie.* vol. 1. (Tübingen, 1879)

Otto, H. "Die Eide und Privilegien Heinrichs VII. und Karls IV. aus ungedruckten Aktenstücken," *Quellen und Forschungen aus italienischen Archiven und Bibliotheken,* 9 (1906).

————. "Zur italienischen Politik Johanns XXII," *ibid.,* 16 (1914).

Perels, E. "Zur Geschichte der böhmischen Kur im 14. und 15. Jahrhundert," ZSSR, Germanistische Abteilung, 45 (1945), pp. 83 ff.

Petrarca, F. *Rime, trionfi e poesie latine,* a cura di F. Neri, G. Martellotti, E. Bianchi, N. Sapegno. (Milan, Naples, 1951)

Pöppelmann, L. *Johann von Böhmen in Italien, 1330-1333.* (AÖG, vol. 35.) (Vienna, 1866)

Preger, W. "Beiträge und Erörterungen zur Geschichte des deutschen Reiches in den Jahren 1330-1334," *Abhandlungen der bayerischen Akademie der Wissenschaften,* Hist. Kl., 15 (1880).

————. "Die Politik des Papstes Johann XXII. in Bezug auf Italien und Deutschland," *ibid.,* 26 (1886).

Puymaigre, T. de. "Une campagne de Jean de Luxemburg, Roi de Bohême," *Revue des questions historiques,* 42 (1882), pp. 168 ff.

————. "Jean l'Aveugle en France," *ibid.,* 52 (1892), pp. 193 ff.

Salzer, E. *Über die Anfänge der Signorie in Oberitalien: Ein Beitrag zur italienischen Verfassungsgeschichte.* (Eberings historische Studien, Heft 14.) (Berlin, 1900)

Schneider, F. *Kaiser Heinrich VII.* 3 vols. (Greiz i. V., Leipzig, 1924-26-28)

Schötter, J. *Johann Graf von Luxemburg und König von Böhmen.* 2 vols. (Luxemburg, 1865)

Sievers, G. *Die politischen Beziehungen Kaiser Ludwigs des Baiern zu Frankreich in den Jahren 1316-1337.* (Eberings historische Studien, vol. 1.) (1896)

Simeoni, L. *Le Signorie.* (Milan, 1950)

Stengel, E. *Avignon und Rhens, Forschungen zur Geschichte des Kampfes um das Recht am Reich in der ersten Hälfte des 14. Jahrhunderts.* (Quellen und Studien zur Verfassungsgeschichte des deutschen Reiches im Mittelalter und Neuzeit, ed. K. Zeumer, vol. 6, Heft 1.) (Weimar, 1930)

Stieber, M. *Böhmische Staatsverträge, I: Seit Přemysl Ottokar II—Gründung des Habsburgischen Reiches.* (Innsbruck, 1912)

Uhlirz, K., and Uhlirz, M. *Handbuch der Geschichte Österreichs und seiner Nachbarländer Böhmen und Ungarn.* vol. 1. (Graz, Vienna, Leipzig, 1927)

Urban, M. "Die staatsrechtliche Stellung Egers zu Böhmen," *Mitteilungen des Vereines zur Geschichte der Deutschen in Böhmen,* 54 (1916), pp. 345 ff.

Viard, J. "La campagne de juillet-août 1346 et la bataille de Crécy," *Le Moyen Âge,* 36 (1926), pp. 1-84.

Vogt, E. *Die Reichspolitik des Erzbischofs Balduin von Trier in den Jahren 1328-1334.* (Gotha, 1901)

Warmski, M. St. *Die grosspolnische Chronik, eine Quellenuntersuchung.* Dissertation. (Cracow, 1879)

Weech, F. von. *Kaiser Ludwig der Bayer und König Johann von Böhmen.* (Munich, 1860)

Zeck, E. *Der Publizist Pierre Dubois, seine Bedeutung im Rahmen der Politik Philipps IV des Schönen und seine literarische Denk- und Arbeitsweise im Traktat "De recuperatione Terrae Sanctae."* (Berlin, 1911)

CHAPTER IV, *Sources* (See also Chapter III.)

Acta camerae apostolicae, ed. J. Ptaśnik. vols. I, II. (Cracow, 1913)
Acta Karoli IV imperatoris inedita, ed. F. Zimmermann. (Innsbruck, 1891).
    Documents from Italian sources.
Annales Mechovienses, MGHS 19, pp. 667 ff.; *MPH* 2, pp. 882 ff.
Annales Sanctae Crucis Polonici, MGHS 19, pp. 678 ff.
Archidiaconi Gnesnensis Chronicon (Janko of Czarnków), ed. Sommersberg,
    SRS 2, pp. 78 ff.; *MPH* 2, pp. 619 ff.
Baluzius, E. *Vitae paparum Avenionensium.* vol. 1. (Paris, 1693, ed. G. Mollat,
    Paris, 1914-22)
Benessius de Waitmül. (Beneš Krabice z Weitmile). *Chronicon, FRB* 4, pp.
    460 ff.
Benessius Minorita, *MBH* IV.
Chronica Cracoviae (Janko of Czarnków), *SRS*, vol. 2, pp. 78-155.
Chronica principum Poloniae, ed. Stenzel, *SRS*, vol. 1, pp. 38 ff.
Codex diplomaticus et epistolaris Moraviae. (Olomouc, 1836 ff.)
Codex diplomaticus Lusatiae superioris, ed. Köhler. (Görlitz, 1857)
Codex diplomaticus Majoris Poloniae, ed. Y. Zakrzewski, F. Piekosiński. 5 vols.
    (Poznań, 1877-1908); *C. D. Minoris Pol.*, ed. F. Piekosiński (1876-87).
Codex diplomaticus Poloniae, ed. L. Rzyszcewski and A. Muzckowski. (War-
    saw, 3 vols., 1847, 1858, vol. 4, 1887)
Codex diplomaticus Regni Poloniae et Lithuaniae, ed. Dogiel. (Wilno, 1758-
    1764)
Codex juris Bohemici, ed. H. Jireček. (Prague, 1867)
Długosz, John. *Opera Omnia*, ed. A. Przezdziecki. Vol. 1-14. (Cracow, 1863-
    1876)
Francisci Pragensis Cronica (Continuatio Cosmae), FRB 4, pp. 347 ff.
Die Goldene Bulle Kaiser Karls IV, ed. K. Zeumer. (Quellen und Studien zur
    Verfassungsgeschichte des Deutschen Reiches, vol. 2.) (Weimar, 1908).
Grünhagen, C. "Die Correspondenz der Stadt Breslau mit Karl IV. in den
    Jahren 1347-1355," *AÖG*, vol. 34, pp. 345-70.
Huber, A. *Die Regesten des Kaiserreiches unter Kaiser Karl IV.* In J. F. Böhmer,
    Regesta Imperii, vol. 8. (Innsbruck, 1877)
Kodeks dyplomatyczny Księstwa Mazowieckiego, ed. T. Lubomirski. (Warsaw,
    1863)
Kodeks dyplomatyczny miasta Krakowa, ed. F. Piekosiński. vol. 1. (Cracow,
    1879)
Lindner, T. *Das Urkundenwesen Karls IV. und seine Nachfolger (1346-1437).*
    (Stuttgart, 1882)
Monumenta Vaticana res gestas Bohemiae illustrantia, vol. 1, *Acta Clementis
    VI (1342-1352)*, ed. L. Klicman (Prague, 1903); vol. 4, *Acta Gregorii
    XI*, part 1 (1370-1372), ed. C. Stloukal. (Prague, 1949)
Neplach. *Chronicon Bohemiae, Epitome*, ed. Dobner, *MHB*, vol. 4, pp. 92 ff.
Palacký, F. *Über Formelbücher, zunächst in Bezug auf böhmische Geschichte.*
    (Abhandlungen der königlichen böhmischen Gesellschaft der Wissen-
    schaften, 5. Folge, vols. 2, 4.) (Prague, 1842)
Petrarca. *Epistolae de rebus familiaribus et variae*, ed. Fracasetti. (Florence,
    1859 ff.)
Petrus Zittaviensis. FRB, IV, pp. 3 ff.
Pomerellisches Urkundenbuch, ed. M. Perlbach. 2 vols. (Danzig, 1881-2)

Preussisches Urkundenbuch, ed. F. Philippi. 3 vols. (Königsberg, 1882-1944)
Summa cancellariae, ed. T. Neumann, *Ein Formelbuch Kaiser Karls IV.* (Görlitz, 1846)
Theiner, A. *Vetera monumenta Poloniae et Lithuaniae.* vol. 1. (Rome, 1860 ff.)
Vita Caroli IV imperatoris, FRB, III, pp. 336 ff.
Werunsky, E. *Excerpta ex registris Clementis VI et Innocentii VI historiam s. Romanii imperii sub regimine Caroli IV illustrantia.* (Innsbruck, 1885)
Wittelsbachische Regesten, ed. J. F. Böhmer. (Stuttgart, 1854)

CHAPTER IV, *Bibliography*

Bittner, K. *Deutsche und Tschechen: Zur Geistesgeschichte des böhmischen Raumes,* I. *Von den Anfängen zur hussitischen Kirchenerneuerung.* (Brünn, 1936)
Bryce, J. *The Holy Roman Empire.* (London, 1922)
Burdach, K. *Vom Mittelalter zur Reformation.* vol. 2, parts 1 and 3. (Berlin, 1912, 1913). Studies on Cola di Rienzo.
Charles IV. For bibliography on Charles IV, see footnote 2 of Chapter IV.
Chaloupecký, V. *The Caroline University of Prague: Its Foundation, Character and Development in the Fourteenth Century.* (Prague, 1948)
Daenell, E. *Blütezeit der deutschen Hanse: Hansische Geschichte von der 2. Hälfte des 14. Jahrhunderts bis zum letzten Viertel des 15. Jahrhunderts.* 2 vols. (Leipzig, 1905-1906)
Fournier, P. *Le royaume d'Arles, 1138-1378.* (Paris, 1891)
Gabriel, A. *Les rapports dynastiques franco-hongrois au Moyen Age.* (Budapest, 1944)
Gerlich, A. *Habsburg-Luxemburg-Wittelsbach im Kampfe um die deutsche Königskrone.* (Wiesbaden, 1960)
Grieser, R. *Das Arelat in der europäischen Politik von der Mitte des 10. bis zum Ausgange des 14. Jahrhunderts.* (Jena, 1925)
Grotefend, S. *Erwerbungspolitik Kaiser Karls IV.* (Eberings histor. Studien, Heft 66). (Berlin, 1909)
Herquet, D. "Beiträge zum Itinerar Karls IV und zu seinem Aufenthalt in Schlesien mit dem König von Cypern im Jahre 1364," *Zeitschrift für Geschichte Schlesiens,* vol. 14. (Breslau, 1878), pp. 521-27.
Hütterbräuker, L. "Die Vikare Karls IV in Deutschland." *Festschrift A. Brackmann.* (Weimar, 1931.), pp. 546-68.
Klein, W. *Kaiser Karls IV. Jugendaufenthalt in Frankreich und dessen Einfluss auf seine Entwicklung.* (Berlin, 1926)
Lindner, T. "Karl IV. und die Wittelsbacher," *Mitteilungen des Instituts für österreichische Geschichte,* 12 (Vienna, 1891), pp. 64-100.
———. "Die Wahl Wenzels zum römischer Könige," *Forschungen zur deutschen Geschichte,* 14 (Göttingen, 1874), pp. 251 ff.
———. *Das Urkundenwesen Karls IV. und seiner Nachfolger (1346-1437).* (Stuttgart, 1882)
Lippert, W. *Wettiner und Wittelsbacher sowie die Niederlausitz im 14. Jahrhundert.* (Dresden, 1894)
Mollat, G. *La collation des bénéfices ecclésiastiques sous les papes d'Avignon.* (Paris, 1921)
Odložilik, O. *The Caroline University, 1348-1948.* (Prague, 1948)

Paulová, M. "L'idée cyrillo methodienne dans la politique de Charles IV et la fondation du monastère slave de Prague," *Byzantinoslavica*, 11 (1950), pp. 174 ff.

Perlbach, M. *Preussisch-polnische Studien zur Geschichte des Mittelalters.* 2 vols. (Halle, 1886). Second volume important for evaluation of Prussian and Polish Annals.

Pirchan, G. *Italien und Kaiser Karl IV. in der Zeit seiner zweiten Romfahrt.* (Deutsche Gesellschaft der Wissenschaften und Künste für die Tschechoslowakische Republik, Historische Kommission. Quellen und Forschungen aus dem Gebiete der Geschichte, vol. 6.) (Prague, 1930)

———. "Karlstein." *Prager Festgabe für Theodor Mayer.* (Salzburg, 1953)

Reincke, H. "Kaiser Karl IV. und die deutsche Hanse," *Pfingsblätter des Hansischen Geschichtsvereines*, Blatt 22 (1931).

Salomon, R. "Zur Geschichte der englischen Politik Karls IV." *Festgabe Karl Zeumer.* (Weimar, 1910), pp. 397-411.

Sanmann, H. von B. *Die Inkorporationen Karls IV: Ein Beitrag zur Geschichte des Staatseinheitsgedankens im späteren Mittelalter.* (Marburger Studien zur älteren deutschen Geschichte, 2. Reihe, 8 Stück.) (Marburg, 1942)

Scheffer, W. *Karl IV. und Innozenz VI., 1355-1360.* (Historische Studien, Heft 101.) (Berlin, 1912)

Schmid, H. *Die rechtlichen Grundlagen der Pfarrorganisation auf westslavischem Boden und ihre Entwicklung während des Mittelalters.* (Weimar, 1938)

Steinherz, S. "Die Beziehungen Ludwigs von Ungarn zu Karl IV.," *Mitteilungen des Instituts für österreichische Geschichtsforschung*, vol. 9 (Innsbruck, 1888)

Studien zur Geschichte der Karls-Universitat zu Prag, ed. R. Schreiber. (Freilassing-Salzburg, 1955)

Sturm, H. *Eger. Geschichte einer Reichsstadt.* (Augsburg, 1951). See especially pp. 103 ff.

Werunsky, E. "Maiestas Karolina," *ZSSR*, Germanistische Abteilung, vol. 9 (1888).

Winter, E. *Rudolf IV.* 2 vols. (Vienna, 1934, 1936)

CHAPTER V, *Sources*

Acta et diplomata Graeca medii aevi sacra et profana, ed. F. Miklosich and J. Müller. 6 vols. (Vienna, 1860-90)

Acta et diplomata res Albaniae mediae aetatis illustrantia, ed. L. v. Thalloczy, K. Jireček, M. Šufflay. 2 vols. (Vienna, 1913-18.) Continued by J. Radonić, *Djuradj Kastriot Skanderbeg i Arbanija u XV. veku.* (Belgrade, 1942)

Actes de Chilandar, Actes grecs, ed. L. Petit, *Vizantijskij Vremennik*, 17 (1911); *Actes slaves*, ed. Korablev, *ibid.*, 19 (1915). For a complete bibliography on editions of Athonite documents see E. Amand de Mendietta, *Le presqu'île des caloyers: Le Mont-Athos* (Bruges, 1955), pp. 360-85.

Actes serbes de Vatopedi, ed. M. Lascaris, *Byzantinoslavica*, 6 (1935).

Acts from Venetian Archives relating to Southern Slavs, ed. S. Ljubić. *Listine o odnošajih izmedju Južnoga Slavenstva i Mletačke Republike.* 10 vols. (Zagreb, 1868-1891)

Anonymous Greek Short Chronicles, ed. S. Lampros and C. Amantos. (Athens, 1933)

Bulgarian Chronicle from 1296 to 1413, ed. I. Bogdan, in *ASPh,* 13 (1891), pp. 526-35. Cf. K. Jireček's remarks, *ibid.,* 14 (1892), pp. 235 ff.

Cecaumeni. *Strategicon,* ed. B. Wassiliewsky and V. Jernstedt. (St. Petersburg, 1896). Transl. by H. G. Beck, *Vademecum des byzantinischen Aristokraten* (Graz, 1956). On Bulgarians and Serbs in the eleventh century.

Chroniques greco-romanes, ed. C. Hopf. (Berlin, 1873). See pp. 270-340 on Albania under the Serbs.

Codex diplomaticus partium regni Hungariae adnexarum, ed. L. v. Thalloczy and A. Aldásy, *MHH, D,* vol. 33 (1907).

Enveri. *The Destan* of Omur, Emir of Aydin. French transl. by I. Mélikoff-Sayar, *Le Destan d'Umur Pacha.* (Paris, 1954)

Demetrius Cydones. *Letters,* ed. R. J. Loenertz, *Correspondence,* I (Vatican City, 1956). Cf. idem, *Les recueils de lettres de Demetrius Cydonès.* (Vatican City, 1947)

Diplomatarium Veneto-Levantinum (1200-1454), ed. G. M. Thomas and R. Predelli. 2 vols. (Venice, 1880-1899)

Ducas. *Chronicle* (from 1341 to 1462), ed. I. Bekker, *CSHB.*

Dušan's *Zakonik,* ed. S. Novaković. (Belgrade, 1898), new edition by N. Radojčić. (Belgrade, 1960). English transl. by M. Burr in the *Slavonic and East European Review,* 28 (1950), pp. 198-217, 516-39.

George Akropolites. *Chronicle,* ed. I. Bekker, *CSHB* (1836).

George Phrantzes. *Chronicle* (from 1258 to 1476), ed. I. Bekker, *CSHB* (1834).

Greek Documents of Serbian Rulers, ed. V. Mošin. *Grčke povolie srpskih vladara.* (Belgrade, 1936)

Innocent III, Pope. Letters, *PL,* vols. 214-15.

John Cantacuzenus. *Historia* (14th century), ed. L. Schopen, 3 vols., *CSHB* (1828).

Laonicus Chalcondyles. *Chronicle,* ed. E. Darkó. 2 vols. (Budapest, 1922-27)

Leunclavius, J. *Historiae Musulmanae Turcorum,* libri XVIII. (Frankfurt, 1591). Most important Turkish sources are included in translation.

Lives of Serbian Kings and Archbishops, ed. D. Daničić. *Životi kraljeva i arhiepiskopa srpskih.* (Zagreb, 1866). See also *Serbische mittelalterliche Herrscher-Viten des 12. und 13. Jh. von Nemanja bis Stefan Lazarević,* with German transl. by S. Hafner. (Berlin, 1959)

Monumenta historica Slavorum meridionalium, ed. V. Makniev. (Belgrade, 1885)

Monumenta Serbica spectantia histor. Serbiae, Bosniae, Ragusii, ed. F. v. Miklosich. (Vienna, 1858)

Monumenta spectantia historiam Slavorum meridionalium, ed. Academy of Zagreb. 33 vols. (Zagreb, 1913)

Nicephorus Gregoras. *Byzantina Historia,* ed. L. Schopen, 3 vols., *CSHB* (1826-1832).

Nicephorus Gregoras. *Correspondence de Nicéphore Grégoras,* ed. R. Guilland. (Paris, 1927)

Serbian Short Chronicles, ed. by L. Stojanović. *Stari srpski rodoslovi i letopisi.* (Belgrad, 1927)

Life of Stephen Lazarević (1389-1427), ed. M. Braun. *Lebensbeschreibung des despoten Stefan Lazarević von Konstantin dem Philosophen.* (The Hague, 1956)

Regesta pontificum romanorum, ed. A. Potthast. 2 vols. (Berlin, 1874-75)

Valenciennes, Henri de. *Histoire de l'empereur Henri de Constantinople*, ed. J. Longnon. (Paris, 1948)

Vetera monumenta historica Hungariam sacram illustrantia, ed. A. Theiner. 2 vols. (Rome, 1859-60)

Vetera monumenta Slavorum meridionalium historiam illustrantia, ed. A. Theiner. vol. 1. (Rome, 1863)

For full account of the sources concerning the southern Slavs see *Historija naroda Jugoslavije* and the works by Zlatarski and Mutafčiev quoted in footnote 1, Chapter V. Sources on the history of the Rumanians are being published by the Rumanian Academy under the title *Documente privind Istoria României* (Bucharest, 1951,, in progress). Useful information on Serbian historiography and sources are given by S. Stanojević, *Istorija srpskog naroda u srednjem veku* (Beograd, 1937).

CHAPTER V, *Bibliography*

Babinger, F. *Beiträge zur Frühgeschichte der Türkenherrschaft in Rumelien 14.-15. Jahrhundert)*. (Brünn-Munich-Vienna, 1944)

Bănescu, N. *Les duchés byzantins de Paristron (Paradounavon) et de Bulgarie.* (Bucharest, 1946)

———. *Un problème d'histoire mediévale: Création et charactère du second empire bulgare (1185).* (Bucharest, 1943)

Borchgrave, E. de. "L'empereur Étienne Dusan de Serbie et la péninsule balkanique au XIIᵉ siècle," *Bulletin de l'Académie Royale des Sciences de Belgique*, 3ᵉ série, 8 (1884), pp. 264-92, 416-45.

Bousquet, G. *Histoire du peuple bulgare depuis les origines jusqu'à nos jours.* (Paris, 1909)

Braun, M., and Schneider, A. *Bericht über die Eroberung Konstantinopels. Nach der Nikon-Chronik übersetzt und erläutet.* (Leipzig, 1943)

Braun, M. *Kosovo, Die Schlacht auf dem Amselfelde in geschichtlicher und epischer Überlieferung.* (Leipzig, 1937)

Buonocore, de Widmann, R. *Storia della Vecchia Serbia e sue relationi con storia italiana.* (Napoli, 1908). Not reliable.

Coquelle, P. *Histoire du Monténégro et de la Bosnie depuis les origines.* (Paris, 1895)

Diehl, C., et al. *L'Europe orientale de 1081 à 1453.* (Paris, 1945)

Dölger, F. "Die dynastische Familienpolitik des Kaisers Michael Palaiologos (1258-1282)." *Festschrift E. Eichmann.* (Paderborn, 1940.), pp. 179-90.

———. "Einiges über Theodora die Griechin, Zarin der Bulgaren (1308-1330)," *Annuaire de l'Institut de philologie et d'histoire orientale et slave*, (1949), pp. 211-21.

Franić, D. "Die Lage auf der Balkanhalbinsel zu Beginn des 13. Jahrhunderts," *WMBH*, 5 (1897), pp. 304-36.

Geanakoplos, D. J. *Emperor Michael Palaeologus and the West.* (Cambridge, Mass., 1959)

Gegaj, A. *L'Albanie et l'invasion turque au XVᵉ siècle.* (Paris, 1937)

Gibbons, H. *The Foundation of the Ottoman Empire.* (Oxford, 1916)

Giurescu, C. C. *Istoria Românilor.* 3 vols. (Bucharest, 1942-1944)

Grégoire, H. "L'opinion byzantine et la bataille de Kossovo," *Byzantion*, 6 (1931), pp. 247-51.

Hilferding, A. *Geschichte der Serben und Bulgaren.* 2 vols. (Bautzen, 1856-64)

Huber, A. *Ludwig I. von Ungarn und die ungarischen Vasallenländer.* (Vienna, 1884)

Hudal, A. *Die serbisch-orthodoxe Nationalkirche.* (Graz, 1922)

Jireček, J. C. (K.) *Geschichte der Bulgaren.* (Prague, 1876)

———. *Geschichte der Serben.* 2 vols. (Gotha, 1911-18)

———. *Die Heerstrasse von Belgrad nach Konstantinopel.* (Prague, 1877)

———. *Die Romanen in den Städten Dalmatiens während des Mittelalters, ibidem,* vols. 48, 49 (Vienna, 1902-04)

———. *Staat und Gesellschaft im mittelalterlichen Serbien.* (*Studien zur Kulturgeschichte des 13.-14. Jhts.,* Denkschriften der kaiserlichen Akademie der Wissenschaften, phil.-hist. Kl., vols. 55, 58.) (Vienna, 1912.) Partial transl. in French, *La civilisation serbe au Moyen Âge.* (Paris, 1920)

———. "Zur Würdigung der neuentdeckten bulgarischen Chronik," *ASPH*, 14 (1892), pp. 255-77. Remarks to I. Bogdan's edition, *ibid.*, 13 (1891), pp. 526-76.

Jorga, N. "Latins et Grecs d'Orient et l'établissement des Turcs en Europe (1342-1362)," *BZ*, 15 (1906), pp. 179-222.

Kanitz, F. P. *Das Königreich Serbien und das Serbenvolk von der Römerzeit bis zur Gegenwart.* 2 vols. (Leipzig, 1904-09)

Klaić, V. *Geschichte Bosniens von ältesten Zeiten bis zum Verfalle des Königreiches.* (Leipzig, 1885)

Komlóssy, F. von. *Das Rechtsverhältnis Bosniens und der Herzegovina zu Ungarn, mit besonderer Rücksicht auf das Mittelalter.* Transl. from the Hungarian by E. K. (Budapest, 1909)

Lascaris, M. "Deux chartes de Jean Uroš, dernier Némanide," *Byzantion,* 215-217 (1955-57), pp. 277-323.

———. "Influences byzantines dans la diplomatie bulgare, serbe et slavoromaine," *Byzantinoslavica,* 3 (1931), pp. 500-10.

Lemerle, P. *L'Emirat d'Ardin, Byzance et l'Occident: Recherches sur "La Gesta d'Umar Pacha."* (Paris, 1957)

Maritch, D. *Papstbriefe an serbische Fürsten im Mittelalter.* (Sremska Karlovci, 1933)

Miklosich, F. v. *Die serbischen Dynasten Crnojević.* (Vienna, 1886). In SbAW, hist. phil. Kl.

Miller, W. "Bosnia before the Turkish Conquest," *English Historical Review,* 13 (1898), pp. 643-66. See also his studies on Greece and the Balkan states in *CMH*, vol. 4, Chapters XV-XVIII, pp. 432-593.

———. "The Medieval Serbian Empire," *Quarterly Review,* 226 (1916), pp. 488-507

Millet, G. *Ancien Art Serbe.* (Paris, 1919)

Milobar, F. *Das geschichtliche Verhältnis Bosniens zu Kroatien und Ungarn.* (Zürich, 1898)

Noli, F. S. *George Castrioti Scanderbeg.* (New York, 1947)

Norden, W. *Das Papsttum und Byzanz.* (Berlin, 1903)

Novak, V. "The Slavonic-Latin Symbiosis in Dalmatia during the Middle Ages," *SEER,* 32 (1953-54), pp. 1-28.

Novaković, St. *Die Serben und Türken im XIV. und XV. Jh. Geschichtliche Studie über die ersten Kämpfe mit dem Türkischen Eindringen vor und nach der Schlacht auf dem Amsfelde.* Transl. by K. Jezdimirović. (Semlin, 1897)

Obolensky, D. *The Bogomils, a Study in Balkan Neo-Manichaeism.* (Cambridge, 1948). See also F. Rački, *Bogomili i Patareni.* (Zagreb, 1869-70)

Ostrogorsky, G. "Étienne Dušan et la noblesse serbe dans la lutte contre Byzance," *Byzantion*, 12 (1952), p. 151 ff.

——. "Historische Entwicklung der Balkanhalbinsel im Zeitalter der byzantinischen Vorherrschaft," *Revue internationale des études balkiniques*, 2 (1936), pp. 389-97.

——. *History of the Byzantine State.* Transl. by J. Hussey. (New Brunswick, N. J.: Rutgers University Press, 1957)

Pauler, J. "Wie und wann kam Bosnien an Ungarn," *WMBH*, 2 (Vienna, 1894)

Purković, M. A. "Two notes on Mediaeval Serbian History," *SEER*, 29 (1950-51), pp. 545-49.

Radojičić, G. "La chronologie de la bataille de Rovine," *Revue historique du sud-est européen*, 5 (1928), pp. 136-39.

Radojčić, N. "Die griechischen Quellen zur Schlacht am Kossovo Polje," *Byzantion*, 6 (1931), pp. 241-46.

Runciman, S. *The Sicilian Vespers: A History of the Mediterranean World in the Later Thirteenth Century.* (Cambridge, 1958)

Ruvarac, H. "Die Regierung des Banus Tvrtko (1353-1377)," *WMBH*, 4 (1896), pp. 324-42.

Sainte-Marie, E. de. *L'Herzégovine: Étude géographique, historique et statistique.* (Paris, 1875)

Songeon, G. *Histoire de la Bulgarie depuis les origines jusqu'à nos jours, 485-1191.* (Paris, 1913)

Soulis, G. "Tsar Dušan and Mount Athos," *Harvard Slavic Studies*, 2 (1956), pp. 125-39. A monograph on Dušan is in preparation by Soulis.

Spinka, M. *A History of Christianity in the Balkans.* (Chicago, 1933)

Stanojević, S. "Die Biographie Stefan Lazarević's von Konstantin dem Philosophen als Geschichtsquelle," *ASPh*, 18 (1896), pp. 409-72.

Stevenson, F. Seymour. *A History of Montenegro.* (London, 1912)

Šufflay, M. v. "Die Grenzen Albaniens im Mittelalter," *Illyrischalbanische Forschungen*, 1 (1916), pp. 289-93.

——. *Städte und Burgen Albaniens hauptsächlich während des Mittelalters.* (Denkschr. der Akad., vol. 63.) (Vienna, 1924)

Temperley, H. *History of Serbia.* (London, 1917)

Thallóczy, L. v. *Studien zur Geschichte Bosniens und Serbiens im Mittelalter.* Transl. from the Hungarian by F. Eckhart. (Munich, Leipzig, 1914)

——. "Untersuchungen über den Ursprung des bosnischen Banates, mit besonderer Berücksichtigung der Urkunden im Körmender Archive," *WMBH*, 11 (1909), pp. 237-85.

Unbegaun, B. "Les relations vieux-russes de la prise de Constaninople," *RES*, 9 (1929), pp. 13-38.

Villari, L. *The Republic of Ragusa.* (London, 1904)

Vojnović, L. *Histoire de la Dalmatie.* 2 vols. (Paris, 1934)

Waring, L. F. "Kosovo," *SEER*, 2 (1923-24), pp. 56-70.

Wittek, P. *The Rise of the Ottoman Empire.* (London, 1938)

Wolff, R. L. "The Second Bulgarian Empire—Its Origin and History to 1204," *Speculum*, 29 (1949), pp. 167-206.

Zlatarski (Slatarski), V. N. *Geschichte der Bulgaren.* 2 vols. (Leipzig, 1917-18)

Chapter VI, *Sources and Bibliography*

Akta grodzkie i ziemskie, ed. A. Liske and A. Prochaska. (Municipal and land acts, vol. 23.) (Lwów, 1868-1928)

Balzer, O. *Les Statuts de Casimir le Grand.* (Studia nad historią prava polskiego, vol. 19.) (Poznań, 1947). In Polish. Posthumus edition.

Burr, M. "The Code of Stephen Dušan," *SEER,* 28 (1949-50), pp. 198-217, 516-39.

Dąbrowski, J. *Corona Regni Poloniae au XIVᵉs.* (Bulletin internat. de l'Academie Polonaise, Classe d'Histoire no. 7.) (Cracow, 1953)

Dèer, J. *L'evoluzione dell' idea dello stato ungherese.* (Rome, 1941.) On the "Holy Crown" of Hungary, pp. 71 ff.

Demel, I. *Geschichte des Fiskalamtes in den böhmischen Ländern.* vol. 1, *Das Fiskalamt des Königreiches Böhmen bis 1620.* (Innsbruck, 1909)

Dopsch, A. *Die ältere Sozial- und Wirtschaftsverfassung der Alpenslaven.* (Weimar, 1909)

Dvornik, F. *The Making of Central and Eastern Europe.* (London, 1949)

Feine, H. E. "Eigenkirchenrechtliche Erscheinungen in Dalmatien im frühen Mittelalter," *ZSSR,* vol. 64, Kanon. Abt., 33 (1944), pp. 265-77.

Fontes rerum Slovenicarum. vols. 1-3: *Urbaria aetatis mediae Sloveniam spectantia,* ed. M. Kos. (Ljubljana, 1939-54.) Commentary in Slovene.

Francastl, P., ed. *Les origines des villes polonaises.* (The Hague, 1961)

Hartung, F. *Die Krone als Symbol der monarchischen Herrschaft im ausgehenden Mittelalter.* (Abhandlungen der preussischen Akademie der Wissenschaften, phil. hist. Kl., vol. 13.) (1940)

Horvat, M. "Das Troginer 'Zavod' Buch vom Jahre 1326," *Studien zur älteren Geschichte Europas, Festschrift für H. F. Schmid,* ed. G. Stökl. (Wiener Archiv für Geschichte des Slaventums und Osteuropas, vol. 2.) (Vienna, 1956), pp. 33-48.

Inchiostri, U. "Contributo alla storia del diritto romano in Dalmazia nel Xᵉ XI secolo," *Archeografo Triestino,* 3 serie 3 (Trieste, 1907), pp. 85-158.

Jireček, C. (K.) *La civilisation serbe au moyen âge.* Transl. by L. Eisenmann. (Paris, 1920)

———. "Die mittelalterliche Kanzlei der Ragusaner," *ASPh,* 26 (1904).

———. *Die Handelsstrassen und Bergwerke von Serbien und Bosnien während des Mittelalters.* (Prague, 1916)

———. *Die Romanen in den Städten Dalmatiens während des Mittelalters.* (Vienna, 1902-09)

———. *Staat und Gesellschaft im mittelalterlichen Serbien.* See Bibl. Chapter V.

Jireček, H. *Codex juris bohemici.* (Prague, 1867 ff.)

Kadlec, K. *Introduction a l'étude comparative de l'histoire du droit public des peuples slaves.* (Paris, 1933). Most important standard book giving complete bibliography on sources and collections of Slavic public law. Pp. 191 ff. Czech; pp. 226 ff. Polish; pp. 290 ff. Croatian; pp. 53 ff. Bulgarian and Serbian political organization and public law.

Koebner, R. "Deutsches Recht und deutsche Kolonisation in den Piastenländern," *Vierteljahrschrift für Sozial- und Wirtschaftsgeschichte,* 25 (1932).

Kutrzeba, S. *Grundriss der polnischen Verfassungsgeschichte.* Transl. by W. Christian. (Berlin, 1912)

Madirazza, F. *Storia e costituzione dei comuni dalmati.* (Spalato, 1911.) Superficial.

Mal, J. *Probleme aus der Frühgeschichte der Slowenen.* (Ljubljana, 1939.) Cf. pp. 127 ff. on the inthronization of Slovene dukes.

Marczali, H. *Ungarische Verfassungsgeschichte.* (Tübingen, 1910)

Matić, T. "Statut der Poljica," *WMBH*, 12 (Vienna, 1912), 329 ff.

Mayer, E. "Die dalmatisch-istrische Munizipalverfassung im Mittelalter und ihre römischen Grundlagen," *ZSSR*, German. Abt., 24 (Weimar, 1903)

Mladenovitch, M. *Le caractère de l'état serbe au moyen âge.* Thèse. (Paris, 1930)

Monumenta Ragusina. 5 vols. (Zagreb, Academy, 1879-1897)

Mošin, V. "Gab es unter den serbischen Herrschaft des Mittelalters eine griechische Kanzlei?," *Archiv für Urkundenforschung*, 13 (1935), pp. 183-97.

Novaković, S. "Villes et citées au moyen âge dans l'Europe occidentale et dans la peninsule balcanique, *ASPh*, 25 (1903), pp. 321-40.

Ostrogorsky, G. "Etienne Dušan et la noblesse serbe dans la lutte contre Byzance," *Byzantion*, 22 (1952), pp. 151-59.

———. *Pour l'histoire de la féodalité byzantine.* Transl. by H. Grégoire. (Brussels, 1954)

Peterka, O. *Rechtsgeschichte der böhmischen Länder.* vol. 1, *Geschichte des öffentlichen Rechtes und die Rechtsquellen in vorhussitischer Zeit.* (Reichenberg, 1923)

———. "Ursachen und Wege der Rezeption des römischen Rechtes in Böhmen und Mähren." In *Prager Festgabe für Th. Mayer, Forschungen zur Rechtsgeschichte und Landeskunde der Sudetenländer*, vol. 1. (Salzburg, 1953.), pp. 37-55.

Pfeifer, W. *Städtewappen und Städtesiegel in Böhmen und Mähren.* (Munich, 1952)

Preux, J. "La loi du Vinodol traduite et annotée," *Nouvelle revue historique du droit français et étranger.* (1896)

Prochno, J. "Terra Bohemiae, regnum Bohemiae, corona Bohemiae." In *Prager Festgabe für Th. Mayer, Forschungen zur Rechtsgeschichte und Landeskunde der Sudetenländer*, vol. 1. (Salzburg, 1953.), pp. 91-111.

Schmid, H. F. "Die Burgbezirksverfassung bei den slavischen Völkern in ihrer Bedeutung für die Geschichte ihrer Siedlung und ihrer staatlichen Organisation," *JKGS*, N.F., 2 (1927), pp. 81 ff.

———. "Dalmatinische Stadtbücher," *Zgodovinski časopis*, 6-7 (1953), pp. 330-90. (Kosov Zbornik)

———. "Das deutsche Recht in Polen." In *Deutschland in Polen.* (Munich, Berlin, 1933)

———. "Die Grundzüge und Grundlagen der Entwicklung des kirchlichen Zehnrechts auf kroatischem Boden während des Mittelalters." *Šišićev Zbornik*, ed. G. Novak. (Zagreb, 1929.), pp. 423-54.

———. "Die sozialgeschichtliche Erforschung der mittelalterlichen deutschreichlichen Siedlung auf polnischem Boden," *Vierteljahrschrift für Sozial- und Wirtschaftsgeschichte*, 20 (Stuttgart, 1928), pp. 301-55. With bibliography of Polish publications.

Schubart-Fikentscher, G. *Die Verbreitung der deutschen Stadtrechte in Osteuropa.* (Weimar, 1942)

Sigel, F. *Lectures on Slavonic Law.* (London, New York, 1902.) Bohemia, pp. 63-99; Poland, pp. 100-36; Croatia, pp. 137-52; Bulgaria and Serbia, pp. 15-25.

Soloviev, A. "Le droit byzantin dans la codification d'Étienne Douchan," *Revue historique de droit,* 7 (1928), pp. 387-412.

———. "Der Einfluss des byzantiuischen Rechts auf die Völker Osteuropas," *ZSSR,* Rom. Abt., 76 (1959), pp. 432-79.

———. "Le patriciat de Raguse au XVᵉ siècle," *Rešetarov Zbornik* (Dubrovnik, 1931.), pp. 59-66.

Timon, A. von. *Ungarische Verfassungs- und Rechtsgeschichte.* Transl. by F. Schiller. (Berlin, 1904)

Tomaschek, J. A. *Das alte Bergrecht von Iglau und seine bergrechtlichen Schöffensprüche.* (Innsbruck, 1897)

Tyc, T. *Die Anfänge der dörflichen Siedlung zu deutschem Recht in Grosspolen (1200-1333).* Transl. by M. Tyc. (Osteuropa Institut, Bibliothek geschichtl. Werke aus den Literat. Osteuropas, vol. 2.) (Breslau, 1930)

Tymieniecki, K. "Les paysans libres (kmiecie) en Pologne à la fin du moyen âge." *La Pologne au VIIᵉ Congrès internat. des sciences histor.* (Warsaw, 1933)

Vlajinats, M. *Die agrarrechtlichen Verhältnisse des mittelalterlichen Serbien.* (Jena, 1903)

Wersche, K. "Das staatsrechtliche Verhältnis Polens zum Deutschen Reich während des Mittelalters," *Zeitschr. der Hist. Ges. für die Provinz Posen,* 3 (1888).

Werunski, E. "Die Maiestas Carolina," *ZSSR,* Germ. Abt., 9 (1888).

Wojciechowski, Z. *Das Ritterrecht in Polen vor den Statuten Kasimir des Grossen.* Transl. by H. Bellee. (Osteuropa Institut, Bibliothek geschichtl. Werke aus den Literat. Osteuropas, vol. 5.) (Breslau, 1930)

Xapalatos, D. *Beiträge zur Wirtschafts- und Sozialgeschichte Makedoniens im Mittelalter, hauptsächlich auf Grund der Briefe des Erzbischofs Theophylaktos von Achrida.* (Munich, 1937)

Zaborski, B. *Über Dorfsformen in Polen und ihre Verbreitung.* Transl. by Schrundbauer. (Osteuropa Institut, Bibliothek geschichtl. Werke aus den Literat. Osteuropas, vol. 3.) (Breslau, 1930)

Zycha, A. *Das böhmische Bergrecht des Mittelalters auf Grundlage des Bergrechts von Iglau.* (Vienna-Berlin, 1900)

———. *Über den Ursprung der Städte in Böhmen und die Städtepolitik der Přemysliden.* (Prague, 1914)

CHAPTER VII, *Bibliography*

Analecta hymnica, ed. G. M. Dreves. (Leipzig, 1886-1906)

L'Art byzantin chez les Slaves. Orient et Byzance (Paris, 1930-32); vol. 4, *Les Balkans,* 2 vols. (1930); vol. 5, *L'ancienne Russie, les Slaves catholiques* (1932).

Blaschka, A. *Die Wenzelslegende Kaiser Karls IV.* (Prague, 1934)

Bosković, G. *L'Art médiéval en Serbie et en Macédoine.* (Belgrade, 1936, reprint, 1952?)

———. "La sculpture de Dečani et la question du développement de quelques cycles iconographiques dans la sculpture médiévale," *Atti del Congresso Internaz. di Studi Byzantini*, vol. 2. (Roma, 1940)

Brückner, A. "Ältere polnische Texte," *ASPh*, 10 (1887), pp. 365-416.

——. "Böhmische Studien, Abhandlungen and Texte," *ASPh*, 2 (1888), pp. 81-104, 189-217, 421-522; 12 (1890), 321-58; 13 (1891), 1-25; 14 (1892), 1-45.

——. *Geschichte der polnischen Literatur.* (Leipzig, 1901.), pp. 1-29.

——. "Neue Quellen zur Geschichte der polnischen Sprache und Literatur: I. Glosar nach 1455, II. Die Tischzucht des Slota und Verwandtes, III. Dorotheenlegende," *ASPh*, 14 (1892), pp. 481-512.

——. "Über die älteren Texte des Polnischen," *ASPh*, 12 (1890), pp. 140-55.

Burdach, K. *Vom Mittelalter Zur Reformation.* (Berlin, 1912-37)

Burjan, M. L. *Die Klosterkirche von Studenica.* (Zenleroda, 1934)

Cronia, A. *Saggi di letteratura bulgara antica.* (Rome, 1926)

Denkstein, V., and Matouš, F. *Gothic Art in South Bohemia.* (Prague, 1955)

Drobna, Z. *Die Gothische Zeichnung in Böhmen.* (Prague, 1956)

Faral, E. *Les arts poetiques du XIIe et du XIIIe siècle.* (Paris, 1924)

Fejfalík, J. "Alttschechische Leiche, Lieder und Sprüche des 14. und 15. Jh.," *SbAW*, 39 (Vienna, 1862), pp. 627-745.

——. *Studien zur Geschichte der altböhmischen Literatur, SbAW*, phil.-hist. Kl., 34 (Vienna, 1861).

——. "Über K. Wenzel von Böhmen als deutschen Liederdichter" *SbAW*, hist. phil. Kl., 25 (1857). Cf. J. Šusta's study in *Český Čas. hist.* ("Czech Histor. Review"), 21 (1912), pp. 217-44.

Filow, B. D. *Early Bulgarian Art.* (Berne, 1919)

Friedel, A. *Magister Theodoricus.* (Prague, 1956)

Friedjung, H. *Kaiser Karl IV. und sein Anteil am geistlichen Leben seiner Zeit.* (Vienna, 1878)

Frind, A. *Geschichte der Bischöfe und Erzbischöfe von Prag.* (Prague, 1873.) Still useful. Also his *Kirchengeschichte Böhmens.* 2 vols. (Prague, 1864-78)

Frova, A. *Pittura romana in Bulgaria.* (Rome, 1943)

Grabar, A. *Peinture religieuse en Bulgarie, Orient et Byzance I.* (Paris, 1928)

——. *Recherches sur les influences orientales dans l'art balkanique.* (Paris, 1928)

Greif, W. *Die mittelalterlichen Bearbeitungen der Trojanersage. Ein neuer Beitrag zur Dares- und Dictysfrage.* (Marburg, 1886)

Havránek, B. "Waren die Handschriften der polnischen Königin Hedwiga polnisch oder tschechisch?," *SR*, 10 (1938).

Heisenberg, A. "Über den Ursprung der illustrierten Chronik des Konstantins Manasses," *Münchener Jahrbuch der bildenden Kunst*, 5 (1928), pp. 81-100.

Hemmerle, J. "Nikolaus von Laun." *Studien zur Geschichte der Karls-Universität zu Prag*, ed. R. Schreiber. (Freilassing-Salzburg, 1957.), pp. 81-129.

Hyma, A. *The Christian Renaissance: A History of the "Devotio moderna."* (Grand Rapids, 1924)

Istrin, V. "Beiträge zur griechisch-slavischen Chronographie," *ASPh*, 17 (1895).

Jackson, T. G. *Dalmatia, the Quarnero and Istria.* 2 vols. (Oxford, 1887)

Jagić, V. "Die Alexius-Legende als serbisches Volkslied," *ASPh*, 9 (1886).

Jagić, V. "Ein Beitrag zur serbischen Annalistik mit literaturgeschichtlicher Einleitung," *ASPh*, 2 (1877), pp. 1-109.

——. "Der weise Akyrios nach einer altkirchenslavischen Übersetzung," *BZ*, 1 (1892).

Jakobson, R. "Medieval Mock Mystery." *Studia Philologica et Literaria in honorem L. Spitzer.* (Berne, 1958.), pp. 245-65: The Quacksalver.

Jakubec, J., and Novák, A. *Geschichte der čechischen Literatur.* (Leipzig, 1909.), pp. 1-38.

Janić, V., and C. T. Hankey. *Lives of the Serbian Saints.* (London, 1921)

Jeanroy, A. *La poésie lyrique des troubadours.* 2 vols. (Toulouse, Paris, 1934)

Jelinek, H. *Histoire de la littérature tchèque des origines à 1850.* 4th ed. (Paris, 1930). Pp. 1-47.

Jireček, J. C. (K.) *La civilisation serbe au moyen âge.* (Paris, 1920.), cf. Chapter V.

——. "Das Gesetzbuch des serbischen Caren Stephan Dušan," *ASPh*, 22 (1900), pp. 144-214.

——. "Eine slavische Alexandergeschichte in Zara 1389," *ASPh*, 25 (1893), pp. 157-58.

John of Jenstein. *Vita Joannis de Jenstein*, *FRB*, I, pp. 439-68; *Relatio de se ipso*, ed. C. Höfler in *Geschichtsschreiber der hussitischen Bewegung*, vol. 2 (Vienna, 1865), pp. 12 ff.; *Codex epistolarius*, ed. J. Loserth in *AÖG*, 55 (1877), pp. 268 ff.; *Die Hymnen Johannes von Jenstein*, ed. G. Dreves (Leipzig, 1886); additional material found in *Analecta hymnica*, 48 (1905), pp. 421-51.

John of Neumarkt. *Die Schriften Johannes von Neumarkt: Das Buch der Liebkosung, Übersetzung des pseudoaugustinischen "Liber soliloquium animae ad Deum,"* ed. J. Klapper (Berlin, 1930). His other works were published J. Klapper and P. Piur in K. Burdach's *Vom Mittelalter zur Reformation,* vol. VI, 1, 2, 4; vol. VII (1931, 1932, 1935, 1937).

Kałużniacki, E. *Aus der panegyrischen Literatur der Südslaven.* (Vienna, 1901)

——. *Werke des Patriarchen von Bulgarien Euthymius (1375-1393), nach den besten Handschriften.* (Vienna, 1901)

Kloss, E. *Die schlesische Buchmalerei des Mittelalters.* (Berlin, 1942)

Kolbuszewski, S. "Influences of Czech Culture in Poland in the Middle Ages," *SEER*, 18 (1939-40), pp. 155-69.

Krofta, K. *Das Deutschtum in der tschechoslowakischen Geschichte.* (Prague, 1934). *Die Deutschen in Böhmen.* (Prague, 1924)

Kunstmann, H. *Denkmäler der alttschechischen Literatur von ihren Anfängen bis zur Hussitenbewegung.* (Berlin, 1955)

Lossnitzer, M. *Veit Stoss: Die Herkunft seiner Kunst, seine Werke und sein Leben.* (Leipzig, 1912)

Lücker, M. A. "Meister Eckhardt und die 'Devotio Moderna,'" *Studien und Texte zur Geistesgeschichte des Mittelalters,* 1 (Leiden, 1950).

Lützow, Count F. v. *Bohemian Literature.* (London, 1911)

——. *A History of Bohemian Literature.* (London, 1899; 2nd ed. 1907.) Translations of some Czech lyric poems on pp. 26-28.

Magoun, E. P. "Stojan Navaković on the so-called 'Serbian Alexander,'" *Byzantion,* 16 (1942-43), pp. 315-38.

Mašin, J. *Romanische Wandmalerei.* (Prague, 1954)

Matějček, A., and Pešina, J. *Gothische Malerei in Böhmen: Tafelmalerei 1350-1450.* (Prague, 1955)

Matl, J. "Die Entwicklungsbedingungen der epischen Volksdichtung bei den Slaven," *JKGS,* 5 (1929), pp. 57-76.

———. "Der heilige Sava als Begründer der serbischen Nationalkirche: Seine Leistung und Bedeutung für den Kulturaufbau Europas," *Kyrios,* 2 (1937), pp. 23-37. Bibliography in Serbian.

Meriggi, B. *Storia delle letterature ceca e slovaca.* (Milan, 1958)

Millet, G. *L'Ancien art serbe.* (Paris, 1915.) Cf. L. Bréhier, "L'architecture serbe au Moyen âge," *Le Moyen âge,* 23 (1921).

———. *La peinture du moyen âge en Yougoslavie (Serbie, Macédoine et Monténégro),* vol. 1 (Paris, 1955); vol. 2 (Paris, 1957). Presented by A. Frolow.

———. *Recherches sur l'iconographie de l'évangile.* (Paris, 1916)

Močul'skij, V. "Zur mittelalterlichen Erzählungsliteratur bei den Südslaven," *ASPh,* 14 (1893).

Monumenta Artis Bulgariae. vol. 1, Grabar, A., *L'Eglise de Boiana* (Sofia, 1924); vol. 2, Rachenov, A., *Eglises de Mesembria* (Sofia, 1932); vol. 3, Filov, B., *Les Miniatures de l'Evangile du roi Jean Alexandre à Londres* (Sofia, 1934); vol. 4, Miatev, K., *Die Keramik von Preslav* (Sofia, 1936).

Murko, M. *Geschichte der älteren südslavischen Literaturen.* (Leipzig, 1908)

———. "Die Geschichte von den sieben Weisen bei den Slaven," *SbAW,* phil.-hist. Kl., 122. (Vienna, 1890)

———. "Die russische Übersetzung des Apollonius von Tyrus und die Gesta Romanorum," *ASPh,* 14 (1892).

Namysłowski, W. "Die Rechtsbestände in den südslavischen Ländern und in Polen," *Przewodnik hist.-prawny,* 2 (1932), pp. 51-66.

———. "Die Teilnahme der Bevölkerung an der Rechtssprechung in den mittelalterlichen kroatischen und serbischen Ländern," *JKGS,* N.F., 3 (1927), pp. 345-64.

Nehring, W. "Altpolnische (Posener) Eidesformeln aus dem 14. Jahrhundert," *ASPh,* 4 (1879), pp. 177-89.

———. *Altpolnische Sprachdenkmäler: Systematische Übersicht, Würdigung, und Texte: Ein Beitrag zur slavischen Philologie.* (Berlin, 1887.) Cf. A. Brückner's review in *ASPh,* 10 (1887), pp. 365-416.

———. "Ein schlesich-polnisches Hochzeitsgedicht aus dem 14. Jahrhundert," *ASPh,* 3 (1878), pp. 637-39.

———. "Über den Einfluss der altčechischen Literatur auf die altpolnische," *ASPh,* 1 (1876), pp. 66-81; 2 (1877), pp. 409-36; 5 (1880), pp. 216-67; 6 (1882), pp. 159-84.

Neuwirth, J. *Geschichte der bildenden Kunst in Böhmen, vom Tode Wenzels III. bis zu den Husitenkriegen.* (Prague, 1893)

———. *Geschichte der christlichen Kunst in Böhmen.* (Prague, 1888)

———. *Zur Geschichte der Miniaturmalerei in Böhmen.* (Mitteilungen der k. k. Central-Commission, vol. 11.) (Vienna, 1885)

Novaković, St. "Zur bulgarischen Alexandersage," *ASPh,* 1 (1888).

Obolensky, D. *The Bogomils.* (Cambridge, 1948), pp. 234-49.

Okunev, N. L., and Mitrović, L. W. "La dormition de la Sainte Vierge dans la peinture médiévale orthodoxe," *Byzantinoslavica,* 3 (1931, pp. 134 ff.).

———. *Monumenta Artis Serbicae.* vols. 1-4. (Prague, 1928-32)

Palacký, F. *Die Vorläufer des Hussitentums.* (Leipzig, 1869.) First edition in 1846 under the name of J. P. Jordan.

Palacký, F. *Würdigung der alten böhmischen Geschichtsschreiber.* (Prague, 1830; 2nd ed., 1869)

Parry, M., and Lord, A. B. *Serbocroatian Heroic Songs.* 2 vols. (Cambridge, Mass., Belgrade, 1953, 1954)

Pešina, J. *Tafelmalerei der Spätgotik und der Renaissance in Böhmen, 1450-1550.* Transl. by E. Winkler. (Prague, 1958)

Petas, F., and Paul, A. *Das jüngste Gericht. Mittelalterliche Mosaik vom Prager St. Veits Dom.* (Prague, 1954)

Petković, V. R. *La peinture serbe du moyen âge.* (Belgrade, 1934)

Pohl, K. *Beiträge zur Geschichte der Bischöfe von Olmütz im Mittelalter.* (Breslau, 1940). Unobtainable to me.

Prohaska, D. *Das kroatisch-serbische Schrifttum in Bosnien und Herzegowina von den Anfängen im 11. bis zur nationalen Wiedergeburt im 19. Jahrhundert.* (Zagreb, 1911)

Prokop, A. *Die Markgrafschaft Mähren in kunstgeschichtlicher Beziehung.* 4 vols. (Vienna, 1904)

Pypine, A. N., and Spasović, W. D. *Histoire des littératures slaves.* French transl. by E. Denis (Paris, 1881). German translation by T. Pech (Leipzig, 1881-83).

Raby, F. J. E. *A History of Secular Latin Poetry.* 2 vols. (Oxford, 1934)

Radojičić, D. S. "Der Roman von Tristan und Isolde in der altserb. Liter." *Die Welt ober Slaven,* 1 (1956), pp. 35-49.

——. "Drei Byzantner, altserbische Schrifsteller. *Akten des XI byzantin. Kongresses* (Munich, 1959), pp. 504 ff.

Ringheim, A. *Eine altserbische Trojasage: Text mit linguistischer und literarhistorischer Charakteristik.* (Prague, Uppsala, 1951)

Šafařík, J. *Geschichte der südslavischen Literatur.* (Prague, 1864, 1865)

Sas-Zalozieeky, W. *Die byzantinische Baukunst in den Balkanländer und ihre Differenzierung unter abendländischen und islamitischen Einwirkungen.* (Südosteurop. Arb. 46.) (Munich, 1956)

Schmaus, A. "Der Neumanichäismus auf dem Balkan," *Saeculum,* 2 (1951).

——. "Zur Frage der Kulturorientierung der Serben im Mittelalter," *Südoststudien,* 15 (1956), pp. 179-201.

Schreiber, R., ed. *Studien zur Geschichte der Karls-Universität zu Prag.* (*Forschungen zur Geschichte und Landeskunde der Sudetenländer,* vol. 2.) (Freilassing-Salzburg, 1954); *ibid.,* studies by J. Bergel, A. Blaschka, J. Hemmerle on the Charles University.

Sharenkoff, V. N. *A Study of Manichaeism in Bulgaria with Special Reference to the Bogomils.* (New York, 1927)

Spina, F. *Die altčechische Katharinenlegende der Stockholm-Brünner Handschrift.* (Prague, 1913)

Spinka, M. *A History of Christianity in the Balkans.* (Chicago, 1933)

Stanojević, St. "Die Biographie Stefan Lazarević's von Konstantin dem Philosophen," *ASPh,* 18 (1890).

Stanoyevich, M. S. *Early Jugoslav Literature (1000-1800).* (New York, 1922.) Too general.

Steinherz, S. *Ein Fürstenspiegel Karls IV.* (Quellen und Forschungen aus dem Gebiete der Geschichte, Historische Kommission der deutschen Gesellschaft der Wissenschaften und Künste für die tschechoslowakische Republik.) (Prague, 1925)

Strzygowski, J. *Die Miniaturen des serbischen Psalters.* (Denkschriften der k. Akademie der Wissenschaften, phil.-hist. Kl., vol. 52.) (Vienna, 1906)

Stwosz, Wit, *Der Krakauer Altar.* (Warsaw, 1953.) With reproductions.

Swoboda, K. M. *Peter Parler: Der Bankünstler und Bildhauer.* (Vienna, 1943)

Syrku, P. "Zur mittelalterlichen Erzählungsliteratur aus dem Bulgarischen," *ASPh,* 7 (1884).

Szydłowski, T. *Le retable de Notre-Dame de Cracovie.* (Paris, 1935)

Tadra, F. *Cancellaria Arnesti: Formelbuch des ersten Prager Erzbischofs Arnest von Pardubic.* (Vienna, 1880)

———. "Cancellaria Iohannis Noviforensis," *Archiv für österreichische Geschichte,* 68 (1886), pp. 1-157.

———, ed. *Summa Cancellariae Caroli IV.* (Prague, 1895)

Thomson, S. H. "Learning at the Court of Charles IV," *Speculum,* 25 (1950), pp. 1-20.

Tintelnot, H. *Die mittelalterliche Baukunst Schlesiens.* (Kitzingen, 1951)

Trautmann, R. *Die alttschechische Alexandreis.* (*Sammlung slavischer Lehr- und Handbücher,* 3. Reihe: Texte und Untersuchungen.) (Heidelberg, 1916)

———. "Die Einleitung der alttschechischen Alexandreis," *ASPh,* 36 (1915), pp. 431 ff.

Trogrančić, F. *Letteratura medioevale degli Slavi meridionali dalle origine al 15 secolo.* (Rome, 1950.), pp. 142-240.

Turdeanu, E. *La littérature bulgare du 14e siècle et sa diffusion dans les pays roumains.* (Paris, 1947)

Valjavec, F. *Geschichte der deutschen Kulturbeziehungen zu Südosteuropa.* 2 vols. (Munich, 1954-55)

Vielhaber, G. "Der 'Libellus do bono mortis' des Erzbischofs Johann von Jenstein." *Festschrift des Vereins für Geschichte der Deutschen in Böhmen.* (Prague, 1902.), pp. 159-65.

Wesselofsky, A. "Die altslavische Erzählung vom Trojanischen Kriege," *ASPh,* 10 (1887), pp. 27-42.

Wilmart, A. *Auteurs spirituels et textes dévots au Moyen Age.* (Paris, 1932)

Winter, E. "Die europäische Bedeutung des Frühhumanismus in Böhmen," *Zeitschr. für deutsche Geistergesch.,* 1 (1935), pp. 232-42.

———. *Tausend Jahre Geisteskampf im Sudetenland.* (Prague, 1938)

Wirth, Z. *Kutná Hora: La ville et son art.* (Prague, 1931)

Wostry, W. "Ein deutschfeindliches Pamphlet aus Böhmen aus dem 14. Jahrhundert," *Mitteilungen des Vereines für Geschichte der Deutschen in Böhmen,* 53 (1915), pp. 193-238.

Xyngopoulos, A. *Thessalonique et la peinture macédonienne.* (Athens, 1955)

Zeissberg, H. "Kleinere Geschichtsquellen Polens im Mittelalter," *AÖG,* 55 (1877).

———. *Die polnische Geschichtsschreibung des Mittelalters.* (Leipzig, 1873)

———. "Vincentius Kadlubek und seine Chronik Polens," *AÖG,* 42 (1869).

CHAPTER VIII, *Sources*

Acta Concilii Constanciensis, ed. H. Finke. (Münster, vol. 1, 1896; vol. 2, 1923).

Aeneas Silvius. *Historia Bohemica, 894-1458,* ed. M. Freher. *SRB* (Hanover, 1602).

Archiv český ("Czech Archives"), vols. 1, 3, 6.

Bachmann, A. *Urkunden und Aktenstücke zur österreichischen Geschichte im Zeitalter Kaiser Friedrich III. und König Georgs von Böhmen. FRA,* vol. 42.

Beneš Krabice. *FRB,* 4 (1884), pp. 460-548.

Cochlaeus, J. *Historia Hussitarum.* (Mainz, 1548)

Documenta Mag. Joannis Hus, vitam, doctrinam, causam in Constantiensi concilio actam et controversias de religione in Bohemia annis 1403-1418 motas illustrantia, ed. F. Palacký. (Prague, 1869)

Finke, H. *Forschungen und Quellen zur Geschichte des Konstanzer Konzils.* (Paderborn, 1889)

Geschichtsschreiber der hussitischen Bewegung in Böhmen, ed. K. Höfler. 3 vols. (Vienna, 1856-66.) (In *FRA,* Abt. I, vols. 2, 6, 7.)

John Hus. *De ecclesia* ("On the Church"), ed. by D. S. Schaff. (New York, 1915.) New edition by S. H. Thompson, *M. Johannis Hus, "Tractatus de ecclesia"* (Boulder, Colo., 1956).

——. *The Letters of John Hus,* ed. H. B. Workman and R. M. Pope. (London, 1904.) V. Novotný, *M. Jana Husa korespondence a dokumenty.* (Prague, 1920)

——. *On Simony.* Transl. by M. Spinka. (Library of Christian Classics, vol. 14, *Advocates of Reform,* Philadelphia, 1953).

——. Latin works published by V. Flajšhans, *M. Joannis Hus, Opera Omnia,* 8 parts (Prague, 1903-08). Czech works published by K. J. Erben, *Sebrané spisy české,* 3 vols. (Prague, 1865-68.) New edition in 25 vols. is planned by the Czech Academy. Vol. 8, *M. Johannis Hus sermones de tempore qui collecta dicuntur,* ed. by A. Schmidtová (Prague, 1959). John Hus's discourses at the University, ed. by A. Schmidtová, *Joannes Hus Mag. Univ. Carolinae Positiones, Recommendationes, Sermones* (Prague, 1958).

Lawrence of Březová, Bartošek. *Chronicles,* K. Höfler, *Geschichtsschreiber der husitischen Bewegung,* vol. 1, pp. 596-620, *FRB,* vol. 5, ed. J. Goll.

Palacký, F. *Staří letopisové čeští* ("Old Czech Annalists"), 1378-1527, *SRB,* 3 (Prague, 1829).

——. *Urkundliche Beiträge zur Geschichte Böhmens und seiner Nachbarländer im Zeitalter Georgs von Podebrad. FRA,* 20 (1860).

Petrus de Mladenowicz. *Opera historica,* ed. V. Novotný. *FRB,* 8 (1932).

Reformatio Sigismundi, Beiträge zum Verständnis einer Reformschrift des 15. Jahrhunderts, L. v. Dohna. (Göttingen, 1959)

Sedlák, J., Neumann, A., and Špaldák, A. *Studie a texty.* vols. 1-4. (Olomouc, 1914-25.) Texts dealing with religious problems of the Hussite period.

Vita Johannis de Jenczenstein, FRB, vol. 1. See Bibl. Chapter VI.

Wratislav, Count. *Diary of an Embassy from King George of Bohemia to King Louis XI of France in the Year of Grace 1464.* (London, 1871)

Žižka, J. *Military Regulation,* ed. by F. Švejkovský and J. Durdík. *Staročeské vojenské řády* ("Ancient Czech Military Regulations"). (Prague, 1952)

CHAPTER VIII, *Bibliography*

Arndt, R. *Die Beziehungen König Sigmunds zu Polen bis zum Ofener Schiedsspruch 1412.* Dissertation. (Halle/Saale, 1897)

Aschbach, J. *Geschichte Kaiser Sigmunds.* 3 vols. (Hamburg, 1838-1845)

Bachmann, A. *Böhmen und seine Nachbarländer unter Georg von Podiebrad*

(1458-1461) und des Königs Bewerbung um die deutsche Krone. (Prague, 1878)

Bartoš, F. M. "Wenceslas Budovec's Defense of the Brethren," transl. by H. Kaminsky, Church History, 28 (1959), pp. 229-39.

Berger, W. Johannes Hus und König Sigmund. (Augsburg, 1871)

Bernard, P. P. "Jerome of Prague, Austria and the Hussites," Church History, 27 (1958), pp. 1-22.

Betts, R. R. "English and Czech Influences on the Hussite Movement," Transactions of the R. Histor. Soc., 21 (1939).

———. "The Influence of Realist Philosophy on Jan Hus and his Predecessors in Bohemia," SEER, 29 (1951), pp. 402-19.

———. "Social and Constitutional Development in Bohemia in the Hussite Period," Past and Present, 7 (1955).

———. "Some Political Ideas of the Early Czech Reformers," SEER, 31 (1952).

Bezold, F. v. König Sigmund und die Reichskriege gegen die Hussiten bis zum Ausgang des dritten Kreuzzeugs. (Munich, 1872)

Boulier, J. Jean Hus. ("Portraits de l'Histoire," no. 15) (Paris, 1958.) Popular.

Caro, J. Aus der Kanzlei Kaiser Sigismunds. Urkundliche Beiträge zur Geschichte des Constanzer Concils. (Vienna, 1879)

Creighton, M. History of the Papacy during the Period of the Reformation. vol. 1. (London, 1881)

Denis, E. Georges de Podiebrad, Les Jagellons, Fin de l'independance de Bohême. vol. 1. (Paris, 1890; 2nd ed., 1930)

———. Hus et la guerre des Hussites. (Paris, 1878)

Dienemann, E. Die Romfahrtfrage in Wenzels Politik. Dissertation. (Halle/Saale, 1909)

Finke, H. König Sigmunds reichsstädtische Politik. (Bocholt, 1880)

Fraknói, W. Mathias Corvinus, König von Ungarn, 1458-1490. (Freiburg i. B., 1891)

Friedrich, O. Helden des Geistes: Jan Hus, Chelčický, Komensky. (Zürich, 1935)

Fries, G. E. Herzog Albrecht V. von Österreich und die Hussiten. (Linz, 1883)

Frind, A. Der heilige Johannes von Nepomuk. (Eger, Prague, 1879.) New edition completed by W. A. Frind, 1929. Czech history by F. Stejskal, 1922.

Gindely, A. Geschichte der böhmischen Brüder. 2 vols. (Prague, 1857, 1858)

Goeller, E. König Sigmunds Kirchenpolitik vom Tode Bonifaz' IX. bis zur Berfung des Konstanzer Konzils (1409-1413). Studien aus dem Collegium Sapientiae, vol. 7.) (Freiburg i. B., 1902)

Goll, J. Quellen und Untersuchungen zur Geschichte der böhmischen Brüder. 2 vols. (Prague, 1878, 1882)

Gottschalk, A. Kaiser Sigmund als Vermittler zwischen Papst und Konzil, 1431-34. Dissertation. (Borna-Leipzig, 1911)

Gullet, E. The Life and Times of John Huss. (London, 1863)

Hauck, A. Studien zu Huss. (Leipzig, 1916)

Haupt, H. Hussitische Propaganda in Deutschland. (Raumers Taschenbuch.) (Leipzig, 1888)

Heeren, J. J. Das Bündnis zwischen König Richard II. von England und König Wenzel vom Jahre 1381. Dissertation. (Halle/Saale, 1910)

Hefele, K. J., and Leclerq, Dom H. Histoire des conciles, vol. 8, 1. (Paris, 1916.) Council of Constance.

Helmke, R. *König Wenzel und seine böhmischen Günstlinge im Reiche.* Dissertation. (Halle/Saale, 1913)

Herben, J. *Huss and his Followers.* (London, 1926.) Popular.

Heyman, F. G. "John Rokycana: Church Reformer between Hus and Luther." *Church History,* 28 (1959), pp. 240-80.

———. *John Žižka.* (Princeton, 1955.) Cf. the review by O. Odložilík in *Speculum,* 31 (1956), pp. 381-83.

———. "The National Assembly of Čáslav," *Medievalia et Humanistica,* 7 (1952).

Höfler, C. A. C. *Magister Johannes Hus und der Abzug der deutschen Professoren und Studenten aus Prag 1409.* (Prague, 1864)

Jacob, E. F. "The Bohemians at the Council of Basel, 1433." *Prague Essays,* ed. R. W. Seton-Watson. (Oxford, 1949)

Jireček, J. K. (C.) "Über die culturellen Beziehungen der Ungarn und Böhmen im 14. und 15. Jahrhundert und die ungarischen Hussiten," *Sitzungsberichte der königlichen böhmischen Gesellschaft* (1885).

Kaminsky, H. "Hussite Radicalism and the Origin of Tabor 1415-1418," *Medievalia et Humanistica,* 10 (1956), pp. 102-30.

———. "Pius Aeneas among the Taborites," *Church History,* 28 (1959), pp. 281-309. Ibid., 26 (1957), pp. 43-71, "Chiliasm and the Hussite Revolution."

Kapras, J. *Un ancêtre de la Société des Nations.* (Prague, 1924)

Kitts, E. J. *Pope John the Twenty-third and Master John Hus of Bohemia.* (London, 1910)

Kluckhuhn, P. *Wenzels Jugendjahre bis zum Antritt seiner Regierung 1378 im Rahmen der Politik seines Vaters Kaiser Karls IV.* Dissertation. (Halle/Saale, 1914)

Koller, H. "Untersuchungen zur Reformatio Sigismundi II.," *Deutsche Arbeit,* 14 (1957), pp. 482 ff.; 14 (1958), pp. 418-64.

Krofta, K. "Bohemia in the Fifteenth Century," *CMH,* 8 (1936), pp. 65-115.

———. "John Hus," *CMH,* 8 (1936), pp. 45-64.

———. *Die Deutschen in Böhmen.* (Prague, 1924)

Krummel, L. *Utraquisten und Taboriten: Ein Beitrag zur Geschichte der böhmischen Reformation im 15 Jahrhundert.* (Gotha, 1871)

Lindner, T. *Geschichte des deutschen Reiches unter König Wenzel.* 2 vols. (Braunschweig, 1875-80)

Loserth, J. *Huss und Wiclif: Zur Genesis der hussitischen Lehre.* 2nd ed. (Munich, Berlin, 1925)

———. "Über die Versuche wiclif-husitische Lehre nach Österreich, Polen, Ungarn und Croatien zu verpflanzen," *Mitteilungen des Vereines für Geschichte der Deutschen in Böhmen,* vol. 24.

———. "Die wiclifitische Abendmahllehre und ihre Aufnahme in Böhmen," *Mitteilungen des Vereines für Geschichte der Deutschen in Böhmen,* 30 (Prague, 1892).

Lützow, F. Count von. *The Life and Times of Master John Hus.* (London, 1909)

Macek, J. *The Hussite Movement in Bohemia.* 2nd ed. (Prague, 1958)

McGowan, J. P. *Pierre d'Ailly and the Council of Constance.* (Washington, 1936)

McNeill, J. T. *Makers of Christianity.* vol. 2. (New York, 1935.), pp. 166-74.

Main, A. *The Emperor Sigismund.* (Oxford, London, The Stanhope Essay, 1903.)

Markgraf, H. "Über Georg's von Podiebrad Project eines christlichen Völkerbundes zur Vertreibung der Türken aus Europa und Herstellung des allgemeinen Friedens innerhalb der Christenheit," *HZ*, 21 (1869), pp. 245-304.

Miebach, A. *Die Politik Wenzels und der Rheinischen Kurfürsten in der Frage des Schismas von der Thronbesteigung des Königs bis zum Jahre 1380.* Dissertation. (Münster i. W., 1912)

Müller, J. T. *Geschichte der böhmischen Brüder.* 3 vols., vols. 1, 2. (Herrnhut, 1922-1931)

Naegle, A., "Der Prager Kanonikus Matthias von Janow," *Mitteilungen des Vereines für Geschichte der Deutschen in Böhmen*, 48 (Prague, 1910).

Odložilík, O. "George of Poděbrady and Bohemia to the Pacification of Silesia—1459," *University of Colorado Studies*, Ser. B, vol. 1, no. 3, pp. 265-88.

————. "Problems of the Reign of George of Poděbrady," *SEER*, 20 (1941), pp. 206-22.

————. *Wiclif and Bohemia.* (Prague, 1937)

————. "Wycliffe's Influence upon Central and Western Europe," *SEER*, 7 (1928-9), pp. 634-48.

————. "The Chapel of Bethlehem in Prague," *Studien zur älteren Geschichte Österreichs*, ed. G. Stökl. (Vienna, 1956), pp. 123-41.

Palacký, F. *Die Geschichte des Hussitentums und Prof. Constantin Höfler.* (Prague, 1868)

Peschke, E. "Die Bedeutung Wiclefs für die Theologie der Böhmen," *Zeitschrift für Kirchengeschichte*, 54 (1935), pp. 462-83.

Říčan, R. *Das Reich Gottes in den böhm. Ländern* (Stuttgart, 1957)

Schaff, D. S. *John Huss, His Life, Teachings and Death after Five Hundred Years.* (New York, 1915)

Schwitzky, E. B. *Der europäische Fürstenbund Georgs von Podebrad.* (Marburg A. L., 1907)

Spinka, M. *John Hus and the Czech Reform.* (Chicago, 1941)

Stubbs, W. *Germany in the Later Middle Ages, 1200-1500*, ed. A. Hassall. 2 vols. (London, 1908)

Thomson, H. S. "Pre-Hussite Heresy in Bohemia," *Engl. Hist. Review*, 48 (1933).

Uhlirz, M. "Die Genesis der vier Prager Artikel," *Sitzungsberichte der k. Akademie der Wissenschaften*, phil.-hist. Kl., vol. 175, Abhandlung 3 (1914).

Uhlmann, P. *König Sigmunds Geleit für Hus und das Geleit im Mittelalter.* (*Hallische Beiträge zur Geschichtsforschung*, ed. T. Lindner, Heft 5.) (Halle/Saale, 1894)

Vetter, H. *Die Beziehung Wenzels zum Deutschen Orden.* Dissertation. (Halle/Saale, 1912)

Vischer, M. *Jan Hus. Aufruhr wider Papst und Reich.* (Frankfurt a. M., 1955). To be used with caution.

Vogel, C. *Peter Cheltschizki, ein Prophet an der Wende der Zeiten.* (Zürich, 1926)

Vogt, C. *Peter Cheltschizki, Das Netz des Glaubens.* (Dachau, 1924)

Vooght, P. de. *L'Hérésie de Jan Huss-Hussiana.* (Louvain, 1960)

Waugh, W. T. "The Councils of Constance and Basel," *CMH*, vol. 8, pp. 1-44.

Workman, H. B. *The Dawn of the Reformation.* vol. 1, Wycliffe; vol. 2, John Hus. (London, 1901-2)

Workman, H. B. *John Wyclif: A Study of the English Medieval Church.* 2 vols. (Oxford, 1926)

Wostry, W. *König Albrecht II.* (1437-39). (Prager Studien aus dem Gebiete der Geschichtswissenschaft, vols. 12, 13.) (Prague, 1906-7)

Wratislaw, A. H. *John Huss.* (London, 1882)

Wulf, M. v. *Die husitische Wagenburg.* Dissertation. (Berlin, 1889)

Young, R. F. "Bohemian Scholars and Students at English Universities, 1347-1750," *English Historical Review* (1923).

Žilka, F. "The Czech Reformation and its Relation to the World Reformation," *SEER*, 8 (1929-30), pp. 284-91.

CHAPTER IX, *Sources*

Akty istoričeskie. vol. 1 (1334-1462). (St. Petersburg, 1841)

Čerepnin, L. V. *Russkie feodal'nye arkhivy XIV-XV vekov.* 2 vols. (Moscow, 1948-51).

Chronicle of Novgorod, 1016-1471. Transl. by Mitchell, R., and Forbes, N. (London, 1914)

Codex epistolaris Vitoldi 1376-1430, ed. A. Prochaska. In *Monumenta medii aevi,* vol. 6. (Cracow, 1882)

Dukhovnye i dogovornye gramoty velikikh i udelnykh knjazej 14-16 vekov, ed. C. V. Bakhrušin and L. V. Čerepnin. (Moscow, Leningrad, 1950)

Henricus Lettus. *Chronicon Livoniae, MGH,* S, vol. 23, pp. 241-332. New ed. by R. Arbusov, and A. Bauer. (Hannover, 1955)

Jasinskij, M. N. *Ustavnye zemskie gramoty litovsko-russkago gosudarstva.* (Kiev, 1889)

Miklosich, F., and Müller, I. *Acta et diplomata graeca medii aevi sacra et profana.* vol. 2. (Vienna, 1860-1890)

Paszkiewicz, H. *Regesta Lithuaniae ab origine usque ad magni Ducatus cum Regni Poloniae unione.* (Warsaw, 1930)

PSRL, vols. 3, 4, "First, Third, Fourth Chronicles of Novgorod." ("Fourth Chronicle," 2nd ed., 1925). ("First Chr., new ed. by A. N. Nasonov, 1950).

Ibid., vol. 17: *Zapadno-russkija Lietopisi.* "West-Russian Chronicles."

Petrus de Dusburg. *Chronica Terrae Prussiae, SRP,* vol. 1, ed. Töpper, pp. 21-219.

Richental, Ulrich v. *Chronik des Constanzer Concils,* ed. M. R. Buck. (Tübingen, 1882)

Theiner, A. *Vetera monumenta Poloniae et Lithuaniae.* 3 vols. (Rome, 1860)

Troitskaja letopisi (to 1408), ed. N. D. Priselkov. (Moscow, 1950)

CHAPTER IX, *Bibliography*

Ammann, A. M. *Kirchenpolitische Wandlungen im Ostbaltikum bis zum Tode Alexander Newskis (1263).* (Studien zum Werden der russischen Orthodoxie, Orient. Christ. Analecta, vol. 105.) (Rome, 1936.) See also the review by L. Arbusov in *Kyrios,* 1 (1936), pp. 294-305.

Baumgarten, N. de. "Polotzk et la Lithuanie: Une page d'histoire," *OCP,* 2 (1936), pp. 223-48.

Bellé, H. *Polen und die römische Kurie in den Jahren 1414-1424.* (Osteuropäische Forschungen, Heft 2.) (Berlin, 1914)

Boswell, A. Bruce. "Poland and Lithuania in the Fourteenth and Fifteenth Centuries," *CMH*, vol. 8, pp. 556-84.

Chudziński, E. *Die Eroberung Kurlands durch den Deutschen Orden im. 13. Jahrhundert.* (Borna, Leipzig, 1917)

Deveike, J. "The Legal Aspect of the Last Religious Conversion in Europe," *SEER*, 32 (1953-54), pp. 117-31.

———. "The Lithuanian Diarchies," *SEER*, 28 (1950), pp. 392-405.

Gersdorf, H. *Der Deutsche Orden im Zeitalter der polnisch-litauischen Union: Die Amtszeit des Hochmeister Konrad Zöllner von Rotenstein (1382-1390).* (Wissenschaftliche Beiträge zur Geschichte und Landeskunde Ost-Mitteleuropas, no. 29.) (Marburg, 1957)

Gnegel-Waitschies, G. *Bischof Albert von Riga: Ein Bremer Domherr als Kirchenfürst im Osten (1199-1229).* (Hamburg, 1958)

Goetz, L. K. *Deutsch-russische Handelsverträge des Mittelalters.* (Abhandlungen des Hamburger Kolonialinstitutes, vol. 37.) (Hamburg, 1916)

Goll, J. "Kaiser Sigismund und Polen 1420-1436," *Mitteilungen des Instituts für österreichische Geschichtsforschung*, 15 (1894).

Grousset, R. *L'empire des steppes: Attila, Gengis-Khan, Tamerlan.* (Paris, 1939).

Grousset, R., and Bouvat, L. *L'empire mongol.* 2 vols. (*Histoire du monde*, vol. 8, no. 3.) (Paris, 1927-41)

Halecki, O. "Imperialism in Slavic and East European History," *The American Slavic and East European Review*, 11 (1951), pp. 1-26.

Hellmann, M. "Der Deutsche Orden und die Königskrönung des Mindaugas," *Zeitschr. fur Ostforshung*, 3 (1954), pp. 387-96.

———. *Das Lettenland im Mittelalter.* (Cologne, 1954)

———. "Die geschichtliche Bedeutung des Grossfürstentums Litauen," *Saeculum*, 9 (1958), pp. 87-112.

———. "Zu den Anfängen des litauischen Reiches," *JGO*, NF, 4 (1956), pp. 162 ff. Answers Pašuto.

Hocij, M. "Die Krone des Mindaugas," *Zeitschrift für Ostforschung*, 3 (1954). Ibid., ff. 360-86, Z. Ivinskis, "Mindaugas und seine Krone."

Höfler, C. R. von. "Der Streit der Polen und der Deutschen vor dem Constanzer Konzil," *SbAW*, phil.-hist. Kl., 95 (Vienna, 1880), pp. 875 ff.

Ivinskis, Z. "Mindaugas und seine Krone," *Zeitschrift für Ostforschung*, 3 (1954), pp. 360 ff.

Jablonowski, H. *Westrussland zwischen Wilna und Moskau.* (Leiden, 1955)

Krollmann, C. *Die Schlacht bei Tannenberg, ihre Ursachen und ihre Folgen.* (Königsberg, 1910)

Lamb, H. *Tamerlane, the Earth Shaker.* (New York, 1928)

Murawski, K. E. *Zwischen Tannenberg und Thorn. Die Geschichte des Deutschen Ordens unter dem Hochmeister Konrad (1441-1449)*, Göttinger Bausteine zur Geschichtswissenschaft, vols. 10-11 (1953).

Osten-Sacken, P. v. "Livländisch-russische Beziehungen während der Regierungszeit des Grossfürsten Witowt von Litauen (1392-1430)," *Mitteilungen aus dem Gebiete der Geschichte Liv-, Est- und Kurland*, 20 (1910), pp. 169-294.

Paszkiewicz, H. *The Origin of Russia.* (London, 1954.), pp. 185-254.

Pfitzner, J. *Groszfürst Witold von Litauen als Staatsmann.* (Brünn, 1930)

Spuler, B. *Die Goldene Horde.* (Leipzig, 1943)

Stökl, G. "Die politische Religiosität des Mittelalters und die Entstehung des Moskauer Reiches," *Saeculum* (1951), pp. 392-412.

——. *Russland von der Mongolenzeit bis zu Peter dem Grossen,* Historia Mundi, vol. 7 (Berne, 1957).

Taube, M. v. "Internationale und kirchenpolitische Wandlungen im Ostbaltikum und Russland zur Zeit der deutschen Eroberung Livlands (12. und 13. Jahrhundert)," *JGO,* 3 (1938), pp. 11 sq.

——. "Russische und litauische Fürsten an der Düna (im 12. u. 13. Jhr.)," *JKGS* (1935), pp. 495 ff.

Vernadsky, G. *The Mongols and Russia.* (New Haven, 1953)

Zegarski, T. *Polen und das Basler Konzil.* Dissertation (Poznań, 1910).

CHAPTER X, *Sources*

Acta Bosnae potissimum ecclesiastica (from 925 to 1752), ed. E. Fermendžin, in *Monum. spect. hist. Slav. meridional,* vol. 23. (Zagreb, 1892)

Acta Bulgariae ecclesiastica (1556-1799), ed. E. Fermendžin, in *Monum. spect. hist. Slav. meridional.,* vol. 18 (Zagreb, 1887)

Acta et diplomata res Albaniae mediae aetatis illustrantia, ed. L. de Thallóczy, C. Jireček, E. de Šufflay, 2 vols. (Vienna, 1913, 1918)

Acta Tomiciana, ed. S. Górski, Z. Celichowski. 12 vols. (Poznań, 1852 ff.) Main source for the reign of King Sigismund I (1507-1530).

Aeneas Silvius Piccolomini. *De statu Europae,* ed. Feher, *RGS,* vol. 2.

Altmann, W. *Eberhart Windeckes Denkwürdigkeiten zur Geschichte des Zeitalters Kaiser Sigismunds.* (Berlin, 1893)

Archivium Jana Zamoyskiego. 4 vols. (Warsaw, Cracow, 1913-1948)

Babinger, F. *Die Geschichtsschreiber der Osmanen und ihre Werke.* (Berlin, 1927.) Critical appraisal of early Turkish historians. Extensive bibliography.

Chalcocondiles, Laonicus. *Historiarum demonstrationes* (from 1298 to 1463), ed. J. Darkó. vols. 1, 2, parts 1, 2. (Budapest, 1922, 1923, 1927)

Chroniques greco-romaines inédites ou peu connues, ed. C. Hopf. (Berlin, 1873.) For Montenegro and Albania in the fifteenth century.

Codex diplomaticus comitum de Frangepanibus, ed. L. v. Thallóczy. 2 vols. (Budapest, 1910)

Codex diplomaticus Hungariae ecclesiasticus et civilis, ed. G. Fejer. vols. 1-40. (Budapest, 1829-44.) Registers in 1866.

Codex diplomaticus partium regno Hungariae adnexarum, ed. L. v. Thallóczy and A. Hodinka. (Budapest, 1903-15)

Comnenus monachus, Proculus monachus, CSHB. On Serbian rule in Epirus and Thessaly in the second half of the fourteenth century. New ed. by Sebastian Cirar Estópañan, *Bizancio y España,* vol. 2 (Barcelona, 1943)

Critobulus, M. *Fragmenta histor, graec.,* vol. 5, ed. C. Müller. Cf. J. Radonić's study of *Glasnik* of the Serbian Academy, vol. 138 (Belgrade, 1930). English translation by T. Riggs, *History of Hehmed the Conqueror.* (Princeton, 1954)

Diplomaterium relationum rei publicae Ragusanae cum regno Hungariae, ed. L. v. Thallóczy. (Budapest, 1887)

Dlugosius, Johannes. *Historiae Polonicae, libri XII, ab antiquissimis temporibus ad a. 1480.* In *Opera omnia,* ed. A. Przeżdziecki. vols. 5-9. (Cracow, 1873-78)

Documents on Skanderbeg, ed. J. Radonić. *Djuradj Kastriot Skenderbeg i Arbanija u XV veku. Istoriska gradja.* (Belgrade, 1942)

Ducas, Michaelus. *Historia* (from 1347 to 1462), *CSHB.*

Ebendorfer, Thomas. *Chronicon austriacum, SRA,* vol. 2.

Fekete, L. *Einführung in die osman-türkische Diplomatik der türkischen Botmässigkeit in Ungarn.* (Budapest, 1926)

Fontes historiae Bulgaricae (Sofia, 1954 ff.), vol. 1 Greek sources, vol. 2 Latin sources, vols. 4, 5 Turkish sources with Bulgarian translation.

Georgii Sirmiensis Epistola de perditione regni Hungarorum, MHH, vol. 1 (Budapest, 1857)

Georgius Phrantzes. *Chronica* (from 1258 to 1476), *CSHB.*

Jorga, N. *Notes et extraits pour servir à l'histoire des croisades au XVᵉs.* 6 vols. (Paris, 1889-1916)

Leunclavius. *Historiae musulmanae Turcorum, libri XVIII.* (Frankfurt, 1591.) Translations of some Turkish sources.

Lezze, Donado da. *Historia turchesca, 1300-1514,* ed. I. Ursu (Bucharest, 1909)

Matricularum Regni Poloniae Summaria, ed. T. Wierzbowski. Parts I-IV, vols. I-III (1447-1548). (Warsaw, 1905-15)

Monumenta vetera Slavorum meridionalium historiam illustrantia, ed. A. Theiner. 2 vols. (Rome, 1863-75)

Neuman, K. F. *Reisen des Johannes Schiltberger aus München 1394-1427.* (Munich, 1859). On the battle of Nicopolis.

Neshri, Mehemmed. *Gihannümā; die altosmanische Chronik,* ed. T. Menzel and F. Taeschner. (Leipzig, 1951-55)

Philippi Callimachi Historia rerum gestarum in Hungaria et contra Turcos per Vladislaum Poloniae et Hungariae regem, MPH, 6, pp. 1-162.

Thuriocz, Johannes de. *Chronica Hungarorum,* ed. Schwandtner, SRH, 1 (1746).

Vetera Monumenta historica Hungariam sacram illustrantia, ed. A. Theiner. 2 vols. (Rome, 1859-60)

Windecke, Eberhart. *Historia vitae imp. Sigismundi vernacula 1386-1442.* ed. W. Altman. (Berlin, 1893)

See also Chapter V, Greek sources. The above listed are main sources.

Chapter X, *Bibliography*

Alexandrescu-Dersca, M. M. *La campagne de Timur en Anatolie (1402).* (Bucharest, 1942)

Andrić, A. *Geschichte des Fürstentums Montenegro von der ältesten Zeit bis zum Jahre 1852.* (Vienna, 1853)

Angelov, D. "Certains aspects de la conquête des peuples balkaniques par les Turcs," *Byzantinoslavica,* 17 (1956), pp. 220-75.

Atiya, S. A. *The Crusade of Nicopolis.* (London, 1934)

Babinger, F. *Mehmed der Eroberer und seine Zeit: Weltenstürmer einer Zeitwende* (Munich, 1953). French transl. by H. E. del Medico, *Mahomet II, le Conquérant et son temps (1432-1481).* (Paris, 1954)

———. "Von Amurath zu Amurath, Vor-und Nachspiel der Schlacht bei Varna (1444)," *Oriens,* 3 (1950), pp. 229-65.

Bain, R. N. "The Siege of Belgrade by Muhammad II, 1456," *English Historical Review,* 8 (1892), pp. 235-52.

Beckmann, G. *Der Kampf Kaiser Sigismunds gegen die werdende Weltmacht der Osmanen 1392-1437.* (Gotha, 1902)

Braun, M. *Lebensbeschreibung des Despoten Stefan Lazarević von Konstantin dem Philosophen: Im Auszug herausgegeben und übersetzt.* (The Hague, 1956)

Brauner, A. *Die Schlacht bei Nikopolis.* 4 vols. (Hamburg, 1838-45)

Dujčev, I. "La conquête turque et la prise de Constantinople dans la littérature slave contemporaine," *Byzantinoslavica,* 14 (1953), pp. 16-54; 16 (1955), pp. 318-29; 17 (1956), pp. 276-340. Important bibliography on Slavic sources.

Fekete, L. "Das Fethnāme über die Schlacht bei Varna," *Byzantinoslavica,* 14 (1953), pp. 258-70.

Fraknói, V. *Mathias Corvinus, König von Ungarn.* (Freiberg i. B., 1891)

Gegaj, A. *L'Albanie et l'invasion turque au XVᵉ siècle.* (Université de Louvain, Recueil de travaux publiés par les membres des conférences d'histoire et de philologie, 2e série, fasc. 40.) (Paris, 1937)

Gopčević, S. *Geschichte von Montenegro und Albanien.* (Gotha, 1914.), pp. 79-124.

Gruber, D. *Kampf der Kroaten mit den Türken seit dem Falle Sigets (1556) bis zum Frieden von Zitva-Darog (1606).* (Agram, 1879)

Gündisch, G. "Die Türkeneinfälle in Siebenbürgen bis zur Mitte des 15. Jahrhunderts," *JGO,* 2 (1937), pp. 393-412.

Halecki, O. *The Crusade of Varna: a Discussion of Controversial Problems.* (New York, 1943)

——. "Angora, Florence, Varna, and the Fall of Constantinople." *Akten des XI byzantin. Kongresses* (Munich, 1959), pp. 217-20.

Hammer-Purgstall. *Geschichte der Chane der Krim unter osmanischer Herrschaft.* (Vienna, 1856)

Huber, A. "Die Kriege zwischen Ungarn und Türken 1440-1443," *Archiv für österreichische Geschichte,* 68 (1886).

——. *Ludwig I. von Ungarn und die ungarischen Vasallenländer.* (Vienna, 1884)

Jorga, N. *La Campagne des Croisés sur le Danube.* (Paris, 1927)

——. *Geschichte des osmanischen Reiches nach den Quellen dargestellt.* vol. 1, to 1451; vol. 2, to 1538. (Gotha, 1908, 1909)

Klaić, V. *Geschichte Bosniens.* (Leipzig, 1889.) Pp. 248-439.

Kohler, I. *Die Schlachten bei Nikopolis und Warna.* (Breslau, 1882)

Kupelwieser, L. *Die Kämpfe Ungarns mit den Osmanen bis zur Schlacht bei Mohács.* (Vienna, 2nd ed. 1899)

Lechat, R. "Lettres de Jean de Tagliacozzo sur le siège de Belgrade et la mort de St. Jean Capistran," *Analecta Bollandiana,* 39 (1921).

Lybyer, A. H. *The Government of the Ottoman Empire in the Time of Suleiman the Magnificent.* (Cambridge, Mass., 1913)

Miklosić, F. "Die serbischen Dynasten Crnojević," *SbAW,* phil.-hist. Kl. (Vienna, 1886)

Miller, W. "The Founder of Montenegro," *English Historical Review,* 25 (1910).

Norden, W. *Das Papsttum und Byzanz.* (Berlin, 1903.), pp. 164-744.

Novaković, St. *Die Serben und Türken.* See Ch. V.

Ostrogorski, G. *History of the Byzantine State.* (New Brunswick, 1957.), pp. 457-509.

Polišenský, J. V. "Bohemia, the Turk and the Christian Commonwealth (1462-1520)," *Byzantinoslavica,* 14 (1954), pp. 82-108.

Popiscu, M. *Die Stellung des Papsttums und des christlichen Abendlandes gegenüber der Türkengefahr vom Jahre 1523 bis zur Schlacht bei Mohacz, 1526.* (1887.) Inaccessible to me.

Radonić, T. *Histoire des Serbes de Hongrie.* (Paris, 1919)

Rosetti, R. "Stephen the Great of Moldavia and the Turkish Invasion (1457-1503)," *SEER,* 6 (1927-28), pp. 87-103.

Šišić, F. "Die Schlacht bei Nikopolis," *WMBH,* 6 (1899), pp. 291-327.

———. *Die Schlacht bei Nikopolis 1396.* (Vienna, 1899)

———. *Die Wahl Ferdinands I. von Österreich zum König von Kroatien.* (Zagreb, 1917)

Skok, P. "L'importance de Dubrovnik dans l'histoire des Slaves," *Le Monde Slave,* 8 (1931), pp. 161-71.

Thallóczy, L. v. "Ungarn und Ragusa," *Ungarische Revue,* 9 (1889), pp. 1-10, 85-96.

———. "Zur Geschichte der Despotenfamilie Branković. Bruchstücke aus der Geschichte der nordwestlichen Balkanländer," *WMBH,* 3 (1895).

Ursu, J. *Die auswärtige Politik des Peter Rareš, Fürst der Moldau.* (Vienna, 1908)

Villari, L. *The Republic of Ragusa, an Episode of the Turkish Conquest.* (London, 1904)

Vlajić, P. W. *Untergang des bosnischen Königreiches.* (Sarajevo, 1926)

Wostry, W. *König Albrecht II. (1437-1439).* 2 vols. (Prague, 1906, 1907).

Zinkeisen, J. W. *Geschichte des osmanischen Reiches in Europa.* 7 vols. (Hamburg, 1840-63.) Still useful.

CHAPTER XI, *Sources*

Dnevnik Ljublinskogo Sejma 1569 goda, ed. M. Kovaljovič. (St. Petersburg, 1869)

Lites ac res gestae inter Polonos Ordinemque Cruciferorum, ed. J. Karwasińska. 2nd ed., 2 vols. (Poznań, 1890-1935)

Paszkiewicz, H. *Regesta Lithuaniae ab origine usque ad magni Ducatus cum Regno Poloniae unionem.* (1930)

Paul Vladimir, Rector of Cracow University. *Scriptum denunciatorium errorum Satyrae J. Falkenberg. Concilio Constantiensi datum,* ed. S. Betch. (Sacrum Poloniae Millenium.) (Rome, 1955.) Vol. 2, pp. 165-192. Text, commentary in English. Good bibliography.

Regesta Historico Diplomatica Ordinis S. Mariae Theutonicorum, ed. E. Joachim and W. Hubatsch. vol. 1, 1198-1454; vol. 2, 1455-1510. (Göttingen, 1948-50)

Rüssow, B. *Livländische Chronik. Aus dem Plattdeutschen übertragen und mit kurzen Anmerkungen versehen von E. Pabst.* (Reval, 1845)

SRP, ed. T. Hirsch, M. Töppen, E. Strehlke. 5 vols. (Leipzig, 1861-74.) To the end of the Teutonic Order. Vol. 1, *Petri de Dusburg Chronicon.*

Töppen, M., ed. *Akten der Ständtage Preussens.* 5 vols. (Leipzig, 1878-1886)

Voigt, J. *Codex diplomaticus Prussicus.* 6 vols. (Königsberg, 1836-61)

More complete indication on sources will be found in the works of F. L. Carsten, A. B. Boswell, and W. Hubatsch (see Bibl., chapters I, III, and XI).

CHAPTER XI, *Bibliography*. Cf. also Chapter III and Chapter IV

Barthold, F. W. *Geschichte der deutschen Hanse.* 2nd ed. (Leipzig, 1909)

Forstreuter, K. "Der Deutsche Orden und Südosteuropa," *Kryrios*, 1 (1936).

——. "Die preussische Flotte im 16. Jahrhundert," *Altpreussische Forschungen*, 17 (1940), pp. 113 ff.

——. "Zu den Kriegsstudien des Herzogs Albrecht von Preussen," *Altpreussische Forschungen*, 19 (1942).

——. *Preussen und Russland.* (Göttingen, 1955)

Gersdorf, H. *Der Deutsche Orden im Zeitalter der polnisch-litauischen Union: Die Amtszeit des Hochmeisters Konrad Zöllner von Rotenstein (1382-1390).* (Wissenschaftliche Beiträge zur Geschichte und Landeskunde Ost-Mitteleuropas, 29.) (Marsburg, 1957)

Halecki, O. "L'évolution historique de l'Union polonolithuanienne," *Le Monde Slave*, 2 (1926).

Hellmann, M. *Das Lettenland im Mittelalter.* (Münster, 1954)

Helm, K., and Ziesemer, W. *Die Literatur des Deutschen Ritterordens.* (Giessen, 1951)

Heyden, H. *Kirchengeschichte Pommerns, Osteuropa und der deutsche Osten.* 2 vols. 2nd ed. (Köln-Braunfeld, 1957)

Hirn, J. *Die Renuntiation des Deutschmeisters Maximilian auf Polen und die damit zusammenhängenden Ereignisse 1587-1603: Ein Beitrag zur Geschichte der österreichisch-nordischen Politik in den Tagen Kaiser Rudolfs II.* Mitteilungen der Institut für österr.-Gesch.-Forsch., Erg. Bd. 4 (1893), pp. 248-96.

Hötsch, O. "Die polnisch-liauische Union," *ZOG*, 1 (1911), pp. 604-10.

Hubatsch, W. *Quellen zur Geschichte des Deutschen Ordens.* (Quellensammlung zur Kulturgeschichte, vol. 5) (Göttingen, Frankfurt, Berlin, 1954.), pp. 191-98: Sources and bibliography.

Joachim, E. *Die Politik des letzten Hochmeisters in Preussen Albrecht von Brandenburg.* (Publikationen aus den preuss. Staatsarchiven, vols. 50, 58, 61.) (Leipzig, 1892-93)

Karge, P. "Herzog Albrecht von Preussen und der Deutsche Orden," *Altpreussische Monatschrift*, 39 (1902).

Kirchner, W. *The Rise of the Baltic Question.* (Newark, 1954)

Lelewel, J. *Histoire de la Lithuanie et de la Ruthénie jusqu'à leur union définitive avec la Pologne conclue à Lublin en 1569.* Transl. by E. Rykaczewski. (Paris, Leipzig, 1861)

Lohmeyer, K. *Geschichte von Ost- und Westpreussen*, Abt. 1, *Bis 1411*, 3rd ed. (Gotha, 1908)

Murawski, K. E. *Zwischen Tannenberg und Thorn: Geschichte des Deutschen Ordens unter dem Hochmeister Konrad von Erlichshansen 1441-49.* (Göttingen, 1953)

Nieborowski, P. *Der Deutsche Orden und Polen in der Zeit des grössten Konfliktes.* 2nd ed. (Breslau, 1924)

Nimmert, B. "Danzigs Verhältnis zu Polen in den Jahren 1466-1492," *Zeitschrift des westpreuss. Geschichtsvereines*, 53 (1912), pp. 109-201.

Oehler, M. *Der Krieg zwischen dem Deutschen Orden und Polen-Litauen 1409-11.* (Elbing, 1910)

Perlbach, M. *Preussisch-polnische Studien zur Geschichte des Mittelalters.* 2 vols. (Halle, 1896)

Rundstedt, H. G. v. *Die Hanse und der Deutsche Orden in Preussen bis zur Schlacht bei Tannenberg 1410.* (Weimar, 1937)
Schienemann, Th. *Russland, Polen, und Livland.* (Berlin, 1887)
Thomson, E. *Baltische Bibliographie 1945-1956.* (Ostdeutsche Beiträge aus dem Göttinger Arbeitskreis, vol. 5.) (Würzburg, 1957)
Thunert, F. *Der grosse Krieg zwischen Polen und dem deutschen Orden 1410 bis 1 Febr. 1411.* Dissertation. (Königsberg, 1886, *Zeitschrift des westpreuss. Geschichtsvereines,* 16, 1886.)
Weise, E. *Staatsverträge des Deutschen Ordens in Preussen im 15. Jh.* 2 vols. (Königsberg, Marburg, 1939, 1955)
——. *Das Widerstandsrecht im Ordenslande Preussen und das mittelalterliche Europa.* (Veröffentlichungen der niedersächsischen Archivverwaltung, Heft 6.) (Göttingen, 1955)
Wittram, R. *Baltische Geschichte: Die Ostseelande Livland, Estland, Kurland 1180-1918: Grundzüge und Durchblicke.* (München, 1954)
——. *Baltische Kirchengeschichte.* (Göttingen, 1956)
Zegarski, T. *Polen und das Basler Konzil.* Dissertation. (Posen, 1910)

CHAPTER XII, *Sources.* Cf. also Chapter IX and Chapter XV

Acta Alexandri regis, Poloniae (1501-06), ed. F. Papée. (Cracow, 1927.) In *Monumenta medii aevi res gestas Poloniae illustrantia,* vol. 19.
Acta et diplomata graeca, see ch. IX, T. Miklosich.
Acta Stephani regis (1576-86), ed. J. Polkowski. In *Acta historica res gestas Poloniae illustr.,* 11 (1889).
Acta Tomiciana, see Sources, ch. X.
Akty istoričeskie ("Historical Acts"). 5 vols. (St. Petersburg, 1841-42). See vol. 1.
Akty juridičeskie ("Juridical Acts"). (St. Petersburg, 1838)
Akty otnosjaščiesja k istorii južnoj i zapadnoj Rossii ("Acts relating to the History of Southern and Western Russia"). 15 vols. (St. Petersburg, 1863-92.) Vol. 1, from 1561 to 1598, Church laws; vol. 2, from 1599 to 1637.
Akty otnosjaščiesja k istorii zapadnoj Rossii ("Acts relating to the History of Western Russia"). 5 vols. (St. Petersburg, 1846-53.) Vol. 1, 1561-1568, Privileges of the Lithuanian princes; vol. 2, 1568-1638; vol. 3, 1544-1587.
Akty rossijskoj imperii. (St. Petersburg, 1836)
Arkhiv jugo-zapadnoj Rossii ("Archives of South-Western Russia") (Kiev), ser. 1, 1-9 (1859-93); ser. 2, 1 (1861); ser. 3, 1, 2, 3, 5 (1863-1902); ser. 6, 1, 2, 4, 6 (1876-1911); ser. 7, 1, 2 (1886-90).
Codex diplomaticus Poloniae . . . , ed. L. Rzyszewski and A. Maczkowski. 3 vols. (Warsaw, 1847-1887). Documents to 1506.
Documenta pontificum Romanorum historiam Ukrainae illustrantia (1075-1953). vol. 1 (1075-1700), ed. A. G. Welykyj. (Rome, 1953)
Giovio, Paolo. *The Historie of the Legation or Ambassade of Greate Basilius, Prince of Moscovia, to Pope Clement the VI.* In P. M. Anglerius, *The Three Decades of the Newe Worlde.* (London, 1555)
Documents on the reign of Stephen Batory. Most of them were published by A. Pawiński in *Żródła dziejowe,* 21 vols. (Warsaw, 1876-94); vols. 2, 3, 4, 8, 9. Vol. 8 on Royal Prussia and Sigismund August.
Herberstein, S. v. *Rerum Moscovitarum commentarii.* (Vienna, 1549). Engl. transl. by O. P. Backus. (Lawrence, Univ. of Kansas, 1956)

Monumenta Poloniae historica. 6 vols. (Lwów, 1869-88, Cracow, 1893). See vol. 5.

Pamiatniki diplomat. snošenij drovnej Rossii. 10 vols. (St. Petersburg, 1851-1871). Vols. 1, 2 (1588-1621).

Pierling, P. *Bathory et Possevino: Documents inédits sur les rapports du Saint-Siège avec les Slaves.* (Paris, 1887)

Poslanija Ivana Groznogo, ed. Likhačev, D., Lur'e. (Moscow, 1951)

Russian Chronicles:

Fourth Chronicle of Novgorod, PSRL, new ed. (St. Petersburg, 1915 ff.), vol. 4; *Russian Chronograph from 1512, PSRL,* vol. 22; *Second Sophia Chronicle, PSRL,* vol. 6; *Stepennaja Kniga, PSRL,* vol. 21; part 2, *Tver' Chronicle, PSRL,* vol. 15; *Voskresenskij Chronicle, PSRL,* vol. 8; *Moskevskij Letopisnyj svod kontsa XV v., PSRL,* vol. 25.

Russkaja istoričeskaja biblioteka ("*Russian Historical Library*"). 39 vols. (St. Petersburg, 1872-1927). Vols. 2, 3, 6. *Litovskaja metrika;* in vols. 20, 27, 32, 33.

Sbornik russkago istor. imp. obščestva. 54 vols. (St. Petersburg, 1867-89). Vol. 35 (Poland, Lithuania 1487-1530); vol. 40 (Crimea, Kazans, Turks 1479-1480); vol. 41 (Tatars); vol. 37 (England).

Theiner, A. *Vetera monumenta Poloniae et Lithuaniae (1217-1775).* vol. 1 (Rome, 1860-64); vol. 2 (Rome, 1861); vol. 3 (1863).

Ziegler, A. W. "Vier bisher nicht veröffentlichte Briefe Isidors von Kijev," *BZ,* 44 (1951), pp. 570-77. Cf. also *OCP,* 18 (1952), pp. 135-42.

CHAPTER XII, *Bibliography*

Alef, G. "The Political Significance of the Inscriptions on Muscovite Coinage in the Reign of Vasili II," *Speculum,* 34 (1959), pp. 1-19.

Amann, A. M. *Ostslavische Kirschengeschichte.* (Vienna, 1950)

Bächtold, R. *Südwestrussland im Spätmittelalter: Territoriale, wirtschaftliche und soziale Verhältnisse.* (Basel, 1951)

Baumgarten, N. de. *Généalogies des branches régnantes des Rurikides du XIVe au XVIe siècle, Orientalia Christiana,* 94 (1934)

Bouvat, L. *L'empire mongol, 2e phase.* (Paris, 1927)

Cherniavsky, M. "The Reception of the Council of Florence in Moscow," *Church History,* 24 (1955), pp. 347-59.

Etienne Batory, Roi de Pologne, Prince de Transylvanie. (Recueil de travaux publiés par l'Académie Polonaise et l'Académie Hongroise.) (Cracow, 1935). Indication of sources and complete bibliography on Batory and his time, pp. 513-64.

Forstreuter, K. *Preussen und Russland von den Anfängen des Deutschen Ordens bis zu Peter dem Grossen.* (Göttingen, 1955). See also Ch. XI.

Geanakoplos, D. "The Council of Florence and the Problem of Union Between the Greek and Latin Churches," *Church History,* 24 (1955), pp. 324-46.

Golder, F. A. *Russian Expansion on the Pacific (1641-1850).* (Cleveland, 1914)

Hofmann, G. "Quellen zu Isidor von Kiew als Kardinal und Patriarch," *Orientalia Christiana Periodica,* 18 (1952), pp. 143-57.

Jablonowski, H. "Die Aussenpolitik Stephan Bathorys," *JGO,* 21 (1937).

———. *Westrussland zwischen Wilna und Moskau: Die politische Stellung und die politischen Tendenzen der russischen Bevölkerung des Grossfürstentums Litauen im 15. Jh.* (Leiden, 1955)

Johansen, P. *Novgorod und de Hanse*, see footnote 13.

Karttunen, K. I. *Jean III et Stefan Batory: Études sur les relations politiques entre la Suède et la Pologne de 1576 à 1583.* (Geneva, 1911)

Lantzeff, G. V. *Siberia in the Seventeenth Century: A Study of the Colonial Administration.* (Berkeley, Cal., University of California Press, 1943)

Lubimenko, I. "England's Part in the Discovery of Russia," *SEER*, 6 (1927-28), pp. 104-18.

———. *Les relations commerciales et politiques de l'Angleterre avec la Russie avant Pierre le Grand.* (Bibliothèque de l'Ecole des Hautes Etudes, Sect. hist. et phil., fasc. 26). (Paris, 1933.) Extensive bibliography.

Malowist, M. "Poland, Russia, and Western Trade in the 15th and 16th Centuries," *Past and Present*, 13 (1958).

Medlin, W. K. *Moscow and East Rome.* (Geneva, 1952)

Müller, G. F. *Conquest of Siberia and the History of Transactions, Wars, Commerce, etc., Carried on between Russia and China from the Earliest Period.* (London, 1842)

Nolde, B. *La formation de l'empire russe, études, notes et documents.* (Paris, 1952). Vol. 1. *Progress on the Volga, in Siberia, in the Urals.* Complete bibliography of sources and studies.

Paczkowski, J. "Sigmund August als Grossfürst-Regent von Litauen (1544-1548)," *ZOG*, 3 (1913), pp. 547-58.

Paszkiewicz, H. *The Origin of Russia.* (London, 1954), pp. 183-254.

Philipp, W. "Ein Anonymous der Tver Publizistik im 15. Jahrhundert." *Festschrift für Dmytro Čyževskij.* (Ost-Europ. Institut der freien Universität Berlin, slavistische Veröffentlichungen, vol. 16.) (Berlin, 1954)

Pierling, P. *Antonio Possevino: Missio Moscovitica.* (Paris, 1882)

———. *Un nouveau nonce du pape en Moscovie.* (Paris, 1884)

———. *Papes et Tsares.* (Paris, 1890)

———. *Rome et Moscou (1547-79).* (Paris, 1883)

———. *La Russie et le Saint-Siège, études diplomatiques.* 5 vols. (Paris, 2nd ed., 1906-1912)

Rahmer, H. *Vom ersten bis zum dritten Rome.* (Rektoratsrede, Innsbruck, 1950)

Ramm-Helmsing, H. v. "Die Moskauer Westpolitik Ivan III. und Ivan IV.," *Deutsche wissenschaftliche Zeitschrift für Polen*, 33 (1937), pp. 61-69.

Schaffgotsch, K. *Iwan der Schreckliche: Geschichte seines Reiches und seiner Zeit.* (Vienna, 1941)

Semjonov, Juri. *Die Eroberung Sibiriens: Ein Epos menschlicher Leidenschaften: Der Roman eines Landes.* (Berlin, 1937). Popular.

Ševčenko, I. "Intellectual Repercussions of the Council of Florence," *Church History*, 24 (1955), pp. 291-323.

Smolitsch, I. *Leben und Lehre der Starzen.* (Vienna, 1936). Reviewed in *BZ*, 38 (1938), p. 180. See also Ch. XIII.

———. "Zur Geschichte der russischen Ostpolitik des 15. und 16. Jhs," *JGO*, 6 (1941), pp. 55-84.

Špidlik, T. *Joseph de Volokolamsk, un chapitre de la spiritualité russe.* (Rome, 1956)

Spuler, B. *Die Goldene Horde.* (Leipzig, 1943)

Stökl, G. "Russland und Europa vor Peter dem Grossen," *HZ*, 184 (1957), pp. 531-54.

Stratonov, I. A. "Die Reform der Lokalverwaltung unter Ivan IV," *ZOG*, 7 (1932), pp. 1-20.
Vernadsky, G. "The Expansion of Russia," *Transactions of the Connecticut Academy*, 31 (New Haven, 1933), pp. 391-425.
————. "The Heresy of the Judaizers and the Policy of Ivan III of Moscow," *Speculum*, 8 (1933), pp. 436-54.
————. *The Mongols and Russia*. (New Haven, 1953)
Waliszewski, K. *Ivan le Terrible*. (Paris, 1904)
Wipper, R. *Ivan Grozny*. Transl. by J. Fineberg. (Moscow, 1947)
Ziegler, A. *Die Union des Konzils von Florenz in der russischen Kirche*, Das östl. Christentum, Heft 4-5. (Würzburg, 1938)
Zivier, E. *Neuere Geschichte Polens*. Vol. 1, *Die zwei letzten Jagellonen (1506-1572)*. (Gotha, 1915)

CHAPTER XIII, *Bibliography*

Ainalov, D. *Geschichte der russischen Monumentalkunst zur Zeit des Grossfürstentums Moskau*. (Berlin, Leipzig, 1933)
Alpatov, M., and Brunov, N. *Geschichte der altrussischen Kunst*. (Augsburg, 1932)
Andreyev, N. "The Pskov-Pechery Monastery in the 16th Century," *SEER*, 32 (1953-54), pp. 318-43.
Backvis, C. "Le renvoi des ambassadeurs grecs, tragédie classique et drame polonais," *Annuaire de l'Institut de Philol. et d'Hist. Orient. et Slaves*, 11 (1951), pp. 31-60.
Badalić, J. "Marko Marulić in Deutschland," *Die Welt der Slaven*, 5 (1960), pp. 245 ff.
Bräuer, H. "Zur Frage der altrussischen Übersetzungsliteratur," *ZSPh*, 27 (1959), pp. 322-347. Deals with philological problems.
Bunt, C. G. E. *A History of Russian Art*. (London, New York, 1946)
Buxton, D. R. *Russian Medieval Architecture*. (Cambridge, 1934)
Conant, K. G. *Medieval Russian Churches*. (Boston, 1949), pp. 65-90.
Ćorović, V. "Serbische Volkslieder über den Abgang des hl. Sava zu den Mönchen," *ASPh*, 28 (1906)
Cronia, A. *Storia della letteratura serbo-croata*. (Milan, 1956), pp. 1-119. To the 17th century, very general.
————. "Marko Marulić," *Wiener slavist. Jahrbuch*, 3 (1953), pp. 5-21.
Deanović, M. *Anciens contacts entre la France et Raguse*. (Zagreb, 1950)
Denissoff, E. *Maxime le Grec et l'Occident*. (Louvain, Paris, 1943)
Filipović, V. "Marko Marulić als Philosopher," *Die Welt der Slaven*, 2 (1957), pp. 259 ff.
Grabar, I. "Die Malerschule des alten Pskow zur Frage der Dezentralisierung des künstlerischen Nachlasses von Byzanz," *Zeitschrift für bildende Kunst*, Heft 1. (Leipzig, 1929-30)
Grumel, V. "La personnalité de Maxime le Grec," *Revue des études byzantines*, 2 (1944), pp. 255-60.
Gudzij, N. K. *History of Early Russian Literature*. Transl. by S. W. Jones. (New York, 1949)
Hamilton, G. H. *The Art and Architecture of Russia*. (Baltimore, 1954)
Hrdina, C. *Commentarius brevis et iucundus itineris atque peregrinationis*

. . . *susceptae ab illustri* . . . *barone de Rosmital et Blatna.* (Prague, 1951). See also Bibl. M. Letts.

Jagić, V. "Die christlich-mythische Schicht in der russischen Volksepik," *ASPh,* 1 (1876).

———. "Der erste Cetinjer Kirchendruck v. J. 1494," *Denkschriften der Wiener Akademie,* 43 (1895).

Jireček, C. (K.) "Beiträge zur ragusanischen Literaturgeschichte," *ASPh,* 21 (1898).

———. "Die mittelalterliche Kanzlei der Ragusaner," *ASPh,* 25, 26 (1903, 1904).

———. "Der ragusanische Dichter Šiško Mencetić," *ASPh,* 19 (1896).

Jugie, M. "Maxime l'Hagiorite, dit le Grec," *Dictionnaire de théologie Catholique,* 10 (Paris, 1928), cols. 460-63.

Kjellin, H. *Ryska Ikoner.* (Stockholm, 1956)

Klonowicz, S. *The Boatman.* Transl. by M. Coleman. (Cambridge Springs, Pa., 1958)

Kloss, E. *Die schlesische Buchmalerei des Mittelalters.* (Berlin, 1942)

Klostermann, R. A. "Maxim Grek in der Legende," *Zeitschrift für Kirchengeschichte,* 53 (1934), pp. 171-228.

Kochanowski, Jan. Works of Kochanowski.
  Die Abfertigung der griechischen Gesandten. Transl. by A. Stylo. (Cracow, 1901)
  Cochanovius, J. *Carmina Latina,* ed. J. Przyborowski. (Warsaw, 1884)
  Jean Kochanowski. *Chants.* Traduits du polonais avec une introduction et un commentaire par J. Langlade. (Paris, 1932)
  Choix de poèmes de Jean Kochanowski. Traduit. par. A. Mary. (Paris, 1931)
  Jan Kochanowski. *Lamenti (Treny),* versione poetica dal polacco di E. Damiani. (Inst. per l'Eur. Orient.) (Rome, 1930)
  Laments by Jan Kochanowski. Versified by D. Prall. (Berkeley, 1920)
  Poems by Jan Kochanowski. Transl. by D. Radin, M. B. Peacock, R. E. Merrill, H. H. Havermale, G. R. Noyes. (Berkeley, 1928.) *Laments, St. John's Eve, The Dismissal of the Greek Envoys.*
  Threnes de J. Kochanowski (1530-1584). Traduits du Polonais par Rognigny. (Paris, 1919)

Kochanowski, Jan. Studies about Kochanowski.
  Bruchnalski, W. "Jan Kochanovski (1529-1584)," *SEER,* 9 (1930-31), pp. 56-78. Cf. *ibid.,* 6 (1927-28), pp. 401-14, *St. John's Eve,* transl. by G. R. Noyes, M. B. Peacock; *ibid.,* 4 (1925-26), pp. 317-20, *Laments,* transl. by D. Prall.
  Jan Kochanowski und das Judentum: Ein Beitrag zur polnischen Literaturgeschichte. Ch. Wolf Steckel. (Breslau, 1937)
  Langlade, J. *Jean Kochanowski, l'homme, penseur, le poète lyrique.* (Paris, 1932.) Bibliography.
  Pietrkiewicz, J. "The Mediaeval Dream-Formula in Kochanowski's *Treny,*" *SEER,* 31 (1952-53), pp. 388-404.
  Weintraub, W. "Kochanowski's Renaissance Manifesto," *SEER,* 30 (1951-52), pp. 412-24.

Kondakov, N. P. *The Russian Icon.* Transl. by E. H. Minns. (Oxford, 1927)

———. *The Russian Icon.* 4 vols. (Prague, 1928-33)

Kot, S. *Five Centuries of Polish Learning.* (Oxford, 1941.), pp. 1-16.

———. "L'Humanisme et la Renaissance en Pologne," *Bibliothèque d'Humanisme et Renaissance,* 15. (Geneva, 1953)

Kot, S. "Le rayonnement de Strassbourg en Pologne à l'époque de l'Humanisme," *RES*, 27 (1951).

Kozak, E. "Bibliographische Übersicht der biblisch-apokryphen Litteratur bei den Slaven," *Jahrbücher für protestantische Theologie*, 18 (1892).

Kowalczyk, G. *Die Denkmäler der Kunst in Dalmatien*. (Berlin, 1910)

Kurbskij, A. M. *The Correspondence between A. M. Kurbsky and Tsar Ivan IV of Russia, 1569-1573*, ed. with a translation and notes by J. L. I. Fennell. (Cambridge, 1955)

Letts, M. *The Travels of Leo of Rožmital through Germany, Flanders, England, France, Spain, Portugal and Italy, 1465-67.* (Publications of the Hakluyt Society, second series.) (Cambridge, 1957)

Loukomski, G. K. *L'architecture religieuse russe du XIe siècle au XVIIe siècle*. (Paris, 1929)

Martel, A. *La langue polonaise dans les pays ruthènes.* (Lille, 1938)

Moravski, K. *Histoire de l'Université de Cracovie.* vol. 1. (Cracow, 1900-05)

Music of the Polish Renaissance: A Selection of Works from the XVIth and Beginning of the XVIIth Century, ed. by J. M. Chromiński and Z. Lissa. (Warsaw, 1955)

Pamjatniki polemičeskoj literatury zapadnoj Rusi ("Polemical literature for and against the Union"), *RIB*, vols. 4, 7, 13.

Pelesz, J. *Geschichte der Union der ruthenischen Kirche mit Rom.* 2 vols. (Würzburg, Vienna, 1881)

Pešina, J. *Painting of the Gothic and Renaissance Periods, 1450-1550.* (Prague, 1958)

Petković, V. R. *L'art dalmate du moyen âge.* (Paris, 1919)

Philipp, W. "Ein Anonymous der Tverer Publizistik im 15. Jahrhundert." In *Festschrift für Dmytro Čyževśkyj.* (Ost-Europa-Institut an der Freien Universität Berlin, slavistische Veröffentlichungen, vol. 5.) (Berlin, 1954), pp. 230-48.

———. "Über das Verhältnis des 'Slovo o pogibeli russkoj zemli' zum 'Žitie Akeksandra Nevskogo,'" *FOG*, 5 (1957), pp. 7-37.

Pollak, O. *Studien zur Geschichte der Architektur Prags 1520-1600.* (Vienna, 1910)

Prohaska, D. *Das kroatisch-serbische Schrifttum in Bosnien und der Herzegowina.* (Zagreb, 1911)

Prokop, A. *Die Markgrafschaff Mähren in kunstgeschichtlicher Beziehung.* 4 vols. (Vienna, 1904). Deals especially with architecture.

Rambaud, A. *La Russie épique.* (Paris, 1876)

Reau, L. *L'art russe.* (Paris, 1920). Standard book.

Russian Icons. UNESCO (1958). Text by V. N. Lazarev and O. Demus; published in English, French, German, and Russian.

The Sacred Art in Poland. Vol. 1, *Architecture, Ars Christiana*, ed. A. Krauze (Warsaw, 1956); vol. 2, *Religious Painting* (Warsaw, 1958). Published also in French and German.

Schweinfurth, P. "Aristotile Fioravanti: Die italienische Forschung und das Buch von V. Snegirev," *JGO*, 2 (1937), pp. 413-32.

———. *Geschichte der russischen Malerei im Mittelalter.* (The Hague, 1930). Standard book.

Serbo-Croatian Heroic Songs, collected by M. Parry, edited and translated by A. B. Lord. 2 vols. (Cambridge, Mass., Belgrade, 1953, 1954)

Setschkareff, V. *Die Dichtungen Gundulićs und ihr poetischer stil.* (Bonn, 1952)

Skarga, P. *Les sermons politiques.* Transl. by A. Berga. (Paris, 1916)
———. *The Eucharist.* Transl. E. J. Dworaczyk. (Milwaukee, 1939)
Smolitsch, I. *Russisches Mönchtum.* (Augsburg, 1953)
———. "Studien zum Klosterwesen Russlands," *Kyrios,* 4 (1939).
Stang, C. S. *Die westrussische Kanzleisprache des Grossfürstentums Litauen.* (Oslo, 1935)
Stanojević, S. "Die Biographie St. Lazarević's von Konstantin dem Philosophen als Geschichtsquelle," *ASPh,* 18 (1896).
Stele, F. *Monumenta artis Slovenicae.* 2 vols. (Ljubljana, 1935-38). Vol. 1: *Medieval mural painting.*
Strojev, V. "Zur Herkunftsfrage der Judaiser," *ZSPh,* 11 (1934).
Szymonowic, S. (Simonides). Selected poems in J. Bowring, *Specimens of the Polish Poet.* (London, 1827)
Trogrančić, F. *Storia della letteratura croata.* (Rome, 1953). From the fifteenth to the nineteenth century. Reviewed by I. Javarek in *SEER,* 32 (1953-54), pp. 550 ff.
Ulbrich, A. *Kunstgeschichte Ostpreussens von der Ordenszeit bis zur Gegenwart.* (Königsberg, 1932)
Unbegaun, B. "Les relations vieux-russes sur la prise de Constantinople," *RES,* 9 (1929), pp. 13-38.
Vaillant, A. *La langue de Dominko Zlatarić, poète ragusain.* 2 vols. (Paris, 1928-31)
———. *Les piesni razlike de D. Zlatarić.* (Paris, 1928)
Vernadsky, G. *Russia at the Dawn of the Modern Age.* (New Haven, 1959)
Voyce, A. *Russian Architecture,* (New York, 1948). Deals more with modern architecture.
Waczynski, B. "Nachklänge der Florentischen Union," see ch. XVIII.
Wesselofsky, A. "Beiträge zur Erklärung des russischen Heldenepos," *ASPh,* 9 (1886), pp. 282-91.
———. "Neue Beiträge zur Geschichte der Salomonsage," *ASPh,* 6 (1882), pp. 393-411, 548-90.
Winfield, D. "Four Historical Compositions from the Medieval Kingdom of Serbia," *Byzantinoslavica,* 19 (1958), pp. 251-78.
Woermann, K. *Geschichte der Kunst.* 2nd ed. (Leipzig, Vienna, 1919). Vol. 4, pp. 313-22, 444-49.
Wolfgramm, "Die osmanische Reichskrise im Spiegel der bulgarischen Haidukengedichte," *Leipziger Vierteljahrschrift für Südostforschung,* 16 (1942), pp. 341-72.
Wollner, W. *Untersuchungen über die Volksepik der Grossrussen.* (Leipzig, 1879)
Woltner, M. "Die altrussische Literatur im Spiegelbild der Forschung," *ZSPh,* 21 (1953), pp. 159 ff., 344 ff.; 23 (1955), pp. 189-200; 27 (1959), pp. 179-198. Extensive bibliography. To be continued.
Żólkiewski, S. *Expedition to Moscow.* Transl. by J. Giertych. (, 1959).

CHAPTER XIV, cf. also Chapter X, *Sources* and *Bibliography*

Alderson, A. D. *The Structure of the Ottoman Dynasty.* (Oxford, 1956)
Backus, O. P. "Die Rechtstellung der litauischen Bojaren 1387-1506," *JGO,* 6 (1958), pp. 1-32. Good bibl. on Lithuanian legal sources.
Balzer, O. *Aus Problemen der Verfassungsgeschichte Polens.* (Cracow, 1916)

Braun, M. *Die Slaven auf dem Balkan bis zur Befreiung von der türkischen Herrschaff.* (Leipzig, 1941), pp. 126-43, 163-200.

Codex iuris municipalis Regni Bohemiae. Vols. 1, 2, ed. J. Čelakovský (Prague, 1886-95), from 1225 to 1419; vol. 3, ed. G. Friedrich (Prague, 1948), from 1420 to 1526; vol. 6/1, *Privilegia non regalium civitatum provincialium ann. 1232-1452,* ed. A. Haas (Prague, 1954).

Conze, W. *Agrarverfassung und Bevölkerung in Litauen.* (Leipzig, 1940)

Dix années d'historiographie yougoslave 1945-1955. (Belgrade, 1955), pp. 209 ff.

Dorošenko, D. "Orthodox-östliche Kirchen- und römisch-westliche Uniongeschichte im neueren polnischen Schrifttum," *Kyrios,* 1 (1936), pp. 402-10. Reviews of works on the Orthodox and Uniat Churches in Poland by the Polish scholars K. Chodynicki, K. Lewicki, M. Andrusiak, J. Woliński, and E. Sakowicz.

Draganović, K. S. "Massenübertritte der Katholiken zur Orthodoxie im kroatischen Sprachgebiet zur Zeit der Türkenherrschaft," *OCP,* 3 (1937), pp. 181-232.

———. "Über die Gründe der Massenübertritte der Katholiken zur Orthodoxie im kroatischen Sprachgebeit," *OCP,* 3 (1937), pp. 550-99.

Dujčev, I. "Die bulgarische Geschichtsforschung während des letzten Vierteljahrhunderts, 1918-1942," *Südost-Forschungen,* 7 (1942), pp. 546-73.

———. "Il cattolicesimo in Bulgaria nel secolo XVII secondo i processi informativi sulla nomina dei vescovi cattolici," *OCA,* no. 111 (1937).

Eichmann, F. *Die Reformen des osmanischen Reiches mit besonderer Berücksichtigung des Vcrhältnisses der Christen des Orients zur türkischen Herrschaft.* (Berlin, 1858).

Elekcs, L. "Die Anfänge einer rumänischen Gesellschaft. Versuch einer rumänischen Entwicklungsgeschichte im XIII-XIV Jh.," *Archivum Europae Centro-Orientalis,* 7 (1941), pp. 361-488.

Fijalek, J. "Le sort reservé à l'Union de Florence dans le Grand-Duché de Lithuanie sous le règne de Casimir Jagellon," *Bulletin internat. de l'Acad. polonaise des sciences et des lettres,* cl. d'hist. et de Philol., 1-3 (Jan.-Mar., 1934).

Filov, B. *Geschichte der bulgarischen Kunst unter der türkischen Herrschaft und in der neueren zeit.* (Berlin, Leipzig, 1933)

Folwarski, H. "Erasmus Ciołek, genannt Vitelius, Bischof von Płock (1503-1522)," *ZOG,* 9 (1935), pp. 38-88.

Gibb, H. A. R., and Bowen, H. *Islamic Society and the West.* (Oxford, 1954)

Giese, F. "Die geschichtlichen Grundlagen für die Stellung der christlichen Untertanen im osmanischen Reich," *Der Islam,* 19 (1931), pp. 264-77.

Hadrovics, L. *Le peuple serbe et son église sous la domination turque.* (Paris, 1947)

———. "Ungarn und die Kroaten," *Ungarische Jahrbücher,* 21 (1941), pp. 136-72.

Hajek, A. *Bulgarien unter der Türkenherrschaft.* (Berlin, Leipzig, 1925)

Halecki, O. "L'évolution historique de l'Union polono-lithuanienne," *Le monde slave* (1926), pp. 279-93.

———. *From Florence to Brest.* (Rome, 1958)

Hammer-Purgstall, J. v. *Geschichte des osmanischen Reiches.* 10 vols. 2nd ed. (Budapest, 1834-36)

Hasluck, F. W. *Christianity and Islam under the Sultans,* ed. M. M. Hasluck. 2 vols. (Oxford, 1929)

Hellmann, M. "Staat und Recht in Altrussland," *Saeculum*, 5 (1954), pp. 41 ff.

Hofmann, G. "Die Wiedervereinigung der Ruthenen mit Rom," *OC*, No. 12 (1924-25), pp. 125-72.

Hudal, A. *Die serbisch-orthodoxe Nationalkirche.* (Graz, 1922)

Ivić, A. "Ansiedlung der Bulgaren in Ungarn," *ASPh*, 31 (1910), pp. 414-30.

Jánossy, D. "Die Territorialfrage der serbischen Woiwodschaft in Ungarn," *Jahrbuch des Institutes für ungarische Geschichtsforschung in Wien*, 3 (1933), pp. 357-74.

Jireček, J. C. (K.) *Die Bedeutung Ragusas in der Handelsgeschichte des Mittelalters.* (Vienna, 1899)

———. *Geschichte der Serben.* vol. 2. (Gotha, 1918)

———. "Der Grossvezier Mehmed Sokolović und die serbischen Patriarchen Makarij und Antonij," *ASPh*, 9 (1886), pp. 291-97. Sixteenth century Serbian history. Cf. H. Ruvarac, "Nochmals Mehmed Sokolović und die serbischen Patriarchen," *ibid.*, 10 (1887), pp. 43-53.

Jorga, N. *Geschichte des osmanischen Reiches nach den Quellen dargestellt.* 5 vols. (Gotha, 1908-13)

———. *Geschichte des rumänischen Volkes im Rahmen seiner Staatsbildung.* 2 vols. (Gotha, 1905)

Kadlec, K. *Intraduction à l'étude comparative de l'histoire du droit public des peuples slaves.* (Paris, 1933.) Sources of Czech jurisprudence, pp. 216-25; Polish-Lithuanian, pp. 272-85.

Kállay, B. v. *Geschichte der Serben.* Transl. from Hungarian by J. H. Schwikker. 2 vols. (Budapest, Vienna, Leipzig, 1878)

Kanitz, F. P. *Das Königreich Serbien und das Serbenvolk von der Römerzeit bis zur Gegenwart.* 3 vols. (Leipzig, 1904-14)

Konopcizynski, L. *Le Liberum Veto.* (Paris, 1930)

Köprülü, M. Fuad. *Alcune osservazioni intorno all' influenza delle istituzioni bizantine sulle istituzioni ottomane.* (Publicazioni dell' Istituto per l'Oriente, no. 50.) (Rome, 1953)

Kretschmayr, H. *Geschichte von Venedig.* 3 vols. (Gotha, 1905-34)

Kukuljević, J. *Jura regni Croatiae, Dalmatiae et Slavoniae.* 3 vols. (Zagreb, 1861-62)

Kupelwieser, L. *Die Kämpfe Österreichs mit den Osmanen vom Jahre 1526 bis 1537.* (Vienna, 1899)

Kutrzeba, S. *Grundriss der polnischen Verfassungsgeschichte.* Transl. by W. Christiani. (Berlin, 1912)

Kutrzeba, S., and Semkowicz, W. *Acta unji Polski z Litwą* ("Acts of Polish-Lithuanian Union"). (Cracow, 1932)

Kyriakos, D. *Geschichte der orientalischen Kirchen.* Transl. by E. Rausch. (Leipzig, 1902)

Langer, W. L., and Blake, R. P. "The Rise of the Ottoman Turks and its Historical Background," *American Historical Review*, 37 (1932), pp. 468-505.

Lascaris, M. "Joachim, métropolite de Moldavie et les relations de l'église moldave avec le Patriarcat de Peć et l'archevêché d'Achris," *Académie Rumaine, Bulletin de la Section Historique*, 13 (1927), pp. 129-59.

Libri citationum et sententiarum, seu Knihy pùhonné a nálezové, ed. V. Brandl. 7 vols. (Brno, 1872-1911). Covers the period from 1374 to 1503.

Lithuanian Statutes, in *Vremmenik* Obščestva istorii i drevnostej, vol. 21 (First St. of 1529); vol. 19 (Second St. of 1566); vol. 18 (Third St. of 1588). Cf. also I. I. Lappo, *Litovskij Statut 1588 goda* (Kaunas, 1934-37).

Ludat, H. *Vorstufen und Entstehung des Städtewesens in Osteuropa.* (Cologne, 1955)

Lybyer, A. H. *The Government of the Ottoman Empire in the Time of Suleiman the Magnificient.* (Cambridge, Mass., 1913)

Marczali, H. *Ungarische Verfassungsgeschichte.* (Tübingen, 1910)

———. *Ungarisches Verfassungsrecht.* (Tübingen, 1911)

Mažuranić, V. *Südslaven im Dienste des Islam (vom 10. bis ins 16. Jh.).* (Ein Forschungsbericht aus kroatisch erschienenen Studien, ed. C. Lucerna.) (Zagreb, Leipzig, 1918)

Nedkoff, B. C. *Die Ğizya (Kopfsteuer) im osmanischen Reich. Mit besonderer Berücksichtigung von Bulgarien.* (Leipzig, 1942)

Nistor, J. *Die auswärtigen Handelsbeziehungen der Moldau im 14., 15. und 16. Jh.* (Gotha, 1911)

Novaković, S. *Die Serben und Türken im 14. und 15. Jh.* Transl. by K. Jezdimirović. (Semlin, 1897)

Okinševič, L. *The Law of the Grand Duchy of Lithuania, Background and Bibliography.* (New York, 1953)

Pejacsevich, J. "Peter Freiherr von Parchevich, Erzbischof von Martianopel, aspostolischer Vikar und Administrator der Moldau, bulgarischer Internuntius am kaiserlichen Hofe und kaiserlicher Gesandter bei dem Kosaken-Hetman Bogdan Chmielnicki (1617-1674). Nach archivalischen Quellen geschildert," *AÖG,* 59 (1880), pp. 337-637.

Radonitch, J. *Histoire des Serbes de Hongrie.* (Paris, 1919)

Rohde, G. *Die Ostgrenze Polens.* 2 vols. (Köln-Graz, 1955)

Rutkowski, J. *Histoire économique de la Pologne avant les partages.* (Paris, 1927)

Scheel, H. "Die staatsrechtliche Stellung der ökumenischen Kirchenfürsten in der alten Türkei: Ein Beitrag zur Geschichte der türkischen Verfassung und Verwaltung," *Abhandlungen der preussischen Akademie der Wissenschaften,* phil.-hist. Kl., no. 9 (1942).

Schwicker, J. *Geschichte der österreichischen Militärgrenze.* (Vienna, Teschen, 1883)

Sigel, F. *Lectures on Slavonic Law.* (London, New York, 1902). Bulgaria, pp. 15-20; Serbia, pp. 20-25; Russia, pp. 26-62; the Bohemian Kingdom, pp. 63-99; Poland, pp. 100-36; Croatia, pp. 137-52.

Šišić, F. *Zrinski et Frankopan, deux martyrs nationaux croates.* (Questions contemporaines, no. 20.) (Paris, 1919)

Stadtmüller, G. *Geschichte Südosteuropas.* (Munich, 1950), pp. 261-84, 334-60.

———. "Osmanische Reichsgeschichte und balkanische Volksgeschichte," *Leipziger Vierteljahrschrift für Südosteuropa,* 3 (1939), pp. 1-24.

Staneff, N. *Geschichte der Bulgaren.* Part 2, *Vom Beginn der Türkenzeit bis zur Gegenwart.* Transl. by H. Kaspar (Swischtoff). (Leipzig, 1917)

Stökl, G. "Die Wurzeln des modernen Staates in Osteuropa," *JGO,* NF 1 (1953), pp. 255 ff.

———. "Die Begriffe Reich, Herrschaft und Staat bei den orthod. Slawen," *Saeculum,* 5 (1954), pp. 104 ff.

Taubenschlag, R. "Gli influssi romano-bizantini sul secondo statuto lituano," *Studia et documenta historiae et juris,* 3 (1937), pp. 42-62.

Temperley, H. W. V. *History of Serbia.* (London, 1917). Pp. 106-161.

Timon, A. v. *Ungarische Verfassungs und Rechtsgeschichte.* Transl. by F. Schiller. 2nd ed. (Berlin, 1909)

Tkalčić, J. B. *Monumenta historica liberae regiae civitatis Zagrabiae.* 19 vols. (Zagreb, 1889-1953). Documents from 1093 to 1669.

Tomaschek, J. A. *Recht und Verfassung der Markgrafschaff Mähren im XV Jh.* (Brünn, 1863)

Vaniček, F. *Spezialgeschichte der Militärgrenze.* 4 vols. (Vienna, 1875)

Vernadsky, G. *Russia at the Dawn of Modern Age.* (New Haven, 1959)

Völker, K. *Kirchengeschichte Polens.* (Berlin, Leipzig, 1930)

Voinovitch, L. de. *Histoire de Dalmatie.* (Paris, 1934). Vol. 2, pp. 495-620.

Wojciechowski, Z. *L'État polonais au moyen âge: Histoire des institutions.* (Paris, 1949), pp. 100 ff.

Xenopol, A. D. *Histoire des Roumains de la Dacie de Trajane depuis les origines jusqu'à l'unification des principautés en 1859.* 2 vols. (Paris, 1896)

CHAPTER XV, *Sources.* Cf. also Chapter XII

Correspondence between A. M. Kurbskij and Ivan IV, original edition, Petrograd, 1914, new edition by D. S. Likhačev and T. S. Lur'e, *Poslanija Ivana Groznogo* (Moscow-Leningrad, 1951). The German translation is by K. Stählin, *Der Briefwechsel Ivans des Schrecklichen mit dem Fürsten Kurbskij (1564-1579)* (Leipzig, 1921). The English translation is by J. L. I. Fennell, *The Correspondence between Prince A. M. Kurbsky and Tsar Ivan IV of Russia, 1564-1579* (Cambridge, 1955). His works (Šočinenija) in *RIB*, vol. 31. Cf. also *Skazanija knjazja Kurbskogo,* ed. N. Ustrialov. 2nd ed. (St. Petersburg, 1842).

Fletcher, G. *La Russie au 16e siécle.* (Paris, 1864)

Heinrich von Staaden. *Aufzeichnungen über den Moskauer Staat,* ed. F. Epstein. (Hamburg, 1930)

Herberstein, S. v. *Rerum moscovit: commentarii.* (Vienna, 1549). Engl. transl. see Ch. XII.

Pamjatniki diplomatičeskikh snošenij drevnej Rossii s deržavami inostrannymi. vol. 1. (St. Petersburg, 1851, ff.)

Pamjatniki drevne-russkago kanoničeskago prava, in *RIB,* vol. 6. (St. Petersburg, 1908)

Sbornik Imper. Russkago Istoričeskago Obščestva. vols. 35, 53, 95. (St. Petersburg, 1867-1916)

Stoglav, ed. D. Kožančikov. (St. Petersburg, 1863)

Sudebnik, ed. G. Telberg. (Harbin, 1926)

Sudebniki 15-16 vekov, ed. B. D. Grekov, R. B. Mjuller, L. V. Čerepnin. (Moscow, 1952)

CHAPTER XV, *Bibliography*

Ammann, A. M. *Ostslavische Kirchengeschichte.* (Vienna, 1950)

Andreyev, N. "Kurbsky's Letters to Vas'yan Muromtsev," *SEER,* 33 (1954-55), pp. 414-36.

Backus, O. P. *Motives of West-Russian Nobles in Deserting Lithuania for Moscow, 1377-1514.* (Lawrence, Okla., 1957)

———. "Die Rechtstellung der litauischen Bojaren 1387-1506," *JGO,* 6 (1958), pp. 1-32.

Behr-Sigel, E. "Nil Sorskij et Joseph de Volokolamsk," *Irénikon*, 14 (1937), pp. 360-77.

Denissoff, E. "Une biographie de Maxime le Grec par Kourbski," *OCP*, 20 (1954), pp. 44-84.

Dvornik, F. "Byzantine Political Ideas in Kievan Russia," *Dumbarton Oaks Papers*, 9-10 (1956), pp. 73-121.

Dewey, H. "The 1497 Sudebnik," *American Slavic and East European Review*, 15 (1956), pp. 325-38.

——. "The White Lake Charter: a Medieval Russian Administrative Statute," *Speculum*, 32 (1957), pp. 74-83.

Eck, A. "L'asservissement du paysan russe." *Le Servage*. (Brussels, 1937), pp. 243-64.

——. "Le grand domaine dans la Russie du moyen âge," *Revue historique au sud-est Européen* (Bucharest, 1944), pp. 82-136.

——. *Le moyen âge russe*. (Paris, 1933), pp. 61-473.

Fennell, J. L. I. "The Attitude of the Josephites and the Trans-Volga Elders to the Heresy of the Judaisers," *SEER*, 29 (1951), pp. 486-509.

Gitterman, V. *Geschichte Russlands*. (Hamburg, 1949). Vol. 1, pp. 133-45 (Ivan III); pp. 147-84 (Ivan IV and his reforms).

Grekov, B. D. *Krestijane na Rusi do 18 veka*. (Moscow, 1946.) German edition. *Die Bauern in der Rus*. Transl. by H. Truhart and K. v. Bergstrasser. (Berlin, 1958-59)

Kadlec, K. *Introduction à l'étude comparée de l'histoire du droit publique des peuples slaves*. (Paris, 1933.), pp. 159 ff.

Kulischer, J. M. *Russische Wirtschaftsgeschichte*. (Jena, 1925). Vol. 1, pp. 158-452.

Leontovitsch, V. *Die Rechtsumwälzung unter Iwan dem Schrecklichen und die Ideologie der russischen Selbstherrschaft*. (Stuttgart, 1947)

Medlin, W. K. *Moscow and East Rome, a Political Study of the Relations of Church and State in Muscovite Russia*. (Geneva, 1952)

Neander, I. "Die Bedeutung der Mongolenherrschaft in Russland." *Geschichte in Wissenschaft und Unterricht*. (Stuttgart, 1954), pp. 257-70.

Obolensky, D. "Byzantium, Kiev, and Moscow," *Dumbarton Oaks Papers*, 11 (1957), pp. 21-78.

——. "Russia's Byzantine Heritage," *Oxford Slavonic Papers*, 5 (1950).

Oljančyn, D. "Aus dem Kultur- und Geistesleben der Ukraine. I. Was ist die Häresie der 'Judaisierenden,'" *Kyrios*, 1 (1936), pp. 176-89. Useful bibliography in Russian and Ukrainian.

Olšr, G. "Gli ultimi Rurikidi e le basi ideologiche della sovranità dello Stato russo," *OCP*, 12 (1946), pp. 322-73.

Philipp, W. *Ivan Peresvetov und seine Schriften zur Erneuerung des Moskauer Reiches*. (Osteuropäische Forschungen, vol. 20.) (Berlin, 1935). Cf. also Sakketi, A. L., and Sal'nikov, J. F. "O vzgljadakh I. S. Peresvetova," *Voprosy istorii*, 1 (1957), pp. 117-24.

Polosin, I. I. "Le servage russe et son origine," *Revue internationale de sociologie*, 36 (1928), pp. 605-45.

Rahner, H. *Vom ersten bis zum dritten Rom*. (Innsbruck, 1950). Inaugural address, a general survey.

Schaeder, H. *Moskau das dritte Rom*. (Hamburg, 1929; reprinted in Darmstadt, 1958).

Ševčenko, I. "A neglected Byzantine Source of Muscovite Political Ideology," *Harvard Slavic Studies*, 2 (1954), pp. 141-79.
Smolitsch, I. "Studien zum Klosterwesen Russlands. II. Zum Problem des Klosterbesitzes im 15. und 16. Jh.," *Kyrios*, 4 (1939), pp. 29-38.
Stratonov, I. A. "Die Reform der Lokalverwaltung unter Ivan IV," *ZOG*, 7 (1932), pp. 1-20.
Struve, P. "Medieval Agrarian Society in its Prime: Russia." In *The Cambridge Economic History*, ed. J. H. Clapham and E. Power. (Cambridge, 1942), pp. 418-37.
Stremooukhoff, D. "Moscow, the Third Rome: Sources of the Doctrine," *Speculum*, 28 (1953).
Szeftel, M. "Aspects of Feudalism in Russian History." In *Feudalism in History*, ed. R. Coulborn. (Princeton, 1956), pp. 166-82.
———. "Le Justicier (Sudebnik) du Grand Duc Ivan III," *Revue historique du droit français et étranger* (1956), pp. 531-68.
———. "The Sudebnik of 1497. Paleographical Analysis, Composition and Sources." *For Roman Jakobson*. (The Hague, 1956), pp. 547-52.
Taube, M. de. "A propos de Moscou, troisième Rome," *Russie et Chrétienté*, 3-4 (1948), pp. 17-24.
Toumanoff, C. "Moscow the Third Rome: Genesis and Significance of a Politico-Religious Idea," *The Catholic Historical Review*, 40 (1955), pp. 411-47.
Vernadsky, G. "Feudalism in Russia," *Speculum*, 14 (1939), pp. 300-23.
———. *The Mongols and Russia*. (New Haven, 1953)
———. "On Some Parallel Trends in Russian and Turkish History," *Transactions of the Connecticut Academy of Arts and Sciences*, 36 (1945), pp. 33 ff.
———. "Serfdom in Russia," *Comitato internaz. di scienze storiche X congresso internaz. di scienze storiche, Relazioni*. (Rome, 1955). Vol. 3, pp. 247-72. Good bibliography.
Wolff, R. L. "The Three Romes: The Migration of an Ideology and the Making of an Autocrat." *Daedalus*. (Boston, 1959), pp. 291-311.
Zernov, N. *Moscow the Third Rome*. (London, 1944). Popular review.

CHAPTER XVI, *Sources and Bibliography*

"Acts and Letters of the Catholic and Utraquist Consistories," *Jednání a dopisy konsistoře katol. i utrakvis.*, ed. K. Borový. (Prague, 1869)
Analecta Romana, quae historiam Poloniae s. XVI illustr., ed. J. Korzeniowski, *SRP*, 15. (Cracow, 1894)
Ball, H. *Das Schulwesen der Böhmischen Brüder*. (Berlin, 1898)
Bednář, F. "Zwei Versuche der alten Brüderunität um einen Aufbau der praktischen Theologie im 16. Jh." *Theologische Zeitschrift*. (Basel, 1952)
Benrath, K. "Dominis de Marcantonio," *RPThK*, 4 (1898), pp. 781-87.
———. "Dudith (Dudić)," *RPThK*, 5 (1898), pp. 54-55.
———. "Vergerio, Pietro Paolo," *RPThK*, 20 (1908), pp. 546-50.
Benz, E. "Wittenberg und Byzanz: Zur Auseinandersetzung der Reformation mit dem Griechentum und der östlich-orthodoxen Kirche. Melanchton und Antonios Eparchos aus Corcyra. Melanchthon und Jakobus Heraklides Despota. Melanchthon und der Serbe Demetrios," *Kyrios*, 4 (1939-40), pp. 1-28, 97-128, 222-61.

Benz, E. *Wittenberg und Byzanz. Zur Begegnung und Auseinandersetzung der Reformation und der östlichen Kirche.* (Marburg/L., 1949)

Berga, A. *Pierre Skarga: Étude sur la Pologne du XVIe siècle et le protestantisme.* (Paris, 1916)

Brandi, K. *Deutsche Geschichte im Zeitalter der Reformation und Gegenreformation.* 2nd ed. (Leipzig, 1942)

Brock, P. *The Political and Social Doctrines of the Unity of Czech Brethren in the 15th and Early 16th Centuries.* (Slavic Printings and Reprintings.) (The Hague, 1957)

Brückner, A. "Aus dem religiösen Leben der Čechen und Polen," *ZOG*, 7 (1933), pp. 491 ff.; pp. 494-99, Hussites; pp. 499-508, Protestants, especially Arianism, and the Polish Brethren.

———. "Die Kultur des alten Polen," *ZOG*, 7 (1933), pp. 161-93.

Caligarii, I. A. nuntii in Polonia epistolae et acta, 1578-81, Monumenta Poloniae Vaticana, ed. L. Boratyński. vol. 4. (Cracow, 1915)

Charvériat, E. *Les affaires religieuses en Bohême au XVe siècle.* (Paris, 1886)

Constant, G. *Concession à l'Allemagne de la communion sous les deux espèces.* (Bibl. des écoles françaises d'Athènes et de Rome, vol. 128, 128 bis.) (Paris, 1923)

Czarnowski, S. *La réaction catholique en Pologne à la fin du 16e et au début du 17e siècle.* (Warsaw, 1933)

Czerwenka, B. *Geschichte der Evangelischen Kirche in Böhmen.* 2 vols. (Bielefeld-Leipzig, 1860, 1870). Vol. I: John Hus (1860); vol. II: Czech Brethren: Protestants to modern time (Leipzig, 1869, 1870).

Daum, H. *Die Verfolgung der Evangelischen in Böhmen.* (Darmstadt, 1860)

Eberlein, H. L. *Schlesische Kirchengeschichte: Das evangelische Schlesien.* vol. 1. (Düsseldorf, 1952)

Elze, T. *Primus Trubers Briefe.* (Tübingen, 1897)

———. *Die slovenischen protestantischen Druckschriften des 16. Jh.* (Venice, 1896)

———. *Die Superintendenten der evangelischen Kirche in Krain während des 16. Jh.* (Vienna, 1863)

———. "Truber Primus," *RPThK*, ed. A. Hauck, 20 (Leipzig, 1908), pp. 136-43.

———. *Die Universität Tübingen und die Studenten aus Krain.* (Tübingen, 1877)

Engels, W. "Tübingen und Byzanz: Die erste offizielle Auseinandersetzung zwischen Protestantismus und Ostkirche im 16. Jh.," *Kyrios*, 5 (1940-41), pp. 250 ff.

Fox, P. *The Reformation in Poland: Some Social and Economic Aspects.* (Baltimore, 1924)

Friedrich, O. *Helden des Geistes: Hus, Cheltschitzki, Komensky.* (Zürich, 1936)

Gindely, A. *Geschichte der Böhmischen Brüder.* 2 vols. (Prague, 1857-68). History to 1609.

Goll, J. *Quellen und Untersuchungen zur Geschichte der Böhmischen Brüder.* (Prague, 1878)

Hočevar, W. "Die Anfänge der Reformation aus dem Gebiete des heutigen Jugoslavien," *Zeitschrift für Kirchengeschichte*, 55 (1936), pp. 615-33.

Holtzmann, R. *Maximilian II. bis zu seiner Thronbesteigung.* (Berlin, 1903)

Hosius. *Stanislai Hosii Epistolae,* eds. Hipler and Zakrzewski. In *Acta histor. res gestas Poloniae illustrantia,* vols. 4, 9. (Cracow, 1878-87)

Hosius, Kardinal Stanislaus, Bischof von Ermland und Herzog Albrecht von Preussen, ihr Briefwechsel über das Konzil von Trent (1560-62), ed. E. Wermter. (Münster, 1957)

Hrejsa, F. *Kirschengeschichte Böhmens*, Ekklesia. Vol. 5. (Leipzig, 1937)

Hutton, J. E. *A History of the Moravian Church.* 2nd ed. (London, 1909)

Jahrbuch der Gesellschaft für die Geschichte des Protestantismus in Österreich. T. Elze's studies on the Slovenian Reformation in vols. 1 (1880), 5 (1884), 12 (1891), 14 (1893), 15 (1894), 20 (1899), 21 (1900), 22 (1901). In vol. 24 (1903), J. Loserth's "Truberiana"; in vols. 23 (1902) and 24 (1903), J. Pindor's study on Slovenian Protestant literature.

Jatzwauk, J. *Sorbische (wendische) Bibliographie.* (Sächsische Akademie der Wissenschaften, phil.-hist. Kl. 98, 3.) 2nd ed. (Berlin, 1952)

Jörgensen, K. *Ökumenische Bestrebungen unter den polnischen Protestanten bis zum Jahre 1645.* (Copenhagen, 1942)

Kahle, W. *Die Begegnung des baltischen Protestantismus mit der russisch-orthodoxen Kirche.* Dissertation. (Marburg, 1956)

Kidd, B. J., ed. *Documents of the Continental Reformation.* (Oxford, 1911)

Kidrič, F. *Die protestantische Kirchenordnung der Slovenen im 16. Jh.* (Heidelberg, 1919)

Kleeberg, G. *Die polnische Gegenreformation in Livland.* (Leipzig, 1931)

Klíma, J. V. "Komenský und Polen," *SR* (1938).

Kostrenčić, J. *Urkundliche Beiträge zur Geschichte der protestantischen Literatur der Südslaven in den Jahren 1559-1565.* (Vienna, 1874)

Kot, S. "Basel und Polen. XV-XVII Jahrh.," *Zeitschrift für schweizerische Geschichte*, 30 (1950).

———. *L'influence de Michel Servet sur le mouvement antitrinitarien en Pologne et en Transylvanie.* (Haarlem, 1953)

———. "Le mouvement antitrinitarien au 16e et au 17e siècle," *Humanisme et Renaissance*, 4 (Paris, 1937).

———. "Opposition to the Pope by the Polish Bishops, 1557-1560," *OSP*, 4 (1953).

———. "Polish Brethren and the Problem of Communism in the 16th Century," *Transactions of the Unitarian Historical Society in London*, 12 (1957).

———. "Polish Protestants and the Huguenots," *Proceedings of the Huguenot Society of London*, 17 (London, 1945).

———. "Le rayonnement de Strasbourg en Pologne à l'époque de l'humanisme," *Mélanges André Mazon, RES*, 27 (1951).

———. *La réforme dans le Grand Duché de Lithuanie, facteur d'occidentalisation culturelle.* (Brussels, 1953)

———. *Socinianism in Poland: The Social and Political Ideas of the Polish Anti-Trinitarians in the Sixteenth and Seventeenth Centuries.* Transl. from Polish by E. M. Wilbur. (Boston, 1957)

———. "Szymon Budny, der grösste Häretiker Litauens im 16. Jahrhundert," *Festschrift H. F. Schmid, Wiener Archiv für Geschichte des Slawentums und Osteuropas*, 2 (1956), pp. 63-124.

Krasiński, W. *Abriss der Geschichte der Entstehung und des Falles der Reformation in Polen.* (Warsaw, 1903). Polish edition by J. Bursche. 2 vols. (Warsaw, 1903-05)

Kroess, A. *Geschichte der böhmischen Provinz der Gesellschaft Jesu.* 2 vols. (Vienna, 1910-27)

Kupsch, E. "Der polnische Unitarismus," *JGO*, 5 (1957), pp. 401-40.

Legrand, E. *Deux vies de Jacques Basilicos.* (Paris, 1889)

Lencz, G. *Der Aufstand Bočkays und der Wiener Friede.* (Debreczen, 1917)

The Letters of Elizabeth, Queen of Bohemia, compiled by L. M. Baker, with an introduction by C. V. Wedgwood. (London, 1953)

Loesche, G. *Geschichte des Protestantismus im vormaligen und im neuen Österreich.* 3rd ed. (Vienna, 1930)

———. *Luther, Melanchthon und Calvin in Österreich-Ungarn.* (Tübingen, 1909)

Lortz, J. *Kardinal Stanislaus Hosius: Beiträge zur Erkenntnis der Persönlichkeit und des Werkes: Gedenkschrift z. 350. Todestag.* (Braunsberg, 1931)

Loserth, J. *Akten und Korrespondenzen zur Geschichte der Gegenreformation in Innerösterreich unter Ferdinand II.* 2 vols. (Vienna, 1906-07). FRA, 58, 60.

———. *B. Hubmaier und die Anfänge der Wiedertäufer in Mähren.* (Brünn, 1893)

———. *Die Reformation und Gegenreformation in den innerösterreichischen Ländern im 16. Jh.* (Stuttgart, 1898)

———. "Zur Geschichte der Reformation und Gegenreformation, Rückblick und Ausschau," *Jahrbuch der Gesellschaft für Geschichte des Protestantismus in Österreich,* 25 (1904), pp. 183-221.

Lubieniecz, S. *Historia Reformationis Poloniae, in qua tum Reformatorum tum anti-Trinitariorum origo et progressus in Polonia et finitimis provinciis narratur.* (Freistadii, 1685)

Martel, A. *La langue polonaise dans les pays ruthènes.* (Lille, 1938)

Martinù, J. *Die Waldesier und die husitische Reformation in Böhmen.* (Vienna-Leipzig, 1910)

Molnár, A. "Luc de Prague et les Vaudois d'Italie." *Bolletino della Società di Studi Valdesi.* (Torre Pellice, 1949)

Monumenta Reformationis Polonicae et Lithuanicae, ed. by the Synod Jednoty Ewang.-Reform. Litewskiej. ser. 1, part 1. (Vilna, 1925)

Müller, J. T. *Die Gefangenschaft des Johann Augusta, Bischofs der Böhmischen Brüder 1548 bis 1564 und seines Diakonen Jakob Bilek von Bilek selbst geschrieben.* (Leipzig, 1895)

———. *Geschichte der Böhmischen Brüder.* 3 vols. (Herrnhut, 1922-31)

———. *Zinzendorf als Erneuerer der alten Brüderkirche.* (Leipzig, 1900)

Müller, L. *Die Kritik des Protestantismus in der russischen Theologie vom 16. bis zum 18. Jh.* (Wiesbaden, 1951)

Murko, M. *Die Bedeutung der Reformation und Gegenreformation für das geistige Leben der Südslaven.* (Prague-Heidelberg, 1927). Also contained in *Slavia,* 4 (1925-27).

Obál, B. *Die Religionspolitik in Ungarn nach dem westfälischen Frieden während der Regierung Leopold I.* Dissertation. (Halle, 1910)

Oberuč, J. *Les persécutions des Luthériens en Slovaquie au 17e siècle.* (Strasbourg, 1927)

Oman Lenanton, C. *Elizabeth of Bohemia.* (London, 1938)

Orechoviana. Opera inedita et epistolae Stanislai Orzechowski, ed. J. Korzeniowski. (Cracow, 1891)

Pescheck, C. A. *Die Auswanderung glaubenstreuer Protestanten aus Böhmen nach Sachsen.* (Löbau, 1858)

———. *Geschichte der Gegenreformation in Böhmen.* 2 vols. (Leipzig, 1850)

Peschke, E. *Die Theologie der Böhmischen Brüder in ihrer Frühzeit.* 2 vols. (Stuttgart, 1935-40)

Petri, H. "Jacobus Basilicus Heraklides, Fürst der Moldau," *Zeitschrift für Kirchengeschichte,* 46 (1927), pp. 705-43.

Petri, H. "Vorbemerkungen zu einer Geschichte der Reformation und Gegenreformation in den Donaufürstentümern," *Südostdeutsche Forschungen,* 2 (1937), pp. 17-35.

Pichler, A. *Geschichte des Protestantismus in der orientalischen Kirche des 17. Jh., oder der Patriarch Cyrillus Lukarys und seine Zeit.* (Munich, 1862)

Pindor, J. *Die evangelische Kirche Kroatien-Slavoniens in Vergangenheit und Gegenwart.* (Esseg, 1902)

Říčan, R. *Das Reich Gottes in den böhmischen Ländern: Geschichte des tschechischen Protestantismus.* Transl. into German by B. Popelaš. (Stuttgart, 1957)

Ruffini, F. *Studi sui Riformatori italiani,* a cura di A. Bertolo, L. Firpo, E. Ruffini. (Torino, 1955)

Šafařík, P. F. *Geschichte der südslavischen Literatur.* 3 vols. (Prague, 1864-65)

Schramm, G. "Nene Ergebnisse der Antitrinitarier-forschung," *JGO,* 8 (1960), pp. 421-36.

Servière, J. de la. "Dominis (Marc-Antoine de)," *Dictionnaire de Théologie catholique,* ed. A. Vacant, E. Mangenot, E. Amann, 4 (1924), cols. 1668-1675.

Skalský, G. A. "Brüder Lukas von Prag und die 'Anweisungen für Priester' vom J. 1527," *Zeitschrift für Brüdergeschichte,* 2 (Herrnhut, 1908).

Sliziński, J. "Über den Aufenthalt der Böhmischen Brüder in Lissa," *Zeitschrift für Slawistik,* 2 (1957).

Šmid, W. "Über Entstehung und Herausgabe der Bibel Dalmatins," *Mitteilungen des Musealvereines für Krain,* 17 (1904), pp. 71-146.

Smith, C. H. *The Story of the Mennonites.* (Newton, Kansas, 1950)

Sommer, E. *Into Exile: The History of the Counter-Reformation in Bohemia (1620-1650).* Transl. by V. Grove. (London, 1943)

Stadtmüller, G. *Geschichte Südosteuropas.* (Munich, 1950), pp. 251-60, 285-308.

Stasiewski, B. *Reformation und Gegenreformation in Polen. Neue Forschungsergebnisse.* (Münster, i W., 1960)

Stökl, G. *Die deutsch-slavische Südostgrenze des Reiches im 16. Jh.* (Schriften des Osteuropa-Institutes zu Breslau, NR, Heft 12.) (Breslau, 1940.) Important for Protestant Slovene Literature.

———. "Das Echo von Renaissance und Reformation in Moskauer Russland." *JGO,* 7 (1959).

Thompson, S. H. "Luther and Bohemia," *Archiv für Reformationsgeschichte,* 44 (1953), pp. 160-81, with bibliography.

Trogrančić, F. *Storia della letteratura croata.* (Rome, 1953). From the 15th to the 19th century. Reviewed by V. Javarek in *SEER,* 32 (1953-54), pp. 550 ff.

Uchansciana, Listy Uchańskiego (1549-81), ed. T. Wierzbowski. 2 vols. (Warsaw, 1884, 1885)

Valjavec, F. *Geschichte der deutschen Kulturbeziehungen zu Südosteuropa.* 2 vols. (Munich, 1954-55.) Vol. 2 on the spread of the Reformation in Hungary, Transylvania, Rumania, Slovakia, and Croatia.

Völker, K. "Die Glaubensfreiheit in den Städten Polens," *ZOG,* 9 (1935), pp. 67-88.

———. *Kirchengeschichte Polens.* (Berlin-Leipzig, 1930.), pp. 133-260.

———. "Stefan Batorys Kirchenpolitik in Polen," *Zeitschrift für Kirchengeschichte,* 56 (1937), pp. 59-86.

Völker, K. "Der Unionsgedanke des Consensus Sendomirensis," *ZOG*, 7 (1933), pp. 508-25.

Whatley, E. J. *The Gospel in Bohemia.* (London, 1878.) Popular.

Wilbur, E. M. *A History of Unitarianism, Socinianism, and its Antecedents.* (Cambridge, Mass., 1945.) *A History of Unitarianism.* 2 vols. (Ibid., 1945-52)

Williams, G. H. "Studies in the Radical Reformation (1517-1618): A Bibliographical Survey of Research since 1939," *Church History*, 27 (1958), pp. 46-69, 124-60.

Winter, E. *Tausend Jahre Geisteskampf im Sudetenraum.* (Salzburg-Leipzig, 1938.), pp. 146-97.

Wittram, R. *Baltische Kirchengeschichte: Beiträge zur Geschichte der Missionierung und Reformation der evang. luth. Landeskirchen und des Volkskirchentums in baltischen Ländern bis zum Ende des 2. Weltkrieges.* (Göttingen, 1956)

Workman, H. B. *The Dawn of the Reformation.* vol. 2. (London, 1902, reprint, 1933)

Wotschke, T. "Polnische Studenten in Wittenberg, Leiden, Heidelberg, Königsberg, Leipzig, Altdorf," *JKGS*, 1 (1926), 2 (1927), 3 (1928), 4 (1929), 5 (1930).

———. "Polnische und litauische Studenten in Königsberg," *JKGS*, 6 (1931), pp. 428 ff.

———. *Urkunden zur Reformationsgeschichte Böhmens und Mährens.* (Jahrbücher des Vereines für die Geschichte der Deutschen in Böhmen.) (Prague, 1929)

Zimmermann, H. "Hans Ungnad, Freiherr von Sonneck, als Förderer reformatorischer Bestrebungen bei den Südslaven," *SF*, 2 (1937), pp. 36-58.

CHAPTER XVII, *Sources*

Akty otnosjašČiesja k istorii Zapadnoj Rossii. 5 vols. (St. Petersburg, 1846-53.) vols. 2, 3, 4.

Archivum domu Radziwiłłow, SRP, 8 (Cracow, 1885). Correspondence of M. K. Radziwiłł, J. Zamoyski, L. Sapieha.

Archivum Jana Zamoyskiego, ed. W. Sobieski and J. Siemieński. (Warsaw, 1904-1913)

Archivum Sapiehów (1575-1606), ed. A. Prochaska. vol. 1. (Lwów, 1892)

Borový, C. *Akta Konsistoře.* (Prague, 1867)

Budovec, V. *Korespondence z let 1579-1619.* Publ. by J. Glücklich. (Prague, 1908)

———. *Nová korespondence z let 1580-1616.* Publ. by J. Glücklich. (Prague, 1912)

Comenius, J. A. (Komenský, J. A.)
  Analecta Comeniana. Publ. by J. Kvačala. (Yur'ev, 1909)
  Continuatio admonitionis fraternae . . . Publ. by J. Kvačala. (Brno, 1913.) An autobiographical fragment.
  Korespondence. Publ. by J. Kvačala. (Prague, 1897-1902)
  Korespondence. Publ. by A. Patera. (Prague, 1892)
  Opera didactica omnia. Editio anni 1657 lucis ope expressa. 5 vols. in 3. (Prague, 1957)

Veškeré spisy. Publ. by J. Novák et al. (Brno, 1910-   .) In progress.
Pampaldia, ed. D. Čyžewskij, H. Geisler, and Schaller. (Heidelberg, 1958)
Documents concerning Transylvania, Wallachia, and Moldavia from the sixteenth and seventeenth centuries are being republished by the Rumanian Academy (1953-56); thus far 19 vols.

Fontes rerum Transylvanicarum, vol. 4 of *Acta et Epistolae relationum Transylvaniae* . . . ed. by A. Veress. 4 vols. (Budapest, 1914-21)
Gindely, A. *Dekrety Jednoty Bratrské.* (Prague, 1865)
————. *Quellen zur Geschichte der Böhmischen Brüder.* (Historische Commission der kaiserlichen Akademie der Wissenschaften.) (Vienna, 1863)
Kollmann, H. *Acta sacrae congregationis de propaganda fide, res gestas Bohemicas illustrantia.* vol. 1. (Prague, 1923)
Moravské korespondence a akta z let 1620-1636. 2 vols. Publ. by F. Hrubý. (Brno, 1934-37.) Moravian correspondence and acts.
Pamjatniki diplomatičeskikh snošenij drevnoj Rossii s deržavami inostrannymi. (St. Petersburg, 1851-1871.) vols. 1, 2.
Pamjatniki diplomatičeskikh snošenij Moskovskago gosudarstva s Krymskoju i Nogajskoju ordami i s Turciej. (Sbornik imperatorskago russkago istoričeskago obščestva, vols. 41 (1884), 95 (1895).) Documents from 1474 to 1521.
Pamjatniki diplomatičeskikh snošenij Moskovskago gosudarstva s nemeckim ordenom v Prussii. (Sbornik imperatorskago russkago istoričeskago obščestva, vol. 53 (1887), ed. G. Karpov.)
Pamjatniki diplomatičeskikh snošenij Moskovskago gosudarstva s Poľsko-Litovskim. (Sbornik imperatorskago russkago istoričeskago obščestva, vols. 35 (1882), 59 (1887), 71 (1892), ed. G. Karpov.) Documents from 1482 to 1571.
Perepiska meždu Rossieju i Poľšeju po 1700 g., ed. N. N. Bantyš-Kamenskij. vols. 1, 2. (Moscow, 1862)
Podlaha, A. *Dopisy reformační komise v Čechách z let 1627-1639. Sbírka pramenů církev. dějin československ., st. 16-18.* (Prague, 1908)
Skála, P. ze Zhoře. *Historie česká od 1602-1632.* 5 vols. (Vienna, Prague, 1865-70)
Slavata, V. *Paměti od r. 1608-1619.* 2 vols. (Prague, 1857-68).
Žerotin, Charles of. *Dopisy* ("Letters"), 1591-1610. Publ. by F. Dvorský. (Prague, 1904)
————. *Spisy* ("Works"). Publ. by V. Brandl. 5 vols. (Brno, 1866-72)

CHAPTER XVII, *Bibliography*

Albrecht, D. *Die deutsche Politik Papst Gregors XV.* (Munich, 1956)
Angyal, A. *Die Slavische Barokwelt.* (Leipzig, 1961)
Baron, H. *Calvins Staatsauffassung und das konfessionelle Zeitalter.* (Berlin-Munich, 1924)
Bourke, J. *Baroque Churches of Central Europe.* (London, 1958)
Brandi, K. *Kaiser Karl V. Werden und Schicksal einer Persönlichkeit und eines Weltreiches.* 2nd ed. (Munich, 1938). Engl. ed. *The Emperor Charles V.* (New York, 1939)
Bretholz, B. *Neuere Geschichte Böhmens (1526-1576).* (Gotha, 1920)
Brunner, O. "Vom Gottesgnadentum zum monarchischen Prinzip," *Das*

Königtum, Vorträge und Forschungen, ed. T. Mayer, 3 (1956), pp. 279-305.

Cambridge Modern History, vol. 4: The Thirty Years' War. (London, 1906)

Charles Quint et son temps: Symposium. (Paris, 1959)

Chudoba, B. *Spain and the Empire, 1519-1643.* (Chicago, 1952)

Čyževskyj, D. "Analecta Comeniana," *Kyrios,* 2 (1937), pp. 313-30.

——. "Comenius' 'Labyrinth of the World': Its Themes and Their Sources," *Harvard Slavic Studies,* 1 (1953), pp. 83-135.

——. "Neue Veröffentlichungen über die tschechische Barockdichtung," *ZSPh,* 11 (1935), pp. 3 ff.; *ibid.,* 12 (1935), pp. 1 ff.; *ibid.,* 13 (1936). Reviews of new Czech discoveries.

Deggeller, G. *Karl V und Polen-Litauen.* (Würzburg, 1939)

Denis, E. *Les premiers Habsbourgs. La défenestration de Prague; Fin de l'indépendance bohême.* vol. 2. (Paris, 1890; 2nd ed., 1930)

Droysen, G. *Geschichte der Gegenreformation.* (Berlin, 1893)

Dvořák, F. *Kupecký Jan, der grosse Porträtmaler des Barocks.* (Prague, 1956)

Fidler, J. "Die Allianz zwischen Kaiser Maximilian I. und Wasilij Ivanovitsch, Grossfürst von Russland von dem J. 1514," *SbAW,* 40 (Vienna, 1860), pp. 27-123.

Franz, H. G. *Die Kirchenbauten des C. Dientzenhofer, Beiträge zur Geschichte der Kunst im Sudenten- und Karpathenraum.* vol. 5. (Brünn, Munich, Vienna, 1942)

Gindely, A. *Die Berichte über die Schlacht auf dem Weissen Berge bei Prag.* (Vienna, 1877)

——. "Die Gegenreformation und der Aufstand in Oberösterreich i. J. 1626," *SbAW,* 118 (1889)

——. *Geschichte des dreissigjährigen Krieges.* 4 vols. (Prague, 1869-80.) Engl. transl. by A. Ten Broek, *History of the Thirty Years War,* 2 vols. (New York, 1884, reprint 1898)

——. *Rudolf II. und seine Zeit.* 2 vols. (Prague, 1863-68)

Goldinger, W. "Das Zeremoniell der deutschen Königskrönung seit dem späten Mittelalter," *Mitteilungen des oberösterr. Landesarchivs,* 5 (1957).

Halecki, O. "Die Beziehungen der Habsburger zum litauischen Hochadel im Zeitalter der Jagellonen," *Mitteilungen des Inst. f. österr. Gesch.,* 36 (1915).

Hankamer, P. *Deutsche Gegenreformation und deutsches Barock.* 2nd ed. (Stuttgart, 1947)

Hantsch, H. *Die Geschichte Österreichs.* 2 vols. 3rd ed. (Graz, 1951-53)

Hegemann, H. W. *Die deutsche Barockbaukunst Böhmens.* (Munich, 1943)

Heyberger, A. *Jean Amos Comenius: Sa vie et son oeuvre d'éducateur.* (Travaux publiés par l'Institut d'Etudes Slaves, vol. 7.) (Paris, 1928)

Hoetzsch, O. "Federation und fürstliche Gewalt (Absolutismus) in der Geschichte Osteuropas im 17. und 18. Jh.," *ZOG,* NR, 4 (1934), pp. 1-38.

Huber, A. *Geschichte Österreichs.* 5 vols. (Gotha, 1885-89.) See vols. 3, 4, 5.

Hurter, F. *Geschichte Kaiser Ferdinands II. und seiner Eltern bis zur Krönung in Frankfurt.* 10 vols. (Schaffhausen, 1850-62)

Jabłonowski, H. "Die Aussenpolitik Stephan Bathorys," *JGO,* 1 (1937).

Kidd, B. J. *The Counter-Reformation, 1550-1600.* (London, 1933)

Krajcar, J. *Bohuslav Balbín S. J. als Geschichtsschreiber.* (Rome, 1956)

Kubíček, A. *The Palaces of Prague.* (Prague, 1946)

Kvačala, J. *Johann Amos Comenius.* (Vienna-Berlin-Leipzig, 1892)

Kvačala, J. "Die pädagogische Reform des Comenius in Deutschland," *Monumenta Germaniae Pedagogica*, 26 (Berlin, 1903).

———. "Thomas Campanella und Ferdinand II," *SbAW*, 159 (1908).

Leitsch, W. *Moskaw und die Politik des Kaiserhofes im XVII. Jh. Teil I, 1609-1654*. (Graz, Cologne, 1960. Wiener Archiv für Geschichte des Slaventums in Osteuropa, vol. 4)

Loesche, G. "Die böhmischen Exulanten in Sachsen," *Jahrbuch der Gesellschaft für die Geschichte des Protestantismus in ehemaligem Österreich*, 42-44 (Vienna-Leipzig, 1923).

Matthews, A. "Comenius and Harvard College," *Publications of the Colonial Society of Massachusetts*, 21 (1919), pp. 146-90.

Noailles, E. *Henri de Valois et la Pologne en 1572*. 3 vols. (Paris, 1867)

Novotný, K., and Poche, E. *The Charles Bridge of Prague*. (Prague, 1947)

Odložilík, O. "Comenius and Christian Unity," *SEER*, 9 (1930-31), pp. 79-93.

———. *Jan Amos Komensky*. (Chicago, 1942)

———. "Karel of Žerotín and the English Court (1564-1636)," *SEER*, 15 (1936-37), pp. 413-25.

Oestrich, G. "Justus Lipsius als Theoretiker des neuzeitlichen Machtstaats," *Historische Zeitschrift*, 181 (1956).

Pekař, J. *Wallenstein 1630-1634: Tragödie einer Verschwörung*. (Berlin, 1937.) A translation of his Czech work, *Valdštejn 1630-1634*. (Prague, 1936)

Piliuski, T. v. *Das polnische Interregnum von 1572-1573 und die Königswahl Heinrichs von Valois*. (Heidelberg, 1861)

Pešina, J. *Tafelmalerei der Spätgotik und der Renaissance in Böhmen*. (Prague, 1959)

Rassow, P. *Forschungen zur Reichsidee im 16. und 17. Jh*. (Cologne, 1955)

———. *Karl V, der letzte Kaiser des Mittelalters*. (Gottengen, 1957)

Redlich, O. *Österreichs Grossmachtbildung in der Zeit Kaiser Leopolds I*. (Gotha, 1921)

———. "Über Kunst und Kultur des Barock in Österreich," *AÖG*, 115 (1943), pp. 333-79.

Rezek, A. *Geschichte der Regierung Ferdinands I. in Böhmen*. (Prague, 1878)

Ritter, M. *Deutsche Geschichte im Zeitalter der Gegenreformation und des Dreissigjährigen Krieges* (1555-1648). 3 vols. (Stuttgart, 1889-1908)

Roberts, M. *Gustavus Adolphus*. 2 vols. (London, New York, 1953-58)

Rutkowski, J. *Histoire economique de la Pologne avant les partages*. (Paris, 1927)

Schaedke, H. *Die Entwicklung des enzyklopädischen Bildungsgedanken und die Pansophie des J. A. Comenius*. (Leipzig, 1930)

Schneider, F. *Die neuren Anschauungen der deutschen Historiker über die deutsche Kaiserpolitik des Mittelalters und die mit ihr verbundene Ostpolitik*. (Weimar, 4th ed. 1940)

Spinka, M. *That Incomparable Moravian*. (Chicago, 1943)

Srbik, H. v. *Wallensteins Ende*. 2nd ed. (Salzburg, 1952)

Stech, V. V. *Die böhmische Barockskulptur*. Transl. from Czech. (Prague, 1958.) Engl. transl. by R. F. Samsour, *Baroque Sculpture*. (London, 1959)

Stele, F. *Monumenta artis Slovenicae*. Vol. 2, *La peinture baroque et romantique*. (Ljubljana, 1935-38)

Stieve, F. *Ferdinand II, deutscher Kaiser: Allgemeine deutsche Biographie*, vol. 6. (Leipzig, 1877), reprinted in his *Abhandlungen Verträge und Reden* (Leipzig, 1900)

Strettiova, O. *Das Barockporträt in Böhmen.* (Prague, 1957)
Sturmberger, H. *Kaiser Ferdinand II. und das Problem des Absolutismus.* (Munich, 1957)
Turnbull, G. H. *Hartlib, Dury and Comenius.* (Liverpool, 1947)
Übersberger, H. *Österreich und Russland seit dem Ende des 15. Jh.* vol. 1, *1489-1605.* (Vienna, 1906)
Ulmann, H. *Kaiser Maximilian I.* 2 vols. (Stuttgart, 1884-1891)
Walsh, W. T. *Philip II.* (New York, 1937)
Wedgwood, C. V. *Thirty Years War.* (London, 1938)
Wittram, R. "Formen und Wandlungen des europäischen Absolutismus." *Festschrift H. Gogarten.* (Giessen, 1948)
Young, R. F. *Comenius in England.* (Oxford-London, 1932)

CHAPTER XVIII, Sources

Acta historica res gestas Polonie illustrantia. Vols. 3, 5, 7 (1879, 1881, 1884), acts from the French Archives concerning King John III, ed. K. Waliszewski; vol. 11 (1887), documents concerning the wars of Stephen Batory, ed. J. Polkowski; vol. 6 (1883), acts concerning John III's expedition of 1683, ed. F. Kluczyski.
Acta Tomiciana, legationum, responsionum et rerum gestarum Sigismundi primi regis Poloniae per St. Górski, ed. Z. Celichowski. 13 vols. (Kórnik, 1852-1916.) Vol. 6, documents on relations between Orthodox and Catholics.
Acts on diplomatic relations between Poland and Moscow, 1598-1615, ed. S. Platonov and S. Belokurov. In *Sbornik imperatorskago rossijskago istoričeskago obščestva,* 137, 142 (Moscow, 1912, 1913).
Akty istoričeskie ("Historical Documents"), 5 vols. (St. Petersburg, 1841-43); *Dopolnenija* ("Supplements"), 12 vols. (St. Petersburg, 1848-75.) Vols. 1 and 2 of the *Akty istoričeskie* cover material pertinent to this chapter.
Akty moskovskago gosudarstva ("Acts of the Muscovite State"). 3 vols. (St. Petersburg, 1890-1901)
Akty otnosjaščiesja k istorii zapadnoj Rossii. Vols. 4, 5. See Chapter XVII.
Akty otnosjaščiesja k istorii južnoj i zapadnoj Rossii ("Acts concerning the History of Southern and Western Russia"). 15 vols. (St. Petersburg, 1862-92.) Vols. 1-13 cover material pertinent to this chapter.
Arkhiv jugo-zapadnoj Rossii ("Archives of Southern and Western Russia"). 8 series in 35 books. (Kiev, 1859-1914.) Series I, vols. 1-12; series II, vols. 1-3; series III, vols. 1, 2; and series VIII, vols. 4, 6 cover material pertinent to this chapter.
Archivum of the Houses Sapieha, ed. A. Prochaska. (Lwów, 1892). See Chapter XVII.
Archivum of John Zamoyski, eds. W. Sobieski and J. Siemieński. 3 vols. (Warsaw, 1904-1913.) See Chapter XVII.
Documents concerning the birth of the Ukraine, ed. O. M. Bodjanskij. In the *Čtenija imperatorskago obščestva istorii i drevnostej ross.* of Moscow University, 24 (1858).
Documents on the "Time of Troubles," ed. S. F. Platonov. (*Pamjatniki*) in the *Russkaja istoričeskaja biblioteka,* 13 (1891).
Listy Stanislava Żólkiewskiego, 1584-1620, ed. T. Lubomirski. (Cracow, 1868)

Reports of papal nuntios in Poland and others on Poland from 1548 to 1690, ed. E. Rykaczewski. 2 vols. (Berlin, Posen, 1864)

Recueil des instructions données aux ambassadeurs et ministres de France depuis le traité de Westphalie, jusqu'à la révolution française. (Paris, 1884-1901.) Vols. 4, 5: L. Farges, Pologne.

CHAPTER XVIII, *Bibliography*

Allen, W. *The Ukraine: A History.* (Cambridge, 1940)

Ammann, A. M. *Abriss der ostslavischen Kirchengeschichte.* (Vienna, 1950)

———. "Zur Geschichte der Geltung der Florentiner Konzilsentscheidungen in Polen-Litauen. Der Streit über die Gültigkeit der 'Griechentaufe,' " *OCP,* 8 (1942), pp. 289-316.

Backus, O. P. *Motives of West Russian Nobles in Deserting Lithuania for Moscow, 1377-1514.* (Lawrence, Kansas, 1957)

Backvis, C. "Some Characteristics of Polish Baroque Poetry," *OSP,* 6 (1955), pp. 51-71.

Battaglia, O. F. de. *Jan Sobieski, König von Polen.* (Zürich, 1946)

Borschak, E. "L'Ukraine dans la littérature de l'Europe occidentale," *Le Monde Slave,* 3, 4 (1933-34).

Cayer, Abbé. *Histoire de Jean Sobieski, roi de Pologne.* 3 vols. (Warsaw-Paris, 1761)

Christensen, A. E. *Dutch Trade to the Baltic about 1600.* (Copenhagen, 1941)

Cyževskij, D. *Die slavische Barockforschung,* see Ch. XVII.

Dorošenko, D. *A Survey of Ukrainian Historiography.* Supplement by O. Ohloblyn, "Ukrainian Historiography, 1917-1956." (New York, 1957)

Drost, W. "Polen und die Kunst des Westens während der Renaissance und der Barockzeit," *Altpreussische Forschungen,* 12 (1935).

Fijalek, J. "Le sort reservé à l'Union de Florence dans le Grand-Duché de Lithuanie sous le règne de Casimir Jagellon," *Bulletin international de l'Académie polonaise des sciences et des lettres,* cl. d'histoire et de philol., 1-3 (January-March, 1934).

Fleischhacker, H. "Die politischen Begriffe der Partner von Perejaslav," *JGO,* NF, 2 (1954), pp. 221-231.

———. *Russland zwischen zwei Dynastien (1598-1613).* (Baden bei Wien, 1933)

———. *Die staats- and völkerrechtlichen Grundlagen der moskauer Aussenpolitik.* (Breslau, 1938)

Fletcher, G. *Russe Common Wealth: Russia at the Close of the Sixteenth Century,* ed. F. A. Bond. (Hakluyt Society, vol. 20.) (London, 1856)

Frommann, T. *Kritische Beiträge zur Geschichte der Florentiner Kircheneinigung.* (Halle, 1872)

Gindely, A. *Die maritimen Pläne der Habsburger und die Teilnahme Kaiser Ferdinands II. am polnisch-schwedischen Kriege während der Jahre 1627-1629.* (Denkschriften der Akademie.) (Vienna, 1891)

Gorgas, S. *Volkswirtschaftliche Ansichten in Polen im 17. Jh.* (Innsbruck, 1905)

Graham, S. *Boris Godunof.* (London, 1933.) To be used with caution.

Guépin, A. *Un apôtre de l'union des églises au XVIIᵉ siècle, St. Josaphat . . .* 2 vols. (Paris, 1897-98)

Günther, O. E. "Der Vertrag von Perejaslav in Widerstreit der Meinungen," *JGO,* NF, 2 (1954), pp. 232-57. Almost complete bibliography to 1954.

Halecki, O. *From Florence to Brest.* (Sacrum Poloniae Millenium.) (Rome, 1958)

——. "La Pologne et la question d'Orient de Casimir le Grand à Jean Sobieski." *La Pologne au VIIe Congrès international des sciences historiques.* (Warsaw, 1933)

——. "Possevino's Last Statement on Polish-Russian Relations," *OCP*, 19 (1953), pp. 261 ff.

——. "Le Problème de l'Union des Églises." *La Pologne au VIe Congrès international des sciences historiques.* (Warsaw, 1930)

Hayden, H. *Kirchengeschichte Pommerns.* 2 vols. (Cologne, 1958)

Hiltebrandt, P. *Die polnische Königswahl von 1697 und die Konversion Augusts des Starken.* (1907). Not available to me.

Hirsch, F. *Die ersten Anknüpfungen zwischen Brandenburg und Russland unter dem grossen Kurfürsten.* (Berlin, 1885-86)

Hrushevsky, M. *A History of Ukraine,* ed. by O. J. Frederiksen. (New Haven, London, Oxford, 1941)

Ionesco, T. *La vie et l'oeuvre de Pierre Movila, métropolite de Kiev.* (Paris, 1944)

Jekel, F. J. *Polens Staatsveränderungen und letzte Verfassung.* 4 vols. (Vienna, 1803-06)

Jörgensen, K. E. J. *Ökumenische Bestrebungen.* See Chapter XVI.

Korduba, E. "Die Entstehung der Ukrainischen Nation." *Contributions à l'histoire de l'Ukraine au VIIe Congrès international des sciences historiques.* (Lwów, 1933)

Krupnyckyj, B. *Geschichte der Ukraine.* (Im Auftrage des ukrainischen wissenschaftlichen Instituts in Berlin.) (Leipzig, 1939)

Krusche, J. *Die Entstehung und Entwicklung der ständigen diplomatischen Vertretung Brandenburg-Preussens am Zarenhofe bis zum Eintritt Russlands in die Reihe der europäischen Grossmächte.* Dissertation. (Breslau, 1932). Also in *Jahrbücher für Kultur und Geschichte der Slawen,* NF, 8 (1932).

Kyriakos, D. A. *Geschichte der orientalischen Kirche von 1453-1898.* Transl. by E. Rausch. (Leipzig, 1902)

Laskowski, O. *Sobieski, King of Poland.* (Glasgow, 1944)

Lehmann. *Brandenburgisch-polnische Türkenzüge von 1671-88.* (Berlin, 1884). Unavailable to me.

Lelewel, J. *Geschichte Polens unter Stanislaus August.* (Braunschweig, 1831)

Malvy, A., and Viller, M. "La confession orthodoxe de Pierre Moghila, métropolite de Kiev 1633-46, approuvée par les patriarches grecs du XVIIe siècle. Texte latin inédit publié avec introduction et notes critiques," *OCP,* 10, no. 39 (1927)

Margeret, Jacques. *Estat de l'empire de Russie et grand duché de Moscovie (1590-1606).* (Paris, 1946)

Massa, I. *Histoire des guerres de la Moscovie 1601-1610.* 2 vols. (Brussels, 1866), ed. by M. Obolenski and A. v. d. Linde.

Meyer, P. *Die theologische Literatur der griechischen Kirche im 16. Jh.* (Studien zur Geschichte der Theologie und der Kirche, eds. N. Bonwetsch and R. Seeberg, vol. 3, Heft 6.) (Leipzig, 1899)

Mjakotin, V. A. "Die Vereinigung der Ukraine mit dem Moskauer Staat," *ZOG,* 7 (1933).

Morton, J. B. *Sobieski, King of Poland.* (London, 1932)

Niitemaa, V. *Der Binnenhandel in der Politik der livländischen Städte im Mittelalter.* (Helsinki, 1952)

Panaitescu, P. P. "L'influence de l'oeuvre de Pierre Mogila archevêque de Kiev dans les principautés roumaines," *Mélanges de l'École Roumaine en France,* 5 (Paris, 1926)

Pärnänen, J. A. *Sigismond Vasa et la succession au trône de Suède, 1592-1594, d'après la correspondance diplomatique du nonce apostolique Germanico Malaspina.* (Genève, 1912)

Pierling, P. *Dmitri le Faux et les Jésuits.* (Paris, 1913)

———. *Rome et Demetrius.* (Paris, 1878)

———. *La Russie et le Saint-Siège.* vol. 3. (Paris, 1901)

Platonov, S. F. *Boris Godunov,* transl. in German by H de Witte. (Paris, 1929)

Poehl, G. v. "Quellenkundliches zur Geschichte des ersten falschen Demetrius: Mosquera-Barezzo Barezzi," *ZOG,* 7 (1933), pp. 73-87.

Polčin, S. "La mission religieuse du P. Antoine Possevin S. J. en Moscovie," *OCA,* no. 150 (Rome, 1957).

Rauch, G. v. "Moskau und die europäischen Mächte des 17. Jhts.," *HZ,* 178 (1954), pp. 25-46.

Rutkowski, J. See Chapter XVII.

Salvandy, N. de. *Histoire du roi Jean Sobieski et de la Pologne avant et sous Jean Sobieski.* 2 vols. (Brussels, 1876)

Savant, J. *Les cosaques: Histoire des cosaques.* (Paris, 1944)

Schiemann, T. *Russland, Polen und Livland bis ins 17. Jh.* (Berlin, 1884)

Schumann, H. "Der Hetmanstaat," *JGO,* 1 (1936).

Skribanowitz, H. *Peudo-Demetrius I.* Dissertation. (Berlin, 1913)

Stökl, G., *Die Entstehung des Kosakentum.* (Munich, 1953)

Tappe, E. D. "Charles II and the Prince of Moldavia," *SEER,* 28 (1950), pp. 406-424. Gheorghe Ştefan, 1653-1658.

Taube, M. v. *Russland und Westeuropa: Russlands historische Sonderentwicklung in der europäischen Völkergemeinschaft.* (Institut für internat. Recht an der Universität Kiel, Erste Reihe, Vorträge und Einzelschriften, Heft 8.) (Berlin, 1928)

Vernadsky, G. "The Death of the Tsarevich Dimitry, a Reconsideration of the Case," *Oxford Slavonic Papers,* 5 (1954), pp. 1-19.

———. "Die Tragödie von Uglič und ihre Folgen," *JGO,* NF, 3 (1955), pp. 41-49.

Waczynski, B. "Nachklänge der Florentiner Union in der polemischen Literatur zur Zeit der Wiedervereinigung der Ruthenen im 16. und Anfange des 17. Jhts.," *OCP,* 4 (1938), pp. 441-72.

Waliszewski, K. *La crise révolutionnaire 1584-1614.* (Paris, 1906). Bibliography, pp. 463-83.

———. *Marysienka, reine de Pologne, Marie de la Grange d'Arguien.* (Paris, 1898)

Willan, T. S. *The Muscovy Merchants of 1555.* (Manchester, 1953)

Chapter XIX, *Sources*

Akty istoričeskie. (See Chapter XVIII.) vols. 4, 5 (St. Petersburg, 1843). Dopolnenija, vols. 1-12.

Akty Otnosjaščiesja Kistorii Zapadnoj Rossii. 5 vols. (St. Petersburg, 1846-53). vols. 4, 5.

Arkhiv Jugo-Zapadnoj Rossii. See Chapter XVIII.
Dejanie moskovskikh soborov 1666 i 1667 godov. (Moscow, 1893)
Documenta pontif. Roman. hist. Ucrainae illustr. vol. 1. (Rome, 1953)
Documents on Razin's uprising. *Krest'janskaja vojna pod predvoditel'stvom Stepana Razina: Sbornik dokumentov* . . . , ed. A. A. Novel'skij. (Moscow, 1957)
Documents concerning the Old Believers. *Pamjatniki istorii staroobrjadčestva v 18 v., RIB,* vol. 39.
Hofmann, G. *Der hl. Josaphat. Quellenscriften in Auswahl, OCP,* 12. (Rome, 1923-25). Indicates other source material on Josaphat and the Union.
Life of Patriarch Nikon written by Ivan Šušerin, ed. in *Russkij Arkhiv,* 3 (1909), pp. 1-144.
Life of Protopope Avvakum, ed. N. K. Gudzij. (Moscow, 1934.) French transl. by P. Pascal, *La Vie de l'archifre Tre Avvakum* (Paris, 1938), with good bibliography. English transl. by J. Harrison and H. Mirrlees, *Avvakum: the Life* (London, 1924).
Ljubimenko, I. "The Correspondence of the First Stuarts with the First Romanovs," *Transactions of the R. Historical Society,* 4th series, 1 (London, 1918), pp. 77-91.
———. "Letters Illustrating the Relations of England and Russia in the 17th Century," *English Historical Review,* 32 (1917), pp. 92-103.
Monuments historiques relatifs aux règnes d'Alexis Michaelovitsch, Fedor III et Pierre le Grand, czars de Russie, ed. A. Theiner. (Rome, 1859)
Muscovite juridical documents. *Sudebniki gosudarstva,* cd. Gorkij. (Moscow, 1939)
Oxford Slavonic Papers, vols. 1 (1950), 2 (1951), 4 (1954), 6 (1955), 7 (1957), 8 (1958), 9 (1960). Documents and letters concerning Anglo-Russian relations, published by S. Konovalov.
Sudebniki XV-XVI vv., eds. B. D. Grekov, R. B. Mjuller, L. V. Čerepnin. (Moscow, 1952)
Pamjatniki diplom. snošenij. See Chapter XII, vols. 3-10.
Polnoe sobranie zakonov. vols. 1, 2. (St. Petersburg, 1830)
Rinhuber, L. *Relation du voyage en Russie fait en 1684.* (Berlin, 1883)
Šmurlo, S. *Le Saint-Siège et l'Orient orthodoxe,* 1609-1654. (Prague, 1928)
Subbotin, N. I. *Materijaly dlja istorii raskola.* 9 vols. (Moscow, 1874-90)
Vetera monumenta Poloniae et Lithuaniae . . . historiam illustrantia, ed. A. Theiner. vol. 3. (Rome, 1863)

CHAPTER XIX, *Bibliography*

Adelung, F. *Kritisch-literarische Übersicht der Reisenden in Russland.* 2 vols. (St. Petersburg-Leipzig, 1846, reprint, Amsterdam, 1960)
Amburger, E. *Die Familie Marselis Studien zur russ. Wirtschaftsgeschichte.* (Giessen, 1957)
Arsenjew, W. K. *Russen und Chinesen in Ostsibirien.* Transl. by F. Daniel. (Berlin, 1926)
Bain, R. N. *The First Romanovs.* (London, 1905)
———. *Slavonic Europe: A Political History of Poland and Russia from 1447 to 1796.* (Cambridge, 1908)
Boresky, Th. *Life of St. Josaphat Martyr of the Union.* (New York, 1955). Popular.

Braun, M. *Der Aufstieg Russlands von Wikingerstaat zur europäischen Gross-macht (1000-1700).* (Leipzig, 1940)
——. "Das Eindringen des Humanismus in Russland im 17. Jahrhundert," *Die Welt der Slaven,* 1 (1956), pp. 35-49.
——. *Die Slawen auf dem Balkan.* (Leipzig, 1941)
Brückner, A. "Die russisch-litauische Kirchenunion und ihre literarischen Denkmäler," *ASPh,* 19 (1897), pp. 189-201.
Burgi, R. *A History of the Russian Hexameter.* (Hamden, 1954)
Champion, P. *Henri III, roi de Pologne (1573-1574).* (Paris, 1943-51)
Čyževskij, D. "Zu den polnisch-russischen liter. Beziehungen," *ZSPh,* 23 (1955), pp. 256-60.
Dorošenko, D. "Die Namen 'Rus,' 'Russland' und 'Ukraine' in ihrer historischen und gegenwärtigen Bedeutung," *Abhandlungen des ukrainischen wissenschaftlichen Instituts in Berlin,* 3 (1931), pp. 3-23.
Fleischhacker, H. "Der politische Antrieb der moskauischen Kirchenreform," *Zwei Dynastien, JGO,* 2 (1937), pp. 224-33.
——. *Die staats- und völkerrechtlichen Grundlagen der moskauischen Aussenpolitik, JGO,* Beiheft 1 (Breslau, 1938).
——. *Russland zwischen (1518-1613).* (Baden, 1933)
Florovskij, A. "Le conflit des deux traditions—la latine et byzantine—dans la vie intellectuelle de l'Europe Orientale aux 16e et 17e ss.," *Bulletin de l'assoc. russe pour les recherches scientifiques à Prague,* 5 (10) (1937), pp. 171-92.
Forstreuter, K. *Preussen und Russland von den Anfängen des Deutschen Ordens bis zum Peter dem Grossen.* (Göttingen Bausteine für Geschichtswissenschaft, vol. 23.) (Berlin, Frankfurt, Göttingen, 1955)
Gerhardi, W. *The Romanovs: Evocation of the Past as a Mirror for the Present.* (New York, 1940.) For general public.
Golder, F. A. *Russian Expansion on the Pacific, 1641-1850.* (Cleveland, 1914)
Hamilton, G. H. *The Art and Architecture of Russia.* (Baltimore, 1954)
Hedenström, A. von. *Die Beziehungen zwischen Russland und Brandenburg während des ersten nordischen Krieges 1655-1660.* Dissertation. (Marburg, 1896)
Ionesco, T. *La vie et l'oeuvre de Pierre Movila, métropolite de Kiev.* (Paris, 1944)
Jakobson, R. "Ivan Fedorov's Primer," *Harvard Library Bulletin,* 9 (1955).
——. "The Kernel of Comparative Slavic Literature," *Harvard Slavic Studies,* 1 (1953), pp. 1-81.
——. "Studies in Comparative Slavic Metrics," *OSP,* 3 (1952), pp. 21-66.
Jensch, G. *Der Handel Rigas im 17. Jh. Ein Beitrag zur livländischen Wirtschaftsgeschichte in schwedischer Zeit. Mitteilungen aus der livländischen Geschichte,* 24, Heft 2 (1930).
Jugie, M. "Moghila Pierre," *Dictionnaire de Théologie Catholique,* 10, cols. 2063-2081.
Karskij, E. *Geschichte der weissrussischen Volksdichtung und Literatur.* (Berlin-Leipzig, 1926)
Köhne, B. v. *Berlin, Moskau, St. Petersburg 1649-1763.* (Berlin, 1882)
Langsch, J. *Die Predigten der "Coena spiritualis" von Simeon Polockij.* (Leipzig, 1940)
——. "Zur Charakteristik Simeon Polockijs als Prediger," *Kyrios,* 5 (1940-41), pp. 82-130.

Lantzeff, G. V. *Siberia in the 17th Century: A Study of the Colonial Administration.* (Berkeley-Los Angeles, 1943)

Laskowski, O. *Sobieski, King of Poland.* (Glasgow, 1944)

Ledit, J. "Nicon," *Dictionnaire de Théologie Catholique,* 11, cols. 646-55.

Leitsch, W. See Chap. XVI.

Lubimenko, I. "The Correspondence of Queen Elizabeth with the Russian Czars," *American Historical Review,* 19 (1913-14), pp. 525-42.

——. *Les relations commerciales et politiques de l'Angleterre avec la Russie avant Pierre le Grand.* (Bibl. de l'École des Hautes Études, sciences hist. et phil., 261.) (Paris, 1933)

——. "The Struggle of the Dutch with the English for the Russian Market in the 17th Century," *Transactions of the R. Historical Society,* Fourth Series, 7 (London, 1924), pp. 27-51.

——. "Trois lettres inédites d'Elisabeth d'Angleterre à la cour de Russie." *Mélanges d'histoire offerts à M. Charles Bémont.* (Paris, 1913.) Pp. 549-57.

Malvy, A., and Viller, M. "La confession orthodoxe de Pierre Moghila, métropolite de Kiev (1633-1646)," *OCP,* 39 (1927).

Martel, A. *La langue polonaise dans les pays ruthènes, Ukraine et Russie Blanche, 1569-1667.* (Lille, 1938)

Mattiesen, H. "Die Versuche zur Erschliessung eines Handelsweges Danzig-Kurland-Moskau-Asien, besonders für Seide," *JGO,* 3 (1938), pp. 533-67.

Mazon, A., and Cocron, F. *La comédie d'Artaxerxes, presentée en 1572 au Tsar Alexis par Gregorii le Pasteur.* (Paris, 1954)

Müller, G. *Die Türkenherrschaft in Siebenbürgen: Verfassungsrechtliches Verhältnis Siebenbürgens zur Pforte 1541-1688.* (Hermannstadt, 1923)

Murko, M. "Die Geschichte von den sieben Weisen," *SbAW,* 72 (Vienna, 1890).

——. "Die russische Übersetzung des Apollonius von Tyrus und der Gesta Romanorum," *ASPh,* 14 (1891), pp. 405-21.

Nolde, B. *La formation de l'empire russe.* vol. 1. (Paris, 1952)

O'Brien, C. Bickford. *Russia under Two Tsars (1682-1689).* (Berkeley, 1952)

Oljančyn, D. "Aus dem Kultur- und Geistesleben der Ukraine, II. Schule und Bildung," *Kyrios,* 2 (1937), pp. 38-69, 143-57, 265-78, 351-66. Deals mostly with Ukrainian teaching from the fifteenth to the eighteenth century. Useful bibliography. List of Ukrainian students at foreign universities.

Ostrogorsky, G. "Das Projekt einer Rangtabelle aus der Zeit des Caren Fedor Alekseevič," *JKGS,* 9 (1933), pp. 86-138.

——. "Zum Stratordienst des Herrschers in der byzantinischslavischen Welt," *Seminarium Kondakovianum,* 7 (1935), pp. 187-204.

Palmer, W. *The Patriarch and the Tsar.* 6 vols. (London, 1871 ff.)

Pascal, P. *Avvakum et les débuts du Raskol.* (Paris, 1938)

Pelesz, J. *Geschichte der Union der ruthenischen Kirche mit Rom.* 2 vols. (Würzburg-Wien, 1881)

Pierling, P. *Rome et Démétrius d'après les documents nouveaux.* (Paris, 1878)

——. *La Russie et le Saint-Siège.* vol. 3. (Paris, 1901)

——. *La Russie et le Saint-Siège: études diplomatiques.* 2 vols. (Paris, 1884)

Podzneev, A. V. "Die geistl. Lieder des Epifanij Slavineskij," *Die Welt der Slaven,* 5 (1960), pp. 356-85.

Psalmon, F. "Un russisant anglais au 16-17e siècle, Richard James (1592-1638)," *Bulletin de géographie historique et descriptive,* 3 (Paris, 1911).

Puls, H. *Die Beziehungen zwischen England und Rusland im 16. und 17. Jh. unter Berücksichtigung des zeitgenössischen englischen Schrifttums über Russland.* Dissertation. (Hamburg, 1941)

Rauch, G. v. "Moskau und die europäischen Mächte des 17. Jh.," *Historische Zeitschrift*, 178 (1954).

Stender-Petersen, A. *Anthology of Old Russian Literature.* (New York, 1954), pp. 325 ff. Notes to be used with caution.

——. *Geschichte der russischen Literatur.* vol. 1. (Munich, 1957)

——. *Tragoediae Sacrae: Materialien und Beiträge zur Geschichte der polnisch-jesuitischen Jesuitendramatik der Frühzeit.* (Dorpat, 1931)

Stief, C. *Studies in the Russian Historical Song.* (Copenhagen, 1953)

Stökl, G. "Russland von der Mongolenzeit bis zu Peter dem Grossen," *Historia Mundi*, 7 (1958), pp. 392-438.

——. "Der Moskauer Zemskij Sobor," *JGO*, 8 (1960), pp. 421-36.

Stremooukhoff, D. "La tiare de Saint Sylvestre et le *Klobuk* blanc," *RES*, 34 (1957), pp. 123-28.

Stupperich, R. "Zur neueren Nikon-Forschung," *ZOG*, 9 (1935), pp. 173-80. Review of works on Nikon before 1914, the unpublished work by A. von Stromberg, and the work by M. V. Zyzykin (Warsaw, 1931).

Übersberger, H. *Russlands Orientpolitik in den letzten zwei Jahrhunderten.* vol. 1. (Stuttgart, 1913)

Unbegaun, B. O. *Russian Versification.* (Oxford, 1956)

Vernadsky, G. V. "Die kirchlich-politische Lehre der Epanagoge und ihr Einfluss auf das russische Leben des 18. Jh.," *Byzantinisch-neugriechische Jahrbücher*, 6 (1928), pp. 119-42.

Waliszewski, K. *Le berceau d'une dynastie, les premiers Romanov (1613-1682).* (Paris, 1909)

Winter, E. "Der Kampf der ecclesia ruthena gegen den Rituswechsel." *Festschrift Eichmann.* (Paderborn, 1940)

Zenovski, S. A. "Die Mönch Epifanij und die Entstehung der altruss. Autobiographie." *Die Welt der Slaven,* 1 (1956), pp. 276-92.

CHAPTER XX, *Sources*

British Diplomatic Instructions, 1689-1789. Vol. 1, *Sweden.* (London, 1922)

Documents of Catherine the Great: The Correspondence with Voltaire and the Instruction of 1797, ed. W. F. Reddaway. (Cambridge, 1931.) Her private correspondence is in the *Sbornik russk. istor. imp. obščestva* (St. Petersburg, 1867 ff.), vols. 1, 2, 4-10, 13-15, 17, 20, 23, 32, 33, 36, 42, 43, 47, 48, 51, 52, 57, 87, 97, 98, 107, 115, 118. *Ibidem,* vols. 3, 5, 6, 11, 15, 22, 25, documents from Peter the Great to Catherine II; vols. 1-6, 21, 30, 31 of the reigns of Alexander I and II.

Documents relatifs à l'histoire du deuxième et troisième partage de la Pologne, ed. B. F. Dembiński. 2 vols. (Lwów, 1902)

Memoirs of Catherine the Great. Transl. by K. Anthony. (New York, London, 1927)

Peter's Letters and Documents. *Pis'ma i bumagi imperatora Petra Velikago.* (St. Petersburg, 1887-95; new ed. by the USSR Academy, 4 vols., Moscow, 1946-52.)

Peter's Military Regulations. *Voennye ustavy Petra Velikago,* ed. P. P. Epifanov. (Moscow, 1946)

Reports on Russia under Peter I. Zeitgenössische Berichte zur Geschichte Russlands, ed. E. Herrmann. Vol. 1, *Russland unter Peter dem Grossen.* (Leipzig, 1872)

Stanislaus Auguste: Mémoires de Stanislaus Auguste et sa correspondence avec l'imperatrice Catherine II. (Posen, 1862)

Theiner, A. *Vetera monum. Poloniae et Lithuaniae.* Vol. 4 (1697-1775). (Rome, 1864)

Tolstoj, D. A. *Le catholicisme romain en Russie.* (Paris, 1864-69.) Documents concerning Peter and Rome, vol. 1, pp. 324-78; the letter of the Sorbonne concerning the union of the churches, *ibid.*, pp. 368-77.

CHAPTER XX, *Bibliography*

Ammann, A. M. *Abriss der ostslavischen Kirchengeschichte.* (Vienna, 1950.), pp. 247-388.

Anderson, M. S. *Britain's Discovery of Russia, 1553-1815.* (London, 1958)

Askenazy, S. *Napoleon et la Pologne.* (Paris, 1925)

Bain, R. N. *Charles XII and the Collapse of the Swedish Empire, 1682-1719.* (New York-London, 1895)

———. *The Daughter of Peter the Great.* (Westminster, 1899)

———. *The First Romanovs, 1613-1725.* (London, 1905.) A history of Muscovite civilization and the rise of modern Russia under Peter the Great and his forerunners.

———. *The Last King of Poland and his Contemporaries.* (London, 1909)

———. *Peter III. Emperor of Russia: The Story of a Crisis and a Crime.* (Westminster, 1902)

———. *The Pupils of Peter the Great: A History of the Russian Court and Empire, 1697-1740.* (Westminster, 1897)

Beer, A. *Die erste Teilung Polens.* (Vienna, 1873)

Bell, J. *Travels from St. Petersburg in Russia to Diverse Parts of Asia.* (Glasgow, 1763.) J. Bell, a Scotsman, was one of Peter's doctors.

Benz, E. *Die abendländische Sendung der östlich-orthodoxen Kirche. Die russische Kirche und das abendländ Christentum im Zeitalter der heiligen Allianz.* (Mainz, 1950)

———. "Ein Unionsversuch unter Peter dem Grossen," *Evangelium und Osten,* 8 (1935), pp. 114-24.

———. *Leibniz und Peter der Grosse.* (Berlin, 1947)

Bilbassow, F. v. *Geschichte Katharina II.* 3 vols. (Berlin, 1891-1893)

Baikalov, V. A. "The Conquest and Colonization of Siberia," *SEER,* 10 (1932), pp. 537-71.

Borschak, E., and Martel, R. *Vie de Mazeppa.* (Paris, 1931). Cf. also O. Ohloblyn, *Het'man Ivan Mazepa ta joho doba* (New York, 1960)

Bratianu, G. J. *La Moldavie et ses frontières historiques.* (Bucharest, 1940)

Braun, M. *Der Aufstieg Russlands zur europäischen Grossmacht.* (Leipzig, 1940)

Bridge, C. A. G., ed. *History of the Russian Fleet during the Reign of Peter the Great by a Contemporary Englishman.* (Navy Records Society's Publications, vol. 15) (1899).

Browning, O. *Peter the Great.* (London, 1898.) A biography not based on primary sources, but superior to those by S. Graham (London, 1929) and G. Ondard (1930).

Brückner, A. *Iwan Possoschkow: Ideen und Zustände in Russland zur Zeit Peters des Grossen.* (Leipzig, 1878)

———. *Katharina die Zweite.* (Berlin, 1883)

Brückner, A. *Peter der Grosse.* (Berlin, 1879.) Still useful.

Burenstam, C. *Retour de la Turquie de Charles XII par la Transylvanie, la Hongrie et l'Autriche.* (Brussels, 1874)

Coquart, A. *Dmitri Pisarev (1840-1868) et l'idéologie du nihilism russe.* (Paris, 1946)

Cordone, C. de. *L'empereur Alexander II: Vingt-six ans de règne.* (Paris, 1883)

Doerries, H. "Dunkle Existenzen und dunkle Machenschaften in Schatten Peters des Grossen," *JGO,* 4 (1939), pp. 111-35.

———. "Peters des Grossen Beziehungen zu Danzig 1716-17 und die Begründung der russischen Agentur," *FOG,* 1 (1954), pp. 23-44.

———. *Ruslands Eindringen in Europa in der Epoche Peters des Grossen.* (Osteuropäische Forschungen, NF, 26.) (Königsberg, Berlin, 1939)

Dorošenko, D. "Hetman Mazeppa." *ZOG,* 7 (1932), pp. 51-73.

Doroshenko, D. (Dorošenko, D). *History of the Ukraine.* (Edmonton, 1939)

Fabre, J. *Stanislas Auguste Poniatowski et l'Europe des Lumières: Étude du cosmopolitisme.* (Publications de la Faculté des Lettres de l'Université de Strasbourg, fasc. 116.) (Strasbourg, Paris, 1952)

Feldman, W. *Geschichte der politischen Ideen in Polen seit dessen Teilungen (1795-1914).* (Munich-Berlin, 1917)

Florovskij, G. "Westliche Einflüsse in der russischen Theologie," *Kyrios,* 2 (1937), pp. 1-22. Good bibliography. A résumé of his Russian work, *Puti russkago bogoslovija ("Development of Russian Theology")* (Paris, 1937).

Forst-Battaglia, O. *Stanislaus Poniatowski und der Ausgang des alten Polenstaates.* (Berlin, 1927)

Galitzin, A. *Mémoirs inédits sur les règnes de Pierre-le-Grand, Cathérine I et Pierre II.* (Paris, 1865)

Golder, F. A. *Russian Expansion on the Pacific, 1641-1850.* (Cleveland, 1914)

Grunwald, C. de. *La Vie de Nicolas I.* (Paris, 1946)

Haintz, O. *König Karl XII von Schweden.* Vol. 1, *Der Kampf Schwedens um die Vormacht in Nord- und Osteuropa,* 1697-1709. (Berlin, 1958)

Hammer-Purgstall, Jr. *Geschichte der Chane der Krim.* (Vienna, 1856). Uses also Crimean sources.

Hassinger, E. *Brandenburg-Preussen, Schweden und Russland 1700-1713.* (Munich, 1953)

Haumant, E. *La Russie au XVIII's.* (Paris, 1904)

Hepner, B. P. *Bakounine et le panslavisme révolutionaire.* (Paris, 1950)

Kerner, R. J. *Bohemia in the Eighteenth Century.* (New York, 1932)

Kersten, K. *Peter der Grosse. Vom Wesen und von den Ursachen historischer Grösse.* (Amsterdam, 1935), 2nd ed., 1951.

Ključevskij, V. O. *A History of Russia.* Transl. by C. J. Hogarth. vols. 4, 5. (London, New York, 1911-31). German transl. by R. v. Walter (Stuttgart, Berlin, 1925), vol. 3.

———. *Peter der Grosse u. andere Porträts aus der russ. Geschichte.* Transl. and ed. by F. Braun. (Stuttgart, 1953)

———. *Peter the Great.* Transl. by L. Archibald. (London, 1958)

———. *Russische Geschichte von Peter d. Grosse bis Nikolaus I.* (Zürich, 1945)

Koch, H. *Die russische Orthodoxie im petrinischen Zeitalter: Ein Betrag zur Geschichte westlicher Einflüsse auf das ostslavische Denken.* (Osteuropa Institut in Breslau, Quellen und Studien, NF, 1.) (Breslau, 1929)

Kohn, H. *Pan-Slavism, its History and Ideology.* (Notre Dame, 1953.) Popular presentation.

Köhne, B. v. *Berlin, Moskau, St. Petersburg 1649 bis 1763: Ein Beitrag zur Geschichte der freundschaftlichen Beziehungen zwischen Brandenburg-Preussen und Russland.* (Schriften des Vereins für die Geschichte der Stadt Berlin, Heft 20.) (Berlin, 1882)

Konenenko, S. *Ukraine and Russia.* (Marquette Slavic Studies, vol. 4.) (Milwaukee, 1958.) Economic relations from 1654 to 1917.

Krupnicky, B. *Hetman, Mazepa, und seine Zeit (1687-1709).* (Leipzig, 1942)

Lappo-Danilevskij, A. *L'Idée de l'état,* see footnote 5.

Lensen, G. *The Russian Push toward Japan, Russo-Japanese Relations, 1697-1895.* (Princeton, 1959)

Leontief, V. "Peter der Grosse, seine Wirtschaftspolitik und sein angeblicher Merkantilismus," *JGO,* 2 (1937), pp. 234-71. Cf. Vernadsky, G., "L'industrie russe sous Pierre le Grand," *Le Monde Slave* (1934).

Lord, R. H. *The Second Partition of Poland: A Study in Diplomatic History.* (Cambridge, Mass., 1915.) The best scholarly account.

——. "The Third Partition of Poland," *Slavonic Review,* 3 (1925).

Lukinich, E. "Der Kaisertitel Peters des Grossen und der Wiener Hof," *JKGS,* NF, 5 (1929), pp. 369-70.

Lutoslanski, K. *Les partages de la Pologne et la lutte pour l'indépendance.* (Lausanne-Paris, 1918)

Manteuffel-Szoege, G. v. *Geschichte des polnischen Volkes während seiner Unfreiheit, 1772-1914.* (Berlin, 1950)

Mavor, J. *An Economic History of Russia.* 2nd ed. (London, 1925.) Vol. 1, pp. 100-63. On economic and financial problems of Peter's time.

Mazour, A. G. *The First Russian revolution: The Decembrist movement.* (Berkeley, 1937)

Miljukov, P., Seignobos, C., and Eisenmann, L. *Histoire de la Russie.* (Paris, 1932.) Vol. 1, pp. 258-427. A critical analysis of Peter's reforms.

Morley, Ch. "Alexander I and Czartoryski," *SEER* (April, 1947).

Mouravieff, B. *Le testament du Pierre le Grand: Légende et réalité.* (Neuchâtel, 1949)

Nolde, B. *La formation de l'empire russe.* vol. 2. (Paris, 1953.) Russian bibliography from Peter the Great on.

Nordmann, C. J. *Charles XII et l'Ukraine de Mazepa.* (Paris, 1958). Thesis, good bibliography.

Petrovich, M. B. *The Emergence of Russian Panslavism, 1856-1870.* (New York, 1956)

Pierling, P. *La Russie et le Saint-Siège.* vol. 4. (Paris, 1907)

Pirenne, J. H. *La Sainte Alliance: Organization Européenne de la paix mondiale.* 2 vols. (Neuchâtel, 1946-49)

Rauch, G. v. "Moskau und die europäischen Mächte des 17. Jhts.," *Historische Zeitschrift,* 178 (1954), pp. 25-46.

Reddaway, W. *Frederick the Great and the Rise of Prussia.* (New York, London, 1904, reprint, 1925)

Redlich, O. *Das Werden einer Grossmacht. Österreich von 1700-1740.* 3rd ed. (Brünn-Munich-Vienna, 1942)

Riasonowski, N. *Russia and the West in the Teaching of the Slavophiles: A study in Romantic Ideology.* (Cambridge, Mass., 1953.) German transl. (Munich, 1954)

Rose, W. J. *Stanislas Konarski, Reformer of Education in 18th Century Poland.* (London, 1929)

Ruffmann, K. H. "England und der russische Zaren- und Kaisertitel," *JGO*, NF, 3 (1955), pp. 217-24.

Sacke, G., and Speranskij, M. M. "Politische Ideologie und reformatische Tätigkeit," *JGO*, 4 (1939), pp. 330-50.

Salomies, J. *Der Hallesche Pietismus in Russland zur Zeit Peters des Grossen.* (Annales Academiae Scientiarum Fennicae, Series B, vol. 31, 2.) (Helsinki, 1936)

Scheibert P. *Von Bakunin zu Lenin. Geschichte der russischen revolutionären Ideologien 1840-95.* (Stud. z. Gesch. Osteur., 3.) (Leiden, 1956)

Schiemann, C. *Geschichte Russlands unter Kaiser Nikolaus I.* 4 vols. (Berlin, 1908-1919)

Schumann, H. "Der Hetmanstaat (1654-1754)," *JGO*, 1 (1936), pp. 499-548.

Schuyler, E. *Peter the Great, Emperor of Russia.* 2 vols. (New York, 1884.) Still useful.

Semjonov, J. *Die Eroberung Sibiriens.* (Leipzig, 1940.) Popular.

Šerech, J. "Stefan Yavorsky and the Conflict of Ideologies in the Age of Peter the Great," *SEER*, 30 (1951), pp. 40-62.

Smolitsch, I. "Katharinas II. religiöse Anschauungen und die russische Kirche," *JGO*, 3 (1938), pp. 568-79.

———. "Die Stellung des russischen Kaisers zur orthodoxen Kirche in Russland vom 18. bis zum 20. Jht.," *FOG*, 2 (1955), pp. 139-64.

Sokolnicki, M. "Le testament de Pierre le Grand: Origines d'un prétendu document historique," *Revue des sciences politiques*, 27 (1912), pp. 88-98.

Sommer, E. F. "Der junge Zar Peter in der Moskauer Deutschen Sloboda," *JGO*, 5 (1957), pp. 67-105.

Stählin, K. *Geschichte Russlands.* vol. 2. (Berlin, 1930.), pp. 1-190. Very good for Peter's reign.

Steinmann, F. K. P. *Pobedonoscevs Leben und Wirken.* (Königsberg, 1933)

Stolypin, P. A., and Krivoschein, W. *Die Kolonisation Sibiriens.* (Berlin, 1912)

Stupperich, R. "Feofan Prokopovič in Rom," *ZOG*, 5 (1931), pp. 335 ff.

———. "Feofan Prokopovičs theologische Bestrebungen," *Kyrios*, 1 (1936), pp. 350-62.

———. "Feofan Prokopovič und Johann Franz Buddeus," *ZOG*, 9 (1935), pp. 341 ff.

———. "Kiev—das zweite Jerusalem," *ZSPh*, 12 (1935), pp. 332-54.

———. *Staatsgedanke und Religionspolitik Peters des Grossen.* (Königsberg-Berlin, 1936)

———. "Zur Geschichte der russischen hagiographischen Forschung (von Ključevskij bis Fedotov)," *Kyrios*, 1 (1936), pp. 47-56.

Sumner, B. *Peter the Great and the Emergence of Russia.* (London, 1956.) Reprint.

———. *Peter the Great and the Ottoman Empire.* (Oxford, 1949.) A thorough study with a good bibliography.

Temperley, H. W. V. *England and the Near East.* (London, New York, 1936.) Crimean war.

Tolstoj, D. *Le catholicisme en Russie.* 2 vols. (Paris, 1863-64)

Tompkins, S. R. *The Russian Mind from Peter the Great through the Enlightenment.* (Univ. of Oklahoma Press, 1953)

Tschiževskij, D. "Das 'Wahre Christentum' Arndts in Russland," *Evangelium und Osten*, 8 (1935), pp. 41-47.

Übersberger, H. *Russlands Orientpolitik in den letzten zwei Jahrhunderten.* Vol. 1, *Bis zum Frieden von Jassy.* (Stuttgart, 1913)

Valjavec, F. *Der Josephinismus: zur geistigen Entwicklung Österreichs im 18. u. 19. Jh.* (Brünn, Munich, Vienna, 1944, 2nd ed. 1945)

Vandal, A. *Louis XIV et Elisabeth de Russie.* (Paris, 1911)

Vassileff, M. *Russland und Frankreich von der Thronbesteigung Peters des Grossen bis . . . 1717.* (Gotha, 1902)

Vernadsky, G. "Alexander Ier et le problème slave," *RSE*, 7 (1927).

——. *Bohdan, Hetman of the Ukraine.* (New Haven, 1941).

——. "L'industrie russe sous Pierre Le Grand," *Le Monde Slave* (1934). Against the thesis of Leontief that Peter the Great supported only war industries.

Waliszewski, K. *Autour d'un thrône: Catherine II de Russie.* 4th ed. (Paris, 1894.) Engl. transl. (London, 1895).

——. *La dernière des Romanovs: Elisabeth de Russie.* (Paris, 1900.) *La Russie au Temps d'Elisabeth Iere, dernière des Romanovs.* (Paris, 1933)

——. *Le fils de la grande Catherine, Paul Ier, Empereur de Russie.* (Paris, 1913.) Engl. transl. (London, 1913)

——. *La Russie il y a cent ans: Le règne d'Alexandre I.* 3 vols. (Paris, 1923-25)

——. (Walischewski, K.). *Pierre le Grand, l'éducation, l'homme, l'oeuvre.* 7th ed. (Paris, 1909). To be used with caution. Engl. transl. (London, New York, 1897)

Winter, E. *Der Josephinismus und seine Geschichte.* (Brünn, Munich, Vienna, 1943)

Wittram, R. *Peter der Grosse; der Eintritt Russlands in die Neuzeit.* (Berlin, 1954)

——. "Peters des Grossen Verhältnis zur Religion und den Kirchen," *HZ*, 173 (1952), pp. 271 ff.

——. "Peter der Grosse und Livland: Zur Kernfrage des Nordischen Krieges." *Deutschland und Europa, Festschrift H. Rothfels,* ed. W. Conze. (Düsseldorf, 1951)

——. "Peters des Grossen erste Reise in den Westen," *JGO*, NF, 3 (1955), pp. 373-403.

Wolf, F. *Preussen und die Protestanten in Polen 1724.* (Berlin, 1894)

Wolkonsky, M. *Die Dekabristen: Die ersten russischen Freiheitskämpfer des 19. Jh.* Transl. by W. Jollos. (Zürich, 1946)

Xenopol, A. D. *Histoire des Roumains.* (Paris, 1896)

TRANSLITERATION AND PRONUNCIATION TABLES

Following are several tables concerning the transliteration and pronunciation of those Slavic languages in use in this book. Four tables are given: one for the Russian language, with additional material noting the divergences from this Belo-Russian, Bulgarian, and Ukrainian; one for Serbo-Croatian, with Slovenian distinctions; one for Polish; and one for Czech, with the Slovak departures. Please note that the system of transliteration is not that of the Library of Congress, but an international one accepted by linguists, with few differences.

1. *Russian*

Cyrillic	Latin Transcription	Approx. Pronun.	Cyrillic	Latin Transcription	Approx. Pronun.
А а	A a	a(continental)	П п	P p	p
Б б	B b	b	Р р	R r	r(trilled)
В в	V v	v	С с	S s	s
Г г	G g	g	Т т	T t	t
Д д	D d	d	У у	U u	u(continental)
Е е	E e	*ye* as in *yet*	Ф ф	F f	f
Ё ё	E e	*yo* as in *yonder*	Х х	Kh kh	German guttural *ch*
Ж ж	Ž ž	*z* as in *azure*	Ц ц	C c	ts
З з	Z z	z	Ч ч	Č č	Eng. hard *ch*
И и	I i	i(continental)	Ш ш	Š š	sh
й	j	Eng. cons. *y* as in *you*	Щ щ	Šč šč	*shch* as in *Ashchurch*
К к	K k	k	ъ	"	mute
Л л	L l	l	ы	y	hard *i*
М м	M m	m	ь	'	Eng. cons. *y* bef. vowel medially
Н н	N n	n	Э э	È è	*e* as in *let*
О о	O o	o	Ю ю	Ju ju	*u* as *you*
			Я я	Ja ja	Germ. *ja.*

1a. The Belo-Russian departures from the above table are:

Cyrillic	Latin Tran- scription	Approximate Pronunciation
Г г	H h	voiced h or ch
I i	I i	i(continental)
Ў ў	U u	w
Э э	E e	e as in *let*

1b. The Bulgarian departures from the above table are:

Cyrillic	Latin Tran- scription	Approximate Pronunciation
Щ щ	Št št	sht
ъ	U ŭ	u as in *but*, mute vowel at the end of a word

1c. The Ukrainian departures from the above table are:

Cyrillic	Latin Tran- scription	Approximate Pronunciation
Г г	H h	voiced h or ch
I i	I i	i(continental)
Ï ï	I i	ye as in *ye*
Є є	E e	ye as in *yet*

2. The following table gives the Serbo-Croatian alphabet:

Cyril- lic	Latin (Croat.)		Approx. Pronun.	Cyril- lic	Latin (Croat.)		Approx. Pronun.
А а	A	a	a(continental)	Н н	N	n	n
Б б	B	b	b	Њ њ	Nj	nj	Eng. soft n
В в	V	v	v	О о	O	o	o(continental)
Г г	G	g	g	П п	P	p	p
Д д	D	d	d	Р р	R	r	r(trilled)
Ђ ђ	Đ, Dj	đ, dj	Eng. *j* as in *Jim*	С с	S	s	s
Е е	E	e	e(continental)	Т т	T	t	t
Ж ж	Ž	ž	Eng. z as in *azure*	Ћ ћ	Ć	ć	Eng. soft *ch*, palatalized *t*
З з	Z	z	z	У у	U	u	u(continental)
И и	I	i	i(continental)	Ф ф	F	f	f

Cyril-lic	Latin (Croat.)	Approx. Pronun.	Cyril-lic	Latin (Croat.)	Approx. Pronun.
Ј ј	J j	Eng. consonantal *y* as in *you*	Х х	H h	Germ. guttural *ch*
К к	K k	k	Ц ц	C c	ts
Л л	L l	l	Ч ч	Č č	Eng. hard *ch*
Љ љ	Lj lj	Eng. soft *l* as in *million*	Џ џ	Dž dž	Eng. *j* as in *John*
М м	M m	m	Ш ш	Š š	sh

2a. The Slovenian departures from the above table are:

Slovenian	Approximate Pronunciation
L l	Finally, and before other consonants usually, as w
V v	As v initially and medially before a vowel, before r and l, and between r and j. Before other consonants, and finally after a vowel as w.

3. The following table gives the Polish alphabet and a guide to the approximate pronunciation:

Polish		Approximate Pronunciation
A	a	a(continental)
	ą	nasal vowel, as French *on*
B	b	b
C	c	ts
Ć	ć	Eng. soft *ch*
D	d	d
E	e	*e* as in *let*
	ę	nasal, as French *fin*
F	f	f
G	g	g
H	h	Germ. guttural *ch*
I	i	i(continental)
J	j	Eng. consonantal *y* as in *you*
K	k	k
L	l	l
Ł	ł	similar to *w*
M	m	m
N	n	n
Ń	ń	Eng. soft *n* as in *lenient*

Polish		Approximate Pronunciation
O	o	o(continental)
Ó	ó	the same as Polish *u*
P	p	p
R	r	trilled **r**
RZ	rz	*zh*, *r* mute
S	s	s
SZ	sz	*sh* in *shall*
Ś	ś	soft *sh*
T	t	t
U	u	u(continental)
W	w	v
Y	y	hard *i*, as *y* in *Mary*
Z	z	z
Ź	ź	Eng. *z* as in *azure*, but softer
Ż	ż	Eng. *z* as in *azure*, but harder

4. The following table gives the Czech alphabet and a pronunciation guide:

Czech		Approximate Pronunciation
A	a	short *a* as in *bat*
Á	á	long *a* as in *father*
B	b	b
C	c	ts
Č	č	Eng. hard *ch*
D	d	d
Ď	ď	soft *d* as in *dew*
E	e	short *e* as in *let*
É	é	long *e* as in *there*
F	f	f
H	h	voiced h
Ch	ch	Germ. guttural *ch*
I	i	short *i* as in *it*
Í	í	long *i* as in *seek*
J	j	Eng. consonantal *y* as in *you*
K	k	k
L	l	l
M	n	m
N	n	n
Ň	ň	Eng. soft *n* as in *lenient*
O	o	short *o* as in *for*
Ó	ó	long *o* as in *door*
P	p	p
R	r	r

Czech		Approximate Pronunciation
Ř	ř	sibilant, vibrant—pron. trilled r and sh simultaneously
S	s	s
Š	š	*sh*
T	t	t
Ť	ť	soft *t* as in *tune*
U	u	short *u* as in *put*
Ú	ú	long *u* as in *boot*
Ů	ů	as long *u*
V	v	v
Y	y	short *i* as in *it*
Ý	ý	long *i* as in *seek*
Z	z	z
Ž	ž	Eng. *z* as in *azure*

4a. The Slovak differences are tabulated below:

Slovak		Approximate Pronunciation
	ä	very open e
Ĺ	ĺ	long vocalic *l* as in *table*
Ľ	ľ	soft l
O	o	*o* in *long*
Ô	ô	*wa* as in *war*

INDEX

Alexius (Alexis), Saint, 155, 169, 301, 520, 521

Alexis, son of Peter the Great, 527, 534, 540

Alexius Strategopulus, Byzantine general, 105

Alexius I Comnenus, Byzantine emperor, 89

Alexius III, Byzantine emperor, 96

Alfonso, King of Aragon and Naples, 236

Alfonso V, King of Portugal, 328

Alfonso X of Castile, the Wise, 9, 30, 31, 327

Alpine lands, 2, 29, 30, 45, 158, 159, 436

Alsace, 456

America (New World, U. S.), 328, 329, 360, 416, 433, 449, 450, 464

Ammann, A., 230, 231, 387

Amsterdam, 457

Amur, 493

Anabaptists, 407, 415, 430, 431

Anchialus, 108

Ančić, I., Croat writer, 426

Ancona, 118, 245

Andex-Meran, German noble family, 132

Andreev, A. I., 555

Andreev, M., 148

Andrejevič, V. K., 282

Andrew Bogoljubskij, Prince, 224, 365, 385

Andrew Kurbskij, *see* Kurbskij

Andrew, St., monastery of, 511

Andrew Alexius of Darazzo, 322

Andrew, Bishop of Prague, 124

Andrew II, King of Hungary, 26, 98, 101, 107, 133, 136, 213, 214

Andrew III, Hungarian king, 33

Andrew Laskarz, Bishop of Poznań, 297

Andrew of Dubá, 335

Andrew of Uglić, 266

Andronicus II, Byzantine emperor, 110, 111

Andrušovo, treaty of, 479, 491

Angelov, D., 148

Angyal, A., 465, 488

Anhalt, 63

Anjou, dynasty of (Angevins), 9, 10, 33, 41, 42, 57, 60, 65, 70, 107-110, 112, 135, 348, 436

Ankara, 233, 245

Annales ecclesiastici, 117, 425

Anne, niece of Peter the Great, 529, 534

Anne, wife of Ferdinand I, 240, 241, 251

Anne, daughter of Peter the Great, 534, 535

Anne, wife of Stephen Bathory, 446

Anne (Aldona), daughter of Gedymin, 48

Anne, wife of Sigismund III, 447

Anne, Czech wife of Richard II of England, 186, 190

Anne, third wife of Emperor Charles IV, 73

Anne, wife of King Radoslav, 99

Anne, Tsaritsa, 543, 544

Anselm, Saint, 153, 156

Antês, Sarmatian tribe, 1

Anthony, Patriarch, 227

Antibari (Bar), 91, 93, 94, 97, 98, 145

Antichrist, 55, 164, 190, 206

Antioch, Patriarch of, 504, 505

Anti-Trinitarians (Socinians), 414-416, 429

Antony Marini of Grenoble, 290

Antwerp, 449

Apenines, 3

Apocrypha in Slavic translations, 173

Aquileia, 132, 208

Arabs, 5, 15, 16, 284

Aragon, Kingdom of, 10, 328

Aragon, Spanish House of, 10, 296

Arctic Ocean, 493

Arezzo, 69

Argirov, St., 116

argosy, 140

Ariosto, L., 285

Aristotle, 17, 151, 284, 535, 536

Arkhangel (Arkhangelsk), 275, 495

Arles, Kingdom of, 7, 41, 42, 46, 64, 69, 70

Armenia, Armenians, 240, 339, 359, 533

Arpáds, Hungarian dynasty, 33, 105, 107, 134, 137

Arsenius, Greek monk, 504

THE GERMAN SLAV BORDERLANDS
13th to 15th CENTURIES

SCALE

50   0   50   100 Miles
50   0   50   100   150 Km.

BALTIC SEA

HOLSTEIN

Hamburg

MECKLENBURG

POMERANIA

○Rügen

○Kolberg

Danzig○

Königsberg○

POLISH FIEF
1466

DUCHY OF
PRUSSIA
1525

VARMIA

○Elbing
○Marienburg

TEUTONIC ORDER

x Grunwald
○Tannenberg

MAZOVIA

ROYAL
TO POLAND
1466
PRUSSIA

○Stettin

BRANDENBURG

Berlin○   ○Küstrin

Magdeburg○

LUXEMBURG
1373-1415

GREAT

KUJAVIA

○Dobrzyn

○Warsaw

POLAND

○Poznań ○Gniezno

LOWER
1368
LUSATIA

SAXONY

Leipzig○

Meissen○
Dresden○

1329
UPPER LUSATIA

○Budissin

SILESIAN DUCHIES

Breslau○

○Sandomierz

GERMANY

TO BOHEMIA
1266
Eger○
(Cheb)   Prague○

LITTLE

○Cracow

TO
POLAND
1457

POLAND

BOHEMIA

○Pizeň

○Kutná Hora

Olomouc○

Nuremberg○

UPPER
1353-73
PALATINATE

KARLŠTYN
LUXEMBURG
1310
○Tabor

○Budějovice

MORAVIA

Brno○

LUXEMBURG
1310

UPPER

HUNGARY

TO POLAND
1412

ZIPS

Danube

River

BAVARIA

○Munich

AUSTRIA

○Salzburg

TO BOHEMIA 1251

STYRIA

TO BOHEMIA
1254

○Graz

Marchfeld
Vienna○   ×

Trnava○ ○Nitra

○Bratislava
(Poszony)
(Pressburg)

○Gran (Esztergom)

HUNGARY

LUXEMBURG   1386

○Budapest

Innsbruck○

TYROL

1335-41LUXEMBURG
1342-63BAVARIAN
1363 HABSBURG

CARINTHIA
1269

VENETIAN

Ljubljana○

CILLI
1260
○Cilli

REPUBLIC

CARNIOLA
1269

○Trieste

ITALY

○Venice

ISTRIA

○Zagreb

CROATIA

m.e.ofrok   1962

FRONTIER OF THE EMPIRE 1378

FRONTIER OF THE EMPIRE 1466

DOMINIONS OF PŘEMYSL OTAKAR II
BEFORE 1282. DATES ARE THOSE
OF ACQUISITION.

DOMINIONS OF THE HOUSE OF LUXEMBURG
WITH DATES OF ACQUISITION

HABSBURG DOMINIONS IN THE 14th and
15th CENTURIES

×   BATTLE

GROWTH OF THE SERBIAN EMPIRE 1282-1355

Deg. E. Long.

HUNGARY

WALLACHIA

MAČVA •Belgrade

BOSNIA

Danube River

Vidin

BULGARIA

(UNDER SERBIAN
SUZERAINTY 1330)

HUM

Niš

Morava River

Sofia

Peć   X Kosovo

Ragusa Kotor
(Dubrovnik)

Zeta   Prizren   Velbužd X   Phillippopolis

42   42

Scutari   Skoplje

Vardar River

BYZANTINE

Durazzo Kroja   Ochrida

Serres

Kastoria   Thessalonica

ADRIATIC

Valona

SEA   Berat

Jannina   Larissa   AEGEAN SEA

CORFU   Trikkala
(ANGEVIN)

NEGROPONTE

CATALAN
DUCHY OF
ATHENS

38   •••••• DOMINIONS OF STEPHEN UROŠ II   38
              MILUTIN   1282-1321   Patras   Athens

      ───── EMPIRE OF STEPHEN DUŠAN   ACHAEA

      ─·─·─ BOUNDARY BY PEACE OF 1350
              -NOT RECOGNIZED BY DUŠAN

      X   BATTLE   SCALE

                                         50   0   50   100 Miles

m.e.otrok   1962   50 0   50   100 150 Km..

Deg. E. Long.

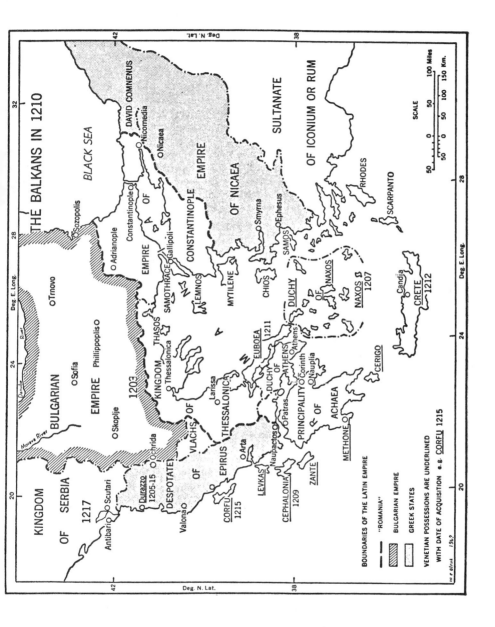

THE BALKANS IN 1210

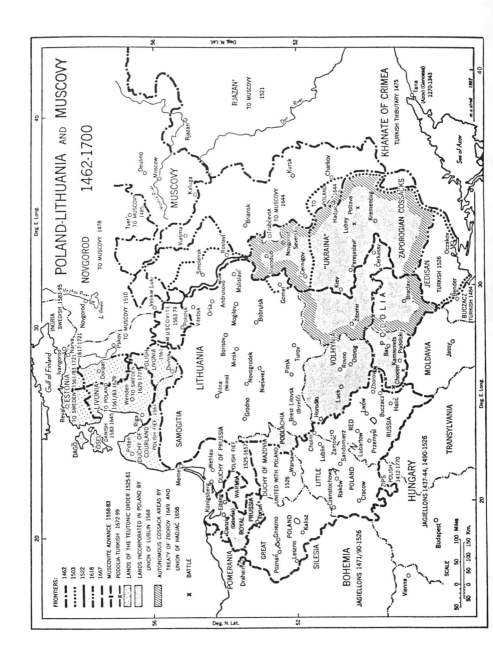

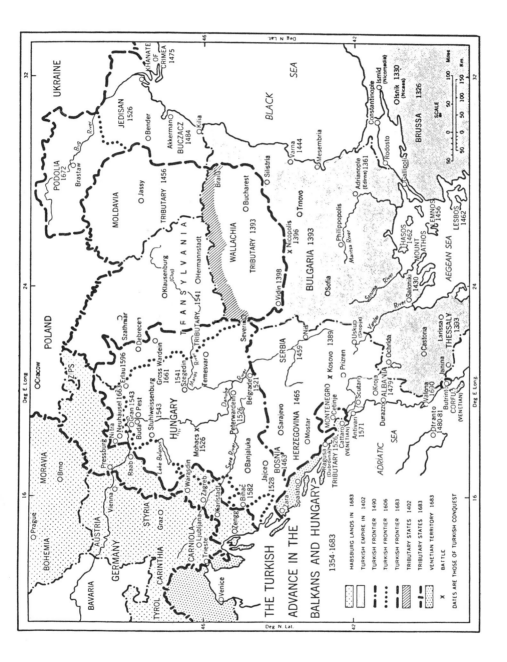

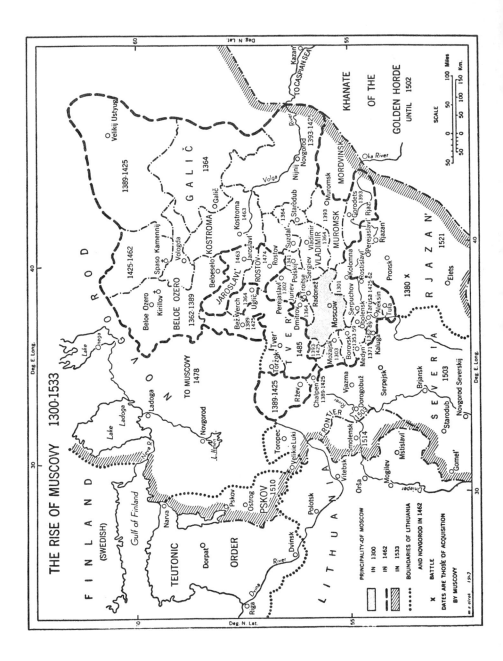

THE RISE OF MUSCOVY 1300-1533

PRINCIPALITY OF MOSCOW

IN 1300
IN 1462
IN 1533

BOUNDARIES OF LITHUANIA
AND NOVGOROD IN 1462

X   BATTLE

DATES ARE THOSE OF ACQUISITION
BY MUSCOVY

SCALE

0 50 100 150 Km.
0 50 100 Miles